The **Guardian**

International Film Guide
2005

the definitive annual review of world cinema
| edited by Daniel Rosenthal
| founding editor Peter Cowie

42nd edition

BUTTON
live communications

London   Los Angeles   Cannes

**Guardian
Books**

58th Locarno International Film Festival.
August 3-13 2005.

GOLDEN LEOPARD, PRIVATE by Saverio Costanzo – Italy
SPECIAL JURY PRIZE, TONY TAKITANI by Jun Ichikawa   Japan
SILVER LEOPARD, EN GARDE by Ayse Polat – Germany
SILVER LEOPARD, DASTAN NATAMAM (Story Undone) by Hassan Yektapanah – Iran/Ireland/Singapore
GOLDEN LEOPARD VIDEO C.P.COMPANY, CONVERSATIONS DE SALON 1-2-3 by Danielle Arbid - France
PRIX DU PUBLIC UBS, HACALA HASURIT/THE SYRIAN BRIDE, by Eran Riklis - Israel/France/Germany

via Ciseri 23
CH-6600 Locarno
tel. +41 91 756 21 21
fax +41 91 756 21 49
info@pardo.ch
www.pardo.ch

Contents
International Film Guide 2005

Editor & Associate Publisher
Daniel Rosenthal
Publisher
Robert Bingham
Founding Editor
Peter Cowie
Consulting Editor
Derek Elley
Editorial Assistant
Sara Tyler
**International Sales &
Marketing Director**
Sandrine Bentata
Sales Managers
*Jacasta Berry (Pacific Asia),
Raquel Escobar (Spain, Latin
America), Mary Rega (UK,
Ireland, Italy), Sara Tyler
(Film Festivals)*
Design
Button Group plc
Photo Consultants
*The Kobal Collection
tel +44 (0) 20 7624 3300
www.picture-desk.com*

Editorial and Business Offices
*Button Group plc
246 Westminster Bridge Road
London SE1 7PD
tel +44 (0) 20 7401 0400
fax +44 (0) 20 7401 0401
e london@buttonplc.com*

*ISBN 0-9548766-0-1 (UK)
British Library Cataloging in
Publication Data
International Film Guide 2005
1. Rosenthal, Daniel 1971-*

*Distributed in the UK by
Gardners Books*

*Published in the UK by
Button Group plc*

*Copyright © 2005 by
Button Group plc*

*Printed and bound in Milan by
Rotolito Lombarda
www.rotolitolombarda.it*

MGM/Kobal

"Friends, Romans, countrymen...": MARLON BRANDO creates one of the great moments in screen Shakespeare, as Mark Antony in Joseph L. Mankiewicz's **Julius Caesar** *(1953). Brando died on July 1, 2004, aged 80.*

International Liaison

Algeria, Morocco, Senegal, Tunisia, rest of West Africa: Roy Armes
Argentina: Alfredo Friedlander
Armenia: Susanna Harutiunian
Australia: Peter Thompson
Austria: Roman Scheiber
Azerbaijan, Belarus, Georgia, Macedonia, Ukraine: Goga Lomidze
Bangladesh: Ahmed Muztaba Zamal
Belgium: Erik Martens
Bosnia & Herzegovina: Rada Sesic
Brazil: Nelson Hoineff
Bulgaria: Pavlina Jeleva
Canada: Brendan Kelly
Chile: Andrea Osorio Klenner
China: Shelly Kraicer
Colombia: Pedro Adrián Zuluaga
Croatia: Tomislav Kurelec
Cuba: Luciano Castillo, Alberto Ramos
Cyprus: Theo Panayides
Czech Republic: Eva Zaoralová
Denmark: Jacob Neiiendam
Ecuador: Gabriela Alemán
Egypt: Fawzi Soliman
Estonia: Jaan Ruus

Finland: Antti Selkokari
France: Michel Ciment
Germany: Peter Körte
Greece: Yannis Bacoyannopoulos
Gulf States, Lebanon, Syria: Mohammed Rouda
Hong Kong: Tim Youngs
Hungary, United States: Eddie Cockrell
Iceland: Skarphédinn Gudmundsson
India: Uma da Cunha
Indonesia: Lisabona Rahman
Iran: Jamal Omid
Ireland: Michael Dwyer
Israel: Dan Fainaru
Italy: Lorenzo Codelli
Japan: Tomomi Katsuta
Kenya: Ogova Ondego
Latvia: Andris Rozenbergs
Lithuania: Grazina Arlickaite
Luxembourg: Jean-Pierre Thilges
Malaysia: Baharudin A. Latif
Malta: Daniel Rosenthal
Mexico: Carlos Bonfil
Namibia, South Africa, Zimbabwe: Martin P. Botha
Nepal: Uzzwal Bhandary
Netherlands: Pieter van Lierop

New Zealand: Peter Calder
Norway: Trond Olav Svendsen
Pakistan: Aijaz Gul
Peru: Isaac León Frías
Philippines: Tessa Jazmines
Poland: Barbara Hollender
Portugal: Martin Dale
Puerto Rico: José Artemio Torres
Romania: Cristina Corciovescu
Russia: Kirill Razlogov
Rwanda: Daddy Youssouf Ruhorahoza
Serbia & Montenegro: Goran Gocic
Singapore: Yvonne Ng
Slovakia: Hana Cielová
Slovenia: Ziva Emersic
South Korea, Taiwan: Stephen Cremin
Spain: Jonathan Holland
Sri Lanka: Amarnath Jayatilaka
Sweden: Gunnar Rehlin
Switzerland: Michael Sennhauser
Thailand: Anchalee Chaiworaporn
Turkey: Atilla Dorsay
United Kingdom: Philip Kemp
Uruguay: Jorge Jellinek

Front Cover
Ernesto Guevara (Gael García Bernal), foreground, and Alberto Granado (Rodrigo de la Serna) cross Chile's Atacama Desert in Walter Salles' superb road movie **The Motorcycle Diaries,** *which in 2004 became one of the 10 most successful foreign-language movies ever at the UK box-office.*
Picture: Paula Prandini/Film Four/South Fork Pictures/Pathé/The Kobal Collection.

Twentieth Century Fox

Let's talk about sex: Liam Neeson, above, as sexual pioneer Alfred Kinsey in Bill Condon's **Kinsey**, one of the most intelligent and compassionate Hollywood biopics ever made. In November 2004, right-wing groups in America absurdly condemned the film's "homosexual agenda". During Cannes 2004, British tabloids had reacted with similarly blinkered outrage to the unsimulated intercourse between actors Margo Stilley (pictured below) and Kieran O'Brien in Michael Winterbottom's intimate **9 Songs** (see p.308).

Optimum Releasing

Notes from the Editor

Regular readers will already have noticed one major change to this *IFG*: it is several months late. Our shift in publication date, from November to March, has enabled contributors to provide a more up-to-date review of the previous year's film-making and festivals than in earlier editions. The later deadline means we have covered many films, including brilliant new works from three of our five Directors of the Year (Kim Ki-duk's *3-iron*, Mike Leigh's *Vera Drake* and Alexander Payne's *Sideways*), whose festival premieres at Venice and Toronto would previously have excluded them until our 2006 edition.

For one year only, therefore, in covering the period from July 2003 to November 2004, we have been obliged to play catch-up. For example, Tomislav Kurelec looks back on two years' worth of features unveiled at Croatia's national festival, held in Pula each July, and our Guide to Film Festivals lists 2003 *and* 2004 award-winners from several important fourth-quarter events, such as Stockholm, Thessaloniki and the Festival des Trois Continents, Nantes.

A wider World

Another significant change to *IFG* this year is geographical. The World Survey section has expanded faster even than the European Union (and with considerably less bureaucracy) and now covers 97 countries, 21 more than our last edition. With additional correspondents being lined up to report from Africa, Eastern Europe and Latin America, we hope to pass the 100-country mark in *IFG 2006*.

Bangladesh, Indonesia, Mali, Senegal and Zimbabwe are some of the nations rejoining the fold, and among those included for the first time are Cyprus, Ecuador, Kenya and Rwanda. On Cyprus, directors such as Christos Georgiou and Christos Siopachas have been exploring the island's divided Turkish/Greek identity through

Daniel Rosenthal

drama and comedy. In Ecuador, Sebastián Cordero (*Crónicas*) and his contemporaries have defied national economic meltdown and may yet join the Latin American *buena onda*, and feature production is on the increase in Kenya, even though the domestic market has only 10 cinemas for a population of 34 million. The legacy of the 1994 genocide in Rwanda dominates the nascent film scene there, in both fiction features and documentaries.

Passion and polemic

As *IFG* still goes to press before full-year charts are available, our World Box-Office Survey looks back to 2003, while the provisional top 20 for 2004 (overleaf) contains the American releases that will, as ever, dominate most of the national top 10s in our next edition, including woeful examples of Hollywood's increasingly dumbed-down, digitalised escapism: *Troy*, *The Day After Tomorrow* and *Van Helsing*.

Also in the list are 2004's least conventional smash hits: *The Passion of the Christ* and *Fahrenheit 9/11*. The ecstatic American Christians pouring out of block-booked screenings for Mel Gibson's biblical horror movie last spring now seem like mass exit polls foretelling the Bush re-election that Michael Moore could not prevent (perhaps Nanni Moretti will have better luck by releasing his *The Cayman*, which he promises will be "a fiction on Silvio Berlusconi, in the best tradition of Italian engaged cinema", in the run-up to the country's election in 2006).

Moore's laboured polemic was the biggest story in a year of remarkable critical and commercial success for non-fiction film-makers at multiplexes and festivals, and in "Documentary Cinema Now" (p.43–52), Thomas White and Carol Nahra reflect on a period in which Kevin Macdonald's *Touching the Void* became one of the few documentaries to have won the Bafta for Best British Film, and Morgan Spurlock's *Super Size Me* helped to change the menus at McDonald's.

In September 2004, one in five movies playing in US cinemas was a non-fiction title, yet this surge of interest extended far beyond English-language releases. I can't recall a year in which so many *IFG* correspondents – from Israel to Norway, Ecuador to Switzerland – have drawn attention to the breadth, quality and popularity of their country's documentaries.

At this distance, *Fahrenheit 9/11* already resembles the documentary equivalent of *Titanic*, a freakish one-off, borne of its divisive times. It grossed an astonishing $220m; yet I was more surprised by a much smaller figure, cited by Michael Sennhauser, *IFG*'s Swiss correspondent. Some 250,000 people in Austria, Germany and Switzerland paid to confront their mortality by watching Stefan Haupt's portrait of a pioneering psychiatrist, *Elisabeth Kübler-Ross – Facing Death*. A documentary that Hollywood marketing experts would dismiss as the ultimate feel-bad movie broke Swiss box-office records; this was perhaps the strangest and, if you care about cinematic diversity, most heartening *IFG* story of the year.
– *Daniel Rosenthal*
(dmr2000@gxn.co.uk)

WORLDWIDE BOX-OFFICE 2004

		$m
1.	Shrek 2	885
2.	The Prisoner of Azkaban	789
3.	Spider-Man 2	784
4.	The Passion of the Christ	609
5.	The Return of the King**	545
6.	The Day After Tomorrow	542
7.	Troy	497
8.	I, Robot*	343
9.	The Last Samurai**	322
10.	Shark Tale*	306
11.	Van Helsing	300
12.	The Incredibles*	275
13.	The Bourne Supremacy*	272
14.	The Village*	255
15.	Fahrenheit 9/11	220
16.	Collateral*	209
17.	King Arthur	201
18.	50 First Dates	195
19.	Garfield: The Movie	194
20.	Scooby-Doo 2	178

*Still in release. **Excludes 2003 gross.
Source: Variety.
Figures are provisional, through November 28, 2004.

Directors of the Year

Kim Ki-duk by Adrien Gombeaud

From *Crocodile*, his first feature, in 1996, to *3-iron* in 2004, Kim Ki-duk has made *at least* one film a year. Because of his strong appetite for filming, Kim relies on instinct rather than intellect and does not try to pursue perfection. By nature, all of his films are imperfect. Instead of avoiding repetition by fighting against his obsessions, he mines them for creative potential. He seems untouched by the commercial failures he has often faced at home in South Korea and inoculated against artist's block. Built like an athlete, Kim looks like a piece of solid rock; yet he creates pieces of art as fragile as porcelain.

KIM KI-DUK was born on December 20, 1960, in the village of Bongwha (Kyongsang province). He entered an agricultural school before starting to work in factories at 17. After five years in the Marines, he decided to become a Catholic priest, spent two years in a monastery and developed an interest in painting. In 1990, the little money he had saved took him to Europe. He travelled from Finland to Greece and settled in France in 1992. Living by selling his paintings on the streets of the Riviera, he slowly became interested in cinema. When he returned to South Korea he was only 34 but had already lived several lives with which to feed many movies. The latter half of the 1990s was the most intense

period in the history of South Korean cinema. Rusted by their years under the military regime, the old studios and established directors had lost touch with the younger audience. Then, for a short period, the doors of the industry opened to people whose determination and ambitions mattered more than their background and connections. Suddenly, vision, a strong personality and a bit of luck were all it took to shoot your first feature: Hong Sang-soo directed *The Day the Pig Fell into the Well* (1996), Lee Chang-dong directed *Green Fish* (1997) and Kim Jee-woon *The Quiet Family* (1998). Kim Ki-duk emerged as Kim Jee-woon had done, by submitting scripts to various competitions. *Painter and Prisoner* won the Creation Prize of the Scriptwriters' Association in 1994 and *Illegal Crossing* won a prize from the South Korean Motion Picture Association the following year. Neither was filmed, but in 1996 he was offered a chance to bring his third script to the screen.

Man as a wild animal

Like most South Korean first films from this period, *Crocodile (Ako)* opens with a very strong scene: a man kills himself by jumping from a bridge into Seoul's Han River; a homeless man takes off his clothes, dives in and swims out with the dead man's wallet. In South Korean classical melodrama, poor characters like Kim's modern vagrant were often reflections of South Korea itself, and the suffering of these naïve figures was a pretext for revealing their inherent generosity and courage. In *Crocodile*, however, Kim shows that when poverty does not actually turn men into animals or automatons (a tramp becomes a living coffee machine to collect a few dimes), it awakens nothing in them but cruelty. *Crocodile* also saw the birth of a rich collaboration between

Kim and actor Cho Jae-Hyeon, who plays the violent homeless man and would later become a star.

It was a confident debut and Kim immediately took on a more ambitious project, *Wild Animals* (*Ya saeng dongmul bohoguyok*, 1997), which tells the story of a South Korean homeless artist who meets a North Korean refugee in Paris. With a soundtrack based on world music (including singer Natacha Atlas, whose voice Kim would use again in *3-iron*) and a detailed exploration of areas like Pigalle and Beaubourg, Kim presented an original vision of the Paris that exists far from the tourist tours. However, he does not speak French and failed in directing his French cast. The acting is so awkward that, despite its obvious merits, *Wild Animals* is scarcely watchable (for a western audience at least). It was also a major disappointment at the South Korean box-office. So when Kim started to write *Birdcage Inn* (*Paran Daemun*, 1998) he thought that he might not be able to raise the money with which to direct this third feature. Eventually, the first prize of the South Korean Film Commission script contest allowed production to start.

Set in a motel on a small harbour, *Birdcage* Inn follows the friendship of two young girls, an art student and a prostitute, who end up swapping identities. Though Kim was in more playful mode here, he did not renounce his obsessions: water, animals, prostitution, dual identity. *Birdcage Inn* fared much better at the box-office during a year in which audiences were open to other disturbing films, such as Im Sang-soo's *Girls' Night Out*, a raw tale of women and sex, E J-yong's *An Affair*, about a young man and an older woman, and Kim Jee-woon's black comedy *The Quiet Family*, in which a decent family has problems disposing of dead bodies.

The late 1990s rebirth of South Korean cinema was encouraged by love of art, by money – and also by patriotism. South Korea needed not only directors such as Kang Jegyu, who could make action-packed blockbusters like *Shiri* (1999), but auteurs to carry the flag around the festival world, and as *Birdcage Inn* was well received

Cho Jae-Hyeon, left, as **Crocodile**, *with Woo Yeun-gyeong*

by international critics at Berlin, Montreal and Karlovy Vary, it became clear that Kim could be one of the latter group. From this point onwards, the publicity surrounding Kim's films would always focus on controversial content and his selection or non-selection for various festivals, rather than box-office millions – a situation in which he was free to stroll the back alleys of the South Korean film industry and leave its grand avenues to others.

Not another cult movie

In 1999, the few minutes of *The Isle* (*Seom*) shown privately to a handful of journalists and distributors at Cannes promised a disturbing film experience. It then competed in Venice, Rotterdam and Toronto and arrived in cinemas in several countries with modern aesthetic and a demonic reputation. *The Isle* is more than another "Asian cult movie" in which, notoriously, people insert fish hooks into their mouth or vagina. Set on a lake far away from civilisation, it tells a passionate love story between a fugitive criminal (Kim Yoo-suk) and a mute occasional prostitute (Seoh Jung).

Kim designed the fantastic set of small houses floating on the lake. Displaying a large range of blue tones, using the sound (or the silence) of water like a musical soundtrack, *The Isle* is hypnotic. However, like his previous films it remained under the influence of French 1980s movies. The monochrome houses of *The Isle* and the nostalgic beach of *Birdcage Inn* come from Beneix's *Betty Blue*; *Crocodile* was obviously inspired by Carax's *Les amants du Pont-Neuf* and in *Wild Animals* the presence of Richard Bohringer in a character similar to the one he plays in Beneix's *Diva*, alongside Denis Lavant, the actor used by Carax in fetish style, was a way for Kim to acknowledge these influences. After *The Isle*, it was time to break away from them.

Kim Ki-yeon, left, and Ju Jin-mo in **Real Fiction**

Portrait of the artist as a boy

After five films, it was clear that Kim's painter characters were tainted by autobiography. But in 2001 he openly faced his childhood in *Address Unknown* (*Suchwiin bulmyeong*). He abandoned the sophisticated lighting of his previous movies for sharp grey tones and focused on three young Koreans living near an American military base. It is Kim's darkest and most brutal piece. The director would later say that the character of the young aspiring artist was himself. The over-acting American soldier who goes crazy is probably inspired by the director's experiences as a marine. The film succeeds in describing Americans and Koreans as two different victims of the same history and was a prelude to a second autobiographical movie the following year, *The Coast Guard*.

Kim Yoo-suk, left, and Seoh Jung in **The Isle**

Shot in 2000, *Real Fiction* (*Siljae sanghwang*) was more a challenge than a movie. It describes the fall of a street painter into schizophrenia. It was shot in Seoul in less than two hours, with 10 video cameras running simultaneously. The difference between this and Agnès Varda's *Cleo from 5 to 7* (among other examples of real-time tales) is that the cameras were part of the story – responsible for the character's crisis because he feels he is being watched all the time. Seoul is a prison under constant surveillance by cameras, in which people don't know if they exist or are characters (hence the ambiguous notion of "real fiction"). Possibly a manifesto about Kim's concept of cinema, *Real Fiction* is also a powerful, fascinating portrait of a modern city, made possible by the strange and frightening performance of star Ju Jin-mo as the artist.

However, in 2001 Kim also shot *Bad Guy* (*Nappeun namja*), the story of a man who prostitutes his own girlfriend. It became Kim's most successful film in South Korea, with 700,000 admissions. In the title role, Cho Jae-yun bravely broke from his clean image as a TV star and Kim gave this performance much of the credit for the film's popularity. Controversy helped, too; feminist groups accused the film of misogyny.

Shot immediately after *Bad Guy*, *The Coast Guard* (*Hae anseon*, 2002) tells the story of a gun-crazy soldier who goes insane after accidentally killing a civilian at the North Korean border. For the second time in his career, Kim used a major star, Jang Dong-gun (as the

Tartan Films

Tartan Films

Cho Jae-yun, left, and So Won in **Bad Guy**

soldier), and again managed to get the best out of him. This is not a war movie, but a portrait of a useless army that invents its own foe. Behind the sadness and violence, there is always a great deal of irony in Kim's films, and it is more prevalent here than ever before. This low-budget movie, in which North Korean spies are pure fantasy, is Kim's sarcastic answer to super-expensive blockbusters like *Shiri*, which succeed by agitating South Korean audiences' fears of their invisible enemy.

In four films and only two years, Kim had totally changed his visual style. His direction had become a practical way to make themes and emotions as clear and readable as possible. The dark aspects and the violence were becoming so visible that they were overshadowing friendship, humour, love and redemption. In 2003, however, *Spring, Summer, Autumn, Winter and... Spring* (*Bom, Yorum, kaeul, kyeoul keurigo bom*) was another change of tack.

Changing with the seasons

To trace the life of a kid raised as a Buddhist monk, Kim came back to an *Isle*-like setting: a temple floating on a lake. Each season is a step of his life, as the film displays the classical Buddhist cycle of constant change: things come back but never repeat themselves. Each spring is the same but also different. Premiered and well

received in Locarno, the film opened successfully in France and in other western countries, helped by its exotic, mystical mood.

This is definitely the work of a mature director. Kim, who also plays the monk in middle age, has total control over his universe, not only mastering visual aspects such as landscape and colour, but also creating a specific sense of time, involving the audience in a slow, coherent rhythm. This creative cycle enlightens us about Kim's concept of artistic creation: the films revolve around the same elements, as the director keeps re-inventing his style.

Tartan Films

Kim Young-min and Ha Yeo-jin in **Spring, Summer, Autumn, Winter... and Spring**

Samaritan Girl (*Samaria*, 2004) was Kim's tenth movie but the first made by his company, Kim Ki-duk Films. Once again he used a familiar pretext: two sweet adolescent Catholic schoolgirls, Jae-young (Seo Min-jung) and Yeo-jin (Kwak Ji-min), try to make enough money through prostitution to buy plane tickets to Europe. Yeo-jin contacts the clients; Jae-young sleeps with them and apparently has no problem with the arrangement. But when she jumps from a window while trying to escape a police raid on a motel she seems willingly to accept her own death. To forgive herself, Yeo-jin has sex with all her friend's Johns and gives them their money back. When her father (Lee Uhl), a cop and a deep believer, discovers his daughter's after-school life, he punishes the clients and takes her on a redemptive countryside journey.

Samaritan Girl revisits themes from Kim's earliest features (prostitution, murder, the need for money), but in less nervous, angry fashion. In soft pastel colours it is inhabited by the quietness of *Spring, Summer…* and both films share a similar tempo, divided into chapters. This strange softness does not dilute the violence of the feelings and actions depicted; it makes the contrast more fluid. Kwak and Lee are wonderful as the leads, as are the actors who play the clients and create convincing individuals in just a few lines. Kim's coherent direction of this fine cast and the simplicity of the storyline, well served by a clear-cut *mise en scène*, make *Samaritan Girl* Kim's finest achievement to date.

When he learned that it had won him the Silver Bear for best director in Berlin in 2004, Kim was having dinner in a restaurant in Paris. He was surprised. *Samaritan Girl* had been shot in just 10 days, when Kim was already focused on *3-iron* (*Bin jib*, 2004), the story of a young drifter, Tae-seok (Jae Hee) who visits houses while the owners are away. He meets a sad and silent model, Seon-hwa (Lee Seung-yeon), who has been beaten by her husband. After Tae-seok beats up the husband (using a 3-iron golf club), the two run away and live from one house to another until they are arrested by the police.

Kim here goes deeper into the quiet territory of *Samaritan Girl* (the two characters never speak

and half the film has no dialogue). In the second half, Kim remakes the end of *The Coast Guard* by introducing a ghost-like character. The device is far more convincing here because Kim does not have to use special effects to create a haunted atmosphere. Completed in time for Venice 2004, *3-iron* won the Silver Lion for Best Director and Kim's consecutive awards at major festivals in the space of nine months were a well-deserved reward after almost 10 years of constant work; though such laurels are perhaps ill suited to a director whose concept of film-making makes the very idea of achievement seem totally foreign.

A secret path

The most important event in Kim Ki-duk's life happened one morning in 1969, when he left for Seoul with his family. The road out of Bongwha would take him from the marines to the streets of France. It is not surprising that his films revolve around the theme of survival. However, this "struggle for life" is just one aspect of his cinema. Kim is mostly interested in our desperate need for shelter; his characters are outcasts looking for a silent place to hide, away from the dangers of the outside world. It can be water (the Han River in *Crocodile*, the aquarium of *The Coast Guard*), it can be a floating temple (*Spring, Summer…*), and it can also be sex or women (the peep-show cabins of *Wild Animals* or *The Isle* as a metaphor for the feminine body).

We are moved by these films not only because of their hard reality, served straight up, but mostly because somewhere in the heart of their chaotic world there is always a shelter, a back door to an "empty house" (the literal meaning of *3-iron*'s South Korean title). Kim is obviously a perceptive observer of his time. The secret path hidden in his films also reveals a modern poet.

ADRIEN GOMBEAUD (AGombeaud@aol.com) is based in Paris, where he writes for *Positif* and the daily financial paper *Les Echos*. He has written a thesis on contemporary South Korean cinema and is director of *Tan'gun*, a bi-annual publication on South Korean culture and society.

Pretty Pictures

Jae Hee in front of a picture of Lee Seung-yeon in **3-iron**

Kim Ki-duk Filmography

1996
AKO (Crocodile)
*Script, Direction and Production
Design: KK-d. Photography: Lee
Dong-sam. Editing: Park Gok-ji.
Music: Lee Mun-hee. Players:
Cho Jae-Hyeon (Crocodile), Woo
Yeun-gyeong (Hyeon-jeon), Jeon
Mu-song (Mr. Oh), Anh Jae-hong
(Aeng Bal). Produced by Kim
Byeong-su for Jo-young Films.
102 mins.*

1997
**YA SAENG DONGMUL
BOHOGUYOK (Wild Animals)**
*Script and Direction: KK-d.
Photography: So Jong-min.
Editing: Park Son-dok.
Production Design: KK-d, Moon
Hye-yeon. Music: Kang In-gu,
Oh Jin-a. Players: Cho Jae-hyun
(Cheong-hae), Jang Dong-jik
(Hong San), Jang Ryun (Laura),
Sacha Rucaniva (Corrine),
Richard Bohringer (Boss), Denis
Lavant (Emile). Produced by
Kwong Ki-yeong for Dream
Cinema. 105 mins.*

1998
PARAN DAEMUN (Birdcage Inn)
*Script and Direction: KK-d.
Photography: So Jeong-min.
Editing: Ko Im-pyo. Music: Lee
Moon-hui. Players: Lee Ji-un (Jin-
a), Lee Hae-un (Hye-mi), Ahn
Jae-mo (Hyun-woo), Jeong
Hyeong-gi (Gek-o), Son Min-seok
(Jin-ho). Produced by Lee Kwang
Min and Yoo Hi-suk for Boogui
Cinema. 105 mins.*

1999
SEOM (The Isle)
*Script, Direction and Production
Design: KK-d. Photography:
Hwang So-shik. Editing: Kyeong
Min Ho. Music: Jeon Sang-yun.
Players Cho Jae-yun (Mang-chee),
Seoh Jung (Hee-jin), Kim Yoo-suk
(Hyun-shik), Park Seung-hee
(Eun-a), Jang Hang-seon (Middle-
aged Man). Produced by Lee Un
for Myung Film. 90 mins.*

2000
**SILJAE SANGHWANG
(Real Fiction)**
*Script, Direction and Production
Design: KK-d. Photography:
Hwang Cheol-hyeon. Editing:
Kyeong Min-ho. Music: Jeon
Sang-yun. Players: Ju Jin-mo
(Painter), Kim Jin-ah, Son Min-
seok, Lee Jae-rak, Kim Ki-yeon.
Produced by Shin Seung-soo for
Shin Seung-soo Production and
Saerom Entertainment. 69 mins.*

2001
**SUCHWIIN BULMYEONG
(Address Unknown)**
*Script, Direction and Production
Design: KK-d. Photography: Seo
Jeong-min. Editing: Ham Seung-
won. Music: Park Ho-jun.
Players: Yang Dong-kun (Chang
guk), Ban Min-jung (Eun-ok),
Kim Young-min (Ji-hum), Cho
Jae-yun (Dog Eyes), Lee In-ok
(Eun-ok's mother). Produced by
Lee Seung-jae for LJ Films. 117 mins.*

2001
NAPPEUN NAMJA (Bad Guy)
*Script and Direction: KK-d.
Photography: Hwang Chol-yeon.
Editing: Hang Seong-won.
Production Design: Kim Sun-ju.
Music: Park Ho-jun. Players: Cho
Jae-hyeon (Han-ki), So Won (Sun-
hwa), Choi Deok-mun (Myeong-
soo), Kim Yun-tae (Yun-tae).
Produced by Lee Seung-jae for LJ
Films. 100 mins.*

2002
HAE ANSEON (The Coast Guard)
*Script and Direction: KK-d.
Photography: Baek Dong-hyun.
Editing: Kim Seon-min.
Production Design: Yun Ju-hun.
Music: Jang Yung-yu. Players:
Jang Dong-gun (Kang), Park Ji-ah
(Mee-young), Kum Yung-hak, Yoo
Hae-jun. Produced by Lee Seung-
jae for LJ Films. 91 mins.*

2003
**BOM, YORUM, KAEUL,
KYEOUL KEURIGO BOM
(Spring, Summer, Autumn,
Winter... and Spring)**
*Script, Direction and Editing: KK-
d. Photography: Park Bong-hyun.
Production Design: Oh Sang-man.
Music: Park Ji-woong. Players:
Oh Young-su (Old Monk), Kim
Ki-duk (Adult Monk), Kim
Young-min (Young Monk), Seo
Jae-kyung (Child Monk), Ha Yeo-
jin (Young Girl), Kim Jung-young
(Mother of the Young Girl), Ji Dae
Han (Ji, Policeman), Choi Min
(Choi, Policeman). Produced by:
Kim So-hee, Karl Baumgartner
and Lee Seungjae for LJ films and
Pandora Film. 103 mins.*

2004
SAMARIA (Samaritan Girl)
*Script, Direction, Editing and
Production Design: KK-d.
Photography: Sun Sang-jae.
Music: Park Ji-woong. Players:
Lee Uhl (Young-gi), Kwak Ji-min
(Yeo-jin), Seo Min-jung (Jae-
young), Kwon Hyun-min
(Salesman 1), Oh Young
(Musician). Produced by KK-d
and Bae Jong-min for Kim Ki-duk
Films. 95 mins.*

2004
BIN JIB (3-iron)
*Script, Direction and Editing: KK-
d. Photography: Jang Song-bak.
Production Design: Kang Chang-
il. Music: Michael Nyman.
Players: Jae Hee (Tae-seok), Lee
Seung-yeon (Seon-hwa), Gweon
Hyeok-ho (Min-gyu). Produced
by KK-d for Kim Ki-duk Films.
95 mins.*

Mike Leigh by Philip Kemp

Simon Mein/Thin Man/Greenlight/Kobal

Over the years one phrase has constantly recurred in discussions of Mike Leigh: 'a prophet without honour'. Admirers of his work have often echoed the director himself when he notes that "the trouble is, the culture of my films is sadly not the prevailing culture in British cinema".

Feted and garlanded abroad, in his native country Leigh is still marginalised, regarded with a mixture of embarrassment and condescension, and denied entry to the pantheon of major British directors where, on any objective assessment, he surely deserves a place. But with the release of *Vera Drake*, his latest – and finest – film, that attitude may at last be about to change.

To understand why he is viewed in this way it is worth remembering that Leigh can be famously prickly in interviews, and his staunch left-wing beliefs – and abiding concern with the English class system – make many people uneasy. Others look askance at his unconventional

approach to film-making, which over the years has often made it hard for him to get funding. Leigh never starts with a script or even an idea for a story. Instead, he assembles a group of actors and asks each to develop a character, often based on someone they know, and improvise situations about them – a process which can take weeks or even months. Using the interactions between the actors, he then creates a text, which, after further extensive rehearsals and discussions, becomes the film script. The title is usually chosen last of all.

Not surprisingly, this tends to disconcert producers, used to being presented with a script – or at least a treatment. As Leigh readily acknowledges: "Producers had a tough decision if they had good scripts and I came along saying, 'I'm going to make a film. I don't know what it will be about.' Sometimes they went with me. Other times I was out of work."

To date he has been able to complete just nine features in a career lasting more than 30 years. Between his first and second features 17 years elapsed, during which he was able to work only in television and theatre. No doubt, given his outstanding skills as a director, he could have secured plenty of assignments if he had been ready to compromise even a little. But "compromise" is not a word for which Leigh has much time. Nor, come to that, is "assignments". He remains stubbornly his own man.

Grammar school boy

MIKE LEIGH was born in Hertfordshire on February 20, 1943 and grew up in Salford, Lancashire, where his father, Abe, was a general practitioner. His grandparents on both sides were Russian Jewish immigrants; the family name was

Liebermann until his father changed it in 1939. Leigh was educated at Salford Grammar; a fellow pupil was Les Blair, later to be the producer of his first feature film, *Bleak Moments*.

He was a less than brilliant pupil, not through any lack of intelligence but because of his instinctive aversion to academic discipline. He found more satisfaction in drawing cartoons and in acting, in school productions of Shaw and Gogol and in revues mounted by the Habonim, the Young Zionist organisation. Abe Leigh took a dim view of his son's theatrical ambitions, dismissing them as "the moonings of a stage-struck girlie", and was scarcely mollified when, at age 17, Leigh won a scholarship to RADA.

Leigh loved London but was unimpressed by RADA, finding the teaching there "sterile, uncreative, prescriptive". After graduating he enrolled in a foundation course at the Camberwell College of Art and a night course in direction at the London School of Film Technique, before embarking on his theatrical career. He soon found that directing other people's plays was not his forte; a 1965 production of David Halliwell's *Little Malcolm and His Struggle Against the Eunuchs* was disastrous. On placement at the Midlands Arts Centre in Birmingham Leigh first began to develop his improvisational methods and explored them further in pieces created while teaching at various drama schools in London.

Discovering Leigh country

Leigh's tenth play, *Bleak Moments*, was commissioned by Charles Marowitz for his Open

Flashbacks

Anne Raitt as a secretary in **Bleak Moments**

Space Theatre in Tottenham Court Road, central London. Marowitz hated the piece when he saw it, as did most of the critics, but Leigh's old schoolfellow Les Blair decided it could make a good film and persuaded Albert Finney, who had been at Salford Grammar a few years before Leigh and Blair, to fund the project through his company, Memorial Films.

Bleak Moments (1971), about a shy, downtrodden secretary who has to look after her mentally deficient sister, immediately explores much of what would become recognisable as Mike Leigh territory. Drab urban settings – south London, in this case; unwittingly self-revealing characters; dialogue and situations based on reality but taken to a level that Leigh calls "heightened realism"; the excruciating comedy of social embarrassment. One scene, where the young woman is taken to an appalling, near-empty Chinese restaurant by a man no less tongue-tied and socially dysfunctional than herself, is almost too painful to watch.

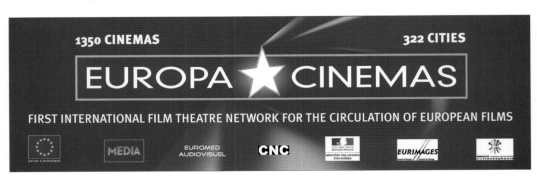

Critical response to the film was generally wary. "A prolonged poem to inhibitions, speechlessness and social unease," observed John Coleman in the *New Statesman*. Unexpectedly, one of the most enthusiastic reviews came from America: in the *Chicago Sun-Times*, Roger Ebert hailed "a masterpiece, plain and simple… its greatness is not just in the direction or subject, but in the complete singularity of the performances."

Despite such praise, no one seemed inclined to finance another Leigh movie. But the film was seen by BBC producer Tony Garnett, of *Cathy Come Home* (1966) fame, who invited Leigh to contribute to his influential "Play for Today" slot. *Hard Labour*, Leigh's first TV play, was transmitted in 1973 and by year's end he had married a young member of its cast, Alison Steadman, whom he had first met while teaching at an east London acting school.

During the early 1970s, Leigh's main outlet was theatre and he has worked extensively for the stage – despite dismissing it as an inferior medium: "There's something worldly, healthy and grown-up about the cinema, in comparison to which the theatre seems insular, up its own arse and full of adolescent petulance."

Sixteen million can't be wrong

Despite these reservations, it was a stage play that – indirectly – brought him widespread fame. Another in the "Play for Today" series, *Nuts in May* (1976), about a London couple on a camping holiday in Dorset, had marked him out as a distinctive voice, but it was *Abigail's Party* (1977) that gave him his breakthrough. Leigh had originally devised the play for the Hampstead Theatre. After its successful run there a TV slot fell vacant when another play was cancelled and Leigh was asked if he could rework *Abigail's Party*, at relatively short notice. "It was broadcast on a very wet night when there was an ITV strike, no Channel 4 and something extremely highbrow on BBC2, so 16 million people watched… I wasn't pleased with the detail because it was filmed so sloppily. Visually it was awful."

Visually awful or not, the play made a huge impact. As the monstrous hostess, Beverly, parading her pretensions, browbeating and hectoring everyone at her suburban soirée, Steadman gave a career-defining performance. Some critics hated the play; Dennis Potter famously lambasted it as "a prolonged jeer, twitching with genuine hatred, about the dreadful suburban tastes of the dreadful lower-middle

Simon Mein/Thin Man/Alain Sarde/Studio Canal/Kobal

Leigh, second left, directs Marion Bailey on location for **All or Nothing,** *watched by cinematographer Dick Pope*

classes". But *Abigail's Party* has remained the most popular of all Leigh's works, and enjoyed a successful theatrical revival in London in 2002.

From then on, Leigh's TV dramas began to attract a lot more attention and, with the advent of the Thatcher government, took on a more pronounced political flavour. Not all the attention was favourable. Accusations of "patronising" his characters and turning them into caricatures, implicit in Dennis Potter's comments, were successively levelled at *Who's Who* (1979) and *Grown-Ups* (1980), at *Home Sweet Home* (1982) and *Meantime* (1984).

Leigh has grown weary of rebutting such charges. "My work is about entertaining and giving glimpses into corners of life, confronting us with the way we live. This class prejudice stuff is facile nonsense and if you watch the films you'll realise that's not what they're about." On another occasion he remarked: "I can tell you that all my pieces are, at one level, a celebration of people in all their detail and filigree, but also about the awfulness of existence which one often talks about by sending it up."

Leigh has never wanted to work with stars, preferring lesser-known actors with the patience and dedication to engage with his demanding methods. But many of those to whom he gave early roles have since become famous, and the list includes some of the brightest talents in British acting: Gary Oldman, David Thewlis, Timothy Spall, Jane Horrocks, Brenda Blethyn, Phil Davis, Tim Roth, Frances Barber, Shirley Henderson, Jim Broadbent, Phil Daniels and the late Katrin Cartlidge. It says a lot for their regard for Leigh that so many of them are still eager to work with him, despite low budgets and long rehearsal periods, when they could be earning far more elsewhere.

Visions of Britain

In 1988, Leigh at last secured backing, partly from Channel 4, to make another feature. *High Hopes* is his anatomy of Thatcher's Britain through three couples – a pair of laid-back,

Ruth Sheen and Phil Davis in **High Hopes**

kindly hippies, Cyril and Shirley, Cyril's yuppie sister, Valerie, and her husband, and an upper-class couple living in a privatised ex-council house next door to Cyril and Valerie's confused elderly mother. Scathing, angry and very funny, the film is far from the simplistic tract some critics took it for.

Leigh's indignation is directed no less at his most likeable characters, Cyril and Shirley; well-meaning they may be, but also lazy and utterly ineffectual. Roger Ebert, hailing Leigh's return to cinema, noted how he "sees his characters and their lifestyles so vividly, so mercilessly and with such a sharp satirical edge, that the movie achieves a neat trick: we start by laughing at the others, and end by feeling uncomfortable about ourselves."

Life Is Sweet (1990) took a gentler, though still sharply observed view of suburban British life, with its tragicomic study of a comfortably married, slightly complacent couple and their contrasted twin daughters. Food provided an ongoing theme, Leigh getting particularly good comic mileage out of Timothy Spall's would-be *nouvelle cuisine* restaurateur, whose menu features, among other things, Tripe Soufflé.

He followed this with his harshest, most violent film to date. In *Naked* (1993) David Thewlis gives a stunning performance as a bitter, fiercely articulate loner, with Lesley Sharp and Katrin Cartlidge as two of the women he battens on. If Leigh's previous films seemed to embody a socialist viewpoint, this one, as he suggested in an interview, slips over into anarchy. Harsh and cheerless, shot in cold, dark tones, it wields disturbing power and was attacked in some quarters for its supposed misogyny. It won Leigh the Best Director prize at Cannes.

David Thewlis in **Naked**

Secrets & Lies (1996) did even better, picking up the Palme d'Or, three Golden Globes and five Oscar nominations among a slew of other awards. The mother (Brenda Blethyn) of a dysfunctional, quarrelsome working-class white family is contacted by a successful young black woman (Marianne Jean-Baptiste) who insists the white woman is her birth mother. Under the impact of this revelation the secrets and lies that have riddled the family start to crumble. Leigh is often described as a profoundly "English" film-maker, and so he is, but *Secrets & Lies*, with its incisive take on issues of class, race and family values, touches a universal nerve.

After so much complex intensity, *Career Girls* (1997) came as a lighter excursion. Virtually

Brenda Blethyn, left, and Marianne Jean-Baptiste in **Secrets & Lies**

a two-hander, it cuts back and forth between the college days of two young women (Katrin Cartlidge and Lynda Steadman) who once shared a London flat and their weekend reunion ten years later. The plot rather overplays its coincidences, but the bittersweet comedy is underpinned by a sense of time's disillusionment.

The very model of a costume drama

That Leigh should choose to make a period drama – about Gilbert and Sullivan, of all things – caused universal astonishment. But Leigh had been a G&S lover since being taken to their operettas as a child, and saw *Topsy-Turvy* (2000) as an opportunity to present a metaphor for the film-making process, "to swing the camera round and do a film about us, us miserable lot who go to hell and back in the cause of entertaining people". It focuses on the tensions and resentments between the irascible Gilbert and the discontented Sullivan (who, as someone once said, "wanted to be another Bach and ended up another Offenbach") when, after two flops (*Princess Ida* and *The Sorcerer*), their partnership is rescued from the brink by the creation of their greatest success, *The Mikado*.

The period reconstruction is meticulously detailed, and Leigh evidently gained huge satisfaction from recreating the mechanics of Victorian stage production. But, as he pointed out, for all the period colour, "ultimately, it's a film about people, and relationships and… all the usual things which skulk around in my films. The real things. The moments in between."

All or Nothing (2002) finds Leigh back on familiar contemporary ground in his gentlest film since *Life Is Sweet*. Set on a south London housing estate and centring round a couple (Lesley Manville and Timothy Spall) whose marriage has lost all meaning, it depicts grim lives seemingly devoid of joy or purpose. Yet, through a chance and initially disastrous event, hope returns. Leigh's love and compassion for his characters are so palpable that, at last, the weary old accusations of "patronising" and "caricaturing" could finally be shown to be way off-beam.

Leigh's compassion is overwhelming in *Vera Drake* (2004). Once again he ventures into period drama, this time to the era in which he grew up, the pinched and embarrassed 1950s. But the Drakes, the central family, though cramped and anything but well off, are happy, close and loving. Vera, the mother (a performance of astounding veracity from Imelda Staunton), is unfailingly cheerful and infinitely kind. Though working all hours as a cleaner in richer folks' homes, she's never too busy to help anyone in need, her bustling, Tiggywinklish little figure forever on the go and beaming with goodwill.

But among those she helps – entirely selflessly – are young women "in trouble", and in 1950s Britain terminating their unwanted pregnancies makes her a criminal. When disaster and the law descend, her face and whole body seem to crumple. Staunton's tear-stained face and inarticulate mumblings are heartbreaking – but so riveting that it is impossible to turn away. As in *Topsy-Turvy*, Leigh's sense of period is impeccable and scrupulously accurate – not just in the sets and props, but in the attitudes, gestures and speech patterns of his characters.

He draws equally outstanding performances from the rest of an outstanding ensemble, not least Phil Davis as her staunchly supportive husband and Eddie Marsan as her inarticulate but good-hearted prospective son-in-law.

Leigh's genius for the commonplace has never been more evident; every detail of the film rings true. Astonishingly, given the appreciation and support – and often financial backing – Leigh has long found in France, *Vera Drake* was rejected for screening at the 2004 Cannes Festival. Cannes' short-sightedness was its great rival's good fortune; the film was selected for Venice and won the Golden Lion, while Staunton picked up the Best Actress award.

With *Vera Drake*, Leigh may at last be accorded the recognition he deserves: not just as one of Britain's most fiercely independent and individualistic film-makers, with a uniquely perceptive vision of life in this country, but also one of its finest.

PHILIP KEMP is a freelance writer and historian and a regular contributor to *Sight & Sound*.

Momentum Pictures

Left to right: Alex Kelly, Daniel Mays, Imelda Staunton and Phil Davis as the Drake family in **Vera Drake**

Mike Leigh Filmography

[Feature film directing credits only]

1971
BLEAK MOMENTS
Script and Direction: ML. Photography: Bahram Manocheri. Editing: Les Blair. Music: Mike Bradwell. Production Design: Richard Rambaut. Players: Anne Raitt (Sylvia), Sarah Stephenson (Hilda), Eric Allan (Peter), Joolia Cappleman (Pat), Mike Bradwell (Norman). Produced by Les Blair. 111 mins.

1988
HIGH HOPES
Script and Direction: ML. Photography: Roger Pratt. Editing: Jon Gregory. Music: Andrew Dickson, Rachel Portman. Production Design: Diana Charnley. Players: Philip Davis (Cyril Bender), Ruth Sheen (Shirley), Edna Dore (Mrs Bender), Philip Jackson (Martin Burke), Heather Tobias (Valerie Burke). Produced by Simon Channing-Williams, Victor Glynn. 112 mins.

1990
LIFE IS SWEET
Script and Direction: ML. Photography: Dick Pope. Editing: Jon Gregory. Music: Rachel Portman. Production Design: Alison Chitty. Players: Alison Steadman (Wendy), Jim Broadbent (Andy), Claire Skinner (Natalie), Jane Horrocks (Nicola), Stephen Rea (Patsy), Timothy Spall (Aubrey). Produced by Simon Channing-Williams. 103 mins.

1993
NAKED
Script and Direction: ML. Photography: Dick Pope. Editing: Jon Gregory. Music: Andrew Dickson. Production Design: Alison Chitty. Players: David Thewlis (Johnny), Lesley Sharp (Louise), Katrin Cartlidge (Sophie), Greg Cruttwell (Jeremy), Claire Skinner (Sandra). Produced

Timothy Spall in Life Is Sweet

by Simon Channing-Williams. 131 mins.

1996
SECRETS & LIES
Script and Direction: ML. Photography: Dick Pope. Editing: Jon Gregory. Music: Andrew Dickson. Production Design: Alison Chitty. Players: Brenda Blethyn (Cynthia Rose Purley), Timothy Spall (Maurice Purley), Phyllis Logan (Monica Purley), Claire Rushbrook (Roxanne Purley), Marianne Jean-Baptiste (Hortense Cumberbatch). Produced by Simon Channing-Williams. 142 mins.

1997
CAREER GIRLS
Script and Direction: ML. Photography: Dick Pope. Editing: Robin Sales. Music: Marianne Jean-Baptiste, Tony Remy. Production Design: Eve Stewart. Players: Katrin Cartlidge (Hannah), Lynda Steadman (Annie), Kate Byers (Claire), Mark Benton (Ricky). Produced by Simon Channing-Williams. 87 mins.

2000
TOPSY-TURVY
Script and Direction: ML. Photography: Dick Pope. Editing: Robin Sales. Music: Arthur Sullivan, Jacques Offenbach, Carl Davis. Production Design: Eve

Stewart. Players: Jim Broadbent (W. S. Gilbert), Allan Corduner (Arthur Sullivan), Timothy Spall (Dickie Temple), Martin Savage (George Grossmith), Lesley Manville (Lucy Gilbert), Ron Cook (Richard D'Oyly Carte), Shirley Henderson (Leonora Braham). Produced by Simon Channing-Williams. 160 mins.

2002
ALL OR NOTHING
Script and Direction: ML. Photography: Dick Pope. Editing: Lesley Walker. Music: Andrew Dickson. Production Design: Eve Stewart. Players: Timothy Spall (Phil), Lesley Manville (Penny), Alison Garland (Rachel), James Corden (Rory). Produced by Simon Channing-Williams. 128 mins.

2004
VERA DRAKE
Script and Direction: ML. Photography: Dick Pope. Editing: Jim Clark. Music: Andrew Dickson. Production Design: Eve Stewart. Players: Imelda Staunton (Vera), Phil Davis (Stan), Richard Graham (George), Eddie Marsan (Reg), Adrian Scarborough (Frank), Heather Craney (Joyce), Sally Hawkins (Susan), Peter Wight (Det. Insp. Webster). Produced by Simon Channing-Williams. 125 mins.

Errol Morris by Eddie Cockrell

Not long into Errol Morris' fanciful yet awestruck profile of theoretical physicist Stephen Hawking, *A Brief History of Time* (1991), the great thinker's sister, Mary, tells Morris an anecdote from their London childhood. "Stephen used to reckon he knew, I think it was, 11 ways of getting into the house. I could only find 10 of them. I'm not sure where the other way was."

With the seven feature-length non-fiction films, one dramatic feature, *First Person* television programme and numerous advertising spots that he has made since 1978, Morris has pioneered a unique "other way" into the documentary form that stylises the cinéma-vérité approach without fundamentally altering its precepts. Some purists have balked at this, yet there is no denying the influence of Morris' vision on a generation of documentary film-makers and advertisers.

Morris is also one loquacious guy, telling indieWIRE in 1997 that he often thought he made films just to be able to appear at festivals and "talk after them". After ingesting these numerous and far-reaching Morris interviews (easily acquired online), one is struck most of all by the sheer restlessness and force of his intellect. "I think what really helps," he told William Phillips in 1998, "is some innate curiosity about the world and about people. But the world is properly considered something of a mystery, and it's our job, if not to solve that mystery, then at least to attempt to explore it." In exploring that mystery, Morris has talked to the serial killer and the secretary of state, the crime scene cleaner and the Holocaust denier.

The truth is out there

Morris constantly pursues what long-time friend Werner Herzog once described as the "Ecstatic Truth", the "deeper strata" of meaning that force one to "read the world differently". Morris does this by combining a patient yet enthusiastic interviewing style and a groundbreaking technique that intertwines found footage of varying texture and quality with subjects who speak directly to the camera. The most recent example of this distinctive methodology, *The Fog of War*, earned Morris not only the Best Documentary Feature Oscar that had eluded him since 1988's *The Thin Blue Line*, but a measure of popular and commercial success commensurate with the critical praise that had greeted the majority of his work.

ERROL MORRIS was born on February 5, 1948, in the Long Island, New York, town of Hewlett (just east of JFK airport). His doctor father died when Errol was two and he was raised by his mother, Cinnabelle, a Julliard graduate and public school music teacher (to this day the music fund in her name supports competitions and recitals in the Hewlett region). He was by all accounts a child prodigy on the cello, studied the instrument at Vermont's Putney School and plays to this day.

Though he claims in Kevin Macdonald's 2000 cable television biography, *A Brief History of Errol Morris*, to have been "incredibly unsuccessful at a number of schools", closer analysis proves this not to be the case. In 1969 he earned a BA in history from the University of Wisconsin (*The Fog of War* is dedicated to two of his professors there), followed by a Masters in physics from Princeton, before settling in to study philosophy at the Berkeley campus of the University of California in the early 1970s.

Throughout these early years, Morris had a keen interest in the macabre, even beginning a book on serial killers. "I'd always been fascinated with murder," he told Macdonald, "and that was sort of the beginning of this twilight world that I was in for a number of years, still hanging on as a graduate student but spending more and more time actually investigating crimes and talking to criminals." He even moved temporarily to Plainfield, Wisconsin, to interview Ed Gein, infamous as the inspiration for *Psycho* and *The Texas Chainsaw Massacre*. "He was very, very, very crazy," Morris said, "and very, very funny. I liked him." This curiosity about the dark side has been a constant theme in Morris' work.

It was back in Berkeley that the headstrong student found his true calling, thanks to the Pacific Film Archive, a full-time repertory cinema where he soon began to spend most of his time. "I'm an obsessional kind of guy," he said in *A Brief History,* "and I became obsessed with watching movies."

Inevitably, Morris started dabbling in moviemaking. "Errol at that time was not taken seriously by anyone," remembers Herzog. "He had a history of abandoned projects behind him." By way of provocation, the German film-maker promised to eat his shoe if the student every actually finished something. That something, finally finished in 1978, was *Gates of Heaven*.

Another pet's grave is prepared in **Gates of Heaven**

Dead pets' society

Inspired by a newspaper article announcing the transfer of hundreds of animal caskets from one pet cemetery to another, *Gates of Heaven*'s odd yet touching story of two clans clashing over the business of burial established Morris' style: the insular logic of its sure-handed rhythm, a keen sense of place, and interviewees speaking almost directly into the camera (Morris crouched so that his cheek touched the side of the lens as he asked questions).

This approach was considered so unusual that Morris went through four cinematographers before finding one who understood what he was trying to do. "I think there was such a strong, prevailing idea of what non-fiction should look like," he told Macdonald, "that it was really difficult for a cameraman to conceive that you could put a non-fiction film together in a different way entirely."

He told author David A. Goldsmith that *Gates of Heaven* is "a very strange film. I am very proud of it." Critic Roger Ebert, who often lectures on the film, recently wrote: "I have seen this film perhaps 30 times, and am still not anywhere near the bottom of it. All I know is, it's about a lot more than pet cemeteries." Morris finished the film and Herzog ingested his footwear, an event immortalised by documentarist Les Blank in the short *Werner Herzog Eats His Shoe* (1979).

The dark side of the sunshine state

Morris next became interested in Vernon, a small town on the Florida panhandle. Nicknamed "Nub City" by insurance investigators for its unusually high number of claims involving mutilated or severed limbs, the burg exerted such a strange force on Morris that he once again relocated to live among his subjects and the result was *Vernon, Florida* (1981).

"[Vernon's residents] literally became a fraction of themselves to become whole financially," Morris has said, with a relish evident even on the page. When the locals threatened to murder him,

Morris shifted the focus of the film to an oddball assortment of residents distinguished in their eccentricities by a strange joy in the bleak world around them. "Quite unforgettable," enthused David Ansen in *Newsweek*. "*Vernon, Florida* isn't sociology at all, it's philosophical slapstick."

Claude Register provided music and opinions in **Vernon, Florida**

After *Vernon*, Morris' funding dried up and he worked as, among other things, a detective. "I think [being a film-maker and a sleuth] have informed each other, because there's a great similarity between the two," he told online humour magazine theonion.com in 1997. "The private detective work I did, I was sort of on the high end of investigation, because I was a Wall Street investigator doing really, really huge cases. But when you clear aside all of the fancy frills about private-detective work, it really comes down to people being willing to give you information about themselves. That's the essence of it."

By 1988, this work led him to the case that would eventually become *The Thin Blue Line*. Morris had initially travelled to Texas to speak with a forensic psychiatrist, who in turn had suggested he interview people on the state's death rows. That was how he met convicted cop killer Randall Dale Adams. After some two years of research, Morris discovered that Adams was innocent and that the real killer was a hitchhiker, David Harris.

Morris takes no writing credit on his films, yet *The Thin Blue Line* illustrates perfectly how he owns and shapes his stories as skilfully as the best screenwriter. In the process, he seems to ask himself as many questions as he throws at his subjects. New to the mix in his account of the Adams case are the elaborate, formal reconstructions illustrating various versions of the shooting and Phillip Glass' hypnotic score, at once tense and serenely elegant. As Morris explained to indieWIRE in 1997: "*The Thin Blue Line* was this attempt to have my cake and eat it, too. Make a film that had journalistic content and at the same time... worked as a movie. It had movie ideas in it."

Randall Dale Adams, subject of **The Thin Blue Line**

Billed in publicity as "the first movie mystery to actually solve a murder", *The Thin Blue Line* was voted the best film of 1988 by more than 250 critics polled by *The Washington Post*, and in 2001 was added to the National Film Registry of the Library of Congress.

Stranger than non-fiction?

In 1989, Morris received a MacArthur Fellowship and established a production company, Fourth Floor. He also began applying his evolving style to television commercials, first for a ubiquitous chain of convenience stores, then for an expanding list of clients that took in an American beer, airline, athletic shoe maker, credit card, television network (that one earned him an

Emmy in 2001), bank and Apple Computers. This work had immediate benefits. "They're very lucrative and they can be done relatively quickly and it leaves me time to do other things," he said in 2003.

The spots also helped him continue to discover the power of his distinctive voice and, perhaps emboldened by his new creative outlet, Morris in 1991 undertook his first and to date only fiction film, an adaptation of Tony Hillerman's novel *The Dark Wind*, a complicated tale of murder and drug smuggling on an Arizona Indian reservation. It was not a positive experience.

"I wasn't really allowed to direct or edit it," he told theonion.com. "It's a very weird experience to work on a movie where you have no control, really, over the outcome. That was a singular experience... and something that I would really never like to repeat." Nevertheless, seen today, *The Dark Wind* is an intermittently atmospheric and entirely competent police procedural, craftily played and punctuated by bits of jet-black humour – and some lovingly detailed corpses. You see at once what drew Morris to the material.

In 1992, Morris' long-gestating *A Brief History of Time* was released. An admiring meditation on wheelchair-bound physicist Stephen Hawking's life and work (as well as Morris' first non-fiction effort to be more or less "about" a single person), the film's numerous awards include the Grand Jury Prize at Sundance. Until *The Fog of War*, it was his most commercially successful project.

Perhaps his most whimsical work, *Fast, Cheap & Out of Control* (1997) weaves the peculiar obsessions of four seemingly unconnected men – a lion-tamer, a topiary gardener, a robotics scientist and a mole-rat specialist – into a fanciful celebration of life and work. "I liked the fact that the stories would form a kind of chronology from past to future," he noted in his theonion.com interview. "So that was part of selecting the material: that I had something going from a version of the Garden of Eden through to the far-distant future."

Stephen Hawking with Morris in **A Brief History of Time**

Once again, music helps stitch together Morris' internal logic; the invigorating and achingly beautiful score is by Caleb Sampson (whose keyboards contributed immensely to the three-piece Alloy Orchestra who had breathed new life into a number of classic silent films). *Fast, Cheap* also marked the first use of Morris' technological breakthrough, the Interrotron. So named by his wife, art historian Julia Sheehan – reportedly because it incorporated the words "interview" and "terror" – the device (patent pending) is like a visual TelePrompter, allowing a two-way audio and visual communication between Morris and his subjects via a monitor that shows the film-maker, mounted directly over the lens; interviewees talk directly to Morris and the camera.

One of the subjects of **Fast, Cheap & Out of Control**

Morris later wrote of *Fog of War* subject Robert McNamara's response to the contraption: "'What is that?' I smiled and said, 'The Interrotron.' He said, 'Well, whatever it is, I don't like it.' But then he sat down, and we proceeded to record over 20 hours of interviews. I guess he came to like it, too."

Singular visions

In 1998, Morris used the Interrotron to make a half-hour profile of an autistic woman, Temple Grandin, who utilised her empathy with livestock to design slaughterhouses (the film was dedicated to Caleb Sampson, who died in mid-1998; Morris, who had enjoyed playing chamber music with his composer friend, called the loss "incalculable"). This short grew into *First Person*, two charmingly eccentric and prodigiously imaginative series of half-hours (save for two hour-long editions) broadcast on the Bravo and IFC channels in the US, which profiled people who are the living embodiments of life's curious mysteries.

While each of the 17 episodes is never less than fascinating – taken sequentially you can almost see Morris tinkering with his style – the best involve affable people in extraordinary positions: the immensely likeable Joan Dougherty talks about how she became a crime scene cleaner; modest pilot Denny Fitch explains how he piloted a disabled airliner and 296 passengers to a fiery yet miraculous Iowa City landing.

The *First Person* experience seems to have energised Morris, both creatively and practically (he expanded the Interrotron into a multi-camera set-up, swiftly dubbed the Megatron). "Technology is making it possible to use all kinds of media," he told an interviewer at the 1998 Toronto Film Festival. "Playing with these differences can become a big part of putting a movie together." Morris was in Toronto to publicise his newest film, *Mr. Death: The Rise and Fall of Fred A. Leuchter, Jr.*

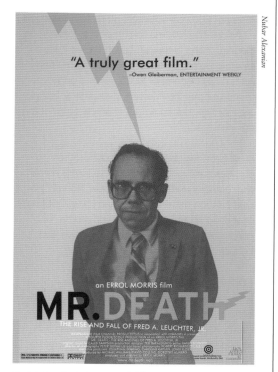

Fred A. Leuchter's, Jr.'s rise and fall is traced in **Mr. Death**

By some accounts one of the subjects originally considered for inclusion in *Fast, Cheap & Out of Control*, Leuchter's back story was right up Morris' alley: the odd little man kind of fell into the manufacturing of execution equipment and was thus exploited by prominent Holocaust deniers into "disproving" the use of poison gas at Auschwitz.

Morris, who completed *Mr. Death* during the *First Person* gestation period, told indieWIRE that the attention-craving Leuchter's story possessed the three essential ingredients of his films: "Sick, sad and funny… I think there's something about [Leuchter's spooky] smile that captures this idea that Fred doesn't quite get it, that he doesn't understand what he's saying."

Affairs of State

One of the subjects Morris had invited to be interviewed for *First Person* was Robert S. McNamara, Secretary of State under Presidents Kennedy and Johnson. Eighty-five when Morris interviewed him and initially agreeing only to promote his conflicted memoir, *In Retrospect*, McNamara ended up spending 20 hours in front of the Interrotron. Morris subsequently uncovered audio tapes revealing that, in contrast to his hawkish reputation, McNamara actually attempted to discourage his presidents from engaging in and escalating the Vietnam war. Thus *The Fog of War* was born.

"For me," Morris told interviewer Brad Schreiber, "the meaning of [McNamara's] story is that when you have a predisposition to see something, you can ignore endless evidence to the contrary. You can even imagine confirming evidence. That's the worst of it. It was in service of this theme, believing is seeing, which as we all know has currency for our particular time in history, because regardless of whether this [occupation of Iraq] is a replay of Vietnam or something very different, there are identifiable themes here. And they relate to many of the things that McNamara is saying."

Robert McNamara in **The Fog of War**

In December 2003, Morris told interviewer Richard Sharp: "Anything that I can do to assure that Bush is not re-elected will make me very happy." When he won his long-coveted Best Documentary Oscar for *The Fog of War* in 2004 (12 months after he had used the Interrotron to create a charming montage of first-person odes to the movies for the Academy Awards broadcast), he brought politics front and centre, concluding his acceptance speech as follows: "Forty years ago this country went down a rabbit hole in Vietnam and millions died. I fear we're going down a rabbit hole once again. And if people can stop and think and reflect on some of the ideas and issues in this movie, perhaps I've done some damn good here."

Later in 2004, in collaboration with the MoveOn PAC (Public Action Committee), Morris interviewed 41 average Americans who were changing their allegiance from George W. Bush to John Kerry. "I'm still a Baptist, but I'm no longer a Republican," claims Shreveport resident Rhonda Nix with a tart practicality that typifies the project. The resulting 30-second television spot, "Real People", ran during the Republican National Convention in August.

There were some notable postscripts to Morris' earlier work in 2004. Stephen Hawking revamped his theory of black holes, and David Harris – one of the very few subjects with whom Morris remained in contact over the years – was finally put to death for a murder he committed during Morris' research for *The Thin Blue Line*. "Harris has always for me remained an enigma," he told Wisconsin Public Radio in July 2004. "I wish I could say that I had some simple explanation for his behaviour."

The future's wide open

Morris lives with Sheehan in Cambridge, Massachusetts. They have a son, Hamilton. The film-maker's base of operations for his Globe Department Store production company is the building of the same name that he bought in 1999, and he has recently revamped his dryly funny website, errolmorris.com. At press time, MGM Home Entertainment was preparing DVD debut releases of *Gates of Heaven*, *Vernon, Florida* and *The Thin Blue Line* (all long out of print on home video). Oddly for a man of so many words, Morris had no plans to record commentary tracks (nor do any appear on the DVDs already available).

Morris has talked of tackling another fiction film (this time on his own terms), describing his *Boots* project as "a dog-trial movie" and alluding to an untitled project – based, perhaps inevitably, on a true story – about an Iowa man whose compulsive theft of books created a private library of 200,000 volumes, stored in a rundown mansion. The film-maker's hope, he told theonion.com, is that any such project "will be as idiosyncratic or as iconoclastic as my non-fiction". By December 2003, he had admitted to at least one interviewer: "I've already started another film, but so as not to jinx it, I try not to talk about it."

Mary Hawking, guessing that her brother Stephen's eleventh route into the family home was a nearly unreachable window, noted: "He was a much better climber than I was." Eternally obsessed and doggedly curious, Morris continues his fine climb towards elusive and Ecstatic Truth.

EDDIE COCKRELL (eddie@nitrateonline.com) is a Maryland-based film critic and programming consultant who reviews for *Variety* from the Berlin, Karlovy Vary and Toronto festivals. His writing has also appeared in *The Washington Post* and on the Nitrate Online and indieWIRE websites.

Thanks to Ann Petrone at The Globe Department Store for invaluable research assistance. Unless otherwise credited, all pictures appear courtesy of Globe Department Store.

Errol Morris Filmography

[Feature film directing credits only]

1978
GATES OF HEAVEN
Direction, Editing: EM. Photography: Ned Burgess. Supervising Editor: Charles Laurence Silver. Contributing Editor: Suzanne Fenn. Associate Editor: Brad Fuller. Assistant Editor: George Csicsery. Additional Photography: Dyanna Taylor. Music: Dan Harberts. Featuring: Lucille Billingsley, Zella Graham, Cal Harberts, Dan Harberts, Phil Harberts, Scottie Harberts, Mike Koewler, Floyd McClure, Ed Quye, Florence Rasmussen. Produced by EM for Gates of Heaven Films. 85 mins.

1981
VERNON, FLORIDA
Direction: EM. Photography: Ned Burgess. Editing: Brad Fuller. Assistant Editor: Robin Katz. Music: Claude Register. With: Albert Bitterling, Claude Register, Snake Reynolds, Henry Shipes. Produced by EM for the Television Laboratory at WNET/THIRTEEN, ZDF and Errol Morris Films, Inc. 56 mins.

1988
THE THIN BLUE LINE
Direction: EM. Photography: Stefan Czapsky, Robert Chappell. Editing: Paul Barnes. Music: Philip Glass. Featuring: Randall Adams, David Harris, Gus Rose, Jackie Johnson, Marshall Touchton, Dale Holt, Sam Kittrell, Hootie Nelson, Dennis Johnson, Floyd Jackson, Edith James, Dennis White, Don Metcalfe, Emily Miller, R.L. Miller, Elisa Carr, Michael Randell, Melvyn Carson Bruder. Re-Enactment Players: Adam Goldfine (Randall Adams), Derek Horton (David Harris), Ron Thornhill (Robert Wood), Marianne Leone (Teresa Turko), Amanda Caprio (Popcorn Lady), Michael Nicoll (Interrogation

Officer), Michael Cirilla (2nd Interrogation Officer), Phyllis Rodgers (Stenographer). An American Playhouse presentation, produced by Mark Lipson for Third Floor Productions, in association with American Playhouse, Public Television Stations, The Corporation for Public Broadcasting, The National Endowment for the Arts, The Chubb Group of Insurance Companies, Channel 4, The Program Development Company. 101 mins.

1991
THE DARK WIND
Script: Neal Jimenez, Eric Bergren, from the novel by Tony Hillerman. Direction: EM. Photography: Stefan Czapsky. Editing: Freeman Davies. Music: Michael Colombier. Players: Lou Diamond Phillips (Officer Jim Chee), Gary Farmer (Cowboy Albert Dashee), Fred Ward (Lt. Joe Leaphorn), Guy Boyd (Agent Johnson), John Karlen (Jake West), Lance Baker (Mr. Archer), Betty C. Barlow (Old Navajo Woman #2), Gary Basaraba (Larry), Billy Beck (Motel Clerk), Arlene Bowman (Edna Nezzie), Charlie Carpenter (Pilot), Blake Clark (Ben Gaines), James Koots (Taylor), Jane Loranger (Gail Pauling), Loren Nahsonhoya (Danny), Ivory Ocean (Curtiss), Timothy Glenn Riley (Man #1), Eugene Sekaquaptewa (Elderly Hopi Man). Produced by Patrick Markey for Seven Arts Productions, North Face Motion Picture Company (released in 1994 by Carolco). 111 mins.

1992
A BRIEF HISTORY OF TIME
Direction: EM, from the book by Stephen Hawking. Photography: John Bailey, Stefan Czapsky. Editing: Brad Fuller. Music: Philip Glass. Featuring: Stephen Hawking, Isobel Hawking, Janet Humphrey, Mary Hawking, Basil King, Derek Powney, Norman Dix, Robert Berman, Gordon

Berry, Roger Penrose, Dennis Sciama, John Wheeler, Brandon Carter, John Taylor, Kip Thorne, Don Page, Christopher Isham, Brian Whitt, Ramond LaFlamme. Produced by Anglia Television, David Hickman, in association with NBC, Tokyo Broadcasting Systems, Channel Four Films (Film Four International/Channel 4 TV), Anglia Television Ltd. 84 mins.

1997
FAST, CHEAP & OUT OF CONTROL
Direction: EM. Photography: Robert Richardson. Editing: Karen Schmeer, Shondra Merrill. Music: Caleb Sampson. Featuring: Dave Hoover, George Mendonca, Ray Mendez, Rodney Brooks. Produced by EM for American Playhouse Theatrical films, in association with Fourth Floor Productions, Inc. 82 mins.

1999
MR. DEATH: THE RISE AND FALL OF FRED A. LEUCHTER, JR.
Direction: EM. Photography: Peter Donahue, Robert Richardson. Editing: Karen Schmeer. Music: Caleb Sampson. Featuring: Fred A. Leuchter, Jr., Robert Jan Van Pelt, David Irving, James Roth, Shelly Shapiro, Suzanne Tabasky, Ernst Zundel. Produced by Michael Williams, David Collins, Dorothy Aufiero for Fourth Floor Productions, Scout Productions. 91 mins.

2003
THE FOG OF WAR: ELEVEN LESSONS FROM THE LIFE OF ROBERT S. MCNAMARA
Direction: EM. Photography: Peter Donahue, Bob Chappell. Editing: Karen Schmeer, Doug Abel, Chyld King. Music: Philip Glass. Featuring: Robert S. McNamara. Produced by EM, Michael Williams, Julie Ahlberg for @radical.media, Senart Films Productions, in association with Globe Department Store. 105 mins.

Alexander Payne by Eddie Cockrell

Claudette Barius/New Line/Avery Pix/Kobal

Writing from the 1996 Sundance festival, Todd McCarthy, *Variety's* Chief Film Critic, praised the unheralded *Precious* as "a rare social satire that takes effective shots at both sides in the abortion battle" and "the closest thing to a Preston Sturges film to have come along in a while". The film, which subsequently saw spotty US release under the title *Citizen Ruth*, was the feature-length directorial debut of Nebraska-born Alexander Payne, then just short of his thirty-fifth birthday. Eight years later, McCarthy cogently summed up the critical response to the world premiere of *Sideways* at the Toronto Film Festival in September 2004 by proclaiming: "Alexander Payne has single-handedly restored humanism as a force in American films."

A proponent of finely drawn studies of true-to-life characters, filmed amongst real people on authentic locations (three of his first four features were shot in and around his mid-western hometown, Omaha), Payne has progressed from late-blooming auteur to critics' favourite, Oscar nominee and arthouse force. It is a story of study, tenacity and vision. These character-driven movies, three of them adapted with long-time writing partner Jim Taylor from other writers' novels, are satirical without being caustic, strong-willed without being partisan or judgmental.

This springs from the duo's love of complex, frequently unsympathetic characters who are, more often than not, their own worst enemies: Laura Dern's fume-huffing mother-to-be, Ruth Stoops, in the abortion debate burlesque *Citizen Ruth* (1996); Matthew Broderick's idealistic yet all-too-human high-school teacher, Jim McAllister, in the socio-political microcosm *Election* (1999); Jack Nicholson's emotionally numb, socially inept widower, Warren Schmidt, in the bittersweet retirement odyssey *About Schmidt* (2002); Paul Giamatti's tighly wrapped yet comically vulnerable oenophile, Miles Raymond, in the keenly perceptive and immensely funny road movie *Sideways* (2004).

That two of these films have their lead character's names in their titles says a lot about Payne's interests as a film-maker. "I just want the [films] to be real and human," he told *Screenwriter* magazine, explaining his desire to emulate the approach of Italian cinema of the 1960s and American movies of the 1970s – his two favourite periods in narrative film. This dovetails nicely with Payne's felicitous talent for directing actors, resulting in films that capture the essence of their times and milieus, while imparting greater truths about the human condition.

ALEXANDER PAYNE was born on February 10, 1961, in Omaha, Nebraska, to Greek parents who, at some point, changed their last name from Papadopoulos. His mother had been a professor and his father ran a restaurant ("We're Greek, [running a restaurant] is the law," Payne joked to the *New Jersey Star-Ledger* while promoting *Sideways*). Payne attended the strict Jesuit high school Creighton Prep, and took a BA in History and Spanish Literature from Stanford University.

Though some sources say that Payne became interested in movies at the age of six, when his father received an 8mm camera, it was not until the early 1980s that cinema began to figure as a career choice. "I told my parents I wanted to be a director," he recalled in the *Star-Ledger* interview. "To which my father said, 'I didn't send you to Stanford to be a waiter.' They pressured me very hard, and although I applied to five film schools I also took the LSATs [Law School Admission Test]. Right until I was 30, 32, my father was offering to pay for law school."

He entered the University of California Los Angeles' graduate film programme in 1984. "It's hard to say that there are any great American movies in the 1980s," he told the web's Film Freak Central in 2003. "I was able to watch older films on nitrate prints that the [UCLA] archive had. Even now, four out of five films I see are old films. Why see new films, new American films, y'know? I always keep up with Iranian films and anything Zhang Yimou does." The 1980s were apparently not a complete wash, as Payne cites William Friedkin's *To Live and Die in L.A.* and Milos Forman's *Amadeus* as "worthwhile".

Passion pays

By 1989, Payne had completed his 49-minute graduation work, *The Passion of Martin*, starring Charley Hayward as an alienated photographer and Lisa Zane as the admirer of his work for whom he tumbles. It "was sort of a loose adaptation of an Argentine novel by Ernesto Sabato, *El Tunel*," Payne told Film Freak Central. "He was to Argentine letters what Camus' *The Stranger* was to French existentialism. Kind of this terse, kind of hilarious, stark, post-war, slim novel." The film's sure hand got it and Payne noticed at the 1991 Sundance festival (perhaps aided by the director's Los Angeles address and phone number as the print source in the festival catalogue), and he soon landed a scriptwriting deal with Universal Pictures, but was stymied by Hollywood contradictions.

"What happens to people like me," he told Stanford's alumni magazine, "is you do a film that attracts the attention of Hollywood, and they say, 'Wow, we love the film you made – it's so new and different! What do you want to do next?' Then you give them a script, and they say, 'Uh, nope, this is just too new and different.'" Among the scripts Payne worked on during this period was *The Coward*, the story of a man on the threshold of retirement. Universal did not like that one, either, so he left the studio after a year.

Around this time Payne met and befriended Jim Taylor. A native of Bellevue, Washington (just east of Seattle), Taylor turned a childhood enthusiasm

Payne, right, directs Jack Nicholson in the wedding sequence from **About Schmidt**

for acting into a lifelong interest in films. "Fellini or Kurosawa or whatever was at [Seattle's venerable arthouse] the Harvard Exit," he told the *Seattle Post-Intelligencer* in 2003. "It thrilled me."

After graduating from California's Pomona College in 1984, Taylor met Czech director Ivan Passer while working as a receptionist at Cannon Films in Los Angeles. A fan of the films Passer had written for Forman during the Czech New Wave of the 1960s (including *Loves of a Blonde* and *The Firemen's Ball*), Taylor worked with him for three years. "We had been working without pay for a long time so that I could no longer afford my apartment," Taylor recalled to the *Post-Intelligencer*. "Alexander was an acquaintance and we ended up being roommates. We wrote some short films together and then we wrote *Citizen Ruth*."

Everybody's got to start somewhere…

These early short films were made for what Payne calls "a low-rent TV show" (the cable TV anthology *Inside Out*, which billed itself as "erotic tales of the unexpected") and also marked the pair's first collaborations with Scotland-born composer Rolf Kent and production designer Jane Ann Stewart, who went on to repeat those roles on Payne's features. These little-seen but memorable shorts shed a good deal of light on this gifted quartet's formative years.

The first, *My Secret Moments*, marks the initial shared screenplay credit of Payne & Taylor (linked by the ampersand that they have used on their subsequent credits) and is a dead-on spoof of the genre, a five-minute, soft-core, masturbatory fantasy seemingly inspired by the stateroom scene in the Marx Brothers' *A Night at the Opera*. As she pleasures herself, a woman (Chana Jael Chiesa) is visited by a series of "secret lovers", from a pair of African Americans to matching Native American Aleutian Islanders, her den mother, various businessmen and even her junior high-school principal. In post-orgasmic slumber, she snores loudly.

The second, *The Houseguest*, from a bizarre script by Ken Rudman, is rendered stunningly poignant by Payne's remarkable way with his two leads. Marilyn Hassett, star of *The Other Side of the Mountain* (1975), plays a Los Angeles career woman who nearly runs down her former fiancé (James Staskel), now a raving and obviously disturbed vagrant. Frantically reminiscing about their time together, she takes him home, cleans him up and beds him, before he staggers back into the city, still mumbling to himself.

Right to laugh issues

About the time the pair finished the first draft of *Citizen Ruth*, Taylor, "30 and deeply in debt", applied to New York University's film school. "I financed it by going on *Wheel of Fortune*. I won a speedboat and sold it. That's how I was able to go to NYU. *Citizen Ruth* was made while I was in my last year there, which was a pretty nice transition."

Citizen Ruth is a decidedly satirical yet deftly balanced look at both sides of the combustible abortion issue. Laura Dern gives a crafty, ambivalent performance as the very irresponsible and very pregnant Ruth Stoops, pulled on one side by conservative couple Norm and Gail Stoney (Kurtwood Smith, Mary Kay Place) and on the other by right-to-life activists Diane Sieglar (Swoosie Kurtz) and her lover, Rachel (Kelly Preston).

Left to right: Kelly Preston, Laura Dern and Swoosie Kurtz in **Citizen Ruth**

Miramax Films

The film has cartoonish elements, particularly in the lifestyle and close-ups of the conservative element. But the script spoofs each side of the debate with equal relish; though barely released in the US (it went through no fewer than four titles), the obvious affection shown by Dern, Payne, Taylor and Stewart in their commentary on the Region 1 DVD reflects the esteem in which the film is held by those who have managed to see it.

"The movie is both really different from the book but quite similar at the same time," Payne told *Screenwriter* magazine, describing *Election*, his second feature and the first of the Payne/Taylor adaptations (though Tom Perotta's novel had yet to see print when Payne read it). With its circular imagery and running visual gag of trash and garbage (Payne articulates this with obvious pride on his easygoing DVD commentary), *Election* sets their career-to-date template for at once pruning and deepening their source material.

In fact, the high-school-set skullduggery of the film – teacher Matthew Broderick locks horns with ambitious student Reese Witherspoon (in her first important role) – represents their most faithful adaptation so far, especially startling when the book reveals itself as a tag-team sequence of first-person accounts by the main characters. *Election* won Independent Spirit awards for film, director and screenplay, while the script was also nominated for an Academy Award.

Matthew Broderick and Reese Witherspoon in **Election**

Following *Citizen Ruth*, Taylor decided to stay in Manhattan, while Payne had already relocated to Los Angeles. To this day the writers refuse to collaborate long-distance and get together on one coast or the other for the "eight or nine months" Payne says it takes to complete each script. Their preferred writing method? Two daisy-chained USB keyboards hooked up to the same computer.

This supremely compatible pair are also known as largely anonymous script doctors. According to one report, they worked on Jay Roach's *Meet the Parents* (2000) and in 2001 took their sole writing credit to date on another director's film, Joe Johnston's *Jurassic Park III*. Though they tried to mix elements of *King Kong* and *The Wages of Fear* their script was largely abandoned. "It was a job," Payne told website FFC. "Four weeks, a nice pay cheque, seemed like a good challenge… We did enough structural changes that we got credit on it, which is good because you get residuals." One would hope the remaining subversive flashes of wit in the dinosaur sequel's shooting script might be traced at least in part to Payne and Taylor's jettisoned draft.

Hit the road, with Jack

Changing what little of Louis Begley's novel *About Schmidt* they did not excise completely, Payne and Taylor wove elements of the former's decade-old script, *The Coward*, into the story of a newly retired insurance company actuary who, after the sudden death of his wife, drives a motor home from Omaha to Denver with a vague notion of preventing his long-neglected daughter from marrying a young man of whom he disapproves. Dominated by Jack Nicholson's very presence and disarmingly low-key performance, *About Schmidt* subsumes the surface humour of *Citizen Ruth* and *Election* in favour of a more organic approach to the marbling of dramatic elements with dry wit.

There were Golden Globe awards for Nicholson and the script, and Nicholson and Kathy Bates (whose fearless nude scene in a backyard hot tub marks a more graceful approach to the piquant sexual element of Payne's work) earned Oscar nominations. Around the time of the Oscars ceremony where both actors missed out on statuettes, Payne told an audience gathered at the Museum of Modern Art, New York, for a career-to-date tribute: "I'm anxious to move out of Omaha." In order to travel forwards, he went *Sideways*.

A daze of wine and noses

For the first time in his career, Payne had the smarts and the clout on *Sideways* to control the casting process (*Election* had been delayed while Tom Cruise considered the Broderick role). Though stars such as George Clooney and Edward Norton expressed interest in Rex Pickett's yet-to-be-published novel about two former college roommates who go on a week-long wine-tasting trip before the wedding of one of them, Payne resisted these pressures and cast *American Splendor* lead Paul Giamatti as Miles, the frustrated novelist and soon-to-be best man, and former TV series star Thomas Haden Church as the priapic groom, Jack.

Add to the mix former B-movie actress Virginia Madsen as the wine country waitress Miles falls for, and Canadian mainstay Sandra Oh (whom Payne had married on New Year's Day 2003) as the winery assistant who has a passionate fling with Jack, and it is the four principal characters in *Sideways*, combined with a palpably 1970s visual scheme, that give the film a warmth and wit that seemed certain to be recognised by Oscar and Golden Globe voters.

When not directing or writing, Payne stays active across a wide spectrum of movie-related activities. He recently interviewed Francis Ford Coppola for the well-received documentary *A Decade Under the Influence* and has filmed a weird but informative introduction to Koch-Lorber's Region 1 DVD of *La Dolce Vita*. He wrote an impassioned treatise on the changing face of American independent film for a *Variety* supplement in September 2004 and retains a fondness for academia that manifests itself in lecturing, teaching and seminar participation. Payne served as an executive producer on close friend Niels Mueller's *The Assassination of Richard Nixon* and also has a credit on Fernando Meirelles' Brazilian powerhouse *City of God*, after working with screenwriter Braulio Mantovani at a Sundance lab in Brazil.

Taylor, having directed three well-received short films since 1995, hopes to direct one of his many solo feature-length scripts, which Payne describes as a comedy about Civil War re-enactors. At press time, the pair were about to embark on another original script, reportedly titled *Nebraska*.

"I am glad that some people think [*Sideways*] is my best film, because I aspire to keep getting better," Payne told the *Star-Ledger*. "But I have pretty high standards, and there's so much to know. I intend to keep learning. Guys like Antonioni and Billy Wilder and Buñuel didn't hit their stride until pretty late in life. So I'm hopeful. I'm hoping that maybe by the time I'm in my fifties I can make a good film."

Alexander Payne Filmography

[Feature film directing credits only]

1996
CITIZEN RUTH
(aka **THE DEVIL INSIDE,**
aka **MEET RUTH STOOPS,**
aka **PRECIOUS**)
Script: AP, Jim Taylor. Direction: AP. Photography: James Glennon. Editing: Kevin Tent. Production

Design: Jane Ann Stewart. Players: Laura Dern (Ruth Stoops), *Swoosie Kurtz* (Diane Sieglar), *Kurtwood Smith* (Norm Stoney), *Mary Kay Place* (Gail Stoney), *Kelly Preston* (Rachel), *M.C. Gainey* (Harlan), *Kenneth Mars* (Dr Charlie Rollins), *David Graf* (Judge Richter), *Kathleen Noone* (Nurse Pat), *Tippi Hedren* (Jessica Weiss), *Burt Reynolds* (Blaine Gibbons), *Lance Rome* (Ruth's Lover), *Jim Kalal* (Tony

Stoops), *Shea Degan* (Arresting Officer), *Marilyn Tipp* (Kathleen), *Lois Nemec* (Sandy), *Sebastian Anzaldo III* (Matthew Stoney), *Alicia Witt* (Cheryl Stoney), *Okley Gibbs* (Norm's Manager), *Roberta Larson* (Briana), *Pam Carter* (Fran), *Steven Wheeldon* (Kirk), *Susan Stern* (Cindy Lindstrom), *Caveh Zahedi* (Peter), *Dennis Grant* (Don Mattox), *Will Jamieson* (Surveillance Guy), *Jeremy Sczepaniak* (Eric), *Delaney*

Driscoll (Ruth's "Sister"), *Judith Hart* (Sarah Schneider), *Katrina Christensen, John Bell* (Ruth's Kids). *Produced by Cary Woods, Cathy Konrad for Independent Pictures. 106 mins.*

1999
ELECTION
Script: AP & Jim Taylor, from the novel by Tom Perrotta. Direction: AP. Photography: James Glennon. Editing: Kevin Tent. Production Design: Jane Ann Stewart. Players: Matthew Broderick (Jim McAllister), *Reese Witherspoon* (Tracy Flick), *Chris Klein* (Paul Metzler), *Phil Reeves* (Walt Hendricks), *Mark Harelik* (Dave Novotny), *Delaney Driscoll* (Linda Novotny), *Molly Hagan* (Diane McAllister), *Colleen Camp* (Judith R. Flick), *Jessica Campbell* (Tammy Metzler), *Franki Ingrassia* (Lisa Flanagan), *Holmes Osborne* (Dick Metzler), *Jeanine Jackson* (Jo Metzler), *Loren Nelson* (Custodian), *David Wenzel* (Tracy's friend Eric), *Joel Parks* (Jerry Slavin), *Matt Malloy* (Vice-principal Ron Bell), *Larry Kaiser* (Chemistry Teacher), *Nick D'Agosto* (Larry Fouch). *Produced by Albert Berger, Ron Yerxa, David Gale, Keith Samples*

for MTV Films, in association with Bona Fide Productions. 104 mins.

2002
ABOUT SCHMIDT
Script: AP & Jim Taylor, from the novel by Louis Begley. Direction: AP. Photography: James Glennon. Editing: Kevin Tent. Production Design: Jane Ann Stewart. Players: Jack Nicholson (Warren Schmidt), *Kathy Bates* (Roberta Hertzel), *Hope Davis* (Jeannie Schmidt), *Dermot Mulroney* (Randall Hertzel), *June Squibb* (Helen Schmidt), *Howard Hesseman* (Larry Hertzel), *Harry Groener* (John Rusk), *Connie Ray* (Vicki Rusk), *Len Cariou* (Ray Nichols), *Mark Venhuizen* (Duncan Hertzel), *Cheryl Hamada* (Saundra), *Phil Reeves* (Minister in Denver), *Matt Winston* (Gary Nordin (Warren's Replacement), *James Michael Connor* (Randall's Best Man), *Marilyn Tipp* (Neighbour Lady), *Reverend Robert Kem* (Priest in Omaha), *Thomas Michael Belford* (Funeral Director), *McKenna Gibson* (Six-year-old Jeannie), *Stephanie Curtis* (Twelve-year-old Jeannie). *Produced by Harry Gittes, Michael Besman for New Line Productions.*

2004
SIDEWAYS
Script: AP & Jim Taylor, from the novel by Rex Pickett. Direction: AP. Photography: Phedon Papamichael. Editing: Kevin Tent. Production Design: Jane Ann Stewart. Players: Paul Giamatti (Miles), *Thomas Haden Church* (Jack), *Virginia Madsen* (Maya), *Sandra Oh* (Stephanie), *Marylouise Burke* (Miles' Mother), *Jessica Hecht* (Victoria), *Missy Doty* (Cammi), *MC Gainey* (Cammi's Husband), *Alysia Reiner* (Christine Erganian), *Shake Toukhmanian* (Mrs. Erganian), *Duke Moosekian* (Mike Erganian), *Robert Covarrubias* (Miles' Building Manager), *Patrick Gallagher* (Gary the Bartender), *Stephanie Faracy* (Stephanie's Mother), *Joe Marinelli* (Frass Canyon Pourer), *Chris Burroughs* (Chris at Sanford), *Toni Howard* (Evelyn Berman-Silverman), *Lee Brooks* (Ken Cortland), *Peter Dennis* (Leslie Brough), *Alison Herson* (Foxen Winery Pourer), *Phil Reeves* (Vacationing Dr. Walt Hendricks), *Lacey Rae* (Los Olivos Waitress), *Natalie Carter* (Siena). *Produced by Michael London for Sideways Productions. 126 mins.*

Merie W. Wallace/Fox Searchlight/Kobal

Paul Giamatti, left, and Thomas Haden Church in **Sideways**

Petr Zelenka by Eddie Cockrell

Negativ Film Productions

" It's our business how we choose to live, not that we have much choice," a leading character reflects near the end of Czech director Petr Zelenka's eccentric, compassionate new romantic comedy, *Wrong Side Up*. "But we mustn't become strangers." This sentiment summarises the practical yet unflaggingly humanistic world view of a film-maker whose four fun-loving features to date have been odes to eccentric humanism and the inspirational power of the rock'n'roll backbeat – both of which justify the distinctive screen credit that reflects his repeated use of the same key technicians and many of the same actors: "A Film by Petr Zelenka and His Friends."

Zelenka has been a key personality in his country's cinema for a decade. His first film, *Mnaga – Happy End*, is the reality-bending saga of a manufactured rock band, starring real Czech musicians, and remains his favourite work. His sophomore effort, the worldwide fest favourite *Buttoners*, is a breezily intricate, off-the-wall and profoundly funny meditation on cosmic coincidence and millennial malaise. The third, *Year of the Devil*, returns to the whimsical template of his debut, while spotlighting one of

his country's most popular musical outfits. And the keenly anticipated *Wrong Side Up*, adapted from his award-winning first stage play, cannonballs into the treacherous yet bracing waters of interpersonal relationships with confidence and mischievous wit.

These award-winning films share a sense of exuberant eccentricity, and the idea that only through role-playing and the adventure of life experience can we perceive more of who we are and our place in an unpredictable, uncontrollable world. Of course, when caught up in the howling winds of chance and change, it helps to have a strong backbeat, so music is the anchoring life force of Zelenka's world.

Like parents, like son

PETR ZELENKA was born on August 21, 1967 in Prague. Screenwriting was apparently embedded in his genes. Dad Otto wrote for the stage and pioneered the long-form series on Czech TV; Mum Bohumila Zelenkova was a dramaturg for Czech TV for three decades and counts among her screen credits the cherished Czech fairytale *Three Wishes for Cinderella*. Husband and wife co-wrote a series of original TV dramas, *Asking Myself*.

Zelenka recalls being galvanised by music at an early age. "I forced my father to record music from [a] television series on an old two-reel tape recorder," he told a Czech radio station. "I must have been like six years of age or something… Somehow this connection of music and film, or pictures and music, was probably very important."

From 1986 to 1991, he studied scriptwriting at Prague's legendary Film Academy of Performing Arts (FAMU), choosing this discipline because his parents were "such a good example". Among his classmates was Jan Hrebejk (best known internationally for *Divided We Fall* and chosen as a Director of the Year in *IFG 2004*), for whom Zelenka wrote three student shorts: *Everything You Always Wanted to Know About Sex and Are Afraid to Experience* (1988), *Year 1948* (1991) and *Don't Do Anything Unless You Have a Good Reason* (1991).

In 1990-91, Zelenka spent nine months as a script editor for Barrandov Film Studios and the BBC on the 50-minute programme *Czech Mate*. During this period he wrote the original screenplays *Witness* and *Pack of Honour*, adapted short stories by Michael Frayn into *The Two of Us* and made his directing debut with a television film, *Hanging Chateau 1982–2007* (1993), all for Czech TV. Though he is dismissive of this early work, the sheer inventiveness and narrative control Zelenka exhibits in the concept and structure of the hour-long *Mnaga – Happy End* (1996) speak of a man who as a student and in his first professional forays had worked hard at his craft.

Anything Rob Reiner can do…

Zelenka deliberately modelled *Mnaga* on Rob Reiner's *This Is Spinal Tap*, using working Czech rockers (including Ivan Kral) to tell the completely fabricated cautionary tale of a manufactured group yearning to become "real" musicians. Or, as the Rotterdam Film Festival catalogue dryly reported: "The film starts with a real imitation band and ends with a false genuine band."

Petr Fiala in **Mnaga – Happy End**

Packed with more in-jokes and cameos than non-Czech audiences could ever hope to digest, the film is nevertheless an accessible and beguilingly affectionate send-up of society's craving for celebrity and the tenuous bonhomie that exists in any artistic discipline where those who feel a creative calling, regardless of their level of talent, mingle with businessmen only in it for the money. *Mnaga – Happy End* won the Plzen festival's Golden Kingfisher award and a prize in Cottbus, and was distributed in the Netherlands and Germany.

Once they get past such high-profile examples as Paul Thomas Anderson's *Magnolia*, future historians in search of authentic evocations of millennial apprehension may find no better dramatic expression of the late 1990s than *Buttoners* (*Knoflikari*, 1997). A dazzlingly structured mosaic of interlinking stories, it ponders a cruel yet absurd world as the narrative moves from a pivotal decision during the Second World War to mid-1990s Prague.

The tales play out as a late-night radio talk-show host drones on about fate and chance. On August 6, 1945 in Kokura, Japan, a group of men curse the weather as, above their heads, a pair of American bomber pilots divert their atomic payload to nearby Hiroshima. Fifty years later, an amorous couple flag down a bemused cabbie, while elsewhere the odd perversion of the title is revealed during a seemingly civilised dinner party (it involves the clandestine plucking of decorative sofa buttons by strategically hidden dentures, manipulated by the muscles of the thighs), cruel chance leads to an automobile accident, and a tired, lonely old couple bicker. Finally, a séance summons one of the long-dead bomber pilots, who speaks on the radio of tolerance and forgiveness.

Low-key and self-assured, *Buttoners* is unlike any other Czech movie of the last 15 years. During its high-profile tour of the world's best film festivals, it won Rotterdam's Golden Tiger, Plzen's grand prize and Czech Golden Lions (the local Oscars) for supporting actor (Jiri Kodet, as the baffled but accommodating dinner host), screenplay, director and film.

Praised by *New York Times* critic Janet Maslin as "artfully subversive", *Buttoners* also codifies a number of Zelenka's ongoing themes, including a fascination with radio as a kind of benevolent power in his protagonists' lives, an enduring fascination with Japanese culture, the presence of divine beings in the world, and, of course, a firm belief in and joyous embrace of the vagaries of chance.

Erotical-philosophical-magical

In 2000, Zelenka was approached by German producer Regina Ziegler to contribute a film to her half-hour anthology series, *Erotic Tales*, which featured internationally acclaimed directors tackling self-penned affairs of the heart, often with tongue firmly in cheek. Zelenka quickly got into the spirit of things, telling Ziegler: "Okay with me, but since you've got enough erotic ones, let's do something philosophically erotic…".

The result was *Powers*, in which Czech actor Ivan Trojan (brother of *Zelary* director and long-time Jan Hrebejk producer Ondrej Trojan) plays Peter, a cabaret magician who suddenly finds that his talent is real and uses it to advance his sister's love life. The first of three films scripted and/or directed by Zelenka in which Trojan plays a character who might be seen as a surrogate for Zelenka's philosophy and desires (think Dario Grandinetti in the films of Eliseo Subiela), *Powers* is a modest but pivotal part of Zelenka's oeuvre.

Also in 2000, the script Zelenka had written from a story dreamed up with Olga Dabrowska was filmed as *Loners* by young director David Ondricek. The son of famed cameraman Miroslav, Ondricek transformed the multi-character, inter-generational story into a sleek meditation on love, personal choices and values, peppered with absurdity and set in a mellow, contemporary Prague. Trojan stars once again, in one of a number of interconnected stories, as a neuro-surgeon who comically stalks an old lover. A resounding commercial success in the Czech Republic, *Loners* earned singer-turned-

actor Jiri Machacek a Supporting Actor Czech Lion and solidified Zelenka's reputation as a screenwriter able to put a distinctively personal stamp on contemporary issues.

Simply put, *Year of the Devil* (*Rok dabla*, 2002) is *Mnaga – Happy End* writ large and twisted in on itself. Czech singer Jaromir Novahica plays himself in the fictional story of a singer and recovering alcoholic who enlists a folk-rock band called Cechomor (played by a folk-rock band called Cechomor) to back him on a summer tour that leads to all manner of bizarre situations and enlightening adventures.

More insular than Zelenka's other films by the very nature of its in-joke concept, *Year of the Devil* still bursts with ideas about fame and identity; few film-makers have ever explored the vibrant world of contemporary music with such immediacy and understanding. "I make films only because of the music," Zelenka wrote in the film's press kit. "If I couldn't put music in my films I wouldn't make them. Images by themselves say nothing to me. I perceive film primarily as a recording medium and I'm convinced the next generation will think about it in this way too."

Jaz Coleman in **Year of the Devil**

The first of his films to be produced by Pavel Strnad's busy, Prague-based Negativ Film Productions, *Year of the Devil* earned a half-dozen Czech Lions (best film, most watched film, director, music, editing and sound, the last for Michal Holubec, another of Zelenka's "friends").

It also won grand prizes at the Trieste and Karlovy Vary festivals. Incidentally, as has become a tradition for Czech film-makers at Karlovy Vary, Zelenka had in 2002 created the latest in a series of witty short films commissioned by the festival to brand each annual edition. Both whimsical and shocking (at least to non-European sensibilities), Zelenka's contribution involved two children discovering a night-watchman dancing nude on the stage of an empty theatre.

The right *Wrong* turn

If *Year of the Devil* amplified established themes in Zelenka's work, *Wrong Way Up* (*Pribehy obcejneho silenstvi*, 2005) definitely marks a new professional chapter. Based on his own popular 2001 stage play, *Tales of Common Insanity*, it's the story of Peter (Trojan again), a morose airport freight employee who pines for his ex-wife, Jana (Sulajova again), even as his stodgy father, David (Miroslav Krobot), finds escape from Peter's flighty mother (Nina Diviskova) via a close friendship with free-spirited sculptor Sylvia (Petra Lustigova).

Negativ Film Productions

Ivan Trojan and Zuzana Sulajova in **Wrong Way Up**

The film's trip from stage to screen offers an interesting glimpse into Zelenka's working methods. A play full of wryly comic despair becomes a movie of mellow eccentricities and cautious hope, suggesting that Zelenka understands and welcomes the differences between his domestic and international audiences. *Wrong Way Up* looked sure to feature prominently on the festival circuit in 2005 and at press time, Zelenka was pursuing a number of new projects. A second play was in the works, and 2005 should see the beginning of production on his long-cherished *The Best Films of Our Lives*, a trio of stories in which a diverse group of average people share an abiding love of movies.

Zelenka is tall, thin and bespectacled and his demeanour belies the rock'n'roll soul bared in his work. He lives in Prague with his second wife, Klara, a dancer. He professes admiration for the work of Woody Allen ("I love him and I think I can do something like him"), Oliver Stone ("I'll never be able to make a film like his films") and Hungarian director Ibolya Fekete ("She is great," Zelenka enthuses about her blending of documentary and fictional elements in such films as *Bolse Vita* and *Chico*).

To date, his films have been under-represented on video and DVD internationally, with only an unsubtitled PAL VHS Czech tape and Dutch disc of *Buttoners* and an extras-laden Region 2 *Year of the Devil* DVD with English subtitles available to the inquisitive enthusiast, plus a fine Region 2 disc of *Loners* with English titles. An enterprising festival programmer could make quite a sidebar of these thematically cohesive and unpretentiously entertaining films.

"Some people that you meet can push you in different directions, which is nice," Zelenka told the Philippines' Cinemanila script lab in 2003. "So if you choose the right people, if you meet the right people, it actually forms the line of your life." On learning that he was to be profiled in *IFG* alongside Mike Leigh, Zelenka e-mailed this author as follows: "We should not pretend I am anywhere near Leigh in terms of achievements or fame or experience. But it is still good to be in the same family." Zelenka may not know Leigh personally, but, united in their commitment to capture the everyday wonder of real people living real lives, they will never be strangers. ■

Petr Zelenka Filmography

[Feature film directing
credits only]

1996
MNAGA – HAPPY END
*Script and Direction: PZ.
Photography: Miro Gabor.
Editing: David Charap. Music:
Mnaga and Zdorp. Players: Petr
Fiala (Himself, Pineapple), Martin
Knor (Himself, Pear), Karel Mikus
(Himself, Lemon), Lukas Philip
(Himself, Apple), Petr Nekuza
(Himself, Banana), Radek Koutny
(Himself, Plum), Chris Clarke
(John Heather), Richard Toth
(Richard I. Brown), Ivan Kral
(Himself), Martin Daniel
(Himself), Martin Schulz
(Himself), Jiri Cerny (Himself),
Zdenek Troska (Himself), Marek
Vasut (Petr Fiala), Marek Brodsky
(Martin Knor). Produced by
Cestmir Kopecky, Alexei Guha,
Helena Vydrova for Czech TV.
62 mins.*

1997
**KNOFLIKARI (Buttoners,
aka The Button-Pinchers,
aka The Button-Pushers)**
*Script and Direction: PZ.
Photography: Miro Gabor.
Editing: David Charap. Music:
Ales Brezina. Players: Pavel
Zajicek (Moderator of Radio 1),
Jan Haubert (Guest of Radio 1),
Seisuke Tsukahara (Japanese with
glasses), Motohiro Hosoya
(Japanese with beard), Junzo
Inokuchi (Young Japanese),
Svetlana Svobodova (Japanese
Woman), David Charap (1st
Pilot), Richard Toth (2nd Pilot),
Frantisek Cerny (Taxi Driver),
Michaela Pavlatova (Woman in
Taxi), Jan Cechticky (Man in
Taxi), Pavel Langer (Client/Pavel),
Zuzana Bydzovska (Wife of Taxi
Driver), Jakub Mejdricky (Lover),
Petr Zelenka (Deviant), Vladimir
Dlouhy (Psychiatrist), Marek
Najbrt (Patient), David Cerny
(Boy), Olga Dabrowska (Girl),
Mirek Wanek (Uz Jsme Doma
Lead Singer/Guitarist), Jiri Kodet
(Host), Inka Brendlova (Hostess),
Borivoj Navratil (Jiri), Alena*

Czech TV/Czech Film Centre

Buttoners

*Prochazkova (Marta), Rudolf
Hrusinsky Jr. (Vrana), Eva
Holubova (Wife of Vrana), Minna
Pyyhkala, Artemio Benki, Siegfried
Markowitz (TV Announcers),
Marian Stojlovova, Bara Brodski,
Julie Stalpovskich, Barbora
Johnova (Girls). Produced by
Cestmir Kopecky, Alexei Guga
for Czech TV. 108 mins.*

2002
ROK DABLA (Year of the Devil)
*Script and Direction: PZ.
Photography: Miro Gabor.
Editing: David Charap. Music:
Jaromir Nohavica, Cechomor,
Karel Holas. Players (all as
themselves, except Jan Prent): Jan
Prent (Jan Holman), Jaromir
Nohavica, Karel Plihal, Karel
Holas, Frantisek Cerny, Radek
Poboril, Michal Pavlik, Radek
Klucka, Jaz Coleman. Produced
by Cestmir Kopecky, Pavel Strnad
for Negativ Film Productions, in
association with Czech TV Brno,
Cestmir Kopecky, Falcon. 88 mins.*

2005
**PRIBEHY OBYCEJNEHO
SILENSTVI (Wrong Way Up)**
*Script and Direction: PZ.
Photography: Miro Gabor.
Editing: David Charap. Music:
Karel Holas. Players: Ivan Trojan
(Peter Hanek), Miroslav Krobot
(Father, David Hanek), Zuzana
Sulajova (Jana), Nina Diviskova
(Mother), Jana Hubinska (Aunt),
Petra Lustigova (Sylvia), Jiri
Babek (Alex), Jiri Bartoska
(Jerry), Zuzana Bydzovska (Alice),
Karel Hermanek (Boss), Marta
Sladeckova (Boss's Wife), Jan
Lepsik (Colleague), Matus
Bukovcan (Colleague 2), Petr
Lafek (Martin), Peter Dubecky
(Waiter), Ida Sovova (Waitress),
Vaclav Strasser (Bubblemann),
Czech Sangsongfah (Young Petr).
Produced by Pavel Strnad, Milan
Kuchynka for Negativ Film
Productions, in co-production
with Pegasus. 108 mins.*

Documentary Cinema Now

How the Documentary Took Flight
by Thomas White

Call it "The *Columbine* Effect" or "The *Fahrenheit* Phenomenon". Since 2002, documentaries have surged in worldwide popularity in unprecedented fashion, running up box-office numbers to rival those for large-format and concert films, not to mention fiction features. Of the top 10 highest-grossing documentaries of all time, according to boxofficemojo.com, eight were released between 2002 and 2004.

Arguably, times of anxiety, war or political polarisation can spur creativity and an urgent desire to explore beyond the traditional parameters of a given form. And in the post-9/11 world, in which the Bush administration's media-military-industrial-fundamentalist complex has split the US along ideological and socio-political lines and alienated many of America's previously staunch international allies, a legion of documentary-makers have leaped into action. In Election Year 2004, a parade of politically oriented non-fiction works was led by Michael Moore's $220m-grossing worldwide phenomenon, *Fahrenheit 9/11*, while Jehane Nouhjaim's *Control Room*, Mark Achbar and Jennifer Abbott's *The Corporation*, Errol Morris' *The Fog of War* and Morgan Spurlock's *Super Size Me* all earned at least $1m at US cinemas.

In an age when such hallowed standard bearers of journalism as *The New York Times*, CBS News, the BBC and *The New Republic* have all suffered various degrees of lapses in ethical turpitude, and when Fox News has worn its "Fair and Balanced Reporting" mantra like a "Kick Me" sign, perhaps the documentary is the new news. Film-makers' collective urge to delve deeper into

Alliance Atlantis/United B'casting/Kobal

Bowling for Columbine *sparked the theatrical resurgence of documentaries*

the issues and report what's not reported by the broadcast and print media has been matched by global audiences' desire to see the results.

Matching form and content

But it's not only Election Year urgency that has driven this box-office surge. You could not assemble a more thematically disparate group of movies than *Winged Migration*, *Spellbound*, *Capturing the Friedmans*, *My Architect*, *The Kid Stays in the Picture* and *Rivers and Tides* – all popular and acclaimed recent documentary releases. But they all tell great stories, both heeding and challenging the dicta of the documentary form. *Winged Migration* is ostensibly a nature film, but by sublimating the narration for the sake of image and music, Jacques Perrin captured the lyricism and poetry of birds in flight. *Spellbound* is a great American story about competition and achievement, but it's also a tale of diversity, immigration and learning.

In re-examining a sex abuse case, *Capturing the Friedmans* looks at the fallibility of memory and the juxtaposition of captured images with the

Tartan Films

Capturing the Friedmans *examined the fallibility of memory*

elusiveness of truth. *My Architect* takes non-fiction tropes – the biography and the personal essay – and fuses them to create a full-bodied, graceful portrait of a complicated artist, architect Louis Kahn. *The Kid Stays in the Picture* subverts the biography form into a cinematic autobiography, where Hollywood mogul Robert Evans is star and story-teller. *Rivers and Tides*, a profile of artist Andy Goldsworthy, exudes the quiet patience and Zen-like process of its subject.

Jonathan Caouette's *Tarnation* caused a sensation at Sundance and Cannes in 2004. As every follower of the film now knows, Caouette made it on iMovie software for $218.32. A kaleidoscopic blend of home videos, audio tapes, answering machine messages, on-camera confessionals, music videos, improvised monologues and *vérité* footage, rendered on just about every shooting format introduced over the past 20 years, *Tarnation* turns the personal documentary genre into what Caouette has described as a "cathartic exorcism and a visual journal" about growing up in a dysfunctional world.

These are just a few examples of the forward-thinking work that's emerging. One should also consider *American Splendor* (2003). Though not a documentary *per se*, its makers, Shari Springer Berman and Robert Pulcini, maintain an allegiance to the form, with Harvey and Joyce Pekar providing a running commentary as their performing counterparts, Paul Giammati and Hope Davis, re-enact their life stories. This hybrid form is not so much a new phenomenon as a zesty new wine in an old bottle.

The digital democracy

The blurring of the boundaries between fiction and non-fiction is, perhaps, a reflection of how documentary makers are trained in certain film schools, where the curricula of documentary and fiction film-making are more fluid and flexible. But there's also the high-octane "cyberverse" of mash-ups, surfing, blogging, list-serving, streaming and synthesising, where access to information, ideas and high and low culture has inspired many to rethink the possibilities of story-telling. Indeed, it has been the digital tools (the DV camera, Final Cut Pro, the iMac, the DVD) introduced in the 1990s that have democratised the art form, lowering the barriers to entry, facilitating the process, changing the economics and broadening the appreciation of the documentary among artists and audiences.

But it wasn't just software that seeded the growth. It was hardware, too: documentary festivals and markets founded in the 1990s have spawned a veritable industry – the festival circuit – of regional, national, genre-specific events. The cable world continues to expand. The DVD has revived classic documentaries and provided a vital ancillary opportunity for distribution. The Internet continues to serve as a dynamic context for convocations and distribution. It's worth looking at all these areas to get a true sense of how the documentary got its wings.

Festivals

As the number of festivals and markets – particularly those focused exclusively on documentaries – has grown, the festival/market circuit (examined in more detail by Carol White later in this section) has become a vital means not only of finding distribution, but of showcasing and marketing documentaries from city to city and country to country. With more and more festivals attracting distributors, commissioning editors, journalists and other festival directors, film-makers are getting savvier, securing publicists, sales agents and producers' reps. The circuit can prove a valuable context for finding a home in theatres, on TV and DVD.

Tentpole festivals such as Sundance and Toronto serve as optimal launch sites, while such showcases as International Documentary Filmfestival Amsterdam (IDFA), Hot Docs in Toronto, Yamagata in Japan, DocPoint in Helsinki, Thessaloniki in Greece, Sheffield in England, Full Frame in North Carolina and Silverdocs in Maryland have also proved viable.

Among wildlife and nature film festivals, Jackson Hole, in Wyoming, and Wildscreen, in Bristol, England, have dominated the genre. What's more, the *grande dame* of festivals, Cannes, which would have balked at giving documentaries a higher profile five years ago, let alone screening more than two or three, has, since *Bowling for Columbine* premiered there in 2002, unfurled the red carpet to more non-fiction fare.

Markets and conferences such as the IFP Market in New York, IDFA Forum in Amsterdam and the Toronto Documentary Forum at Hot Docs have also provided more opportunities. MIPDOC in Cannes, NATPE in Las Vegas, RealScreen in Washington, DC, and Sunny Side of the Doc in Marseilles have been slightly harder on the pocket book for independent film-makers than for commissioning editors and distributors, but nonetheless provide a valuable window into what's selling, who's buying, who's watching and what's being made.

Theatrical exhibition

The spike in the popularity of documentaries has meant more have found distribution and staying power beyond the week-long four-wall. Arthouses, alternative venues and universities continue to champion the form, but multiplexes have also opened a screen or two to non-fiction. With the continued promise of digital cinema, which has grown faster in Europe than in the US, independent documentary-makers will increasingly be able to showcase their work more cost-effectively.

While the major studios by and large continue to shy away from docs, their specialty divisions, particularly Sony Pictures Classics (*Riding Giants*,

The Fog of War, *Winged Migration* and *Dogtown and Z-Boys*) and Universal's Focus Features (*The Kid Stays in the Picture*) have been willing to put more marketing muscle behind non-fiction releases in the US. Mid-sized distributors like Lions Gate (*Fahrenheit 9/11*), THINKFilm (*Spellbound*, *Festival Express*), IFC Films (*Touching the Void*, *Metallica: Some Kind of Monster*) and Magnolia Pictures (*Capturing the Friedmans*, *Control Room*) have found success with their non-fiction releases, as have smaller companies like Roadside Attractions (*Super Size Me*), New Yorker Films (*My Architect*, *Etre et avoir*) and Zeitgeist Films (*The Corporation*).

Television has taken notice – and tentatively ventured into theatrical distribution. Discovery Channel launched its Discovery Docs division in 2004, with the intention of releasing two to three titles per year for limited theatrical release, before airing them on Discovery Channel or Discovery Times. HBO partnered with THINKFilm, Magnolia Pictures and New Yorker Films for their respective successes, *Spellbound*, *Capturing the Friedmans* and *My Architect*. *NOVA*, the long-running science series on America's Public Broadcasting Service (PBS), produced *Shackleton's Antarctic Adventure* for the IMAX market and *Shackleton's Voyage of Endurance* for television.

Television

In a field where sources of funding have always been limited, television has consistently provided a large part of documentary financing. Such leading figures as HBO's Sheila Nevins and the BBC's Nick Fraser have over the past 20 years overseen a remarkable slate of non-fiction programmes. They have pushed the art form forward, giving viewers a rich range of provocative stories. The HBO imprimatur has, arguably, inspired other cable channels to follow suit with their own singular, edgy style. In addition, such PBS programmes as *Independent Lens* and *P.O.V.* continue to provide homes for progressive documentary programming.

Many of these TV-funded documentaries have

earned Academy Award nominations. In 2002, in an effort to encourage theatrical exhibition of documentaries, however, the Academy modified the eligibility rules for Oscar consideration to include a blackout period between cinema exposure and broadcast on television or the internet. This restriction has caused some consternation among broadcasters in Europe and elsewhere, given the extent to which topicality often drives non-fiction programming decisions.

My Architect: *critically acclaimed in the US and UK*

So-called "Reality TV" has dominated the airwaves over the past five years, and pundits and documentary purists alike have been wringing their hands over the popularity of this trend-turned-juggernaut. There's "Reality TV" – essentially game shows, increasingly scripted and directed – and then there's the documentary series. Wall to Wall Television's *1900 House*, *Frontier House* and *Colonial House*, for example, brought an element of drama – and reality – without the grand prizes and wannabe celeb contestants. While these series, and others like Actual Reality Pictures' *Freshman Diaries* and *American Candidate*, make for fascinating television, they haven't achieved the high ratings of *The Apprentice*, *The Amazing Race* or *Survivor*.

Whether the ongoing popularity of "Reality TV" has contributed to the surge in popularity of the documentary form is open to discussion. If anything, it has captured an audience that, it is hoped, will "graduate" to what we might call true

reality TV. The US networks, which have shied away from documentary programming since the advent of cable, have made only tentative forays into opening their programming choices.

One of the earliest documentaries about the terrorist attacks, *9/11*, aired to huge ratings on CBS in March 2002, but that did not inspire the network to develop a documentary division. Similarly, it was big news in the documentary community when NBC aired *Deadline*, about death penalty cases in Illinois, on the network's news magazine programme *Dateline* as a two-hour special last summer. But that has not opened the door for more long-form non-fiction programming on NBC, either.

The Internet

The Internet has proved a vital tool for documentary-makers to reach audiences and one another. A website for a film can serve not only as a cyber press-kit, but as an ancillary art form. For PBS, the website is a necessary component to continue the viewing experience, with interactive forums, additional information, links and so on. The Web has also served as a dynamic meeting place for the documentary community, with TheD-word.com, DocuLink.com and others serving as virtual Algonquin Roundtables for discussions of issues ranging from ethics to aesthetics.

The New York-based MediaRights.org has proved itself with its online "Media That Matters" Festival, as well as an extensive database of social issue documentaries. Witness.org and OneWorld.org have further democratised the form, giving cameras to individuals in far-away places to document human rights concerns for the world to see – and do something about. MoveOn.org has utilised the Web as a means of communicating with and mobilising a community around specific political issues and, over the past year or so, has expanded into documentary distribution, recognising the art form's long-standing renown for instigating change. MoveOn.org sold hundreds of thousands of DVDs of Robert Greenwald's *Uncovered: The*

Tartan Films

Whole Truth About the Iraq War and *Outfoxed: Rupert Murdoch's War on Journalism* to its subscribers, encouraging them to organise screening parties and discussion sessions in their homes. Cinema Libre then distributed both films to theatres across the US.

This strategy of reaching the core audience first, then taking the film to theatres, could well be a new model for independent distribution. Something along these lines was posited by media consultant Peter Broderick in an article in *DGA* magazine and at a panel that he moderated at the 2004 IFP Market. With home video and DVD, film-makers can opt to retain rights to this ancillary stream and target their core audience via the Web. Of course, this means that the film-makers become the middleperson, immersing themselves in the field of e-commerce distribution and all that it entails – marketing, fulfilment, shipping and so on.

The DVD

Since the DVD player was introduced in 1996, this format has been the fastest growing technology in media history. Netflix, the online DVD rental service, offers its two million members more than 25,000 titles, including 1,600 documentaries. DVD is a boon to sales – and an opportunity to think creatively about how this format, like the website, can serve a documentary, enhancing it and giving it a life beyond the film itself.

The DVD has also helped to revive the classics. Companies like Docurama, The Criterion Collection and Facets Multimedia have reissued films like *Grey Gardens*, *Primary* and *Salesman*, bolstering appreciation for documentaries – and creating new revenue for the film-makers.

Looking Ahead

Will 2005 be "The Year of the Documentary IV"? The sceptics determined that *Bowling for Columbine* was the exception to the rule in 2002. Michael Moore was and is synergy in action, with not only hit movies, but also best-selling books,

a one-man show in London, a couple of television series and a sold-out lecture tour to bolster his celebrity status. But Moore pushed the door open, and with a steady stream of documentaries sustaining their theatrical runs beyond expectations – including the Moore-esque *Super Size Me* – the door never closed.

Does this mean audiences, exhibitors and distributors will be looking for the next Moore, just as studios were clamouring in the mid-1990s to replicate Quentin Tarantino? After Morgan Spurlock, will other film-makers try to be like Mike? As long as the documentary form continues to grow well beyond its previously marginalised status, it seems certain that the public will continue to engage with these works as films rich with possibilities. But documentaries will still be required to compete hard for cinemagoers' money, just like fiction films.

At the Doc Salon at the 2004 Toronto International Film Festival, participants in "The Sellers" panel discussion attested to a post-*Fahrenheit 9/11* spike in interest from audiences and buyers. Whether this is a trend or a genuine awakening to an art form that's been around since the beginning of cinema will depend, of course, on the whims of the marketplace and on the key players in the documentary community – film-makers, exhibitors, distributors, commissioning editors, festival programmers, funders – who will need to work together to keep the documentary thriving for everyone.

THOMAS WHITE (tom@documentary.org) is editor of *International Documentary* magazine.

Michael Moore, right, confronts Congressman John Tanner in **Fahrenheit 9/11**

The Rise of the Documentary Festival by Carol Nahra

I f you want to escape from the world, head for a Hollywood release at the nearest multiplex. If you'd rather engage with it, head for a documentary film festival. And these days there's a good chance that there will be one near you.

When Ally Derks decided to start a documentary festival in Amsterdam almost 20 years ago, the situation was very different. Derks wanted to celebrate Holland's tradition of creative documentaries, pioneered by legends such as Joris Ivens, Bert Haanstra and Johan van der Keuken. While documentaries were screened as part of the nearby Rotterdam Film Festival, she felt that they were often unjustly overshadowed by the fiction selection. It was time for a festival all about docs: the International Documentary Filmfestival Amsterdam (IDFA).

Initially, Derks and her colleagues had to hunt diligently for docs; finding truly creative examples proved hard going. "There were a lot of nature films and *reportages* sent to us," recalls Derks. "But [now] we really do get creative documentaries." She still oversees IDFA's programme, which in 2003 received a staggering 1,850 submissions, despite its insistence on premieres. Each year the festival has grown; in 2003 it screened 200 documentaries over 10 days and sold 110,000 tickets, making it the world's largest documentary festival.

Since IDFA's first edition, the notion of a doc film festival has grown from unusual to commonplace: they are now found in every shape and size in most parts of the world. The documentary component of general film festivals has also become increasingly important. The past year saw two firsts: a documentary opened Sundance 2004 (Stacy Peralta's surfing homage, *Riding Giants*), and Michael Moore's *Fahrenheit 9/11* took the Palme D'Or at Cannes. Having witnessed the huge box-office success of

Fahrenheit 9/11, *Etre et avoir* and *Super Size Me*, theatrical distributors are showing up at festivals looking for the next big documentary money-spinner, watching keenly how the non-fiction titles play to the crowds.

Super Size Me *has drawn distributors to documentary festivals*

Have doc, will travel

For film-makers, festivals offer a number of advantages, not least professional development of a very enjoyable kind. You get the chance to bring your documentary to the attention of distributors and buyers and you also raise your profile. "It's good for your ego to go to these festivals," says veteran German director Christian Bauer. "People might not have seen your films but they've read about them, seen the title, seen your name pop up here and there. So in the long run it's important to your career."

Bauer's latest feature, *The Ritchie Boys*, tells the story of German Jews who formed an elite US intelligence unit during the Second World War. It was the opening film at the 2004 Hot Docs festival in Toronto (second in size only to IDFA). "To have a film with 800 people [watching] is fantastic," he says. "You get a direct response. When the audience is laughing at the right places you know you've done your job. You don't get that on television."

Phil Grabsky's feature documentary *The Boy Who Plays on the Buddhas of Bamiyan* has played more that 40 festivals, winning a handful of awards for its observation of a cheeky young Afghan boy and his family, who live amidst the ruins of the Buddhas destroyed by the Taleban. Based in Brighton, England, Grabsky used to be a prolific maker of television documentaries, but now spends his energies on cinematic work. He sees the festival circuit as vital to building the credibility of documentary-makers as artists: "You actually meet a community of film-makers. It's a much more outwardly co-operative environment than television."

Having self-funded *The Boy...*, shot entirely by the director on DV over three seasons in Afghanistan, Grabsky left a nine-month window for it to play at festivals before television showings or theatrical release. "I could have a better income from making [TV] films on ancient Egypt, but I wouldn't be attending festivals [and] meeting other film-makers, I wouldn't be doing something that I think has value."

Blitz/Welch/Kobal

Spellbound's theatrical success followed festival screenings

He adds that festivals play a very important role in "breaking the hegemony of broadcasters" and cites the number of broadcasters who haven't had the courage to commission documentaries on seemingly ho-hum topics – like spelling bees or French one-room schoolhouses (as featured in *Spellbound* and *Etre et avoir*) – who have then bought such films after seeing them at festivals.

Show them the money

The downside of the festival circuit for directors is that it depletes your energy, time – and wallet. While they often will cover travelling expenses, the fact that nearly all festivals remain unwilling to pay to screen documentaries is a particular thorn in film-makers' flesh. Says Bauer: "They're expecting us to give them our films, in which we have invested a lot of time, energy and love – and sometimes a lot of our money – for free. I think it's just not fair."

The benefits of having your documentary at a festival such as Sundance or IDFA can far outweigh the costs. Sundance's documentary programmer, Diane Weyermann, says buyers are turning out in big numbers to watch docs, particularly since the festival opened its doors to non-American documentaries in 2003. "Most of the world documentaries we screened were subsequently broadcast on US television," she says. "A few even broke out theatrically – such as *The Corporation* (Canada) and *Bus 174* (Brazil)."

When Sundance screened Weijun Chen's *To Live Is Better Than to Die*, about HIV-Aids in a family in rural China, the response was astonishing. "Virtually every commissioning editor attending the screening picked [it] up for broadcast and international distribution," recalls Weyermann. The film was bought by HBO/Cinemax and has since garnered prizes around the world.

Importantly for many directors, premiering at a festival abroad can also bring much-wanted attention back home. In 2004, Sundance screened the world premiere of the South Korean documentary *Repatriation*, in which director Kim Dong Won follows long-term political prisoners as they are released and repatriated to North Korea. The film won the Freedom of Expression prize and was taken on by a Korean distributor, who bore the cost of converting it to film for theatrical release. It became the highest-grossing documentary ever at South Korean cinemas and one of the country's top 10 independent films.

Israeli director Yoav Shamir's *Checkpoint*, depicting the grim realities of the endless checkpoints in the occupied territories, has played at more than 80 festivals and picked up many awards. Its world premiere was at IDFA, where it filled the 670-seat cinema for several screenings and won the Joris Ivens Award.

During the premiere's Q&A there was heated discussion about the minuscule number of Israelis expected to catch the film on the niche channel it was headed for at home. "There was a debate about how come these kinds of films, no matter how successful they are abroad, are going to get a small Israeli audience," recalls Shamir. The pressure from the audience helped convince the watching buyer from Israel's Channel Two to acquire the film. "It was very important to me," says Shamir, "because basically it was made for Israelis. It's nice to do well at festivals, but the most important target audience was Israelis."

Despite the prestige that comes with premiereing at the biggest festival, Shamir has found some of the smaller festivals to be the most enjoyable and it was at a relatively small documentary conference in Bardonecchia, Italy, that Shamir met Caroline Leth of Zentropa Real, who became co-producer of his next documentary, on anti-semitism.

Many of the smaller festivals springing up around the world start as the vision of one person. Typical is Docudays in Beirut, founded by

Mohamad Hashem in 1999. That it exists at all is remarkable: Lebanon has little television tradition of documentaries beyond wildlife programming, and no history of film festivals. Hashem himself comes from a background in animation but always loved documentaries. So he decided to start up a festival, self-funding it the first year. "It was my very expensive hobby," he notes. Six years on, he has secured substantial sponsorship, including support from Arab broadcaster Al-Jazeera. The festival has proved hugely popular, with screenings normally full to overflowing.

Docudays is the largest doc festival in the Arab world, and Hashem is determined to make it a must-attend industry event. "We have a lot of untold stories in the Arab world, concerning history, religion and politics," says Hashem. "In most Arab countries you can't tell what you are feeling, you can't speak out. Documentaries are a way for people to speak out."

Human rights, right now

The need to speak out remains the raison d'être for a huge proportion of documentaries globally, something reflected by festivals in their programming of more and more human rights films. "With what's happening in the world everywhere, there are a lot of anti-globalisation films, films on Iraq, Afghanistan and Chechnya, the refugee camps, and, above all, migration," says IDFA's Derks. "People are trying to leave

Hollywood's response to the surging popularity of documentaries, as imagined in **The Pitchers,** *the weekly cartoon strip from* The Guardian

their country for a better future in other countries – that's a worldwide phenomenon."

Many festivals have been created with an explicit human rights agenda, most notably Amnesty International Film Festival and the Human Rights Watch International Film Festival (HRWIFF). John Biaggi, Deputy Director of New York-based HRWIFF, says the festival has been a catalyst for highlighting issues important to the organisation. "Nobody is going to read through our reports, which can be 100 pages," he says. "We're able to put the whole story of this particular human rights incident or situation up on the screen in under two hours in a compelling manner."

When it was founded in 1988, HRWIFF aimed to split its programming evenly between dramas and documentaries, but quickly realised the latter was by far the more powerful genre. "You can count the good dramas made a year on your hand," says Biaggi. The festival, which runs in London and New York as well as on tour in North America, now selects documentaries to make up about 80% of its programme.

Savvy film-makers are combining festival appearances with other media exposure to campaign for the message in their films – a strategy that has evolved gradually. Says Biaggi: "It was really kind of sad when I first came here, because we would show the film and it was [the film-makers'] one little moment in New York and

there was not going to be anything else: it came and went very quietly." Biaggi estimates that 80% of documentaries HRWIFF screens now have a built-in campaign before they arrive.

A good example is *Born into Brothels*, a hit on the festival circuit in 2003–04, which had an HBO broadcast and theatrical release. The film, which won 16 awards, including Sundance's Audience Award, is closely tied to a foundation set up by co-director Zana Briski, which empowers marginalised children through photography.

Beyond the screens

The most successful festivals create their own non-fiction universe by holding events alongside the public screenings. Dimitri Eipidis, head of the thriving Thessaloniki Documentary Festival, focuses on a different social issue each year; past years chose terrorism and the human rights of children. "In this part of the world, news and television networks and the press are mainstream, with very little independent information," says Eipidis. "We like to break through that monopoly of news somehow, and bring out more independent voices."

Although more documentaries are breaking into cinemas, there is no denying that the sales potential of most documentaries is still in television markets. Recognising this, the largest and most successful documentary festivals hold

industry events to bring together television executives and film-makers to talk deals.

The most entertaining and dramatic example is the pitching forum, where producers and directors have a few minutes to pitch their ideas to broadcasters in front of a crowd. Initiated in 1992 by IDFA, which hosts the three-day Amsterdam Forum alongside the festival, the format has been copied by festivals eager to bring in international decision-makers.

Hoping to turn a previously domestic event into an international one, Toronto's Hot Docs Festival launched its pitching forum in 1998, and it quickly became North America's premier documentary event. Two recent doc hits, *Weather Underground* and *The Corporation*, were originally pitched at the Toronto Documentary Forum, which raises up to $1.5m worth of funding a year for its projects, according to Hot Docs director Chris MacDonald. "It's been extremely helpful to Canadian film-makers, because we've now created this marketing event where broadcasters from around the world come into our back yard," says MacDonald.

Look on the Sunny Side

Documentary film-makers determined to make connections to support their next big project are increasingly forking out money to attend one of the world's biggest documentary events, which includes no festival at all: Marseilles' annual Sunny Side of the Doc. Launched in 1990 by television station France 2's Yves Jeanneau, the four-day event has grown enormously.

"We succeeded in the idea we had 16 years ago, which was to create a place where the documentary world could meet, where commissioning editors, producers and distributors can work on the future, work on co-production deals," recounts Jeanneau. "I'm proud that 300 commissioning editors from all around the world are coming." While Sunny Side focuses on the networking necessary to get docs made, Jeanneau says festivals have been vital in saving documentaries from a long, slow death. "In France in 1984 there were no more slots on TV. Festivals helped a lot to bring back the genre."

So is there a danger that there could ever be too many doc festivals? Emphatically not, says Derks. "There are still a lot of countries who have no idea what documentary really is." She adds that because of censorship it's impossible for some of the films that IDFA screens to be shown on television in their country of origin. Secure in its position of primacy, IDFA has taken to helping other countries build their own festivals, and in 2004 brought in programmers from more than a dozen developing countries to learn the tricks of the trade.

CAROL NAHRA (carol@stampede.co.uk) is a London-based documentary film critic, journalist and producer.

RUTH DISKIN, *of Jerusalem-based Ruth Films, on taking a documentary to the international market.*

"When I opened my company in 2001, I decided to focus on documentaries. The first film in my catalogue was *It Kinda Scares Me* by Tomer Heymann, about a youth leader confessing the fact that he is gay. It took 10 international [festival] prizes. I try to focus [initially] on the leading festivals, like IDFA, Berlin or Hot Docs. The first 12 months after the film is released is the time to really work intensively. Usually I pick up a film in Israel just before it screens in one of the Israeli festivals. The biggest challenge is to be able to select the docs with the highest international potential.

One of the most successful films was *Detained*, directed by Anat Even and Ada Ushpiz. It's a political film about three Palestinian widows living in a house where the front of the house is in Israeli territory and the back is in Palestinian territory. It was sold to over 10 networks, including Sundance. Films dealing with politics and the Israeli–Palestinian conflict are the most successful."

– *Interview by Carol Nahra.*

DVD Round-Up
by Daniel Rosenthal

The work of John Cassavetes and Robert Altman – two giants of post-war American cinema in terms of artistic achievement and influence, though never commercial success – received deservedly outstanding DVD treatment in 2004. The box set **John Cassavetes: Five Films** (Criterion, Region 1) devotes loving attention to the godfather of independent film across eight discs, dominated by new transfers of *Shadows* (1959), whose shocking revelation of racism is still unsurpassed, *Faces* (1968), *A Woman Under the Influence* (1974), with career-best performances from Gena Rowlands and Peter Falk, *The Killing of a Chinese Bookie* (1976; and the shorter re-edit from 1978) and *Opening Night* (1977). The final disc offers Charles Kiselyak's 200-minute documentary, *A Constant Forge – The Life and Art of John Cassavetes*.

The set makes one wish Cassavetes were still alive, defiantly retaining quality control into his mid-seventies, like Altman, four years his senior. Never available on VHS, Altman's entertaining **California Split** (1974; Columbia TriStar, Region 1) makes its DVD debut, while the Criterion Collection's extensive mining of his back catalogue (all Region 1) kicks off with **Three Women** (1977), a deeply unsettling tale of identity theft that looks like a dry run for Barbet Schroder's more conventional and exploitative take on the same concept, *Single White Female* (1992).

Sissy Spacek is the vulnerable country girl increasingly obsessed with imitating every detail of flatmate Shelly Duvall's self-deluded and banal life. The third woman is Janice Rule, as the pregnant wife of an unfaithful bar owner. Gerald Busby's oboe and cello-heavy score adds to the unease; Altman supplies a strong commentary.

There were also timely Election Year reissues of the claustrophobically intense **Secret Honor** (1984), with Philip Baker Hall as Nixon, and **Tanner '88** (1988, two discs), the six-hour Altman/Garry Trudeau 'docu-TV news-soap opera', which pitted Michael Murphy's presidential candidate against real-life politicians, and now seems a precursor to both the satirical comedy-drama of Altman admirer Tim Robbins' *Bob Roberts* (1992) and the politician-ambushing stunts of Michael Moore and Ali G.

Robbins plays the philandering Los Angeles cop in the magnificent **Short Cuts** (1993). Criterion's two-disc set includes a special paperback edition of the Raymond Carver stories so skilfully edited and stitched together by Altman and co-writer Frank Barhydt into the 23-character mosaic which was animated by a flawless cast and provided a template customised by Paul Thomas Anderson in the more operatic *Magnolia* (Altman builds up to an earthquake; Anderson to a shower of frogs).

Watched soon after the Altman, Richard Linklater's ultra low-budget **Slacker** (1991, Criterion, Region 1), feels like *Short Cuts* with an

Spelling/Fine Line/Kobal

Anne Archer and Tim Robbins in **Short Cuts**

Attention Deficit Disorder, as we encounter and then swiftly abandon more than 100 "aggressive nonparticipants" in Austin, Texas. The appeal of film and characters escapes me, but its devotees will find everything they could want to know about its production on this two-disc set.

Hollywood Classics

The supplementary material for the reissue of **Casablanca** (Warner Home Video, Regions 1 and 2) is fairly ordinary, but a superb transfer restores Bergman to her matchless radiance and the pleasure of hearing Bogart and Claude Rains delivering their waspish dialogue never fades. From an unproduced stage play, for which Warners paid a then record $20,000, emerged, in Peter Bogdanovich's apt phrase, "one of the great accidental masterpieces in movies".

The immediate response to the enjoyable two-disc reissue of David Niven and Cantinflas' antics in the original **Around the World in 80 Days** (1956; Warner, Regions 1 and 2) and the simultaneous, abject failure of 2004's Steve Coogan/Jackie Chan remake is to think not only that "They don't make 'em like they used to" but that today's producers were misguided even to try emulating a globe-trotting extravaganza that belongs to an irretrievable era; as do George Cukor's **My Fair Lady** (1964) and **Seven Brides for Seven Brothers** (Stanley Donen, 1954; both Warner, Regions 1 and 2), given sumptuous two-disc treatment on their fortieth and fiftieth birthdays respectively.

Great Adaptations

In its silver jubilee year, Volker Schlöndorff's Oscar-winning treatment of Günter Grass' **The Tin Drum**, with David Bennent unforgettable as the boy who refused to grow, has been reissued in two editions (Criterion, Region 1; Nouveaux Pictures, Region 2). The two-disc Criterion set includes a documentary, *Banned in Oklahoma*, reminding us that the stunted hero's sexual awakening sparked a child pornography lawsuit. Schlöndorff's 1984 take on Proust, **Swann in Love** (Home Vision Entertainment, Region 1), is a lesser work, but boasts Jeremy Irons at his glacial best as Swann.

David Bennent in **The Tin Drum**

The twisted imagination of William S. Burroughs found an ideal cinematic counterpart in David Cronenberg in **Naked Lunch** (Criterion, Region 1), and Joseph Strick made an admirable and moving feature from a still more 'unfilmable' novel, James Joyce's **Ulysses** (1967; Arrow Films, Region 0), which makes a belated UK debut on DVD, with Milo O'Shea, Barbara Jefford and Maurice Roeves coming closer to the complexity of Leopold and Molly Bloom and Stephen Dedalus than their counterparts in Sean Walsh's 2003 Irish film version. Arrow has also reissued Strick's **The Balcony** (1963), a briskly eccentric adaptation of Jean Genet's 1957 play, with Shelley Winters on domineering form as the sharp-suited madame of a *Westworld*-like brothel that continues catering to middle-aged male fantasies even while the rest of a nameless country is being torn apart by revolution.

Milo O'Shea as Leopold Bloom in **Ulysses**

Just one of the three major phases of Lampedusa's novel was sufficient for Luchino Visconti to create his three-hour masterpiece, **The Leopard** (1963, Criterion, Region 1; bfi, Region 2). Criterion's three-disc set includes the 185-minute original Italian version and the 161-minute English-language version released in the US, which allows one to appreciate Burt Lancaster as the prince in his own voice. Here, as with his equally memorable portrayals in *Sweet Smell of Success* and *Atlantic City*, Lancaster's finest acting is borne of truly great writing. Both transfers showcase the glorious opulence of the production design. Visconti directed an equally fine film from a much slimmer, more intimate source, with **Death in Venice** (1971; Warner, Region 2), reissued with a fine transfer but few extras.

Luchino Visconti, left, and Burt Lancaster shooting **The Leopard**

The restored fiftieth anniversary reissue of John Halas and Joy Batchelor's animated **Animal Farm** (Home Vision Entertainment, Region 1) has the harshness of Orwell's allegory, badly missed by the *Babe*-like live-action television version from 1999. Liv Ullman's epic film of Sigrid Unset's fourteenth-century-set love story, **Kristin Lavransdatter** (1995, Home Vision Entertainment, Region 1), comes to DVD with a new interview with Ullman and a fine transfer of Sven Nykvist's ever-brilliant cinematography.

Silent Shakespeare (bfi, Region 2) brings together films condensing entire plays into one or two reels, including Percy Stow's movingly simple *The Tempest* (UK, 1908) and a delightful

A Midsummer Night's Dream (US, 1909), shot on location in title-contradicting daylight; both feature primitive but effective special effects.

European Classics

Jean Vigo's death at 29 means that his complete works can fit onto a single disc, **The Complete Jean Vigo** (Artificial Eye, Region 1), containing *A propos de Nice* (1930), *Taris* (1931), *Zéro de conduite* (1933) and the enduringly erotic *L'Atalante* (1934). Extras on a second disc include a feature-length documentary from 1964 by Jacques Rozier.

The latest Fellini reissues include his autobiographical portrait of dead-end provincial life and his own escape from it, **I vitelloni** (1953), and **La strada** (1954; both Criterion, Region 1). The latter includes a video introduction by Martin Scorsese in which he cites the influence of Anthony Quinn's brutal circus strongman on the 'me against the world' anti-heroes of his own work, notably *Raging Bull*'s Jake la Motta.

The final shots of both films are among the most powerful in all cinema: Quinn's solitary howl of anguish, and the breathtaking editing that sees the train carrying Fellini's alter ego (Franco Interlenghi) steam through the bedrooms of the friends he is leaving behind. **La dolce vita** (1960) makes its Region 2 debut in a remastered transfer from Nouveau Pictures, with a new interview with Anita Ekberg.

Only a film-maker with Ingmar Bergman's equal command of theatre and cinema could have

Giulietta Masina and Anthony Quinn in **La Strada**

THE CRITERION COLLECTION/JANUS FILMS

THE GREATEST FILMS FROM AROUND THE WORLD

 **JANUS FILMS**

THE CRITERION COLLECTION
www.criterionco.com

produced a feature with the verbal wit and all-round vigour of **Smiles of a Summer** (1955; Criterion, Region 1). The construction is worthy of Sheridan or Molière; the sexually frank dialogue sounds like Wilde liberated from the need for innuendo and the action proceeds at a pace to match Howard Hawks in screwball mode. This is 108 minutes of sheer delight.

Peter Lorre as the child killer in **M**

Jean-Pierre Melville's 1970 heist-gone-wrong thriller **Le cercle rouge** (Criterion, Region 1, two discs; bfi, Region 2, one disc) remains a cool and soulless film, one to admire rather than enjoy. Fritz Lang's serial killer masterpiece, **M** (1931), has been reissued in excellent two–disc editions (Criterion, Region 1; Eureka Video, Region 2); the former features Lang in conversation with William Friedkin, the latter has him talking to Peter Bogdanovich.

The **Werner Herzog/Klaus Kinski** box set (Anchor Bay, Regions 1 and 2) is a must-own tribute to the most tempestuous of all cinema's great director/actor partnerships. It includes *Woyzeck*, *Nosferatu* (including a Herzog commentary and "Making of" documentary), *Aguirre, the Wrath of God* (with commentary by Herzog and Norman Hill), *Cobra Verde* and Herzog's moving feature documentary on Kinski, *My Best Fiend*.

Klaus Kinski as **Nosferatu**

Japanese Masters

Yasujiro Ozu's centenary in 2003 was marked by retrospectives all over the world and in 2004 by several reissues (all Criterion, Region 1), the best of which are perhaps his greatest portraits of the strains and pleasures of ordinary family life: **Tokyo Story** (1953; two discs), which is backed by a two-hour documentary on the director, *I Lived, But...*, and **Early Summer** (1951), with commentary by that great scholar of Japanese cinema, Donald Richie.

As in all of Akira Kurosawa's films, the consequences of violence for victims and perpetrators are dramatised with immense force and compassion in **Stray Dog** (1949, Criterion, Region 1), which is both a gripping chase thriller and a socially acute portrait of post-war Tokyo and its sprawling black markets. Takashi Shimura is the veteran detective who must help Toshiro Mifune's soldier-turned-rookie cop track down the volatile young criminal who has killed using Mifune's stolen gun.

The film is reissued with a feature-length commentary by Stephen Prince, covering a wealth of technical, historical and thematic points about this "existential and moral parable about

choice in a time of chaos". There's also a Japanese television documentary, taken from the series *Akira Kurosawa: It Is Wonderful to Create,* in which actors and crew members reveal their great respect and affection for their director, the "Emperor".

An innovative double-bill pairs Kurosawa's 1957 adaptation of Gorky's play **The Lower Depths** (Criterion, Region 1) with Jean Renoir's 1936 version. Finally, **Ran** (1985; Warner, Region 2), Kurosawa's epic transposition of *King Lear,* boasts a transfer that does greater justice to the film's extraordinary colour scheme and battle scenes than last year's disappointing Region 1 release. The extras include Chris Marker's "Making of" documentary, *A.K.*.

Criterion's DVD reissue of **Stray Dog**

Asian Gangster Classics

Though UK companies have long championed Chinese-language cinema on home video, collectors have largely had to rely on US labels for Japanese genre classics and Home Vision Entertainment (HVE; all Region 1) has been leading the way, with swathes of titles from the 1960s and 1970s by directors like Kinji Fukasaku and Seijun Suzuki, plus the marvellous ongoing reissue of the entire 26-part series featuring **Zatoichi** the blind swordsman.

Fans of Fukusaku's anarchic final movie, *Battle Royale*, won't be disappointed by HVE's selections from his classic period at Toei studio, especially the five-part gangster saga, **The Yakuza Papers** (1973–76, in a boxed set, or individually), covering 25 years of post-war Japanese society, and the rage-filled **Street Mobster** (1972) and **Graveyard of Honor** (1975), centred on individual hoods taking on the system. There's a vigour about these films – a high-quality tabloid approach reminiscent of Sam Fuller – that sets Fukasaku apart from most other studio journeymen. He's certainly more consistent than the over-rated Seijun Suzuki, whose genre twists are thinly spread throughout **Underworld Beauty** (1958) and the

period dramas **Kanto Warrior** (1963) and **Tattooed Life** (1965).

Far more interesting is Masahiro Shinoda's bleak, existential, Melville-ish yakuza tale, **Pale Flower** (1964), stunningly shot in chiaroscuro black-and-white. Though the widescreen ratios aren't quite the full 2.35:1, HVE's transfers and individual notes are superb; *The Yakuza Papers* even comes with a helpful genealogy of the gangster families, and each *Zatoichi* adventure includes the original poster.

It's tempting to see the legacy of Fukasaku's intense, stylised realism in a Hong Kong classic like John Woo's **Bullet in the Head** (1990, Hong Kong Legends, Region 2), arguably his most ambitious and involving film. This edition does the movie proud, with masses of extras (including the original ending) and a standard-setting commentary by genre expert Bey Logan. Unfortunately Woo was "too busy" to contribute. All the main survivors pitch up for a two-disc Special Edition of **Enter the Dragon** (Warner, Regions 1 and 2), with a transfer that looks better than the original movie did in 1973, plus enough documentary footage of Bruce Lee (and scenes from his uncompleted *Game of Death*) to satisfy any chop-socky fan. – *Derek Elley*.

Other Recent Releases

Reviewed by Eddie Cockrell (EC), Erik Martens (EM) and Daniel Rosenthal (DR).

Key to Abbreviations: [R1: Region Code; ACI: Archive Cast/Crew Interview; AD: Archive Documentary; ADI: Archive Director Interview; CC: Cast/Crew Commentary; DC: Director's Commentary; NCI: New Cast/Crew Interview; ND: New Documentary; NDI: New Director Interview; NDT: New Digital Transfer; NST: New Subtitle Translation; RC: Restoration Comparison; SC: Scholar/Critic's Commentary; SG: Stills Gallery; TT: Theatrical Trailer.]

La Balance (Bob Swaim, 1982) [Home Vision Entertainment (HVE), R1. TT; NDT.] Swaim's brutal and sexy *policier* boasts fine work from Nathalie Baye and Philippe Léotard. – *DR*

Brussels by Night (Marc Didden, 1983) [MMG, R1&2. ACI; ADI; NCI; ND; NDI; NDT; NST; TT.] Welcomed in the 1980s as the first Flemish film noir in an urban setting. The hero is killer Max, wandering a bleak Brussels. – *EM*

Carmen Jones (Otto Preminger, 1954) [bfi, R2. TT.] Dorothy Dandridge and Harry Belafonte shine in energetic version of Hammerstein's great reworking of Bizet. – *DR*

Castle Keep (Sydney Pollack, 1969) [Columbia TriStar, R1. NDT; TT.] This hallucinatory Second World War dramedy starring Burt Lancaster and Peter Falk has finally been restored to widescreen glory. – *EC*

City of Men (Various directors, 2003) [Optimum Releasing, R2.] Entertaining TV mini-series spin-off from the *favela* phenomenon *City of God*; follows the further adventures of the young gangsters. – *DR*

The Conscript (Roland Verhavert, 1973) [MMG, R1&2. ACI; ADI; NCI; ND; NDI; NDT; NST; TT.] Story of Jan and girlfriend Katrien, who are put to the test by gloomy fate after Jan's conscription. Based on a popular novel by Hendrick Conscience. – *EM*

The Diary of Anne Frank (George Stevens, 1959) [Twentieth Century Fox, R1. AD; CC; ND; NDT; SG.] Perhaps Stevens' most powerful late-period work, lovingly restored to its original, velvety widescreen black-and-white beauty. The mellow commentary interplay between Stevens' son, George Jr., and star Millie Perkins is a sentimental delight. – *EC*

Don't Die Without Telling Me Where You're Going (Eliseo Subiela, 1995) [Facets Video, R1.] Though bare-bones and full-frame, this moving meditation on movies and individuality is one of the very best films of the 1990s. – *EC*

Easy Rider (Dennis Hopper, 1969) [Columbia TriStar, R1. DC; ND, NDT; 2 discs.] Definitive release of the road movie that marked a sharp turn in the course of American cinema. – *EC*

Ed Wood (Tim Burton, 1994) [Touchstone, R1. CC; DC; ND; NDT; TT.] Burton's mischievously reverential approach and Johnny Depp's unflaggingly enthusiastic performance as the king of the Z pictures renders this a career highlight for both. – *EC*

Edge of the World, The (Michael Powell, 1937) [bfi, R2. AD; CC.) The R2 debut of Powell's account of bleak island life in the Shetlands features commentary by Ian Christie and Thelma Schoonmaker and a 1978 documentary following Powell's *Return to the Edge of the World*. – *DR*

Fallen Angel (Otto Preminger, 1945) [bfi, R2. TT.] Entertaining if second-division noir, with Dana Andrews as the gold-digging drifter falling for small-town siren Linda Darnell. – *DR*

Fahrenheit 9/11 (Michael Moore, 2004) [Columbia TriStar, R1; Optimum Releasing, R2. ND.) Includes a featurette on the film's controversial release, updates on people and events and even a segment on Arab-American comedians in a post-9/11 world. – *EC*

Film Noir Classic Collection (Various Directors, 1944-1950) [Warner Home Video, R1. ADI; DC; NDT; SC; TT; 5 discs.] The DVD debut of Jacques Tourneur's *Out of the Past* is the main reason to own this essential set of post-war noir, which also features pristine transfers of *The Asphalt Jungle*, *Gun Crazy*, *Murder, My Sweet* and *The Set-Up*. All titles available separately. – *EC*

Gone with the Wind (Victor Fleming, 1939) [Warner, R1&2. NCI; ND; NDT; RC; SC; TTx5;

4 discs.] A set for the ages of a fervently loved studio-era classic, with five-plus hours of extras. – *EC*

Grave of the Fireflies (Isao Takahata, 1988) [Optimum Releasing, R2. ND; NDI; TT; 2 discs.] Powerful, sentimental *anime* tale of a young Japanese cadet and his moppet-like sister enduring Second World War hardships after their mother is killed in a US air raid. – *DR*

The Early Films of Peter Greenaway – Volumes 1 and 2 (Peter Greenaway, 1964–1980) [bfi, R2. DC.] Five hours' worth of sometimes baffling avant-garde work that precedes Greenaway's breakthrough with the dazzling *The Draughtsman's Contract* (1983, also a bfi reissue). – *DR*

Alfred Hitchcock – 1940–1959 [Warner, R1&2. AD; ADI; CC; ND; NDT; SG; TT; 10 discs.] Box set with fine new transfers of *Dial M for Murder*, *Foreign Correspondent*, *Mr. & Mrs. Smith*, *North by Northwest*, *Stage Fright*, *Strangers on a Train* (2 discs), *Suspicion* and *The Wrong Man*. Most titles include new "Making-of" featurettes, and all are available separately. – *EC*

Journey to Italy (Roberto Rossellini, 1953) [bfi, R2. SC.] Ingrid Bergman and George Sanders are outstanding as a middle-aged couple caught in a stagnant marriage. – *DR*

Legong: Dance of the Virgins (Henry de la Falaise, 1935) [Milestone Film & Video, R1.] New Jersey-based distributor Milestone delivers one of the year's best discs with this UCLA-led restoration of a two-color Technicolor oddity made by an eccentric wannabe mogul on Bali. – *EC*

The Marx Brothers Collection (Various directors, 1937–1946) [Warner, R1&2; ND; SC; TT; 5 discs R1; 6 discs R2.] Seven comedies in a box set: *At the Circus*, *The Big Store*, *A Day at the Races*, *Go West*, *A Night at the Opera*, *A Night in Casablanca* and *Room Service*. – *EC*

Memento (Christopher Nolan, 2000) [Pathé, R2; AD; ADI; NCI; NDI; 3 discs.] Deluxe edition of Nolan's atmospheric, time-shifting noir, including a reverse version Easter egg and an excellent Sundance Channel *Anatomy of a Scene* documentary. – *DR*

The Merchant–Ivory Collection (James Ivory, 1963–1983) [Criterion, R1] Individually released single discs of *The Householder* (1963), the beautiful, bittersweet *Shakespeare Wallah* (1965), the tragic, Bollywood-set love story *Bombay Talkie* (1970), *Savages* (1972), *Hullabaloo over Georgie* and *Bonnie's Pictures* (1978) and *Heat and Dust* (1983). All feature new interviews with Merchant, Ivory and key collaborators – *DR*

Mystic River (Clint Eastwood, 2003) [Warner, R1. CC; ND; TT; 3 discs.] Economical in both style and content, the magnificent *Mystic River* employs everything from Eastwood's distinctive character POV shots to the patented aerial overviews of his lawless lands. Disc three is the soundtrack CD. – *EC*

F. Murray Abraham and Sean Connery in **The Name of the Rose**

Name of the Rose, The (Jean-Jacques Annaud, 1986) [Warner R1&2. AD; DC; NDI; TT.] Sean Connery on fine form in Umberto Eco's fourteenth-century detective story. – *DR*

Pumping Iron (George Butler, Robert Fiore, 1977) [HBO Video, R1 & 2. ND; NCI] Compelling portrait of Arnold Schwarzenegger and his fellow body-

Arnold Schwarzenegger poses in **Pumping Iron**

builders seems innocent in this age of steroid-abuse. New documentary offers 'Where are they now?' updates on Arnie's competitors and the scariest moment comes when someone asks the 28-year-old: "When are you running for President?" – *DR*

The Rapture (Michael Tolkin, 1991) [New Line, R1. CC; DC; TT.] Screenwriter Michael Tolkin's little-seen but immensely powerful drama about a woman (Mimi Rogers) convinced a religious apocalypse is upon us. – *EC*

The Saddest Music in the World (Guy Maddin, 2003) (MGM, R1; NCI; ND; NDI; TT.] Melodrama about the musical competition mounted in Depression-era Manitoba by a legless beer baroness (Isabella Rossellini); features three startling new shorts from the iconoclastic Maddin. – *EC*

Seagulls Die in the Harbour (Kuypers, Verhavert & Michiels, 1955) [MMG, R1&2. ACI; ADI; NCI; ND; NDI; NDT; NST; TT.] Lost soul with guilty mind desperately tries to escape from Antwerp harbour. Like *Brussels by Night* and *The Conscript*, it has subtitles in English, French and Dutch and all three titles are available from www.filmarchief.be. – *EM*

The Martin Scorsese Collection (Martin Scorsese, 1968-1990) [Warner, R1; AD; CC; DC; ND; NDT; TT; 6 discs.] Long-overdue box set collects *After Hours*, *Alice Doesn't Live Here Anymore* (both new to DVD), *GoodFellas* (a two-disc special edition that's also a R2 release), *Mean Streets* (newly remastered) and *Who's That Knocking at My Door*. Each title features a Scorsese commentary. – *EC*

The Shawshank Redemption (Frank Darabont, 1994) [Warner, R1&2. DC; ND; SG; 2 discs.]

Frank Darabont's **The Shawshank Redemption**

Michael Weinstein/Castle Rock/Kobal

Darabont's prison tale was recently named the best movie never to have picked up an Oscar by British voters and the R2 set sports an extra disc of bonus features. The R1 transfer is equally pristine, and extras include a comic spoof, *The Sharktank Redemption*. – *EC*

Smile (Michael Ritchie, 1975) [MGM, R1. TT.] One of the most scathing social comedies of the 1970s makes its DVD debut with every ounce of its teen beauty pageant satire intact. – *EC*

Sunrise (F.W. Murnau, 1927) [Eureka R2. CC; DS; RC; SG; TT; 2 discs.] The camera moves, dissolves and lyrical storytelling still take the breath away in this wonderful restoration of a silent classic. – *DR*

THX-1138 (George Lucas, 1971) [Warner, R1&2. AD; DC; ND; NDT; TT; 2 discs.] Lucas' first feature survives today as a modest, visually startling but remarkably prescient meditation on privacy, thought control and the bleakest of futures. Includes the original USC film school short on which Lucas based the feature. – *EC*

Tomorrow (Joseph Anthony, 1972) [HVE, R1. NCI; NDT.] Adaptation of a Faulkner short story, notable for one of Robert Duvall's least-seen performances, as a slow-witted deep South caretaker. – *DR*

Trilogy (Lucas Belvaux, 2003) [Tartan Video, R2. DC; 4 discs.] Belvaux's uneven but formally adventurous trilogy in a box set, with sequential edits of key scenes fragmented in the individual films. *On the Run*'s account of an escaped terrorist's last days grips, but the simultaneous comedy and melodrama of *An Amazing Couple* and *After Life* stretch patience and credulity. – *DR*

Wisconsin Death Trip (James Marsh, 1999) [HVE, R1. CC; DC; ND.] One of the strangest, most macabre documentaries ever made, examining the misfortunes of Black River Falls, Wisconsin, in the 1890s. Ian Holm supplies the grim narration. – *DR*

Correction
IFG 2004 – DVD Round-UP (p.56): *Il posto* and *I fidanzati* are both released by Criterion for R1, not, as stated, R2. *Rififi* is released by Arrow Films in R2, not R1, where it is a Criterion title.

Books Round-Up

by Daniel Rosenthal

Alexander Mackendrick, left, with Burt Lancaster, recalls Sweet Smell of Success *in* **On Film-making**

H ow fortunate the film students at the California Institute of the Arts were to have Alexander Mackendrick, director of *The Ladykillers* and *Sweet Smell of Success*, as their tutor from 1969 until his death in 1993. How fortunate we are that hundreds of pages of his class notes have now been turned into **On Film-making – The Art of the Director** (Faber, London; Farrar, Straus, Giroux, New York), impressively edited and introduced by Paul Cronin.

Mackendrick's examples and exercises carry a common-sense authority borne of decades of practical experience, underpinned by his devout belief that a director is "nothing but the centripetal force" holding together the disparate elements of the film-making process. He incorporates witty "Slogans for the Screenwriter's Wall", an extended examination of his collaboration with Ernest Lehman and Clifford Odets on *Sweet Smell of Success* and a dazzling exercise in reducing 12 pages of dialogue for a two-handed scene to half a page.

Lindsay Anderson's **Diaries** (Methuen, London), edited by Paul Sutton with clear contextual notes, begin with his army medical exam in 1942 and end shortly before his death in 1994, when he was hoping finally to make an *If...* sequel with Malcolm McDowell. There are banal details about home-cooked meals, some star-gazing, instances and self-criticism of his intellectual snobbery and all too many "melancholy periods of wasted time and squandered opportunities", whether professional or personal. His prose talents are shown to much greater effect in **Never Apologise – The Collected Writings of Lindsay Anderson** (Plexus, London), edited by Paul Ryan: more than 600 pages on British and American cinema, theatre, critics and

criticism. Ryan notes that Anderson always resisted the idea of such a collection, asking "Do you honestly think anyone will want to read this stuff?" They certainly should.

Biography and History

Anderson called Humphrey Jennings "the only true poet of the English cinema" and with **Humphrey Jennings** (Picador, London), Kevin Jackson cements his position as the leading authority on the life and work of the director whose documentary portraits of Britain during the Second World War are, Jackson writes, "now part of that collective ancestral past which we must know about in order to know who we are".

John Schlesinger's stroke in 2001 put paid to his long-planned memoirs and he turned instead to William J. Mann to write an authorised biography. **Edge of Midnight: The Life of John Schlesinger** (Hutchinson, London), published a year after Schlesinger's death, benefits hugely from Mann's unrestricted access to diaries and production notes, as well as lengthy interviews with the director and Michael Childers, his partner of more than 35 years. Mann shows considerable but far from uncritical affection for a film-maker

United Artists/Kobal

who, after the failure of *Yanks* (1979), came to realise that he would never better *Sunday, Bloody Sunday* or *Midnight Cowboy*.

Icons in the Fire (Orion, London), subtitled *The Decline and Fall of Almost Everybody in the British Film Industry, 1984–2000*, is the posthumously published final volume in Alexander Walker's three-part history of British cinema. He writes in sorrow and anger of the terminal rot that he believed set in with the sale of Elstree Studios and the EMI film library and cinema chain to Menahem Golan and Yoram Globus' Cannon Films in 1985, and includes a riveting examination of David Puttnam's short-lived tenure at Columbia. When Walker considers *My Beautiful Laundrette* or Branagh's *Henry V* one recalls the stylish, passionate critic who was a key draw for the London *Evening Standard*'s readers for 40 years.

Walker famously engaged in "argy-bargy" with Ken Loach at a Cannes press conference in 1991, attacking *Hidden Agenda*, and the incident is recalled in *Icons in the Fire* and Anthony Hayward's **Which Side Are You On? Ken Loach and His Films** (Bloomsbury, London), a solid account that is strong on the director's close working relationships with writers Jim Allen, Barry Hines and Paul Laverty.

The European new wave that influenced Loach is analysed and celebrated by *IFG* founding editor Peter Cowie in **Revolution! The Explosion of World Cinema in the 60s** (Faber, London and New York). Cowie, whose life was transformed by seeing *The Seventh Seal* in 1958, combines his own recollections of the decade (including being caught up in the demonstrations at Cannes in 1968) and its films with extensive new interviews with 20 key directors, among them Boorman, Forman, Makavejev and former Paris film school classmates Schlöndorff and Tavernier.

Hollywood

After the best-selling *Easy Riders, Raging Bulls*, Peter Biskind again demonstrates his ability to tap the interview sources other writers cannot

reach in **Down and Dirty Pictures** (Bloomsbury, London), his weighty and abrasive history of Miramax, Sundance and the rise of independent film. Sundance founder Robert Redford features as somewhat of a fallen idol and the domineering anti-hero is Harvey Weinstein, beloved patron saint and detested sinner of the indie movement. As Miramax workers liken their jobs to "factory labour in a Third World country" and film-makers bear witness to Harvey's "most base kind" of creative interference, the cumulative effect is of a never-ending screening room row between arrogant millionaires screaming "Go fuck yourself!" This makes the book simultaneously unreadable and (in very small doses) impossible to put down.

In Joe Eszterhas' autobiography, **Hollywood Animal** (Knopf, New York; Hutchinson, London), the status of the man who gave us *Flashdance* and *Basic Instinct* as the hero of every story (even when admitting marital infidelity) is summed up by his chapter headings: "I Kill Rocky Balboa", "I Coldcock Ovitz", "I Redeem Myself". At 730 pages, the book desperately needed an icepick-wielding editor, but there are many priceless tales, notably an early battle with Sylvester Stallone over the writing credit for *F.I.S.T.*.

Hardboiled Hollywood – The Origins of the Great Crime Films (No Exit Press, Harpenden) presents a splendid idea stylishly executed, as Max Décharné traces the journey from page to screen of 11 great crime films, including *Psycho*, *Point Blank* and *L.A. Confidential*. The best of the 25 portraits of Hollywood stars in Peter Bogdanovich's **Who the Hell's in It** (Faber, London; Knopf, New York) is also the most personal, as he assesses the talent and mourns the loss of River Phoenix, who died soon after they worked together on the little-seen drama *The Thing Called Love*.

Interviews

The "Conversations with Film-Makers" series from the University Press of Mississippi, Jackson, continues with **Fritz Lang**, edited by Barry Keith Grant, and **Pedro Almodóvar**, edited by Paula Willoquet-Maricondi, the latter including welcome

English translations of several lively interviews originally published in Spanish. In **Robert Aldrich**, edited by Eugene L. Miller, Jr. and Edwin Arnold, there are no-nonsense reflections on a hardboiled oeuvre.

Kevin Jackson's revised **Schrader on Schrader** (Faber, London) adds *Light Sleeper, Affliction, Auto Focus* and the director's misadventures on *Exorcist: The Beginning* to the powerful body of work covered by the original edition. **Trier on von Trier**, edited by Stig Björkman, covers the co-founder of Dogme's ceaselessly provocative and inventive career up to pre-production on *Manderlay*. In **Minghella on Minghella**, editor Timothy Bricknell lets the director of the over-praised *The English Patient* and the unfairly maligned *Cold Mountain* do all the talking, and while Minghella is occasionally prone to gush about his collaborators, he's fascinating on his use of landscape and Gabriel Yared's music in trying "to create operas using prose".

David A. Goldsmith's beautifully and extensively illustrated **The Documentary Makers** (RotoVision, Hove) brings to life the working methods and films of Barbara Koppel, Ken Burns, Errol Morris, Jürgen Leth and a dozen other leading exponents of cinema and television non-fiction. Pascal Pinteau's **Special Effects: An Oral History** (Harry N. Abrams, New York and London) highlights many of the quantum leaps in SFX technology, with 1,000-plus illustrations.

Film Studies

Recent additions to the Modern Classics series (bfi, London) include Manhola Dargis' earnest take on **L.A. Confidential** and a superb **Unforgiven** by Edward Buscombe. Ryan Gilbey's enjoyable **Groundhog Day** features revealing comments from screenwriter Danny Rubin. Two compact and user-friendly entries to the bfi's Screen Guides series see Jason Wood write brief essays on **100 American Independent Films**, while Philip Brophy does the same for **100 Modern Soundtracks**. Wood's alphabetical selection rounds up the usual suspects (*Being John Malkovich, Boogie Nights,*

Easy Rider), and encourages readers to seek out unsung works such as Lizzie Borden's *Born in Flames* (1983). Gönül Dönmez-Colin provides a timely analysis of the relationship between **Women, Islam and Cinema** (Reaktion Books, London), concentrating mainly on films from Turkey and Iran.

Art and Photography

Damian Pettigrew's **I'm a Born Liar – A Fellini Lexicon** (Harry N. Abrams, New York) collects the maestro's observations on everything from Epiphanies to Hype and Flash Gordon, with a magnificent assortment of colour and black-and-white photos. Karl French's eclectic **Art by Film Directors** (Mitchell Beazley, London) combines the familiar (Kurosawa and Jarman's paintings, Alan Parker's cartoons) and the revelatory (Mike Figgis' black-and-white photos of female nudes; a Chagall-like painting by John Huston).

Western devotees should derive equal pleasure from the text and illustrations of Peter Cowie's utterly absorbing **John Ford and the American West** (Harry N. Abrams, New York and London), which shows how Ford's screen vision was influenced by Albert Bierstadt, Frederic Remington and Charles M. Russell's paintings of cowboys, wagon trains and cavalry charges. **Twentieth Century Fox – Inside the Photo Archive** (Harry N. Abrams, New York and London) is a treasure trove of mainly black-and-white images. Some are poignant (the doomed Sharon Tate shooting *Valley of the Dolls*), others iconic (Fonda in *The Grapes of Wrath*)

Hollywood Horror: from Gothic to Cosmic (Harry N. Abrams, New York) has 260 immaculately reproduced black-and-white photographs to complement Mark A. Vieira's comprehensive survey of the genre. **Horror Poster Art**, edited by Tony Nourmand and Graham Marsh (Aurum, London), has an admirably international flavour pulling together Gothic, slasher, suspense and comic imagery. Finally, Taschen's bargain-priced, picture-led surveys of decades now includes Jürgen Müller's **Movies of the 60s** and **Movies of the 70s**.

Other Recent Publications

Alfred Hitchcock – A Life in Darkness and Light – Patrick McGilligan (Wiley, Chichester). Mammoth biography of the master of suspense.

Alice Guy Blaché – Lost Visionary of the Cinema – Alison McMahan (Continuum, New York and London). Biography of the first woman-film-maker, whose output in the early 1900s totalled approximately 1,000 films (mostly lost).

Bollywood – A Guidebook to Popular Hindi Cinema – Tejaswini Ganti (Routledge, New York and London). Concise, very readable primer on the world's most prolific movie industry.

Buster Keaton – Tempest in a Flat Hat – Edward McPherson (Faber, London). Concise, tersely written biography of the comic genius who "created a silent poetry of camera and limb".

Cinema's Illusions, Opera's Allure – David Schroeder (Continuum, New York, London). Lively study of "the operatic impulse in film". Ranges from 'Opera Snobbery in *Hannah and Her Sisters*' to *Apocalypse Now*.

The Cinema of Latin America – Edited by Alberto Elena & Marina Díaz López (Wallflower Press, London). Twenty-four academic essays.

The Cinema of Terrence Malick – Edited by Hannah Paterson (Wallflower Press, London). Fourteen academic essays.

Contemporary Cinema of Latin America – Deborah Shaw (Continuum, New York and London). Includes a penetrating chapter comparing Hector Babenco's *Pixote* and Walter Salles' *Central Station* as Brazilian allegories.

The Films of Peter Weir – Jonathan Rayner (Continuum, New York and London). Academic study of Australia's most versatile director.

Get Your Film Funded – UK Film Finance Guide 2005 – Caroline Hancock and Nic Wistreich (Shooting People Press, London).

Getting Into Films & TV – Robert Angell (How To Books, Oxford). Nuts and bolts explanations of production; also pragmatic advice on "Selling Yourself".

Godard – A Portrait of the Artist at 70 – Colin MacCabe (Bloomsbury, London). MacCabe presents "a series of angles on Godard's life and work", including a memoir of his own collaborations with the director in the 1980s and 1990s.

The Guerrilla Film-Makers' Hollywood Handbook – Genevieve Jolliffe and Chris Jones (Continuum, New York and London). Interviews with 100 US film industry personnel; engrossing case studies, including *thirteen* and *Donnie Darko*.

Horizons West – Jim Kitses (bfi, London). Essays on Ford, Mann, Boetticher, Peckinpah, Leone and Eastwood.

Hungarian Cinema – From Coffee-House to Multiplex – John Cunningham (Wallflower Press, London). István Szabó, Miklós Jancsó and Marta Mészaros loom large in this fine history.

Natalie Wood – Gavin Lambert (Faber, London). Lambert's elegant prose, insider's knowledge of Hollywood and 20-year friendship with Wood make for an exceptionally rewarding biography.

Paul Newman – Daniel O'Brien (Faber, London). Workmanlike biography. The most astute comments come second-hand from Newman.

Projections 13 – Edited by Isabella Weibrecht and John Boorman (Faber, London and New York). Typically diverse edition of the Faber journal, on "Women film-makers on film-making".

The Seven Basic Plots – Why We Tell Stories – Christopher Booker (Continuum, New York and London). Spielberg and *The Terminator* rub shoulders with Proust and Wagner in Booker's monumental study of narrative through the ages.

Shooting Stars – Harry Shapiro (Serpent's Tail, London). Shapiro's title plays on "Action!" and injections as he examines drugs in movies, from *Reefer Madness* to *Trainspotting*.

The Stats (bfi Information Services, London). User-friendly statistics on the British film, TV and home video industries from 1990–2001. (Available direct only. Tel: +44 [0]20 7255 1444).

Very Naughty Boys – Robert Sellers (Metro, London). Entertaining history of Handmade Films, the company behind *Life of Brian*.

World Survey

6 continents | 97 countries | 1,000s of films…

Algeria Roy Armes

Recent Films

MON AMIE MA SOEUR
(My Friend, My Sister)
[Drama, 2003] Script and Dir:
Mohamed Lebcir. Prod:
Wahid Films.

CHOUCHOU
[Comedy, 2003] Script and Dir:
Merzak Allouache. Phot: Laurent
Machuel. Players: Gad Elmaleh,
Alain Chabat, Claude Brasseur,
Roschy Zem, Catherine Frot.
Prod: Les Films Christian
Fechner/France 2 Cinéma/KS2
Productions (France).

VIVA LALDGÉRIE
[Drama, 2003] Script and Dir:
Nadir Moknèche. Phot: Jean-
Claude Larrieu. Players: Lubna
Azabal, Biyouna, Nadia Kaci.
Prod: Sunday Morning
(Paris)/Need (Brussels)/
BL (Algiers).

LE SOLEIL ASSASSINÉ
(The Murdered Sun)
[Drama, 2003] Script and Dir:
Abdelkrim Bahloul. Phot: Charlie
Van Damme. Players: Charles
Berling, Mehdi Dehbi, Ouassini
Embarek, Abbes Zahmani,
Clotilde de Bayser, Alexis Loret.
Prod: Mact Productions
(France)/Les Films du Fleuve
(Belgium).

B oujemaa Karèche, director of the Algerian Cinémathèque, was not exaggerating when he noted: "Algerian cinema in 2000: zero production, zero film theatres, zero distributors, zero tickets sold." No Algerian features were made between 1997 and 2002. There was simply no finance available in the country after the state production organisation was completely shut down in 1998.

Though director Yamina Bachir-Chouikh remained in Algeria, her internationally acclaimed *Rachida* (see *IFG 2004*), which ended the production drought, was made totally with French money. A funding scheme based on a tax on box-office receipts dried up (there were virtually no box-office receipts to tax) and had to be supplemented by the Ministry of Culture, with the aim of producing five films to celebrate the thousand year history of Algiers.

But only when this was supplemented again, by joint Algerian-French funding to celebrate the Year of Algeria in France (2002), did the first of these five films emerge, *The Neighbour* (see *IFG 2004*). The funding of nine further projects to celebrate the Year of Algeria has proved more successful – four of the films discussed here were backed with modest sums – but the bulk of all budgets must still come from state funds in Europe (mostly various French sources).

The only Algerian-based film-maker to produce a feature in 2003 was Mohamed Lebcir, who had worked in local television. **My Friend My Sister** (*Mon amie ma soeur*) is a familiar tale of the Algerian War, dealing with a hospital cleaner who is persuaded to steal medical aid supplies and smuggle them to the resistance. The other two fictional features set in Algeria were made by exiles and take lighter approaches to contemporary themes. Abdelkrim Bahloul, who had been totally identified with immigrant cinema in France since his debut with *Mint Tea* in 1974, made **The Murdered Sun** (*Le soleil assassiné*), the tale of two theatre students, ejected from a competition because their play is in French and then befriended by the (real) French-language Algerian poet, Jean Sénac.

Nadir Moknèche had set his commercially successful debut *The Harem of Mme Osmane* in Algiers, but felt constrained to shoot it in Morocco. This time, for **Viva Laldgérie**, he did shoot in Algiers, but again used French rather than Arabic dialogue. The film follows the unfulfilled lives of three women living in the same hotel: a mother who longs nostalgically for the past, her daughter who leads a liberated, Westernised life and her friend, who works as a prostitute.

War stories

Two other Algerian-born but foreign-based directors also returned to film in Algeria, both making documentaries reflecting on the Algerian War. Jean-Pierre Lledo, who had earlier directed two features for the state organisations of the 1980s and 1990s, made **An Algerian Dream** (*Un rêve algérien*). This is an exploratory journey to the lost dreamworld of a colonial childhood, made by the director along with Henri Alleg, author of *The Question*, the classic study of French torture in Algeria.

Mohamed Soudani's previous feature-length documentary, *Waalo fendo*, was set among the Senegalese illegal immigrant community in Milan. Now, returning home for the first time since he settled in Switzerland in 1987, Soudani made **War Without Images** (*Guerre sans images*), which looks at Algeria's past and present and the interplay between reality and the photographic image.

By contrast, Merzak Allouache's **Chouchou** is set in the immigrant community in Paris and marks his return to the field of comedy, following the pattern of the highly successful *Salut cousin!* and reuniting the director with the star of that film, Gad Elmaleh. Again, a young Algerian arrives in Paris, this time disguised as a Chilean refugee, and discovers the dazzling world of Clichy. Chouchou is so successful in his assumed role of transvestite dancer that one of the customers, Stanislas, falls in love with him, provoking farcical consequences. The film was a box-office hit in France in 2003.

ROY ARMES (roy@royarmes.freeserve.co.uk) is Emeritus Professor of Film at Middlesex University, London, and has written widely on Third World and, especially, African cinemas. His latest book is *Post Colonial Images: Studies in North African Film* (University of Indiana Press).

A victim shows her scar in
War Without Images

GUERRE SANS IMAGES
(**War Without Images**)
[Documentary, 2002] Script and Dir: Mohamed Soudani. Phot: Paul Nocol, Mohamed Soudani, Michael von Graffenried. Prod: Soudani, von Graffenried, Amka Films.

UN REVE ALGERIEN
(**An Algerian Dream**)
[Documentary, 2003] Script and Dir: Jean-Pierre Lledo. Phot: Jean-Jacques Mrejen. Prod: Maha Productions/Nawel Film (France, Algeria)/Tarentula (Belgium).

Quote of the Year

"The absence of images robs Algeria of its reality. It constructs a fantasy country that doesn't exist."
BENJAMIN STORA,
Algerian-born historian.

Les Films Christian Fechner

Gad Elmaleh, left, as **Chouchou** *with Alain Chabat*

Argentina Alfredo Friedlander

The Year's Best Films

Alfredo Friedlander's selection:

Valentín
(Alejandro Agresti)
Bar El Chino
(Daniel Burak)
I Don't Know What Your Eyes Have Done to Me
(Docu. Lorena Muñoz, Sergio Wolf)
Roma (Adolfo Aristarain)
Good Life Delivery
(Leonardo Di Cesare)

Boy Olmi and Gimena La Torre in **Bar El Chino**

Recent and Forthcoming Films

BAR EL CHINO
[Comedy-drama, 2003] Script: Mario Lion, Beatriz Pustilnik, Daniel Burak. Dir: Burak. Phot: Sergio Dotta. Players: Boy Olmi, Jimena La Torre, Juan Pablo Baillinou, Lucas Santa Ana, Ernesto Larrese, Néstor Sánchez, Pasta Dioguardi, José Sacristán. Prod: Mario Lion.
Encouraged by a 26-year-old woman, a 47-year-old film-maker resumes work on his unfinished documentary about Bar El Chino, which is rooted in tango music.

Argentina's Silver Condor Awards are listed on p.95

Although 53 Argentine features were released in 2003 – the highest number for 50 years – local movies claimed only 9% of the box-office. Public and critics agreed that quantity did not necessarily mean quality, and few domestic features made an impression, not helped by an uneven distribution schedule. In the first four months of 2003 only five Argentine films opened, then 16 opened between May and August and 32 in the last four months, and in several weeks three simultaneous local releases inevitably led to disastrous results for distributors.

Happily, the picture in 2004 was completely different, with 25 local releases in the first six months and the general improvement in quality highlighted by the success at Berlin 2004 of **A Lost Embrace** (*El abrazo partido*), which received two Silver Bears, for the picture and lead actor Daniel Hendler.

Daniel Hendler in **A Lost Embrace**

Best of the fests

In March 2004, the 19th International Film Festival of Mar del Plata chose for the first time a local production, **Good Life Delivery** (*Buena vida delivery*), as its Best Film. The name and design of the award (called Ombú in the past) was changed to the Astor, in honour of Astor Piazzola, the late tango composer, who was born in Mar del Plata. Among the distinguished guests visiting the city were Bob Rafelson, Ken Russell, Phillip Noyce, Alan Rickman and Hector Babenco, whose *Carandiru* opened the festival out of competition. The director of the festival, Miguel Pereira, emphasised the orientation towards Latin American cinematography. President Néstor Kirchner attended a ceremony honouring Pino Solanas, followed by a screening of his recent **Memoría del saqueo** (literally, *Memories of the Plundering*).

In April 2004, the sixth Buenos Aires International Film Festival (BAFICI) brought more good news for Argentine movies, its jury unanimously choosing Ana Poliak's Pin Boy (*Parapalos*) as best movie. The festival dedicated retrospectives to Raul Ruiz, who attended, Glauber Rocha and Jonas Mekas among others. But overall at this BAFICI, quantity (more than 300 films, including shorts) outpaced quality for local and international movies.

Argentina had two films in the main competition at Cannes in 2004, Lucrecia Martel's **The Holy Girl** (*La niña santa*) and, as a co-producer, Walter Salles' **The Motorcycle Diaries** (*Diarios de motocicleta*). Lisandro Alonso's second feature, **The Dead** (*Los muertos*), took part in the Directors' Fortnight.

Among the 2004 releases from established directors, Adolfo Aristarain's **Roma**, a co-production with Spain, was well received by the critics, unlike another Spanish co-production, **The Whore and the Whale** (*La puta y la ballena*), directed by Luis Puenzo (*The Official Story*). Juan Carlos Campanella's **Avellaneda Moon** (*Luna de Avellaneda*) teams him again with lead actor Ricardo Darín from *Son of the Bride* and became a major hit. Other important directors such as Alejandro Agresti and Pablo Trapero were scheduled to release new films in the second half of 2004.

The number of films from new Argentine directors awaiting release has been steadily increasing and an important new law has been passed obliging every screen in Argentina to exhibit a local film for at least one week per quarter. This will give many anxious directors an opportunity to show their movies. It will also encourage students at the various film schools, such as the Universidad del Cine, which has almost 800 students.

The lack of art theatres in Argentina means that there is an increasingly two-tiered distribution structure, between blockbusters from the US and independent Argentinean releases. Films from countries other than the US and Argentina will mostly screen only at the two film festivals in March and April, which may not satisfy a public that has traditionally enjoyed foreign films all year round.

ALFREDO FRIEDLANDER (fredyfriedlander@ciudad.com.ar) is a member of the Asociación de Cronistas Cinematograficos de Argentina. He is a regular columnist on www.leedor.com, presents movies at the Cine Club Nucleo and is, above all, a film buff.

YO NO SÉ QUÉ ME HAN HECHO TUS OJOS
(I Don't Know What Your Eyes Have Done to Me)
[Documentary, 2003] Script and Dir: Lorena Muñoz, Sergio Wolf. Phot: Segundo Cerrato, Federico Ransenberg, Marcelo Lavintman. Prod: Marcelo Céspedes, Carmen Guarini.
In 1942, Ada Falcón, one of the great legends of tango, retired prematurely and took up residence in a convent, vowing never to sing or be interviewed again. Now she tells her story.

EL ABRAZO PARTIDO
(A Lost Embrace)
[Comedy-drama 2003] Script: Marcelo Birmajer, Daniel Burman. Dir: Burman. Phot: Ramiro Civita. Players: Daniel Hendler, Adriana Aizemberg, Jorge D'Elía, Sergio Boris, Diego Korol, Norman Erlich, Rosita Londner. Prod: BD Cine.
An encounter between a father and his estranged son (Hendler).

LOS GUANTES MÁGICOS
(The Magic Gloves)
[Comedy, 2003] Script and Dir: Martín Rejtman. Phot: José Luis García. Players: Gabriel "Vicentico" Fernández Capello, Valeria Bertucelli, Fabián Arenillas, Cecilia Biagini, Susana Pampín. Prod: Martín Rejtman, Rizoma Films/Artcam International (France)/Pandora Film Produktion (Germany).
When his girlfriend dumps him, the chauffeur of a Renault 12 gets involved in what he thinks is a promising business venture: selling imported gloves.

EL JUEGO DE LA SILLA
(Musical Chairs)
[Comedy-drama, 2002] Script and Dir: Ana Katz. Phot: Paola Rizzi. Players: Raquel Bank, Diego de Paula, Ana Katz, Luciana Lifschitz, Verónica Moreno, Nicolás Tacconi. Prod: Universidad del Cine/ Tresplanos Cine.
Many years after emigrating to Canada, Victor (de Paula) returns

to Argentina. Various games, songs and meals demonstrate how distant his family and friends have become.

BUENA VIDA DELIVERY
(Good Life Delivery)
[Drama, 2004] Script: Leonardo Di Cesare, Hans Garrino. Dir: Di Cesare. Phot: Leandro Martínez. Players: Ignacio Toselli, Moro Anghileri, Oscar Núñez, Alicia Palmes, Sofía da Silva, Ariel Staltari, Pablo Ribba, Marcelo Nací, Gabriel Goity. Prod: La Normanda Prods./INCAA/Tu vas voir (Paris).
Since his family emigrated to Spain, Hernán (Toselli), a delivery boy, has lived alone in his parents' house. When he invites a girl to move in, her entire family comes too, and chaos ensues.

MEMORIA DEL SAQUEO
(literally, **Memories of the Plundering**)
[Documentary, 2003] Script and Dir: Fernando Ezequiel Solanas. Phot: Alejandro Fernández Muján, Solanas. Prod: Cinesur/Thelma Film AG (Zurich)/ADR Productions (Paris)/Télévision Suisse Romande.
An analysis of the economic, social, political and moral decadence in Argentina between 1976 and 2001.

Mercedes Morán in **The Holy Girl**

LA NIÑA SANTA
(The Holy Girl)
[Drama, 2004] Script and Dir: Lucrecia Martel. Phot: Felix Monti. Players: Mercedes Morán, Carlos Belloso, Alejandro Urdapilleta, María Alché, Julieta Zylberberg, Mónica Villa, Mía Maestro. Prod: Lita Stantic, El Deseo (Spain)/Senso/ La Pasionaria/Teodora (Italy),

Miguel Angel Solá in **The Whore and the Whale**

R&C (Italy).
A chance encounter between Amalia and Dr Jano, who is attending a medical conference at a hotel owned by Amalia's family, enables the young girl to find her vocation: to save a man from sin.

18-J
[Political drama, 2004] Script and Dir: Adrián Caetano, Daniel Burman, Lucía Cedrón, Alberto Lecchi, Juan B. Stagnaro, Marcelo Schapces, Mauricio Wainrot, Adrián Suar, Alejandro Doria, Carlos Sorín. Prod: Aleph Media/BD Cine/Cinema Digital/ Cinetauro/El Puente/Kaos/ Patagonik Film Group/Pol-Ka/ Universidad Nacional de Tres de Febrero/Zarlek.
On July 18, 1994, a bomb exploded at the Argentine-Israeli Mutual Association, killing 85 people. 18-J is a compilation of 10 shorts conceived as tributes to the victims.

LUNA DE AVELLANEDA
(Avellaneda Moon)
[Social drama, 2004] Script: Fernando Castets, Juan Pablo Domenech, Juan José Campanella. Dir: Campanella. Phot: Daniel Schulman. Players: Ricardo Darín, Mercedes Morán, Eduardo Blanco, Valeria Bertucelli, Silvia Kutica, Daniel Fanego, Atilio Pozzobón. Prod: Pol-ka Producciones/100 Bares Producciones/Tornasol Films (Spain).
Members of the almost bankrupt

Luna de Avellaneda social and sports club struggle to keep it alive. Then an old member comes up with the perfect solution: sell the club and turn it into a casino.

LA PUTA Y LA BALLENA
(The Whore and the Whale)
[Drama, 2003] Script: Luis Puenzo, Lucía Puenzo, Ángeles González-Sinde. Dir: Luis Puenzo. Phot: José Luis Alcaine. Players: Aitana Sánchez-Gijón, Leonardo Sbaraglia, Miguel Ángel Solá, Mercé Llorens, Edward Nutkiewicz. Prod: Wanda Vision (Spain)/Patagonik Film Group/Historias Cinematográficas.
We cut between the arrival of a whale in Patagonia in the 1930s and its reappearance seven decades later at a hotel that was once a brothel and belongs to a tango player and composer.

EL NÚREMBERG ARGENTINO
(The Argentine Nuremberg)
[Documentary, 2003] Script: Fredy Torres, Miguel Rodríguez Arias. Dir: Rodríguez Arias. Phot: Carpo Cortés. Prod: Metrópolis Media Group/Anola Films/Plural.
Examination of the 1985 trial of members of the military junta that had ruled Argentina 1976-83.

TAN DE REPENTE
(So All of a Sudden)
[Road movie, 2003] Script: Diego

Lerman, María Meira. Dir: Lerman. Phot: Luciano Zito, Diego del Piano. Players: Carla Crespo, Tatiana Saphir, Verónica Hassan, Beatriz Thibaudin, Marcos Ferrante, María Merlino. Prod: Diego Lerman, Lita Stantic, Nylon Cine/Hubert Bals Fund (Netherlands).
Two punk girls bump into virgin and embark on a breathtaking, fantastical journey.

ROMA
[Drama, 2004] Script: Adolfo Aristarain, Mario Camus, Kathy Saavedra. Dir: Aristarain. Phot: José Luis Alcaine. Players: Juan Diego Botto, José Sacristán, Susú Pecoraro, Marcela Kloosterboer, Luis Luque, Gustavo Garzón. Prod: Tesela P.C. (Spain)/Aristarian P.C.
The relationship between a writer and the young journalism student hired to transcribe his memoirs.

CLEOPATRA
[Comedy, 2003] Script: Silvina Cahgue. Dir: Eduardo Mignogna. Phot: Marcelo Camorino. Players: Norma Aleandro, Natalia Oreiro, Leonardo Sbaraglia, Héctor Alterio, Alberto de Mendoza. Prod: Carlos Luis Mentasti, Telefé/Pablo Bossi, Patagonik.
A retired teacher and a famous soap-opera actress go on the weekend trip of a lifetime.

EL POLAQUITO
(The Little Pole)
[Social drama, 2003] Script: Juan Carlos Desanzo, Ángel O. Espinoza. Dir: Desanzo. Phot: Carlos Torlaschi. Players: Abel Ayala, Marina Glezer, Fernando Roa, Roly Serrano, Laura Spínola, Lucas Lasarich, Fabián Arenillas. Prod: Desanzo, José María Calleja de la Fuente.
A 13-year-old urchin who makes a living singing tangos at Buenos Aires Central Station in the style of famous singer "Polish" Goyeneche falls in love with a young prostitute.

AY JUANCITO
[Historical drama, 2004] Script:

José Pablo Feiman, Héctor Olivera. Dir: Olivera. Phot: Willi Benisch. Players: Adrián Navarro, Inés Estévez, Leticia Bredice, Laura Novoa, Jorge Marrale, Norma Aleandro, Atilio Pozzobon, Roberto Carnaghi. Prod: Tercer Milenio, Aries Cinematográfica Argentina
Juan "Juancito" Duarte was Evita's only brother and Peron's private secretary. He was the most sought-after bachelor in the country, but Evita's death and his own incurable syphilis led him to a tragic end.

PARAPALOS (Pin Boy)
[Drama, 2004] Script: Ana Poliak, Cis Bierinckx. Dir: Poliak. Phot: Victor "Kino" González, Alejandro Fernández Mouján. Players: Adrián Suárez, Nancy Torres. Prod: Viada Producciones s.r.l./Desire Productions A.S.B.L. (Belgium).
A young country boy finds work as a parapalos (pin boy), putting up bowling pins in one of Buenos Aires' few remaining manual bowling alleys.

ADIOS QUERIDA LUNA
(Goodbye, Dear Moon)
[Comedy, 2003] Script: Sergio Bizzio, Javier Diment, Alejandro Urdapilleta, Alejandra Flechner, Fernando Spiner. Dir: Spiner. Phot: Claudio Beiza. Players: Flechner, Horacio Fontova, Gabriel Goity, Urdapilleta, Rita Morchio, Manu Soler. Prod: Azpeitía Cine.
In 2068, Earth is threatened by constant typhoons and floods. When an Argentine scientist determines that this is due to the gravitational pull of the moon, the government launches space mission "Goodbye, Dear Moon" to destroy it and establish Argentina as a world leader.

Quote of the Year
"Our young film-makers are prophets in foreign lands, recognised by international juries and critics."
NÉSTOR KIRCHNER,
President of Argentina, in his speech during the 2004 Mar del Plata Film Festival.

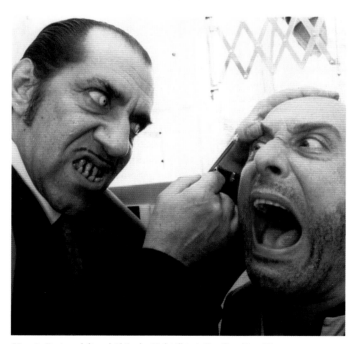

Horacio Fontova, left, and Alejandro Urdapilleta in **Goodbye, Dear Moon**

Armenia Susanna Harutyunyan

Recent and Forthcoming Films

JEANO (Jeano)
[Drama, 2004] Script and Dir: Suren Babayan, Phot: Ashot Movsisyan. Players: Jean-Pier Nshanian, Anna Laray, Matsak Hovhannisyan. Prod: Hayfilm Studio.

ARAHET (Path)
[Drama, 2005] Script: Rouben Kochar, Eduard Khald. Dir: Kochar. Phot: Armen Khachatrian, Ashot Movsesyan, Robert Balasanyan. Players: Harutyun Movsisyan, Ashot Adamyan, Armen Elbakyan. Prod: Hayfilm/Armenfilm/Blue Lion Entertainment (US).

TAK ERKIR – TSURT DZMER (Hot Country, Cold Winter)
[Drama, 2004] Script: David Safaryan, Yana Drouz. Dir: Safaryan. Phot: Jarek Raczek, Armen Khachatryan, Ashot Mkrtchyan. Players: Ashot Adamyan, Yana Drouz, Karen Janibekyan. Prod: Studio DS/Armenfilm/NFM Production (The Netherlands)/Studio 217 (Russia)/HFF Potsdam-Babelsberg Production (Germany).

MARIAM
[Drama, 2004] Script and Dir: Edgar Baghdasaryan. Phot: Vahagn Ter-Hakobyan. Players: Janet Harutyunyan. Prod: Hayfilm Studio.

LOVEMBER
[Lyrical drama, 2004] Script and Dir: Tigran Xmalyan. Phot: Samvel Amirkhanyan. Players: Sergey Danielyan, Lilit Stepanyan, Karen Janibekyan. Prod: Yerevan Film Studio.

Armenian cinema celebrates its eightieth birthday in 2005. It was in 1925 that the first state-run studio, Armenkino, produced the country's first feature, Hamo Bek-Nazarov's *Namus*, the melodramatic story of a young couple who fall victim to prejudices and *namus*, the stagnant Armenian notion of honour. Renamed Hayfilm, this studio remains in state hands (despite recent, widespread rumours about its possible privatisation or even sale to foreigners) and shared subsidy of around $800,000 (432m drams) for 2004 with another state-run studio, Hayk, of which slightly more than half is allocated to live-action fiction feature production, the balance going to animation, documentaries, preservation and festival/market promotion.

Matsak Hovhannisyan as Matso, left, and Jean-Pier Nshanian as Jeano in **Jeano**

This is enough for Hayfilm to make around a dozen projects – features and shorts – in 2004, one of which, Suren Babayan's **Jeano**, had its premiere in July. Jeano is a photographer and cameraman, who, like many other artists during the recent, economically strained "times of transition", no longer has a chance to follow his vocation. Forced to earn money doing something which is incompatible with both his soul and talents, he decides to fake news of his death through the mass media and leaves for the "paradise" of his childhood, where he will stay forever.

A strange way home

In a rare example of Armenian/US co-production (Hayfilm/Armenfilm and Blue Lion Entertainment), Rouben Kochar directed the fantastical psychological drama **Path** (*Arahet*). The hero, Avetik, is an Armenian who's gone to America and works as a petrol station employee and night-shift taxi driver. One night, beside the freeway, Avetik finds a little path that miraculously leads him back to Armenia to visit his parents. Nobody believes him, but he makes the trip several times, before the path disappears as he chooses to embrace the new goals and hopes that America offers him.

Based on Bellini's classic opera, the Russian-Armenian **Norma** is another interesting co-production. Armenian-born, Moscow-based Boris Hayrapetyan directs several famous Armenian singers against a backdrop of marvellous Armenian locations and Hellenic and early Christian architecture.

Two films exploring the story of the Virgin Mary and reviewed in *IFG 2004*, Edgar Baghdasaryan's *Mariam* and Tigran Xmalyan's *Lovember* were still awaiting release in September 2004. Among new projects started in 2004 are Vigen Chaldranian's large-scale historical drama, *Full Moon* (*Lialousin*), which takes us back to when Armenia adopted Christianity in 301AD, and two short debuts: psychological drama *Following the Light* (*Louysi Hetkov*) by Vrezh Petrosyan and Gagik Harutyunyan's social drama *Yarkhoushta* (named after the Armenian folk dance traditionally presented by men who are about to leave for war).

In Yerevan from June 30 to July 4, 2004, audiences attended the first International Film Festival Golden Apricot ("apricot" in Latin is *prunus Armeniaca*, meaning Armenian plum). It was a vital development in helping to put the country on the world cinema map and included a competition with 61 films made by Armenian film-makers or film-makers of Armenian origin, a non-competitive section and retrospectives dedicated to three eightieth anniversaries: the founding of Armenian cinema, Sergey Parajanov and Charles Aznavour.

The festival became a symbolic unification of film-makers from Armenia and its diaspora, including many young participants at the festival making their first visit to the country and, in some cases, deciding to prolong their stay or promising to return to work on a future project. For example, Toronto-based director Garine Torossian shot important scenes of her new film just after the festival. The second Golden Apricot will be held from July 12 to 17, 2005 under the slogan "Armenia as a Cultural Crossroads", with two competition sections, for fiction and documentary films, and Pan-Armenian Panorama section (details at www.gaiff.am).

SUSANNA HARUTYUNYAN graduated in film criticism from Moscow's State Cinema Institute in 1987. She has been film critic of the daily *Respublika Armenia* since 1991 and is president of Armenia's Association of Film Critics and Cinema Journalists.

Love story of an odd young couple, a street musician and a nurse, who in the year 2000 try to give birth to God.

LIALOUSIN (Full Moon)
[Historical drama, 2005] Script: Vigen Chaldranyan, Anahit Aghasaryan. Dir: Chaldranyan. Phot: Vahagn Ter-Hakobyan. Players: Ruzanna Vit, Karen Janibekyan, Marine Sargsyan, Karen Jangirov. Prod: Hayfilm/Armenfilm/Symphony Pictures (US).
A Russian report of the discovery of a wooden structure on Mt. Ararat sends an international expedition up its slopes. Among them is Hayk Armenian, a historian who stumbles onto a cave inhabited by an ancient Priestess. We flash back to her story in 301AD, when she prophesies the country's conversion from pagan rituals to Christianity by Gregory the Illuminator.

Ruzanna Vit as a priestess in **Full Moon**

Quote of the Year

"I am so proud! Of all the attention *Ararat* received, this award is the most meaningful."
ATOM EGOYAN *accepts his Grand Prix at the first Golden Apricot Film Festival.*

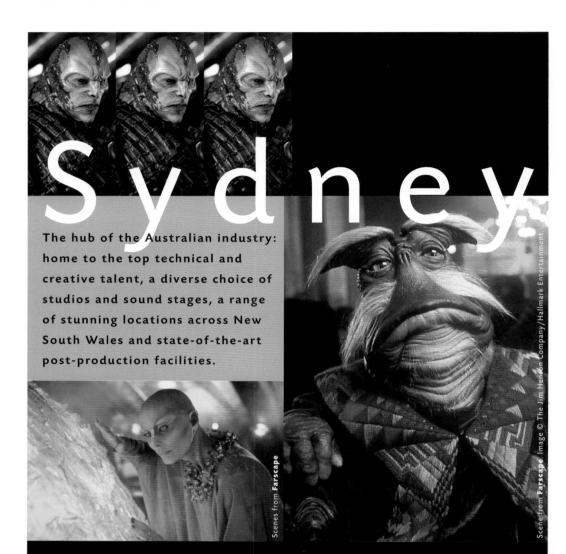

Sydney

The hub of the Australian industry: home to the top technical and creative talent, a diverse choice of studios and sound stages, a range of stunning locations across New South Wales and state-of-the-art post-production facilities.

Scenes from **Farscape**

Scene from **Farscape**. Image © The Jim Henson Company/Hallmark Entertainment.

If you're planning to shoot in Australia, you can't afford to overlook Sydney and New South Wales.

New South Wales Film and Television Office
Level 7, 157 Liverpool Street, Sydney NSW 2000, Australia
TEL 612 9264 6400 **FAX** 612 9264 4388
EMAIL fto@fto.nsw.gov.au **WEB** www.fto.nsw.gov.au

fto 212

Australia Peter Thompson

The Year's Best Films

Peter Thompson's selection:

Tom White
(Akinos Tslimidos)

Somersault
(Cate Shortland)

The Finished People
(Khoa Do)

Recent and Forthcoming Films

TOM WHITE

[Social drama, 2004] Script: Daniel Keene, based on his play. Dir: Alkinos Tsilimidos. Phot: Toby Oliver. Players: Colin Friels, Loene Carmen, David Field, Bill Hunter, Dan Spielman, Angela Punch McGregor, Rachael Blake, Jarryd Jinks. Prod: Rescued Films Pty Ltd/Fandango.

STRANGE BEDFELLOWS

[Comedy, 2004] Script: Dean Murphy, Stewart Faichney. Dir: Murphy. Phot: Roger Lanser. Players: Paul Hogan, Michael Caton, Pete Postlethwaite. Prod: David Redman, Nigel Odell/Instinct Entertainment Pty Ltd.

Two old-timers in a small country town declare themselves a homosexual couple on a tax return and then have to learn how to appear gay.

PEACHES

[Romantic social drama, 2004] Script: Sue Smith. Dir: Craig Monahan. Phot: Ernie Clark. Players: Jacqueline McKenzie, Hugo Weaving, Emma Lung, Matthew Le Nevez, Sam Healy, Tyson Contor. Prod: Craig Monahan, Don Reynolds/Peach Films Pty Ltd.

At the games of the 28th Olympiad in 2004, Australian athletes were wreathed in glory. Drawing from a population of less than 20 million, they came fourth in the medal tally, ahead of dozens of larger countries. How can a nation produce such outstanding results in one field and yet fail to speak proudly to the world with its own voice through a medium as universal as motion pictures?

This is obviously not a dilemma unique to Australia, but one that is relevant to the current crisis in our national film culture. The point is not just that Australia is an affluent country blessed by good weather, where athletic activity comes naturally. It's a question of priorities. As the happily inebriated Aussie cheer squads demonstrated in Athens, Australian identity can be celebrated with ferocious enthusiasm. Australians know who they are and look at the world with remarkable confidence and optimism.

And yet, for the most part, we let Hollywood define our dreams and supply our role models. Australians love American movies and consume them with gusto. Of course, we're not alone in this. Even in film-crazy France, Hollywood dominates the box-office, but if Australians made films in proportionate numbers to the French, we would make 60 films a year, not the pitiful 15 in 2004. More to the point, none of these was an outstanding popular success.

Some are saying it's just cyclical and that the present slump will be followed by an inevitable boom. Others point to structural failings. But 2004 gave little cause for optimism. Not for many years have there been so many voices singing in unison about the parlous state of a so-called industry that currently looks more like a sheltered workshop.

Australian cinema would look a lot better if we kidnapped Peter Jackson from across the Tasman Sea. But unlike New Zealand-born Russell Crowe and Sam Neill (whom we claim as our own), Jackson remains firmly rooted in his native country. His phenomenal success with *The Lord of the Rings* nevertheless makes Australians face up to the discomfiting fact that big ideas are not limited by geographical isolation or population base. In sharp contrast, Australian film-making remains locked mostly in the low-budget ghetto, with only occasional breakouts like the

A love story that deals with accepting loss and change, and learning to move on.

ORANGE LOVE STORY
[Romance, 2004] Script: Adam Bowen, Tom Cowan. Dir: Cowan. Players: Kay Nankervis, John Mercel, Ellen Rossi, Banjo Fitzsimons, Trevor Dawe. Prod: Tom Cowan/Local Emotion Pictures.
A rural romance whose heroine braves love, longing, lust and loss.

ONE PERFECT DAY
[Social drama, 2004] Script: Paul Currie, Chip Richards. Dir: Currie. Phot: Gary Ravenscroft. Players: Kerry Armstrong, Daniel Spielman, Leeanna Walsman, Andrew Howard, Nathan Phillips, Abbie Cornish, Rory Williamson, Frank Gallacher. Prod: Phil Gregory, Paul Currie, Charles Morton/ Lightstream Films.
Gifted young musician Tommy Matisse, torn from the obsessive pursuit of his classical music career by the freak overdose of his younger sister, embarks on a path of self-discovery.

LIQUID BRIDGE
[Adventure, 2003] Script: Pim Hendrix. Dir: Phillip Avalon. Phot: Roger Buckingham. Players: Ryan Kwanten, Jeremy Sims, Tony Bonner, Jarrod Dean, Simone Kessell, Carmen Duncan, Nathaniel Lee, Damen Stephenson. Prod: Phillip Avalon, Avalon Film Corporation/3 Spears Pty Ltd.
Nick dreams of joining the professional surfing ranks

internationally financed *Moulin Rouge* and *Babe*, years ago. More typical are the mid-budget films, such as Ray Lawrence's *Lantana* and Phillip Noyce's *Rabbit-Proof Fence*, that connect with larger-than-expected audiences.

Heidi in the mountains, Aussie-style

Standing as it does in such a barren field, Cate Shortland's **Somersault** looks perhaps rather better than it would otherwise. It's a tightly focused treatment of a familiar theme – a girl's rite of passage towards sexual maturity – executed with great passion and a persuasive poetic sensibility. Heidi (Abbie Cornish) is 16 but throws herself into casual sexual encounters like someone much older. After a bruising confrontation with her mother, she leaves home and ends up at a ski resort in the Snowy Mountains, near Canberra. Desperate for human contact, she's easy prey for any predatory male, but has the qualified good luck to cross paths with Joe (Sam Worthington). They fall into bed and while Joe recoils from her deep emotional hunger, there's enough empathy there to unravel Heidi's isolation and teach her the difference between sex and love. Cornish gives a startling, strongly committed and moving performance. *Somersault* was well received at Cannes 2004 and swept the board at the 2004 AFI Awards.

Abbie Cornish and Sam Worthington in **Somersault**

It's often said that Australian films are let down by inadequately developed scripts but, if that's true, then **Tom White** is an exception. In filming a play by Daniel Keene (whose work has been performed mostly outside Australia), director Alkinos Tsilimidos successfully opens out Keene's story of a middle-class man's crisis, making good use of Melbourne locations shot mainly at night. Tom has a loving family and an adequate career, but when he's demoted he disappears without trace. He becomes an anonymous street person travelling through a contemporary underworld that is as unexpectedly funny as it is tragic. The richly developed characters are given dialogue that rises far above the utilitarian grunts that pass for speech in many Australian films.

Colin Friels, left, and Dan Spielman in **Tom White**

Veteran actor Colin Friels is wonderfully engaging as Tom, conveying both strength and wild confusion, and the cast is filled out with comparable performances from actors clearly relishing their superior material. Beyond that, the film explores the insecurity of contemporary Western life, especially for men in their later years, hanging onto their social status by their fingernails.

Khoa Do's **The Finished People** is a kind of "behind the tabloid headlines" drama, made, like *Tom White*, with tremendous passion by all concerned. An awkward combination of documentary and fiction, rough as guts in places, it nevertheless presents a group of undeniably real people. Cabramatta, a suburb of western Sydney, has been populated by immigrants over the last 30 years. For complex reasons, including that many Vietnamese coming here in the wake of the war (in which Australia fought alongside the Americans) were traumatised by the conflict, it's been plagued by social problems and is regarded as Australia's drugs capital.

As three stories of love, family and friendship play out amidst homelessness, drugs and crime, Do blurs the boundaries between fiction and reality. We glimpse the lives of young people as anonymous as the brick walls that surround them. Do's protagonists are locked in a vicious circle but *The Finished People* focuses the audience on their shared humanity.

alongside his friend and mentor, Dane.

THE FINISHED PEOPLE
[Social drama, 2003] Script: various. Dir: Khoa Do. Players: Rodney Anderson, Jason McGoldrick, Joe Le, Shane McDonald, Daniela Italiano, Mylinh Dinh, Sarah Vongmany, Ivan Topic, Viet Dang, Miriam Marquez, Steve Kourouche, Anh Do. Prod: Khoa Do, Anh Do/Post 75 Productions Pty Ltd.

THREE DOLLARS
[Comedy-drama, 2004] Script: Robert Connolly, Elliot Perlman, from Perlman's novel. Dir: Connolly. Phot: Tristan Milani. Players: David Wenham, Frances O'Connor, Sarah Wynter. Prod: John Maynard/Arenafilm Pty Ltd.
An honest, compassionate man finds himself with a wife, a child and three dollars.

SOMERSAULT
[Drama, 2004] Script and Dir: Cate Shortland. Phot: Robert Humphreys. Players: Abbie Cornish, Sam Worthington, Erik Thomson, Lynette Curran, Nathaniel Dean. Prod: Anthony Anderson/Red Carpet Productions Pty Ltd.

THE OYSTER FARMER
[Romantic comedy, 2004] Script and Dir: Anna Reeves. Phot: Alun Bollinger. Players: Alex O'Lachlan, Diana Glenn, Kerry Armstrong, David Field, Jim Norton, Jack Thompson. Prod: Anthony Buckley, Piers Tempest, Anthony Buckley Films Pty Ltd/Oyster Farmer Ltd.
Jack, 23, robs fish markets and sends the money to a remote location north of Sydney. Trying to recover the money, he discovers a world of eccentrics including Pearl, a local girl with a reputation.

RIGHT HERE RIGHT NOW
[Social drama, 2004] Script: Matthew Newton, Toby Schmitz. Dir: Newton. Phot: Hugh Miller. Players: Dai Peterson, Matthew

Newton, Toby Schmitz, Tim Draxl, Tim Richards, Geoff Morell, Brooke Satchwell, Pia Miranda, Genevieve O'Reilly. Prod: David Gross, Big Kid Films. To save their suicidal pal, Dan, five friends escape to a small coastal town where they once partied hard to celebrate the end of their school days. They try to revive that spirit but a lot has changed. And what they don't know is that Dan has a very different reason for having this weekend away.

A MAN'S GOTTA DO
[Comedy, 2004] Script and Dir: Chris Kennedy. Players: John Howard, Rebecca Frith, Alyssa McClelland, Gyton Grantley. Prod: Chris Kennedy, John Winter/Oilrag Productions. What a guy's gotta do …
is marry off his daughter.

THE HUMAN TOUCH
[Erotic romance, 2004] Script and Dir: Paul Cox. Players: Jacqueline McKenzie, Aaron Blabey, Chris Haywood, Rebecca Frith, Aden Young, Terry Norris, Simon McBurney. Prod: Cox, Illumination Films Pty Ltd/Mark Patterson, Go Patterson Films Pty Ltd.
The relationship between Anna and David is tested when a wealthy man enters Anna's life. His worldliness and seductive charm open her up to the sensual world of touch and she embarks on an intimate journey of self-discovery and physical fulfilment.

THE EXTRA
[Romantic comedy, 2005] Script: Jimeoin. Dir: Kevin Carlin. Phot:

Who will run the gauntlet?

Of the many films that I reviewed enthusiastically in last year's *IFG*, few connected strongly with audiences, which is one of the reasons for the present soul searching. *Danny Deckchair*, for example, proved anything but a goofy, feel-good comedy for most critics. They also hurt another film, *Strange Bedfellows*, which I judged had a good chance of finding an appreciative audience and, in spite of the bad press, it did respectable business.

Generally speaking, Australian film-makers seem unwilling to run the gauntlet of the mainstream marketplace. Memorable films of earlier times such as *Gallipoli*, *Breaker Morant*, *Muriel's Wedding* and *Strictly Ballroom* managed to appeal to a wide spectrum as well as connecting internationally. But contemporary directors seem much more restricted in their reach.

Debate rages on several fronts about the future of our national cinema. One focus of conflict is the free trade agreement with the United States, which might allow Hollywood to dictate Australian audiovisual policy and restrict government financial support. In 2002-03, total film and TV production reached $405m (AU$588m) but $171m was American money spent by runaway Hollywood productions taking advantage of comparatively low production costs. Opponents of tax breaks and incentives given to foreign producers have long argued that these inflated figures disguise the shrinking commitment to local production. Their warnings have proved correct.

The fatuous argument that the free market will decide the future to everyone's satisfaction is still peddled by some, despite overwhelming evidence to the contrary. Australian political parties, left and right, genuflect to private entrepreneurship but also subsidise and protect the "industry". Mark Latham's Labor Party had promised greatly increased film funding but, in the election of October 2004, lost again to John Howard's conservatives and any hope of creative leadership disappeared.

Back to where we started: Australians do well at the Olympics because we spend a lot of money on sport and think the Games

are exciting and important. Australian cultural expression doesn't generate the same heat; it's still regarded as a bit of a luxury. Counteracting this are the huge number of young people committing to media careers. Film schools and tertiary communications faculties are bursting. And several new films that went into production late in 2004 could spark a star-led recovery. Leading directors including Ray Lawrence, Jocelyn Moorhouse, Rowan Woods and Neil Armfield took charge of casts led by Australians Russell Crowe, Cate Blanchett, Geoffrey Rush, Heath Ledger and Guy Pearce. So, just possibly, 2004 may have been the bust before the boom.

PETER THOMPSON (summerfilms9msn@iprimus.com.au) is a writer, film-maker and critic who appears regularly on Australian television.

Cindy Nitipaisalkul

Sarah Vongmany in **The Finished People**

Mark Wareham. *Players: Jimeoin, Rhys Muldoon, Katherine Slattery, Colin Lane, Shaun Micallef, Kristy Hinze. Prod: Charlesworth Josem Partners, Stephen Luby, Mark Ruse/Ruby Entertainment /Republica Films/Extra Extra.* An average guy sees movie stars making big money and getting the girls, thinks he has what it takes to do the same and makes his way to the big city.

THE ILLUSTRATED FAMILY DOCTOR
[Comedy, 2004] Script: Kriv Stenders, David Snell. Dir: Stenders. Phot: Kevin Hayward. Players: Samuel Johnson, Sacha Horler, Colin Friels, Jessica Napier. Prod: Kriv Stenders, Catherine Kerr/Pod Film Pty Ltd. A dark, irreverent comedy about illness, work, death and a young man who learns to survive them all.

DECK DOGZ
[Adolescent adventure, 2005] Script and Dir: Steve Pasvolsky. Phot: Denson Baker. Players: Sean Kennedy, Richard Wilson, Tony Hawk. Prod: Bill Bennett, Jennifer Cluff/Deck Dogz Films. Fast-paced story tracks three adolescent boys as they go to meet their hero, a legendary skateboard champion

BONDI TSUNAMI
[Adventure, 2004] Script and Dir: Rachael Lucas. Players: Taki Abe, Keita Abe, Nobu-Hisa Ikeda, Miki Sasaki. Prod: Anthony Lucas-Smith, Naomi Lucas-Smith /Burlesque Productions. Four Japanese surfers travel up the spectacular east coast of Australia on a psychedelic road trip. Shark is an urban cowboy being pursued by his femme fatale ex-girlfriend, Kimiko. Things get

very weird when they pick up the mysterious Gunja Man.

DARK LOVE STORY
[Romantic thriller, 2004] Script: Belinda McClory, Jon Hewitt. Dir: Hewitt. Phot: Franc Biffone. Players: Aaron Pedersen, Belinda McClory. Prod: Gregory J Read/ Paper Bark Films/Rough Beast. Gil and Gretchen, two star-crossed lovers, chase a happy ending. Desperate for cash, Gil has a fake gun and a crazy plan, but the omens are bad as they plunge into the underworld.

JOSH JARMAN
[Romantic comedy, 2004] Script and Dir: Pip Mushin. Phot: Jaems Grant. Players: Marcus Graham, Daniela Farinalli, Damien Richardson, Kestie Morassi, Kym Gyngell. Prod: Eva Orner, Pip Mushin/ Red Rover Productions. Josh Jarman is a passionate playwright whose only desire is to get his play produced in a proper theatre with a decent audience.

Quotes of the Year

"The Australian film industry is stuffed."
STEPHEN SMITH, *President, Australian Screen Producers Association.*

"Audiences don't want a continuing procession of outdated, stereotypical characters that are somehow seen as quintessentially Australian."
BRIAN ROSEN, *CEO, Australian Film Finance Corporation.*

The AFI Awards 2003 and 2004 are listed on p.89.

Austria Roman Scheiber

The Year's Best Films

Roman Scheiber's selection:
Hotel (Jessica Hausner)
Antares (Götz Spielmann)
Darwin's Nightmare
(Docu. Hubert Sauper)
The Souvenirs of Mr X
(Docu. Arash T. Riahi)
The Edukators
(Hans Weingartner)

Recent and Forthcoming Films

ANTARES
[Drama, 2004] Script and Dir: Götz Spielmann. Phot: Martin Gschlacht. Players: Petra Morzé, Andreas Patton, Hary Prinz, Susanne Wuest, Dennis Cubic, Martina Zinner. Prod: Lotus Film/Teamfilm.

Lotus Films

Susanne Wuest in **Antares**

BÖSE ZELLEN (Wicked Cells)
[Drama, 2003] Script and Dir: Barbara Albert. Phot: Martin Gschlacht. Players: Kathrin Resetarits, Ursula Strauss, Georg Friedrich, Gabriela Schmoll. Prod: coop 99 Filmproduktion.

DARWIN'S NIGHTMARE
[Documentary, 2004] Script and Dir: Hubert Sauper. Phot: Alexander Rieder. Featuring: Fishermen. Prod: coop 99 Filmproduktion/Mille et une production (France)/Saga Film (Belgium).

They appeared suddenly and their impact has just begun to spread: young Austrian directors with spirit and vision, gaining attention in the wake of the groundbreaking success of Barbara Albert's feature debut, *Northern Skirts* (*Nordrand*). Thus, no fewer than four Austrian films were invited to the prestigious Toronto Festival in 2004, among them Jessica Hausner's fascinating mystery thriller, **Hotel**.

coop99 Filmproduktion

Franziska Weisz in **Hotel**

Hausner, acclaimed for her feature debut, *Lovely Rita*, is another of Austrian cinema's rising stars and *Hotel* is a headstrong study of the mystery genre – a bizarre, bloodless and in a way very Austrian version of *The Shining*. It follows a young woman, Irene (Franziska Weisz), in her first career steps as a receptionist at a remote hotel in the mountain woods. Frightened by the hotel's obscure atmosphere and the strange disappearance of her predecessor, she begins to mix up fantasy and reality.

Also invited to Toronto, and opening the competition at Locarno in 2004, was **Antares** by Götz Spielmann, which deals with intense emotions through sequential episodic drama. Love is the driving force behind the characters' experiences. You may call Antares the Viennese *Magnolia*: three interconnected tales that are in a sense "Scorpio stories" (Antares is the name of the largest star in the constellation of Scorpius), with a wide range of emotional aspects: sex, jealousy, boring routine, violence, crisis and death. In a way, Spielmann seems to be influenced by other Austrian *auteurs* like Hausner or Albert, but sticks to his own, simple visual style.

The Edukators (*Die fetten Jahre sind vorbei*, literally: The prosperous years are over; see also Germany report) by Hans Weingartner is an energetically shot triangular story about youthful idealism, revolutionary passion and uneasy confrontation between two generations. Jan, Peter and Jule share a burning desire for political change. Jan is a quiet thinker; Peter, his best friend, a man of action and charmer of Croatian descent, is full of drive; and Jule, Jan's shy but politically committed girlfriend, can, if pushed, be more courageous than the two men put together. *Jules et Jim* step aside, Jule and Jan rule.

Young guns, new fish

Weingartner's second feature was produced by one of Austria's promising, newer film companies, coop 99 Filmproduktion, which since 1999 has given young film-makers and craftspeople the chance to create high quality movies away from the mainstream. It is the artistic home of, among others, directors Hausner and Albert and cinematographer Martin Gschlacht, who shot *Antares* and *Hotel*. Another young production company is Amour fou, founded in 2002, which has already gained great success, focusing not only on features but also experimental, short and animated films.

Highly recommended for all video and film freaks working on their own filmography is the amusing – and touching – documentary **The Souvenirs of Mr X** (*Die Souvenirs des Herrn X*) by Arash T. Riahi. Ostensibly a search for clues relating to the life and work of an unknown film-maker, it can easily be read as an homage to amateur directors everywhere, their vision of cinema and their desire to find the extraordinary in everyday life. It is also about amateur film prize juries judging the unjudgable.

Another Austrian documentary presented at Venice in 2004, winner of the 2004 Vienna Film Prize Festival, should be mentioned: **Darwin's Nightmare** by Hubert Sauper is a true story about globalisation – and fish. The main characters are fishermen from Lake Victoria and the pilots of huge, rusty, ex-Soviet cargo planes who fly from Africa's poorest countries to America and Europe with a bizarre cargo: tonnes of the artificially introduced but fast-breeding Victoria Perch. Planes come daily to collect the latest catch in exchange for their southbound cargo: Kalashnikovs and ammunition bound for the countless wars in the dark centre of the continent. The film shows how this booming multinational trade has created an ungodly globalised alliance on the shores of the world's biggest tropical lake: an army of young fishermen, Indian factory owners, African ministers, EU commissioners, Russian pilots and Tanzanian prostitutes. Survival of the fittest, somehow.

ROMAN SCHEIBER (ro.scheiber@chello.at) is an editor of Austria's monthly movie magazine, *RAY*.

DER GLÄSERNE BLICK (**Dead Man's Memories**)
[Thriller, 2003] Script and Dir: Markus Heltschl. Phot: Christian Berger. Players: Sylvie Testud, Miguel Guilherme. Prod: TTV Film/Agora Film (Germany).
Death, lies and videotape, west of Lisbon. A man's body is washed ashore on the Portuguese coast. Detective Pinto interrogates a young woman about her apparent involvement in his death.

DONAU, DUNAJ, DUNA, DUNAV, DUNAREA (**Danube**)
[Drama, 2003] Script and Dir: Goran Rebic. Phot: Jerzy Palacz. Players: Otto Sander, Robert Stadlober, Anabelle Mandeng. Prod: Lotus Film/Wega Film.
A modern odyssey, a fairy tale river movie. A diverse group of people flee down the Danube towards the Black Sea.

HOTEL
[Thriller, 2004] Script and Dir: Jessica Hausner. Phot: Martin Gschlacht. Players: Franziska Weisz, Birgit Minichmayr, Regina Fritsch, Peter Strauss, Marlene Streeruwitz. Prod: coop 99 Filmproduktion/Essential Film (Germany).

NACKTSCHNECKEN (**Slugs**)
[Comedy, 2004] Script: Michael Ostrowski, Michael Glawogger. Dir: Glawogger. Phot: Wolfgang Thaler. Players: Raimund Wallisch, Michael Ostrowski, Pia Hierzegger, Iva Lukic, Sophia Laggner, Georg Friedrich, Detlev Buck. Prod: Dor Film.
Three college dropouts try to shoot an amateur porn video.

DIE SOUVENIRS DES HERRN X (**The Souvenirs of Mr X**)
[Documentary, 2004] Script and Dir: Arash T. Riahi. Phot: Marco Zimprich. Featuring: Amateur Filmmakers. Prod: Nikolaus Geyrhalter Filmproduktion/Peter Stockhaus Filmproduktion (Germany).

Azerbaijan Goga Lomidze

Recent and Forthcoming Films

MYAKANYN MELODIYASY
(Melody of Space)
[Drama 2003] Script: Ramiz Rovshan, Gusein Mehtiev. Dir: Mehtiev. Phot: Nadir Mehdiev. Players: Aladin Abbasov, Ayan Mirgasymova, Mehriban Zeki. Prod: Azerbaijanfilm.

QYUCHYALYARYA SU SYAPMISHYAM
(I Will Sprinkle the Streets)
[Drama, 2004] Script: Isi Melikzade, Nijad Feizullaev, based on Melikzade's novel. Dir: Feizullaev. Phot: Kenan Mamedov. Players: Fuad Poladov, Rasim Babaev, Megriban Zaki. Prod: Azerbaijanfilm.

NATSIONALNAYA BOMBA
(National Bomb)
[Drama 2004] Script and Dir: Vagif Mustafaev. Phot: Jimsher Qristesashvili and Lomer Akhvlediani. Players: Avtandil Makharadze, Yashar Nuri, Saida Kulieva, Nuria Akhmedova. Prod: Valeri Ruzin, Azerbaijanfilm.

Vagif Mustafaev on location for **National Bomb**

Quote of the Year

"I'm very proud that Azerbaijan has taken part in this festival for the first time."

VAGIF MUSTAFAEV,
director of National Bomb,
screened at Moscow 2004.

Hollywood blockbusters continue to dominate the box-office in Azerbaijan, while local films are mostly confined to festival screenings before resurfacing on national television. In 2004 the state contributed around $700,000 (3.5 billion manat) to production, and the main studio, Azerbaijanfilm, produced four features and one short.

Baku, the capital, hosted the sixth International Film Festival East-West in May 2004, screening work by popular names from former Soviet countries, including Bakhtyar Khudoinazarov, Stanislav Govorukhin and Sergey Soloviev. Visiting Russian stars Aleksandr Abdulov and, especially, Aleksandr Kalyagin, who has appeared in several Azerbaijani films, were the biggest public attractions.

August 2, 2004 was National Film Day, organised by the Ministry of Culture at the Nizami Cinema, where state awards were given to prominent film-makers and, after the ceremony, the audience watched the premiere of Nidzhat Feyzullayev's **I Will Sprinkle the Streets** (*Qyuchyalyarya su syapmishyam*). This is a psychological drama based on the novel by Isa Meliqzade, in which a teenager takes the blame upon himself for an accidental killing during a shooting trip and enters prison for many years. This is the first fiction feature from Feyzullayev, a graduate of the Leningrad Film Institute who previously worked in documentaries.

Melody of Space (*Myakanyn melodiyasy*) is a new drama by Husseyn Mehdiyev, one of the country's most popular directors. It focuses on Murad, an 80-year-old violoncellist who, dissatisfied with his life and the choices he has made, is contemplating suicide. He meets Rena, a younger woman suffering from cancer, who changes his life. At the Moscow International Film Festival 2004 critics praised Vagif Mustafaev's **National Bomb** (*Natsionalnaya bomba*), a collage of short stories about a woman who is a professional mourner at funerals, a prominent film editor who wants to protest on public radio about the loss of his job and a man preparing the bomb of the title, to be used not against an external enemy but his own country.

GOGA LOMIDZE (gnl_98@hotmail.com) works in the Netherlands as a freelance translator.

Belarus Goga Lomidze

Recent and Forthcoming Films

ANASTASYA SLUCKAYA
[Historical drama, 2004] Script:
Anatoly Delendik. Dir: Juri
Elkhov. Phot: Tatyana Loginova.
Players: Svetlana Zelenkovskaya,
Gennady Davydenko, Anatoly
Kot, Nikolai Kirichenko. Prod:
Sergei Mosin, Belarusfilm.

Svetlana Zelenkovskaya as
Anastasya Sluckaya

OKKUPATSIA. MISTERII
(Mysteries. Occupation)
[War drama, 2004] Script:
Aleksander Katchan. Dir: Andrei
Kudinenko. Phot: Pavel
Zubritsky. Players: Aleksander
Kolbyshev, Anatoly Kot,
Aleksander Molchanov, Zvetlana
Zelenkovskaya. Prod: Alexander
Debaliok, UP Extrans.

BALNOE PLATIE (Ball Dress)
[Children's drama, 2003] Script:
Fedor Konev. Dir: Margarita
Sasymova and Irina Volokh.
Phot: Aleksandr Abadovski.
Players: Lena Borushko, Kolia
Raevski, Violetta Nesterovich,
Tatyana Bovkalova, Marina
Mogilevskaya. Prod: Belarusfilm.

F ilm distribution in Belarus remains in state ownership but most of the imported foreign films shown at the country's 150 cinemas are imported by Russia-based companies. Annual admissions are around 11 million, mostly for Hollywood films and some Russian productions. State subsidy of around $1m a year funds about two or three features annually. Dozens of episodes of Russian TV series are shot in Belarus.

At Russia's Kinoshok Festival in 2004, Belarus presented two feature films. Juri Elkhov's **Anastasya Sluckaya** was a costume drama about the fifteenth-century Byelorussian princess who marries Prince Semion Olelkovich. After he is killed in the war against the Crimean Tatars she takes command of the army. In the children's drama **Ball Dress** (*Balnoe platie*), Vika (Lena Borushko), an orphan and her best friend, Mitia (Kolia Raevski), who are both brought up by stepmothers, must deal with the various problems brought on by adolescence.

Kolia Raevski and Lena Borushko in **Ball Dress**

Andrei Kudinenko secured a grant from the Netherlands' Hubert Bals Fund that helped him finance his three-part Second World War drama, **Mysteries. Occupation** (*Okkupatsia. Misterii*), which had its premiere at Rotterdam in 2004. The film comprises three short stories, "Adam & Eve", "Mother" and "Father", and goes against traditional and official accounts of the partisan movement. In "Adam & Eve", a partisan searches for new recruits and meets a former fighter who deserted for love. In "Mother", a woman whose son has been killed meets a wounded enemy soldier and brings him to her house and "Father" follows a boy's search for his missing dad. The film has strong camerawork and an impressive soundtrack and Kudinenko, who has won international prizes for his short films, addresses the complexities and horrors of war without passing moral judgments.

Belgium Erik Martens

The Year's Best Films

Erik Martens' selection:

Steve + Sky
(Felix Van Groeningen)

The Missing Half
(Benoît Mariage)

The Alzheimer Case
(Erik Van Looy)

Sea of Silence
(Stijn Coninx)

The Rachevski Tango
(Sam Garbarski)

Phillipe Grand'Henry in
The Missing Half

Recent and Forthcoming Films

DE ZAAK ALZHEIMER
(The Alzheimer Case)
[Thriller, 2003] Script: Erik Van Looy, Carl Joos, based on a novel by Jef Geeraerts. Dir: Van Looy. Phot: Danny Elsen. Players: Carl Joos, Koen De Bouw, Werner De Smedt, Jan Decleir, Jo Demeyere. Prod: Erwin Provoost, MMG.
Inspectors Vincke and Verstuyft hunt a contract killer who appears to be suffering from Alzheimer's.

PLOP EN DE TOVERSTAF
(Plop and the Magic Wand)
[Children's comedy adventure, 2003] Script: Gert Verhulst, Danny Verbiest, Hans Bourlon, Sander De Regt. Dir: Matthias Temmermans. Players: Walter De

According to the European Audiovisual Observatory, only 6.3% of all cinema tickets bought in Europe in 2003 were for a European film – an all-time low. In Belgium, however, and especially in Dutch-speaking Flanders, statistics have moved in the opposite direction: local Flemish production quadrupled its market share, thanks to one film, **The Alzheimer Case** (*De zaak Alzheimer*). Erik Van Looy's adaptation of a novel by popular author Jef Geeraerts is an efficiently told horror/crime thriller about a hitman (Flanders' most popular actor, Jan Decleir) who suffers from Alzheimer's. The film's only defect is that it is too obviously aware of its famous predecessors in the genre, such as *Se7en* and *The Silence of the Lambs*.

Jan Decleir as a hitman in **The Alzheimer Case**

It had drawn more than 600,000 Flemings by the end of December 2003, with a further 150,000 admissions by June 2004, making it the fourth most successful Belgian film ever, behind three films by Stijn Coninx, two featuring local comedian Urbanus (*Koko Flanel* registered 1.08 million visitors and *Hector* drew 933,000) and the period piece *Daens* (848,000), about the socialist priest. In May 2004, *Alzheimer* took five of the annual Joseph Plateau Awards: Best Film, Director, Actor (Decleir), Screenplay and, by some distance, the Box-Office Prize.

Small-screen influences

The *Alzheimer* phenomenon was one of several indications that Flemish films are increasingly tied in with local public and commercial television. People go to cinemas to see familiar TV faces in movies that are variations on television programmes. Though *Alzheimer* was based on a novel, its stars and director were well known from television, which shows popular crime series such as *Cops* and *Windforce 10* – both produced, like *Alzheimer*, by MMG (formerly Multimedia), Erwin Provoost's company, which was responsible for films that helped create a modest Belgian cinema revival in the 1980s, including titles by Marc Didden and Dominique Derudder and Coninx's Urbanus hits.

The second biggest hit of 2003, Jan Verheyen's **Team Spirit II** (350,000 admissions), is very simple entertainment, though well crafted, and closely related to TV soap opera. It brings together the old bunch of footballing friends from the original *Team Spirit*, though all kinds of problems hinder their reunion.

Some 55,000 young children and their parents went to see Studio 100's **Plop and the Magic Wand** (*Plop en de toverstaf*), the new film about Plop the dwarf, originally a TV character. Even though this film targets a very specific audience, it's part of a wider trend: little by little, a more commercial attitude is gaining ground in Flemish film production – probably the legacy of Belgium's first decade of commercial television.

Plop and the Magic Wand was also notable as the first Belgian feature to have been digitally produced, distributed and projected. The Kinepolis group owns 10 multiplex sites with one digital projection system each and *Plop* was on show throughout the Kinepolis digital network only. Artistically speaking the film about the little men has little merit, but as a prototype for this new kind of distribution it is important.

The most interesting and original Flemish project is Felix Van Groeningen's first feature, **Steve + Sky**. The story of two colourful young lovers who wander around the desolate semi-industrial neighbourhoud of Ghent demonstrates a lively imagination and a gift for style and atmosphere.

In 2004, popular youth author Marc De Bel finally lost his cinematic appeal. **The Fearless Triplets** (*De zusjes kriegel*), directed by Dirk Beliën, who was nominated for an Oscar for his short, *Fait d'hiver*, drew only 45,000 visitors, far fewer than the two previous De Bel adaptations (*Blinker I* and *II*). Equally disappointing, both critically and in terms of admissions, was the live action adaptation of **The Dark Diamond** (*De duistere diamant*), based on Willy

Donder, Aimé Anthoni, Chris Cauwenberghs, Agnes De Nul, Hilde Vanhulle, Luc Caals. Prod: Michel Verlinden, Studio 100. Dwarves Plop and Klus embark on a journey to recover the magic wand and return it in time for dwarf Christmas.

TEAM SPIRIT II
[Comedy, 2003] Script: Dimitri Leue, Jan Verheyen, Ed Vanderweyden. Dir: Verheyen. Phot: Frank Van den Eeden. Players: Tom Van Landuyt, Michaël Pas, Dimitri Leue, Mathias Secru, Geert Hunaerts, Axel Daeseleire, Warre Borgmans. Prod: Verheyen, Dirk Impens, Favourite Films.

Evelien Apers, Kathleen Apers and Dorien Janssens as **The Fearless Triplets**

DE ZUSJES KRIEGEL
(The Fearless Triplets)
[Adventure, 2003] Script: Johan Verschuren. Dir: Dirk Beliën. Phot: Philip Van Volsem. Players: Evelien Apers, Kathleen Apers, Dorien Janssens, Victor Löw, Liesbeth Kamerlinck. Prod: Eric Caroen, Front-line.
Lien, Sien and Fien Kriegel are junior witches whose school psychiatrist decides to put a stop to the terrible threesome's antics once and for all by putting them in an institution.

DE DUISTERE DIAMANT
(The Dark Diamond)
[Adventure, 2004] Script: Rudi Van den Bossche, Ilse Somers. Dir: Van den Bossche. Phot: Gerd Schelfhout. Voices: Dirk Roofthooft, Celine Verbeeck, Joeri Busschots, Peter Van den Begin, Stany Crets. Prod: Antonio Lombardo, Cine 3. Spike and Suzy spend their

summer holidays on a mysterious estate in the Netherlands, where Auntie Sidonia succumbs to the influence of a dark diamond with unsuspected powers.

STEVE + SKY
[Drama, 2004] Script and Dir: Felix Van Groeningen. Phot: Ruben Impens. Players: Titus De Voogdt, Delfine Bafort, Johan Heldenbergh, Romy Bollion. Prod: Dirk Impens, Favourite Films.
Steve, 22, is in jail because of an ecstasy deal that went wrong. Sky is 22, likes to eat banana splits and talk to her fish. Jean Claude is in a wheelchair. Three people stuck in a moment.

LE TANGO DES RACHEVSKI
(The Rachevski Tango)
[Comedy, 2003] Script: Philippe Blasband, Sam Garbarski. Dir: Garbarski. Phot: Jean-Paul Kieffer. Players: Natan Cogan, Tania Garbarski, Hippolyte Girardot, Michel Jonasz, Daniel Mesguich, Ludmila Mikaël, Rudi Rosenberg. Prod: Archipel/ Entre Chien et Loup/Samsa Film (Luxembourg).

J'AI TOUJOURS VOULU ETRE UNE SAINTE
(I Always Wanted to Be a Saint)
[Drama, 2003] Script: Philippe Blasband, Geneviève Mersch, Anne Fournier. Dir: Mersch. Phot: Séverine Barde. Players: Marie Kremer, Thierry Lefevre, Janine Godinas, Barbara Roland. Prod: Claude Waringo, Patrick Quinet/Samsa Film (Luxembourg)/Artemis Productions/Media Services/RTBF.

L'AUTRE (The Missing Half)
[Drama, 2003] Script and Dir: Benoît Mariage. Phot: Philippe Guilbert. Players: Dominique Bayens, Philippe Grand'Henry, Laurent Kuenhen, Jan Decleir, Colette Emmanuelle. Prod: Dominique Janne/K2/RTBF.

VERDER DAN DE MAAN
(Sea of Silence)
[Drama, 2004] Script: Jacqueline

Vandersteen's popular *Suske and Wiske* comics (known to English-language readers as Spike and Suzy) .

Titus De Voogdt and Delfine Bafort as **Steve + Sky**

Mariage tackles marriage

Compared to the fruitful Flemish season, the French-speaking part of Belgium had some difficulty in leaving any footprints. Prolific screenwriter Philippe Blasband participated in two feature films, but this was not his best year. **The Rachevski Tango** (*Le tango des Rachevski*), Sam Garbarski,s debut feature, is a feel-good movie about a Belgian Jewish family brooding about its Jewish roots. The second Blasband-scripted film, **I Always Wanted to Be a Saint** by Geneviève Mersch (see also *IFG 2004*, Luxembourg), is the story of Norah, who is still struggling with the fact that she was abandoned by her mother at an early age.

In Benoît Mariage's **The Missing Half** (*L'autre*), small aspects of everyday life are observed with a sense of wonder. There is hardly any dialogue. Pierre, an eye doctor, is married to Claire. Nothing seems to be able to disturb their daily routine, but then Claire falls pregnant with twins and nothing will ever be the same again. The minimalist approach – one image, one idea – makes this a small film for a small audience, but its universe is unique.

It seems only right to conclude this survey with the man who has been dominating the Belgian box-office for more than ten years: Stijn Coninx. His latest film, **Sea of Silence** (*Verder dan de maan*), was presented as Belgian contender for the Academy Awards, even though, apart from the director and a few cast and crew members, everything about it is Dutch. The press slaughtered the story of Kato's youth at her parents' pig farm, and barely 10,000 visitors turned out; quite a drop from the million who saw Coninx's *Koko Flanel*.

Animation student Jonas Geirnaerts saved the day by winning a jury prize at Cannes in 2004 for his snappy short, *Flatlife*, a glance at the daily routines in four neighbouring flats, which augurs well for his future. In 1997, Lieven Debrauwer won a similar prize for *Leonie*, which led to his first feature, *Pauline and Paulette*, and his second film, *Jam*, was eagerly awaited at press time.

ERIK MARTENS (e.martens@skynet.be) is a freelance film critic and editor-in-chief of the Belgian Film Archive's Flemish film history DVD project.

Epskamp. Dir: Stijn Coninx. Phot: Walther Vanden Ende. Players: Bert André, Anneke Blok, Jappe Claes, Neeltje de Vree, Annet Malherbe, Wim Opbrouck, Huub Stapel, Johanna ter Steege. Prod: Broadcasting Agency/Isabella Films/KRO/Lichtblick Film-und Fernsehproduktion (Germany)/Sophimages/Zentropa Productions (Denmark).
In 1960s Holland a Catholic farmer's family try to cope with setbacks in their daily life.

ELLEKTRA
[Drama, forthcoming] Script:
Rudolf Mestdagh, Daniel Lamberts. Dir: Mestdagh. Phot: Danny Elsen. Players: Julien Schoenaerts, Matthias Schoenaerts, Axelle Red. Prod: Rudolf Mestdagh, Cosmo Kino.

CINEASTES A TOUT PRIX (Born to Film)
[Documentary, 2004] Dir: Frédéric Sojcher. Phot: Michel Houssiau. Prod: Saga Films/ Flight Movie/RTBF/WIP.
Film historian Sojcher shows three dedicated amateur film-makers in their home environments.

CONFITUUR (Jam)
[Drama, forthcoming]. Script:

Lieven Debrauwer, Jacques Boon. Dir: Debrauwer. Phot: Philippe Guilbert. Players: Marilou Mermans, Rik Van Uffelen, Chris Lomme, Ingrid De Vos. Prod: Dominique Janne, K2.

DE KUS (The Kiss)
[Drama, forthcoming] Script and Dir: Hilde Van Mieghem. Phot: Jan Vancaille. Players: Marie Vinck, Jan Decleir, Fedja van Huêt. Prod: Michel Houdmont, Signature Films.
Sarah, 15, beautiful and gifted, dreams of running away to become a ballet dancer.

Quote of the Year

"Now that I'm 41, I know that nobody knows anything, especially when we're talking about film or TV. But I know that if you work harder, the result will be better."

ERIK VAN LOOY *tries to explain what made* The Alzheimer Case *a hit.*

Australian Film Institute Awards 2003

Film: *Japanese Story*.
Director: Sue Brooks (*Japanese Story*).
Actress: Toni Collette (*Japanese Story*).
Actor: David Wenham (*Gettin' Square*).
Supporting Actress: Sacha Horler (*Travelling Light*).
Supporting Actor: David Ngoombujarra (*Black and White*).
Original Screenplay: Alison Tilson (*Japanese Story*).
Adapted Screenplay: Tony McNamara (*The Rage in Placid Lake*).
Editing: Jill Bilcock (*Japanese Story*).
Cinematography: Ian Baker (*Japanese Story*).
Sound: Livia Ruzic, Peter Grace, Peter Smith (*Japanese Story*).
Original Music Score: Elizabeth Drake (*Japanese Story*).
Production Design: Steven Jones-Evans (*Ned Kelly*).
Costume Design: Anna Borghesi (*Ned Kelly*).
Global Achievement: Geoffrey Rush.

Australian Film Institute Awards 2004

Film: *Somersault*.
Director: Cate Shortland (*Somersault*).
Actress: Abbie Cornish (*Somersault*).
Actor: Sam Worthington (*Somersault*).
Supporting Actress: Lynette Curran (*Somersault*).
Supporting Actor: Erik Thomson (*Somersault*).
Original Screenplay: Cate Shortland (*Somersault*).
Editing: Scott Gray (*Somersault*).
Cinematography: Robert Humphreys (*Somersault*).
Sound: Mark Blackwell, Peter Smith and Sam Petty (*Somersault*).
Original Music Score: 'Decoder Ring' (*Somersault*).
Production Design: Melinda Doring (*Somersault*).
Costume Design: Emily Seresin (*Somersault*).
Global Achievement: Naomi Watts.

Bosnia and Herzegovina Rada Sesic

The Year's Best Films

Rada Sesic's selection:

Days and Hours
(Pjer Zalica)

Summer in the Golden Valley
(Srdjan Vuletic)

Recent and Forthcoming Films

KOD AMIDZE IDRIZA
(Days and Hours)
[Family drama, 2004] Script:
Namik Kabil. Dir: Pjer Zalica.
Players: Senad Basic, Mustafa
Nadarevic, Semka Sokolovic
Bertok. Prod: Ademir Kenovic,
Refresh.

Nedzad Begovic, top left, and family
in **Strictly Personal**

SASVIM LICNO
(Strictly Personal)
[Experimental docu-fiction,
2004] Camera, Script and Dir:
Nedzad Begovic. Featuring:
Begovic, his family and friends.
Prod: Ismet Nuno Arnautalic and
Nedzad Begovic, SaGa Company.
Combining home video footage
with animation, this witty and
contemplative low-budget project
begins in the time of Tito, covers
the tragic Bosnian war and ends
in the recent past.

T en years after the Dayton agreement ended the war, the film industry in Bosnia and Herzegovina is at last on a roll, thanks to an exceptionally dynamic and successful season in 2003-04. Despite the perennial problems – chiefly the shortage of money and technical facilities – cinema professionals, from riggers to actors, composers and producers, rediscovered their zest for film-making.

Even the government, which had hitherto given only sporadic financial support, changed its tune and began to emphasise cinema's role in promoting the country's international profile. Practically, this means that four or five fiction features, with an average budget of approximately €1m, can expect some financing from the state, which also gives substantial grants to the country's best organised cultural event, the Sarajevo Film Festival. The shortage of screens remains a problem; a population of three million is served by only 30 cinemas.

The year began well at the Rotterdam Film Festival, which selected both of the Bosnian films produced in 2003. Pjer Zalica's debut, **Fuse** (*Gori vatra*; see *IFG 2004*), had already won the Silver Leopard at Locarno and was well received in Rotterdam, while **Summer in the Golden Valley** (*Ljeto u zlatnoj dolini*), from another debutant, Srdjan Vuletic, won the prestigious Tiger Award, which guaranteed its theatrical distribution in the Netherlands.

Zana Marjanovic and Haris Sijaric in **Summer in the Golden Valley**

Set in Sarajevo, Vuletic's drama depicts youngsters confused and disillusioned by post-war society. The main character, Fikret, is a well-mannered teenager who at his dad's funeral is shocked by another man's accusations that his late father owes him a lot of money. Family honour can be restored only by collecting money and paying the debt in a hurry, leading Fikret into dubious company. When a rich man's daughter is kidnapped, Fikret is assigned to watch over her, but falls in love with his captive.

Vuletic introduces surreal elements and the tragic and poetic opening and closing sequences suggest that rich and happy people live in another world, while the film's marginalised heroes are doomed to be losers in a life full of crooks and corrupt cops. Sarajevo's subculture and street life had not previously been explored on film in this way. The two young leads, making their debuts, give exceptional performances which, allied to the despairing atmosphere created by Vuletic, make for a movie that's hard to forget.

Mourning becomes Zalica

In August 2004 Pjer Zalica's second film, the family drama **Days and Hours** (*Kod amidze idriza*), successfully opened the tenth Sarajevo Film Festival. This chamber piece, written by Namik Kabil (who at press time was preparing to direct his first feature), tackles an issue of great importance in post-war Sarajevo: how one deals with unforgettable, tragic loss.

Fuke (Senad Basic), left, visits his uncle (Mustafa Nadarevic) and aunt (Semka Sokolovic) in **Days and Hours**

Fuke sometimes visits his old uncle, Idriz, and aunt, Sabira, who have lost all hope since their son was killed in the war. Fuke drops by to repair the water heater but stays overnight and ends up fixing broken family bonds, too. At the end, the dead son's wife returns with her daughter and her second husband-to-be and the old couple finally accept the necessary changes in their lives, embracing the prospect of their daughter's remarriage and new relations with their neighbours. Zalica builds each character's inner drama and their relationships with a marvellous eye for detail. Almost in the style of Bollywood melodramas, the climax unites the whole neighbourhood in a song and dance sequence.

DOBRO USTIMANI MRTVACI
(**Well-Tempered Corpses**)
[Drama, 2004] Script and Dir: Benjamin Filipovic. Players: Lazar Ristovski, Emir Hadzihafizbegovic, Tanja Sojic. Prod: Dunja Klemenc, Cedo Kolar, Danis Tanovic.

GO WEST
[War drama, 2004] Script: Almir Imsirovic and Ahmed Imamovic, based on a novel of Enver Puska. Dir: Imamovic. Players: Tarik Filipovic, Marko Drmac, Rade Serbedzija, Mirjana Karanovic. Prod: Ismet Nuno Arnautalic and Faruk Serdarevic, SaGa.

SNIJEG (Snow)
[Post-war drama, 2005] Script and Dir: Aida Begic. Prod: Pascal Judelewicz, Elma Tataragic, Azra Camo, Mama Film (Sarajevo)/Les Films de Cinéma (Paris).
A small group of Bosnian women return to live in their war-ravaged village following the deaths of many of their relatives and friends. The government has no interest in supporting them but they hang on to their dreams.

KROVNI TALAS (Roof Wave)
[War satire, 2005] Script and Dir: Jasmin Durakovic. Prod: F.I.S.T.
The story follows several characters during and after the war, beginning when Jennet Hugh, a black American woman, falls into one of the numerous holes in besieged Sarajevo on the evening of December 31, 1992. There she meets Red Eye, a soldier who suffered a terrible tragedy in a Bosnian country town at the beginning of the war, since when he's lost his identity.

ZIVI I MRTVI (Alive and Dead)
[War drama, 2005] Script: Josip Mlakic. Prod: Miro Barnjak, Porta (Mostar).
The story follows one family's destiny, flashing back from the recent war to the Second World War.

JEMIN
[Genre tbc, 2005] Script and Dir: Srdjan Vuletic. Prod: Ademir Kenovic, Refresh.

GRBAVICA
[War drama, 2005] Script and Dir: Jasmila Zbanic. Prod: Deblokada.

Quotes of the Year

"The world doesn't see us as poor Bosnians destroyed by war but as dangerous competition: film-makers that everybody wants to present at his festival."

ADEMIR KENOVIC,
producer of Fuse, Summer in the Golden Valley *and* Days and Hours.

"The war did not destroy life, but even now, nine years later, it still challenges its sense of purpose."

PJER ZALICA,
director, on the theme of his Days and Hours.

All three films mentioned above were produced by Refresh, the most prolific and successful company in Bosnian cinema. But others are doing their utmost, too. SaGa has completed the debut of Ahmed Imamovic, **Go West**, a love story covering something very new in Bosnian cinema: a gay affair. The problem, however, is not that the lovers are of the same sex, but, with the war raging, the fact that one is Muslim and the other Serb (the homosexual relationship is just a frame for the complex political drama).

Flash has finished the Slovenian co-production **Well-Tempered Corpses** (*Dobro ustimani mrtvaci*). Benjamin Filipovic's absurdist drama unites the destinies of several people in post-war Sarajevo, including mortuary workers, intellectuals and small-time crooks, who are played by actors from all over the former Yugoslavia, including the great Lazar Ristovski, a Serb, as well as Bosnian star Emir Hadzihafizbegovic.

Encouragingly, production has begun in cities outside the capital, including Banja Luka in the northern Republic of Srpska, where young film-makers Dejan Strika and Danijela Majstorovic have produced intriguing documentaries. Strika's **Once There Was a Champion** (*Bio jednom jedan sampion*) is about a former world boxing champion, a Croat who lives in the Serbian part of Bosnia. Majstorovic's **Counterpoint for Her** (*Kontrapunk Zanju*) tells the stories of girls forced into prostitution. In the south a handful of documentary and video productions emerge from Mostar and Konjic. Even in the small town of Siroki Brijeg in Herzegovina, enthusiasts have started a new festival for documentaries from Mediterranean countries.

Finally, the Sarajevo Film Festival continues to be an amazing success story. Its tenth edition presented the largest ever selection of Balkan cinema and drew 70,000 spectators (3,000 per night at the open-air screenings) and a significant media presence. Reporters were drawn by visitors such as John Malkovich, Gérard Depardieu, Carole Bouquet and Mike Leigh. At the newly renovated National Theatre, the red-carpet treatment given to local directors, actors, producers and composers helped turn them into genuine stars and the festival plays a pivotal role in exposing the country's films to global attention.

RADA SESIC (sesic@worldonline.nl) makes short films, writes for *Skrien* and *Dox* and lectures at the University of Amsterdam. She also collaborates on the programmes of the IDFA and Rotterdam festivals.

Brazil Nelson Hoineff

Os Normais *was a big hit in 2003*

Recent and Forthcoming Films

CONTRA TODOS
(Up Against Them All)
[Drama, 2004] Script and Dir: Roberto Moreira. Phot: Adrian Cooper. Players: Leona Cavalli, Ailton Graça, Silvia Lourenço, Giulio Lopes. Prod: Fernando Meirelles, Roberto Moreira, Georgia Costa Araujo, Andrea Ribeiro, Bel Belinck.
Teodoro, a professional killer, lives with his teenage daughter, Soninha, and his second wife, Claudia, in a barren neighbourhood on the outskirts of São Paulo. When Claudia's lover is murdered, she destroys the family home and runs away.

O DIABO A QUATRO O
(Four for None)
[Comedy, 2004] Script: Alice de Andrade, Joaquim Assis, Cláudio McDowell, Pauline Alphen, Jacques Arhex, Jean-Vincent Fournier. Dir: de Andrade. Phot: Pedro Farkas, Jacques Cheuiche. Players: Marcelo Farias, Maria Flor. Prod: Flavio R. Tambellini, Jacques Arhex, Yannick Bernard, Francois Dartemere, Maria Joao Mayer.
The destinies of four characters become entwined in Copacabana, Rio de Janeiro.

o fewer than seven Brazilian films sold over 1.5 million tickets each in 2003, led by *Carandiru* (4.7 million) and *Lisbela and the Prisoner* and the comedy *Os Normais* (both more than 3.5 million). Market share for the 40 local releases more than doubled compared to 2002, thanks in no small measure to the local distribution operations of the Hollywood majors (among the year's top ten Brazilian films, five were released by Columbia, two by Warners, and one each by Fox and Buena Vista) and the investments of Globo Filmes as co-producer of six of the 10 biggest local hits.

Guel Arraes' **Lisbela and the Prisoner** (*Lisbela e o prisioneiro*) was one of the best Brazilian films of recent few years. Arraes had already adapted the famous play by Ariano Suassuna for television, and returned to its folk tale of the young daughter of a judge who falls in love with a wise outlaw, building a magical atmosphere in which every component enchanted the audience.

The local successes continued in 2004 when **Cazuza – Time Never Stops** (*Cazuza – o tempo não para*), directed by Walter Carvalho and Sandra Werneck, drew nearly three million admissions. This long-awaited biopic tells the story of Brazilian rock star Cazuza, who was struck down by Aids in the mid-1990s when his career was at its peak. *Cazuza* was not only fluently adapted from a biography written by the star's mother, Lucia Lins, but photographed with customary mastery by co-director Carvalho, whose many credits as a cinematographer include *Behind the Sun* and *Carandiru*.

Daniel de Oliveira as the eponymous rock star in **Cazuza – Time Never Stops**

FEMINICES (Woman Talk)
[Comedy, 2004] Script and Dir: Domingos Oliveira. Phot: Dib Lufti. Players: Priscila Rozenbaum, Dedina Bernadelli, Clarice Niskier, Caca Mourthe, Oliveira. Prod: Sergio Rossini.
Four actresses in their forties write a play called *Confessions of a 40-Year-Old Woman*, but its director is not satisfied with the text because he says women do not confess at that age.

FILHAS DO VENTO
(Daughters of the Wind)
[Drama, 2004] Script and Dir: Joel Zito Araujo. Phot: Jacob Sarmento Solitrenick. Players: Milton Ghonçalves, Ruth de Souza, Lea Garcia, Tais Araujo, Maria Ceiça, Thalma de Freiras, Danielle Ornallas. Prod: Marcio Curi, Carla Gomide.
A girl leaves her home town to become an actress, leaving her sister to look after their father. When they are reunited years later, their home town's ghosts shape the drama.

LOST ZWEIG
[Drama, 2004] Script: Sylvio Back, Nicholas O'Neill. Dir: Back. Phot: Antonio Luiz Mendes. Players: Rudiger Vogler, Ruth Rieser, Renato Borghi, Daniel Dantas, Ney Piacentini, Claudia Netto, Juan Alba, Ana Carbatti, Odilon Wagner. Prod: Margit Richter.
The story of the famous Austrian Jewish author Stephan Zweig (*Brazil – Land of the Future*), his young wife, Lotte, and his descent into a world of loss and betrayal.

TAINÁ 2 – A AVENTURA CONTINUA (Tainá 2 – A New Amazon Adventure)
[Children's adventure, 2004] Script: Claudia Levay. Dir: Mauro Lima. Phot: Uli Burtin. Players: Eunice Baia, Vitor Morosini, Arilene Rodrigues, Kadu Moliterno, Chris Couto, Aramis Trindade. Prod: Pedro Carlos Rovai.
In this sequel to *Tainá – An Amazon Adventure*, the heroine

Another local blockbuster, **Olga**, launched in August 2004, sold a million tickets in its first three weeks. The debut feature of Jayme Monjardim (like Guel Arraes, one of the most successful directors of local *telenovelas*), it tells the story of Olga Benario, a German Jew who in the 1930s lived with Brazilian communist leader Carlos Prestes and was deported by President Getulio Vargas and killed by the Nazis after her return to Germany. Suffering from an excess of melodramatic clichés, it was nevertheless a winner with audiences who enjoy TV dramas.

Historical drama **Olga** *drew more than one million admissions*

High quality: who needs it?

Some of the best films flopped at the box-office. Hugo Carvana's **Apolonio Brasil**, an enjoyable comedy about the end of a romantic period in Rio de Janeiro's nightlife, was seen by fewer than 13,000 viewers. Sergio Rezende's **Onde Anda Você** (literally, *Where Have You Been?*), a romantic story about the rise and fall of a popular TV star, was seen by about 50,000 spectators, while Alain Fresnot's **Desmundo**, a strong account of the Portuguese colonisation of Brazil in the sixteenth century, managed to sell 100,000 tickets. An amazing new film by cult director Carlos Reichembach, **Garotas do ABC**, about the lowlife in one of the best-known industrial areas of São Paulo, fared poorly after its premiere in August 2004.

Other under-achievers included **Benjamin**, directed by Monique Gardenberg from a best-selling novel by Chico Buarque de Hollanda about a man in seacrch of his memories, and **Eternal Pelé** (*Pelé eterno*), the biggest documentary ever made about the great Brazilian soccer genius. Directed by Anibal Massaini, it features more than 400 of Pelé's goals and its failure confirmed the old market view that sports documentaries are better received on TV than in the cinema.

That failure apart, however, 2004 was a strong year for Brazilian documentaries in cinemas, helped in part by the expansion of the arthouse circuit (now around 130-strong) and the growth of digital distribution (almost 50 screens), whose lower costs suit independent non-fiction fare. Notable examples were Silvio Tendler's **Glauber Rocha – Labirinto do Brasil** (literally, *Glauber Rocha – Labyrinth of Brazil*), about the late film-maker, and Maria Augusta Araujo's **Justice** (Justiça), which examined the struggle of working-class Brazilians to gain access to justice in an environment of complex bureaucracy and corruption.

On the industry front, the most important development was the Ministry of Culture's proposal, unveiled in July 2004, to transform the National Agency for Cinema (Ancine) into the new National Agency for the Audiovisual (Ancinav), which would control not only cinema but also television, mobile phone content and the internet. The Ancinav proposal immediately became the focus of an intense media debate and at press time was still the subject of prolonged scrutiny by the National Council of Cinema, whose recommendations must be made before the government can send the measure to Congress.

NELSON HOINEFF (nelson@comalt.com) is president of the Association of Film Critics of Rio de Janeiro and film critic for the daily *Jornal do Brasil*.

faces a dangerous gang who are trying to destroy jungle trees and rare species.

REDENTOR (The Redeemer)
[Drama, 2004] Script: Elena Soarez, Fernanda Torres, Claudio Torres. Dir: Claudio Torres. Phot: Ralph Strelow. Players: Pedro Cardoso, Miguel Falabella, Camila Pitanga, Stenio Garcia, Fernanda Montenegro, Fernanda Torres. Prod: Claudio Torres, Leonardo Monteiro de Barros. A journalist is convinced by an old friend to become involved in an illegal business.

Regiane Alves in **Onde Anda Você**, *which underperformed at cinemas*

The 52nd Silver Condor Awards (Argentina)

Presented by the Asociación de Cronistas Cinematográficos de Argentina, Buenos Aires, May 4, 2004.

Film: *Valentín* (Alejandro Agresti).
First Film: *Bar El Chino* (Daniel Burak).
Director: Alejandro Agresti (*Valentín*).
Original Screenplay: Alejandro Agresti (*Valentín*).
Adapted Screenplay: Ariel Sienra, Luis César D'Angiolillo (*Potestad/Legal Authority*).
Actor: Tato Pavlosky (*Potestad*).
Actress: Marina Glezer (*El polaquito/The Little Pole*).
Supporting Actor: Gustavo Garzón (*El fondo del mar/The Bottom of the Sea*).
Supporting Actress: Beatriz Thibaudin (*Tan de repente/So All of a Sudden*).
Male Newcomer: Rodrigo Noya (*Valentín*)
Female Newcomer: Raquel Bank (*El juego de la silla/Musical Chairs*).
Cinematography: Carlos Torlaschi (*El polaquito*).

Julieta Cardinali and Rodrigo Noya in the award-winning **Valentín**

Music: Paul Van Brugge (*Valentín*).
Sound: Daniel Márquez (*Raúl Barboza*).
Editing: Alejandro Bordersohn (*Valentín*).
Art Direction: Floris Vos (*Valentín*).
Documentary: *Yo no sé que me han hecho tus ojos/I Don't Know What Your Eyes Have Done to Me* (Lorena Muñoz, Sergio Wolf).
Videofilm: *Oscar Alemán – Vida con swing/Oscar Alemán – Life with Swing* (Hernán Gaffet).
Foreign Film: *Russian Ark* (Alexander Sokurov).

Bulgaria Pavlina Jeleva

The Year's Best Films

Pavlina Jaleva's selection:

Alphabet of Hope
(Docu. Dir: Stefan
Komandarev)

You Are So Pretty, My Dear
(Georgy Diulgerov)

Burning Out (Stanimir Trifonov)

Mila from Mars
(Zornitsa Sophia)

Crazy Day (Sylvia Pesheva)

Kosta Tzonev in **Crazy Day**

Recent and Forthcoming Films

[In production credits
BNT indicates Bulgarian
National Television]

ISPEPELIAVANE (Burning Out)
*[Drama, 2004] Script: Yordan
De Meo. Dir: Stanimir Trifonov.
Phot: Emil Hristov. Players:
Paraskeva Djukelova, Stefan
Valdobrev, Deyan Donkov. Prod:
Parallax, with the support of
National Film Centre
(NFC)/BNT/FS Vreme/Doli
Media Stidio/Camera Ltd.*

MILA OT MARS
(Mila from Mars)
*[Experimental drama, 2004]
Script and Dir: Zornitsa Sophia.
Phot: Rumen Vassilev. Players:
Vessela Kazakova, Assen
Blatechki, Zlatina Todeva. Prod:
All Things – Zornitsa
Sophia/Kirov Consult/Doli Media
Stidio/Camera Ltd/Art Service
Sarajevo/Boyana Film.*

Following the passing of the long-awaited new Film Law in late 2003, the renamed Executive Agency – National Film Centre created a new umbrella body for the industry, the National Film Council (NFC). The NFC has 12 members, selected on a fixed quota basis from professional associations and state bodies, who serve for three years. In addition, four new commissions began two-year investigations into artistic, financial, technical and promotional aspects of the national film industry.

The new legislation has given the NFC €3m a year for film support, including production finance for a minimum of five features annually. Bulgarian National Television (BNT) provides another €2.3m per year and the NFC is also introducing positive measures concerning the local distribution and promotion of European films. However, some within the industry argue that the level of funding is far too low. The Association of Bulgarian Film Producers was among the professional organisations to suggest that the government had missed an excellent opportunity to introduce a film industry levy on distributors and commercial television operators. The establishment of a film fund drawing on public and private revenues remains an important goal.

The eighth edition of the Sofia Film Fest, in March 2004, screened 144 features from 40 countries in Sofia and the beautiful Black Sea port city of Bourgas. Highlights included a special tribute to a 'living legend' of Bulgarian cinema, 75-year-old Rangel Valchanov, and a Wong Kar-Wai retrospective. Among the nicest surprises was the feminine sensibility of Svetla Tsotsorkova, whose 20-minute diploma film *Life with Sophia* (*Jivot s Sofia*) was about a village wife waiting in vain for her husband to return from abroad. In August 2004 the twenty-sixth National Film Festival "Golden Rose" was combined with the twelfth "Love Is Folly" festival. Among the 16 new Bulgarian features shown, six were debuts and the line-up again highlighted the indispensable role of BNT, which had commissioned seven of the films.

Mila's miles from home

Mila from Mars, directed by Zornitsa Sophia (b. 1972), shared the festival's main prize with *Burning Out*, from Stanimir Trifonov (b. 1958) – two directors showing very different images of Bulgaria.

In **Mila from Mars** (*Mila ot Mars*), a pregnant 16-year-old (Vessela Kazakova) runs away from her dangerous lover, full of fear and disgust. She reaches a poor village near the Greek border. Its elderly inhabitants make their living growing marijuana and she learns that their huge plantation belongs to her boyfriend. The film is a strong interpretation of the nightmares of a lost generation.

Left to right: Deyan Donkov, Paraskeva Djukelova and Stefan Valdobrev in **Burning Out**

Burning Out (*Ispepeliavane*) takes in the end of the Second World War and the first two decades of communist rule in Bulgaria. Young and romantic Italian doctor Enrico falls in love with a beautiful Bulgarian, Kalina (Paraskeva Djukelova). After he is arrested by the boss of the secret service, Metody Stoev, and sent to a camp, Kalina is forced to become both lover of and an informer for Stoev. Enrico escapes but his attempt to be reunited with Kalina leads to diplomatic scandal and, ultimately, tragedy.

Sylvia Pesheva's debut feature **Crazy Day** (*Shantav den*) took two awards and elegantly portrayed the relationship between Ina (Vessela Kazakova), 18, a painter and aspiring children's book illustrator, and her ailing and eccentric grandfather (Kosta Tzonev), whom she tries and fails to help in a day that is filled with unpleasant incidents but ends hopefully, thanks to a young architect.

Georgi Djulgerov's **You're So Pretty, My Dear** (*Hubava si, mila moya*) is an unusual experiment, poetically binding together the confessional stories of four jailed prostitutes, each of which contains an extraordinary mixture of lies and truth as the women build themselves new biographies that they all sincerely believe. Finally, the moving and impressive documentary **Alphabet of Hope** (*Azbuka na nadejdata*), by young director Stefan Komandarev, shows the courageous efforts of children, parents and teachers to survive in one of the poorest regions in southern Bulgaria.

PAVLINA JELEVA (geopoly@techno-link.com) has been a film critic since 1978, contributing to leading Bulgarian publications. Formerly Bulgaria's representative on the boards of Eurimages and FIPRESCI, she runs her own film company.

SHANTAV DEN (Crazy Day)
[Romantic drama, 2004] Script: Sylvia Pesheva, Ina Braneva. Dir: Pesheva. Phot: Stefan Kutzarov. Players: Vessela Kazakova, Kosta Tzonev, Stoyo Mirkov, Elena Atanassova. Prod: Geopoly, with BNFC/BNT/Boyana Film.

DRUGIAT NASH VAZMOJEN JIVOT (The Other Possible Life of Ours)
[Drama, 2004] Script: Nevelina Popova. Dir: Rumiana Petkova. Phot: Svetla Ganeva. Players: Vania Tzvetkova, Ivan Ivanov. Prod: Doli Media Studio, with BNFC/BNT.

I GOSPOD SLEZE DA NI VIDI (And God Came Down To See Us)
[Drama, 2004] Script: Stanisslav Stratiev. Dir: Petar Popzlatev. Phot: Emil Hristov, Eli Yonova-Mihailova. Players: Katya Paskaleva, Itzko Finzi, Svetlana Yancheva. Prod: Post Scriptum 2/NFC(Bulgaria) /Mact Production /CNC (France)/Eurimages.

HUBAVA SI, MILA MOIA (You Are So Pretty, My Dear)
[Experimental docu-fiction, 2004] Script and Dir: Georgy Diulgerov. Phot: Georgy Chelebiev. Players: Liubov Liubcheva, Iliana Kitanova, Radena Valkanova. Prod: Diulgerov and friends.

SLEDVAI ME (Follow Me)
[Drama, 2004] Script: Marin Damianov, Docho Bodjakov. Dir: Bodjakov. Phot: Ivan Varimezov. Players: Hristo Shopov, Biliana Petrinska, Stoicho Mazgalov. Prod: BNT.

Quote of the Year

"At a difficult moment in my life I cut all my links with Bulgaria. But when I received the invitation to play the main part in *The Other Possible Life of Ours* I immediately asked: 'When does shooting start?'"

VANIA TZVETKOVA,
US-based Bulgarian actress.

Canada Brendan Kelly

The Year's Best Films

Brendan Kelly's selection:
The Corporation
(Docu. Mark Achbar,
Jennifer Abbott)
Gaz Bar Blues
(Louis Bélanger)
Love and Magnets
(Yves Pelletier)
**Love, Sex and Eating
the Bones**
(David "Sudz" Sutherland)
A Silent Love
(Federico Hidalgo)

Marlyne N. Afflack and Hill Harper in
Love, Sex and Eating the Bones

Recent and Forthcoming Films

LES AIMANTS
(Love and Magnets)
*[Romantic comedy, 2004] Script
and Dir: Yves Pelletier. Phot:
Pierre Jobin. Players: Isabelle
Blais, Sylvie Moreau, Stéphane
Gagnon, Emmanuel Bilodeau,
David Savard. Prod: Nicole
Robert, Gabriel Pelletier, Go Films.*

AURORE
*[Drama, 2004] Script and Dir:
Luc Dionne. Phot: Louis de
Ernsted. Players: Marianne
Fortier, Stéphanie Lapointe, Serge
Postigo, Hélène Bourgeois-
Leclerc, Rémy Girard, Yves
Jacques. Prod: Denise Robert,
Daniel Louis, Cinémaginaire.*

I f it had not been for Denys Arcand, it would have been tempting to write off the past year as among the worst ever for Canadian film since its movie industry first developed in the 1960s. That industry is going through rough times, to put it politely, but, with his inspired **The Barbarian Invasions** (*Les invasions barbares*), Arcand, virtually single-handed, reminded everyone that Canada can make a film that appeals to critics and audiences at home and abroad. It won Canada's first Foreign-Language Oscar and several categories at the Genie Awards, the Quebec Jutra Awards and, most surprisingly, the French Césars and grossed more than $20m worldwide, one of the highest takes for a Canadian picture.

Interestingly, Arcand achieved all this by returning to filming in French after failing with a pair of English-language pics (*Stardom* and *Love and Human Remains*) and by focusing on his own personal obsessions rather than trying to ape Hollywood. He kept things original, close to his roots – a lesson other Canadian film-makers could do well to heed.

It was another dismal year for film in English Canada. Telefilm Canada, the funding agency, is still on its push to finance more commercial pics, but there are still far too few English–Canadian hits. Alliance Atlantis, the country's only well-financed film company, threw all kinds of marketing money at the caper heist flick **Foolproof** and it still tanked. There were high hopes for the horror sequel **Ginger Snaps 2** and it also bombed. Worse still, Alliance Atlantis then shut down its feature production and international sales activities, leaving a gaping hole; at press time there was no major international distributor focused on selling Canadian pics.

Many now wonder if Telefilm's plan is misguided. Clearly, trying to follow American commercial formulae does not work for Canadian film and it could be argued that the old, auteur-driven policy at least fostered a wave of internationally renowned film-makers like Atom Egoyan, Patricia Rozema and François Girard. French-language Quebec film continues to thrive on its home turf, however. Quebec directors have a captive audience keen to see domestically produced fare. The province also has its own star system and a media machine always willing to give massive coverage to local releases – precisely the elements missing in the rest of Canada, where Hollywood dominates.

THINK Film

And now, the good news...

Artistically, there were outstanding films produced on both sides of the linguistic divide. First-time feature director Federico Hidalgo crafted a smart, mature look at cross-cultural relationships with **A Silent Love**, a superbly acted film in English and Spanish about a middle-aged Montreal professor who finds and marries a young Mexican woman via an internet agency. Noel Burton makes the lonely, repressed prof seem like a loser but it is a tribute to his skills that we still root for him. Vanessa Bauche is very good as the confused, pouting young Mexican, but the real revelation is Susana Salazar, who makes what could have been a stock character – the dreaded mother-in-law – into the film's most intriguing figure.

Ewan Christie, left, and Noel Burton in **A Silent Love**

Another promising debut came courtesy of actor-turned-director Jacob Tierney with **Twist**, his radical update of *Oliver Twist*. Tierney transfers Dickens' poor-house classic to the lurid world of male hustlers on the gritty streets of downtown Toronto. Like *A Silent Love*, *Twist* works largely thanks to outstanding performances and the sure hand of its director. Nick Stahl plays Dodge (equivalent to the Artful Dodger) and makes you love and hate this mess of complexes and emotions. Newcomer Joshua Close gives Oliver just the right blend of vulnerability and flirtatiousness and Tygh Runyan is suitably tortured as Dodge's troubled brother, David.

Louis Bélanger, one of Quebec's most exciting newish film-makers, followed his riveting debut feature, *Post-Mortem*, with the even more impressive **Gaz Bar Blues**, a moving, down-home autobiographical story about Le Boss (Serge Thériault), who runs a small, gas station in Quebec City, suffers from Parkinson's Disease and has strained relations with his sons. It is moving chiefly because of Thériault, who gives the performance of his career.

Love and Magnets (*Les aimants*) is a refreshingly inventive romantic comedy from Yves Pelletier that is worth the price of admission simply to bask in the glow of lead actress Isabelle Blais, as a hippie-dippie do-gooder struggling with her cynical older sister (played with gusto by Sylvie Moreau). Set in Toronto, David "Sudz" Sutherland's **Love, Sex and Eating the Bones** is a hip-hop-flavoured urban – and urbane – comedy about a young guy who can't get it on without a little help from porn images and Sutherland deftly deals

Horrifying story of a young child abused by her stepmother in 1900s Quebec.

LIE WITH ME
[Drama, 2004] Script: Clement Virgo, Tamara Faith Berger, based on Berger's novel. Dir: Virgo. Phot: Barry Stone. Players: Eric Balfour, Lauren Lee Smith, Polly Shannon, Kate Lynch, Kristin Lehman, Don Francks. Prod: Damon D'Oliveira, Virgo, Conquering Lion Pictures.
Sexually voracious Leila and decent, uncertain David, both attractive young people, play with casual and daring sex.

LE SURVENANT
(The Outlander)
[Drama, 2004] Script: Diane Cailhier. Dir: Erik Canuel. Phot: Bernard Couture. Players: Jean-Nicolas Verreault, Anick Lemay, Gilles Renaud, François Chénier. Prod : Jacques Bonin, Claude Veillet, Films Vision 4.
In the early 1900s, a stranger stirs up trouble in a small, isolated rural community.

LOVE, SEX AND EATING THE BONES
[Comedy, 2004] Script and Dir: David "Sudz" Sutherland. Phot: Arthur E. Cooper. Players: Hill Harper, Marlyne N. Afflack, Mark Taylor, Kai Soremekum, Jennifer Baxter, Kardinal Offishall, Ed Robertson. Prod: Jennifer Holness, Eating the Bones Productions.
Michael (Harper), a handsome black photographer, 26, has an obsessive porn habit. He falls for Jasmine (Afflack), 28, a market researcher.

MAMAN LAST CALL
[Comedy, 2004] Script: Nathalie Petrowski, based on her novel. Dir: François Bouvier. Phot: Allen Smith. Players: Sophie Lorain, Patrick Huard, Stéphane Demers, Patricia Nolin. Prod: Pierre Gendron, Christian Larouche, Christal Films.
Newspaper columnist Alice Malenfant, 37, dates a radio host

and is worried by the ticking of her biological clock.

MÉMOIRES AFFECTIVES
(Looking for Alexander)
[Drama, 2004] Script: Francis Leclerc, Marcel Beaulieu. Dir: Leclerc. Phot: Steve Asselin. Players: Roy Dupuis, Rosa Zacharie, Guy Thauvette, Nathalie Coupal. Prod: Barbara Shrier, Palomar.
Alexandre comes out of a long coma after a hit-and-run accident and begins trying to piece together his past life.

Noémie Godin-Vigneau and David La Haye in **Nouvelle-France**

NOUVELLE-FRANCE
[Drama, 2004] Script: Pierre Billon. Dir: Jean Beaudin. Phot: Louis de Ernsted. Players: Noémie Godin-Vigneau, David La Haye, Gérard Depardieu, Irène Jacob, Pierre Lebeau, Johanne Marie Tremblay. Prod: Richard Goudreau, Melenny Productions.
Eighteenth-century Nouvelle-France (now Quebec). A young peasant woman (Godin-Vigneau) falls in love with an audacious adventurer (La Haye) who has returned from studying in Paris.

WHERE THE TRUTH LIES
[Drama, 2004] Script Atom Egoyan, based on the novel by Rupert Holmes. Dir: Egoyan. Phot: Paul Sarossy. Players: Kevin Bacon, Colin Firth, Alison Lohman, David Hayman. Prod: Robert Lantos, Serendipity Point Films/First Choice Films.
Legendary showbiz duo Lanny and Vince's partnership is torn apart when a dead beauty turns up in their hotel suite. Twenty years later, a writer begins researching this tale of treachery.

with the idea of porn addiction in mostly light, funny fashion. Shame about the film's enigmatic title, though.

Le dernier tunnel (literally, *The Last Tunnel*) coud have been a paint-by-numbers bank heist thriller, but director Erik Canuel and writers Paul Ohl and Mario Bolduc make this true-life tale something much more interesting by focusing on the tense group dynamics among the crooks tunnelling their way into a bank in Old Montreal. It is a familiar plot, but still enthralling.

Canada contributed to the current cinema renaissance of the feature documentary with **The Corporation**, a Michael Moore-esque blast at mega-multinationals' influence on today's world. It turned out to be one of the biggest – and, at 165 minutes, longest – recent home-grown hits, ringing-up more than C$1m (US$792,000) at the Canadian box-office. Directors Mark Achbar and Jennifer Abbott did not really tell audiences anything they did not already know but somehow managed to make their case – that big corporations are psychopaths – in highly entertaining fashion.

Moore becomes less

There were of course disappointments. Norman Jewison's **The Statement**, starring Michael Caine, was touted as an awards season hopeful but Jewison and adapter Ronald Harwood took a fine, intelligent thriller by Brian Moore and transformed it into a dull, meandering movie. Moore's book is all about the tangled ties between the Catholic Church in France and the country's Nazi sympathisers, but Jewison's film loses that nuance and becomes little more than a routine cops-chase-fugitive flick.

After making a highly original debut with *Last Night*, Don McKellar stumbled with his sophomore effort as writer-director, **Childstar**, a less than insightful look at the life of a teen Hollywood star filming in Toronto. Bruce McDonald followed the major misfire *Picture Claire* with the minor misfire **The Love Crimes of Gillian Guess**, based on the true story of a woman juror who becomes romantically entangled with the accused in a high-profile murder trial. It is "Movie of the Week" material and McDonald only makes things more opaque by trying to turn it into a hip, experimental flick.

The most offensive Canadian movie of 2003-04 was Pierre Falardeau's deliberately idiotic "comedy", **Elvis Gratton XXX – La Vengeance d'Elvis Wong**, an odious attack on Falardeau's favourite targets, notably all ethnic groups who are not old-stock French-Canadians.

BRENDAN KELLY (brendank@mlink.net) reports on the Canadian film scene for *Variety*, writes about entertainment for *The Montreal Gazette* and is a columnist on CBC Radio.

Chile Andrea Osorio Klenner

The Year's Best Films

Andrea Osorio Klenner's selection:

B-Happy
(Gonzalo Justiniano)

Bad Blood
(León Errázuriz)

Average Red
(Nicolás López)

Recent and Forthcoming Films

SUB-TERRA

[Drama, 2003] Script: José Manuel Fernández, Carlos Doria, Jaime Sepúlveda, based on the book by Baldomero Lillo. Dir: Marcelo Ferrari. Phot: Esteban Courtalon. Players: Francisco Reyes, Paulina Gálvez, Héctor Noguera, Consuelo Holzapfel, Alejandro Trejo. Prod: Pablo Bulo, Daniel Pantoja, Televisión Nacional de Chile/Cine Sur.
Chile, 1900s. Thousands of miners and a powerful Spanish aristocratic family, the Cousiño-Goyenechea, offered their blood and lives for a dream. The hardships of the coal miners' lives and the family's attempts at industrial revolution flow into a story of strong social and human content.

B-HAPPY

[Drama, 2003] Script: Gonzalo Justiniano, Fernando Aragón, Sergio Gómez, Daniela Lillo. Dir: Justiniano. Phot: Andrés Garretón. Players: Manuela Martelli, Ricardo Fernández, Lorene Prieto, Eduardo Barril. Prod: Carlo Bettin, Cinecorp/Igeldo Comunicaciones/Joel Films Producción.
Katty, 14, lives with her mother

elped considerably by more concerted and innovative marketing of local movies, 2003-04 was a very good period for Chilean cinema. Although fewer domestic titles were released than in 2002, they attracted 1,697,003 viewers (412,961 in 2002), led by Boris Quercia's lively comedy **Sex with Love** (*Sexo con amor*), whose 990,000 spectators not only established a new local box-office record (profits of more than $3m), but also surpassed *The Return of the King* and other international blockbusters – an achievement that would have been unthinkable a few years ago.

Remarkably, a second Chilean film featured in the 2003 top ten: Marcelo Ferrari's debut, **Sub-Terra**, based on the novel by Baldomero Lillo depicting Chilean coal mines in the early twentieth century, ranked sixth with 470,343 admissions. With a budget of more than $1m, the film was immensely expensive by local standards.

Héctor Noguera, left, as the head of a mining family in **Sub-Terra**

Don't worry...

"I'm not afraid of anything," Katty, the leading character in Gonzalo Justiniano's **B-Happy**, keeps repeating to herself. Manuela Martelli was just 18 and finishing school when Justiniano cast her as the heroine whose life is marked by abandonment (absent father, sick mother), and portrays her as an increasingly lonely, yet somehow immutable character. "One gets used to living with fear," she says. A few fade-outs fragment the story in a simply shot film whose value lies in the strength shown by Katty in Martelli's brilliant screen debut. It won her the Second Coral for Best Actress at the La Havana festival in 2003 – one of 10 international awards for the film, including Best Film in the Forum section at Berlin 2004. Unfortunately, *B-Happy* could gather only 38,000 viewers, only half the number and elder brother in a low-class rural neighbourhood. Abandonment and the forces of destiny push her into undreamed-of experiences.

MALA LECHE (Bad Blood)
[Crime thriller, 2004] Script: León Errázuriz, Matías Ovalle. Dir: Errázuriz. Phot: Andrés Garcés. Players: Juan Pablo Ogalde, Mauricio Diocares, Ramón Llao, Adela Secall, Luis Dubó. Prod: Matías Ovalle,León Errázuriz,Cine FX.

MACHUCA
[Drama, 2004] Script: Roberto Brodsky, Mamoun Hassan, Andrés Wood. Dir: Wood. Phot: Miguel Joan Littin. Players: Matías Quer, Ariel Mateluna, Manuela Martelli, Aline Kuppenheim, Federico Luppi, Ernesto Malbrán. Prod: Gerardo Herrero,Mamoun Hassan,A. Wood Producciones/Tornasol Films/Paraíso/Chilefilms. Chilean politics in the 1970s, seen through the eyes of two 11-year-old boys in Santiago, one from a well-off family and neighbourhood, the other from a humble, illegal new settlement just two blocks away.

PROMEDIO ROJO (Average Red)
[Black comedy, 2004] Script and Dir: Nicolás López. Phot: Chechu Graf. Players: Ariel Levy, Benjamín Vicuña, Xenia Tostado, Nicolás Martínez. Prod: Javier Valiño,Santiago Segura,Nicolás López,Miguel Asensio,Aldea Films/Amiguetes Entertainment /Sobras Producciones.

Quote of the Year

"Do I look like a director or just a decadent fat guy?"
NICOLAS LOPEZ, *while shooting* Average Red.

Manuela Martelli and Eduardo Barril in **B-Happy**

drawn by **The Nominee** (*El Nominado*), whose only merit was its opportunistic exploitation of the success of reality TV shows.

In 2004 it became clear that greater access to audio-visual technology and the integration of new narrative techniques have been opening new territory in Chilean cinema, especially for young film-makers. Although it chooses an overly familiar topic for national productions, marginality, León Errázuriz's debut, **Bad Blood** (*Mala Leche*), is admirably realistic, with well-mounted action scenes. It's the story of two marginal youngsters who, after a drug deal goes wrong, have just two days to recover the money they've lost and find themselves risking death as they sink deeper and deeper into the world of crime. Its predictable finale and the problem that some viewers may not understand every word of the street slang used by the characters are minor drawbacks in the face of good direction, editing and acting.

Another debut, **Average Red** (*Promedio rojo*), made for about $1m by 20-year-old Nicolás López, also stands out. It is a mixture of superheroes, grandparents who reappear after death à la Obi Wan Kenobi and a fat, bespectacled 17-year-old schoolboy, Roberto Rodríguez, who's always dressed in black and who draws comics portraying his pathetic existence. In the words of its director, this is an "adolescent romantic comedy with superpowers". It is also remarkable for the participation of the Spanish star Santiago Segura (from *Torrente*), as producer and actor, playing a doctor who performs illegal abortions.

ANDREA OSORIO KLENNER (cineclub@uach.cl) is a journalist and Executive Producer and Programme Co-ordinator of the Valdivia International Film Festival.

China Shelly Kraicer

The Year's Best Films

Shelly Kraicer's selection:
Peacock (Gu Changwei)
Letter From an Unknown
Woman (Xu Jinglei)
Tang Poetry (Zhang Lu)
Jiang Jie (Zhang Yuan)
South of the Clouds
(Zhu Wen)

Li Xuejian in **South of the Clouds**

Recent and
Forthcoming Films

KANSHANG QU HEN MEI
(Beautiful)
[Drama, 2004] Script: Ning Dai,
Zhang Yuan, based on the novel
by Wang Shuo. Dir: Zhang. Phot:
Yang Tao. Players: Dong Bowen,
Ning Yuanyuan, Chen Manyuan,
Zhao Rui, Li Xiaofeng. Prod:
Zhang,Marco Müller,CITIC
Cultural and Sports Industry/
Century Hero Film Investment/
Cinovision Productions.

LUCHENG (Passages)
[Drama, 2004] Script and Dir:
Yang Chao. Phot: Zhang Xigui.
Players: Geng Le, Chang Jieping,
Gao Hu, Maizi. Prod: Yang
Haijun,Infinitely Practical
Prods./Century Hero Film
Investment/CITIC Culture
and Sports Industry/Asian
Union Film.

Film-making in China over the last year has continued to take advantage of the groundwork laid by recent trends: especially a welcome diversification in the industry's basic structure. While art films continued to win awards overseas, films made by independent producers for home consumption held their own, without exactly thriving.

Nostalgia has been a powerful impulse in Chinese cinema since its inception. In 2003-04, the drive to explore China's recent past (the 1960s to 1980s) had a new sophistication. Perhaps the dizzying pace of economic and social development in China's cities evokes a need to see alternatives on screen; many of today's most significant films offer either a glimpse of a contrasting past or a continued harsh critique of the present.

The late 1970s/early 1980s is one of the most fertile periods for Chinese cinema to (re)create: not long ago, but utterly unlike today. Perhaps the most significant of these films, and certainly the most beautiful, is Gu Changwei's debut, **Peacock** (*Kongque*). It tells the interlocking stories of three misfit siblings and their extraordinarily sad families. Each finds a way to excavate a private space, if not of pleasure, then at least of momentary peace, in a still-collectivised society. With a perfect eye for formally astonishing, emotionally staggering images, Gu (formerly d.p. for Zhang Yimou and Chen Kaige) instantly establishes himself as a new major voice in Chinese cinema.

Zhang Jingchu in Gu Changwei's **Peacock**

Less successful aesthetically, but more immediately accessible, Lu Yue's second film, **The Foliage** (*Mei ren cao*), evokes the late

**YU NI TONG ZAI DE
XIATIAN (Summer)**
*[Drama, 2004] Script: Xie Dong,
Liu Huidong. Dir: Xie. Phot:
Yang Tao. Players: Jiang Yan, Xu
Tao. Prod: Zhang Hongxin,Philip
Lee,Huawei Time
Entertainment/Huawei Film &
Television Performing Art/Beijing
October Pictures Cultural
Development.*

XIANGRIKUI (Sunflower)
*[Drama, 2004] Script and Dir:
Zhang Yang. Phot: Jong Lin.
Players: Joan Chen, Sun Haiying,
Liu Zifeng, Gao Ge. Prod: Peter
Loehr,Han Sanping,Ming
Productions/Fortissimo Film
Sales/China Film Group.*

SHIJIE (The World)
*[Drama, 2004] Script and Dir:
Jia Zhangke. Phot: Yu Lik-wai.
Players: Zhao Tao, Cheng
Taisheng, Wang Hongwei. Prod:
Zhou Qiang,Shanghai Film
Studio/Hong Kong Xinghui.*

RIRI YEYE (Day and Night)
*[Drama, 2004] Script and Dir:
Wang Chao. Phot: Yihuhewula.
Players: Liu Lei, Wang Lan,
Xiao Ming, Wang Zhen, Sun
Guilin. Prod: Fang Li,Sylvain
Bursztejn,Laurel Films/
Rosem Films.*

DELAMU
*[Documentary, 2004] Dir: Tian
Zhuangzhuang. Phot: Wang Yu,
Wu Qiao. Prod: Takahiro
Hamano,Yang Zhao,BDI
Films/Beijing Time United
Culture Developing.*

**ZAO'AN BEIJING
(Good Morning, Beijing)**
*[Drama, 2004] Script and Dir:
Pan Jianllin. Phot: Zou Qin,
Peng Zhe, Liu Caiyun, Fan Qi,
Wu Shiyou. Players: Sun Peng,
Chen Nanxuan, Ben Hui, Yu
Xiaolei. Prod: Chen Wei,Pan
Jianlin Image Studio.*

**JI FENG ZHONG DE MA
(Season of the Horse)**
*[Drama, 2004] Script and Dir:
Ning Cai. Phot: Jong Lin.
Players: Ning Cai, Na Renhua.
Prod: Neimenggu Chengjisihan*

stages of the Cultural Revolution. Though compromised by its obvious play for commercial appeal, the film is still a gentle, thoughtful romance between two adolescents (played by mainland heartthrob Liu Ye and Taiwanese star Shu Qi) "sent down" to the countryside by government policy. The film contrasts the richness of their young lives with the spiritual emptiness eating away at contemporary existence. Which is exactly the preoccupation of Zhu Wen's splendid **South of the Clouds** (*Yunde nanfang*). This, Zhu's second feature, is explicitly cast as a false-nostalgia film. It limns a subtle, deeply felt portrait of a retired pensioner (Li Xuejian) who, dissatisfied with his life in a northern big city, yearns to recreate the imaginary "past" he never had as a youth in Yunnan province. He arrives only to find an uncanny mixture of rhapsodic fantasy wish fulfilment and absurdist modern farce.

Zhang Yuan's opera film **Jiang Jie** is in a class by itself. Though it looks like a Cultural Revolution nostalgia film – it's a virtually "straight" adaptation of the 1964 model opera based on the life of a Communist heroine – its straight-up idealism, gorgeously lyrical music and the power of the brilliant central performance by opera star Zhang Huoding make it one of the most provocative and moving Chinese films this year.

Opera star Zhang Huoding, centre, in **Jiang Jie**

Moving further back in time, director-writer-producer-actress Xu Jinglei sets her second film, **Letter From an Unknown Woman** (*Yige mosheng nürende lai xin*), in 1940s Beijing. Xu's transposition of Stefan Zweig's Viennese novella is a marvel of atmosphere and tempo. Ostensibly about the unrequited life-long love of a young woman (Xu) for a rakishly narcissistic journalist (Jiang Wen), its inspiration is both lyrical and radical. Abetted by Mark Lee's luminous cinematography, Xu's exquisite tone poem is ruled by a subversively female gaze.

Daggers fly, *Warriors* fall

Reaching back to ninth-century Tang dynasty China, Zhang Yimou's **House of Flying Daggers** (*Shimian maifu*) is an unabashed visual feast. Lighter than **Hero** (*Yingxiong*), its exhilaratingly mounted set-pieces (star Zhang Ziyi's mesmerising drum dance, and a lengthy combat gracefully suspended at the top of sublimely green bamboo forest) decorate a somewhat more earthbound romantic triangle of a plot, which sets Chinese superstar Andy Lau and Taiwanese heartthrob Takeshi Kaneshiro as two Tang cops vying for the love of Zhang Ziyi's blind singer/rebel spy. At press time it looked set to emulate *Hero* and lead the annual box-office chart.

Ge You as an adulterous TV host in **Cell Phone**

Other than Zhang Yimou, the commercial sector's production was largely unexceptional. Best of the lot, by far, is perennial hit-maker Feng Xiaogang's New Year's hit, **Cell Phone** (*Shouji*). Ge You plays a TV host unable to juggle wife, mistress and lover, even with the benefit of advanced cell phone technology. While giving the local audience the snappy laugh lines and sharp contemporary references that it expects from him, Feng produces a surprisingly acidic black comedy about the corrosive effects of mendacity in nouveau riche Beijing.

Nuan, Huo Jianqi's Golden Rooster-winning drama, reprises his usual fine craftsmanship and picturesque photography, but adds little that's new to the well-worn struggling-rural-woman genre. **Warriors of Heaven and Earth** (*Tiandi yingxiong*) is Columbia Pictures' martial arts epic misfire. The usually reliable He Ping and a big budget can't rescue this stillborn desert pic (starring Jiang Wen and Zhao Wei). Its Gobi desert panoramas and expensively costumed exoticism fail to hide a basic narrative incoherence and inadequately realised special effects.

Yingshi Wenhua/Neimenggu Tiandi Tong Gonglu Jianshe Fazhan.

KEKEXILI (Mountain Patrol)
[Drama, 2004] Script and Dir: Lu Chuan. Phot: Cao Yu. Players: Duo Bujie, Zhang Lei, Qi Liang, Zhao Xueying, Ma Zhanlin. Prod: Wang Zhongjun,Huayi Brothers & Taihe Film Investment/Columbia Pictures Film Production.

HAODA YIDUI YANG (Two Great Sheep)
[Drama, 2004] Script and Dir: Liu Hao. Phot: A Bing. Players: Sun Yunkun, Jiang Zhikun. Prod: Lola/Studio of New Film Project of China Youth Directors/Beijing Starlight Int'l Media.

LIANAIZHONG DE BAOBER (Baober in Love)
[Drama, 2004] Script: Li Shaohong, Zheng Zhong, Wang Yao. Dir: Li. Phot: Zeng Nianping. Players; Zhou Xun, Huang Jue, Chen Kun, Liao Fan. Prod: Li Xiaowan,Beijing Rosat Film & TV Production.

MOLIHUA KAI (Jasmine Women)
[Drama, 2004] Script: Zhang Xian, Hou Yong, based on a novel by Su Tong. Dir: Hou. Phot: Yao Xiaofeng. Players: Zhang Ziyi, Joan Chen, Jiang Wen, Liu Ye, Lu Yi. Prod: Li Xudong,Han Sanping,Beijing Wan Ji Communications/Century Hero Film Investment/Asian Union Film/Beijing Jing Ying Ma.

MANYAN (Pirated Copy)
[Comedy, 2004] Script: He Jianjun, Cui Zi'en. Dir: He. Phot: Yuan Deqiang. Players: Yu Bo, Wang Yamei, Hu Xiaoguang, Naren Qimuge, Su Fang. Prod: Liu Xinghai,Chen Jinliang,Lu Zhixin,Fanhall Studio.

TIANXIA WUZEI (A World without Thieves)
[Comedy, 2004] Script: Feng Xiaogang, Wang Gang, Lin Lisheng, Ah Lu. Dir: Feng. Phot: Zhang Li. Players: Andy Lau, René Liu, Ge You. Prod: Chen

Kuofu, Wang Zhonglei, Huayi Brothers & Taihe Film Investment/Media Asia Films/Topman Global (B.V.I.).

DUZI DENGDAI
(Waiting Alone)
[Comedy, 2004] Script and Dir: Dayyan Eng. Phot: Toby Oliver. Players: Xia Yu, Gong Beibi, Gao Qi, Li Bingbing. Prod: Eng, Colordance Pictures.

XINGXING XIANG XIXI
(Star Appeal)
[Fantasy, 2004] Script and Dir: Cui Zi'en. Phot: Zhang Huilin. Players: Yu Bo, Wang Guifeng, Zhang Xiwen. Prod: Xiao Wu, Cuizi DV Studio.

WU JI (The Promise)
[Action-fantasy, 2004] Dir: Chen Kaige. Phot: Peter Pau. Players: Cecilia Cheung, Nicholas Cheung, Hiroyuki Sanada, Jang Dong-Kun. Prod: Chen, Chen Hong, China Film Group/21st Century Shengkai Film/Show East/Moonstone Entertainment.

Zeng Xueqiong, left, and Liang Hongli in Uniform

SHANG SHAN
(On the Mountain)
[Drama, 2003] Script and Dir: Zhu Chuanming. Phot: Zhu. Players: Sun Congwang, Sun Zhitong, Chen Yongyun, Hu Xilin, Chen Licai. Prod: Zhu, Ming Liang, Bright Brothers.

LU CHA (Green Tea)
[Romantic comedy, 2003] Script: Zhang Yuan, Jin Renshun, from a novel by Jin. Dir: Zhang. Phot: Christopher Doyle. Players: Zhao Wei, Jiang Wen, Fang Lijun, Wang Haizheng. Prod: Dong Ping, Asian Union Film.

Into the open at last

All the films mentioned above are "authorised", i.e. approved for release in China by the Film Bureau, the official film censors. Lu Yue and Zhu Wen had previously made underground films, accessible only at informal screenings or on VCD or DVD. This move – out from the underground – is the biggest industry news story of the past year. In addition to Lu and Zhu, most of the major Chinese underground directors have "come out" this year, including Jia Zhangke, Wang Chao, Wang Xiaoshuai, He Jianjun and Liu Hao.

Representatives of this "sixth generation" of directors had met with the Film Bureau in 2003. A resulting hope for a new openness and co-operation was mitigated by the fact that, of this writing, Film Bureau control seems to have tightened yet again. But official control has always been cyclical, and the general trend is positive. What's certainly more important is that many of the directors who came of age in the 1990s have become fed up with the underground cinema "system". They want a chance to compete on the local market with local investment to try to win a local audience.

That does not mean that no interesting work is being done in the underground sector. In the last year, several noteworthy DV features gained attention at film festivals abroad. Although Diao Yi'nan's debut feature, **Uniform** (*Zhifu*), owes its laconic, dispassionate style to Jia Zhangke, its tale of a loser who wears a stolen cop's uniform to impress his new girlfriend is nonetheless fascinating, and was a winner at Vancouver. More bracing in its formal demands, and ultimately packing more of a punch, is Gao Xiao'er's **The Only Sons** (*Shanqing shuixiu*), the first Cantonese (and Catholic) mainland underground feature. The amateur actors may mumble their lines, but with cinematography this beautiful, and a shocking story – of a poor and desperate rural labourer whose need for money prompts him to contemplate the most awful sacrifices and undergo Job-like suffering – that's virtually Biblical in scope, the film is unexpectedly mesmerising.

Of cops and karma

Popular screenwriter Liu Fendou's first film, **Green Hat** (*Lü maozi*), won two top prizes at the 2004 Tribeca Film Festival. It follows the story of an amateur bank robber trapped with a hostage, then switches to a tale of the cuckolded cop who tries to arrest him. Under its narrative jolts, sexual frankness and violent tension lurks a North American indie sensibility that probably won't hurt it in the international market.

Ning Hao's quirky graduation project, **Incense** (*Xianghuo*), tells the story of a destitute Buddhist monk's encounters with prostitutes, cops and karma, as he attempts to raise money for his decrepit temple. Its droll, oddly humorous style won top prizes in Tokyo and Hong Kong. Andrew Cheng's luridly night-light-drenched portrait of the urban underground, **Welcome to Destination Shanghai** (*Mudidi Shanghai*), won prizes in Hong Kong and Rotterdam. But the strongest and most demanding of recent underground DV features is Zhang Lu's brilliant debut, **Tang Poetry** (*Tangshi*). Rigorously minimal in its means, it employs a rigidly fixed camera, two locations (inside and outside an apartment) and about 15 lines of dialogue to sketch the bleak relationship between two petty thieves, once lovers, who share nothing but despair.

Wang Xiang, left, and Cui Yuemei as petty thieves in **Tang Poetry**

Amidst a general rebound in film production after 2003's SARS-related slowdown, key developments include the Closer Economic Partnership Arrangement (CEPA) implemented between Hong Kong and the mainland in 2004. Subject to certain conditions, CEPA gives Hong Kong film-makers direct access to the mainland market through co-production arrangements. No longer will such films count towards the 20-film annual import quota.

As already indicated, there has also been more give and take at the Film Bureau: looser censorship regulations for features (the Bureau need approve only plot synopses, rather than full screenplays) are balanced by the loss of the DV loophole (public screenings of DV features and docs now also require Bureau approval). On the other hand, the Culture Ministry, which has authority over DVDs while the stricter State Administration of Radio, Film and Television handles the Film Bureau, has started to allow – or at least turn a blind eye towards – the legal release of underground films on DVD in shops around the country.

SHELLY KRAICER (shelly@chinesecinemas.org) is the Beijing-based editor of the *Chinese Cinema Digest* and China consultant for the Udine Far East Film Festival.

Quote of the Year

"The relationship between film-makers and censors in China means you are always 'dancing with chains around your legs', as Milan Kundera said in *The Unbearable Lightness of Being*."
ZHANG YUAN, *director.*

The 23rd Annual Golden Rooster Awards

Film: *Nuan* (Huo Jianqi); *Stormy Waves* (Qu Junjie).
Screenplay: Qiu Shi (*Nuan*).
Director: Zhang Yimou (*Hero*).
Actor: Xia Yu (*Policeman Has a Date*).
Actress: Yu Nan (*Jingzhe*).
Supporting Actor: Zhao Jun (*The Parking Attendant in July*).
Supporting Actress: Xu Jinglei (*Far from Home*).
Cinematography: Mu Deyuan (*Stormy Waves*).
Debut Film: *Me and Dad* (Xu Jinglei); *Nuan chun* (Wulan Tana).
Animation: *Remembering*.
Documentary: *The Piano Dream*.
Co-production Feature: *Hero*.
Special Mention Feature: *Deng Xiaoping* (Ding Yinnan).
Special Mention Actor: Li Min (*When Ruoma Was Seventeen*).

The 26th Annual Hundred Flowers Awards (2003)

Voted by the readers of *Popular Cinema* magazine
Film: *Charging out Amazon* (Song Yeming), *Hero, Deng Xiaoping* (Ding Yinnan).
Actor: Lu Qi (*Deng Xiaoping*).
Actress: Xu Jinglei (*Spring Subway*).
Supporting Actor: Wang Zhiwen (*Together*).
Supporting Actress: Yuan Quan (*Pretty Big Feet*).

Colombia Pedro Adrián Zuluaga

The Year's Best Films

Pedro Adrián Zuluaga's selection:

Small Voices
(Short. Eduardo Carrillo)
María Full of Grace
(Joshua Marston)
The Supreme Uneasiness...
(Docu. Luis Ospina)
From Palenque de San Basilio
(Docu. Erwin Goggel)
Ensalmo
(Short. Sara Harb Said)

Fernando Vallejo, subject of
The Supreme Uneasiness

Recent and Forthcoming Films

LA DESAZÓN SUPREMA. RETRATO INCESANTE DE FERNANDO VALLEJO (The Supreme Uneasiness. Incessant Portrait of Fernando Vallejo)
[Documentary, 2003] Script, Dir, Phot and Prod: Luis Ospina. Documentary about Fernando Vallejo, the polemical Colombian writer living in Mexico.

MARÍA LLENA ERES DE GRACIA (Maria Full of Grace)
[Drama, 2003] Script and Dir: Joshua Marston. Phot: Jim Denault. Players: Catalina Sandino, Jenny Paola Vega, Guilied López, John Alex Toro.

August 7, 2003, witnessed the commercial premiere of **The Supreme Uneasiness. Incessant Portrait of Fernando Vallejo** (*La desazón suprema. Retrato incesante de Fernando Vallejo*) in Medellín, the country's second city. Luis Ospina's documentary is about the controversial author of the novel *Our Lady of the Assassins* (*La virgen de los sicarios*), which was filmed by Barbet Schroeder in 2000. Although it went practically unnoticed, this event was a dual milestone: the first time that a DVD was accepted as an appropriate exhibition format in a commercial theatre, and the first time an auteur documentary had caught the Colombian public's attention.

Months later, in 2004, another documentary, **The Private Files of Pablo Escobar** (*Los archivos privados de Pablo Escobar*), about the head of the Medellín Cartel, was playing successfully around the country. Director Marc de Beaufort did everything he could to clean the image of the criminal. Both documentaries are determined to deal with uncomfortable issues, but do so from obliging standpoints. Escobar and Vallejo are portrayed as monolithic heroes, little gods capable of eclipsing their own directors (aesthetically, Ospina's is the much better film).

A third documentary, **From Palenque de San Basilio** (*Del Palenque de San Basilio*), directed by Erwin Goggel, received a very limited release but almost unanimous approval. It focuses on the rituals, music, customs and everyday life of the black inhabitants of Palenque de San Basilio, a village on Colombia's Caribbean coast. Very carefully shot and with a very precise anthropological view, Goggel's film is simultaneously cold and distant, limited by its own virtuosity. Beside this happy coincidence of three documentaries premiered in less than a year, national films continued to have a marginal presence in cinemas.

Christmas gifts disappoint

On December 25, 2003, a traditional date for Colombian premieres, two completely different films opened. **The Car** (*El Carro*), a comedy by Luis Ortega, with support from renowned scriptwriter and producer Dago García, is a disposable popcorn product, not far removed from TV comedies. Confusion abounds when a typically peaceful and humble family in Bogotá acquires a car. Popular culture is treated in stereotyped, laughable fashion – a popular style pioneered by the influential García and warmly welcomed by the large audiences for *The Car* and earlier titles such as *I Look for You* (*Te busco*) or *Maximum Penalty* (*La pena máxima*).

Confusion reigns when a Bogotá family acquires **The Car**

The other Christmas day premiere was Guillermo Rincón's **Bolivar, the Hero** (*Bolivar, el héroe*), erroneously promoted as Colombia's first animated feature (ignoring the work of pioneers such as Fernando Laverde and Carlos Santa). It was poorly received by the public and drew very negative comments about the poor quality of the drawing and the deficiencies of its argument, based on the image of Simon Bolivar as hero and liberator during the independence movement.

A Colombo-American production, **Maria Full of Grace** (*María llena eres de Gracia*), by the American film-maker Joshua Marston, won the Golden Bear for Best Actress (Catalina Sandino) at Berlin and became perhaps the biggest story in Colombian cinema in 2004 in terms of number of spectators and mass media attention. Tackling the controversial issue of Colombian women used by dealers as "mules" to carry drugs to the US in their bodies, the film has great emotional impact and is a shocking document, thanks largely to Marston, who restrains himself from making a movie with a sordid and miserable tone.

Christobal Corral Vega/Icon

Joshua Marston, right, directs Catalina Sandino Moreno in **Maria Full of Grace**

Prod: Paul Mezey, Jaime Osorio, Tucán Producciones.

DEL PALENQUE DE SAN BASILIO (From Palenque de San Basilio)
[*Documentary, 2004*] *Script, Dir and Prod: Erwin Goggel. Phot: Goggel, Jorge Echeverri, Carlos Gaviria.*

An inhabitant of **Palenque de San Basilio**

MALAMOR (Bad Love)
[*Drama, 2003*] *Script, Dir and Prod: Jorge Echeverri. Phot: Oscar Bernal, Echeverri. Players: Cristina Umaña, Fabio Rubiano.* Portrait of the last ten days in the life of a 17-year-old girl who risks everything to win the love of her mother's boyfriend, Hache.

EL CARRO (The Car)
[*Comedy, 2003*] *Script: Dago García. Dir: Luis Orjuela. Phot: Juan Carlos Vasquez. Players: Fenando Arévalo, César Badillo, Luly Bosa, Diego Cadavid. Prod: García, Carolina Barrera, Dago García Producciones.*

LOS ARCHIVOS PRIVADOS DE PABLO ESCOBAR (The Private Files of Pablo Escobar)
[*Documentary, 2004*] *Script and Dir: Marc de Beaufort. Phot: Luigi Baquero. Prod: Françoise Nieto, Yezid Production Company/Centauro Films.*

SUMAS Y RESTAS (Additions and Subtractions)
[*Drama, forthcoming*] *Script: Hugo Restrepo, Víctor Gaviria. Dir: Gaviria. Phot: Rodrigo Lalinde. Players: Juan Uribe, Fabio Restrepo. Prod: La Ducha Fría (Colombia)/A.T.P.I.P. (Spain).* Santiago, a well-off engineer, is seduced into a get-rich-quick world of random violence by his

childhood friend, El Duende (The Goblin), now a drug dealer.

BOLIVAR, EL HÉROE (Bolivar, the Hero)

[Animation, 2003] Script: Ricardo Pachón, Guillermo Rincón, María Teresa Gámez. Dir and Prod: Rincón. Voices: Manuel Cabral, Edgardo Román, Luis Fernando Orozco, Flor Vargas.

Local audiences did not warm to **Bolivar, the Hero**

APOCALIPSUR

[Drama, forthcoming] Script and Dir: Javier Mejía. Phot: Juan Carlos Orrego. Players: Andrés Echavarría, Marisela Gómez, Pedro Pablo Ochoa. Prod: Perro a Cuadros Producciones.
In 1992, Medellín is a dangerous place. "The Flaco" has to flee to London because his mother is threatened. After a few months he returns but things have not changed.

EL REY (The King)

[Drama, forthcoming] Script and Dir: Antonio Dorado. Phot: Paulo Andrés Pérez, Juan Cristóbal Cobo. Players: Fernando Solórzano, Cristina Umaña, Marlon Moreno, Vanesa Simon. Prod: Daniel Lesoeur, Alina Hleap, Fundación Imagen Latina/ Eurocine/Club de Técnicas de Producción.
The transformation of Cali, Colombia's third city, during the 1960s, is described through the reminiscences of "El Grillo", a popular hero.

ROSARIO TIJERAS

[Drama, forthcoming] Script: Marcelo Figueras, based on the novel by Jorge Franco. Dir: Emilio Maillé. Phot: Pascal Martí. Players: Flora Martínez, Manolo Cardona, Unax Ugalde,

Several forthcoming features deal with contemporary social conflict and its violent consequences from different viewpoints. Directed by Mexican Emilio Maille, *Rosario Tijeras* is based on the novel of the same name by Jorge Franco and looks at the social consequences of the drug business in Medellín, as does Sergio Cabrera's *Citizen Escobar* (*El Ciudadano Escobar*), another documentary looking at the mythic *capo*.

While Colombian production and exhibition remain full of uncertainty and difficulties, all sectors of the industry have high hopes for the new cinema law, the product of four years of negotiations and operating fully since early in 2004. It will distribute development and production funds collected through a tax on cinema tickets. However, the state will never be the sole producer of a film. The three announcements of funding for 2004 pledged support to features, shorts and documentaries, plus an additional percentage for audience development.

It is too soon to evaluate the impact of the law, but it will undoubtedly be positive. Future revision, however, must legislate for contributions from television and video companies, who were exempted from the new law to ensure its passage through Congress (private television in Colombia is controlled by two powerful monopolies which, exert a strong influence on political decisions).

Beside these legal and political issues, other areas of the audio-visual sector are improving. Universities are opening new cinema courses or consolidating their existing film programmes, while cinema clubs, specialist exhibitors and large and small themed festivals continue to offer a viable alternative to short-sighted commercial exhibition of imported blockbusters.

PEDRO ADRIÁN ZULUAGA (pzuluaga@colomboworld.com) is a journalist and editor of *Kinetoscopio* magazine, published by the Centro Colombo Americano in Medellín.

Rodrigo Oviedo. Prod: Matthías Ehrenberg, Gustavo Ángel, Clara María Ochoa, Mano Producciones/United Angels Production/Maestranza Films/Dulce Compañía.
Antonio and Emilio, friends and members of high-class society, meet and fall in love with Rosario, a beautiful and sexy young assassin who works for the *capos* of the Medellín Cartel.

Quote of the Year

"Movies show us how we are, but also how we would like to be in our dreams."
MARIA CONSUELO ARAUJO, *President of the National Council for Arts and Culture in Cinematography, announcing the first allocation of funds from the new cinema law.*

Croatia Tomislav Kurelec

The Year's Best Films

Tomislav Kurelec's selection:
Witnesses
(Vinko Bresan)
A Wonderful Night in Split
(Arsen Anton Ostojic)
Here
(Zrinko Ogresta)
Sorry for Kung Fu
(Ognjen Svilicic)
Under the Line
(Petar Krelja)

Coolio and Marija Skaricic in
A Wonderful Night in Split

Recent and Forthcoming Films

INFEKCIJA (Infection)
[Fantasy thriller, 2003] Script: Mate Matisic, Krsto Papic. Dir: Papic. Phot: Goran Trbuljak. Players: Leon Lucev, Lucija Serbedzija, Sven Medvesek, Filip Sovagovic, Ivo Gregurevic. Prod: Ben Stassen, Krsto Papic, Ozana film/nWave Pictures/HRT – Croatian Television.

ISPOD CRTE (Under the Line)
[Drama, 2003] Script: Petar Krelja, Drago Kekanovic. Dir: Krelja. Phot: Karmelo Kursar. Players: Rakan Rushaidat, Leona Paraminski, Filip Sovagovic, Jasna Bilusic, Dubravka Ostojic. Prod: Veljko Krulcic, Vedis/HRT – Croatian Television.

The national festival centred around the 7,500-seat Roman arena in Pula each July is the most important event for Croatian cinema, hosting the premieres of almost all the new features, and *IFG*'s new deadline means that this report covers two years' production, for 2003 (Pula's fiftieth anniversary) and 2004.

The 2003 crop, the best in the 12 years since independence, was dominated by Vinko Bresan's **Witnesses** (*Svjedoci*) and Zrinko Ogresta's *Here* (*Tu*). In Bresan's provocative film about the 1990s war of independence, three young Croatian soldiers return from the action in which the father of one of them was killed. They mine the house of a Serbian civilian in a small town near the front line, killing him, without knowing that his little daughter is the sole witness who can accuse them – if they let her live. Bresan (b. 1964) builds a very original spiral dramatic structure, repeating key moments in different contexts. The meaning changes every time, but is not dependent, as in *Rashomon*, on the storyteller's viewpoint but on how much the audience has learned. This is an impressive picture of the disaster of war, with complex, tormented protagonists.

Zrinko Ogresta (b. 1958) shows equally impressive skill in **Here**, made up of six short tales, the first about a short ceasefire during the war, in 1992, the other five set in the present and connected by the presence of one or more of the ex-soldiers from the first episode and an interest in marginalised people, including a pensioner and a junkie. Each story is a rather gloomy but very convincing slice of life, creating an original mosaic of Croatian life.

Peace-time conflicts

After a break of 13 years, one of the country's best documentary directors, Petar Krelja, returned to fiction with **Under the Line** (*Ispod crte*), about the conflicts between three generations of one family. The grandparents know how to keep their place in upper-class society. Their son, a traumatised ex-soldier who dislikes his parents' lifestyle, has married a working-class woman, and the rebellious, hopeless grandson's stupid mistakes lead him into crime. Krelja creates strong drama and his documentary work is evident in his presentation of social problems through everyday situations. Branko Ivanda (b. 1941) has waited even longer (22 years) to make his fifth movie, **Konjanik**, a historical action drama (an extremely

KONJANIK (The Horseman)
[Period drama, 2003] Script:
Branko Ivanda, Ivan Aralica.
Dir: Ivanda. Phot: Slobodan
Trninic. Players: Niksa Kuselj,
Zrinka Cvitesic, Goran Grgic,
Mladen Vulic, Borko Peric. Prod:
Stanislav Babic, Luka
Babic/Telefilm/HRT – Croatian
Television.

MERCY OF THE SEA
[Drama, 2003] Script: Paul
Gronseth. Dir: Jakov Sedlar,
Dominik Sedlar. Phot: Igor
Sunara. Players: Martin Sheen,
Renée Estevez, Mike Bernardo,
Bozidar Alic, Bozidar Smiljanic.
Prod: Jakov Sedlar, Ron
Assoulin, Orsat Zovko/Orlando
film/Filmmind (Tel Aviv).

ONAJ KOJI CE OSTATI
NEPRIMJECEN (*literally,* **The**
One Who Will Be Unnoticed)
[Drama, 2003] Script and Dir:
Zvonimir Juric. Phot: Vjeran
Hripka. Players: Daria Lorenci,
Natasa Dangubic, Bojan
Navojec. Prod: Boris T.
Matic,Propeler film/HRT –
Croatian Television.

SVJEDOCI (Witnesses)
[Drama, 2003] Script: Vinko
Bresan, Jurica Pavicic, Zivko
Zalar. Dir: Bresan. Phot: Zivko
Zalar. Players: Leon Lucev, lma
Prica, Mirjana Karanovic,
Drazen Kühn, Kresimir Mikic.
Prod: Ivan Maloca,Interfilm/
HRT – Croatian Television.

SVJETSKO CUDOVISTE
(The World's Greatest Wonder)
[Black comedy, 2003] Script:
Goran Rusinovic, Aris
Movsesijan, Tena Stivicic. Dir:
Rusinovic. Phot: Tomislav Pinter.
Players: Goran Susljik, Mirta
Haramina, Gorica Popovic, Ivica
Vidovic, Slobodan Milovanovic.
Prod: Mario Romulic,Mlijecni
put/Romulic/Jadran film/HRT –
Croatian Television/Gama studio.

TU (Here)
[Drama, 2003] Script: Zrinko
Ogresta, Josip Mlakic. Dir:
Ogresta. Phot: Davorin Gecl.
Players: Jasmin Telalovic, Marija

Three soldiers commit an atrocity in **Witnesses**

rare breed in Croatia's chronically underfunded film industry). The skills of director, cinematographer and production design team make it look far more expensive than its actual budget. It is set in the eighteenth century, in a part of Croatia that bordered the Venetian and Turkish empires. The resulting ethnic tensions resemble the hatreds that led to the 1990s Yugoslav war, and the film's *Romeo and Juliet*-like affair between a Catholic warrior and the Muslim daughter of the leader of the Turkish province sets off political and armed struggles.

Krsto Papic's **Infection** (*Infekcija*) is a very interesting, updated remake of his *The Redeemer/Izbavitelj* (1976). The fantastic story about men becoming giant rats and taking power was originally a metaphor for the birth of 1930s fascism but is now set in the present, to show how democratic state mechanisms can give rise to totalitarian dictatorship, helped by the power of television.

Youthful follies

Two younger directors disappointed with their arthouse movies. After a brilliant start with *Mondo Bobo* (1997), Goran Rusinovic (b. 1969) made **The World's Greatest Wonder** (*Svjetsko cudoviste*), whose only genuine merit is the wonderful cinematography (mostly in black-and-white) of the greatest Croatian director of photography, Tomislav Pinter (b.1926). The movie switches incoherently between two very different stories, set just before and during the Second World War, one following the "greatest wonder" (a young girl whose hands were eaten by swine in childhood) and the other a man who has made his fortune in the US and comes home to save his communist brother from police persecution. Zvonimir Juric (b. 1971) works from an improvised script for his very uneven first feature, **The One Who Will Be Unnoticed** (*Onaj koji ce ostati neprimjecen*), which unconvincingly tries to make audiences believe that asexual, angelic creatures live unnoticed among us, their sole intention being to do good.

The most prolific but in my view least talented Croatian film-maker of the last decade, Jakov Sedlar (b. 1952), has co-directed with his son, Dominik (b. 1972), probably his best movie, **Mercy of the Sea**, in English. Americans Martin Sheen and Renée Estevez appear in a typical Croatian post-war story about a mother seeking the son taken away by the Serbs after the fall of Vukovar. The directors blend reality and hallucinations with some success, but unfortunately believe more in big words and direct messages than the power of images.

Neither *Here* (winner of Pula's Great Golden Arena for Best Film) nor *Under the Line* (winner of the Public Award) could attract more than 10,000 viewers in cinemas, but the situation improved in 2004, when *Witnesses* was the first Croatian film in competition at Berlin, winning the unofficial Peace Film Prize, and *Here* won the Special Prize at Karlovy Vary (Croatia's first award at an A-grade festival). This success helped Bresan's film sell more than 10,000 tickets and boosted other local films. Ivanda's *Horseman* sold 15,000 tickets and 25,000 saw Igor Mirkovic's feature documentary **Lucky Kid** (*Sretno dijete*), a very original look at the vibrant rock'n'roll scene in Zagreb in the early 1980s.

A village epic

At a national level, 2004 belonged to Antun Vrdoljak (b. 1931) and his three-and-a-half-hour epic (drawn from a TV serial of 13 one-hour episodes), **Long Dark Night** (*Duga mracna noc*). It is set in a village in north-east Croatia, where for centuries many Germans had lived happily with their Croatian neighbours, from the beginning of the Second World War until the end of the first and most cruel phase of the Yugoslav communist regime in the 1950s.

Long Dark Night attracted 50,000 viewers at cinemas and at Pula, where it took all the major prizes, 7,500 seats were not enough to satisfy demand. However, many critics attacked the film, and media stories suggested that the Pula jurors had been chosen because they were likely to favour Vrdoljak, who had been Croatia's first post-independence vice-president, president of its Olympic Committee and the man who ran Croatian cinema in the 1990s. Some of the negative criticism may well have had more to do with the man than his movie. However, although undoubtedly a good storyteller, Vrdoljak sometimes appears to use the story primarily to illustrate his political opinions, which makes the characters and events less convincing than they should be.

Also it would be better to divide *Long Dark Night* into two movies. In the superior first part some of the German villagers become Nazis and the rest join the anti-fascist partisans, while one Jew and two Croats (one nationalist and the other anti-fascist) try to maintain

Tadic, Zlatko Crnkovic, Ivo Gregurevic, Ivan Herceg. Prod: Ivan Maloca,Interfilm/HRT – Croatian Television.

100 MINUTA SLAVE
(100 Minutes of Glory)
[Romantic drama, 2004] Script: Robert Perisic. Dir: Dalibor Matanic. Phot: Branko Linta. Players: Sanja Vejnovic, Predrag Miki Manojlovic, Vili Matula, Natasa Lusetic, Darko Rundek. Prod: Goran Mecava, Sanja Vejnovic,Fos Film/HRT – Croatian Television/Jadran film.

DOKTOR LUDOSTI
(The Doctor of Craziness)
[Comedy, 2003] Script and Dir: Fadil Hadzic. Phot: Slobodan Trninic. Players: Pero Kvrgic, Igor Mesin, Elizabeta Kukic, Damir Loncar, Zarko Potocnjak. Prod: Jozo Patljak,Alka film.

DRUZBA ISUSOVA
(The Society of Jesus)
[Period drama, 2004] Script: Silvije Petranovic, based on the novel by Jiri Sotola. Dir: Petranovic. Phot: Miso Orepic. Players: Leona Paraminski, Milan Plestina, Ivica Vidovic, Livio Badurina, Galliano Pahor. Prod: Silvije Petranovic, Maydi film.

DUGA MRACNA NOC
(Long Dark Night)
[Drama, 2004] Script and Dir: Antun Vrdoljak. Phot: Vjekoslav Vrdoljak. Players: Goran Visnjic, Katarina Bistrovic-Darvas, Mustafa Nadarevic, Ivo Gregurevic, Goran Navojec, Tarik Filipovic. Prod: Mirko Galic, Antun Vrdoljak, Goran Visnjic,Mediteran film/HRT – Croatian Television.

JERUZALEMSKI SINDROM
(Syndrome Jerusalem, 2004)
[Docu-drama, 2004] Script: Jakov Sedlar Dir: Jakov Sedlar, Dominik Sedlar. Phot: Mario Kokotovic. Players: Bozidar Alic, Boris Miholjevic, Elvis Lovic and (as themselves) Macaulay Culkin, Charlotte Rampling, Martin Sheen. Prod: Jakov Sedlar, Ron

Assouline, Stephen
Ollendorf, Orlando
film/Filmmind (Tel Aviv).

OPROSTI ZA KUNG FU
(Sorry for Kung Fu)
[Comedy, 2004] Script and Dir:
Ognjen Svilicic. Phot: Vedran
Samanovic. Players: Daria
Lorenci, Filip Rados, Vera Zima,
Vedran Mlikota, Luka Petrusic.
Prod: Vesna Mort, HRT –
Croatian Television.

SEX, PICE I KRVOPROLICE
(Sex, Booze and Short Fuse)
[Portmanteau film, 2004] Script
and Dir: Boris T. Matic,
Zvonimir Juric, Antonio Nuic.
Phot: Vjeran Hrpka. Players:
Admir Glamocak, Matko
Fabekovic, Kreso Mikic, Leon
Lucev, Bojan Navojec, Franjo
Dijak.

SLUCAJNA SUPUTNICA
(literally, **Accidental**
Fellow-Traveller)
[Road movie, 2004] Script:
Srecko Jurdana, Drazenka
Polovic. Dir: Jurdana. Phot:
Silvijo Jasenkovic. Players: Dora
Fister, Zlatko Ozbolt, Cintija
Asperger, Ante Prkacin, Nenad
Cvetko. Prod: Ivan
Maloca, Interfilm.

TA DIVNA SPLITSKA NOC
(A Wonderful Night in Split)
[Drama, 2004] Script and Dir:
Arsen Anton Ostojic. Phot:
Mirko Pivcevic. Players: Dino
Dvornik, Marinko Prga, Mladen
Vulic, Marija Skaricic, Coolio.
Prod: Jozo Patljak, Alka
film/HRT – Croatian Television.

LIBERTAS
[Period drama, 2005] Script:
Mirko Kovac, Ivo Bresan, Feda
Sehovic, Veljko Bulajic. Dir:
Bulajic. Players: Sven Medvesek,
Livio Badurina, Sandra
Ceccarelli, Goran Grgic, Radko
Polic. Prod: Aleksandar
Crcek, Produkcija Libertas/Tuna
film, HRT – Croatian
Televison/DDC Film.

their friendship. The second part concentrates on the tragic destiny of the partisan major (Goran Visnjic), who after the war quickly finds himself in conflict with the communist dictatorship.

Goran Visnjic, left, and Goran Navojec in **Long Dark Night**

The Critics' Prize deservedly went to **A Wonderful Night in Split** (*Ta divna splitska noc*), the debut of Arsen Anton Ostojic (b. 1965), winner of many international awards for his short films. Ostojic masterfully interweaves the tragic love stories of three couples during the last two hours of New Year's Eve: an ex-soldier turned small-time dealer and the widow of his best friend, who was killed in the war; a young addict and a suicidal American sailor (Coolio); adolescents trying to find a room for their first night together. The hopelessness of the young emerges in the shadow of a rock concert that tries to present Split (beautifully shot in black-and-white by Mirko Pivcevic) as a cheerful Mediterranean city.

Also very accomplished is Ognjen Svilicic's **Sorry for Kung Fu** (*Oprosti za kung fu*), about a young woman's return to her patriarchal, poor village after spending the war in western Europe. She is pregnant by an absent Chinese man and her shame-filled family tries to find her a local husband. But her time abroad has changed her and she is no longer willing to accept their traditional ways, provoking a series of funny and sometimes tragic situations that show how xenophobia deforms human relations.

Slava to love

Following his excellent *Nice Dead Girls* (2002), Dalibor Matanic (b. 1975) made **100 Minuta Slave** (*100 Minutes of Glory*), a 100-minute account of the affair between one of the greatest Croatian painters of the late 1800s, Slava (meaning 'glory') Raskaj, and her teacher. To this impressive love story the director unwisely adds superficial, redundant scenes connecting the story with the present.

Silvije Petranovic (b. 1959) made a belated feature debut with **The Society of Jesus** (*Druzba Isusova*), a very personal adaptation of the novel by Czech writer Jiri Sotola (1924-1989) about Jesuits who in the mid-1600s want to obtain the castle of a young widow, Countess Maria, and send one of their number, the devout Had, to be her confessor and win her over. Maria is attracted to him after years of loneliness, but he stays faithful to his vows. The period is beautifully recreated and while the audience is most interested by the frustrated love story, Petranovic's main goal appears to have been an exploration of Jesuit politics, which unbalances the film.

After a break of 19 years, the veteran Fadil Hadzic (b. 1922), returned with an unpretentious comedy, **The Doctor of Craziness** (*Doktor ludosti*), about patients in the wating room of an old psychiatrist, but failed to convince critics or attract the public. A former critic and influential political columnist, Sreko Jurdana (b. 1950), became one of the oldest feature debutants in Croatian cinema, following his 1980s short films with **Slucajna suputnica** (literally, *Accidental Fellow-Traveller*). A pretty, good-hearted young woman leaves her low-paid job and hits the road, living off accidental encounters with men. Most of the characters are so predictable that this movie reveals only commonplaces about Croatia.

TOMISLAV KURELEC (tomislav.kurelec@hrt.hr) has been a film critic since 1965, mostly on radio and television. He has directed five short films and many television items.

Quotes of the Year

"I haven't done this movie for a special kind of audience, nor for the festivals. I felt a necessity to talk about the moral problems of my own society."

VINKO BRESAN
discusses *Witnesses*.

"This is a tragicomedy. It's based on tragedy, but the people laugh at somebody else's misery, recognising their own wickedness."

OGNJEN SVILICIC
on his *Sorry for Kung Fu*.

RKO/Kobal

Beauty meets the beast: FAY WRAY *screams her way into movie history in* King Kong *(1933). She died on August 8, 2004, aged 96.*

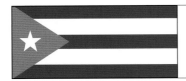

Cuba Luciano Castillo and Alberto Ramos

The Year's Best Films

Luciano Castillo and
Alberto Ramos' selection:
Three Times Two
(Pavel Giroud, Lester Hamlet,
Esteban G. Insausti)
Love by Mistake
(Gerardo Chijona)
Utopia
(Short. Arturo Infante)
Freddy or Noel's Dream
(Short. Waldo Ramírez)

Martha del Río in Lila
(*part of* **Three Times Two**)

Recent and Forthcoming films

AUNQUE ESTÉS LEJOS
(**So Far Away**)
[Comedy-drama, 2003] Script: Arturo Arango, Juan C. Tabío. Dir: Tabío. Phot: Hans Burmann. Players: Antonio Valero, Mirtha Ibarra, Bárbaro Marín. Prod: ICAIC/Tornasol Films (Spain)/DMVB (France).
Spanish actor Alberto, film producer Mercedes and her lover, screenwriter Pedro, are looking for a plot to make a movie. Pedro proposes a story about his colleagues' personal experiences, and they all agree.

In March 2004, the Cuban Institute of Film Art and Industry (ICAIC), created three months after the Revolution, austerely celebrated its forty-fifth birthday. In a nostalgic tribute to the pioneers of new Cuban cinema, Julio G. Espinosa, director of the International Film and Television School at San Antonio de los Baños (EICTV) and theorist of "imperfect cinema", became the second recipient of the National Prize of Cinema. ICAIC also co-produced **The Cuban Revolution**, a series of seven documentaries on its audiovisual memory, directed by three Cuban film-makers and containing previously unseen archive footage.

The anniversary came as this renowned institution appears to have recovered from the devastating 1990s crisis, when the withdrawal of Soviet finance from the Cuban economy pulled the film industry to the brink of collapse. New films are still in comparatively short supply, but some directors have been turning to traditionally neglected genres, as with Manuel Herrera's forthcoming **Dancing the Chachachá** (*Bailando el chachachá*), his second move into the musical after his groundbreaking hit, *Zafiros: locura azul* (1997), and the debut feature of Jorge Luis Sánchez, **Benny Moré**, a biopic of a popular singer (both scheduled for release in 2005).

Rigoberto López's **Scent of an Oak** (*Roble de olor*), whose melodramatic story of doomed love encompasses racism, xenophobia and political intolerance, did well, with 129,930 tickets sold. Juan Padrón's animated **More Vampires in Havana** (*Más vampiros en la Habana*), a sequel to his popular *Vampires in Havana* (1985), had 2003's highest tally (284,919), although in this second instalment the visuals are hampered by a slightly contrived, almost expressionist concept and a confusing plot.

The comedies that blossomed in the past decade, their elusive humour peppered with covert social criticism, remain the best barometer of the times. Juan C. Tabío draws inspiration from the film-making world in the insipid, rather affected **So Far Away** (*Aunque estés lejos*). As a scriptwriter, an actor and a film producer try to set up a Cuban Spanish co-production, characters and stories that mirror their own lives join a harmless cinematic *ménage* that overcame critical indifference to attract 185,862 moviegoers.

Mónica Alonso, Luis A. García and Susan Pérez in **Love by Mistake**

A higher achievement was **Love by Mistake** (*Perfecto amor equivocado*), Gerardo Chijona's bittersweet, ironic account of Cuban society's two-faced morality. A famous writer and unrepentant liar finds his middle-class world (wife, daughter, lover and job) close to collapse, setting off a frantic, amusing parade of unsentimental manipulation as he strives to preserve his status.

The best of youth

ICAIC's hegemony has finally been challenged by the emergence of new creative poles at EICTV and the Faculty of Communication at the Institute of Art, providing fresh talent that escapes the ideological constraints of the state-ruled giant. In general, these young directors have some academic training and experience in advertising, music videos and documentary. Theirs is a fresh, open and uncompromising generation that disregards loyalties – political strictures included – and looks around with irony.

A typical case is *Utopia*, a short in which Arturo Infante (an EICTV writing graduate) pokes fun at an increasingly marginalised society. With a nod to the Czech New Wave's anarchic approach, he shows the violent effects of cultural indoctrination on four hot-tempered domino players, a retarded student struggling with Borges and two vulgar young ladies engaged in an absurd, hilarious squabble about Italian opera composers.

The spontaneous if transient friendship between a little country girl and a boy who suddenly leaves with his parents for the US is the subject of *Na-Na*, a fine short by Patricia Ramos (another EICTV writing graduate) that taps into the national obsession with exile. Coincidentally, Juan C. Cremata (*Nothing More*, reviewed in *IFG 2004*) takes the side of the kids in his second feature, **Viva Cuba**, a children's adventure driven by the little ones' reluctance to embrace the legacy of ideological antagonism that marks their parents' lives.

MÁS VÁMPIROS EN LA HABANA
(**More Vampires in Havana**)
[Animation, 2003] Script: Juan Padrón. Dir: Padrón. Prod: ICAIC/Estudios ISKRA S.L.
In 1923, the scientist Von Dracula invented "Vampisol", a formula allowing vampires to be safely exposed to sunshine. After discovering "Vampisol", his Cuban nephew Pepe must face a Nazi vampire.

TRES VECES DOS
(**Three Times Two**)
[Portmanteau drama, 2003] Episode One: Flash *[Romantic thriller] Script: Pavel Giroud. Dir: Giroud. Phot: Luis Najmías Jr. Players: Georbis Martínez, Verónica López, Susana Tejera. Prod [all episodes]: ICAIC. Episode Two:* Lila *[Musical] Script: Alejandro Brugués, Lester Hamlet. Dir: Hamlet. Phot: Luis Najmías Jr. Players: Olivia Manrufo, Martha del Río, Caleb Casas.*
Lila is an old woman haunted by memories as she learns that an old flame is back in town. *Episode Three:* Red Light *[Drama] Script: Xenia Rivery, Esteban Insausti. Dir: Insausti. Phot: Alejandro Pérez. Players: Zulema Clares, Alexis Díaz de Villegas.*
A psychiatrist and a blind radio announcer have a brief encounter.

FREDDY O EL SUEÑO DE NOEL
(*literally,* **Freddy or Noel's Dream**)
[Short drama, 2003] Script: Waldo Ramírez. Dir: Ramírez. Phot: Luis A. Guevara. Players: Noel Nieto. Prod: Televisión Serrana.

UTOPÍA (Utopia)
[Short comedy, 2004] Script and Dir: Arturo Infante. Phot: Diego Marín. Players: Jorge Molina, Beatriz González, Alicia Alén. Prod: Guagua & Co.

PERFECTO AMOR EQUIVOCADO
(**Love by Mistake**)

[Comedy-drama, 2004] Script: Gerardo Chijona, Eduardo del Llano. Dir: Chijona. Phot: Raúl Pérez. Players: Luis A. García, Susana Pérez, Beatriz Valdés. Prod: ICAIC/Wanda Vision (Spain)/Fénix PC (Spain).

BAILANDO EL CHACHACHÁ
(*literally,* **Dancing the Chachachá**)
[Musical drama, 2004] Script: Manuel Herrera, Alejandro Brugués. Dir: Herrera. Phot: Raúl Rodríguez. Players: Eslinda Núñez, Sandy Marquetti, Goya Toledo. Prod: ICAIC/Castelao Productions S.A.+ (Spain).
Against a tense political backdrop, three youngsters try to make a living in 1952 Havana, while their mother lives her own fantasies in a society swept by a new musical rhythm.

Teherán Aguilar in **Dancing the Chachachá**

FRUTAS EN EL CAFÉ
(*literally,* **Fruits in the Coffee**)
[Tragi-comedy, 2004] Script: Alejandro Brugués, Humberto Padrón. Dir: Padrón. Phot: Oscar Valdés. Players: Jorge Perugorría, Gilda Bello, Yailene Sierra. Prod: Producciones Habana Adentro.
A whore, a communist and an artist face the possibility of sexual debasement.

GENTE DE PUEBLO
(*literally,* **Common People**)
[Drama, 2004] Script: Humberto Solás, Elia Solás, Sergio Benvenuto. Dir: H. Solás. Phot: Rafael Solís. Players: Jorge Perugorría, Isabel Santos, Adela Legrá. Prod: ICAIC.3

A child's innocence is the ultimate affirmation of life in *Freddy or Noel's Dream* (*Freddy o el sueño de Noel*) by Waldo Ramírez. In a region ravaged by drought, a kid's fantasy of joyous, plentiful life is conveyed by his vision of water bursting the banks of an empty dam and impoverished neighbours arriving for a baptismal fishing trip under the falling waters.

Definitive proof that Cuban cinema renaissance is inextricably attached to the fate of young newcomers came with *Three Times Two*, a milestone in Cuban cinema which gave three debutants the chance to create two stories each, shot on digital video. Pavel Giroud's virtuoso *Flash* deals with the doomed fascination of a young photographer for the unknown woman who haunts the spectral images he takes of Havana. Giroud has crafted a fantastic thriller where the romantic necrophilia of Hitchcock's *Vertigo* meets the esoteric, manipulative look of M. Night Shyamalan. In *Lila*, Lester Hamlet uses the nostalgic musical genre to address guerrilla insurrection without heroic overtones. The glamorised love story between a partisan and a maiden turns into an abridged version of Demy's *The Umbrellas of Cherbourg*. As for *Red Light*, the hectic and stagy editing of director Esteban G. Insausti brings a typically contemporary pessimism to a tale of loneliness and urban neurosis.

Days of being digital

Prompted by the need for fresh money to revitalise native cinema, the industry has encouraged co-productions and servicing foreign films, a practice that dates back to the 1980s, and partnerships with Peru, Bolivia, Venezuela and Spain have led to the completion of eight pictures with the involvement of ICAIC in 2004, including Spanish director Benito Zambrano's **Habana Blues**, a vibrant and colourful homage to the city rendered through the lives of two young musicians.

In response to the chronic shortage of production finance, the greatest living Cuban director, Humberto Solás (*Lucía*, 1968), has shifted from expensive period pieces to low-profile, contemporary features made according to "poor cinema" rules: digital technology, minimal staff and an unpaid cast and crew. After *Honey for Ochún* (2001), the first Cuban film shot according to Solás' guerrilla manifesto, comes *Common People* (*Gente de pueblo*), an ambitious portrait of life in Havana.

LUCIANO CASTILLO (lcastillo@eictv.org.cu) is a film critic and scholar, director of the mediatheque at the EICTV film school in Havana and editor-in-chief of *Cine Cubano* magazine. **ALBERTO RAMOS** (arzhabana@cocc.co.cu) is a film critic and editor of *ECOS* magazine

Cyprus Theo Panayides

Recent and Forthcoming Films

TO TAMA (Word of Honour)
[Comedy-drama, 2001] Script: Andreas Pantzis, Aleksandr Adabachian. Dir: Pantzis. Phot: Nikolay Lazarov. Players: Georges Corraface, Valeria Golino, Elias Aletras, Yannis Voglis. Prod: Andreas Pantzis,Greek Film Centre/PA Stephania Film Productions Ltd./Cyprus Cinema Advisory Committee/Kourion Films/ERT S.A./Bulgarian National Film Centre/Cinemax (Bulgaria)/Sigma TV/Lumière Prods. Ltd.

KATO APO T'ASTRA (Under the Stars)
[Drama, 2001] Script and Dir: Christos Georgiou. Phot: Roman Osin. Players: Myrto Alikaki, Akis Sakellariou, Stella Fyrogeni, Andros Kritikos. Prod: Pantelis Mitropoulos,Yorgos Lykiardopoulos - Attica S.A. (Greece)/Sam Taylor, Christos Georgiou, Lychnari (Cyprus)/Film and Music Entertainment (UK)/Prooptiki S.A. (Greece)/Lumière Prods. Ltd./Greek Film Centre.

Akis Sakellariou and Myrto Alikaki in **Under the Stars**

The de facto division of Cyprus since the Turkish invasion of 1974 looms large over the country's fledgling film industry. In the north is a Turkish-occupied, Turkish-speaking pseudo-state, not recognised by the international community. In the south is the Greek-speaking Republic of Cyprus, where film production was for a long time sketchy and disorganised. However, things have changed significantly over the past decade.

One factor has surely been the emergence of privately owned TV channels (there was only a single state channel until the early 1990s), which has boosted local production of shows and commercials and allowed a new generation of craftsmen to make their living from film. Another factor was undoubtedly the establishment in 1994 of the Cinema Advisory Committee, which is the main source of local film funding, allocating 500,000 Cyprus pounds (approximately $1m) a year to production, distribution and festival support.

Saint and sinner

As in most countries, audiences are in thrall to the multiplex (another relatively new development). The ten top-grossing films in 2003 were wholly or partly American and the market share for local films is insignificant. Nonetheless, there is some hope. The Greek film *Politiki Kouzina* was a major hit (with around 50,000 admissions) at the beginning of 2004, while three Cypriot films have had commercial releases in the past two years. **Word of Honour** (*To Tama*) by veteran Andreas Pantzis, is set in 1940s Cyprus, where a peasant treks across the island to fulfil a vow he made to a local saint. The pilgrimage requires him to be "pure", but he falls into temptation and sin at every step. The film is handsome and smoothly crafted, but let down by some rather heavy ironies and the shaky Cypriot accent of Franco-Greek lead actor Georges Corraface.

Christos Georgiou's **Under the Stars** (*Kato apo t'astra*) played for a month in the capital Nicosia after winning awards on the festival circuit. The story of a refugee who meets a young woman who smuggles goods to and from the occupied north and pays her to take him to the village he fled as a child 25 years earlier tackles the "Cyprus problem" (the island's divided status), but in a way that is

BAR
[Drama, 2003] Script and Dir:
Aliki Danezi-Knutsen. Phot:
Cornelius Schultze-Kraft. Players:
Stella Fyrogeni, Michael McKell,
Achilleas Grammatikopoulos,
Yannis Stankoglou. Prod: Anna
Tsiarta,Roads & Oranges Film
Productions Ltd./Cyprus Cinema
Advisory Committee/ERT
S.A. /Nicholas St Moller/XL
Films (Uruguay).

KALABUSH
[Comedy, 2003] Script: Adonis
Florides. Dir: Florides,
Theodoros Nikolaides. Phot:
Constantinos Othonos. Players:
Marios Ioannou, Semeli
Economou, Spyros Stavrinides,
Sofoklis Kaskaounias. Prod:
Adonis Florides,Nikos Kanakis,
Cyprus Cinema Advisory
Committee/ERT/Camera Stylo
Ltd./Sigma TV(Cyprus)/Hyperion
(Greece)/Greek Film Centre.

KOKKINI PEMPTI
(Red Thursday)
[Drama, 2003] Script and Dir:
Christos Siopachas. Phot:
Rostislav Pyroumov. Players:
Paschalis Tsarouchas, Clare Day,
Dimitra Zeza, Sergei Vinogradov,
Patrick Myles. Prod: Christos
Siopachas,Cyprus Cinema
Advisory Committee/Greek Film
Centre/ERT/Arctinos Ltd.
(Cyprus)/Studio Classica (Russia).
A small-time smuggler falls in
with a shady but charismatic
Russian, and shelters his new
friend from gangsters after a
killing. Complicating matters is
his wife, who falls in love with
his younger brother.

Paschalis Tsarouchas and Clare Day in
Red Thursday

VAREA ANTHYGIINA
(Hazardous and Unhealthy)
[Comedy-drama, 2003] Script:
Antonis Papadopoulos, G.

allusive and never didactic, with a sensual feel for the local
landscape and the sea at night. Most interesting, perhaps, is
its sympathetic portrayal of the north, making the righteous
nationalism of its Turk-hating hero seem outdated and a little
ridiculous. Whether this is conscious political baiting or
unconscious subtext is a moot point; still, there's no avoiding the
contrast between the protagonist's dour, obsessive mien and the
playful, humane situations around him.

The clash of cultures

Political change is bound to have an impact on Cypriot film. In April
2003 the border between north and south was opened – albeit
only at a few checkpoints – for the first time since the invasion,
and in May 2004 Cyprus joined the EU. The island is becoming
less insular and film-makers who were children in 1974 are less
likely to make films about the "Cyprus problem". Many are based
in Greece, like Yiannis Economides who received acclaim for his
debut, *Matchbox*. Those who stay strive to reflect a new, multi-
cultural Cyprus.

Marios Ioannou as a Syrian immigrant in **Kalabush**

The hero in **Kalabush**, a bright and skilful comedy directed by
Adonis Florides and Theodoros Nikolaides, is a Syrian immigrant
who winds up in Limassol thinking that it's Naples. He is an
innocent forced into a hand-to-mouth existence and caught up in
increasingly outlandish adventures, with a dash of magical realism
and a view of the island unlikely to be endorsed by the Cyprus
Tourist Board. Russian girls pole-dance in cabarets while foreign
workers try to dodge the cops, working in pig farms or picking
oranges. The film tries to do too much, leaving some strands
unresolved, but is sharp and timely; above all, with its emphasis
on comedy and local TV stars in key roles, it could well be the
box-office shot in the arm that Cypriot movies need.

Red Thursday (*Kokkini pempti*) also mixes cultures, set partly in
the no-man's-land between north and south where smugglers from
both sides meet to do business. An English wife and a shady

Russian adventurer also feature in this good-looking drama from director Christos Siopachas; alas, the script is rambling and increasingly hysterical, a heavy-breathing melodrama set in the cliché of an archetypal rural Cyprus. Nonetheless, like *Kalabush*, it reflects the industry's newfound commitment to making local films attractive for the mass audience.

The cryptic, moody **Bar** is directed by Aliki Danezi-Knutsen, whose debut *Roads and Oranges* was a fresh-faced drama about a Cypriot girl setting out to find her missing-in-action father (Danezi-Knutsen's own father is among those missing since the invasion). *Bar* also revolves around absence, but is a more ambitious though also more pretentious film, playing Borgesian games with reality and imagination in two stories linked by the figure of a young Cypriot woman who sees the image of her long-lost brother in a photo on the wall of a bar in Montevideo, Uruguay. The film is in English, Greek and Spanish, set in Cyprus and Uruguay and offers another Cypriot perspective on a culture of borders.

Yiannis Stankoglou and Stella Fyrogeni in **Bar**

Finally, mention should be made of Paschalis Papapetrou, whose documentaries seek to chronicle vanishing traditions in a rapidly changing society. His latest, **The Last Kerchief-Maker of Cyprus**, is subtitled "Before Memories Fade". Despite its title, it studies an entire cottage industry, now in terminal decline along with the old village society that spawned it. "Everything in life has a beginning and an end," offers one of its subjects at the very end. "It's sad, but life goes on."

The most heartening industry news is the number of projects under development at the Cinema Advisory Committee, which has tripled from the corresponding number in the mid- or late 1990s. With veterans like Yiannis Ioannou and Michael Papas as well as younger film-makers preparing their second or third features, the result should be a decent crop of Cypriot films.

THEO PANAYIDES (0529p@spidernet.com.cy) reviews films for the *Cyprus Mail* and his personal website: http://leonardo.spidernet.net/Artus/2386.

Papadoyannis, D. Spyrou, A. Kakavas. Dir: Papadopoulos. Phot: Polydefkis Kyrlidis. Players: Paschalis Tsarouchas, Nena Mendi, Antonis Antoniou. Prod: C. Lambropoulos, Greek Film Centre/ERT/CL Productions/Cyprus Cinema Advisory Committee.
A former Second World War soldier returns to the town in Greece where he saved 70 people from the Nazis 30 years ago.

O TELEFTAIOS MANTILARIS TIS KYPROU
(**The Last Kerchief-Maker of Cyprus**)
[Documentary, 2004] Script and Dir: Paschalis Papapetrou. Phot: Nicos Avraamides. Prod: Anadysis Films/Cultural Services of the Ministry of Education and Culture (Cyprus).

AKAMAS
[Drama, 2005] Script and Dir: Panicos Chrysanthou. Phot: Andres Gero. Players: Chris Greco, Agni Tsangaridou. Prod: Artimages (Cyprus)/Marathon (Turkey)/Creator 4 (Hungary)/Cyprus Cinema Advisory Committee.

HI! AM ERICA!
[Comedy-drama, 2005] Script and Dir: Yiannis Ioannou. Phot: Andreas Bellis. Players: Alexis Ioannou, Manfred Andrae, Angel Torres. Prod: Cyprus Cinema Advisory Committee/O Circo A Vapor Film Productions/Akreon Films/Moviemakers International Ltd.

Quote of the Year

"If you ask permission to film in a house in London, the owner will be on the phone to his accountant in five minutes. In Athens, they might slam the door in your face. Here, at least it's possible they'll say: 'Making a film! You crazy guy – come inside...'"
CHRISTOS GEORGIOU,
director, on the advantages of shooting in Cyprus.

Czech Republic Eva Zaoralová

The Year's Best Films

Eva Zaoralová's selection:
Bored in Brno
(Vladimír Morávek)
Champions
(Marek Najbrt)
Up and Down
(Jan Hrebejk)
Zelary (Ondrej Trojan)
Feelings
(Tomás Hejtmánek)

Recent and Forthcoming Films

BOLERO
*[Crime drama, 2004] Script:
Markéta Zinnerová. Dir and
Phot: Frantisek A. Brabec.
Players: Borislav Polívka, Martin
Stropnicky, Juan Potmesil, Barbora
Seidlová, Jan Kacer, Jirí Bartoska,
David Kraus. Prod: Diamant
Film Praha/Czech Television.*

Borislav Polívka in **Bolero**

CESKY SEN (Czech Dream)
*[Documentary, 2004] Script and
Dir: Vít Klusák, Filip Remunda.
Phot: Klusák. Prod: Hypermarket
Film/Czech TV/Studio
Mirage/FAMU.*

CHOKING HASARD
*[Horror comedy, 2004] Script:
Stepán Kopriva. Dir: Marek
Dobes. Phot: Martin Preiss.*

The Czech Republic joined the EU on May 1, 2004 and, having been a member of Eurimages since 1993 and having enjoyed access to grants from the MEDIA programme since 2002, its film industry can thus now make full use of support from European funds. In their local environment, however, Czech film-makers have more and more reasons to complain about dwindling support from the state. Because of financial problems, Czech Television, which until 2003 was an important co-producer of the majority of Czech films, has discontinued its support.

Czech producers, distributors and exhibitors have joined directors in calling for an amendment to the law on the State Fund for Cinematography. They propose that all companies profiting from the distribution and promotion of films (video, DVD and TV operations, not only cinemas, as has hitherto been the case) should share in the financing of Czech films, using the resources channelled into the state fund. The financial squeeze is reflected in the fall in production, with only 14 films made in 2003 (down from a peak of 23 in 1995), and the average cost per film was around €660,000 (20m marks). Conversely, the number of documentaries has risen, mainly thanks to televised series.

More positively, 2003 saw cinema attendance rise by 13% and the popularity of home-grown films also increased, led by Jan Hrebejk's comedy *Pupendo*. The Oscar-nominated village war drama *Zelary*, by Ondrej Trojan, was the fourth most popular local film.

Anna Geislerova and György Cserhalmi in the Oscar-nominated **Zelary**

Chairman of the *Bored*

The greatest number of Czech Lions, the Film Critics' award and the main prize at the national screenings in Plzen all went to the original debut by distinguished stage director Vladimír Morávek, **Bored in Brno** (*Nuda v Brno*). The somewhat intellectual humour in this gentle black comedy about the troubled love affairs of several inhabitants of the Moravian capital during one summer night did not capture the hearts of a mass audience, but it still ranked eighteenth in the year's chart – a good result against so much competition from Hollywood.

Marek Daniel and Ivana Uhlirova in **Bored in Brno**

Comedy continues to be the most popular local genre. The third film by David Ondrícek, the black comedy **One Hand Can't Clap** (*Jedna ruka netleská*), which plays with the detective genre and is full of absurd situations and dialogue, was extremely well received in 2003. Former director of the Barrandov Film Studios, producer Václav Marhoul, introduced himself to cinemagoers with the appealing, small-scale **Smart Philip** (*Mazany Filip*), an affectionate parody of Chandler's detective stories. Among the more debased examples of the genre was the vulgar **Good One** (*Kamenák*) by the experienced Zdenek Troska, which plays to the lowest common denominator with some stereotypical Czech characters.

Several new directors whose films opened in the first half of 2004 also put their money on the comic genre. Unquestionably the most remarkable of these was the bittersweet comedy by Marek Najbrt, about typical Czech vices, whose title, **Champions** (*Mistri*), is an ironic reference to passionate hockey fans found crowded round the pub television. Marek Dobes' zombie parody, **Choking Hazard**, is admirable more for the enterprising spirit of its makers than for its actual merits, and the same applies to Martin Kotík's family comedy **Men's Show** (*Pánská jízda*).

Players: Jan Dolansky, Jaroslav Dusek, Eva Nadazdyová, Kamil Svejda, Anna Fialková. Prod: Marek Dobes, Brutto/A.C.E. a.s./Cinemasound s.r.o.

HOREM PÁDEM
(Up and Down)
[Satirical comedy, 2004] Script: Petr Jarchovsky. Dir: Jan Hrebejk. Phot: Jan Malír. Players: Petr Forman, Emilia Vasáryová, Jirí Machácek, Jan Tríska, Natasa Burger, Ingrid Timková, Pavel Liska, Jaroslav Dusek, Jan Budar. Prod: Total HelpArt T.H.A./Czech Televison/Barrandov Studio/Falcon.

JEDNA RUKA NETLESKÁ
(One Hand Can't Clap)
[Black comedy, 2003] Script: David Ondrícek, Jiri Machácek. Dir: Ondrícek. Phot: Richard Rericha. Players: Machácek, Ivan Trojan, Marek Taclík, Klára Pollertová, Isabela Bencová. Prod: Lucky Man Films/Czech Television/CinemArt/Barrandov Studio.

Jiri Machacek in **One Hand Can't Clap**

KRÁL ZLODEJU
(King of Thieves)
[Psychological drama, 2003] Script and Dir: Ivan Fíla. Phot: Vladimír Smutny. Players: Lazar Ristovski, Yasha Kultiasov, Katharina Thalbach, Julia Khanverdievová, Oktay Ozdemir. Prod: Lichtblick Filmproduction/Charlie's/Slavia Capital/In Film/ Ivan Fíla Filmproduction/Mact Productions/Helga Baehr, Wega Film.

MAZANY FILIP (Smart Philip)
[Crime comedy, 2003] Script and

Dir: *Václav Marhoul. Phot: Vladimír Smutny. Players: Tomás Hanák, Vilma Cibulková, Frantisek Skála, Pavel Liska, Bohumil Klepl, Viktor Preiss. Prod: Silver Screen s.r.o.*

MISTRI (Champions)
[Black comedy, 2004] Script: Robert Geisler, Benjamin Tucek, Marek Najbrt. Dir: Najbrt. Phot: Miloslav Holman. Players: Jan Budar, Klára Melísková, Jirí Ornest, Leos Noha, Tomás Matonoha. Prod: Negativ s.r.o./Czech Television/Barrandov Studio.

NUDA V BRNO (Bored in Brno)
[Black comedy, 2003] Script: Jan Budar, Vladimír Morávek. Dir: Morávek. Phot: Divis Marek. Players: Budar, Katerina Holánová, Miroslav Donutil, Martin Pechlát, Jaroslava Pokorná. Prod: Cestmír Kopecky, První verejnoprávní/Czech Television.

PÁNSKÁ JÍZDA (Men's Show)
[Comedy, 2004] Script: Petr Nepovím, Tomás Koncinsky, Martin Kotík. Dir: Kotík. Phot: Miroslav Ctvorsjak. Players: Martin Dejdar, Vladimír Skultéty, Ondrej Vetchy, Josef Abrhám. Prod: Major K. International/Ateliéry Bonton Zlín.

POST COITUM
[Erotic black comedy, 2004] Script: M. Bystron, Juraj Jakubisko. Dir: Jakubisko. Phot: Ján Duris. Players: Eva Elsnerová, Richard Krajco, Jirí Langmajer, Beata Greneche, Franco Nero. Prod: Jakubisko film s.r.o.

SENTIMENT (Feelings)
[Docu-fiction, based on films by Frantisek Vlácil, 2003] Script: Tomás Hejtmánek, Jirí Soukup. Dir: Hejtmánek. Phot: Jaromír Kacer, Divis Marek. Players: Jirí Kodet. Prod: Filio/Bionaut/Czech Television.

Jan Budar in **Champions**

Another debut director was Prague-based Icelander Börkur Gunnarsson, whose minimalist acidic comedy **Bitter Coffee** (*Silny kafe*; see also Iceland section), about several young couples struggling to communicate, attracted attention for the fine performances by an international cast of unknowns. The successful cycle of comedies about the thwarted love affairs of a young doctor continued with the fourth in the series, **Poets Never Lose Hope** (*Jak básníci neztrácejí nadeji*), directed by Dusan Klein.

Crime, perversion and a real *Dream*

F. A. Brabec's **Bolero** was inspired by the still unsolved murder of a female Slovak student during the 1970s. It unsuccessfully combines detective elements, set in contemporary nouveau-riche society, with ostentatious symbolic dance numbers. Despite being directed by the experienced Juraj Jakubisko, **Post coitum** did not fare much better with audiences or critics. This "chilling comedy" about the debauched morals of modern neo-capitalist society is set in an environment of sexual perversion and starred Italian actor Franco Nero. Considerably more intimate and effective was Michaela Pavlátová's feature debut about a marital crisis, **Faithless Games** (*Neverné hry*; see also Slovakia section), awarded a Special Mention at San Sebastian in 2003. Ivan Fíla's international co-production **King of Thieves** (*Král zlodeju*) tells the story of children who are victims of an international crime ring.

Of the documentaries aimed at cinema audiences, *No Regrets* (*Niceho nelituji*), by young director Theodora Remundová, and *Czech Dream* (*Cesky sen*), by two recent graduates from FAMU, Filip Remunda and Vít Klusák, were particularly noteworthy. The first part of **No Regrets** examines the relationships between mother, daughters and granddaughters who reveal everything that infuriates them about one another. The other part, about the relationship between an original woman and her two sons, has a more positive emotional charge. **Czech Dream** is based on an unusual, cynical idea: the implementation of an advertising campaign for a new but in reality non-existent hypermarket.

At press time there were high hopes for the satirical comedy *Up and Down* (*Horem pádem*), reteaming Jan Hrebejk with screenwriter Petr Jarchovsky, and by David Jarab's debut, *Vaterland – A Hunting Diary* (*Vaterland – lovecky deník*), with its elements of surrealist mystification. Milan Cieslar's *Soul like Caviar* (*Duse jako kaviár*) steps on the thin ice of sexual deviation and, for teenaged winter sports lovers, comes the debut by Karel Janák, *Snowboarders* (*Snowboard'áci*).

The majority of the directors discussed so far are in their thirties or forties. Nevertheless, representatives of the older generations continue to fight for their projects, sometimes with much originality, like Jan Nemec who, while waiting to find co-producers for a film about the famous Czech surrealist painter Toyen, filmed and produced another essay, **Landscape of My Heart** (*Krajina mého srdce*), an exploration of the conscious and unconscious thoughts of a man as he undergoes lengthy heart surgery. Co-producers are also being sought by one of the most eminent figures on the Czech scene, celebrated surrealist Jan Svankmajer, for his planned horror story based on the tales of Edgar Allan Poe, *Madness* (*Sílení*).

EVA ZAORALOVÁ (e.zaoralova@volny.cz) is Artistic Director of the Karlovy Vary International Film Festival, editor of the magazine *Film a doba* and the author of several books on Czech, French and Italian cinema.

SPRÁVCE STATKU
(**Manager of the Farm**)
[Family film, 2004] Script, Dir and Phot: Martin Duba. Players: Adam Stivín, Jarmila Dubová, Anna Veselá, Luicie Vendlová, Petr Duba, Jirí Duba, Martin Duba. Prod: Vestfilm o.s.
A simple family story written, shot and edited by Duba on his family farm, with characters played by himself, his wife, children and friends.

Denmark Jacob Neiiendam

The Year's Best Films

Jacob Neiiendam's selection:

Brothers (Susanne Bier)

With Blood on My Hands – Pusher II (Nicolas Winding Refn)

Aftermath (Paprika Steen)

Kings' Game (Nikolaj Arcel)

Terkel in Trouble (Stefan Fjeldmark et al)

Mikael Birkkjær and Sophie Gråbøl as bereaved parents in **Aftermath**

Recent and Forthcoming Films

TERKEL I KNIBE
(Terkel in Trouble)
[Animated comedy, 2004] Script: Mette Heeno, based on an idea by Anders Matthesen. Dir: Stefan Fjeldmark, Kresten Vestbjerg Andersen, Thorbjørn Christoffersen. Voices: Matthesen. Prod: Thomas Heinesen, Trine Heidegaard, Nordisk Film/A. Film.

STRINGS
[Puppet fantasy-adventure, 2004] Script: Naja Maria Aidt, Anders Rønnow Klarlund. Dir: Rønnow Klarlund. Phot: Kim Hattesen, Jan Weincke. Voices: James McAvoy, Catherine McCormack,

enmark's film industry continues to be the envy of its Nordic neighbours because of its high local market share, the level of government support and its international successes. However, talk to Danish producers and it's clear that not everything is plain sailing. The Danish Film Institute, the major backer of all feature films, lost $3.2m in state funding in 2003 and protracted negotiations between national broadcasters and film producers caused several movies to be delayed or scrapped.

However, though no films were really huge at the box-office in 2003, production increased from 19 to 24 features, and market share was 26%, just 1% down from 2002. At press time, 2004 looked likely to have produced just 22 home-made releases, but after a slow first half the autumn saw market shares of up to 60% several weeks in a row.

No more English, please, we're Danish

While 2003 saw Danish directors try their hands at English-language projects, with little or no luck (Lars von Trier's *Dogville* was, as usual, the notable exception), 2004 proved that local audiences still choose home-made films over most Hollywood product. This has been evident for years, but in 2004 it became obvious that Danes were ready for a change, having grown tired of the contemporary family dramas, with a touch of tragedy but plenty of heart and humour, which dominated the Danish Dogme movement and Dogme-like follow-ups.

Fortunately, film-makers felt the same way, and began exploring a wider variety of genres. However, the new wave of youth-oriented films – Aage Rais-Nordentoft's **Kick'n Rush** (*2 ryk og en aflevering*), Anders Gustafsson's **Scratch** (*Bagland*) and Linda Krogsøe Holmberg's **Count to 100** (*Tæl til 100*) – failed to stir audiences when they came out in late 2003 and early 2004, even though critics praised the return of a genre which used to be a trademark of Danish cinema.

Feel-bad movies

Instead, a change of direction that seemed like probable commercial suicide turned out to be moderately successful.

Erik Aavatsmark

Per Arnesen

Prisoners are at the heart of **In Your Hands**

Introduced by the clever provocateurs at Zentropa at the release of Annette K. Olesen's Dogme drama **In Your Hands** (*Forbrydelser*), the term "feelbad movie" suited the new serious streak in Danish films. Olesen's film follows a young theology graduate (Ann Eleonora Jørgensen, the hairdresser from Italian For Beginners), who becomes a substitute priest in a women's prison. She has been trying to have a child with her husband for years, and against all odds becomes pregnant after meeting an inmate (Trine Dyrholm) who might have supernatural powers. This brooding tale of faith and forgiveness was praised by critics and surprised at the box-office, with a solid 131,445 admissions.

It was written by the prolific Kim Fupz Aakeson, who appeared to be reacting against his crowdpleasing scripts for *Okay, Old, New, Borrowed and Blue* and *The One And Only*. In addition to In Your Hands, he delivered Paprika Steen's **Aftermath** (*Lad de små børn…*) and Jacob Thuesen's **Accused** (*Anklaget*). All three dig deep into the lives of ordinary middle-class parents, and though the characters and environments do not differ much from his previous films, he toned down the humour and turned up the tragedy. The first is about not being able to have children, the second about recovering from the death of a young child and in the third, which marked the directing debut of editor Thuesen (*The Kingdom*), a father is accused of sexually abusing his daughter.

Steen, an acclaimed actress (*Festen, Okay* and *Open Hearts*), impressed critics with her firm grip on the actors in *Aftermath*, her directing debut, but it disappointed commercially, with just 52,061 admissions, not least due to its overlap with veteran Erik Clausen's **Villa Paranoia**, in which a wealthy middle-aged man hires an unemployed actress to take care of his old father. Clausen, the old working-class satirist, was here in more serious mood than usual, painting a picture of a land of material wealth and mental poverty, but that did not deter his regular audience.

Julian Glover, Derek Jacobi, Ian Hart. Prod: Niels Bald, Bald Film

A.J. Donsby

One of the puppet heroes of **Strings**

LAD DE SMÅ BØRN…
(Aftermath)
[Drama, 2004] Script: Kim Fupz Aakeson. Dir: Paprika Steen. Phot: Erik Zappon. Players: Sofie Gråbøl, Mikael Birkkjær, Laura Christensen, Karen-Lise Mynster, Søren Pilmark. Prod: Thomas Heinesen, Nordisk Film.

BRØDRE (Brothers)
[Drama, 2004] Script: Anders Thomas Jensen, based on an original idea by Jensen and Susanne Bier. Dir: Bier. Phot: Morten Søborg. Players: Ulrich Thomsen, Nikolaj Lie Kaas, Connie Nielsen, Solbjørg Højfeldt, Bent Mejding. Prod: Sisse Graum Olsen, Peter Aalbæk Jensen, Zentropa Productions/Two Brothers Ltd.

KONGEKABALE (Kings' Game)
[Political thriller, 2004] Script: Nikolaj Arcel, Rasmus Heisterberg, based on a novel by Niels Krause Kjær. Dir: Arcel. Phot: Rasmus Videbæk. Players: Anders W. Berthelsen, Søren Pilmark, Nastja Arcel, Nicolas Bro, Lars Mikkelsen. Prod: Meta Louise Foldager, Nimbus Film.

PUSHER II (With Blood on My Hands – Pusher II)
[Drama, 2004] Script and Dir: Nicolas Winding Refn. Phot: Morten Søborg. Players: Mads Mikkelsen, Leif Sylvester. Prod: Henrik Danstrup, NWR Productions.

ANKLAGET (Accused)
[Drama, 2005] Script: Kim Fupz

Aakeson. Dir: Jacob Thuesen.
Phot: Sebastian Blenkov. Players:
Troels Lyby, Sofie Gråbøl, Paw
Henriksen, Louise Mieritz. Prod:
Thomas Heinesen, Nordisk Film
Production.

KINAMAND (Chinaman)
*[Comedy-drama, 2005] Script:
Kim Fupz Aakeson. Dir: Henrik
Ruben Genz. Players: Bjarne
Henriksen, Vivian Wu, Charlotte
Fich, Paw Henriksen, Johan
Rabeus. Prod: Thomas
Gammeltoft, Fine & Mellow
Productions.*

DEAR WENDY
*[Drama, 2005] Script: Lars von
Trier. Dir: Thomas Vinterberg.
Phot: Anthony Dod Mantle.
Players: Jamie Bell, Chris Owen,
Mark Webber, Michael
Angarano, Danso Gordon,
Alison Pill, Bill Pullman. Prod:
Sisse Graum, Lucky Punch
(Zentropa Productions/Nimbus
Film).*

ADAMS ÆBLER
(Adam's Apples)
*[Black comedy, 2005] Script and
Dir: Anders Thomas Jensen.
Phot: Sebastian Blenkov. Players:
Mads Mikkelsen, Ulrich
Thomsen, Paprika Steen, Nicolas
Bro, Ole Thestrup. Prod: Tivi
Magnusson, Mie Andreasen,
M&M Productions.*

MANDERLAY
*[Drama, 2005] Script and Dir:
Lars von Trier. Phot: Anthony
Dod Mantle. Players: Bryce
Dallas Howard, Isaach De
Bankole, Danny Glover, Willem
Dafoe. Prod: Vibeke Windeløv,
Zentropa Entertainments 13.*

FLUERNE PÅ VÆGGEN
(literally, The Flies on the Wall)
*[Political thriller, 2005] Script
and Dir: Åke Sandgren. Players:
Trine Dyrholm, Lars Brygmann,
Kurt Ravn, Henrik Prip. Prod:
Thomas Heinesen, Nordisk Film
Production.*

ALLEGRO
*[Drama, 2005] Script: Christoffer
Boe, Mikael Wulff. Dir: Boe.*

At Christmas 2004, Nicolas Winding Refn delivered **With Blood on My Hands – Pusher II** (*Pusher II*), a sequel to his breakthrough film, which follows a petty criminal (Mads Mikkelsen) from the original movie, fresh out of jail and trying to get a life. The first big box-office surprise in 2004 had been the very politically incorrect **Terkel in Trouble** (*Terkel i Knibe*), a low-budget comedy whose *South Park*-like humour and animation united audiences and critics. It was the brainchild of stand-up comic Anders Matthesen, who voiced all the characters and wrote the radio series on which the film was based. It provided Danes with countless catchphrases and drew 380,781 admissions.

A new political age

Things turned more serious in the autumn, when three very different films reintroduced politics to Danish cinema for the first time in a decade. Lotte Svendsen's **What's Wrong with this Picture?** (*Tid til forandring*) never really found its footing in its attempt to paint a satirical image of modern Danish society, but Susanne Bier's *Brothers* (*Brødre*) and Nikolaj Arcel's *Kings' Game* (*Kongekabale*) widened the definition of what a Danish film can be.

Bier's second collaboration with versatile writer Anders Thomas Jensen following *Open Hearts*, **Brothers** explored how war can change a family. Danish-born Connie Nielsen (*Gladiator*) made her debut in her own language opposite two of the country's most acclaimed actors, Ulrich Thomsen and Nikolaj Lie Kaas, as the wife of a professional soldier (Thomsen) who falls for his ex-con younger brother (Lie Kaas), when the husband is reported missing, presumed dead, in Afghanistan. The gripping drama brought international conflicts into the living room and confirmed that the multi-award-winning Bier is at the top of her game.

Erik Aavatsmark

Nikolaj Lie Kass, left, and Ulrich Thomsen as **Brothers**

Newcomer Arcel took a different route in his feature directing debut, the political thriller **Kings' Game**. Loosely based on a factual novel about a power struggle in the Danish parliament, it is an extremely well crafted *All the President's Men*-like story, which, like *Brothers*, took critics and audiences by storm, passing 450,000 admissions. In years to come, *Kings' Game* will most likely be seen as the film that revived the political thriller in Denmark, and at least two more were due for release in 2005, Åke Sandgren's *Fluerne på Væggen* (literally, *The Flies on the Wall*) and Gert Fredholm's *Dommeren* (literally, *The Judge*).

Nicolas Bro, left, and Anders W. Berthelsen as political reporters in **King' Game**

Manslaughter (*Drabet*), the highly anticipated new film from Per Fly, who took all the major national awards with his two previous features, *The Bench* and *Inheritance*, also deals with political issues in the story of a 50-year-old man who falls for a young former student and fights to clear her of the murder of a policeman at a political rally. Von Trier is expected to cause controversy again in 2005, first with his script for Thomas Vinterberg's *Dear Wendy*, about a group of young American pacifists who share a dangerous infatuation with guns, and with *Manderlay*, virtually certain to premiere at Cannes, which picks up where *Dogville* left off, and follow Grace (Bryce Dallas Howard, replacing Nicole Kidman) to an Alabama plantation where the slaves are unaware that slavery was abolished 70 years earlier.

JACOB NEIIENDAM (neiiendam@film.dk) is a Danish film critic and journalist who has been Nordic correspondent for *Screen International* since 1999. He is also head of programming for the Copenhagen International Film Festival.

Phot: Manuel Claro. Players: Ulrich Thomsen, Henning Moritzen, Nicolas Bro. Prod: Tine Grew Pfeiffer, AlphaVille Productions Copenhagen.

DOMMEREN
(*literally,* **The Judge**)
[Drama, 2005] Script: Mikael Olsen. Dir: Gert Fredholm. Phot: Jørgen Johansson. Players: Peter Gantzler, Jens Okking, Sarah Boberg, Peter Schroeder, Samanta Gomez. Prod: Mikael Olsen, Zentropa Entertainments 7.

PUSHER III (I'm the Angel of Death – Pusher III)
[Action drama, 2005] Script and Dir: Nicolas Winding Refn. Phot: Morten Søborg. Players: Zlatko Buric, Slavko Labovic. Prod: Henrik Danstrup, NWR Productions.

DRABET (Manslaughter)
[Drama, 2005] Script: Kim Leona, Per Fly, Dorte Høegh, Mogens Rukov. Dir: Fly. Phot: Harald Paalgard. Players: Jesper Christensen, Beate Bille, Charlotte Fich, Pernilla August. Prod: Ib Tardini, Zentropa Entertainments 12.

Quote of the Year

"I expect [*Manderlay*] will unite the Ku-Klux-Klan and the coloured, because both parties will want to kill me afterwards."

LARS VON TRIER, *anticipating American responses to his* Dogville *follow-up.*

Ecuador Gabriela Alemán

The Year's Best Films

Gabriela Alemán's selection:

At the Edge of the Boudoir
(Short. Andrés Crespo)
Crónicas (Sebastián Cordero)
A Man and a River
(Franklin Briones)
**Ecuador vs. The Rest
of the World**
(Docu. Pablo Mogrovejo)
Orgiastic Sunday
(Short. Sandino Burbano)

Recent and
Forthcoming Films

FUERA DE JUEGO (Offside)
*[Drama, 2004] Script: Luis and
Victor Arregui. Dir: Victor
Arregui. Phot: Germán Valverde.
Players: Manolo Santillán, Dany
Bustamante, Ximena Ganchala,
Fabián Velasco. Prod: Productora
Bochinche.*
A group of jobless middle-class
teenagers try to find some sense
to their lives while the country
falls apart.

**MIENTRAS LLEGA EL DIA:
1809-1810** (*literally*, **Until the
Day Arrives: 1809-1810**)
*[Historical drama, 2004] Script:
Mauricio Samaniego, Camilo
Luzuriaga. Dir: Luzuriaga. Phot:
Daniel Andrade. Players: Marilú
Baca, Gonzalo Gonzalo,
Arístides Vargas, Victor Hugo
Gallegos, Aitor Merino. Prod:
Alcaldía de Quito/FONSAL/
Gobierno de Pichincha.*
The Creole patriots' preparations
for the uprising against the
Spanish monarchy serve as a
backdrop for a love story
between one of the revolutionary
intellectuals and his student.

After the virtual demise, in the early years of the new century, of ASOCINE (Association of Ecuadorian Film-makers), the only national body that had vainly lobbied for a film law since the 1980s, Ecuadorian film-makers lost all institutional support. The switch from the sucre to the dollar as national currency in 2000 had a devastating effect on cinemagoing, as the average price of a ticket went from $0.40 in 1999 to $1.50 in 2000 and now $3.50. Despite these problems, and the worst economic crisis in Ecuador's history, there has been a small boom in production.

Two international shoots, for *Proof of Life* and *The Dancer Upstairs*, first roused the hibernating industry in 2002, providing work for dozens of technicians. The arrival of new digital technologies, the creation of the first film school, in Quito, and the return of young film-makers who had been studying abroad woke it up fully. In 2002-03, a number of Ecuadorian projects won international prizes: Sebastián Cordero's *Crónicas* screenplay won the Sundance/NHK Award and the FondSud post-production award and Victor Arregui's **Offside** (*Fuera de juego*) won the Cine en Costrucción Section at San Sebastián. The post-production award from the Poor Cinema Festival of Gibara, Cuba, went to Fernando Miele's *Deported Prometheus* (*Prometeo deportado*), due in 2006, which follows the fortunes of Ecuadorians held in immigration limbo at a European airport.

With no state or institutional support, commercial producers are at the forefront, led by Cabeza Hueca Productions and the Cine Memoria Corporation. Cine Memoria has also, since 2003, organised the Encuentros del Otro Cine Documentary Festival, which has stimulated interest in non-fiction cinema. Among the most interesting recent documentary releases are Javier Izquierdo's

Teenagers face a hopeless future in the award-winning **Offside**

debut, **Augusto San Miguel Died Yesterday** (*Augusto San Miguel ha muerto ayer*), which explored the myths surrounding the first Ecuadorian film-maker; **Personal Problems** (*Problemas personales*) by Lisandra Rivera and Manolo Sarmiento, which followed three Ecuadorian immigrants in Spain for one year; Juan Martin Cueva's **The Place Where the Poles Meet** (*El lugar donde se juntan los polos*), which weaves together the histories of Ecuador, Cuba and Nicaragua through personal memories, and Pablo Mogrovejo's **Ecuador vs. The Rest of the World** (*Ecuador vs. el resto del mundo*), which recounts Ecuador's first participation in the soccer World Cup.

Helped by Mexican co-producers, Cordero's **Crónicas** (literally, *Chronicles*) had the largest budget ever for an Ecuadorian film (about $3m), and the most international and star-studded cast. It received the dubious honour of being pirated and out on the streets two days before its commercial release. Mateo Herrera's long awaited second feature, **Threat** (*Jaque*), whose leitmotif is the identity crisis of Ecuador, was shot in seven days without a screenplay. His actors had to improvise in actual locations during the city-wide celebration of the founding of Quito by the Spaniards 500 years ago, and all the action occurs in real time.

Collective endeavours

Conceptual video artists the Sapo Inc. Collective are the guerrillas of the audio-visual sector. Shooting on video they shun all conventions and have produced more than 20 interesting shorts. Sapo director and editor Pancho Viñachi and producer-director Juan Rhon are both names to watch. Other noteworthy shorts include Andres Crespo's *At the Edge of the Boudoir* (*Filo de tocador*), which explores the reactions of an astonished TV audience which learns that an Ecuadorian porno flick has just won at Cannes, and Sandino Burbano's *Orgiastic Sunday* (*Domingo orgiástico*), which achieves something close to cinematic poetry by spending a lazy Sunday afternoon with retired Bolshoi dancers at a Moscow park.

Franklin Briones, a maverick of Ecuadorian production, produced four different cuts of **A Man and a River** (*Un hombre y un rio*). Two competed in festivals (Cuenca and Quito), one was shown in the theatres of his native Manabi, and he hoped to sell the fourth, six-hour version to TV as a mini-series. The movie dissects the mores of Manabi society while following a woman's search for her father.

GABRIELA ALEMÁN (gabrielaa@usfq.edu.ec) is a journalist with a PhD from Tulane University, where she specialised in Latin American Cinema. She lectures at the universities of San Francisco de Quito and Andina in Ecuador.

CRÓNICAS
(*literally*, **Chronicles**)
[Drama, 2004] Script and Dir: Sebastián Cordero. Phot: Enrique Chediak. Players: Leonor Watling, Damián Alcázar, John Leguizamo, José María Yazpick. Prod: Cabezahueca/Anhelo (Mexico)/Tequila Gang (Mexico).
A child murderer (Alcázar) jailed for the wrong crime tries to wrestle free by feeding information to an ambitious news reporter (Leguizamo) from Miami.

JAQUE (Threat)
[Drama, 2004] Dir: Mateo Herrera. Phot: Daniel Andrade. Players: Cristian Arroyo, Juan Francisco Racines, Natalia Mendoza. Prod: El Otro Lado Films.
Despite their differences, Cristian and Juan Fernando have been friends since childhood. During the celebrations of the founding of Quito one of them puts their friendship on the line.

Threat

ISLA DE PAZ aka **MALDITA PRIMAVERA** (*literally*, **Island of Peace** aka **Damn Spring**)
[Political comedy-thriller, 2005] Script and Dir: Mauricio Samaniego. Phot: Enrique Chediak. Prod: Cabeza Hueca/Tequila Gang (Mexico)/Enrique Chediak.
Teenager Adriana falls in love with Ignacio. She slowly realises he is part of a guerrilla movement.

DEL SUEÑO AL CAOS
(*literally*, **From Dreams to Chaos**)
[Documentary, 2005] Dir: Isabel Dávalos. Phot: Iván Mora. Prod: Cabeza Hueca.
Exploration of the Alfaro Vive Carajo! uprising. What led upper middle-class Ecuadorian youngsters to fight social injustice in the 1980s?

Egypt Fawzi Soliman

The Year's Best Films

Fawzi Soliman's choice:
Sleepless Nights
(Hani Khalifa)
I Love Cinema
(Ossama Fawzi)
Girls' Love
(Khaled El Hagar)
Best Times (Hala Khalil)
Everything Is Gonna Be Alright
(Docu. Tamer Ezzat)

Best Times

Recent and Forthcoming Films

SAHAR AL-LAYALI
(Sleepless Nights)
[Social drama, 2003] Script: Tamer Habib. Dir: Hani Khalifa. Phot: Ahmad Abdel Aziz. Players: Mona Zaki, Hanan Turk, Gihan Fadel. Prod: Al Arabia for Production and Distribution.

HOBB AL-BANAT (Girls' Love)
[Social drama, 2003] Script: Tamer Habib. Dir: Khaled El Hagar. Phot: Samir Bahzan. Players: Leila Elwi, Hana Turk, Hana Sheha. Prod: Media City for Film Production.

Although the ministry of culture made 2003 "The Year of Egyptian Cinema" to mark the seventy-fifth anniversary of the country's first feature film, the industry's crisis continued, with only 21 films completed, far below the 1980s and 1990s average. The National Film Festival jury deplored the lack of artistic achievement and thought in most new films, but praised some newcomers. Others took hope from the presence of Youssef Chahine's *Alexandria – New York* and Yousri Nasrallah *Sun's Gate* in the official programme at Cannes 2004.

The first-time director/writer pairing of Hani Khalifa and Tamer Habib on **Sleepless Nights** (*Sahar al-layali*) produced an acclaimed box-office hit. It is a very courageous look at the social and emotional problems faced by a group of old male friends in their married lives, and broke taboos by depicting the sexual frustration of a young wife. The eight lead actors, none of them stars, shared the award for best acting at Damascus.

By contrast, Hala Khalil's **Best Times** (*Ahla al-awqat*) takes a feminist view of the friendship between three nostalgic young women. Alongside Khalil, another new female director tackling fiction for the first time after working in documentaries is Kamla Abou Zikri with **First Year in Swindling** (*Sana oula nasb*). It was written and produced by Samira Mohsen who had eyes firmly on the box-office in combining social problems and entertainment in this story of young men looking for work and love.
In his first film as director, writer and set designer, **From First Sight** (*Men nazret ein*), Ihab Lamei experimented with computer technology. The protagonist is a photographer who composes the image of his dream girl via computer and finds her, just as he imagined, as his bride.

My father the fanatic

Ossama Fawzi's **I Love Cinema** (*Bahib al-sima*) was considered by some critics as one of the most important films of the last 20 years. It deals with the life of middle-class Coptic families (orthodox and protestant) in 1966-67, in the time of Nasser. The main theme is religious, social and political oppression as a 40-year-old man narrates flashbacks to his childhood, dominated by his love of cinema and his rejection by his fanatical father. Although Fawzi, his scriptwriter and producer are Copts, there were claims before the film's release that it might offend the Coptic church and society, but intellectuals rejected the censors' suggestion that it should be viewed by the clergy.

In **Alexandria – New York**, Chahine completes his autobiographical *Alexandria* quartet. Joe, a famous Alexandria-born film director, encounters his first love, Ginger, when he is honoured at Lincoln Center, New York, in 2001. We flash back to the 1940s when they were both 19 and students at the Institute of Dramatic Art, California, and pledged to love each other forever. Reunited, the American Dream is no longer what it used to be, but Joe finds out that he had an American son. In this boisterous epic in which heroes love, sing, dance, laugh and cry, Chahine re-evaluates his ambiguous relationship with the nation he once loved so much.

Yousri Nasrallah explores Palestinian suffering in **Sun's Gate**

Yousri Nasrallah **Sun's Gate** (*Bab el shams*) deals with the Palestinian tragedy from 1943 to 1992 through the daily life of Palestinians and a love story in two parts: "The Departure" and "The Return". Unable to raise money from international co-producers, Mohamed Khan was obliged to make his twentieth film, **Klephty**, meaning "little thief" or "con man", as cheaply as possible on digital. It follows a street guy who lives off odd-jobs, sometimes swindles, and portrays a city, Cairo, where honesty is becoming a mirage.

A new wave of documentaries and shorts is being made with state and private finance. For example, SEMAT, set up by six young directors, aims to give young talents the chance to create with DV technology. SEMAT produced **Everything Is Gonna Be Alright** (*Kul shei hayebka tamam*), directed and shot in New York by Tamer Ezzat. It deals with different Egyptian generations, their identities and their attitudes towards September 11. Hala Galal's **Women's Chitchat** (*Dardasha nessayiat*) deals with the problems of women as experienced by several generations of the same family. Emad Ernest's **Cactus of the City** (*Sabbar al medina*) examines Alexandria through the eyes of an Alexandrian painter.

FAWZI SOLIMAN (adifwzgm@hotmail.com) is a film journalist and critic who has contributed to magazines and newspapers in Egypt and the Arab world.

SANA OULA NASB
(First Year in Swindling)
[Romantic comedy, 2004] Script: Samira Mohsen. Dir: Kamla Abou Zikri. Phot: Ahmad Morsi. Players: Ahmad Ezz, Nour, Dalia El-Beheiri. Prod: Al-Adl Group.

BAHIB AL-SIMA
(I Love Cinema)
[Social drama, 2004] Script: Hani Fawzi. Dir: Osama Fawzi. Phot: Tarek El Telmissany. Players: Leila Elwi, Mahmoud Hemeida, Yousef Osman. Prod: Hani Guirguis/Al Arabia for Production and Distribution.

AHLA AL-AWQAT (Best Times)
[Social drama, 2004] Script: Wissam Soliman. Dir: Hala Khalil. Phot: Ahmad Morsi. Players: Hanan Turk, Hind Sabri, Menna Shalabi. Prod: Al Adl Group.

MEN NAZRET EIN
(From First Sight)
[Social drama, 2003] Script and Dir: Ihab Lamei. Phot: Walid Nabil. Players: Amr Waked, Mona Zakri. Prod: Nihad Farid Shawki Films.

ALEXANDRIA – NEW YORK
[Drama, 2004] Script: Youssef Chahine and Khaled Youssef. Dir: Chahine. Phot: Ramsis Marzouk. Players: Mahmoud Hemeida, Ahmad Yahia, Yousra El Louzi. Prod: Misr International/H. Balzan (Paris).

Quote of the Year

"I have to remind Americans of a time when they were not hated throughout the Arab world. I have returned to the late 1940s, when as a virile youth, I was studying at the Pasadena Playhouse but also getting my apprenticeship in sex and love."

YOUSSEF CHAHINE *talks about* Alexandria – New York.

Estonia Jaan Ruus

The Year's Best Films

Jaan Ruus' selection:

Somnambulance
(Sulev Keedus)

Made in Estonia
(Rando Pettai)

A Living Force
(Docu. Jaak Kilmi,
Andres Maimik)

Frank and Wendy
(Animated shorts.
David Snowman)

Instinct
(Animated short.
Rao Heidmets)

Madis Milling in **Made in Estonia**

Recent and Forthcoming films

SIGADE REVOLUTSIOON
(Revolution of Pigs*)*
[*Coming-of-age tragicomedy,*
2004]. Script and Dir: *Jaak*
Kilmi, René Reinumägi. Phot:
Arko Okk. Players: Jass
Seljamaa, Uku Uusberg, Evelin
Kuusik, Vadim Albrant, Lilian
Alto, Mikk Tammepõld,
Arvo Kukumägi. Prod: Anu
Veermäe,Rudolf Konimõis Film
Production/OÜ Sigade
Revolutsioon/Mikko Räisanen,
Crea Video (Finland).

For a small country, Estonia's film industry is developing well. In 2003, the number one box-office hit was the sketch comedy **Made in Estonia** (*Vanad ja kobedad*), made by TV advertising director Rando Pettai, with popular local comics Henrik Normann and Madis Milling each playing three male and three female roles. In part, it owed its popularity to *Names in Marble* (*Nimed marmortahvlil*), the account of schoolboys fighting in the Estonian War of Independence of 1918, which in 2002 brought Estonians back to a domestic production after a 10-year break.

Sulev Keedus' demanding **Somnambulance** (*Somnambuul*) sought to entertain arthouse audiences. This slow-moving, claustrophobic and heavily symbolic drama captures the existential dissociation of a young woman, Eetla (the brilliant Katariina Lauk), in the end of the Second World War. It masochistically presents the rape of Eetla and the growing madness of her father, a lighthouse keeper, as a metaphor for the psychic breakdown of the entire nation under Soviet occupation, but it lacks catharsis.

Katariina Lauk as Eetla in **Somnambulance**

The third feature (the average annual output) of 2003, Esa Illi's **Brothers** (*Broidit*), is a Finnish chamber film with a modest Estonian contribution. It presents improvisational psychological studies of two brothers, the younger fatally ill and in love with a girl from an Estonian summer resort. **A Living Force** (*Elav jõud*) by Jaak Kilmi and Andres Maimik is a lively feature documentary that considers the personal and social choices of losers and winners in present-day Estonia.

Welcome to camp kitsch

In 2004, **Revolution of Pigs** (*Sigade revolutsioon*) marked the fiction feature debut of young directors Jaak Kilmi and René Reinumägi. It is a kitschy, clamorous and fast-moving youth comedy about political and sexual awakening in a Soviet student summer camp in 1986. Young audiences enjoyed it. The historic discourse, however, is naïve, and the direction has flaws.

Ilmar Taska, a 50-year old producer, directed his debut, the half-hearted criminal drama **Set Point** (*Täna öösel me ei maga*). Estonian fashion model Carmen Kass took a leading role and Taska broke the rules of the thriller genre to satisfy his artistic ambitions but the result was neither art nor a hit.

Andres Maimik's documentary feature *Welcome to Estonia* was widely debated. Made in the form of a political sketch, it ridicules the activities of the ruling party, Res Publica, and takes its near-fascist election slogan "Choose order!" to extremes. One of the few Baltic children's films of recent years, the Latvian–Estonian co-production **Waterbomb for the Fat Tomcat** (*Veepomm paksule kõutsile*), was made with great warmth by eminent Latvian master Varis Brasla and favourably received by audiences.

There is a healthy production scene for short films, led by Andres Tuisk's surrealistic thriller *Family Business* (*Perebisnes*; shorts Grand Prix at Mannheim 2003) and the animated *Instinct* (*Instinkt*) by director Rao Heidmets and artist Navitrolla, which depicts the Creator losing control over the world he made and has won 10 festival prizes. Priit Pärn, the Grand Old Man of Estonian animation, and his colleagues Priit Tender, Ülo Pikkov and Kaspar Jancis (working under the collective pseudonym David Snowman) delivered a series of shorts, about American super agents trying to save the world, *Frank and Wendy*.

Estonian film production depends primarily on state subsidies, which were $3.6m in 2003 (EEK 48.6m) and $4.3m in 2004, of which the Estonian Film Foundation contributed $2.9m. Estonian film is represented internationally, alongside Latvia and Lithuania, by Baltic Films, the regional umbrella organisation. Of great concern is the shortage of cinemas, with only 12 operating in 2004, and the government has assigned funds to establish cinemas in every large town. Ticket prices went up by 7% in 2003, to an average $4.64; admissions fell by 18% to 0.94 per capita and box-office by 14%.

JAAN RUUS (jaan@ekspress.ee) works as a film critic for the biggest Estonian weekly, *Eesti Ekspress*, and is president of Estonian FIPRESCI.

MALEV (Men at Arms)
[*Absurd comedy, 2004*] Script: Tõnis Leht, Kaaren Kaer, Erik Moora, Lauri Lippmaa. Dir: Kaer. Phot: Andrus Prikk. Players: Ott Sepp, Mirtel Pohla, Raivo E. Tamm. Prod: Anneli Ahven, Exitfilem/Tõnis Leht, Erik Moora, Lauri Lippmaa, Õ-Fraktsioon.
Estonians fight foreign invaders in the thirteenth century.

KONTSERTREIS (Concert Trip)
[*Road movie, 2005*]. Script: Valentin Kuik, Peeter Simm. Dir: Simm. Phot: Rein Kotov. Players: Heio von Setten, Thomas Smausser. Prod: Artur Talvik, Allfilm/ Hans Honert, Saxonia Media (Germany).

Ott Sepp in **Martin from the Robbers' Rock**

RÖÖVLIRAHNU MARTIN (Martin from the Robbers' Rock)
[*Children's film, 2005*] Script: Mihkel Ulman. Dir: René Vilbre. Phot: Manfred Vainokivi. Players: Ott Sepp, Madis Ollikainen, Andry Zhagars, Kadi Sink. Prod: Manfred Vainokivi/Parunid & Von'id.
The friendship between a boy and a human-like cat.

STIILIPIDU (Open Dresscode)
[*Drama, 2005*] Script: Valentin Kuik, Mo Blackwood. Dir: Peeter Urbla. Phot: Mait Mäekivi. Players: Maarja Jakobson, Anne Reemann, Evelin Pang. Prod: Anneli Ahven, Exitfilm (Estonia)/Mika Ritalahti, Silva Mysterium OY (Finland).
Three women establish a new business renting out costumes.

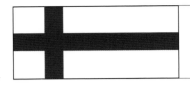

Finland Antti Selkokari

The Year's Best Films

Antti Selkokari's selection:
Eila (Jarmo Lampela)
Dog Nail Clipper
(Markku Pölönen)
War Children
(Erja Dammert)

Recent and Forthcoming Films

PAHAT POJAT
(Bad Boys – A True Story)
[True crime comedy-drama, 2003] Script: Pekka Lehtosaari, based on an original idea by Anssi Miettinen and Lehtosaari. Dir: Aleksi Mäkelä. Phot: Pini Hellstedt. Players: Peter Franzén, Niko Saarela, Lauri Nurkse, Jasper Pääkkönen, Vesa-Matti Loiri. Prod: Solar Films.

EILA
[Social drama, 2003] Script: Tove Idström. Dir: Jarmo Lampela. Phot: Harri Räty. Players: Sari Mällinen, Ilkka Koivula, Hannes Suominen, Kristiina Halkola, Kari Hietalahti. Prod: Tero Kaukomaa, Blind Spot Pictures.

SIBELIUS
[Biopic, 2003] Script and Dir: Timo Koivusalo. Phot: Pertti Mutanen. Players: Martti Suosalo, Miina Turunen, Seela Sella, Vesa Vierikko, Jarmo Mäkinen. Prod: Koivusalo, Artista Filmi.

LAPSIA JA AIKUISIA
(Producing Adults)
[Drama, 2003] Script: Pekko Pesonen. Dir: Aleksi Salmenperä. Phot: Tuomo Hutri. Players: Minna Haapkylä, Minttu Mustakallio, Kari-Pekka Toivonen. Prod: Tero Kaukomaa, Blind Spot Pictures.

One of 2003's best Finnish films was Jarmo Lampela's **Eila**. The story of a cleaning woman and single mother, Eila (Sari Mällinen), who must support her ex-con son and sues her employer for unlawful dismissal, it presents very well aspects of everyday Finnish life. After Eila and her colleagues receive pink slips on Christmas Eve they gradually come together to take on the government. Lampela, whose previous films include *Freakin' Beautiful World* and *The River*, refuses to take the obvious routes, neither pumping the drama up into soap opera nor lowering the tone to that of a banal TV "Movie of the Week" and he draws aptly low-key performances; Mällinen fills a gutwrenching part without a hint of sentimentality and she and her director won Jussi awards.

Sari Mällinen faces harsh reality as the title character in **Eila**

Writer-director Timo Koivusalo had worked overtime to get all the details of the maestro's life correct in the biopic **Sibelius**, which arrived in September 2003, but the facsimile approach prevented the film from rising above the level of pretty period drama (although it still became the year's seventh biggest hit). The story follows two timelines, one for the composer's younger, active years, the other with the old maestro recounting his early days. The acting was moderate; Martti Suosalo was the best as the young Sibelius.

Two views of the Finnish male

Human dignity took centre stage when Markku Pölönen dramatised Veikko Huovinen's novel **Dog Nail Clipper** (*Koirankynnen leikkaaja*), a heartwarming drama about a brain-damaged war veteran, Mertsi (played by Pölönen mainstay Peter Franzén), a reclusive, shy fellow who works as a carpenter's assistant and does not meet the macho standards set by the mocking lumberjacks around him.

Peter Franzén, rear centre left, as Mertsi in **Dog Nail Clipper**

His naivety allows him to be deceived twice: first in the war, by militaristic propaganda, then by a co-worker's tall tale about a dog desperately in need of nail-clipping. The film lovingly recreates post-war Finland, where hard, physical labour equates to honesty and human kindness, and Pölönen blends schmaltz and nostalgia. Though it romanticises the past, *Dog Nail Clipper* serves as a timely reminder of values long forgotten.

Free market economics entered Finland relatively late and the recent replacement of the distinctively Finnish currency, the *markka*, by the euro has created a wave of longing, previously expressed in the films of Aki Kaurismäki and now in Veikko Aaltonen's adaptation of an immensely popular Finnish novel by Kari Hotakainen, **Trench Road** (*Juoksuhaudantie*), which premiered in August 2004 to mostly favourable reviews. The film tells the story of a man's doomed attempts to win back his family after tempers have flared. His trick is to purchase the house of their dreams, no matter what.

Aaltonen has emphasised the tragic elements of Hotakainen's witty, sarcastic tragicomedy. The writer-director understands the dilemmas and fears of the modern Finnish male, obliged to be both 'soft' family man and hard-nosed go-getter, and his actors all deliver fine performances.

Selin's Midas touch

When audiences for Finnish films declined during the 1980s and early 1990s, producers, in tandem with the Finnish Film Foundation, decided to bring the public back by investing in mainstream genre pictures. The continued results of this policy were very clear in 2003-04: eight of the ten most popular Finnish titles of 2003 were genre films, while those designed to give viewers more than just one night's fun faced a tougher ride. Finnish films' market share in 2003 rose by 4% to 21% and admissions rose to 7.9 million, up 200,000 on 2002. Hollywood continues to dominate the box-office consistently, however, whereas the

Two lesbians working at the same fertility clinic develop a ménage à trois with a married man.

YSTÄVÄNI HENRY
(My Friend Henry)
[Children's drama, 2003] Script and Dir: Auli Mantila. Phot: Heikki Färm. Players: Ylva Ekblad, Pertti Sveholm, Helle Willberg, Ninni Ahlroth, Aleksi Rantanen. Prod: Anna Heiskanen, Do Films.UOM.
A 12-year-old girl makes friends with Henry, who may or may not be imaginary.

HYMYPOIKA (Young Gods)
[Teen drama, 2003] Script: Jukka Vieno, from an idea by Jaajo Linnonmaa. Dir: Jukka-Pekka Siili. Phot: Jarkko T. Laine. Players: Jussi Nikkilä, Reino Nordin, Jenni Banerjee, Laura Malmivaara, Ville Virtanen, Kari Hietalahti. Prod: Aleksi Bardy, Olli Haikka/Helsinki Filmi.
Adolescents dare each other to videotape themselves having sex and bring in the tapes for all the boys to see, with the best performance winning a trophy.

KOIRANKYNNEN LEIKKAAJA
(Dog Nail Clipper)
[Drama, 2004] Script: Markku Pölönen, based on the novel by Veikko Huovinen. Dir: Pölönen. Phot: Kari Sohlberg. Players: Peter Franzén, Taisto Reimaluoma, Ville Virtanen, Ahti Kuoppala. Prod: Kari Sara, Fennada-filmi.

VARES
[Crime thriller, 2004] Script: Pekka Lehtosaari, based on the novel by Reijo Mäki. Dir: Aleksi Mäkelä. Phot: Pini Hellstedt. Players: Juha Veijonen, Laura Malmivaara, Jorma Tommila, Jari Halonen, Samuli Edelmann. Prod: Markus Selin, Solar Films.

JUOKSUHAUDANTIE
(Trench Road)
[Drama, 2004] Script: Veikko Aaltonen, from a novel by Kari Hotakainen. Dir: Aaltonen. Phot: Pekka Uotila. Players: Eero Aho, Tiina Lymi, Kari Väänänen. Prod: Lasse Saarinen, Kinotar.

Eero Aho as Matti Virtanen in **Trench Road**

SOTALAPSET (War Children)
[Documentary, 2003] Script and Dir: Erja Dammert. Phot: Marita Hällfors.
The remarkable evacuation of 70,000 Finnish children to Sweden, Denmark and Norway in 1939-44 is condensed into the stories of just seven of them.

HELMIÄ JA SIKOJA
(Pearls and Pigs)
[Drama 2003] Script and Dir: Perttu Leppä. Phot: Jyrki Arnikari. Players: Mikko Leppilampi, Laura Birn, Unto Helo, Jimi Pääkallo, Amanda Pilke. Prod: Jarkko Hentula, Talent House.
A family of petty criminals stumbles into good intentions and old habits.

Quote of the Year

"I'd make at least three films. Then I would have nice budgets."

ANNA HEISKANEN, *producer of* My Friend Henry, *when asked what would she do with* € *10m in a country where films very rarely cost more than* € *2m.*

fortunes of local movies are always likely to fluctuate from season to season.

In this climate, producer Markus Selin's populist features have become a brand of their own, including 2003's **Bad Boys – A True Story** (*Pahat pojat*), directed by Aleksi Mäkelä. The eponymous heroes are four none-too-clever brothers who rob self-service petrol stations by ripping out the pumps with chains and tractors, then smashing their way to the money inside and blowing it on expensive home cinema equipment, flashy cars and motorbikes. Based on real-life events, featuring Hollywood-style product placement and heavily marketed (by Finnish standards), *Bad Boys* was an extremely successful popcorn flick and its 614,000 admissions made it the year's biggest hit.

Selin generally produces boys' flicks, but he broadened his slate with **Addiction** (*Levottomat 3*), hiring a woman, Minna Virtanen, to direct the story of an unhappily married career woman who becomes a sex addict. The subject matter was guaranteed to generate media interest and although the film was an unsatisfactory treatment of an interesting idea, it became a hit early in 2004.

Selin's profitable partnership with Aleksi Mäkelä continued with **Vares**, based on a best-selling series of novels about a private detective. Vares (played by Juha Veijonen with sloppy charm) turns 40 promising never to drink again. He meets a beautiful woman army sergeant (Laura Malmivaara) who's been deceived into marrying a crook, and ends up on the trail of the Russian mob. The emphasis was all on action and violence and by September, *Vares* was on course to be the best-selling film of 2004.

ANTTI SELKOKARI (antti.selkokari@welho.com) works as a freelance film critic and journalist in Helsinki, contributing to *Aamulehti*, Finland's second best-selling daily newspaper.

Miina Turunen and Martti Suosalo as Aino and Jean Sibelius in **Sibelius**

France Michel Ciment

The Year's Best Films

Michel Ciment's selection

5 x 2 (François Ozon)
Intimate Strangers
(Patrice Leconte)
L'Esquive
(Abdel Kechiche)
Red Lights
(Cedric Kahn)
Not on the Lips
(Alain Resnais)

Recent and Forthcoming Films

PAS SUR LA BOUCHE
(Not on the Lips)
*[Operetta, 2003] Script: André
Barde. Dir: Alain Resnais. Phot:
Renato Berta. Players: Sabine
Azema, Pierre Arditi, Isabelle
Nanty, Audrey Tautou, Lambert
Wilson, Darry Cowl. Prod: Arena
Films.*

Serge Renko in **Triple Agent**

TRIPLE AGENT
*[Historical drama, 2004] Script
and Dir: Eric Rohmer. Phot:
Diane Baratier. Players: Serge
Renko, Katerina Didaskalou,
Amanda Langlet, Cyrielle Clair,
Grigori Manoukov, Dimitri
Rafalsky. Prod: Rezo
Productions.*

French cinema remains in good health, particularly in a European context. It produced in 2003 the largest number of films of any European country (212, including 183 with majority French backing, a rise of 6%) and 218 French films were released (20 more than in 2002 and the highest level for 20 years). The market share for Hollywood films is the lowest in Europe and the audience for local releases the highest. Though down by 5.4%, total admissions of 174.15 million are also a European peak. Small wonder, then, that David Kessler, former culture adviser to socialist prime minister Lionel Jospin, was in serene mood when in September 2004 he stepped down as managing director of the Centre national du cinema (CNC), where he had enjoyed an exceptionally good relationship with the industry.

However, a few clouds prevent total optimism. As in other countries, piracy is a source of increasing worry, especially online. The success of DVD, with films now released only six months after their theatrical opening, has undoubtedly contributed to the small decline in cinema attendance. The closure of 134 screens in 2003 was offset by the opening of 167 new ones, but 121 of these were in the multiplexes, which favour blockbusters over more valuable films that struggle to find exposures in independent theatres. Finally, French film export revenues declined, particularly in Europe (–54% in Italy, –48% in Germany and Switzerland, –20% in Spain; the trend bucked only by Britain +166%). France's best clients outside Europe remain Japan and the US.

Furthermore, while France remains a privileged country for auteur cinema there are growing signs of unease. Many directors, actors, producers and distributors agree that financing for high-quality films is becoming harder to find. Claude Berri, a producer and director who has for a long time maintained a delicate balance between purely commercial projects such as the *Astérix* series and more artistically ambitious work with the likes of Polanski, Chéreau, Forman and Rivette, admits that this equilibrium is no longer possible and that, for example, he had to give up a project with Jacques Doillon because of the shortage of financial partners.

Many other films have been similarly aborted and budgets have been cut. One reason for the crisis is the increasing preoccupation of TV channels – without whose involvement no film of a certain

NOTRE MUSIQUE
(Our Music)
*[2004] Script and Dir: Jean-Luc
Godard. Phot: Julien Hirsch.
Players: Sarah Adler, Nade Dieu,
Rony Kramer, George Aguilar,
Leticia Gutierrez, Jean-
Christophe Bouvet. Prod:
Avventura Films.*

Notre Musique

HISTOIRE DE MARIE ET JULIEN
(The Story of Marie and Julien)
*[Drama, 2003] Script: Jacques
Rivette, Pascal Bonitzer,
Christine Laurent. Dir: Rivette.
Phot: William Lubtchansky.
Players: Emmanuelle Béart, Jerzy
Radziwilowicz, Anne Brochet,
Bettina Kee, Olivier Cruveiller,
Mathias Jung. Prod: Pierre Grise
Productions.*

HOLY LOLA
*[Drama, 2004] Script:
Dominique Sampiero, Bertrand
Tavernier, Tiffany Tavernier. Dir:
Bertrand Tavernier. Players:
Isabelle Carré, Jacques Gamblin.
Prod: Little Bear.*

CONFIDENCES TROP INTIMES (Intimate Strangers)
*[Drama, 2004] Script: Jérôme
Tonnerre. Dir: Patrice Leconte.
Phot: Eduardo Serra. Players:
Fabice Luchini, Sandrine
Bonnaire. Prod: Alain Sarde.*

A TOUT DE SUITE
(Right Now)
*[Drama, 2004] Script and Dir:
Benoît Jacquot. Phot: Caroline
Champetier. Players: Isild Le Besco,
Ouassini Embarek, Nicolas
Duvauchelle, Laurence Cordier,
Fotini Kodoukaki, Catherine
Davenier. Prod: Natan Productions.*

budget can be produced – with ratings. This is true of the private channel (TF1) and the public ones (Antenne 2, FR3), though Arte is an exception. Of the 100 most popular programmes, 32 were feature films in 2001, 23 in 2002 and only 17 in 2003. Therefore, to boost the audience, the channels have favoured popular comedies and politically correct scripts. Cinema producers have also hired stand-up comedians, favourites of the small screen, to embody characters in big-screen fictions. Michael Youn, whose trash humour is inspired by America's *Jackass*, sold two million tickets with **La Beuze** and three million with **The Eleven Commandments**. Jamel Debbouze, in a vein close to America's Chris Tucker, with his sense of rap rhythm and wild improvisations, was a key reason why *Astérix & Obélix: Mission Cléopâtre* attracted 14 million spectators.

Resnais, Varda still in the vanguard

Despite these problems, some excellent personal films have had considerable success (around one million seats), such as Noemie Lvovsky's *Les sentiments*, Claude Chabrol's *La fleur du mal*, Pierre Salvadori's *Après vous*, Jean-Paul Rappeneau's *Bon Voyage* or François Ozon's *Swimming Pool*. One of the comforting aspects of the French system – together with the impressive amount of first features, 37% of the year's output – is the presence of directors in their seventies or eighties, still active, still inventive.

The first of these is Alain Resnais with **Not on the Lips** (*Pas sur la bouche*), a 1920s operetta, which he had always dreamed of seeing and which he has revived for his pleasure (and ours too). It is an exercise close in spirit to his **Melo** and confirms Resnais' taste in his late period for the theatre and actors, for a lighter inspiration, though it is also linked to his lifelong addiction to music and the games of the past. Known for his interest in intellectual constructions (*Last Year in Marienbad, Providence*), he has also been a constant fan of popular culture.

Thierry Valletoux/Arena Films

1920s operetta **Not on the Lips**

Agnès Varda (whose first feature, *La Pointe courte,* Resnais edited) has directed a 34-minute short *Ydessa, les ours et etc…*, where her playful virtuosity excels in one of her favourite subjects: the proliferation of objects and images. This time the photos of teddy bears collected by an artist, Ydessa Hendelens, and accompanied by the usual brilliant commentary of Varda, are the source of her inspiration. Another immersion into the past was Eric Rohmer's **Triple Agent**, a Conradian tale of a White Russian exiled in 1930s Paris with his Greek wife, who works for several foreign powers at the time of the Spanish Civil War and the Soviet Nazi pact. As always with Rohmer, the sinuous, abundant, complex speeches give an opacity to the clarity of his images.

Jean-Luc Godard has never been overly concerned with the past (except for innumerable cultural references), preferring to confront contemporary problems. In **Our Music** (*Notre musique*), divided into three parts – very loosely based on Dante's Hell, Purgatory, Paradise – he offers one of his least arcane meditations, this time on Sarajevo and the Israeli Palestinian conflict which has involved him for many years (and not without debatable aphorisms).

Artificial Eye

Jerzy Radziwilowicz and Emmanuelle Béart in **The Story of Marie and Julien**

With **The Story of Marie and Julien** (*Histoire de Marie et Julien*) Jacques Rivette follows the steps of Jacques Tourneur with his tales of phantoms but remains close to his own interest in conspiracies. He lacks the light touch and suggestive ability of the director of **Cat People** to give a new life to lost loves, and his characters seem for too long to be bloodless. But thanks to the talent of Emmanuelle Béart and Jerzy Radziwilowicz they come to life in the last section.

Cambodia: fiction and fact

The generation that succeeded the New Wave, caring less about imposing its auteurist touch, more eclectic in its formal and thematic options, was no less prolific. Once more Bertrand

CHEMINS DE TRAVERSE
(Byways)
[Road movie, 2004] Script and Dir: Manuel Poirier. Phot: Christophe Beaucarne. Players: Sergi López, Kevin Miranda, Lucy Harrison, Mélodie Marcq, Jacques Bosc, Alain Bauguil. Prod: Pan Européenne Production.

Franco Zecchin

Sergei López in **Byways**

CLEAN
[Melodrama, 2004] Script and Dir: Olivier Assayas. Phot: Eric Gautier. Players: Maggie Cheung, Béatrice Dalle, Laura Smet, Jeanne Balibar, Ian Brown, Tricky. Prod: Elizabeth Films

EXILS (Exiles)
[Drama, 2004] Script and Dir: Tony Gatlif. Phot: Céline Bozon. Players: Romain Duris, Lubna Azabal, Leila Makhlouf, Zouhir Gacem, Habib Cheik. Prod: Princes Films.

FOLLE EMBELLIE
(A Wonderful Spell)
[Drama, 2004] Script: Dominique Cabrera, Antoine Montperrin. Dir: Cabrera. Phot: Hélène Louvart. Players: Miou-Miou, Jean-Pierre Léaud, Morgan Marinne, Marilyne Canto, Julie-Marie Parmentier, Yolande Moreau. Prod: Films de la Croisade (Les).

Lola Neymark in **A Common Thread**

BRODEUSES
(A Common Thread)
[Drama, 2004] Script: Eléonore

Faucher, Gaëlle Mace. Dir:
Faucher. Phot: Pierre Cottereau.
Players: Lola Neymark, Ariane
Ascaride, Marie Félix, Jackie
Berroyer, Thomas Laroppe,
Arthur Quehen. Prod: Sombrero
Productions.

QUI A TUE BAMBI?
(Who Killed Bambi?)
[Horror, 2003] Script: Gilles
Marchand, Vincent Dietschy.
Dir: Marchand. Phot: Pierre
Millon. Players: Sophie Quinton,
Laurent Lucas, Catherine Jacob,
Yasmine Belmadi, Michèle
Moretti, Valérie Donzelli. Prod:
Haut et Court.

LES CHORISTES (The Choir)
[Drama, 2004] Script and Dir:
Christophe Barratier. Phot:
Dominique Gentil, Carlo Varini.
Players: Gérard Jugnot, François
Berléand, Kad Merad, Jean-Paul
Bonnaire, Marie Bunel, Jacques
Perrin. Prod: Galatée Films.

L'ESQUIVE
[Drama, 2004] Script: Abdel
Kechiche, Ghalya Lacroix. Dir:
Kechiche. Phot: Lubomir
Bakchev. Players: Osman
Elkharraz, Sara Forestier, Sabrina
Ouazani, Nanou Benahmou,
Hafet Ben-Ahmed, Aurélie
Ganito. Prod: Lola Films/Noé
Productions Int.

Osman Elkharraz in L'Esquive

APRES VOUS (After You)
[Comedy, 2003] Script: Pierre
Salvadori, Benoît Graffin. Dir:
Salvadori. Phot: Gilles Henry.
Players: Daniel Auteuil, José
Garcia, Sandrine Kiberlain,
Marilyne Canto, Michèle

Fabrice Luchini and Sandrine Bonnaire in Intimate Strangers

Tavernier confirmed his risk-taking and his constant need to renew himself. With **Holy Lola**, which follows the journey to Cambodia of a couple looking for a child to adopt, he has avoided all the trappings of his subject: picturesque exoticism, sentimentality, sociological demonstration. With his inspired actors Jacques Gamblin and Isabelle Carré he once more confirms himself as a lucid observer of our time and a sensitive analyst of intimate relationships.

Patrice Leconte is also prone to experiment and also went to Cambodia, to shoot **D'ogora**, a documentary made without commentary and with a dazzling kaleidoscope of images. But it is with **Intimate Strangers** (Confidences trop intimes) that Leconte shows himself at his best. His long-standing taste for encounters between people who are worlds apart this time selects a married woman (Sandrine Bonnaire) who looks for a psychoanalyst and accidentally finds herself talking to the financial adviser (Fabrice Luchini) next door instead. The leads are brilliant and Leconte subtly orchestrates their misunderstandings.

It was also a pleasure to see two talented directors back on form after more ambitious but flawed films, Benoît Jacquot with **Right Now** (A tout de suite) and Olivier Assayas with Clean. Jacquot traces the journey of a young girl (excellent Isild le Besco) from a bourgeois family who houses a burglar before running away with him around the Mediterranean and finally finding herself alone and stranded. Shot with a small camera, in black-and-white with a voice-over commentary, the film – set in the 1970s – harks back to the mixture of romanticism and realism characteristic of the New Wave.

It is another portrait of a woman that Olivier Assayas draws in **Clean**, a melodrama without the excesses (often rewarding) of the genre. Maggie Cheung won the Best Actress prize in Cannes for her sensitive performance as an ex-pop star and former drug addict who wants to lead a new life to be closer to her child.

Fathers and sons

Manuel Poirier explores a father-son relationship in **Byways** (*Chemins de traverse*), a road movie dear to his taste, which follows the peregrination of an odd couple, Victor (Sergi López), who lives on small tricks and swindles, and Félix (Kevin Miranda), maintained in a stubborn silence. Around these wanderings Poirier creates a strange melancholy tinged with humour. The theme of the journey is also central in **Exiles** (*Exils*) by Tony Gatlif (an undeserved Best Director prize at Cannes), in which the son of a former French settler in North Africa and a young Algerian girl leave Paris to go back to the land of their ancestors. As usual with the author of *Gadjo Dilo*, music and dance and the constant agitation of the camera are intended to create a trance-like state in the audience. The undeniable energy does not, however, hide a number of clichés.

An odd journey is also the core of Dominique Cabrera's **A Wonderful Spell** (*Folle embellie*), in which a group of escaped lunatics at the time of the German invasion in 1940 drift on a barge or wander the banks of the Loire. This uneven work succeeds through comedy, lyricism and a poetic realism reminiscent of the French films of the 1930s.

Several first and second features confirmed the arrival of new blood. Among the beginners, Eléonore Faucher was singled out in the Cannes Critics Week for her **A Common Thread** (*Brodeuses*), the portrait of a young supermarket cashier (Lola Neymark) who feels isolated and starts to embroider stories (inventing a cancer, hiding her pregnancy) until she meets a real embroiderer (Ariane Ascaride) who helps her overcome her inhibitions.

Gilles Marchand, well-known for his scripts, including Laurent Cantet's *Ressources humaines*, also attracted attention with his first feature, **Who Killed Bambi** (*Qui a tué Bambi?*), a genre film pitched between horror and fairy tale. In the spirit of George Franju he tells with masterful skill the story of a young hospital nurse who discovers the strange behaviour of a surgeon who takes advantage of his patients. They could not rival, at least in terms of box-office, Christophe Barratier and his **Les choristes**, a remake of a cult film of the 1940s, *La cage aux rossignols*, which seduced seven million people, as many as *Harry Potter* and *The Lord of the Rings*. This tale of a reform schoolteacher and his choir in a village confirms the audience appeal of the life of *la France profonde*.

Second time lucky

The artistic success of a second feature is even more satisfying yet it is often a stumbling-block for young directors. One such was

Moretti, Garance Clavel. Prod: Films Pelléas (Les).

Carole Bouquet in **Red Lights**

FEUX ROUGES (Red Lights)
[Drama, 2004] Script: Cédric Kahn, Laurence Ferreira Barbosa. Dir: Kahn. Phot: Patrick Blossier. Players: Jean-Pierre Darroussin, Carole Bouquet, Vincent Deniard, Charline Paul, Jean-Pierre Gos. Prod: Alicéléo.

Valéria Bruni-Tedeschi and Stéphane Freiss in **5 x 2**

5x2
[Drama, 2004] Script and Dir: François Ozon. Phot: Yorick Le Saux. Players: Valéria Bruni-Tedeschi, Stéphane Freiss, Géraldine Pailhas, Françoise Fabian, Michael Lonsdale. Prod: Fidélité Productions.

COMME UNE IMAGE (Look at Me)
[Comedy drama, 2004] Script: Agnès Jaoui, Jean-Pierre Bacri. Dir: Jaoui. Phot: Stéphane Fontaine. Players: Marie-Lou Berry, Agnès Jaoui, Jean-Pierre Bacri, Laurent Grevill, Virginie Desarnauts, Keine Bouhiza. Prod: Films A4 (Les).

POURQUOI (PAS) LE BRESIL?
[Drama 2004] Script: Dir: Laetitia Masson. Phot: Crystel Fournier. Players: Elsa Zylberstein, Marc Barbé, Daniel Auteuil, Pierre Arditi, Bernard Lecoq, Francis Huster. Prod: Rezo Productions/Salomé.

10e CHAMBRE, INSTANTS D'AUDIENCE
[Documentary, 2004] Dir: Raymond Depardon. Phot: Depardon, Fabienne Octobre, Justine Bourgade. Prod: Palmeraie et Désert.

S.21 LA MACHINE DE MORT KHMER ROUGE (S.21 The Khmer Rouge Killing Machine)
[Documentary, 2004] Dir and Phot: Rithy Panh. Prod: Institut National de l'Audiovisuel.

LE CHIEN, LE GENERAL ET LES OISEAUX (The Dog, the General and the Birds)
[Animation, 2003] Script: Tonino Guerra. Dir: Francis Nielsen. Prod: Solaris Productions/Roissy Films.

LA PROPHETIE DES GRENOUILLES (Raining Cats and Frogs)
[Animation, 2003] Script: Jacques-Rémy Girerd, Antoine Lanciaux, Iouri Tcherenkov. Dir: Girerd. Prod: Folimage Valence Production.

Raining Cats and Frogs

L'Esquive by Abdellatif Kechiche (another bright talent of Maghreb origin), an unconventional portrayal of the youngsters of a popular Parisian suburb as they rehearse a Marivaux play in and outside the classroom, while struggling with their own sentimental problems. The contrast between Marivaux's classical language and the kids' home-made slang is brilliant and Kechiche is a master at getting the best from his cast of young Arab, black and white amateurs.

The appearance in the last decade of a group of talented young directors has been one of the most conspicuous features in French cinema. Pierre Salvadori, for example, has established himself as the best director of comedies of his generation. **After You** (*Après vous*) has all the qualities of classical screwball, with its absurd situations, sizzling dialogue and inspired actors: Daniel Auteuil as a *maître d'* who wants to save a stranger from committing suicide and José Garcia, who becomes a burden after being rescued.

Just as rigorous, but on the tragic side, **Red Lights** (*Feux rouges*) was Cedric Kahn's intense adaptation of the Simenon novel about a man (haunting Jean-Pierre Darroussin) whose journey with his wife (Carole Bouquet) on the roads of France becomes a descent into hell. In **5 x 2**, François Ozon also examines the disintegration of a couple by showing in reverse chronological order five key moments, from divorce to first encounter. Once more using the scalpel of a surgeon or the magnifying glass of the entomologist, he shows his talent at drawing the best from his performers (Valéria Bruni-Tedeschi and Stéphane Freiss).

After *The Taste of Others*, Agnès Jaoui appears the true heiress of Claude Sautet in **Look at Me** (*Comme une image;* Best Script at Cannes), another wry look at dissatisfied characters: a male chauvinist publisher, a disillusioned song teacher (played by Jaoui), a young girl full of complexes and a novelist who is becoming the talk of the town. The social comment matches the psychological study.

Jean-Paul Dumas (Grillet/Corbis)/Pathé

Jean-Pierre Bacri and Virginie Desarnauts as husband and wife in **Look at Me**

Laetitia Masson in **Pourquoi (pas) le Brésil?** questions the state of auteur cinema today by showing the economic and artistic impossibility of adapting a novel by Christine Angot. Avoiding the cerebral artefact (the making of a film), she manages with the help of her alter ego (Elsa Zylberstein) to prove the contrary of her thesis by creating a piece of cinema at once original and intelligent.

For the first time Cannes selected in competition two documentaries and two animated films, giving these forms the status they deserve outside specialised events. Two of the best films of the year were indeed documentaries: **10e Chambre, instants d'audience** by Raymond Depardon, a fascinating examination of the proceedings in a law court for petty crimes, which becomes a real human comedy, and **S.21 The Khmer Rouge Killing Machine** (*S.21 la machine de guerre Khmer Rouge*) by Rithy Panh, a chilling and devastating investigation into the Cambodian genocide, as told by the executioners themselves.

The imaginary dimension, not often explored in French cinema, was powerfully present thanks to animation. In Francis Nielsen's **The Dog, the General and the Birds** (*Le chien, le général et les oiseaux*) the superb drawings of Serguei Barkhin illustrate the poetic tale of a bitter, retired general hunted by birds he had used as living torches to burn Moscow under the orders of Napoleon. Of an almost biblical dimension – but funny – Jacques-Remy Girard's **Raining Cats and Frogs** (*La prophétie des grenouilles*) gathers zoo animas in an ark after a group of frogs announce an imminent 40-day flood.

MICHEL CIMENT is president of FIPRESCI, a member of the editorial board of *Positif*, a radio producer and author of 15 books on cinema.

Quotes of the Year

"This isn't a particularly fashionable subject."

CHRISTOPHE BARRATIER, *first-time director, struggles to explain why* Les Choristes, *his tale of a reform school choir, sold 7.5 million tickets.*

"The cops had a tip-off from a former member with a grudge."

LAZAR, *spokesman for urban explorers La Mexicaine de Perforation, following the police's discovery of* the secret cinema built by the group in a cave beneath the streets of Paris.

"I've taken this decision following an unprecedented media lynching. For years the critics have attacked my films, and for years the public has come to my rescue."

CLAUDE LELOUCH *explains why he offered free screenings of his* Les Parisiens *across France for one evening in 400 cinemas in September 2004 – at a personal cost of €153,000.*

French César Academy Awards 2004

Film: *The Barbarian Invasions/Les invasions barbares.*
Director: Denys Arcand (*The Barbarian Invasions*).
Actress: Sylvie Testud (*Fear and Trembling/Stupeur et tremblements*).
Actor: Omar Sharif (*Monsieur Ibrahim*).
Supporting Actress: Julie Depardieu (*La petite Lili*).
Supporting Actor: Darry Cowl (*Not on the Lips*).
Female Newcomer: Julie Depardieu (*La petite Lili*).
Male Newcomer: Gregori Derangare (*Bon voyage*).
Foreign Film: *Mystic River.*
Film from the EU: *Good Bye, Lenin!*.
Screenplay: Denys Arcand (*The Barbarian Invasions*).
First Film: *Since Otar Left/Depuis qu'Otar est parti …*
Short Film: *L'homme sans tête.*
Score: Benoît Charest (*Belleville Rendez-Vous/Les triplettes de Belleville*).
Costumes: Jackie Budin (*Not on the Lips*).
Cinematography: Thierry Arbogast (*Bon voyage*).
Set Design: Jacques Rouxell and Catherine Leterrier (*Bon voyage*).
Editing: Danielle Anezin, Valerie Loiseleux and Ludo Troch (*Trilogy*).
Best Sound: Jean-Marie Blondel, Gérard Hardy and Gérard Lamps (*Not on the Lips*).

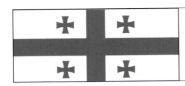

Georgia Goga Lomidze

Recent and Forthcoming Films

DEPUIS QU'OTAR EST PARTI... (Since Otar Left)
[Drama, 2003] Script: Julie Bertuccelli, Bernard Renucci. Dir: Bertuccelli. Phot: Christophe Pollock. Players: Esther Gorintin, Nino Khomassouridze, Dinara Droukarova, Temur Kalandadze, Rusudan Bolqvadze, Sasha Sarishvili, Duta Skhirtladze. Prod: Les Films du Poisson/Arte France Cinéma/Entre Chien et Loup/Studio 99.

SCHUSSANGST (Gun-Shy)
[Drama, 2003] Script: Dirk Kurbjuweit, Dito Tsintsadze. Dir: Tsintsadze. Phot: Manuel Marck. Players: Fabian Hinrichs, Lavinia Wilson, Johan Leysen, Ingeborg Westphal. Prod: Selma Brenner, Chritine Ruppert,Tatfilm.

**CHERI ANU MASALA DAUMTAVREBELI PILMISATVIS
(The Ceiling, or Materials for an Unfinishing Film)**
[Drama, 2003] Script: Rezo Esadze, Rezo Kveselava. Dir: Esadze. Phot: D.Gujabidze. Prod: Merab Tskhakaia for National Centre of Cinematography (NCC).

6 & 7
[Fantasy, 2002] Script and Dir: Geno Tsaava. Phot: Mikheil Mednikov. Players: Gogola Kalandadze, Mikheil Gomiashvili. Prod: NCC.

**COMME UN NUAGE
(Like a Cloud)**
[Drama, 2003] Script and Dir: Mikheil Kobakhidze. Players: Tina Kobakhidze, Cyr Chevalier, Pierre Belot, Patricia Colin, Frederic Lagnau. Prod: Hugues Desmichelles/Parabole S.A.

Two new cinemas have recently opened in Tbilisi, bringing to five the total of theatres in the capital that have the same standards as Western multiplexes. The new Amirani and Rustaveli cinemas immediately became popular hang-outs for Georgian youths, drawn by the latest Hollywood productions, which dominate the box-office (the biggest hits of 2003 were *Tomb Raider 2* and *Pirates of the Caribbean*). In the rest of the country there are a few renovated modern cinemas, including in the seaside resort of Batumi and the high-altitude spa resort of Oni, but the national total is still far below its 1957 peak of 1,000 cinemas.

Arthouse films struggle to gain exhibition but are showcased at the Tbilisi International Film Festival, which in 2003 included three Georgian films alongside works from France, Russia and the rest of eastern Europe. They were Erekle Badurashvili's long-delayed historical drama *One More Georgian History* (*Kidev erti qartuli istoria*; see *IFG 2004*), Rezo Esadze's *The Ceiling, or Materials for an Unfinishing Film* (*Cheri, anu masala daumtavrebeli pilmsatvis*) and Geno Tsaava's *6 & 7*, a mystery in which the director tries to locate a border zone between reality and a dream world. The heroine (played by one of Georgia's most popular actresses, pretty and subtle Gogola Kalandadze) enters a world where time does not exist and the beautiful production design and costumes help to create a fairy tale atmosphere.

Strangers on a tram

Georgian director Dito Tsintsadze's latest German film, **Gun-Shy** (*Schussangst*), winner of the Grand Prix at San Sebastian in 2003, is a drama about Lukas (Fabian Hinrichs), a twentysomething eco-activist who leads an isolated life, only coming into contact with the housebound old people to whom he delivers meals. Then he falls in love with a girl, Isabella (Lavinia Wilson), he meets on a tram and their relationship develops very quickly. With minimalist technique, Tsintsadze creates an atmosphere of despair and emotional crisis and his focus on outsiders is also a critique of modern society.

The biggest surprise of the year was the bittersweet, beautifully made **Since Otar Left** (*Depuis qu'Otar est parti...*) by Julie Bertuccelli, who won the 2004 César for Best First Film. The main characters of this Georgian-language drama are three generations

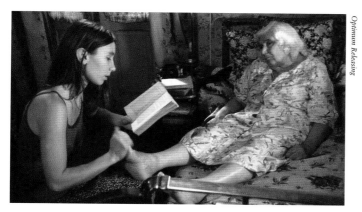

Optimum Releasing

Dinara Droukarova, left, and Esther Gorintin in **Since Otar Left**

of one family who share a flat in Tbilisi: grandma Eka (Esther Gorintin), widowed daughter Marina (Nino Khomassouridze) and granddaughter Ada (Dinara Droukarova). The differences between their mentalities and behaviour are often hilarious.

Eka, who adores Otar, the son who has left to live in Paris, is a Stalinist and at the same time aristocratic, refined. Marina is flexible about principles and a rationalist, but the most vulnerable of the three. Ada, a student, dreams of leaving for a Francophone world. Marina's bitter remark to her boyfriend – "It would be great if I was in love with you" – sums up the essence of the movie. The characters' economically strained lives leave almost no space for romantic feelings.

With **A Gift from Heaven** Dover Kosashvili enjoyed more success at the Israeli box-office. This hilarious tragi-comedy looks at Georgian expatriates in Israel in the early 1970s and, like his arthouse success *Late Marriage* (2001), explores Jewish morals and manners.

The National Centre of Cinematography planned to use its annual subsidy of around $450,000 (900,000 lari) to support seven feature films in 2004, but that left film-makers struggling to find alternative funding for their projects. New DVDs released for local distribution included popular folk comedy *Merry Romance* and classic TV shorts from the 1970s. RUSCICO's continuing reissues of Soviet classics included *Repentance* by Tengiz Abuladze, with films by Aleqsandre Rekhviashvili, Giorgi Shengelaya and Rezo Chkheidze also set for release.

SARKMELI (The Window)
[Drama, 2003] Script: J. Aqimidze, Tina Menabde and Kakha Melitauri. Dir: Menabde, Melitauri. Phot: K. Chelidze. Prod: M. Alavidze/NCC.

PORTRETI (The Portrait)
[Drama, 2003] Script and Dir: G. Ckonia. Phot: T. Erqomaishvili. Prod: T. Glonti/NCC.

MGLIS AGSAREBA (Confession of the Wolf)
[Drama, 2003] Script and Dir: R. Nanaeishvili. Phot: M. Sturua. Prod: Tamaz Laitidze/NCC.

Quote of the Year

"Fear does not exist in nature. We create it ourselves and give it different names."
DITO TSINTSADZE, *director, on the theme of his* Gun-Shy.

Germany Peter Körte

The Year's Best Films

Peter Körte's selection:
Wolfsburg (Christian Petzold)
Head-On (Fatih Akin)
Nightsongs
(Romuald Karmakar)
Kroko (Sylke Enders)
Berlin Blues
(Leander Haussmann)

Peripherfilm

Christian Petzold, director of **Wolfsburg**

Recent and Forthcoming Films

AGNES UND SEINE BRÜDER
(*literally,* **Agnes and
His Brothers**)
*[Drama, 2004] Script and Dir:
Oskar Roehler. Phot: Carl-
Friedrich Koschnik. Players:
Moritz Bleibtreu, Martin Weiss,
Herbert Knaup, Vadim Glowna,
Katja Riemann. Prod: X-Filme
Creative Pool.*

DAS WUNDER VON BERN
(**The Miracle of Bern**)
*[Historical drama, 2003] Script:
Rochus Hahn, Sönke Wortmann.
Dir: Wortmann. Phot: Tom
Fährmann. Players: Louis
Klmaroth, Peter Lohmeyer,
Johanna Gastdorf, Mirko Lang,
Peter Franke, Sascha Göpel.
Prod: Little Shark
Entertainment/Senator Film
Produktion/Seven Pictures.*

When Leninism ruled in Germany for the second time, the outcome was more delightful than in the days of the DDR, bringing good entertainment and box-office gold. No German film for a decade had triggered such intense public debate as Wolfgang Becker's *Good Bye, Lenin!*. It reconciled people in East and West by humorously reenacting their shared recent history. The film's multiple triumphs culminated in Rome in December 2003, when it won three European Film Awards, including Best Film.

In some ways, *Lenin!* was the symbol of a broader cultural pattern, as a new, self-confident generation of writers and film-makers went down memory lane to come to terms with their recent past, in some way closing off the era of 1968 and all that – and accepting, without too much nostalgia, that they had grown up. Leander Haussmann's **Berlin Blues** tackles a similar subject to Becker's film. Based on a novel, it's set in 1989 and depicts a bartender in Kreuzberg, Berlin's then hip neighbourhood, idly living through the years. The day the Wall comes down, he is sitting in a pub watching it on TV and just says: "Better finish your beer first." Haussmann's charming and well-cast film was joined by Hendrik Handloegten's **Learning to Lie** (*liegen lernen*), about a young man trying to finish with his current girlfriend by turning back to his past love. He arrives in Berlin on his mission just as the Wall tumbles, but his private love story overshadows history.

Play It Loud (*Verschwende deine Jugend*), by promising director Benjamin Quabeck, went further back, to the short spring of the German punk and new wave scene in 1980. It's a funny and also somewhat melancholy film about a young bank clerk who tries to put together a big gig for a band and can only pull it off by robbing his bank, eventually recognising that his youth is now over.

Achim von Borries' **Love in Thoughts** (*Was nützt die Liebe in Gedanken*) travelled back to the 1920s for an intense, fatal love story about four young people in Berlin. Based on a true story, with young stars Robert Stadlober and August Diehl giving striking performances, the film was invited to Sundance. Though it was rather old-fashioned and uninspired, Margarethe von Trotta's **The Women of Rosenstrasse** (*Rosenstrasse*), yet another look at Nazi Germany, won Katja Rieman the Best Actress prize at Venice in 2003.

Senator Film

Father and son bond through football in **The Miracle of Bern**

The period piece **The Miracle of Bern** (*Das Wunder von Bern*) recreated a crucial moment in German post-war history: the national soccer team winning the World Cup in 1954. Even Chancellor Schröder attended the premiere and shed tears. Sönke Wortmann's film intertwines a father-son relationship with the upcoming *Wirtschaftswunder*. Having been a soccer professional himself in his early twenties, Wortmann delivers an excellent reenactment of the decisive soccer match, but though sometimes emotionally gripping the connection between family story and soccer is not very subtle and the performances are quite wooden.

Some fresh air came from first films. **Quiet Like a Mouse** (*Muxmäuschenstill*) offers a satirical view of a young philosopher who turns into a self-appointed vigilante. **Kroko** tells the story of a young proletarian Gucci-bitch in Berlin, sentenced to work with handicapped people. The excellently cast **Hierankl** delivers a dark and incestuous renaissance of the old *heimat* films.

Among the documentaries, **The Story of the Weeping Camel** (*Die Geschichte vom weinenden Kamel*), set among nomads in Mongolia, did surprisingly well at the box-office in Germany (and later in the UK, too), and Aelrun Goette's courageous and disturbing **The Children Are Dead** (*Die Kinder sind tod*), based on a true crime story in East Germany, follows a young mother who let her two children die of thirst.

In love and grief

The only film to come close to matching *Lenin!*'s impact was Fatih Akin's **Head-On** (*Gegen die Wand*) – appropriately characterised by a British magazine as "a full-blooded Turkish-Hamburg punk melodrama". Sibel Kekilli and Birol Ünel give stunning performances as a German-Turkish couple who only fall in love for real after marrying to help her escape her traditional family. The film won the Golden Bear at Berlin 2004 and its success confirmed that stories

DER NEUNTE TAG
(*literally,* **The Ninth Day**)
[Historical drama, 2004] Script: Daniel Pflüger, Eberhard Görner. Dir: Volker Schlöndorff. Phot: Tomas Erhart. Players: Ulrich Matthes, August Diehl, Bibiana Beglau, Hilmar Thate. Prod: Provobis.

DIE FETTEN JAHRE SIND VORBEI (The Edukators)
[Drama, 2004] Script: Kathrina Held, Hans Weingartner. Dir: Weingartner. Phot: Daniela Knapp, Matthias Schellenberg. Players: Daniel Brühl, Julia Jentsch, Stipe Erceg, Burghart Klaussner. Prod: Y3 Film (Berlin)/Coop 99 (Vienna).

Julia Jentsch in **The Edukators**

DIE GESCHICHTE VOM WEINENDEN KAMEL
(**The Story of the Weeping Camel**)
[Documentary, 2003] Script and Dir: Byambasuren Davaa, Luigi Falorni. Phot: Falorni. Prod: Hochschule für Film und Fernsehen.

UGC Films UK

The Story of the Weeping Camel

DIE KINDER SIND TOT
(**The Children Are Dead**)
[Documentary, 2003] Script and Dir: Aelrun Goette. Phot: Bernd Meiners. Prod: Zero Film.

DIE NACHT SINGT IHRE LIEDER (Nightsongs)
[Drama, 2004] Script: Martin Rosefeldt. Dir: Romuald Karmakar. Phot: Fred Schuler. Players: Frank Giering, Anne Ratte-Polle, Manfred Zaptaka, Marthe Keller. Prod: Pantera Film/Studio Babelsberg Motion Pictures GmbH.

ERBSEN AUF HALB SECHS (Peas at Half-Past Five)
[Comedy-drama, 2004] Script: Ruth Toma, Lars Büchel. Dir: Büchel. Phot: Judith Kaufmann. Players: Fritzi Haberlandt, Hilmir Snaer Gudnason, Hilmar Schrott, Tina Engel. Prod: Mr Brown Entertainment Filmproduction/Senator Film Produktion.

FARLAND
[Drama, 2004] Script: Undine Damkoehler, Michael Klier. Dir: Klier. Phot: Hans Fromm. Players: Laura Tonke, Richy Müller, Daniel Brühl, Karina Fallenstein. Prod: Zero Film.

GEGEN DIE WAND (Head-On)
[Drama, 2004] Script and Dir: Fatih Akin. Phot: Rainer Klausmann. Players: Birol Ünel, Sibel Kekilli, Catrin Striebeck, Güven Kirac. Prod: Wüste Filmproduktion/Corazon International.

HERR LEHMANN (Berlin Blues)
[Comedy, 2002] Script: Sven Regener. Dir: Leander Haussmann. Phot: Frank Griebe. Players: Christian Ulmen, Detlev W. Buck, Katja Danowski, Tim Fischer. Prod: Boje Buck Produktion.

Delphi Filmverleih

Christian Ulmen in **Berlin Blues**

Kerstin Stelter/WÜSTE Film

German Film Prize winners Birol Ünel and Sibel Kekilli in **Head-On**

from second-generation immigrants can find their market and show what's happening in contemporary Germany. The emotional impact and the raw power of the film-making also convinced audiences.

The arthouse market was dominated by Christian Petzold's **Wolfsburg**, which eventually made its way into theatres after being produced originally for television. It's a story about guilt and remorse, as a man kills a child in a car accident and later falls in love with the grieving mother. Subtly performed, with a cool *mise-en-scène*, it generates enormous emotional heat.

After years of being neglected, Germany finally had a contender in competition at Cannes in 2004. In Austrian director Hans Weingartner's **The Edukators** (*Die fetten Jahre sind vorbei*; see also Austria section), three young rebels who try to "educate" the rich by ravaging their mansions kidnap a victim who surprises them. With no specific political axe to grind, it precisely depicts the general unease of a young generation.

Maverick film-maker Romuald Karmakar's **Nightsongs** (*Die Nacht singt ihre Lieder*), based on a play by Jon Fosse, split audiences. For some it was a typical film you love to hate, for others, like the critic of *Le Monde*, the director was the new hope for German cinema. Karmakar's chamber piece about a young couple with a baby, frozen in their relationship, hurting each other with words, revived the tradition of theatre-film crossover that has been dormant in Germany since Fassbinder.

Banking on "Bully"

Though admissions fell significantly from 163.9 million in 2002 to 149 million in 2003, the year was not all bad. It was marked by a certain ambivalence. A new federal film funding law came into effect on January 1, 2004, designed to guarantee economic consolidation. Movie theatres, public and private television and home video companies are now obliged to pay a higher annual contribution to the film industry, and the position of the FFA, Germany's only federal film funding institution, has been strengthened. Additional funding for films will no longer only depend on their box-office results, but also on their participation in international festivals.

A new German film academy has been founded. Its main goal is to build a real home for the film industry, as academies and institutes in other countries have done for decades. After some negotiations, the government finally agreed that the academy would not only host the annual German Film Awards, but also replace the former, government-appointed awards jury. The academy will dispense the €3m prize fund (the biggest cultural awards in Germany), which must be invested in new films. Some professionals and commentators fear the new academy might lean too heavily towards mainstream pictures and ignore arthouse work.

The question of how good a year 2004 would turn out to be was always going to be answered by the performance of one home-made summer blockbuster, and Michael "Bully" Herbig's **(T)Raumschiff Surprise – Period 1** surpassed expectations with 3.4 million admissions in its first week, the best result ever in German cinema, and a gross of more than $55m after five weeks (more than double the take for *Spider-Man 2*). The *Star Trek* parody follows the recipe of Herbig's previous smash, *Manitou's Shoe*, by spoofing a well-known pop culture form with unsubtle but always punchline-aware comedy, appealing to older viewers who remember the original and to youngsters who enjoy pure fun.

The Downfall – Hitler and the End of the Third Reich (*Der Untergang*), the Bernd Eichinger-produced and written film on Hitler's last days, which opened in mid-September, was one of the most expensive German films of recent decades with a budget of

Constantin Film

Juliane Köhler (Eva Braun), Bruno Ganz (Hitler) and Heino Ferch (Speer) in **The Downfall**

HIERANKL
[Drama, 2003] Script and Dir: Sebastian Steinbichler. Phot: Bella Halben. Players: Josef Bierbichler, Johanna Wokalek, Barbara Sukowa, Peter Simonischek, Frank Giering. Prod: Avista Film.

KROKO
[Comedy-drama, 2003] Script and Dir: Sylke Enders. Phot: Matthias Schellenberg, Katrin Vorderwühlbecke. Players: Franziska Jünger, Hinnerk Schönemann, Alexander Lange. Prod: Luna-Film.

LAUTLOS (Soundless)
[Thriller, 2004] Script: Lars-Olaf Beier. Dir: Mennan Yapo. Phot: Torsten Lippstock. Players: Joachim Król, Nadja Uhl, Christian Berkel, Lisa Martinek, Peter Fitz. Prod: X-Filme Creative Pool.

LIEGEN LERNEN
(Learning to Lie)
[Comedy-drama, 2003] Script and Dir: Hendrik Handloegten. Phot: Florian Hoffmeister. Players: Fabian Busch, Fritzi Haberlandt, Susanne Bormann, Sophie Rois, Florian Lukas. Prod: X-Filme Creative Pool.

LICHTER (Distant Lights)
[Drama, 2003] Script: Hans-Christian Schmid, Michael Gutmann. Dir: Schmid. Phot: Bogumil Godfrejow. Players: Devid Striesow, Maria Simon, Alice Dwyer, August Diehl, Herbert Knaup.

MUXMÄUSCHENSTILL
(Quiet Like a Mouse)
[Comedy, 2004] Script: Jan-Henrik Stahlberg. Dir: Marcus Mittermeier. Phot: David Hofmann. Players: Stahlberg, Fritz Roth, Wanda Perdelwitz. Prod: Schiwago Film.

SCHULTZE GETS THE BLUES
[Comedy, 2003] Script and Dir: Michael Schorr. Phot: Axel Schneppat. Players: Horst Krause, Harald Warmbrunn, Karl Fred Müller. Prod: Filmkombinat.

**(T)RAUMSCHIFF SURPRISE –
PERIOD 1** (*literally*, **Spaceship
Surprise – Period 1**)
[Star Trek parody, *2004] Script:
Michael "Bully" Herbig, Alfons
Biedermann, Rick Kavanian. Dir:
Herbig. Phot: Stephan Schuh.
Players: Rick Kavanian,
Christian Tramitz, Til Schweiger,
Herbig. Prod: Bavaria Film.*

ROSENSTRASSE
(The Women of Rosenstrasse)
*[Historical drama, 2002] Script
and Dir: Margarethe von Trotta.
Phot: Franz Rath. Players: Maria
Schrader, Katja Riemann, Juergen
Vogel. Prod: Meyer Film/Get Reel
(Netherlands)/Studio Hamburg.*

DER UNTERGANG
**(The Downfall – Hitler and the
End of the Third Reich)**
*[Historical drama, 2003] Script:
Bernd Eichinger. Dir: Oliver
Hirschbiegel. Phot: Rainer
Klausmann. Players: Bruno
Ganz, Alexandra Maria Ladra,
Juliane Köhler, Ulrich Noethen,
Corinna Harfouch, Daniel Brühl.
Prod: Constantin Productions.*

**VERSCHWENDE DEINE
JUGEND (Play It Loud!)**
*[Comedy-drama, 2003] Script:
Ralf Hertwig, Kathrin Richter.
Dir: Benjamin Quabeck. Phot:
David Schultz. Players: Tom
Schilling, Robert Stadlober,
Jessica Schwarz, Denis
Moschitto. Prod: Claussen &
Wöbke Filmproduktion.*

**WAS NÜTZT DIE LIEBE IN
GEDANKEN (Love in Thoughts)**
*[Drama, 2004] Script: Annette
Hess, Hendrik Handloegten.
Dir: Achim von Borries. Phot:
Players: Daniel Brühl, August
Diehl, Thure Lindhardt, Jana
Pallaske. Prod: X-Filme Creative
Pool.*

WOLFSBURG
*[Drama, 2003] Script and Dir:
Christian Petzold. Phot: Hans
Fromm. Players: Benno
Fürmann, Nina Hoss, Antje
Westermann, Astrid Meyerfeldt;
Matthias Matschke. Prod:
teamWorx Televison & Film.*

€14.5m. Bruno Ganz gives a striking performance as Hitler, supported by an A-list cast of German talent, and director Oliver Hirschbiegel is always crosscutting between the claustrophobic atmosphere in the *Führerbunker* and the fights in the streets of Berlin.

The film tries – not always convincingly – to give the monster a human face by telling the story mostly from the perspective of Hitler's secretary, Traudl Junge. By October, *The Downfall* had taken more than $18m at German cinemas and been sold to more than 25 territories, but even with this success, and new films by Volker Schlöndorff, Oskar Roehler and Michael Klier due in the fourth quarter, it was *(T)Raumschiff* alone that made the industry dream of a happy 2004.

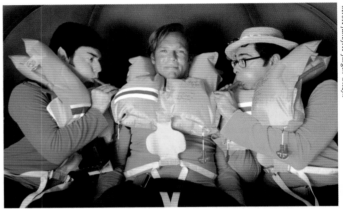

*Left to right: Michael "Bully" Herbig (Mr Spuck), Christian Tramitz (Käpt'n Kork)
and Rick Kavanian (Schrotty) in* **(T)Raumschiff Surprise – Period 1**

PETER KÖRTE (p.koerte@faz.de) is a cultural editor of the *Frankfurter Allgemeine Sonntagszeitung* in Berlin, and the author of books on Humphrey Bogart, Quentin Tarantino, the Coen Brothers and Hedy Lamarr.

Correction
In the Germany report
in *IFG 2004*, the still
from *Angst* (p.147)
shows Andre Hennicke,
not Ben Becker.

Quote of the Year

"Everybody feels offended all the time, because he gets no money or no prizes or no distributor. That makes me sick to my stomach. You cannot always put the blame on somebody else."

BERND EICHINGER, *producer,
at a German Film Academy
meeting entitled "What I Hate
About German Film".*

German Film Prizes 2004

Film: *Head-On*.
Documentary: *The Children Are Dead*.
Actress: Sibel Kekilli (*Head-On*).
Actor: Birol Ünel (*Head-On*).
Supporting Actress: Fritzi Haberlandt (*Learning to Lie*).
Supporting Actor: Detlev W. Buck (*Berlin Blues*).
Director: Fatih Akin (*Head-On*).
Screenplay (Filmed): Sven Regener (*Berlin Blues*).
Screenplay (Unfilmed): Marei Gerken (*The Far Side of the Sea*).
Cinematography: Rainer Klausmann (*Head-On*).
Editing: Sarah Clara Weber (*Quiet Like a Mouse*).

Part of the award-winning production design for **Schultze Gets the Blues**

Music: Dirk Reichardt and Stefan Hansen (*Peas at Half-Past Five*).
Production Design: Natascha E. Tagwerk (*Schultze Gets the Blues*).

Prize of Honour: Mario Adorf.
Audience Award (German Film): *The Miracle of Bern*.
Foreign Film: *Lost in Translation* (Sofia Coppola).

Phil Nijhuis

Dutch film-maker THEO VAN GOGH, above, was murdered in Amsterdam on November 2, 2004. He was 47. IFG Netherlands correspondent Pieter van Lierop, who describes van Gogh's life and death on p.220, writes: "His body of work as a film-maker was as loud and uneven as the man himself – though always interesting. Day at the Beach *(1984),* Terug Naar Oegstgeest *(1987),* Blind Date *(1996) and* Interview *(2003) were among his finest achievements."*

Meet the production executives in Greece

75 Feature Films
14 TV series
20 Documentaries
7 Productions for Cultural Olympiad
300 events took place within the scope of the "Herodes Atticus"
Theater Festival and the "Ancient Epidaurus" Theater Festival,
in summers 2002, 2003, 2004

The "Acropolis Millennium Show"

International co-productions
"Brides", a film by Pantelis Voulgaris
Executive producer: Martin Scorseze
"Trilogy: The weeping Meadow", a film by Theo Angelopoulos

+ Opening & Closing ceremony
Of the Olympic Games 2004 in Athens
Major associate of the JACK MORTON Public Events

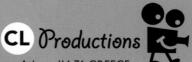

65 Vrilissou st, Poligono, Athens 114 76 GREECE
T. 0030 2106412700 F. 0030 2106412709
M: info@clproductions.gr W. www.clproductions.gr

Espresso Studio

Greece Yannis Bacoyannopoulos

The Year's Best Films

Yannis Bacoyannopoulos'
selection:

Eyes of Night
(Pericles Hoursoglou)

The Way to the West
(Kyriakos Katzourakis)

Trilogy The Weeping Meadow
(Theo Angelopoulos)

To the Inn (Giorgos Bakolas)

Totally Married
(Dimitris Indares)

Recent and
Forthcoming films

[In Production credits, GFC
indicates Greek Film Centre]

I SKONI POU PEFTI (Dust)
*[Drama, 2004] Script and Dir:
Tassos Psarras. Phot: Nikos
Kavoukidis. Players: Sophocles
Peppas, Themis Bazaka, Giorgos
Armenis, Marika Tziralidou,
Thodoros Boyiadjis, Katia Yerou,
Emily Koliandri, Anestis Vlachos.
Prod: GFC/Hellenic Broadcasting
Corp. ERT S.A./Nikos
Kavoukidis/Screenladia s.r.o.
Praha Chez/Tassos Psarras.*
Chronis, a successful journalist
in his fifties, living an orderly and
conventional life in Athens, sees
in a documentary on the civil war
a man who looks like his father,
fighting for the rebels. Since his
father was presumed dead while
serving in the national army, Chronis
begins an exhaustive investigation.

Greek Film Centre

Katia Yeron in **Dust**

The recent steady increase in production volume and a huge increase in total attendance for domestic films could lead to bursts of euphoria in the Greek industry, but this would be a deluded reaction. The increase in production was the result of the systematic use of DV cameras in low-budget films, often with poor visual aesthetics. The increase in audience stemmed solely from the phenomenal success of *A Touch of Spice*, with 1.3 million admissions.

With the exception of Stamatis Tsarouchas' **The Valiants of Samothrace** (*I yenei tis Samothrakis*), a farcical comedy about the adventures of a military unit stationed on a remote Greek island, which garnered 140,000 admissions, the 'hits', including Theo Angelopoulos' *Trilogy – The Weeping Meadow*, covered a span of between 20,000 and 120,000 admissions. Unfortunately, several of the better award-winning films met with audience indifference (between 1,000 and 10,000 admissions).

Once again audiences flocked to American productions. The multiplexes continued to spread, particularly to previously 'barren' country towns. They are increasingly linked to other forms of entertainment and are meeting points for young people. *The Return of the King* and *Troy* dominated the box-office in 2004. A much smaller, discriminating audience once again singled out remarkable films from the rest of the world, including *Dogville*, *Good Bye, Lenin!*, *21 Grams* and, very belatedly, *Atanarjuat, the Fast Runner*.

Greek Film Centre

The lovers flee their flooded village in **Trilogy – The Weeping Meadow**

The first part of Theo Angelopoulos' long-awaited, **Trilogy – The Weeping Meadow** (*To livadi pou dakirizi*), is a summing up of his cinematic art and of modern Greek history. In 1919, Greek refugees from Odessa arrive in Macedonia and settle in a lakeside village. It's a difficult life, which hits a crisis when the love of a boy and the lost girl his family took in as a child clashes with his father's love for her and we see the neverending flight of the young couple.

This deep-seated conflict with traditional patriarchy attains the bounds of timeless social conflict. The new, the healthy, the honest, the progressive constantly clash with the rigid structures of conservatism and the turbulent history of modern Greece up to the middle of the twentieth century, racked by civil and other wars. Angelopoulos also retraces his own successive themes, his obsessions and his stylistic artistry, constantly charging his evocative images and balancing between epic retrospection and drawn-out melancholy elegy.

Boulmetis' perfect recipe

At the other end of the scale, Tassos Boulmetis' smash hit **A Touch of Spice** (*Politiki kouzina*) is a clear vote of confidence from Greek society and constitutes the closest example of a Greek film made with the mentality of American cinema. A lavish production, filmed in 70mm, it couples a political-historical theme with memories of culinary pleasures and unfulfilled childhood loves. The yearning for the lost homeland of Constantinople (Istanbul) among Greeks forced to leave by the Turks, despite international treaties, touched a sensitive chord. The reference to their extraordinary culinary tradition and the return of the hero to Constantinople, where he meets his childhood love for the last time, add charm and tender drama as real-life experiences are retold with glossy affectation.

Village Roadshow

Traditional Greek cuisine is at the heart of **A Touch of Spice**

DELIVERY
[Drama, 2004] Script: Nikos Panayotopoulos, Michel Fais. Dir: Panayotopoulos. Phot: Costis Gikas. Players: Thanos Samaras, Alexia Kaltsiki, Dimitris Imelos, Errikos Litsis, Spyros Stavranidis, Fotini Baxevani, Christos Loulis, Angela Brouskou, Vassilis Andreou, Nikos Kordonis. Prod: GFC/Marianna Films/New Star/Graal S.A./Hellenic Broadcasting Corp. ERT S.A.
A young pizza delivery boy experiences the reality of the megacity that is modern Athens, meeting the homeless, immigrants and others whom even God appears to have forgotten. Competed at Venice in 2004.

Greek Film Centre

Alexia Kaltsiki in **Delivery**

HERETA MAS TON PLATANO
[Drama, 2004] Script and Dir: Dimitris Makris. Phot: Akis Safaris. Players: Betty Valassi, Dimitra Hatoupi, Panayotis Filipeos, Panos Kranidiotis, Vana Zakka, Makis Papadimitratos, Maria Constantaki, Michalis Enatzoglou, Eleni Tzortzi, Makis Arvanitakis, Ioakim Enatzoglou, Costas Darlassis. Prod: GFC/Dimitris Makris.
Four months in the life of young Makis: from New Year's Eve 1967 to Easter Sunday, 1968, and the first anniversary of the "National Rebirth", when, according to the Colonels, "Greece was resurrected". Makis lives with his grandmother and father (an admirer of dictator Papadopoulos) in a working-class Athens suburb. Through his eyes we see the adult world of intrigue, joy and conflicts.

2004

THE YEAR
of Greece

GREEK FILM CENTRE
10, PANEPISTIMIOU AVE., 106 71 ATHENS, GREECE
TEL.: (+30 210) 3648.007, 3678.500 - FAX: (+30 210) 3614.336
e-mail:info@gfc.gr   www.gfc.gr

Pericles Hoursoglou delivered powerful, realistic drama with **Eyes of Night** (*Matia apo nichta*). The slow-burning romance between a truck driver (Yannis Karatzoyannis) and a working middle-aged woman (Vangelio Andreadaki), desperate to have a child, becomes explosive when a lost young girl comes between them. The outcome is unexpectedly bold, but justified. The director's methods are acutely observational and low-key, building up human tension and sudden clashes through a strong screenplay, and the drama relies on the excellent balance between instinct, weakness and free will.

Yannis Karatzoyannis and Vangelio Andreadaki fall in love in **Eyes of Night**

Girogos Bakolas' first film, **To the Inn** (*Hani*), shows remarkable maturity as regards substance and style. The film-maker revives the atmosphere and ethos of rural life in Turkish-occupied Greece, circa 1900, the primitive savagery but also the deep-rooted religiousness. Two young men attempt to escape on horseback towards the civilised West after committing a crime for money, and they meet their fate in an inn in the forest. The film follows the style of old narrators and makes constant reference to the metaphysics of human responsibility and guilt.

In the comedy **Totally Married** (*Gamilia narki*), Dimitris Indares handles the subject of modern urban life in Athens and the emotional problems of a young working couple, with accuracy, tenderness and grace. Two male friends and the wife of one (once the other friend's lover) face dramatic existential conflicts and love choices and the couple face a crisis as a beautiful immigrant comes between them.

Finally, Kyriakos Katzourakis made a very important contribution to the field of the drama-documentary with **The Way to the West**, which gives voice to the illegal immigrants (Russians, Bulgarians, Pakistanis) who struggle to survive in today's Greece or continue their journey towards other developed countries. The imagery is

ALITHINI ZOI (Real Life)
[Drama, 2002] Script: Panos Koutras, Panos Evangelidis. Dir: Koutras. Phot: Elias Konstantakopoulos. Players: Nikos Kouris, Themis Bazaka, Marina Kaloyirou, Anna Mouglalis, Maria Panourgia, Odysseas Papaspiliopoulos, Yannis Diamandis. Prod: GFC/ Argonaut S.A. – Program 33/Hellenic Broadcasting Corp. ERT S.A./Strada Productions/ Filmnet/PPV S.A./STAR TV.
Aris is young, handsome, rich. He returns to Athens after a long period in detox abroad, determined to steer clear of his old life while also trying to shed light on his forgotten childhood and remember his father, who died under mysterious circumstances while Aris was still a child. He meets and falls madly in love with Alexandra, a beautiful, penniless fashion student, but his old girlfriend, Joy, drags him into his old habits.

AGAPE STA 16 (Love at 16)
[Drama, 2004] Script and Dir: Costas Haralambous. Phot: Katerina Marangoudaki. Players: Giorgios Gerontidakis, Betty Vallasi, Vassilis Andreopoulos, Dina Michailidou, Antonis Loudaros, Petros Xekoukis, Stelios Kalathas. Prod: GFC/Hellenic Broadcasting Corp. ERT S.A./AB SEAHORSE Ltd. (Cyprus)/Betty Valassi/ Costas Haralambous/FILMNET/NOVA.
Magazines and TV shows such as *Charlie's Angels* and *Happy Days* influence the daily life and characters of teenagers in a village in the 1980s.

Giorgios Gerontidakis in **Love at 16**

MARATHON

[Drama, 2004] Script: Antonis Kokkinos, Costas Koronidis. Dir: Kokkinos. Phot: Costis Gikas. Players: Yannis Kokiasmenos, Maria Zorba, Sylvia Venizelea, Eleana Tachiaou, Stella Kazazi, Emilia Valvi, Giorgos Giannopoulos, Michalis Goussis. Prod: GFC/Thalassa S.A.

A man reaches emotional dead-ends in his relationships with women as he tries to train the Greek marathon champion for the 2004 Olympics.

METEORITES (Meteors)

[Drama, 2004] Script and Dir: Yannis Mavrogenis. Phot: Giorgos Argiroiliopoulos. Players: Michalis Iatropoulos, Markella Yannatou, Yannis Bostantzoglou, Vangelis Mourikis, Marilee Mastrantoni, Costas Baras, Kalliopi Takaki, Ektoras Kaloudis. Prod: GFC/S.M. Art Media.

A remote bay with a deserted canteen is the ideal observation post from which to watch a meteor shower, but a flasher is on the prowl and the case is assigned to an ace cop who is very close to solving another difficult case that is sure to get him a promotion. A troubled woman, pursued by a hysterical homosexual, enters the story.

NYFES (Brides)

[Drama, 2004] Script: Ioanna Karystiani. Dir: Pantelis Voulgaris. Phot: Giorgos Arvanitis. Players: Damian Lewis, Victoria Charalambidou, Andrea Ferreol, Evi Saoulidou, Dimitris Katalifos, Steven Berkoff. Prod: Cappa Productions/ Alco Films/Cinegram SA./GFC/CL Productions/K.G. Productions/ Alpha Tv/Lexicon/Filmnet.

Summer, 1922. American photographer Norman Harris (Lewis) is returning home from Asia Minor. Also on board are a spinster chaperoning orphans, a famous fortune-teller and 700 mail-order brides from Greece, Romania, Russia, Turkey and Armenia. Norman wants to

devastating (Katzourakis is a distinguished painter), as are the sound and music, and the director interposes a written monologue performed by an actress and attributed to a Russian who kills herself. He orchestrates everything with skill, dynamism, humanity and lyricism.

YANNIS BACOYANNOPOULOS has written about film since 1960 in many newspapers and books. He was film critic of the Athens daily *Kathimerini* (1974-2003), and since 1975 has been a critic for the Hellenic Broadcasting Corporation.

photograph them and falls in love with one, Niki (Charalambidou), a seamstress. Premiered at Toronto in 2004.

TO PERASMA (The Crossing)

[Drama, 2004] Script: Thanassis Scroubelos, Dimitris Stavrakas. Dir: Stavrakas. Phot: Vangelis Kalambakas. Players: Safiulach Bari Adam, Hasna Banu Eti, Thanos Grammenos, Costas Xykominos, Erikkos Litsis, Hilda Iliopoulou. Prod: GFC/Sarmasik Sanatlar/Baran Seyhan-Jale Onanc (Turkey).

Young lovers Jahid and Jasmine try to make a life for themselves in difficult circumstances in a village in Bangladesh. Jahid leaves to try his luck elsewhere and, after a series of adventures, reaches Athens. When the police deport him he returns home to many unpleasant surprises.

TO POULI TOU PARADISSOU (The Bird of Paradise)

[Drama, 2004] Script: Petros Hadzopoulos, George Panoussopoulos. Dir and Phot: Panoussopoulos. Players: Betty Livanou, Dimitra Matsouka, Natalia Dragoumi, Katy Papanika, Maria Zorba, Vangelio Andreadaki, Dimitris Liakopoulos. Prod: GFC/Graal S.A.

Petros, a sailor on his first shore leave, is forced to return to his island for a day, where he starts finding all the women around him attractive. Strangely, they succumb to his advances.

TO ONIRO TOU SKILOU (The Dog's Dream)

[Drama, 2004] Script and Dir: Angelos Frantzis. Phot: Evgenios Dionyssopoulos. Players: Constantinos Markoulakis, Peggy Trikalioti, Aris Servetalis, Lina Sakka, Christos Stergioglou, Markos Lezes, Argyris Xafis, Fotini Baxevani, Evangelia Samiotaki. Prod: GFC/C.L. Productions.

One night in Athens. A man hears a work colleague describe a dream of a strange robbery, and returns home to find that his belongings have been stolen in an equally strange manner. As an experienced cop tries to solve the case by unorthodox means, the mystery spreads.

OUTOPIA (Utopia)

[Drama, 2004] Script: S. Valoukos, N. Kanakis. Dir: Giorgos Karypidis. Phot: Lefteris Paavlopoulos. Players: Takis Spyridakis, Niki Pallikaraki, Themis Panou, Arto Apartian, Anna Makraki, Rania Brilaki, Maria Katsanari, Elias Asproulis. Prod: GFC/Kanakis.

Greece, the future. Hector and Anna discover a common, dark past linked to extreme political situations.

RAKUSHKA (Life Is Elsewhere)

[Drama, 2004] Script and Dir: Fotini Siskopoulou. Phot: Tassos Zafiropoulos. Players: Constantinos Kalokerinos, Milana Yussupova, Irina Boiko, Vangelis Mourikis, Dorothea Nikiporczyk, Gennadios Patsis. Prod: GFC/Vlassis.

Stathoulias/Fotini Siskopoulou. Vassilis, a lawyer-turned-pawnbroker, picks up from the airport his Russian mother-in-law, who has come for the funeral of her 18-year-old daughter, who has committed suicide. During the wake, Vassilis, tries to explain the sudden death of his wife, a cellist, forcing himself to dredge up painful memories and humiliating confessions.

INE O THEOS MAYIRAS
(Like Chef, Like God)
[Comedy, 2004] Script: Stergios Niziris, Vassilis Raissis. Dir: Niziris. Phot: Spyros Papatriantafylou. Players: Giorgos Karamichos, Giorgos Nakos, Theodora Tzimou, Alexia Kaltsiki, Ioanna Tsirigouli, Eftichia Pakoumi. Prod: GFC/Niziris.
Vassilis changes jobs and wanders around the streets observing women. His light-hearted and humorous disposition diminishes when he discovers his talent for cooking, joins a semi-secret chefs' club and starts searching for the perfect dish and the perfect woman.

ALEMAYA
[Drama, 2004] Script and Dir: Elias Yannakakis. Phot: Giorgos Argiroiliopoulos. Players: Dimitris Katalifos, Yvonne Maltezou, Ekavi Douma, John Dritsas, Panayotis Thanassoulis, Michelle Valley, Thanos Samaras, Anna Mascha, Rania Economidou. Prod: GFC/Yannakakis.
The Greek community in Ethiopia, 1960. Isabella grows up like a princess in a closed, affluent society. When she is 18, Dimitris falls madly in love with her, but when her father opposes the relationship their plan to elope to Lake Alemaya is foiled and Isabella is "exiled" to Greece where she marries and has two children. Thirty-five years later, Dimitris, sick with diabetes, rents an apartment opposite Isabella's now rundown family home.

Quotes of the Year

"Greek cinema might have told us for yet another year: 'I have the best of intentions but I am incapable of realising them.'"
CHRISTOS MITSIS, *film critic.*

"What grade would I give my sense of humour? I would give it an 'A'. I look at myself in the mirror, apply face cream and mutter: 'What a waste of money.'"
MARTHA KARAYANNI, *sex bomb of the Greek movies of the 1970s.*

Hong Kong Tim Youngs

The Year's Best Films

Tim Youngs' selection:
Running on Karma
(Johnnie To, Wai Ka-fai)
One Nite in Mongkok
(Derek Yee)
Love Battlefield (Soi Cheang)
Men Suddenly in Black
(Pang Ho-cheung)
Herbal Tea (Herman Yau)

Niki Chow in **Love Battlefield**

Recent and Forthcoming Films

A-1 TAU TIN (A-1)
[Thriller, 2004] Script and Dir:
Gordon Chan, Chung Kai-
cheong. Players: Lee Sinje,
Anthony Wong, Edison Chen,
Gordon Lam. Prod: Panorama.

LUNG FUNG DAU
(Yesterday Once More)
[Drama, 2004] Script: The
Hermit, Au Kin-yee. Dir: Johnnie
To and Wai Ka-fai. Players: Andy
Lau, Sammi Cheng. Prod: Media
Asia/Sil-Metropole.

GUNG JIU FOOK SAU GEI
(Beyond Our Ken)
[Drama, 2004] Script: Pang Ho-
cheung, Wong Wing-sze. Dir:
Pang Ho-cheung. Players: Gillian
Chung, Tao Hong, Daniel Wu.
Prod: Making Film/Mei Ah Film

Hong Kong's film-making community was hoping for a brighter year after a continued slump in productions during 2003 and the first half of 2004. Only 77 local movies reached cinemas in 2003, down from 92 in 2002, reflecting the slowdown caused by the SARS health crisis. Although the release schedule rebounded with summer hits like local vampire slayer blockbuster *The Twins Effect* and an upbeat run moving into early 2004, the pace lost steam after Easter 2004, against stiff competition from Hollywood big-hitters.

The drop in output did not prevent local directors from raising the quality bar with challenging and entertaining fare. The standout in 2003 was Johnnie To and Wai Ka-fai's fascinating **Running on Karma** (*Dai jek lo*). In a radical departure from the co-directors' high-season comedy successes, they crafted a bravura mainstream hit based around karma. Packaging a difficult topic alongside police action, the supernatural, martial arts and a marketing-friendly prosthetic muscle suit for leading man Andy Lau, *Running on Karma* was intelligent and thought-provoking viewing.

Director To separately continued his acclaimed work in the crime genre with 2004's **Breaking News** (*Dai si gin*), a high-concept siege thriller in which the police and a heavily-armed gang play media games with each other. He quickly followed *Breaking News* with **Throw Down** (*Yau dou lung fu bong*), a quirky and highly stylised judo-themed affair that paid tribute to Akira Kurosawa. Late in 2003, *Infernal Affairs* (a huge hit in 2002) spawned the colourful prequel **Infernal Affairs II** (*Mou gan do II*), which took viewers

Andy Lau wears a muscle suit in **Running on Karma**

back to flesh out characters from the first film and introduce other key players, and then the sequel **Infernal Affairs III** (*Mou gan do III*), which brought back the first film's lead actors in lengthy flashbacks, and added intrigue with shady new characters (and outperformed *II* at the box-office).

Yee's *Nite* owls

Derek Yee contributed a landmark crime drama, **One Nite in Mongkok** (*Wong gok hak yeh*). Set largely over a single night, and drawing first-rate performances from stars Daniel Wu, Cecilia Cheung and Alex Fong, Yee's movie followed policemen on a breathtaking race to quell a gangland flare-up in the city's most crowded district. Soi Cheang departed from his string of successful horror movies with a crime thriller, **Love Battlefield** (*Oi jok sin*). Buoyed by Cheang's tense atmospherics, it pitched a couple on the verge of a break-up into a tangle with drug runners who initially steal their car. Stars Niki Chow and Eason Chan excelled alongside mainland actors Qin Hailu and Wang Zhiwen as the drama brewed towards an uncompromising romantic finale.

Cecilia Cheung and Daniel Wu in **One Nite in Mongkok**

After several nostalgic productions in 2002, some dramatic works in late 2003 investigated the process of moving on – an attractive post-SARS topic amid ongoing economic woes. Derek Yee's uplifting **Lost in Time** (*Mong but liu*) saw a young woman (Cecilia Cheung) lose her fiancé, take over his job as a minibus driver and cling to the past by speaking to his phone answering service. When she befriends a fellow driver (Lau Ching-wan) she finally moves on. The lead pair's performances prompted strong word-of-mouth. Similar themes turned up in Carol Lai's mainland-set **The Floating Landscape** (*Luen ji fung ging*), in which a Hong Kong girl heads north searching for the landscape drawn by her dead boyfriend but instead finds closure.

Nostalgia managed to crop up in Wai Ka-fai's crazed comedy, **Fantasia** (*Gwai ma kong seung kuk*), inspired by audience favourites of the 1970s and 1980s, with stars Lau Ching-wan, Cecilia Cheung and Louis Koo reworking material chock full of pop

Production/ *Beijing Jinyingma Movie.*

SIU BAK LUNG
(**The White Dragon**)
[*Action, 2004*] *Script: Wilson Yip, Law Yiu-fai. Dir: Yip. Players: Cecilia Cheung, Francis Ng, Andy On. Prod: One Hundred Years of Film/China Star.*

SUN GING CHAK GOO SI
(**New Police Story**)
[*Action, 2004*] *Script: Alan Yuen. Dir: Benny Chan. Players: Jackie Chan, Charlie Young, Daniel Wu, Charlene Choi, Nicolas Tse. Prod: JCE Movies.*

AH MA YAU LAN
(**Leave Me Alone**)
[*Action comedy, 2004*] *Script: Danny Pang, Sam Lung, Curran Pang. Dir: Danny Pang. Players: Ekin Cheng, Charlene Choi, Chapman To. Prod: Universe.*

SUN GIU YUK GWAI
(**The Attractive One**)
[*Comedy, 2004*] *Script: Matt Chow, Lau Ho-leung. Dir: Chow. Players: Lau Ching-wan, Joey Yung, Chapman To, Yumiko Cheng. Prod: One Hundred Years of Film/China Star.*

WU DIP (**Butterfly**)
[*Drama, 2004*] *Script and Dir: Yan Yan Mak. Players: Josie Ho, Tian Yuan, Isabel Chan, Eric Kot, Joman. Prod: Lotus Film/Filmko.*

SAM CHA HAU (**Divergence**)
[*Action drama, 2004*] *Script: Ivy Ho. Dir: Benny Chan. Players: Aaron Kwok, Daniel Wu, Ekin Cheng. Prod: Universe.*

2046
[*Drama, 2004*] *Script and Dir: Wong Kar-wai. Players: Tony Leung Chiu-wai, Gong Li, Faye Wong, Takuya Kimura, Zhang Ziyi, Carina Lau, Chang Chen, Maggie Cheung. Prod: Jet Tone.*

TIM SI SI (**My Sweetie**)
[*Comedy, 2004*] *Script and Dir: Yip Nim-sum. Players: Sammy Leung, Stephy Tang, Gaile Lok. Prod: Mei Ah/Gold Label.*

SEI MONG SEH JUN
(Ab-normal Beauty)
*[Thriller, 2004] Script: Oxide
Pang, Curran Pang. Dir: Oxide
Pang. Players: Roseanne Wong,
Race Wong. Prod: Universe.*

JEH BING (Set To Kill)
*[Action, 2004] Script: Tai Tak-
kong. Dir: Marco Mak. Players:
Raymond Wong, Johnny Lo,
Ning Jing, Marco Lok, Isabel
Chan. Prod: S&W
Entertainment/China Star.*

BAU LIT DOU SI
(Explosive City)
*[Action 2004] Script: Sam Leong,
Paul Chung. Dir: Leong. Players:
Simon Yam, Alex Fong, Hisako
Shirata, Sonny Chiba, Edwin Siu,
Crystal Kwok. Prod: Same
Way/Art Port.*

TAU MAN JI D (Initial D)
*[Action, 2004] Dir: Andrew Lau,
Alan Mak. Players: Jay Chou,
Edison Chen, Anne Suzuki,
Anthony Wong, Chapman To,
Jordan Chan. Prod: Media Asia.*

Quote of the Year

"Nowadays, without
mainland China, Hong Kong
would hardly make any films."

JOSEPH LAI, *Vice-Chairman
of the Movie Producers' and
Distributors' Association of
Hong Kong, on the increase
in co-production.*

The 23rd Hong Kong
Film Awards

Best Film: *Running on Karma.*
Best Director: Johnnie To Kei-
fung (*PTU*).
Best Screenplay: Wai Ka-fai, Yau
Nai-hoi, Au Kin-yee, Yip Tin-sing
(*Running on Karma*).
Best Actor: Andy Lau Tak-wah
(*Running on Karma*).
Best Actress: Cecilia Cheung
Pak-chi (*Lost in Time*).
Best Supporting Actor: Tony
Leung Ka-fai (*Men Suddenly
in Black*).
Best Supporting Actress: Josie
Ho Chiu-Yi (*Naked Ambition*).

Eric Tsang, front, in **Men Suddenly in Black**

culture references and an uplifting sensibility. Promising young
director Pang Ho-cheung's **Men Suddenly in Black** (*Dai jeung foo*)
borrowed gangster genre conventions for a clever black comedy
about foolhardy men who find themselves free for a day and stage
elaborate plans to snare women across the territory, not realising
that their savvy wives are on their tails.

Herman Yau blended sentimentality and warm humour in two offbeat comedies. In **Herbal Tea** (*Lam seung lui ha*), one of the most
unexpected charmers of 2004, Yau infused a low-budget production
centred on a teashop with a cheery district community spirit, while
Papa Loves You (*Jeh gor ah ba jung bau ja lit*) was a paean to a
parent's love within a cheery send-up of gangland bluster.

The huge success of Dante Lam's **The Twins Effect** (*Chin gei bin*)
in summer 2003, taking in $3.6m (HK$28.4m), highlighted the
continued appeal of lead actresses and pop sensations Twins
(Charlene Choi and Gillian Chung), while enlivening the action genre
for younger audiences as local heroes save the world from Western
vampires raising hell in Hong Kong. A name-only sequel, the Corey
Yuen and Patrick Leung-directed **The Twins Effect II** (*Chin gei bin II*),
followed a year later to less success. Chung and Choi returned,
but the enjoyably choreographed battles of the first *Twins Effect*
were replaced by less appealing period fantasy.

Among a reduced number of horror productions, Fruit Chan's
Dumplings... Three – Extremes (*Gau ji: Sam gan ji*) hit cinemas as
an extended cut from pan-Asian horror omnibus *Three – Extremes*.
An adults-only, low-key feature about a middle-aged celebrity eating
aborted foetuses to regain her youthful looks, it moved star Miriam
Yeung into darker territory than her normal lightweight fare.

Cross-border partnerships

Positive developments have come through Hong Kong/mainland
China co-productions. Buoyed by the Closer Economic

Partnership Arrangement signed early in 2003, producers are increasingly looking across the border for partners offering them quota-free access to mainland theatres. However, access is only granted if a co-production has at least a third of the cast from the mainland, a China-related plot or characters, and a script approved before shooting.

Censorship restrictions cover sexual and political themes, tales of the supernatural and stories in which the bad guys win. Some film-makers have responded by making dual versions for mainland and Hong Kong release; others play safe in both territories. Soi Cheang's **The Death Curse** (*Goo jat sum fong fong*) chose the latter route, becoming the first Hong Kong horror film simultaneously released on the mainland, despite featuring what appear to be ghosts.

Summer 2004 closed on a more positive note, with local release schedules promising highly anticipated features, including Johnnie To's romantic caper *Yesterday Once More*, Wong Kar-wai's long-awaited *2046* and Jackie Chan's *New Police Story*.

TIM YOUNGS is a Hong Kong-based writer who serves as Hong Kong consultant to the Far East Film Festival, Udine.

Best New Actor: Andy On Chi-kit (*Star Runner*).
Best Cinematography: Arthur Wong Ngok-tai (*The Floating Landscape*).
Best Editing: Chan Kei-hop (*The Twins Effect*).
Best Art Direction: Bill Lui Chor-hung (*The Twins Effect*).
Best Costuming and Makeup: Yee Chung-man (*The Twins Effect*).
Best Action Choreography: Donnie Yen Ji-dan (*The Twins Effect*).
Best Original Score: Peter Kam Pui-tat (*Lost in Time*).
Best Original Song: "Cheung Hung" from *Infernal Affairs II*.
Best Sound Effects: Kinson Tsang King-heung (*The Twins Effect*).
Best Special Effects: Eddy Wong, Yee Kwok-leung (*The Twins Effect*).
Best Asian Film: *The Twilight Samurai* (Japan).
New Director Award: Pang Ho-cheung (*Men Suddenly in Black*).

Paramount/Kobal

Anthony Perkins and JANET LEIGH in Psycho *(1960), the film that defined both their careers. Leigh, who had made one of her final screen appearances alongside daughter Jamie Lee Curtis in* Halloween: H2O *(1998), died on October 3, 2004, aged 77.*

Hungary Eddie Cockrell

The Year's Best Films

Eddie Cockrell's selection:
After the Day Before
(Attila Janisch)
Control (Nimrod Antal)
Dealer (Benedek Fliegauf

Felician Keresztes in **Dealer**

Recent and Forthcoming Films

MASNAP (After the Day Before)
[Metaphysical thriller, 2004]
Script: Andras Forgach. Dir:
Attila Janisch. Phot: Gabor
Medvigy. Players: Tibor Gaspar,
Denes Ujlaki, Kati Lazar, Bori
Derzsi, Sandor Czeczo. Prod:
Peter Miskolczi, Eurofilm Studio.

ARGO
[Historical action-comedy, 2004]
Script: Bence Trunko, Peter
Huszar. Dir: Attila Arpa. Phot:
Christoph Vitt. Players: Lajos
Kovacs, Sandor Oszter, Laszlo
Gorog, Laura Ruttkay, Peter
Scherer. Prod: Peter Bruno
Gyorgy, Attila Arpa, Legend
Film/A2 Media/Tivoli Film.
Three gangs scour the
Hungarian countryside for a
historical treasure.

A MOHACSI VESZ
(The Battle of Mohacst)
[Historical comedy, 2004] Script:
Miklos Jancso, Ferenc
Grunwalsky, Gyula Hernadi. Dir:

By the time Hungary and nine neighbours officially joined the European Union on May 1, 2004, all the elements of the long promised and even longer anticipated film renaissance were in place: an enticing new law aimed at generating an influx of foreign (and particularly American) productions had been implemented; a National Film Office had been created to work alongside existing domestic bureaus to handle the anticipated demand; and the foreign press had been dazzled at the 35th Hungarian Film Week in February 2004 by no fewer than three world-class dramatic features, very different in tone but each signaling a potentially saleable blend of the arthouse sensibilities for which Hungarian cinema is known and the commercial savvy it must acquire to become competitive and respected. The international mainstreaming of Hungarian cinema seemed finally to be at hand.

The shift began in earnest with the passage of the Film Law in December 2003. Conceived as a direct response to similar enticements in Prague, Bucharest and elsewhere, it offers a hefty 20% rebate on all production costs incurred in Hungary by local and foreign productions (provided international producers partner with a local company).

"This is a very good law. You can't lose," Laszlo Sipos, owner of Hungarian Film Connection, told *Variety*. While the highest profile film to date to use the incentive was Hallmark Entertainment's *A Christmas Carol*, starring Kelsey Grammer, hundreds of companies have expressed interest in the scheme and by press time at least 40 productions had begun the application process. Andras Erkel, vice-president of the Hungarian Producers Association, marvelled early in 2004: "My e-mail box is full of people asking about this."

Domestic film production followed the prevalent regional trend by dipping slightly, from 24 produced features in 2002 to 21 in 2003. Like the rest of Europe, ticket prices were up (by roughly $1), while at the multiplex local productions lost a bit of ground to Hollywood juggernauts. Bottom line: the industry kept pace.

Antal's tubeway army

Just as the ink was drying on the new law, the first of three films that have since travelled extensively on the international festival circuit opened in Budapest. **Control** (*Kontroll*) is a supple and kinetic action comedy set entirely in the city's dank, Soviet-built subway system and following a ragtag group of ticket inspectors who help solve a series of murders. It marks an audacious feature bow for Nimrod Antal, who was born in the US before studying in Budapest. With its pulsing techno score and nimble storytelling savvy, the film topped the annual box-office chart, hauling in 257,528 admissions – a figure eclipsed in 2004 by the 453,063 tickets sold for **Hungarian Vagabond** (*Magyar Vandor*), a comedy steeped in local history and lore (and thus much less likely to ride the international rails).

Though its list of festival appearances and awards is too extensive to detail here, *Control* was chosen as Hungary's official Oscar entry and beat off American dramatic heavyweights such as *The Woodsman* and *Undertow* to take the Gold Hugo at the Chicago International Film Festival in October 2004. Antal was scheduled to participate in the first-ever "New Faces in European Cinema" event launched by European Film Promotion at November's AFI Fest in Los Angeles. ThinkFilm was scheduled to open *Control* in the US in the first half of 2005, and at press time rumours of a Hollywood remake continued to circulate.

Left to right: Zoltan Mucsi, Sandor Csanyi, Zsolt Nagy, Sandor Badar and Csaba Pindroch in **Control**

The most emotionally distant of the accomplished new trio is **Dealer**, writer-director Benedek Fliegauf's widescreen, DV-to-35mm follow-up to the critically lauded *Forest* (*Rengeteg*). So impersonal that its eponymous protagonist-in-crisis is never even named, it follows the last day in the life of a pusher as he cycles from client to client, almost completely detached from the woes of those in the crumbling metropolis around him. It's a technically remarkable piece, but lacks a narrative framework that resonates with the human tragedy of three-dimensional characters, and tangible emotional involvement remains elusive. In the end, it's a quintessential "love-it-or-hate-it" experience.

Janisch's *Day* trip

Combining the rigour of *Dealer* with *Control*'s palpable love of cinema's potential for distinctive visual grammar, Attila Janisch's

Jancso. Phot: Grunwalsky. Players: Peter Scherer, Zoltan Mucsi, Judit Schell, Emese Vasvari, Attila Racz, Gyula Bodrogi.
Everyman heroes Kapa and Pepe take their fifth foray into Hungarian history.

PESTI HARLEM
(Budapest Harlem)
[Comedy, 2004] Script: Csaba Novak. Dir: Akos Takacs. Players: Endre Beleznay, Zita Gorog, Majka, Gabriella Gubas. Prod: Gyorgy Dora, New Balance.
A smug building contractor finds his world crumbling after a mistake.

VILAGSZAM!
(Colossal Sensation)
[Comedy, 2004] Script: Peter Horvath, Robert Koltai. Dir: Koltai. Phot: Balazs Marton. Players: Koltai, Sandor Gaspar, Orsolya Toth, Peter Scherer. Prod: Gabor P. Koltai, Filmsziget.
Twins become successful circus performers in the early 1900s.

KONTROLL (Control)
[Action comedy-thriller, 2003] Script and Dir: Nimrod Antal. Phot: Gyula Pados. Players: Sandor Csanyi, Zoltan Mucsi, Sandor Badar, Csaba Pindroch. Prod: Tamas Hutlassa, Café Film/Bonfire.

Boglarka Csosz, left, and Kata Gaspar in **Dad Goes Nuts**

APAM BEAJULNA!
(Dad Goes Nuts)
[Teen comedy, 2004] Script: Richard Salinger, based on his novel. Dir: Tamas Sas. Phot: Elemer Ragalyi. Players: Kata Gaspar, Boglarka Csosz, Andras Kern, Janos Kulka, Mari Kiss, Janos Koos. Prod: Gabor Kalomista, Megafilm.
Two young women who meet working tourist traps at Lake

Balaton take off for adventures in Crete, Barcelona and Rome.

DEALER
[Drama, 2004] Script and Dir: Benedek Fliegauf. Phot: Peter Szatmari. Players: Felician Keresztes, Lajos Szakacs, Barbara Thurzo, Aniko Szigeti, Edina Balogh. Prod: Andras Muhi, Inforg Studio/Filmteam.

NYOCKER (The District)
[Animated feature, 2004] Script: Erik Novak. Dir: Aron Gauder. Voices: Sandor Badar, Andrea Fullajtar, Karoly Gesztesi, Dorka Gryllus. Prod: Erik Novak, Lichthof.
A mixed-race group of young boys in Budapest's notorious eighth district attempt to broker peace among their parents.

Dorka Gryllus in **Mix**

MIX
[Drama, 2004] Script and Dir: Steven Lovy. Phot: Janos Vecsernyes. Players: Alex Week, Janos Kulka, Jeffrey Schecter, Olga Koos, Dorka Gryllus, Krisztian Kolovratnik. Prod: Robert Lovy, Steven Lovy, Jozsef Cirko/mixpix/HCC Happy Crew Company.
An aspiring Los Angeles DJ connects with his Hungarian roots during a stay in Budapest.

RAP, REVU, ROMEO (Rap, Revue, Romeo)
[Crime action-comedy, 2004] Script: Gabor Olah J., Gabor Revesz. Dir: Olah J. Phot: Zoltan Janossa. Players: Janos Galvolgyi, David Csanyi, Huang Phong, Andras Stohl, Lili Monori. Prod: Kornel Sipos, Zsofia Kende/Laurinfilm.
A new Chinese shop sends ripples through a neighbourhood.

breathtakingly unclassifiable **After the Day Before** (*Masnap*), probably best tagged as a metaphysical thriller, invokes memories of both Maya Deren and *The Shining* in its story of a befuddled stranger adrift in a shifting wilderness that may or may not exist entirely between his own ears. Janisch, whose similarly creepy *Long Twilight* (1996) was a feature-length adaptation of a Shirley Jackson short story, "The Bus", injects the genre element of a sad and brutal murder into proceedings. However, he claimed to one stunned Hungarian Film Week audience: "I'm not making scary movies. I'm not interested in brutality, [but] a reaction to daily hatred."

Director Attila Janisch, left, and cinematographer Gabor Medvigy shooting **After the Day Before**

After the Day Before deservedly took the Week's main prize, and there were also wins for cinematographer Gabor Medvigy (*ex aequo* with *Control's* Gyula Pados), lead actor Tibor Gaspar and supporting actress Kati Lazar. Like *Dealer*, *After the Day Before* was set for a fall 2004 domestic release. This pair and *Control* collectively mark the start of an exciting new chapter in the way Hungarian films are made and the subjects they address.

ALLITSATOK MEG TEREZANYUT! (Stop Mommy Theresa!)
[Romantic comedy, 2004] Script: Bela Rigo, Zsuzsanna Racz, based on Racz's novel. Dir: Rigo. Phot: Gyula Pados. Players: Judith Schell, Gabriella Hamori, Eszter Onodi, Melinda Major. Prod: Istvan Bodzsar, Unio Film.
A woman in her early thirties encounters men, jobs and everyday adventures.

A TEMETETLEN HALOTT – NAGY IMRE NAPLOJA (The Unburied Man: The Diary of Imre Nagy)
[Historical drama, 2004] Script: Marta Meszaros, Eva Pataki. Dir:
Meszaros. Phot: Nyika Jancso. Players: Jan Nowicki, Lili Horvath, Marianna Moor. Prod: Attila Csaky, Michal Kwiecinski, Igor Hudec, Cameofilm/Akson Studio/ARS Media.

Quote of the Year
"I'm not saying that all [subway] inspectors are saints, but it's pretty heavy if you're told on a daily basis 'Go fuck your mother.' Even the passengers who have a ticket say that."
NIMROD ANTAL, director, on his subterranean research for *Control*.

Iceland Skarphédinn Gudmundsson

The Year's Best Films:

Skarphédin Gudmundsson's
selection:
Cold Light (Hilmar Oddsson)
Niceland
(Fridrik Thór Fridriksson)
Strong Coffee
(Börkur Gunnarsson)
A Shining Star
(Docu. Ólafur Jóhannesson)
The Last Farm
(Short. Runar Runarsson)

Ingvar E. Sigurdsson in Cold Light

Recent and Forthcoming Films

KALDALJÓS (Cold Light)
*[Drama, 2004] Script: Freyr
Thormodsson, Hilmar Oddsson.
Dir: Oddsson. Phot: Sigurdur
Sverrir Pálsson. Players: Ingvar
E. Sigurdsson, Kristbjörg Kjeld.
Prod: Icelandic Film Corporation.*

NÆSLAND (Niceland)
*[Drama, 2004] Script: Huldar
Breidfjörd. Dir: Fridrik Thór
Fridriksson. Phot: Morten Søborg.
Players: Gary Lewis, Martin
Compston, Peter Capaldi, Kerry
Fox. Prod: Zik Zak Filmworks/
Nimbus Film (Denmark)/
Tradewind Pictures (Germany)/
Film & Music Entertainment (UK).*

The Icelandic film industry continues to become increasingly global, as more local directors choose to work abroad after completing their film studies, and more international projects are shot in Iceland, often as co-productions. It has, however, been a relatively disappointing period for Icelandic features, with no major commercial successes in 2003-04 (the market share for local films was only 3% in 2003). Some in the industry have laid part of the blame for this lack of interest at the door of television stations, saying they do not produce and broadcast enough local films.

The best received film of 2004 was Hilmar Oddsson's **Cold Light** (*Kaldaljós*). Based on a novel by Vigdís Grímsdóttir, it is an intense, spiritual family drama set in a small fishing town and starring one of Iceland's leading actors, Ingvar E. Sigurdsson. It won five EDDA awards (Icelandic Oscars), including Best Picture and Actor, as well as prizes at festivals in Slovakia, Argentina and Portugal. It was also Iceland's entry for the Academy Awards.

Fridrik Thór Fridriksson's latest study of human isolation and the meaning of life, **Niceland** (*Næsland*), was warmly received by some Icelandic critics but failed at the home box-office. Martin Compston plays a simple lad desperately looking for answers to difficult questions about life, death and happiness. The eponymous heroine of **Dís**, a young university student in downtown Reykjavik, also searches for some meaning to her life, in a light comedy based on a bestseller by three girlfriends and directed by one of them, Silja Hauksdóttir. It did quite good business and Hauksdóttir showed promise in her feature debut.

Martin Compston, left, and Gary Lewis in Niceland

DÍS
[Comedy, 2004] Script: Silja
Hauksdóttir, Birna Anna
Björnsdóttir, Oddny Sturludóttir.
Dir: Hauksdóttir. Players: Álfrún
Örnólfsdóttir, Ilmur
Kristjánsdóttir. Prod: Sögn ehf.

Álfrún Örnólfsdóttir, centre, as **Dís**

OPINBERUN HANNESAR
(The Revelation of Hannes)
[Comedy, 2004] Script and Dir:
Hrafn Gunnlaugsson. Phot:
Jakob Ingimundarson. Players:
Vidar Víkingsson, Helga Braga
Jónsdóttir, Jóhanna Vigdís
Arnardóttir. Prod: F.I.L.M.

Í TAKT VID TÍMANN
(In Tune with Time)
[Comedy, 2004] Script: Ágúst
Gudmundsson and players. Dir:
Gudmundsson. Players: Eggert
Thorleifsson, Egill Ólafsson,
Jakob F. Magnússon, Ragnhildur
Gísladóttir, Tómas R. Tómasson,
Thórdur Árnason, Ásgeir
Óskarsson. Prod: Ísfilm.

STRÁKARNIR OKKAR
(11 Men Out)
[Comedy, 2005] Script: Jón Atli
Jónasson, Róbert I. Douglas. Dir:
Douglas. Prod: Icelandic Film
Company/Solarfilm Inc./ Borealis
Production AS (Norway)/ Film &
Music Entertainment (UK).

A LITTLE TRIP TO HEAVEN
[Thriller, 2005] Script and Dir:
Baltasar Kormákur. Players:
Forest Whitaker, Julia Stiles,
Jeremy Remner, Peter Coyote.
Prod: Palomar Pictures (US).

BJÓLFSKVIDA
(Beowulf & Grendel)
[Drama, 2005] Script: Andrew
Rai Berzins. Dir: Sturla
Gunnarsson. Phot: Jan Kiessel.
Players: Gerard Butler, Sarah
Polley, Ingvar E. Sigurdsson,
Stellan Skarsgård, Benedikt
Clausen. Prod: Arclight Films

Hrafn Gunnlaugsson delivered yet another highly controversial work with the low-budget satirical comedy **A Revelation for Hannes** (*Opinberun Hannesar*). Based on a short story by Iceland's foreign minister, Davíd Oddsson, it takes some well-aimed shots at twenty-first century bureaucracy. In neurotic, raw style, Gunnlaugsson follows a dedicated employee at the Institute for State Supervision, who secretly develops the SuperCode Databank, containing ID numbers through which everyone's behaviour can be monitored. When his office computer is stolen, he desperately tries to solve the case but becomes the prime suspect.

On the move

It becomes harder to pin down the number of genuinely Icelandic films produced annually as more Icelanders opt to make films set in other countries and languages. **Third Name** (*Thridja nafnid*), released in 2003, was directed by Einar Thor, who is based in England but made this low-budget romantic thriller in Iceland with English and Icelandic actors. María Sólrún Sigurdardottir lives and works in Berlin, and the award-winning **Jargo**, her debut fiction feature following the acclaimed documentary *Two Girls and a War*, deals in an objective but passionate way with today's multi-cultural German society. It is the story of two young friends, a German who has returned home after growing up in Saudi-Arabia, and a Turk raised in Berlin.

Börkur Gunnarsson's debut, **Strong Coffee** (*Silny kafe*), is a low-budget, DV gem made with a largely Czech cast and crew in Prague, where Gunnarsson studied film-making. It is an intelligent drama dealing with modern-day relationships between the sexes and did well at the box-office in the Czech Republic and parts of eastern Europe. **A Royal Smile** (*Konunglegt bros*) was another small, humble but effective feature, a surreal comedy by the promising Gunnar B. Gudmundsson, who won the EDDA for best short in 2003. It was produced by Óskar Axelsson, who is based in New York.

Documentary *Star*

Arguably, 2004 was the year of shorts and documentaries in Iceland. The best evidence for the growing interest in these often under-rated forms was the success of two festivals in Reykjavik: Reykjavik Shorts & Docs and the Nordisk Panorama (for shorts and documentaries). The latter, which rotates annually between five Nordic countries, had the most successful edition in its 15-year history and the jury chose *The Last Farm* (*Sídasti bærinn*) by Icelander Rúnar Rúnarsson as Best Nordic Short.

In late 2004, Ólafur Jóhannesson's **A Shining Star** (*Blindsker - Saga Bubba Morthens*) became one of the most successful documentaries in Icelandic cinema history. Its subject is Bubbi Morthens, the country's biggest rock star for the last 25 years, and it won the EDDA for Best Documentary. Ólafur Sveinsson made the second documentary in his Berlin trilogy, **Schräge Zeit** (*Múrinn*), which looks at East Berlin in the years before the Wall came down, through the eyes of rebellious punks who opposed the communist authorites.

Ragnars Bragason's **Love Is in the Air** is a thoroughly enjoyable, spot-on documentary about the exceptionally successful young Icelandic theatre group, Vesturport, whose acrobatic production of *Romeo and Juliet* has recently had two runs in London's West End. Veteran director Páll Steingrímsson, who received the Honorary Prize at the 2004 EDDAs, won a prize at the Green Vision Festival, St Petersburg, for *World of Solitude* (*Öræfakyrrd*), in which Magnus Magnusson, famous as the presenter of the BBC's *Mastermind* quiz, explores Europe's largest glacier, Vatnajökull.

Two major projects are scheduled for 2005 release. Baltasar Kormakur's *A Little Trip to Heaven* is a $12m thriller, shot in Iceland with American leads and set in the US, about a husband and wife who tangle with an investigator over the insurance policy of the wife's late brother. *Beowolf and Grendel* (*Bjólfskvida*) is Sturla Gunnarsson's $13m take on the Anglo-Saxon epic poem, the blood-soaked tale of a Norse warrior's battle against the murderous troll, Grendel (a heavily disguised Ingvar E. Sigurdsson).

In Tune with Time (*Í takt vid tímann*) is Ágúst Gudmundsson's sequel to the musical comedy *On Top* (*Med allt á hreinu*, 1982), Iceland's most succesful film of all time. Gudmundsson will reunite audiences with the hoplessly dedicated pop group Studmenn (for 30 years one of Iceland's most popular real-life combos) as they experience mid-life crises on a comeback tour. *Grown-Up People* (*Voksne Mennesker*) is Dagur Kári's second feature, shot in Denmark with Danish actors and funding. Its hero is a graffiti artist in Copenhagen who suddenly finds true love.

SKARPHÉDINN GUDMUNDSSON (skarpi@mbl.is) is a journalist and a film and music critic for Iceland's best-selling newspaper, *Morgunbladid*.

(US)/Spice Factory Ltd. (UK)/ The Film Works Ltd. (Canada)/ Icelandic Film Corporation.

ÓVINAFAGNAOUR
[*aka* **THORDUR KAKALI**]
(**A Gathering of Foes**)
[Drama, forthcoming] Script: Einar Kárason. Dir: Fridrik Thór Fridriksson. Prod: Icelandic Film Corporation.

JARGO
[Drama, 2004] Script and Dir: María Sólrún Sigurdardóttir. Players: Constantin von Jascheroff, Oktay Özdemir, Udo Kier. Prod: oe-Film.

SILNY KAFE (**Strong Coffee**)
[Drama, 2004] Script and Dir: Börkur Gunnarsson. Phot: Tony Gresek. Players: Kaisa El Ramly, Marketa Coufalova, Martin Hofman. Prod: Bionaut Films (Czech Republic)/ Zik Zak Filmworks.

Jean Loose in **Strong Coffee**

Quote of the Year

"The first rule about a movie is that it's a lie. I've never believed there is more truth to a dogma, it's all a lie."
BALTASAR KORMÁKUR,
director, who set his forthcoming A Little Trip to Heaven *in the US but shot it in Iceland.*

India Uma da Cunha

The Year's Best Films

Uma da Cunha's selection:

Maqbool (Fair Is Foul)
(Vishal Bhardwaj)
I Found Someone
(Rakesh Roshan)
Raincoat (Rituparno Ghosh)
Dev (Govind Nihalani)
Emotions of Being
(Satish Menon)

Recent and Forthcoming Films

BLACK FRIDAY
[Hindi. Historical drama, 2004]
Script: Anurag Kashyap, based on
S. Hussain Zaidi's novel. Dir:
Kashyap. Phot: N. Nataraja
Subramanian. Players: Kay Kay
Menon, Aditya Srivastava, Pawan
Malhotra, Vijay Maurya, Gajraj
Rao. Prod: Sanjaay Routray, Mid
Day Multimedia Ltd.

SWAPNER DIN
(Chased by Dreams)
[Bengali. Social drama, 2004]
Script and Dir: Buddhadeb
Dasgupta. Phot: Venu. Players:
Prasenjit, Rima Sen. Prod: J.
Sughand Prods. Pvt. Ltd.

KISNA
[English and Hindi versions.
Historical drama, 2005] Script:
Subhash Ghai, Farookh Dhondy,
Margaret Glover. Dir: Ghai. Phot:
Ashok Mehta. Players: Vivek
Oberoi, Antonio Bernath, Isha
Shravani, Michael Maloney,
Caroline Langrish, Amrish Puri,
Om Puri. Prod: Mukta Arts Ltd.

SWADESH
[Hindi. Social drama, 2004] Script
and Dir: Ashutosh Gowarikar.
Phot: Mahesh Aney. Players:
Shahrukh Khan, Gayatri Joshi,

I n mid-2003, just when a sinking box-office suggested that some soul-searching was overdue, the marquee lights flared on again and hope of revival was kindled in countless industry hearts. New releases were suddenly going well, at home and better abroad. Five films earned over $2m in the US and UK markets alone: *Chalte, Chalte*, *Koi Mil Gaya*, *Andaz*, *Munnabhai MBBS* and *Baghban* (the last two were even hits at home). Early 2004 started with a modest success, *Murder*, then a crescendo of commercial triumphs with *Main Hoon Na*, *Hum Tum*, *Kyon Ho Gaya Na*, *Fida*, *Mujhse Shadi Karoge*, climaxing with *Dhoom*, which did splendidly at home and abroad. Morale picked up after the spate of failures that had gone with a frenzy of production. On top of theatrical revenues, DVD sales continued to grow rapidly.

An ever-superstitious industry thanked its lucky stars for exorcising its demons. In 2003, India's entertainment business took in revenues estimated at $1 billion, a figure predicted to increase by more than 100% by 2008, at an annual growth rate of 18%. Government backing is available and banks are lending to the film business (accorded official industry status only at the start of the new century), so there is more stability and regulation. Big entertainment names such as UTV, Sahara, Ram Gopal Varma's The Factory and the Pritish Nandy Corporation are funding features.

There is one more key factor: Indian films are doing great business abroad. The overseas market for film, video and television brings back to India 15-20% of total earnings. The ethnic Indian market worldwide has been estimated at 20 million people (18% of them in the UK and US). Add in the audience in Bangladesh and Pakistan and you have a vast diaspora, an audience more affluent and dependable than the fickle domestic one.

Meet the new bosses

The industry is re-modelling itself to fit new realities. The old modus operandi – essentially person-to-person contact among traders and directors given to "mood" and temperament – is making way for new techniques of management and film-making. Younger professionals like Karan Johar, Aamir Khan, Sooraj Bharjatiya, Shahrukh Khan and Aditya Chopra are building into their production companies such unfamiliar concepts as branding, corporate sponsorship and merchandising.

Much is changing in response to the "Bollywood" buzz abroad. Aishwarya Rai, Indian temptress, was courted by Cannes, turned the heads of Hollywood honchos and helped Gurinder Chadha bring Jane Austen to India, turning the Bennets into Bakshis in *Bride and Prejudice*. Mira Nair soars from triumph with her India-set *Monsoon Wedding* to the Indo–Brit audacity of *Vanity Fair*. Advertising guru Tarsem Singh was set to shoot scenes for *The Fall*, his latest feature, in India, replete with home-brewed song and dance. But these expat directors of Indian origin, who now have a truly international sensibility, are a hard act to follow for those living in and attuned to Indian styles of filming.

At home, the box-office remains an enigma. Some 54% of India's one billion population is under 25. Their tastes, feeding more and more on television, veer towards westernised entertainment. They are not stirred, as their elders were, by the melodramatic angst and family themes that were once the hallmark of Indian cinema. They want topical urban plots that relate to their world and slick films that surprise them.

So, current successes go from schizophrenics in psychedelic drama (*Dhoom*) to fortune tellers (*Rakht*) and ghosts from the past (*Bhoot*), to tales of sexy, liberated new Indian women breaking all the rules (*Jism and Paap*). On another plane, producers have found profitable territory in nationalist films about India's border wars (Pakistan is the enemy in *Lakshya* and *Khaki*), with heroic portrayals of the country's army and police.

More than 50 debut film-makers flooded the marketplace in 2003-04, and one of the most promising was Chicago-based Satish Menon, with **Emotions of Being** (*Bhavam*), a Kerala-set reworking of *A Streetcar Named Desire*, in which a disillusioned journalist and his college lecturer wife are visited by the wife's mysterious sister.

Yet despite all these positives, the world's most prolific film-producing nation makes fewer and fewer features: 1,013 in 2001, 973 in 2002 and only 877 in 2003. As usual, Hindi films led (246), followed by releases in the four south Indian language belts, Telugu (155), Tamil (151), Kannada (109) and Malayalam (64). By the end of June 2004, only 414 new films had been made. India has more than 20 languages, each with its own script. Increasingly, certain American films are released in English and in versions dubbed into the main Indian languages to increase regional business. In 2003, 44 films were dubbed in Hindi, 32 in Telugu and 28 in Tamil. There are more imported films, too: 282 in 2003, mostly from the US.

Lekh Tandon, Raja Awasthi, Vishwa S. Badola, Kishori Balal. *Prod: UTV Motion Pictures/Ashutosh Gowariker Productions.*
A young Indian gives up his lucrative job with NASA and returns to rural India to confront social issues.

1857 – The Rising
[Hindi. Patriotic drama, 2004] Script: Farrukh Dhondy. Dir: Ketan Mehta. Phot: Santosh Sivan. Players: Aamir Khan, Amisha Patel, Rani Mukherjee, Toby Stephens. Prod: Bobby Bedi, Kaleidoscope Films/Mehta, Maya Movies.
Patriot Mangal Pandey triggers India's fight for independence.

BOSE –
THE FORGOTTEN HERO
[Hindi, English. Historical drama, 2005] Script: Shama Zaidi, Atul Tiwari. Dir: Shyam Benegal. Phot: Rajan Kotari. Players: Sachin Khedekar, Partap Sharma, Yashwant Sinha, Jishu Sengupta, Divya Dutta. Prod: Sahara India Ltd.
Five key years in the life of Bengali freedom fighter Netaji Subhash Chandra Bose, who raised an Indian National Army and formed a government in exile against the British.

Rani Mukherjee, left, and Abhishek Bachchan shooting **Yuva**

YUVA (Youth)
[Hindi. Social Drama, 2004] Script: Mani Ratnam, Anurag Kashyap. Dir: Ratnam. Phot: Ravi Chandran. Players: Ajay Devgan, Abhishek Bachchan, Vivek Oberoi, Rani Mukherjee, Esha Deol, Kareena Kapoor, Om Puri. Prod: Madras Talkies.

In Kolkata, three interlocking stories convey the violence-tinged lives of today's aspirational youths.

NAVARASA (Nine Emotions)
[Tamil. Social drama, 2004] Script: Santosh Sivan, Raajaa Chandrasekar, K. Vishnu Vardhan. Dir and Phot: Sivan. Players: Sweta, Bobby Darling, Harea Krishna, Ejji K. Umamahesh, Kushbu. Prod: Handmade Films/Santosh Sivan Productions.
Shweta, 13, follows her uncle – a man by day and woman by night – into the myth-ridden world of transsexuals.

Victor Banerjee and Lillete Dubey in **Bow Barracks Forever**

BOW BARRACKS FOREVER
[English, Hindi, Bengali. Social drama, 2004] Script and Dir: Anjan Dutt. Phot: Indranil Mukherjee. Players: Lillete Dubey, Victor Banerjee, Neha Dubey, Moonmoon Sen, Sabyasachi Chakravarty, Avijit Dutt, Rupa Ganguly. Prod: Tapan Biswas.
Drama about the Anglo-Indian residents of Bow Barracks.

AKALE (At a Distance)
[Malayalam. Social drama, 2004] Script and Dir: S. Shyamprasad. Phot: S. Kumar. Players: Prithviraj, Sheela, Geetu Mohandas, Tom George, Sreelekha Mitra. Prod: Kolath Films.
Tennessee Williams' *The Glass Menagerie* evocatively transposed to a seaside shanty-town in Kerala in the 1970s.

STRUGGLER
[Hindi. Social drama, 2004] Script and Dir: Mahesh V. Manjrekar. Phot: Vijay Arora.

Going global

The globalisation of Indian cinema manifests itself in three ways. First, films strain after foreign settings or a story that connects India with another country, foreign actors will mingle with Indians, or India becomes the meeting ground between west and east. Second, English or Indian–English dialogue is here to stay, with even popular Hindi films constantly featuring English. More and more films are shot entirely in English with an eye on the global audience – a dozen such were in the pipeline in mid-2004.

Antonio Bernath and Vivek Oberoi in **Kisna**: *shot in Hindi and English versions*

Third, blockbusters are being shot back-to-back in Hindi and English, including Subhash Ghai's **Kisna**, which harks back to India's independence struggle as an Englishwoman looks back on her dangerous and romantic escapades 50 years ago, and **1857 – The Rising**, starring Aamir Khan, set during India's nineteenth-century fight for freedom.

Outside India, the so-called 'diaspora film' is gaining ground, with at least ten scheduled to be completed in 2004 in the US alone. Mira Nair is returning to her Indian roots to film Pulitzer Prize-winner Jhumpa Lahiris' novel, *Namesake*, starring Rani Mukherjee, who in her twenties has suddenly emerged as the top young actress in India. Deepa Mehta completed *Water* in Sri Lanka (in English and Hindi), with top-drawer talents John Abraham, Lisa Ray and Seema Biswas. Ismail Merchant is making his next film with singing diva Tina Turner playing an Indian goddess.

Indian actors are now sought for films in the US, UK and beyond. Jackie Chan has taken two Indians to Hong Kong for his next action film and German director Florian Gallenberger's **Shadows of Time**, which premiered at Toronto 2004, is entirely Indian. The story of a doomed love that begins with child labour in a carpet factory, it is in Bengali, has an Indian cast and is set in Kolkata.

Truly Indian?

Fewer and fewer established film-makers do original work that is genuinely Indian. The never-say-die stalwarts include Rituparno Ghosh, whose latest, **Raincoat**, was his first in Hindi. Premiered at Karlovy Vary, it is a romance between a married entrepreneur (Ajay Devgan) and a woman (Aishwarya Rai), who are reunited in Kolkata years after they first met. Anurag Kashyap's **Black Friday**, about the 1993 bomb blasts that shook Mumbai, competed in Locarno; Buddhadeb Dasgupta's **Chased by Dreams** premiered at the Toronto Festival. At press time, eagerly awaited titles were Shyam Benegal's bio-pic *Bose – The Forgotten Hero*, Ashutosh Gowarikar's *Swadesh* and Ketan Mehta's *1857–The Rising*.

Alco picked up by festivals was Vishal Bhardwaj's innovative **Maqbool** (**Fair Is Foul**), which transposed *Macbeth* to the underworld of today's Mumbai, where the young mistress of an ageing don, Abbaji, conspires with his second-in-command, Maqbool, to murder him. In **Dev**, Govind Nihalani, the leading Hindi director, known for his tough stand on current issues, examined the growing communal divide widened by self-seeking politians and the police force as they strive to maintain law and order in the land. Packed with special effects, Rakesh Roshan's much-hyped Hindi blockbuster **I Found Someone** (*Koi mil gaya*) was the tale of a young man with the heart and IQ of an 11-year-old and the extra-terrestrial friend he meets when aliens come to earth on a giant spaceship.

As it looked ahead to 2005, the challenge to Indian cinema was to capitalise on potential revenues abroad while maintaining control at home. In attempting this, Indian film-makers run a risk. The uniqueness of Indian cinema lies in its rooted folk idiom, devil-may-care style, song and dance and exaggeration. Straining to become universal, it may lose sight of its individuality. Screenwriters and directors must satisfy changing audience tastes. In the struggle for the golden egg, the goose may die.

UMA DA CUNHA (ugmedius@hathway.com) heads Medius (India) Services, which provides casting and executive services for films shot in India. She edits *Film India Worldwide* magazine and is a film festival programmer.

Players: Manjrekar, Lala Deshmukh, Atul Kale. Prod: Shreya Creations Pvt. Ltd.
Story about the many sad souls who come to Mumbai to look for a break in its fabled film world.

KHAMOSH PANI (Silent Waters)
[Urdu and Punjabi. Social drama, 2003] Script: Paromita Vohra, Sabiha Sumar. Dir: Sumar. Phot: Ralph Netzer. Players: Kirron Kher, Aamir Malik, Arshad Mahmud, Salman Shahid, Shilpa Shukla. Prod: Vidhi Films/ Unlimited/Flying Moon/ZDF.

Page Three

PAGE THREE
[Hindi. Social drama, 2004] Script: Nina Arora, Manoj Tyagi. Dir: Madhur Bhandarkar. Phot: Michale Anderson. Players: Konkona Sen Sharma, Atul Kulkarni, Boman Irani, Tara Sharma, Suchitra Pillai. Prod: Rahul Pushkarna.
Symbiotic power games involving the rich and famous and the media.

KAL, TODAY AND TOMORROW
[English and Hindi. Social suspense drama, 2004] Script and Dir: Ruchi Narain. Phot: Prakash Kutti. Players: Shiney Ahuja, Chitrangda Singh, Smriti Mishra, Sarika, Boman Irani, Ram Kapoor. Prod: Raas Entertainment.
Murder among five college friends.

WHITE NOISE
[English. Social drama, 2004] Script: Mozez Singh, Vinta Nanda, Uday Watsa. Dir: Nanda. Phot: Inderjit Bansal. Players: Rahul Bose, Koel Purie, Aryan Vaid, Mona Ambegaonkar, Jatin Syal. Prod: Troiiika Picture Company.
In Mumbai, the city of dreams,

talent is often replaced by ego and judgment.

Rahul Bose and Koel Puri in **White Noise**

BRIDES WANTED
[English. Social drama, 2004] Script and Dir: Girish Acharya. Phot: I. Andrews. Players: Waheeda Rahman, Girish Karnad, Anuj Sawhney, Sarah Jane. Prod: O2 Pix Productions.
A young US-based Indian returns home to seek a bride and discovers love through serendipity.

WHITE RAINBOW
[English. Social drama, 2004] Script and Dir: Dharan Mandrayar. Phot: B. Kannan. Players: Sonali Kulkarni, M.S. Jha, Virendra Saxena, Gaurav Kapoor. Prod: Dharlin Entertainment.
Four remarkable women fight the stigma attached to their widowhood.

CHAI PANI ETC...
[English and Hindi. Social drama, 2004] Script and Dir: Manu Rewal. Phot: Pushan Kripalani. Players: Zafar Karachiwala, Konkona Sen Sharma, Sinia Jain, Gaurav Kapoor. Prod: Duniya Vision Pvt. Ltd.
The coming-of-age of Satya, a film-maker who returns to India from the US.

Vijay Raaz as **Hari Om**

HARI OM
[English, Hindi, French. Romantic drama, 2004] Script and Dir: G. Bharat Bala. Phot: Angus Hudson. Players: Vijay Raaz, Jean-Marie Lamour, Camille Natta. Prod: Tips Films/Bharat Bala Productions.
An unlikely trio go on a romantic caper through Rajasthan.

SINS
[English. Psychological thriller, 2004] Script and Dir: Vinod Pande. Phot: Jogendra Panda. Players: Shiney Ahuja, Seema Rehmani, Uttara Baokar, Nitesh Pande, Rishi Khurana. Prod: Rainspirit Films for Vinod Pande Entertainment Organisation.
Obsessive love leads to crimes of passion.

Director Vinod Pande shooting **Sins** *with Seema Rehmani*

SAU JHOOTH EK SACH
(The Uninvited)
[Hindi. Thriller, 2004] Script: Pankaj Kapoor, Bappaditya Roy. Dir: Roy. Phot: Amitabha Singh. Players: Mammothy, Lilette Dubey, Neha Dubey, Joy Sengupta. Prod: Think 16/Homecoming Pictures.
When a pregnant girl kills herself, an uninvited police inspector uncovers dark secrets in the home of a rich industrialist.

ITI SRIKANTA
(Your Truly, Srikanta)
[Bengali. Period drama, 2004] Script: Rajarshi Roy, Shantasree Sarkar. Dir: Anjan Das. Phot: Sirsha Roy. Players: Adil Hussain, Soha Ali Khan, Reema Sen, Nirmal Kumar, Piyush Ganguly, Debesh Mukherjee, Adil. Prod: Beyond Reels.
Philosophical drifter Srikanta's

Soha Ali Khan in **Iti Srikanta**

plans to return to Burma are overcome by his love for two utterly different women.

AUTOGRAPH
[Tamil. Drama, 2004] Script and Dir: Cheran. Phot: Ravi Varman, Vijay Milton, Dwarahanath, Sankhi Mahendra Players: Cheran, Sneha, Kanika, Gopika, Mallika, Karuppaiah, Rajesh, Vijayasingh. Prod: Adream Theatres.
On his wedding anniversary, a man looks back at the people and events that have shaped his life.

PARZANIA
[English. Social drama, 2004] Script: David Donihue, Rahul Dholakia. Dir: Dholakia. Phot: Robert Eras. Players: Naseeruddin Shah, Corin Nemec, Sarika, Parzan Dastoor, Pearl Barsiwalla, Raj Zutshi. Prod: Circles Motion Pictures.
Parzan, 10, invents an imaginary world, Parzania, where buildings are made of chocolate and no-one is killed over religion.

Quote of the Year

"My knowledge of India comes primarily from Mahatma Gandhi's writings and Satyajit Ray's films. When I think of Gandhi, I think I belong to India as much as to Iran."
MOHSEN MAKHMALBAF, director, while on the jury of the Cinefan Festival, *Delhi.*

Indonesia Lisabona Rahman

The Year's Best Films

Lisabona Rahman's selection:
Arisan! (Nia diNata)
The Birdman's Tale
(Garin Nugroho)
Mengejar Matahari
(Rudy Sujarwo)
Kwaliteit 2
(Dennis Adhiswara)
Abrakadabra
(Docu short. Aryo Danusiri)

Recent and Forthcoming Films

BIOLA TAK BERDAWAI
(The Stringless Violin)
[Drama, 2003] Script and Dir:
Sekar Ayu Asmara. Players:
Nicholas Saputra, Ria Irawan,
Jajang C. Noer. Prod: Afi
Shamara, Nia diNata, Kalyana
Shira Film.

TUSUK JELANGKUNG
(Pierce the Ouija Board)
[Horror, 2003] Script: Erwin
Arnada, Upi Avianto. Dir:
Dimas Jayadiningrat. Players:
Marcella Zalianty, Dinna Olivia,
Samuel Rizal, Azuzan. Prod:
Arnada, Rexinema.

KIAMAT SUDAH DEKAT
(*literally*, Armageddon is Coming)
[Religious drama, 2003] Script:
Musfar Yasin. Dir: Deddy Mizwar.
Players: Andre Stinky, Deddy
Mizwar, Ayu Pratiwi. Prod:
Mizwar, Demi Gisela Citra Sinema.

KAFIR (Satanic)
[Religious drama, 2003] Script
and Dir: Mardali Syarief.
Players: Meriam Bellina Sudjiwo
Tejo, Subarkah. Prod: Chand
Parwez Servia, Kharisma
Starvision Sempurna.

D espite suffering a severe economic crisis since the late 1990s, Indonesian cinema has awoken from its decade-long hibernation and increased annual film production. National newspaper *Kompas* noted that 50 films were in production in August 2004, although less than half this number will make it to local cinemas, which are dominated by Hollywood films.

The success of children's film *Sherina's Adventure* (*Petualangan Sherina*) and teenage drama *What's Up with Love* (*Ada apa dengan Cinta*) in 2002 proved audiences' interest in Indonesian fare and producers quickly responded by delivering more of the same. *Sherina's Adventure* was followed by a surprising and sudden drop in the audience for children's movies, but teen flicks, often adapted from or inspired by popular television shows, continue to be a gold mine.

An extended, 195-minute cut of **Eiffel, I'm in Love**, a puppy-love romance written by 15-year-old Rachmania Arunita, was released within six months of its initial 122-minute version. They drew a combined total of 2.2 million viewers, whereas the majority of domestic releases are lucky to register more than 150,000 admissions. For example, Nia diNata's **Arisan!** (literally, *Gathering*), a friendship drama which targeted older viewers, had good reviews but could not compete with *Eiffel*. DiNata raised issues of homosexuality, a rare theme in Indonesian cinema.

Another popular genre is horror, with stories adapted from local tales, such as **Pierce the Ouija Board** (*Tusuk jelangkung*) and **The Coffin** (*Peti mati*). Based on the horrific exploits of a real-life Indonesian cannibal serial killer, **Kanibal Sumanto** (literally, *Sumanto the Cannibal*) had limited success on its cinema release in 2003.

Rachel Maryam, right, in **Arisan!**

Stefanny Imelda

EIFFEL, I'M IN LOVE
*[Drama, 2003] Script: Rachmania
Arunita. Dir: Nasry Cheppy.
Players: Samuel Rizal. Prod: Sunil
Soraya, Soraya Intercine Film.*

ARISAN! (*literally,* **Gathering**)
*[Drama, 2003] Script: Joko
Anwar, Nia diNata. Dir: diNata.
Players: Rachel Maryam, Cut
Mini Theo. Prod: diNata, Afi
Shamara, Kalyana Shira Films.*

MENGEJAR MATAHARI
(*literally,* **Chasing the Sun**)
*[Drama, 2004] Script: Titien
Wattimena. Dir: Rudi Sujarwo.
Players: Winky Wiryawan, Fedi
Nuril, Ade Habibie. Prod: Leo
Sutanto/SinemArt.*

KANIBAL SUMANTO (*literally,*
Sumanto the Cannibal)
*[Thriller, 2004] Script: Naryono
and Taufik Daraming Tahir. Dir:
Christ Helweldery. Players:
Jeremias Nyagoen, Sujiwo Tedjo,
Anna Tairas. Prod: Chand
Parwez Servia, Kharisma
Starvision Sempurna.*

BURUAN CIUM GUE
(**Kiss Me Quick!***)*
*[Drama, 2004] Script: Ve
Handojo. Dir: Findo HW.
Players: Masayu Anastasya,
Hengki Kurniawan. Prod: Rizal
Mantovani, Raam
Punjabi/Multivision Plus Picture.*

Kiss Me Quick!

**KUTUNGGU (KAU) DI
SUDUT SEMANGGI**
(*literally,* **I'll Wait for You at the
Corner of Semanggi Bridge**)
*[Drama, 2004] Script and Dir:
Lukmantoro DS. Players: Tengku
Firmansyah, Slamet Rahardjo
Jarot, Dede Yusuj. Prod: Griya
Sembada Group/MM Audia
Visual Production.*

With **The Birdman's Tale**, Garin Nugroho directed a poetic portrayal of the contemporary situation in Papua New Guinea and its cry for independence from Indonesia, told through the growing pains of four teenagers. Dennis Adhiswara's **Kwaliteit 2** was a fresh, experimental comedy about the conflict between freshmen and seniors in an Indonesian college.

Politics makes a comeback

Trying not to be taken aback by the commercial failure of *Eliana, Eliana* in 2002, Riri Riza was at press time working on *Gie*, a biopic about Soe Hok Gie, the enigmatic 1960s student activist who was prominent when the Indonesian military took power through a gradual coup. Three other political films were set for release in the second half of 2004, including **Kutunggu kau di sudut Semanggi** (literally, *I'll Wait for You at the Corner of Semanggi Bridge*), a drama set during the 1998 student protests against President B.J. Habibie's transitional government, and *Angels Cry*, the story of a Balinese child's survival after losing her mother in the 2002 night-club bombing.

Nicholas Saputra as a 1960s student activist in the forthcoming biopic **Gie**

Apart from the problem of distribution, Indonesian film-makers continue to complain about high taxes on production. Very few directors dare shoot on celluloid, and opt instead for cheaper digital technology. There is an alternative independent distribution circuit for shorts and features, mainly through road shows and screenings in universities or art spaces. Apart from the circuit of the main importer of Hollywood movies, 21 Cineplex, very few cinemas remain open and many independent theatres are closing because of non-payment of tax. The government's response to vehement calls for support from the industry was a plan to revive the dormant Indonesian Film Festival late in 2004.

In August 2004, the public was surprised when **Kiss Me Quick**! (*Buruan cium gue*), about an adolescent girl dreaming of her first kiss, was withdrawn from cinemas by the Board of Film Censorship after Muslim groups accused this spin-off from a teen TV series of encouraging kissing – the first step to adultery. Film-makers reacted angrily to a move that recalled the despotic regime which regularly banned films from the 1970s to the early 1990s. At press time, Multivision Plus Picture was planning to launch a toned-down cut of the movie in 2005.

Late in 2004, two directors made their feature debuts. Faozan Rizal created **Yasujiro Journey**, a visual poem about Yasujiro Yamada (played by Suzuki Nobuyuki) and his search for his grandfather, a Japanese fighter pilot who went missing during the Second World War. The other debut was **Rainmaker** (*Impian kemarau*) by Ravi Bharwani, about a village surviving a long dry season and hoping for rain. Despite their low budgets, both films offer attractive imagery and are interesting contributions to recent Indonesian cinema. Bharwani and Rizal show considerable promise.

LISABONA RAHMAN (lisabona@centrin.net.id) is a Jakarta-based freelance writer on film, literature and visual arts. She took part in the film journalism and criticism section of the Berlin Talent Campus 2004.

GIE
[Historical Drama, 2004] Script and Dir: Riri Riza. Players: Nicholas Saputra, Wulan Guritno, Tutie Kirana, Robby Tumewu. Prod: Riza, Mira Lesmana, Miles Production.

RINDU KAMI PADA-MU
[Religious drama, 2004] Script: Armantono, Garin Nugroho. Dir: Nugroho. Players: Didi Petet, Neno Warisman. Prod: Geger, Nugroho/Sinekom.

IMPIAN KEMARAU (Rainmaker)
[Drama, 2004] Script: Armantono, Ravi Bharwani, M. Abduh Azis. Dir: Bharwani. Players: Levie Hardigan, Clara Sinta, Ria Irawan. Prod: Shanty Harmajn, M. Abduh Azis, Novialita/Cinemasphere.

YASUJIRO JOURNEY
[Experimental drama, 2004] Script: Ariansyah. Dir: Faozan Rizal. Player: Suzuki Nobuyuki. Prod: Faozan Rizal, Sastha Sunu/Kotak Hitam.

European Film Awards 2004

Film: *Head On/Gegen die Wand* (Fatih Akin, Germany).
Director: Alejandro Amenabar (*The Sea Inside/Mar* adentro, Spain).
Actor: Javier Bardem (*The Sea Inside*).
Actress: Imelda Staunton (*Vera Drake*, UK).
Screenwriter: Agnès Jaoui and Jean-Pierre Bacri (*Look at Me/Comme une image*, France)
Cinematographer: Eduardo Serra (*Girl With a Pearl Earring*, UK).
Composer: Bruno Coulais (*The Chorus/Les choristes*, France).
Discovery – Fassbinder Award: *Stolen Children/Certi bambini* (Andrea and Antonio Frazzi, Italy).
Documentary: *Darwin's Nightmare* (Hubert Sauper, Austria).
Prix *Screen International* (Non-European Film): *2046* (Wong Kar-wai, Hong Kong).

Wong Kar-wai's **2046** *won the Prix Screen International*

Tartan Films

European Short Film: *I'll Wait for the Next One/J'attendrai le suivant* (Philippe Orreindy, France).
Prix FIPRESCI: Theo Angelopoulos (*Trilogy – The Weeping Meadow*, Greece).
Achievement in World Cinema: Liv Ullman.
Lifetime Achievement: Carlos Saura.

People's Choice Awards
Director: Fatih Akin (*Head-On*).
Actor: Daniel Bruehl (*Love in Thoughts/Was nutzt die Liebe in Gedanken*).
Actress: Penélope Cruz (*Don't Move/Non ti muovere*).

Iran Jamal Omid

Recent and Forthcoming Films

BAR-E DIGAR ZENDEGI
(Life Once Again)
[Drama, 2004] Script and Dir: Majid Majidi. Phot: Mohammad Davudi, Mahmud Kalari. Players: Parviz Parastui, Roya Teymurian, Mahmud Behraznia, Afarin Obeisi. Prod: Majidi, Fuad Nahas. A man regains his eyesight after many years and starts a new life.

KHEILI DUR, KHEILI NAZDIK
(Too Far, Too Close)
[Drama, 2004] Script: Reza Mirkarimi, Mohammad Reza Gowhari. Dir and Prod: Mirkarimi. Phot: Hamid Khozui Abyaneh. Players: Masud Rayegan. Dr. Alem, a neurology specialist, suddenly decides to abandon his successful career and visit his only son, who is busy observing the stars in the desert.

BEH RANG-E ARGHAVAN
(In Purple)
[Social drama, 2004] Script and Dir: Ebrahim Hatamikia. Phot: Hassan Karimi. Players: Hamid Farrokhnezhad, Khazar Masumi, Farhad Qaemian, Mehrdad Zia'ie. Prod: Bestra Film.

ZAN-E ZIADI
(The Other Woman)
[Social drama, 2004] Script and Dir: Tahmineh Milani. Phot: Faraj Heidari. Players: Merila Zare'ie, Amin Hia'ie, Parsa Piruzfar, Elsa Firuz-Azar. Prod: Mohammad Nikbin.

BABA AZIZ (Father Aziz)
[Historical drama, 2004] Script and Dir: Mohammad Naser Khamir. Phot: Mahmud Kalari. Players: Golshifteh Farahani, Nasim Kamlul, Maryam Hamid, Parviz Shahinkhu. Prod: Alireza Shojanoori, Auriol Circus (Iran,

I n 2003-04, Iranian cinema experienced a period of welcome stability. It was too early for film-makers to adopt a clear stance towards the newly appointed film authorities, who had yet to spell out their policies but did their best to create an atmosphere of trust and encouragement, and their efforts ushered in one of the busiest years of recent times. Well-known directors such as Rakhshan Bani-etemad, Dariush Mehrjui, Majid Majidi, Mohammad Bozorgnia, Masud Kimia'ie, Ahmad Reza Darvish and Puran Derakhshandeh all went to work, as did directors creating their first or second films. Around 80 films were produced, including action-packed detective stories, family melodramas, comedies and intellectual art films.

Yet the underlying crisis persisted, and the new films failed to arouse much response from spectators. Local critics and film-makers continued to bemoan the shortage of cinemas in many parts of Tehran, the outdated technology and worn condition of those theatres still open, spectators' reluctance to watch inordinately long Iranian films and the need to increase imports of foreign films.

The *Lizard* king

Most Iranian films flopped, with comedy the only successful genre (though most examples sadly lacked redeeming artistic features). The most popular comedies addressed unorthodox subjects that are still taboo on television. Kamal Tabrizi's **The Lizard** (*Marmoulak*) was an exceptional success commercially and artistically. Tabrizi emerged from war movies and gained a prominent position with his very popular *Leily Is with Me*, establishing a reputation for satirising subjects normally accorded serious treatment. After making two more conventional films (*Carpet of the Wind* and *Take a Look at the Sky Sometimes*), he returned to satirical ways – and regained his status as Iran's most controversial film-maker – with the attractive *The Lizard*, in which Reza, alias the Lizard (a fine performance from Parviz Parastui), is gaoled for armed robbery. He escapes by donning the cloak and turban of a cleric and accidentally becomes a very popular mullah. How to get rid of the cloak and turban that helped him escape?

Tabrizi adroitly and intelligently treads the thin line between political controversy and audience preference, never overstepping the permissible boundaries, and creates a delightful film out of a

Parviz Parastui, left, as the eponymous hero of **The Lizard**

depressing story of armed robbery and cold prison life. He
successfully communicates the message that love and happiness
are not reprehensible and that one can enjoy earthly delights
without forgetting God or necessarily committing sin. However, the
film aroused great controversy because of the basic premise and
the behaviour of the disguised criminal, and was pulled with the
producer's consent a month after its release, when it had already
become the year's top-grossing film and audience demand was still
as high as on opening night. Had it been allowed to run its normal
course it could have set an unsurpassable box-office record

To stay or not to stay?

The next most popular film was Arash Moayerian's debut feature,
Coma, whose pseudo-social, superficial story was calculated to
appeal to the young. Amir Moradian, the only child of a wealthy
family, has relationship problems, especially with his father, a
staunchly traditional, high-ranking government official. His divorced
mother has emigrated and wants Amir to join her in the US, but the
plan is opposed by the father. Moayerian and his screenwriter,
Peyman Moadi, boldly put forward a number of social criticisms
(notably the brain drain of talented Iranians away from the country),
but they are simplistically treated and the dramatic structure is
loose. Nonetheless, this was a promising debut.

Amin Hayai, left, and Atila Pesiyani in **Coma**

France, Tunisia, Germany and
UK co-production).
The life of Ebrahim Adham,
the great eleventh-century
Iranian mystic.

RASTEGARI DAR 8:20
(Salvation at 8:20)
[Drama, 2004] Script:
Mohammad-Hadi Karimi. Dir
and Prod: Sirus Alvand. Phot:
Ali Allahyari. Players: Bahram
Radan, Mahtab Keramati, Shahab
Hosseini, Afarin Obeisi.
Young religious residents of a
city district are suspicious of a
newly arrived woman's
mysterious connections.

HASHTPA (The Octopus)
[Social drama, 2004] Script, Dir
and Prod: Alireza Davudnezhad.
Phot: Asghar Rafi'ie-Jam. Players:
Mohammd-Reza Forutan, Mahtab
Keramati, Vishka Asayesh, Ahmad
Najafi, Mahaya Petrosian.
The leader of a gang of criminals
tries to drag several young men
and women into a plot to
embezzle a financial institution.
One of the youths tries to stand
up to the criminals, while a
policewoman follows the case.

SALAD-E FASL (Season's Salad)
[Melodrama, 2004] Script:
Fereydun Jeyrani, Khosro
Shakibaie. Dir: Jeyrani.
Phot: Hossein Malaki. Players:
Khosro Shakibaie, Leyla Hatami,
Mohammad-Reza Sharifinia,
Mahnaz Afshar, Reza
Karamrezaie. Prod: Seyed
Kamal Tabatabaie.
Leyla's accidental acquaintance
with Hamid opens up a new path
in her life, but Adel, who is in
love with her, affects her plans.

JANG-E KUDAKANEH
(Children's War)
[Melodrama, 2004] Script and
Dir: Abolqassem Talebi. Phot:
Hassan Puya. Players: Maliheh
Rangzan, Yalda Qashqaie, Foad
Ahmadi-Saber. Prod: Mohsen
Ali-Akbari.
Ali, a small Iraqi boy whose
parents have been killed during
the American invasion, searches

for his one-year-old brother and finally arrives at a refugee camp set up near the border by the Iranian Revolutionary Guards.

GHORUB SHOD BIA
(Come at Sundown)
[Social drama, 2004] Script and Dir: Ensieh Shah-Hosseini. Phot: Mohammad Ahmadi. Players: Ladan Mostofi, Farhad Aslani, Farhad Qaemian. Prod: Jozan Film.
A group of friends remain faithful in the midst of shady commercial deals.

CHAYE TALKH (Bitter Tea)
[Social drama, 2004] Script and Dir: Nasser Taqvaie. Phot: Farhad Saba. Players: Hossein Yari, Morteza Ahmadi, Marzieh Vafamehr. Prod: Said Haji-Miri.
At the start of the Iran-Iraq war, a family refuses to be evacuated from their border village, partly to protect their palm grove.

JAEE BARAYE ZENDEGI
(A Place to Live)
[Drama, 2004] Script: Mohammad Bozorgnia, based on a story by Jamal Omid. Dir: Bozorgnia. Phot: Hossein Jafarian. Players: Ezatollah Entezami, Hedyeh Tehrani, Reza Kianian, Atila Pessyani. Prod: Hassan Beshkufeh, Sima Film.
Eidi Mohammad's large family is dispersed after the Iraqis capture his estate at the start of the war. As each member awaits Iran's liberation, fear, hope and the will to resist affect their decisions.

BIDARSHO AREZU
(Wake Up, Arezu)
[Drama, 2004] Script, Dir and Prod: Kianush Ayari. Phot: Mansur Azargol. Players: Behnaz Jafari, Mehran Rajabi.
An hour after the Bam earthquake, a 24-year-old teacher emerges from the rubble in a nearby village. She heads for Bam to get help for the buried villagers but cannot persuade anyone to go with her.

GOL-E YAKH (Frost Flower)
[Melodrama, 2004] Script and Dir: Kiomars Purahmad. Phot:

Another, less commercially successful debut, Hamid Nematollah's **Boutique**, is a surprisingly fine and intelligent analysis of young people's lives in the tense atmosphere of Tehran. It delves compassionately into a group of youths, centred around two principals, a girl named Etti and a shop window designer, whose relationship sparks a series of events. Despite occasional lapses into sentimentality and indulgent social rhetoric, Nematollah admirably avoids gratuitous action, provides careful characterisation and attention to detail, with uniformly fine performances.

Also promising is Asghar Farhadi, whose second film, **The Beautiful City** (*Shahr-e ziba*), offers engaging and entertaining social comment, very much in the vein of his debut, *Dance in the Mist* (acclaimed at Moscow in 2003). Akbar, 16, has been sentenced to death for murder. He is held in a reformatory school until he can be executed lawfully, after his eighteenth birthday. When Akbar's friend is released after serving a sentence for robbery, he meets Akbar's sister and they try to persuade the murder victim's family to save Akbar from the death penalty. Farhadi's convoluted script avoids emotional excess and, as in his debut, presents a rather optimistic vision of poverty and social corruption.

Another brilliant second feature is Mohammad Mahdi Asgarpur's **The Sacred Footsteps**. After 15 years engaged in various government functions, Asgarpur created a surprisingly effective picture about Rahman, who has grown up among villagers believing that he is a foundling, but, as he prepares to fulfil a religious vow, has a dream that reveals traces of his parents. The director's intelligent use of viewpoints and characterisation has produced one of the finest films on religious and social themes.

Chronicles of war

Rakhshan Bani-etemad's *Mother Gilaneh*, an episode from the three-part portmanteau film, **Triple Chronicles**, tells the story of a young boy, wounded in the war, who along with his mother awaits the arrival of a passenger from the south. Alongside costly war movies such as Ahmad-Reza Darvish's *The Duel* and Rasul Mollaqolipur's *The Family Farm*, *Mother Gilaneh* shines like a small jewel, eschewing the man-to-man combat and shrapnel explosions favoured by other directors. Instead, Bani-etemad manages to portray the lofty sentiments of a wounded combatant's mother without the usual war movie clichés. Bolstered with fine performances by Fatemeh Motamed Aria and Bahram Radan, the film is the best tribute imaginable to all soldiers' mothers.

Behruz Afkhami was another veteran who defied cinemagoers' expectations. After four years away from film-making as a member of parliament, Afkhami abandoned his previously classical approach with an experimental but faithful adaptation of Jafar Modarres Sadeghi's novel, **Gavkhuni (The Marsh)**. A young man leaves Isfahan and takes refuge in Tehran in the hope of forgetting his sad childhood and his father's death. He describes a recurrent dream in which his dead father tries to drag him into Gavkhuni marsh. Memories of his father's strange attachment to the Zayandeh-Rood River, which flows through Isfahan and ends in Gavkhuni, also disturb the narrator.

Afkhami's film is undoubtedly a cut above the normal commercial cinema, but offers nothing more than a pictorial depiction of characters and situations. Many of those who have read the original novel believe it is a perfect piece of literature, and that its film adaptation offers nothing to enhance the text.

Dariush Mehrjui's **Mama's Guest** (*Mehman-e maman*) is a more intelligent literary adaptation, based on Hushang Moradi Kermani's delightful novel. After years of making films on philosophical, mystic themes, Mehrjui has returned to real people with an entertaining and engrossing comedy of situations, similar to his *The Lodgers* (1989). Mother is expecting two dear guests, a newlywed couple on their first visit. But father, a cinema projectionist, returns home to tell his family the theatre has been closed down. Mother is embarrassed because now their financial situation will make it impossible for her to receive the guests in the style dictated by tradition. But the neighbours, despite being equally stretched, come to her aid and throw a splendid party. Mehrjui depicts quiet, tense relationships, and with fine acting and a tight script delivers one of his best works.

Along with this crop of good films, new policy announcements offered hope. The first measure exempts producers from the 5% tax on production costs levied on signature of contracts. In the overall film policy, the major points include the construction of 100 new screening halls and a new, $1.5m private studio complex in Hashtgerd (about 60 kilometres west of Tehran), with construction scheduled to begin in November 2004 and last two years. The government has also set up a state-backed production investment guarantee fund, with the collaboration of insurance firms. It remains to be seen whether Iranian cinema can finally shake off the menacing shadow of crisis.

JAMAL OMID (fcf2@dpi.net.ir) has been a film critic and author for more than 40 years (16 books, including the three-volume *History of Iranian Cinema*). He is also a screenwriter and executive producer and a founding member of Iran's Museum of Cinema.

mir Karimi. Players: Mohammad-Reza Golzar, Gohar Kheirandish, Vishka Asayesh, Alma Oskuie. Prod: Purahmad, Gholam-Reza Musavi.
Abbas leaves his young wife, Targol, and travels to Kish Island in search of a well-paid job. Believing his wife has died in an earthquake, he meets Marjan, who helps him become a popular singer. Then he discovers Targol is alive.

EZDEVAJ BEH SABK-E IRANI (Marriage, Iranian Style)
[Melodrama, 2004] Script: Minu Farsh-Chi. Dir: Hassan Fat'hi. Phot: Kazem Shahbazi. Players: Dariush Arjmand, Fatemeh Gudarzi, Said Kangarani, Shila Khodadad, Ladan Tabatabaie. Prod: Ali Moalem.
A visiting American, David, falls in love with an Iranian girl, Shirin, asks for her hand and complies with traditional rites.

IFG 2004
"Iranian Cinema Now"
Corrections
(p.41) Majid Majidi's *Baran* is set on a construction site, not in a factory. The director of *Djomeh* is Hassan Yektapanah, not Yekapanah.
(p.42) Nasser (not Naser) Taghvai's previous fiction feature before *Blank Page* (2002) was *Oh Iran!* (1990), not *Captain Korshid* (1987). The picture on this page was taken from Rasul Sadr Ameli's *The Girl in the Sneakers*, not the same director's *I'm Taraneh, 15.*
(p.43) The director of *Red* is Fereydoun Jeyrani, not Geyrabni.

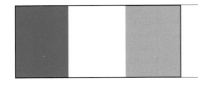

Ireland Michael Dwyer

The Year's Best Films

Michael Dwyer's selection:

Inside I'm Dancing
(Damien O'Donnell)
Adam & Paul
(Lenny Abrahamson)
Man About Dog
(Paddy Breathnach)
Timbuktu (Alan Gilsenan)
Cowboys & Angels
(David Gleeson)

Mark O'Halloran, right, and Tom Jordan Murphy as **Adam & Paul**

Recent and Forthcoming Films

ADAM & PAUL
[Drama, 2004] Script: Mark O'Halloran. Dir: Lenny Abrahmson. Phot: James Mather. Players: O'Halloran, Tom Jordan Murphy. Prod: Porridge Pictures.

BLOOM
[Literary adaptation, 2003] Script: Sean Walsh, based on Ulysses *by James Joyce. Dir: Walsh. Phot: Ciaran Tanham. Players: Stephen Rea, Angeline Ball, Hugh O'Conor. Prod: Odyssey Pictures.*

BOY EATS GIRL
[Comedy-horror, 2004] Script: Derek Landy. Dir: Stephen Bradley. Phot: Players: Samantha Mumba, David Leon, Deirdre O'Kane, Bryan Murray. Prod:

Throughout 2003 the Irish film industry was consumed by a cliff-hanger scenario: the looming real-life threat that the Section 481 tax incentive scheme would be discontinued from the end of 2004. The representative body, Screen Producers Ireland, led the relentless lobbying campaign that intensified in the run-up to the December Budget, highlighting a clear and present danger that killing Section 481 could kill the film industry, with the loss of hundreds of jobs and substantial revenue to the government. To a collective sigh of relief, the government extended the scheme to the end of 2008 and raised the cap on total investment in any one film from €10.48m to €15m.

However, during this extended period of uncertainty, producers were reluctant to risk gambling, so not a single feature was shot in Ireland in the first half of 2004. Ironically, the industry was dormant while local productions were enjoying an all-time high at the box-office. Released in a blaze of publicity – albeit to generally qualified reviews – Joel Schumacher's thriller **Veronica Guerin**, featuring Cate Blanchett as the Irish crime journalist murdered by gangsters in 1996, became the year's box-office champion. Its success was remarkable given that an earlier film dealing with Guerin's life and death, John Mackenzie's *When the Sky Falls* (2000), starring Joan Allen, had done merely average business.

Buena Vista International (Ireland), the distributors of Schumacher's film, scored another big hit with John Crowley's vibrant directing debut, *Intermission* (see *IFG 2004*), and made it a hat-trick with the successful release of the micro-budget Dublin comedy *Spin the Bottle*, a spin-off from a popular Irish TV sitcom.

Jim Sheridan's delightful, semi-autobiographical *In America* took more than €2m in Ireland and received three Oscar nominations. Aisling Walsh's *Song for a Raggy Boy*, released by Irish distributor Abbey Films, took more than €800,000 as the boom for the Irish exhibition sector continued apace, with cinema admissions for 2003 reaching a record 17.4 million (up 4.7% on the previous year). Given the general decline in European admissions, the Irish figures were boosted by the success of home-made productions.

In a decision warmly welcomed by distributors, censorship legislation was amended to allow for films going on limited release to pay substantially lower censorship fees than movies intended for general release. Previously, all films were charged at the same rate, based on their running times. Now fees for a general release picture are €12 per minute, while the charge for a film showing on six prints or fewer is €3 per minute. This new policy has broadened the availability of non-mainstream cinema in Ireland, notably foreign-language productions, US and UK indies and lower-budget Irish movies.

Dubliners and first-timers

The majority of more recent Irish productions have been micro-budget films made by first-time directors. Released to coincide with the centenary of the publication of James Joyce's *Ulysses*, Sean Walsh's **Bloom** marks the second screen treatment of that ostensibly unfilmable novel, following Joseph Strick's *Ulysses* (1967). Walsh bravely grapples with the novel's torrents of dialogue, aided by a sturdy performance from Stephen Rea as Leopold Bloom and Angeline Ball's thoroughly sensual portrayal of his wife, Molly.

Odyssey Pictures

Stephen Rea and Angeline Ball as Leopold and Molly Bloom in **Bloom**

In Lance Daly's punchy comedy **The Halo Effect**, Rea plays the inaptly named Fatso, the owner of a struggling Dublin chip shop whose gambling debts spiral out of control. Daly, who makes resourceful use of a very low budget, peppers his screenplay with sharp Dublin humour. Karl Golden's ironically titled romantic comedy **The Honeymooners** draws together a jilted, emotionally uptight young Dubliner (Jonathan Byrne) and a feisty waitress (Alex Reid) fed up with the false promises of her married lover. Their mutual antagonism gradually thaws in this confident first feature, a bittersweet entertainment featuring refreshingly natural performances from the two leads.

Writer-director David Gleeson, the son of an Irish cinema owner, made a distinctive feature debut with **Cowboys & Angels**, a breezy, sweet-natured comedy-drama engagingly played by Michael Legge and Allan Leech, as two young men who share a flat for economic reasons. Leech plays an assured, openly gay fashion student who takes a shy, bored young civil servant (Legge) on a journey of self-discovery that is charted with wit and insight.

Element Films/Lunar Films.
A teenage date goes disastrously wrong, causing mayhem in suburbia.

BREAKFAST ON PLUTO
[Drama, 2004] Script: Neil Jordan, based on the novel by Patrick McCabe. Dir: Jordan. Phot: Declan Quinn. Players: Cillian Murphy, Liam Neeson, Stephen Rea, Brendan Gleeson. Prod: Parallel Films.
A young transvestite from an Irish border county sets out to become a supermodel in London.

COWBOYS & ANGELS
[Comedy-drama, 2003] Script and Dir: David Gleeson. Phot: Volker Tittel. Players: Michael Legge, Allen Leech, Amy Shiels, Frank Kelly. Prod: Wide Eye Films.

THE HALO EFFECT
[Drama, 2003] Script and Dir: Lance Daly. Phot: Ivan McCullough. Players: Stephen Rea, Grattan Smith, Kerry Condon. Prod: Fastnet Films.

THE HONEYMOONERS
[Comedy, 2003] Script and Dir: Karl Golden. Phot: Darren Tiernan. Players: Jonathan Byrne, Alex Reid, Justine Mitchell. Prod: Samson Films.

Karl Golden, writer-director of **The Honeymooners**

INSIDE I'M DANCING
[Comedy-drama, 2004] Script: Jeffrey Caine. Dir: Damien O'Donnell. Phot: Peter J. Robertson. Players: James McAvoy, Steven Roberston, Romola Garai, Gerard McSorley, Tom Hickey, Brenda Fricker. Prod: Octagon Films/Working Title.

Alan Gilsenan, an adventurous director who moves comfortably between cinema, television and theatre, has produced a characteristically stylish and uncompromising drama in **Timbuktu**, featuring Eva Birthistle as a young Irishwoman aided by a precocious transvestite friend (Karl Geary) on a quest to find her brother, a monk abducted by Algerian rebels in the Sahara. This edgy road movie acutely captures the culture clashes encountered by strangers in a strange land.

Breathnach enjoys his *Dog* days

After the disappointment that was *Blow Dry*, Paddy Breathnach returns to form – and the road movie format of his earlier *I Went Down* – with the pacy and very funny **Man About Dog**. It features Allen Leech, Tom Jordan Murphy and Ciaran Nolan as opportunistic Belfast friends falling foul of a corrupt bookie (Sean McGinley). The comic consequences in Pearse Elliott's nifty screenplay involve forged £20 notes, on which Gerry Adams' features have replaced the Queen's, and a laboratory experiment that produces sexual enhancements to rival anything offered in internet spam.

Treasure Films

Man About Dog

Tom Jordan Murphy demonstrates his range as one of the eponymous duo in **Adam & Paul**, in which he co-stars with the film's writer, Mark O'Halloran, as longtime friends – scruffy, glazed-eyed junkies observed over the course of one eventful day as they stumble around Dublin, desperately scrounging for drugs to feed their addiction. Most people would cross the road to avoid them, but the film finds humour in the most unlikely places and skilfully draws the viewer into the pair's hapless, anxiety-ridden lives. This is an auspicious feature debut for director Lenny Abrahamson after years of working on commercials.

Having made two engaging and serious comedies in the North and Midlands of England (*East Is East* and *Heartlands*), Irish director Damien O'Donnell has, with **Inside I'm Dancing**, made his first film on home turf and his most accomplished work. Stamped with his trademark blend of humanity and humour, it brings together two young men in a home for the disabled. Michael (Steven Robertson),

INTERMISSION
[Drama, 2003] Script: Mark O'Rowe. Dir: John Crowley. Phot: Ryszard Lenczewski. Players: Colin Farrell, Cillian Murphy, Colm Meaney, Kelly MacDonald, Shirley Henderson, Brian F. O'Byrne, Ger Ryan. Prod: Parallel Films/ Company of Wolves.

MAN ABOUT DOG
[Comedy, 2004] Script: Pearse Elliott. Dir: Paddy Breathnach. Phot: Cian de Buitlear. Players: Allen Leech, Tom Jordan Murphy, Ciaran Nolan, Sean McGinley, Fionnula Flanagan. Prod: Treasure Entertainment.

MICKYBO AND ME
[Drama, 2004]
Script: Terry Loane, based on the play Mojo Mickybo *by Owen McCafferty. Dir: Loane. Phot: Roman Osin. Players: Niall Wright, John Jo McNeil, Julie Walters, Ciaran Hinds, Adrian Dunbar, Gina McKee, Susan Lynch. Prod: New Moon Pictures.*
Two young boys escape the sectarianism of 1970s Northern Ireland by imagining they are Butch Cassidy and the Sundance Kid.

THE MIGHTY CELT
[Drama, 2004] Script and Dir: Pearse Elliott. Phot: Seamus Deasy. Players: Robert Carlyle, Gillian Anderson, Ken Stott, Tyrone McKenna, Sean McGinley. Prod: Treasure Entertainment.
Coming-of-age drama about a 14-year-old Northern Irish boy and his greyhound.

OMAGH
[Drama, 2004] Script: Guy Hibbert, Paul Greengrass. Dir: Pete Travis. Phot: Donal Gilligan. Players: Gerard McSorley, Michele Forbes, Brenda Fricker, Stuart Graham. Prod: Hell's Kitchen International/ Tiger Aspect.
Dramatic reconstruction of the Real IRA's bombing of Omagh in 1998 and the long campaign for justice by the families of the victims.

TIMBUKTU
[Road movie, 2004] Script: Paul Freaney. Dir: Alan Gilsenan. Phot: P.J. Dillon. Players: Eva Birthistle, Karl Geary, Liam O'Maonlai. Prod: Yellow Asylum Films/MR Films.

TRISTAN & ISOLDE
[Period drama, 2004] Script: Dean Georgaris. Dir: Kevin Reynolds. Phot: Arthur Reinhart. Players: James Franco, Sylvia Myles, Rufus Sewell, David O'Hara, Dexter Fletcher, Bronagh Gallagher. Prod: Octagon Films/ Scott Free Productions.
The latest screen treatment of the much-filmed story dealing with the doomed relationship between a young guerilla and an Irish princess.

VERONIC GUERLIN
[Drama, 2004] Script: Mary Agnes Donoghue. Dir: Joel Schumacher. Phot: Brendan Galvin. Players: Cate Blanchett, Ciaran Hinds, Brenda Fricker, Gerard McSorley. Prod: Jerry Bruckheimer Films.

Quotes of the Year

"It's not a camp film and it's not really about cross-dressing, but about someone trying to find an alternative to a tough, tragic world."
NEIL JORDAN *on the transvestite hero of his forthcoming* Breakfast on Pluto.

"The film is neither social commentary nor symbolic of other aspects of social or psychological isolationism or exclusion. It did not set out to be overtly a 'political' film."
DAMIEN O'DONNELL *on his disability comedy-drama,* Inside I'm Dancing.

Steven Robertson, left, and James McAvoy in **Inside I'm Dancing**

who has cerebral palsy and has effectively been abandoned by his barrister father, is taken under the wing of Rory (James McAvoy), a brash, coarse newcomer with muscular dystrophy. With the help of Siobhán (Romola Garai), a beautiful supermarket employee-turned-carer, they move beyond institutionalised life and begin to experience independence.

Working from an incisive screenplay by Jeffrey Caine, O'Donnell sensitively explores the impediments faced by the disabled – lack of wheelchair access, social prejudice and condescension, sexual frustration – in an essentially unsentimental film, which proves as witty as it is touching and is graced with terrific performances from its two young leading actors.

MICHAEL DWYER has been film correspondent with *The Irish Times* in Dublin since 1988. He is co-founder and artistic director of the Dublin International Film festival, which had its third edition in February 2005.

Stephen Rea as chip shop owner Fatso in **The Halo Effect**

Israel Dan Fainaru

The Year's Best Films

Dan Fainaru's selection:
Thirst (Tawfik Abu Wael)
Or (Keren Yedaya)
Campfire (Josef Cedar)
Walk on Water (Eytan Fox)
Year Zero (Josef Pitchadze)

Recent and Forthcoming Films

AVANIM (Stones)
[Drama, 2004] Script and Dir:
Raphael Nadjari. Phot: Laurent
Brunet. Players: Assi Levy, Uri
Gavriel, Florence Bloch, Shaul
Mizrahi, Danny Steg, Gaby
Amrani. Prod: Marek Rozenbaum,
Itai Tamir, Geoffroy Grison,
Transfax Film Productions/
BVNG Prod./Compagnie des
Phares et Balises/2.1 Films.

AHAVA COLOMBIANITH
(Colombian Love)
[Comedy, 2004] Script: Reshef and
Regev Levi. Dir: Shay Kanot,
Reshef Levi. Phot: Ofer Harari,
Sasha Franklin. Players: Mili
Avital, Assi Cohen, Shmil Ben Ari,
Nir Levi, Osnat Hakim, Einat
Weizman. Prod: Mosh Danon,
Eilon Ratchkovski, Mirit Tuvi, JCS
Content/Metro Communications.
The pleasures, heartbreaks and
tribulations of getting married.

OR
[Drama, 2004] Script: Keren
Yedaya, Sari Ezouz. Dir: Yedaya.
Phot: Laurent Brunet. Players:
Ronit Elkabetz, Dana Ivgi,
Meshar Cohen, Shmuel Edelman.
Prod: Marek Rozenbaum, Itai
Tamir, Emmanuel Agneray,
Jerome Bleitrach, Transfax/Bizibi.

Thanks to the Cinema Law passed in 2000, the Israeli film industry has made a sharp turn for the better. More films are produced every year. Domestic audiences went back to see them in greater numbers in 2003-04, after decisively rejecting Hebrew-language movies for years (though the 439,000 admissions for Israeli pictures in 2003 represented less than 5% of total admissions), and the list of festivals screening and garlanding Israeli films grows daily.

More importantly, they are beginning to attract investors at home and abroad. United King Films not only provides screens for its Israeli productions but gives them massive advertising campaigns that have no doubt boosted attendance for *Bonjour M. Shlomi* (50,000 admissions in 2003) and *Turn Left at the End of the World* (the year's biggest local hit, with more than 200,000 admissions by August 2004). Abroad, independent producers, international film funds and broadcasters who in the past displayed limited interest, and even then mostly in topical documentaries, are now co-producing Israeli fiction, and five of the films premiered at the Jerusalem Film Festival in 2004 boasted hefty foreign investment.

But all these positive developments may be short-lived if the Treasury has its way (and it usually does) and the funds pledged by the afore-mentioned law (half the commercial television channels' license fees) gradually dwindle into nothing; already they have shrunk by about 60%. No wonder that the Jerusalem festival, which with an all-time record of 14 new Israeli features was originally intended as a grand celebration, turned into one long protest against the latest cut in subsidy, announced on the eve of the event.

Until a solution is found, there is no denying the higher artistic quality and the emergence of new film-makers with clear ideas of what they want to talk about and how. Classic subjects are still around. The success of Avi Nesher's deftly devised **Turn Left at the End of the World**, which throws together in a new town immigrants from India and Morocco, and tops it all with a coming-of-age romance, shows ethnicity remains a favourite subject. But instead of traditional, compare-and-contrast meetings between ethnic opposites, directors are more likely to explore one community's specific problems.

USHPIZIN (Guests)
*[Comedy-drama, 2004] Script:
Shuli Rand. Dir: Gidi Dar. Phot:
Amit Yasur. Players: Rand,
Michal Bat-Sheva Rand, Shaul
Mizrahi, Ilan Ganani. Prod: Dar,
Rafi Bukaee, Gilgamesh
Prod./Eddie King.*
During the Feast of Tabernacles,
when no guest should be turned
out by true believers, the home of
a destitute but devout observant
family is invaded by a couple of
escaped convicts, friends from the
husband's dubious past.

Guests

DISTORTION
*[Drama, 2004] Script: Hami
Bouzaglo, Yoram Milo. Dir:
Bouzaglo. Phot: Milo. Players:
Bouzaglo, Smadar Kilchinski,
Amos Lavie, Tzofit Grant, Avi
Gilor, Haim Znati. Prod:
Bouzaglo, Milo.*
A playwright in crisis tries to
incorporate in a new work his
personal problems in dealing
constantly with the threat of
terrorism, moral and
economic decline.

Ronit Elkabetz in **To Take a Wife**

VELAKAKHTA LEKHA ISHA
(To Take a Wife)
*[Drama, 2004] Script and Dir:
Ronit and Shlomi Elkabetz. Phot:
Yaron Scharf. Players: Ronit
Elkabetz, Simon Abkarian, Sulika
Sabag, Omer Moskovich. Prod:
Marek Rozenbaum, Itai Tamir,
Jean-Philippe Reza, Transfax.*

*Left to right: Mariano Edelman-Moshe, Rotem Abuhave-Jose, Israel Katorza-Josi and
Nadav Abuksis-Gabi in* **Turn Left at the End of the World**

Women's rights, and wrongs

Amos Gitai's *Kadosh* opened the door for further examination of
the orthodox world and women's status within it in no fewer than
four new features. Inspired by one of the country's major recent
economic scandals, Rafael Nadjari's **Stones** (*Avanim*) has a young
married woman from an observant family reveal to the law how her
father and an orthodox politician defrauded the Treasury and used
the money to build a religious college. The script tackles admirably
the sexual rights of a woman in a community that does not
recognise such things, and the double standards of people who
pretend to be symbols of probity.

To Take a Wife (*Velakakhta lekha isha*) is far more focused. A sort
of *Woman under the Influence* in a family of Moroccan immigrants,
it has Ronit Elkabetz, one of the country's best-known actresses,
directing for the first time with her brother, Shlomi, and playing as
if in a trance a woman who can no longer stand the passive
oppression of family life dictated by Moroccan traditions, without
quite bringing herself to escape into the unknown. A claustrophobic
picture which seems to suffocate its characters with tight camera
angles, its fate will hang on audience reaction to Elkabetz's over-
exalted performance (she's in every scene).

In **Campfire** (*Medurath hasheveth*), Josef Cedar's second foray into
the National Religious camp, the widow of a nationalist religious
activist with two adolescent daughters intends to join a new West
Bank colony and finds out the people who surrounded her late
husband with sympathy are less enthusiastic about her. This
understated film's main strength is in the things it implies rather than
states, particularly that the fanatical views of West Bank settlers are
a pretext for obtaining bigger, more comfortable houses (largely at
the state's expense).

As if to answer Gitai's indictment of orthodox rituals, Gidi Dar's
Guests (*Ushpizin*), written by Shuli and Michal Bat-Sheva Rand,

both actors who left the secular world for the religious community, focuses on faith rather than procedure, with surprising results. Dar gives this comedy of manners earnest, almost missionary undertones, and elicits soulful leading performances. It's a sincere attempt to reveal a usually secluded world that rejects movies.

Bride at the border

The Middle East conflict has taken a back seat cinematically since the advent of the second Intifada, but still surfaces, for example in **The Syrian Bride** (*Hakala hasurith*), Eran Riklis' neatly packaged melodrama about a young Druze woman whose family has decided to marry her to one of their own people, living across the border in Syria. The preparations for the wedding and border crossing cause bureaucratic, political and personal crises, highlighting Druze traditions and attitudes to women, and Israeli-Syrian border skirmishes. Well-acted, nicely shot and politically correct to a fault, it will probably appeal to larger audiences abroad than at home (Audience Award, FIPRESCI and Ecumenical prizes at Montreal 2004).

The Syrian Bride

Eytan Fox's remarkably successful **Walk on Water** (120,000 admissions) deals with the sexual and national identity crisis of an Israeli macho man and sends him to Germany, whose youths also have identity problems. Dan Verete offers a different take on these issues in **Metallic Blues**, a dark, rather predictable comedy in which two Israeli car dealers think they can make a fortune by selling an American stretch limo in Germany. One is Ashkenazi and carries the traumas of a second-generation Shoah survivor, the other is Sephardi and less personally affected by being in Germany.

Having already experimented with multi-layered storytelling, Josef Pitchadze in **Year Zero** (*Shnath efes*) presents a leisurely, *Short Cuts*-style composite portrait of contemporary Israel, starting with an egotistic real estate agent and his wife, a radio broadcaster, then moving on to a student who prostitutes herself to feed her son, a sound engineer paying tribute to his dead punk father, a shady wheeler-dealer and a blind physiotherapist, amongst others.

HAKALA HASURITH
(The Syrian Bride)
[*Drama, 2004*] *Script: Suha Arraf, Eran Riklis. Dir: Riklis. Phot: Michael Wiesweg. Players: Hiam Abbas, Makhram Khoury, Clara Khoury, Ashraf Barhoum, Eyad Sheety, Evelyn Kaplun, Adnan Trabshi, Marlene Bajjali, Julie-Anne Roth, Uri Gabriel, Alon Dahan. Prod: Riklis, Bettina Brokemper, Antoine de Clermont-Tonnerre, Michael Eckelt.*

MEDURATH HASHEVETH
(Campfire)
[*Drama, 2004*] *Script and Dir: Josef Cedar. Phot: Ofer Inov. Players: Michaela Eshet, Hani Furstenberg, Moshe Ivgy, Maya Maron, Assi Dayan, Yehoram Gaon, Idith Teperson, Oshri Cohen. Prod: David Mandil, Eyal Shirai, Cinema Prod.*

METALLIC BLUES
[*Comedy-drama, 2004*] *Script and Dir: Danny Verete. Phot: Yoram Milo. Players: Avi Kushnir, Moshe Ivgy. Prod: Verete, Suzanne Girard, Klaus Rettig.*

ATASH (Thirst)
[*Drama, 2004*] *Script and Dir: Tawfik Abu Wael. Phot: Asaf Sudry. Players: Hussein Yassin Mahajne, Amal Bweerat, Roba Blal, Gamila Abdul Hussein, Ahmed Abdel Algani, Muhammad Shafik Kahawish. Prod: Avi Kleinberger, Baher Agbaria, Atash Partnership.*

SHNATH EFES (Year Zero)
[*Drama, 2004*] *Script: Josef Pitchadze, Dov Steuer. Dir: Pitchadze. Phot: Itay Neeman. Players: Menashe Noy, Keren Mor, Sara Adler, Moni Moshonov, Exra Kafri, Dani Geva, Dan Toren, Tzuki Ringart, Uri Klauzner, Roman Kricheli, James Gonsalves. Prod: Pitchadze, Steuer, Lior Shefer, Year Zero Ltd.*

HAKOACH LISKHOTH
(Watermarks)
[*Documentary, 2004*] *Script and Dir: Yaron Zilberman. Phot: Tom Hurwitz. Prod: Zilberman, Yonatan Israel, Paul Rozenberg,*

Philippa Kovarsky, Cinephil
Tel Aviv.

ODESSA MAMA
*[Documentary, 2004] Script and
Dir: Michal Boganim. Phot:
Jakob Ihre. Prod: Marek
Rozenbaum, Itay Tamir, Frederic
Niedermayer, Transfax Film
Productions.*
Reviews the history of the
vanishing Jewish community of
Odessa, now spread all over the
world. Shot in Ukraine, New
York and Ashdod in Israel, it
was one of the year's best
documentaries.

MEKUDESHSETH
(Sentenced to Marriage)
*[Documentary, 2004] Script and
Dir: Anath Zuria. Phot: Ron
Katzenelson. Prod: Amit Breuer,
Amythos Films.*

ARNA'S CHILDREN
*[Documentary, 2003] Script and
Dir: Daniel Daniel, Juliano Mer-
Khamis. Phot: Mer-Khamis,
Hanna Abu Saada, Uri Steinmetz.
Featuring: Arna Mer-Khamis.
Prod: Osnat Trabelsi, Pieter van
Huystee.*
Study of Arna Mer-Kahmis,
the co-director's mother, who
founded an alternative school for
Palestinian children. It looks at
what happened to these children
once they grew up. Best
Documentary at Tribeca 2004.

MAKHSOMIM (Checkpoints)
*[Documentary, 2003] Script, Dir
and Phot: Yoav Shamir. Prod:
Amit Breuer, Edna Kowarsky,
Elinor Kowarsky, Amythos Films.*

The year's best films were the Cannes prize-winners. Keren
Yedaya's rigorous **Or** (Camera D'Or for best first feature) pits a
middle-aged prostitute (intensely played by Ronit Elkabetz) against
the adolescent daughter desperately trying to get her off the streets.
Grim, painful, uncompromising and stark, this is a remarkable
achievement, matched only by **Thirst** (*Atash*; FIPRESCI Award),
Tawfik Abu Wael's tragedy of the Palestinian people, metaphorically
dramatised in the father-son conflict inside an Arab family living out
in a wasteland, rejected by their own people and harassed by the
unseen Israeli presence. It is superbly performed by non-actors and
stunningly shot in widescreen.

Transfax Film Productions

Dana Ivgy, left, as the daughter of a prostitute (Ronit Elkabetz) in **Or**

Documentary is now so fertile that it becomes increasingly difficult
to see every new film. The more controversial items included Yoav
Shamir's **Checkpoints** (*Makhsomin*), which makes unsettling points
about the Israelis manning the infamous barriers to and from the
Palestinian territories. Giuliano Mer's **Arna's Children** may be the
first Israeli-produced film partially to legitimise Palestinian terrorism.

Sentenced to Marriage is Anath Zuria's sequel to her much-
praised *Purity*, and is another searing portrait of victimised orthodox
women denied the right to divorce. **Watermarks** focuses on
Hakoach Vienna, the legendary pre-Second World War women's
swimming team, and throws in troubling remarks on the conduct
of the Viennese that Austrian Television asked to have cut before
broadcast. Israeli Television has proved unwilling to show Shiri
Tzur's **I Wanted to Be a Hero**, about Israeli conscientious
objectors. Avi Nesher's **Oriental** tries to explain the Middle East
crisis through the vagaries in the relations between a Russian-born
belly dancer and her Arab accompanists.

DAN FAINARU (dfainaru@netvision.net.il) is co-editor of Israel's only
film magazine, *Cinematheque*, and a former director of the Israeli
Film Institute. He reviews regularly for *Screen International*.

Italy Lorenzo Codelli

The Year's Best Films

Lorenzo Codelli's selection:

Good Morning, Night
(Marco Bellocchio)

The Consequences of Love
(Paolo Sorrentino)

The Scent of Blood
(Mario Martone)

First Love (Matteo Garrone)

A Particular Silence
(Docu. Stefano Rulli)

Recent Films

**L'AMORE È ETERNO
FINCHÉ DURA**
(Love Is Eternal Until It Lasts)
*[Comedy, 2004] Script: Carlo
Verdone, Pasquale Plastino,
Francesca Marciano. Dir:
Verdone. Phot: Danilo Desideri.
Players: Verdone, Laura Morante.
Prod: Vittorio Cecchi Gori,
Cecchi Gori Group.*

L'AMORE RITROVATO
(Love Found Again)
*[Drama, 2004] Script: Carlo
Mazzacurati, Doriana Leondeff,
Claudio Piersanti, from Carlo
Cassola's novel. Dir: Mazzacurati.
Phot: Luca Bigazzi. Players:
Stefano Accorsi, Maya Sansa.
Prod: Donatella Botti, Bianca
Film/Medusa Film/
Pyramide (France).*

BALLO A TRE PASSI
(Three-Step Dancing)
*[Drama, 2003] Script and Dir:
Salvatore Mereu. Phot: Renato
Berta, Tommaso Borgstrom,
Renato Bravi, Nicolas Frank.
Players: Caroline Ducey,
Yaël Abecassis. Prod:
Gianluca Arcopinto, Andrea
Occhipinti, Eyescreen.*

A transitional year preceded a predictable doomsday. In January 2004, the state cut off the cash flow that had been keeping the film industry breathing. A further €26m cut was threatened by the conservative government, which simultaneously tried to impose bombastic, scarcely enforceable reform on the subsidy system. This was a triple setback in line with the widespread depression affecting several major companies (Fiat, Alitalia, Parmalat) – but not Prime Minister Silvio Berlusconi's expanding media empire.

From August 2003 to August 2004, 70 national features were released, securing around 25% of the gross. Two titles only reached the top ten for this period: **Unexpected Paradise** (*Il paradiso all'improvviso*), Leonardo Pieraccioni's comic vehicle for his own *bon vivant* persona, and **Christmas in India** (*Natale in India*), tycoon Aurelio De Laurentiis' usual lowbrow holiday farce.

The Venice Mostra's two latest instalments were at the core of the crisis. In 2003, Rai Cinema, the public television network's film arm, pushed with all its might to secure the Golden Lion for Marco Bellocchio's *Good Morning, Night*, failed, then swore never to swim back to Lido island. It later appeared elated by the culture ministry's dismissal of Venice director Moritz de Hadeln. Just before Venice 2004, Rai Cinema and almost every other film company (including Berlusconi's mighty Medusa!) signed a full-page ad in the daily newspapers complaining of mistreatment by the government.

Back at Venice 2004, Rai Cinema was pushing hard for Gianni Amelio's *The House Keys,* but once more the Golden Lion eluded the company. Despite its long history of progressive and cultivated

Stefano Damadio/01 Distribution

Luigi Lo Cascio in **Good Morning, Night**

BARZELLETTE (Jokes)
[Comedy, 2004] Script: Enrico Vanzina, Carlo Vanzina. Dir: Carlo Vanzina. Phot: Claudio Zamarion. Players: Luigi Proietti, Carlo Buccirosso. Prod: Aurelio De Laurentiis, Filmauro.

BUONGIORNO, NOTTE
(Good Morning, Night)
[Drama, 2003] Script and Dir: Marco Bellocchio. Phot: Pasquale Mari. Players: Maya Sansa, Roberto Herlitzka. Prod: Marco Bellocchio, Sergio Pelone, Filmalbatros/Rai Cinema/Sky.

CANTANDO DIETRO I PARAVENTI
(Singing Behind Screens)
[Drama, 2003] Script and Dir: Ermanno Olmi. Phot: Fabio Olmi. Players: Bud Spencer, Jun Ichikawa. Prod: Luigi Musini, Roberto Cicutto, Cinema 11/Rai Cinema/Sky/Pierre Grise Productions (France)/Lakeshore Entertainment (UK).

IL CARTAIO (The Cardmaker)
[Thriller, 2004] Script: Dario Argento, Franco Ferrini. Dir: Argento. Phot: Debie Benoît. Players: Stefania Rocca, Liam Cunningham. Prod: Claudio Argento, Opera Film/ Medusa Film.

CATERINA VA IN CITTÀ
(Caterina Goes to Town)
[Comedy, 2003] Script: Paolo Virzì, Francesco Bruni. Dir: Virzì. Phot: Arnaldo Catinari. Players: Alice Teghil, Sergio Castellitto. Prod: Riccardo Tozzi, Cattleya/Rai Cinema.

CERTI BAMBINI
(Some Children)
[Drama, 2004] Script: Antonio Frazzi, Andrea Frazzi, Marcello Fois, Ferdinando Vicentini Orgnani, Diego De Silva, from De Silva's novel. Dir: Andrea and Antonio Frazzi. Phot: Paolo Carnera. Players: Gianluca Di Gennaro, Carmine Recano. Prod: Rosario Rinaldo, Pequod.

CHE NE SARÀ DI NOI
(What Will Happen to Us)

management, Rai is becoming more commercially oriented. In partnership with Cattleya, Bianca, Mikado, Sacher and a cluster of so-called 'independents' bold enough to face hard times, it used regularly to handle ambitious film-makers such as Ermanno Olmi, Paolo Virzì, Francesca Comencini, Pupi Avati, Giuseppe Piccioni and Nanni Moretti.

Bellocchio sees Red

Bellocchio's **Good Morning, Night** (*Buongiorno, notte*), a rageful remembrance of Christian Democrat leader Aldo Moro's kidnapping and murder by the Red Brigades in 1978, achieves a complex psychoanalytical exposé of extremism, and doubles as a bitter metaphor for the current imprisonment of ideas and individual freedoms. Amelio's affectionate look at a troubled father and son relationship, **The House Keys** (*Le chiavi di casa*), draws its lymph from physically handicapped Andrea Rossi, a witty, Harry Potter-ish boy more appealing than any able-bodied professional actor.

Claudio Iannone/01 Distribution

Kim Rossi Stuart, left, and Andrea Rossi as father and son in **The House Keys**

Ermanno Olmi's lavish extravaganza, **Singing Behind Screens** (*Cantando dietro i paraventi*), set in a fantasy Middle Ages on a Chinese pirate ship with a female warrior captain, propels a hymn to peace. Its astonishing views à la Méliès are sometimes blurred by talky sermonising. Paolo Virzì's crackling dialogues for **Caterina Goes to Town** (*Caterina va in città*) enliven his topical satire of a nation sternly divided into left and right-wing factions, permanently assaulting each other from schooldays onwards.

Francesca Comencini found trade union support for **I Like Working – Mobbing** (*Mi piace lavorare*), starring a dignified Nicoletta Braschi (Mrs Roberto Benigni), a neorealist pamphlet about the practice known in Italy as white-collar 'mobbing' (managers sidestep the unions by harassing staff earmarked for dismissal into quitting). Notwithstanding its propagandist happy ending, Comencini's low-budget blitz helped invigorate the engaged cinema movement. Limited distribution in the arthouse normally fixes the destiny for this kind of 'feel-bad' fare. Eugenio Cappuccio's **To Sleep Next to Her**

(*Volevo solo dormirle addosso*, 2004) brings off a zanier variant on Comencini's denounciation, by laying bare a rampant executive's soul.

Young and dangerous

Talented Neapolitan Vincenzo Marra's **Land Wind** (*Vento di terra*), his second uncompromising opus, deals in the style of Zavattini with a destitute soldier contaminated by gases on a mission to Bosnia. Racism against underprivileged immigrants is finely analysed in Roman newcomer Francesco Munzi's **Saimir**. Michelangelo Frammartino's **The Gift** (*Il dono*), a wordless observation of a dying Calabrian village, is an ageless parable. Grotesque hyper-realism is former painter Matteo Garrone's favourite playground. In **First Love** (*Primo amore*) he pokes fun at a goldsmith's vampiric manipulation of an anorexic girl and presents probably the blackest and most vengeful lampoon of opulent, self-satisfied North-East provinces since Pietro Germi's masterful *Ladies and Gentlemen* (1966).

Paolo Sorrentino's **The Consequences of Love** (*Le conseguenze dell'amore*) is a miniature about an apparently wealthy financier (Toni Servillo) living alone in a lousy Swiss hotel. His hidden secrets surface through a suspenseful circle of coincidences. A compassionate novelist as well as an innovative stylist – as his 2001 debut, *One Man Up* (*Un uomo in più*), had already revealed – Sorrentino ranks among the leading Italian hyphenates.

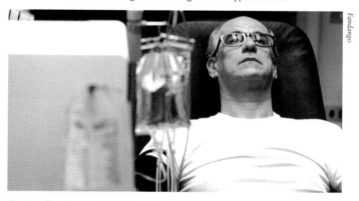

Fandango

Toni Servillo in **The Consequences of Love**

Like Garrone himself, Sorrentino was lucky enough to join offbeat producer Domenico Procacci and his Fandango multi-media company. This long-haired impresario has also sponsored Gabriele Muccino, Luciano Ligabue and Emanuele Crialese: the "Fandango Wave". Guido Chiesa came lately under Procacci's umbrella to direct **Working Slowly** (*Lavorare con lentezza*, 2004), about an anarchic student radio station in the rebellious 1970s. This is a generational fresco unfortunately drowned by a torrent of ideological artifice.

[Comedy, 2004] Script: Giovanni Veronesi, Silvio Muccino. Dir: Veronesi. Phot: Fabio Zamarion. Players: Muccino, Violante Placido. Prod: Aurelio De Laurentiis, Filmauro.

LE CHIAVI DI CASA
(The House Keys)
[Drama, 2004] Script: Gianni Amelio, Sandro Petraglia, Stefano Rulli, from Giuseppe Pontiggia's novel. Dir: Amelio. Phot: Luca Bigazzi. Players: Kim Rossi Stuart, Andrea Rossi. Prod: Elda Ferri, Jean Vigo Italia/Achab Film/Rai Cinema/Pola Pandora Produktion (Germany)/Arena Films (France).

LE CONSEGUENZE
DELL'AMORE
(The Consequences of Love)
[Drama, 2004] Script and Dir: Paolo Sorrentino. Phot: Luca Bigazzi. Players: Toni Servillo, Olivia Magnani. Prod: Domenico Procacci, Fandango/Indigo Film/Medusa Film.

IL DONO (The Gift)
[Drama, 2004] Script and Dir: Michelangelo Frammartino. Phot: Mario Miccoli. Players: Angelo Frammartino, Gabrielle Maiolo. Prod: Letizia Dradi, Santamira Produzioni/Coop. Ca.Ri.Na.

THE DREAMERS
[Drama, 2003] Script: Gilbert Adair, from his novel. Dir: Bernardo Bertolucci. Phot: Fabio Cianchetti. Players: Michael Pitt, Eva Green, Louis Garrel. Prod: Jeremy Thomas, Recorded Picture Company (UK)/Peninsula Films (France)/Medusa Film.

THE HEART IS DECEITFUL...
ABOVE ALL THINGS
[Drama 2004] Script: Asia Argento, Alessandro Magania, from J.T. Leroy's novel. Dir: Argento. Phot: Eric Alan Edwards. Players: Argento, Jimmy Bennet. Prod: Gianluca Curti, Minerva/Metro-Tartan (UK)/Wild Bunch (France)/Artist Film Inc. (Japan).

**MI PIACE LAVORARE
(I Like Working – Mobbing)**
*[Drama, 2004] Script and Dir:
Francesca Comencini. Phot: Luca
Bigazzi. Players: Nicoletta
Braschi, Camille Dugay
Comencini. Prod: Donatella
Botti, Bianca Film/Rai Cinema.*

**NATALE IN INDIA
(Christmas in India)**
*[Comedy, 2003] Script: Fausto
Brizzi, Lorenzo De Luca, Marco
Martani, Neri Parenti. Dir:
Parenti. Phot: Gianlorenzo
Battaglia. Players: Christian
De Sica, Massimo Boldi. Prod:
Aurelio De Laurentiis, Filmauro.*

**NON TI MUOVERE
(Don't Move)**
*[Drama, 2004] Script: Sergio
Castellitto, Margaret Mazzantini,
from Mazzantini's novel. Dir:
Castellitto. Phot: Gianfilippo
Corticelli. Players: Castellitto,
Penélope Cruz. Prod: Riccardo
Tozzi, Cattleya/Medusa
Film/Alquimia Cinema (Spain).*

**L'ODORE DEL SANGUE
(The Scent of Blood)**
*[Drama, 2004] Script: Mario
Martone, from Goffredo Parise's
novel. Dir: Martone. Phot: Cesare
Accetta. Players: Michele Placido,
Fanny Ardant. Prod: Donatella
Botti, Bianca Film/Mikado
Film/Arcapix (France)/Babe
(France).*

**IL PARADISO
ALL'IMPROVVVISO
(Unexpected Paradise)**
*[Comedy, 2003] Script: Leonardo
Pieraccioni, Giovanni Veronesi.
Dir: Pieraccioni. Phot: Italo
Petriccione. Players: Pieraccioni,
Angie Cepeda. Prod: Pieraccioni,
Levante Film/Medusa Film.*

PRIMO AMORE (First Love)
*[Drama, 2004] Script: Matteo
Garrone, Vitaliano Trevisan,
Massimo Gaudioso. Dir:
Garrone. Phot: Marco Onorato.
Players: Trevisan, Michela
Cescon. Prod: Domenico
Procacci, Fandango.*

Andrea and Antonio Frazzi's **Some Children** (*Certi bambini*) champions Neapolitan boys' violent deeds using dull clichés but won a prize at Karlovy Vary 2004. Locarno 2004 prize-winner **Private**, a dreary *kammerspiel* by newcomer Saverio Costanzo, champions a Palestinian family's right to survive. Sicilian Roberto Andò's sophomore movie, **Under a False Name** (*Sotto falso nome*), starring Daniel Auteuil as a secretive novelist, exhibits Gallic sophistication. Debutant Salvatore Mereu, from Sardinia, celebrates in **Three-Step Dancing** (*Ballo a tre passi*) his island's archaic rites.

Winners and losers

Unfairly snubbed by critics and audiences, Mario Martone's **The Scent of Blood** (*L'odore del sangue*) studies a married couple's sexual inferno. The husband (a very convincing Michele Placido) embodies late writer and journalist Goffredo Parise's peculiar mythology. A kind of outmoded intellectual cynicism gets parachuted into today's degraded Roman elite by Martone's carnal oratorio. This dynamic director works too seldom in cinema but remains a shining star of stage and opera.

Fanny Ardant and Michele Placido as a married couple in **The Scent of Blood**

Bernardo Bertolucci wished obviously to dance another tango in Paris with **The Dreamers**. Three student cinéphiles make love and revolution inside a bourgeois apartment while May '68 explodes outside their windows. Some brilliantly executed choreographies warm up this stagnant sexcom, which lacks truthful confessions. In **Don't Move** (*Non ti muovere*), a big hit, popular actor-director Sergio Castellitto exploits his wife Margaret Mazzantini's megaselling pulp: a coldhearted weepie about a wealthy doctor who rapes a penniless, hideous immigrant named Italia (an unbelievably camouflaged Penélope Cruz).

Carlo Mazzacurati's **Love Found Again** (*L'amore ritrovato*), a meticulous adaptation of Carlo Cassola's romance, cannot really hide its basic instinct of capitalising on divo Stefano Accorsi's fame. Baptised "Mastroianni Redux", Accorsi was acclaimed by fans for baring all in Michele Placido's pap **Wherever You Are** (*Ovunque sei*, 2004). Breakneck star Silvio Muccino (director Gabriele's younger brother) displays his rough charms in Giovanni Veronesi's teen summer romp **What Will Happen to Us** (*Che ne sarà di noi*).

Among seasonal sleepers, **Love Is Eternal Until It Lasts** (*L'amore è eterno finché dura*) is a pleasantly familiar entertainment directed by and starring ageing Roman idol Carlo Verdone. Carlo Vanzina's portmanteau **Jokes** (*Barzellette*) raises broad laughs, thanks especially to chameleon comedian Luigi Proietti. Daniele Ciprì and Franco Maresco, a Sicilian duo scorned by censors, reconvene with two uneven mockumentaries: **The Return of Cagliostro** (*Il ritorno di Cagliostro*) and **How We Wreaked Havoc on Italian Cinema** (*Come inguaiammo il cinema italiano*, 2004), the former devoted to an imaginary old movie, the latter to Franco Franchi and Ciccio Ingrassia, those once-lionised folksy clowns. Giuseppe Piccioni returns to top form with **The Life I Would Like** (*La vita che vorrei*, 2004), a personal reshuffling of themes from *The French Lieutenant's Woman,* as two co-stars (sparkling Sandra Ceccarelli and Luigi Lo Cascio) fall in love on set and in the costume movie they are shooting.

With **Christmas Rematch** (*La rivincita di natale*), prolific Pupi Avati offers an emotional sequel to his successful **Christmas Gift** (*Regalo di Natale*, 1986), as the same bunch of disillusioned card-sharps are reunited for their final contest. Veteran Michelangelo Antonioni may have bidden a sad, dragging farewell with his documentary short, *Michelangelo's Look* (*Lo sguardo di Michelangelo*, 2004), promoting Michelangelo Buonarroti's restored Moses, followed by *The Dangerous Thread of Things* (*Il filo pericoloso delle cose*, 2004), his voyeuristic contribution to the portmanteau **Eros**.

Argento family values

Shockmaster Dario Argento has recently left behind horror for giallo pulp, and **The Cardmaker** (*Il cartaio*) looks short of his former punch and thrills. His Hollywood-based daughter, Asia, concocted **The Heart Is Deceitful... Above All Things**, a baaad-mommy recital hammily performed by the director-star. SFX wizard Sergio Stivaletti's **Three Faces of Terror** (*I tre volti del torrore, 2004)* resuscitates Mario Brava's gothic universe.

The documentary pasture generates zero profits and gets almost no help from television networks too fearful of breeding any potential Michael Moore. Yet it attracts a few daring explorers such as acclaimed screenwriter Stefano Rulli (*The Best of Youth*, *The House Keys*). In **A Particular Silence** (*Un silenzio particolare*, 2004) he assembles an extraordinarily intimate journal covering 20 years of his retarded son Matteo's pains.

**IL RITORNO DI CAGLIOSTRO
(The Return of Cagliostro)**
[Comedy, 2003] Script: Daniele Ciprì, Franco Maresco, Lillo Iacolino. Dir: Ciprì, Maresco. Phot: Ciprì. Players: Robert Englund, Luigi Maria Burruano. Prod: Giuseppe Bisso, Cinico Cinema.

**LA RIVINCITA DI NATALE
(Christmas Rematch)**
[Drama, 2004] Script and Dir: Pupi Avati. Phot: Pasquale Rachini. Players: Diego Abatantuono, Alessandro Haber. Prod: Antonio Avati, Duea Film/Medusa Film.

**SOTTO FALSO NOME
(Under a False Name)**
[Drama, 2004] Script: Roberto Andò, Salvatore Marcarelli. Dir: Andò. Phot: Maurizio Calvesi. Players: Daniel Auteuil, Greta Scacchi. Prod: Fabrizio Mosca, Titti Film/Vega Film (Switzerland).

VENTO DI TERRA (Land Wind)
[Drama, 2004] Script and Dir: Vincenzo Marra. Phot: Mario Amura. Players: Vincenzo Pacilli, Edoardo Melone. Prod: Tilde Corsi, R & C Produzioni.

Quote of the Year

"Currently Berlusconi and his alliance are doing things so unfairly, so selfishly that in some ways they are reanimating the opposition."
MARCO BELLOCCHIO, director.

Corrections
In Lorenzo Codelli's *IFG 2004* report, the still from *A Heart Elsewhere* shows Neri Marcorè, not Marcoreè (p. 189); the picture shows The *Best of Youth*'s Sonia Bergamasco, not Berganasco (p. 192); *Respiro* was directed by Emanuele Crialese, not Grialese (p. 194).

David di Donatello Awards 2004

Film: *The Best of Youth* (*La meglio gioventù*).
Director: Marco Tullio Giordana (*The Best of Youth*).
Debuting Director: Salvatore Mereu (*Three-Step Dancing/Ballo a tre passi*).
Producer: Angelo Barbagallo (*The Best of Youth*).
Actress: Penélope Cruz (*Don't Move/Non ti muovere*).
Actor: Sergio Castellitto (*Don't Move*).
Supporting Actor: Roberto Herlitzka (*Good Morning, Night*).
Supporting Actress: Margherita Buy (*Caterina Goes to Town/Caterina va in città*).
Script: Sandro Petraglia, Stefano Rulli (*The Best of Youth*).
Cinematography: Italo Petriccione (*I'm Not Scared/*

Finally, some interesting volumes on Italy's film heritage, including Vittorio Storaro's outstanding English-language trilogy, *Writing with Light*, and Dante Ferretti's parallel coffee table tome, *The Art of Production Design* (all Electa/Accademia dell'Immagine). Marsilio Editori has published a collection of Rai Cinema's produced scripts, from the likes of Amelio, Bellocchio and Virzì. Gremese Editore has produced national genre-by-genre filmographies (*Fantascienza, fantasy, horror,* and *Gialli, polizieschi, thriller*) and Dino Risi has written a spellbinding autobiography, *I miei mostri* (Mondadori).

LORENZO CODELLI (codelli@interware.it) is on the board of Cineteca del Friuli and is a regular contributor to *Positif* and other periodicals.

Io non ho paura).
Music: Banda Osiris (*First Love/Primo amore*).
Art Direction: Luigi Marchione (*Singing Behind Screens*).
Costume Design: Francesca Sartori (*Singing Behind Screens*).
Editing: Roberto Missiroli (*The Best of Youth*).
Sound: Fulgenzio Ceccon (*The Best of Youth*).

Short Film: *Sole* (Michele Carrillo), *Zinana* (Pippo Mezzapesa).
Foreign Film: *The Barbarian Invasions*.
European Film: *Dogville; Rosenstrasse*.

Orion/Kobal

CARLO DI PALMA, *left, shooting* September *(1987) with* Woody Allen. *The Italian cinematographer, who described his decade-long collaboration with Allen as "the most enjoyable period of my professional life", died on July 9, 2004, aged 79.*

Japan Tomomi Katsuta

The Year's Best Films

Tomomi Katsuta's selection:
Nobody Knows
(Hirokazu Kore-Eda)
Vibrator (Ryuichi Hiroki)
Jose, Tiger and Fish
(Isshin Inudo)
**Kamikaze Girls –
Shimotsuma Story**
(Tetsuya Nakajima)
**Akame 48 Waterfalls –
Shinju** (Genjiro Arato)

Shinobu Terajima in **Vibrator**

Recent and Forthcoming Films

TOKYO GODFATHERS
*[Animation, 2003]
Script: Satoshi Kon, Keiko
Nobumoto. Dir: Kon. Prod:
Madhouse/Tokyo Godfathers
Production Committee.*
An ex-bicycle racer, a homosexual
and a runaway girl, all homeless,
discover an abandoned baby and
try to find its mother.

RIARIZUMU NO YADO
(Ramblers)
*[Drama, 2003] Script: Kosuke
Mukai, Nobuhiro Yamashita. Dir:
Yamashita. Phot: Tatsuhito Kondo.
Players: Keishi Nagatsuka, Kouji
Yamamoto. Prod: Yuji Sadai,
Kunihiko Tomioka, Haruo
Okamoto, Bitters End/Vap.*

In 2003, Japanese cinemas took a record $1.87 billion (203.3 billion yen), up from $1.81 billion in 2002. The major film companies and the media hailed a revival and annual admissions of 200 million were in sight for the first time since 1971, reflecting the steady rise from 119.6 million in 1996.

After years of negligence, the Japanese government finally dipped its hand deep into the public purse to boost the previously perfunctory support for local films, assigning $22.9m for the 2004 fiscal year, an increase of 34% on 2003, despite the still troubled state of the economy. Vivid memories of the Second World War, when the fascist government forced the industry to make propaganda films, coupled with the relative commercial success of Japanese cinema after the war, have traditionally made politicians and film-makers wary of official subsidy. However, the prolonged recession has reawakened the government to the value of films as commercial and cultural exports, while anxiety at the rise of other Asian cinemas, notably South Korea, has spurred the need to foster new talents.

Recent international approval for Japanese films and actors may help revive local audience interest. Yoji Jamada's *The Twilight Samurai (Tasogare seibei)* was nominated for Best Foreign-Language film at the Oscars, as was *The Last Samurai's* Ken Watanabe in the Best Supporting Actor category (he was then cast in *Batman Begins*). After the success of *The Ring*, remakes of several other Japanese films have been greenlit, including Takashi

Yuji Oda, centre, in **Bayside Shakedown 2**

An offbeat road movie about the meeting between an indie director and a scriptwriter.

CHI TO HONE
(*literally,* **Blood and Bone**)
[Drama, 2004] Script: Chong Wui Sin, Yoichi Sai. Dir: Sai. Phot: Tsuyoshi Hamada. Players: Beat Takeshi, Kyoka Suzuki. Prod: Chi to Hone Production Committee.
During and after the Second World War, a strong and selfish Korean–Japanese man tortures those around him with his violence and egoism.

ODORU TANUKI GOTEN
(*literally,* **Dancing Raccoon Castle**)
[Musical comedy, 2004] Script: Yoshio Urasawa. Dir: Seijun Suzuki. Players: Zhang Ziyi, Joe Odagiri. Prod: Geneon Entertainment/Dentsu/Nippon Herald Films/Ogura Jimusyo.
Veteran's remake of a classic Japanese operetta is a story of love between a human prince and a raccoon princess in human form.

UMINEKO
(*literally,* **Japanese Gull**)
[Drama, 2004] Script: Tomomi Tsutsui. Dir: Yoshimitsu Morita. Phot: Minoru Ishiyama. Players: Misaki Ito, Toru Nakamura, Koichi Sato. Prod: Toshiya Nomura, Yoshihiro Kojima, Kazuko Misawa.
When Kaoru's marriage to a fisherman turns sour, she is overwhelmed by love for her brother-in-law.

SEMISHIGURE
(*literally,* **Shower of Cicada Buzz**)
[Drama, 2004] Script and Dir: Mitsuo Kurotsuchi. Phot: Shinji Kugimiya. Players: Somegoro Ichikawa, Yoshino Kimura. Prod: Tateo Mataki.
At the end of the Edo era, a lower-class samurai, whose father must commit harakiri after he is accused of taking part in a conspiracy to overthrow the regime, is torn between loyalty to his family name, his belief in justice and his forbidden love for a noblewoman.

Shimizu's remake of his *Grudge* (*Juon* and *Juon 2*), which opened at number one at the US box-office in October 2004. Takeshi Kitano was named Best Director at Venice 2003 for **Zatoichi**. His eleventh film was an entertaining reworking of the popular 1970s film and TV series and became his biggest local hit.

The market is still dominated by a few mega-hits. In 2003, Katsuyuki Motoki's **Bayside Shakedown 2** (*Odoru Daisousasen the Movie 2*), took $158.7m, a record for live-action films, beating *Harry Potter and the Chamber of Secrets* and *The Matrix Reloaded*. These three grabbed 22% of the entire market, while the share for Japanese films was 33%, up from 27.1% in 2002 (in 1984 the figure was 50.9%, but it has not exceeded 40% since 1998). *Bayside Shakedown 2*, a sequel to the 1998 hit spin-off from a popular TV series, offered a unique combination of serial-killer thriller and satire on police bureaucracy, but was enjoyable only for those carrying background information from the TV series (TV is becoming an increasingly important source of material for features).

Death becomes them

The most celebrated film of 2003 was **Akame 48 Waterfalls – Shinju** (*Akame shijuya taki shinju misui*), directed by Genjiro Arato (producer of cult films such as Seijun Suzuki's *Zigeunerweisen*), which won many prominent national awards. Based on a novel by Chokitsu Kurumatani, it is the story of a young writer who escapes from the real world and drifts into the underground, where he meets a prostitute (Shinobu Terajima) who also wants to flee and they end up attempting a double suicide. Though too long, the film is incomparably passionate and intense, with a fascinating performance from Terajima, a well-known stage actress making a sensational screen debut.

Shinobu Terajima in **Akame 48 Waterfalls Shinju**

Terajima immediately demonstrated her talent again in **Vibrator**, as a neurotic freelance writer who jumps into the truck driven by a man she happens to meet in a convenience store. During a three-day journey she is healed through the union of their bodies and souls. Director Ryuichi Hiroki, using three types of narratives – the woman's actual voice, her interior monologue and subtitles – brilliantly focuses on the woman's gradual transformation, delicately portrayed by Terajima.

Following 1998's *Tomorrow*, Kazuo Kuroki, a maestro now in his mid-seventies, released the second and third parts of his war trilogy: **Kirishima 1945** (*Utsukushii natsu Kirishima*) and **Face of Jizo** (*Chichito Kuraseba*), in which he describes the distorted nature of daily life in wartime and expresses his truthful and persuasive anti-war feelings. As seen through the eyes of a 15-year-old boy, *Kirishima 1945* is Kuroki's faithful reproduction of his life in a small village when Japan faced defeat. Adapted from a play by Hisashi Inoue, *Face of Jizo* is set in Hiroshima several years after the war. Its heroine is a young girl suffering from survivors' guilt, who is cheered up by the ghost of her father, who was killed by the atomic bomb. Their conversations forcefully express the brutality and inhumanity of the atomic bomb

High school hijinks

A new type of young film-maker is emerging. Unlike their elders, they seem able delicately to balance the demands of art and commerce, winning critical and audience approval. **69/sixty-nine** (*69/silty nine*), the third feature by Lee Sang-Il (b. 1974) and his first to secure nationwide release, is a high-speed, piquant comedy-drama about high–school boys' hijinks. **Joze, Tiger and the Fish** (*Joze to tora to sakanatachi*), the third feature by 40-year-old Isshin Inudo, taps into the frailty and recklessness of youth in the sad love story between a disabled girl and a lukewarm male student.

Based on a true story, **Nobody Knows** (*Daremo shiranai*) by Kazuhiro Kore-Eda, 40, is one of the few films successfully to engage with social reality. Four siblings who have different fathers and who have never been to school try to survive in an apartment after they have been abandoned by their mother. In dramatising this extraordinary situation, Kore-Eda extracts the universal strength and weakness of children. Yuya Yagira, 14, who plays the oldest brother, won Best Actor at Cannes.

Isao Yukisada caused a box-office sensation with **Crying Out Love, In the Centre of the World** (*Sekai no chushin de ai wo sakebu*). Based on a bestselling novel, it's an old-fashioned, clichéd and excessively sentimental love story between a high–school boy and a girl with leukaemia in 1980s urban Japan. Yukisada's shrewd narrative skills helped it take more than $64m.

SHIMOTSUMA MONOGATARI (Kamikaze Girls – Shimotsuma Story)
[Comedy, 2003] Script and Dir: Tetsuya Nakajima. Phot: Shoichi Ado. Prod: Yuji Ishida, Takashi Hirano, Satoru Ogura, Shimotsuma Story Film Partners.
Friendship between two girls, a Lolita type and a delinquent, in a provincial high school.

The Taste of Tea Prod. Committee

Maya Banno in **The Taste of Tea**

CHA NO AJI (The Taste of Tea)
[Comedy, 2003] Script and Dir: Katsuto Ishi. Phot: Kosuke Matsusima. Players: Tadanabu Asano, Takahiro Sato, Satomi Tezuka, Maya Banno. Prod: Grasshoppa!.
All five members of the Haruno family have their own worries, including the youngest, Sachiko (Banno), eight, who must get rid of her giant double. Ishi's mix of surreal images and peaceful atmosphere creates irresistible humour.

SWING GIRLS
[Comedy, 2004] Script and Dir: Shinobu Yaguchi. Phot: Takahide Shibanushi. Players: Juri Ueno, Shihori Kanjiya, Yuika Motokariya. Prod: Chihiro Kameyama, Yoshishige Shimatani, Ryuichi Mori.
Music starts to colour the idle days of lazy high–school girls when they discover the joys of big-band jazz.

KAKUSHI KEN ONI NO TSUME (*literally*, **Hidden Sword, Nail of Demon**)
[Drama, 2004] Script: Yoji Yamada, Yoshitaka Asama. Dir: Yamada. Phot: Rokuo Naganuma. Players: Masatoshi Nagase, Hidetaka Yoshioka,

Takako Matsu. Prod: Shochiku Co.
A low-class samurai's hidden love
for a married maid is stirred up
again by news of her illness.

LADY JOKER
*[Thriller, 2004] Script: Chong
Wui Sin. Dir: Hideyuki
Hirayama. Players: Tetsuya
Watari, Kyozo Nagatsuka, Koji
Kikkawa. Prod: Nikkatsu.*
Railing against social injustice, a
group of men call themselves
"Lady Joker" and kidnap the
president of a giant beer company.

KANARIA (Canary)
*[Drama, 2004] Script and Dir:
Akihiko Shiota. Phot: Yutaka
Yamazaki. Players: Hidetoshi
Nishijima, Houshi Ishida, Mitsuki
Tanimura, Ryo. Prod: Shiro
Sasaki, Tomiyasu Ishikawa,
Kazumi Kawashiro.*
A boy whose mother holds high
office in a fanatical cult and a
girl who has run away from her
oppressive family meet and start
to search for the boy's lost sister.

*Rie Miyazawa as a Hiroshima survivor
in* **Face of Jizo,** *which completed
Kazuo Kuroki's war trilogy*

Toho Co.

Kou Shibasaki, left, and Takao Osawa in **Crying Out Love, in the Centre of the World**

Return of the giants

The three titans of Japanese animation, Mamoru Oshii, Katsuhiro
Otomo and Hayao Miyazaki, finished long-awaited new features
in 2004. First came Ohii's **Ghost in the Shell 2: Innocence**
(*Innocence*), the sequel to his legendary cyber-punk action hit. Its
CG images are dazzlingly beautiful and the intricate, philosophical
dialogue is profound, but the mixture is too complex for moviegoers
to accept. Otomo's **Steamboy** is a well-made action-adventure set
in London during the industrial revolution that failed to match the
audience expectations created by his *Akira*, the epoch-making cult
hit of 1988. Both performed disappointingly at the local box-office.

Miyazaki's **Howl's Moving Castle** (*Hauruno ugoku shiro*), which
won the Osella Prize at Venice, is based on a British fantasy novel.
It's the story of Sophie, 18, who is transformed into a 90-year-old
woman by an ill-tempered witch and settles in the moving castle of
a handsome wizard, Howl. Against the background of war Sophie
and Howl fall in love. Miyazaki spurs his magnificent imagination
again and even though there is more romance and less of the
entertainment and philosophy of his Oscar-winning *Spirited Away*,
which set a Japanese box-office record of $275m, vivid and
overwhelming images still surge out from the screen.

TOMOMI KATSUTA (katsuta@b-star.ne.jp) writes on film for
The Minichi Shimbun, one of Japan's major daily newspapers.

Quotes of the Year

"If only we continue to make
films in character with Japan,
some day the world might
turn its eyes on us."
YOJI YAMADA, *director
of the Oscar-nominated*
The Twilight Samurai.

"I don't believe cinemas exist
to make the world better, but
at least I try to make films
that let people think about
themselves and society."
HIROKAZU KORE-EDA,
director, talks about his
Nobody Knows.

Kenya Ogova Ondego

The Year's Best Films

Ogova Ondego's selection:
Asekon's Journey
(Alessandro Sermoneta)
Spurts of Blood
(Short. Willie Owusu)
Dangerous Affair
(Judy Kibinge)
**Lamu: A Splendour
of Heritage** (Docu short.
Susan Wamburi)
The Epilogue
(Short. Willie Owusu)

Willie Owusu, director of **The Epilogue**

Recent and
Forthcoming Films

DANGEROUS AFFAIR
*[Thriller, 2003] Script: Njeri
Karago, Judy Kibinge. Dir:
Kibinge. Phot: Fabian Muhire.
Players: Nini Wacera, Serah
Mwihaki, Lornah Irungu, Toni
Njuguna, Leonard Ogembo.
Prod: Njeri Karago, Baraka
Films/Kenya Film & Television
Professional Association.*

LUCKY YOU
*[Comedy-thriller, 2004] Script:
Mark Mutahi. Dir: Bob Nyanja.
Prod: Njeri Karago, Baraka
Films/Kenya Film & Television
Professional Association.*

SPURTS OF BLOOD
[Abstract drama, 2003] Script,

Although Kenya was exposed to film-making as long ago as 1935, when the British colonial government established the Bantu Educational Cinema Experiment (later the Colonial Film Unit), aimed at 'civilising' Africans, cinema never really took root. Consequently, there are no formal bodies offering production finance. However, organisations like the Ford Foundation, the Goethe-Institut and the French Embassy have limited funds for training. Film technologies available locally include Digi-Beta, BetaSp, DVCam, 16mm, 35mm and High Definition.

Kenya has no filmgoing culture and only 10 cinemas (eight in Nairobi, with a total of 15 screens, and two in Mombasa) cater to a population of 34 million. There are two official distributors for Hollywood releases (Fox Film Distributors and Nu-Metro) and three for Bollywood titles (Fox, Unicine and Nyalimax). At $2.5 (200 shillings), even the lowest-priced cinema ticket is beyond the reach of most people in a country with 40% unemployment and average annual income of less than $300.

Domestic productions make absolutely no impact at Kenyan cinemas and most film-makers produce documentaries with little theatrical appeal, some using grants from organisations interested in getting messages across to society through non-commercial production. Documentaries produced recently include the short *Lamu: A Splendour of Heritage*, a study of the rich cultural heritage in Lamu, the only Swahili settlement in East Africa that has defied modern influence. The few local producers who do make feature films target television as their primary distribution medium. About 300 audio-visual productions are made in Kenya annually; this total includes shorts, commercials, TV series, documentaries and fiction features.

Kenya remains a very popular location for international films requiring shots of the African savannah (the most celebrated examples include *Out of Africa* and *Nowhere in Africa*). After a quiet 2003 on this front, 2004 was busy thanks to the John le Carré adaptation *The Constant Gardener* and *The White Maasai*, a German production directed by Hermine Hunthgeburth and based on a novel by Corine Hoffman about a German woman who marries a Samburu man but after four years finds cultural differences driving them apart. Television features and series such as *Survivor Lebanon*, *The Last Breakthrough* and *Brothers of the Head* were also made in Kenya,

Prod and Dir: Willie Owusu.
Players: Aleks Kamau, Telley
Savalas Otieno, Emily Wanja.
A woman demands that her
boyfriend go for an HIV test,
causing tension between them.

ASEKON'S JOURNEY
[Drama, 2003] Dir: Alessandro
Sermoneta. Players: Veronica
Nambu, Wyclif Ekal, Natiwa
Ebenyo. Prod: AMREF.

THE EPILOGUE
[Abstract short, 2003] Script,
Prod and Dir: Willie Owusu.
Two friends engage in heated
discussion in a public toilet.

**LAMU: A SPLENDOUR OF
HERITAGE**
[Documentary short, 2003] Script
and Dir: Susan Wamburi. Prod:
Film Production Department.

PROJECT DADDY
[Romantic comedy, 2004] Script
and Dir: Judy Kibinge. Phot:
Martin Munyua. Players:
Wangechi Murage, Bruce
Odhiambo, June Gachui,
Damaris Agweyu. Prod: Prod:
Bob Nyanja, Baraka Films/Kenya
Film & Television Professional
Association.

REKE TUMANWO
(literally, **Let's Part Peacefully**)
[Drama, 2004] Script and Dir:
Kibaara Kaugi. Phot: Gadson
Waweru. Players: Simoricious
Wangare, Jans Karsholt, Peter
Ndung'u, Paul Gatonye. Prod:
Kaugi, Film Production
Department.
Drama examining the role of the
Mau Mau in Kenya's struggle for
independence. Shot in the Gikuyu
language.

Quote of the Year

"To make a film in Kenya,
you've got to be rich or
know bosses of funding
organisations. Creativity is
not needed – as you'll have
noticed from our productions."
WILLIE OWUSU, award-winning
abstract film director.

helping to generate $17m for the local economy.

Kibinge takes the lead

Despite the shortage of funding, there has been an increase in
feature film production. Full-length titles completed in 2003 included
Driving to Glory, Behind Closed Doors and Alessandro Sermoneta's
Asekon's Journey, shot in the Turkana language, which follows the
trials of a Turkana woman dropped by potential suitors when they
learn that she suffers from lotobor (hydatidosis), a dreaded disease
that renders women barren.

Judy Kiginge's **Dangerous Affair** (2003) featured a group of fun-
loving young men in Nairobi who fear commitment in relationships,
and Kibinge's new romantic comedy, **Project Daddy**, was
completed in 2004. It tells the story of a high-flying 29-year-old
woman in Nairobi who searches for the happiness and love she
believes will come through having a baby before she turns 30.
Reke tumanwo, shot in phases over two years, was set finally to
be launched in December 2004.

Lornah Irungu, Toni Njuguna and Serah Mwihaki, the stars of **Dangerous Affair**,
attend its premiere in Nairobi

Having carved a niche as the leading entertainment house, Baraka
Films was at press time preparing to film Lucky You, a comedy-
thriller about a pastor who wins $61,000 in a beer raffle. The
company is lobbying for new measures to help create more low-
budget films about Kenyans for Kenyans, and make copies
available cheaply. Efforts continue to establish a film commission
and set quotas for the broadcast of local content. ComMattersKenya
hopes to publish a Kenya film guide. Throughout 2003 and 2004
Kenyans continued to be increasingly active in areas like production,
management, scripting, networking and infrastructure using the
support of the French Embassy.

OGOVA ONDEGO (oondego@artmatters.info) is publisher of
www.artmatters.info and an arts and lifestyle writer, specialising in
African film and television.

Latvia Andris Rozenbergs

Recent and Forthcoming Films

TA STUNDA NAK
(The Hour Is Near)
[Documentary, 2004] Script and Dir: Juris Poskus. Phot: Poskus, Andrejs Rudzats, Igors Stads, Peteris Tidrikis, Oskars Poikans, Janis Eglitis, Peteris Cirulis. Prod: Poskus, Laima Freimane, FA Filma.

A girl wears a Second World War relic unearthed in **Keep Smiling!**

KEEP SMILING!
[Documentary, 2004] Script: Viktors Duks, Askolds Saulitis, based on Duks' novel, Diggers. Dir: Saulitis. Phot: Saulitis, Mikus Meirans, Uldis Jancis. Prod: Saulitis, Subjektiv Filma.

ROMEO UN DZULJETA
(Romeo and Juliet)
[Documentary musical, 2004] Script and Dir: Viesturs Kairiss. Phot: Gints Berzins. Players: Rita Fedotova, Armands Slempers. Prod: Guntis Trekteris, Kaupo Filma.

LEIJPUTRIJA (Dreamland)
[Documentary, 2004] Script and Phot: Maris Maskalans. Dir: Laila Pakalnina. Prod: Vides Filmu Studija/NDR in association with ARTE.

UDENSBUMBA RESNAJAM RUNCIM (Waterbomb for the Fat Tomcat)
[Family drama, 2004] Script: Alvis Lapins. Dir: Varis Brasla. Phot: Uldis Jancis. Players: Baiba

The year 2004 began with an unpleasant surprise: the State Chancellery "in order to optimise state management" decided to dissolve the National Film Centre of Latvia. In practice this would have meant the governments renouncing all support for film production. Only the collapse of the coalition government saved Latvian film-making and the incoming Minister of Culture even promised to double state aid by 2006.

Film-makers responded to this better news with some charming pictures that praise diversity and life itself. Mention goes first to a paradoxical documentary by Juris Poskus, **The Hour Is Near** (*Ta stunda nak*), about two young men who preach on the streets like biblical evangelists. Their gospel is a strange mixture of Christianity and consumerism. One of them claims that wearing clothes from internationally known fashion houses is a sign of God's love. Doubling as travelling salesmen who offer leather purses and bags, they evidently earn enough to justify these blessings; one sequence shows their hands full of high-value banknotes.

Askolds Saulitis' documentary, **Keep Smiling!**, is based on the novel *Diggers* by Viktors Duks, which was electronically published in the US. It also tells an uncommon story: four men are looking for the unidentified graves of Second World War soldiers. Sometimes they find identity papers and thus return individuality to a soldier killed in action many years ago. Saulitis gradually reveals how "great historical events" make people lose their identity. By coincidence, the story unfolds as the 2003 war in Iraq drags on.

This is Saulitis' second film dedicated to the controversial issues surrounding the war. The first, *The Red and the Brown*, was an attempt to throw light on one of the most controversial points in our history: Latvian soldiers during the last century several times have fought, as they believed, for the independence of their fatherland under foreign flags and in foreign uniforms, sometimes even one against another.

Bernstein reunited with the Bard

Viesturs Kairiss' **Romeo and Juliet** (*Romeo un Dzuljeta*) tells the classic tale in unconventional fashion, with deaf mutes performing the play in contemporary Riga. Shakespeare's text is expressed

Broka, Undine Viksne, Zane Leimane, Gundars Abolins. Prod: Gatis Upmalis/F.O.R.M.A. (Latvia) /Artur Talvik, ALLFILM (Estonia). To earn a living, a woman has to leave her daughters, Martha, eight, and Linda, four, with her authoritarian sister for a while. After several misunderstandings, the girls realise their aunt's strict attitudes are the product of loneliness and they try to reconcile her with her suitor.

PITONS (The Python)
[Absurd drama, 2003] Script and Dir: Laila Pakalnina. Phot: Gints Berzins. Players: Mara Kimele, Juris Grava, Januss Johansons, Ilze Pukinska, Intars Janbergs. Prod: Pakalnina/Hargla. Somebody has defecated in the school attic and the tyrannical headmistress investigates. Uproar results when a photographer's python escapes.

RIGAS SARGI (Guards of Riga)
[Historical drama, 2005] Script: Andris Kolbergs. Dir: Aigars Grauba. Phot: Vladimirs Basta. Players: Janis Reinis, Elita Klavina, Andris Keiss, Arturs Skrastins, Girts Kesteris, Ivo Martinsons. Prod: Andrejs Ekis, Platforma Filma. A love story against the background of a crucial moment for Latvian independence: November 11, 1919, when 11,000 riflemen, mostly inexperienced volunteers, defeated 51,000 German and Russian mercenaries.

TRIS MUSKETIERI (Three Musketeers)
[Puppet animation, 2005] Script: Maris Putnins, based on Dumas' novel. Dir: Janis Cimmermanis. Phot: Evalds Lacis. Prod: Putnins, ABOOM Ltd./Peter Garde, Zentropa (Denmark)/Bob Last, Three Musketeers Films Ltd. (UK).

D'Artagnan in **Three Musketeers**

through the plastic symbols of sign language (subtitled) and Bernstein's music for West Side Story, and Kairiss cuts between the story and rehearsals, in which he appears in the role of director. He and his cast create an astonishing and rich performance.

Armands Slempers and Rita Fedotova as **Romeo and Juliet**

Laila Pakalnina, whose Python was the first Latvian film chosen for Venice and who has become something of a brand name within national cinema, has made an enchanting documentary, **Dreamland** (Leijputrija). It is conceived as a movie about the rubbish dump as a metaphor for human life. In this habitat, rats, snails, bugs and other creatures find their dreamland. Yes, we live in dirt but the dawns with their dissolving wraps of golden mist are so beautiful; yes, every minute we run the risk of being devoured by somebody bigger and stronger but even the dead corpses projecting against pure snow have a sad magnificence.

It is amazing how much beauty the camera of Maris Maskalans catches in this ostensibly unpleasant environment. Marvellous close-ups and wide shots are interspersed with glorious morning landscapes and sunsets in non-linear fashion, supported by a soundtrack on which music by Japanese composer Shigeru Umebayashi imperceptibly segues into noises arranged by Anrijs Krenbergs. This looks like another festival contender for Pakalnina.

Finally, and most remarkably, Latvia, despite its unpredictable and fragile film policy, has gained a modern, well-equipped studio facility. Producer and TV channel manager Andrejs Ekis is using it for what by national standards is a mega-production, The Guards of Riga, while production company Platforma Filma is planning to use the studio for co-productions and is already servicing foreign film crews, including some from the BBC. These are good omens for the future of Latvian film-making.

ANDRIS ROZENBERGS (Andris.Rozenbergs@nfc.gov.lv) has directed seven fiction films and a dozen documentaries. He is Head of the Film Registry at Latvia's National Film Centre.

Lebanon Mohammed Rouda

The Year's Best Films

Mohammed Rouda's selection:

Girdle of Fire (Bahij Hojeij)

In the Battlefields
(Daniel Arbied)

Recent Films

ZINNAR EL-NAR
(Girdle of Fire)
[Drama, 2004] Script and Dir:
Bahij Hojeij. Phot: Maxime
Herot. Players: Nidaa Wakim,
Hasan Farhat, Bernadette Hdeib,
Julia Kassar, Abdullah Homsi.
Prod: OnlineFilm.

MAARAIK HOBB
(In the Battlefields)
[Drama, 2004] Script and Dir:
Daniel Arbied. Phot: Helen
Lofort. Players: Marian Fgaly,
Rawya Elshab, Lody Arbied,
Ouni Quass, Carmen Loubos.
Prod: Que Vadi Cinema/Versus
Prods (Belgium)/Taxi Films (France).
A young girl living with her
traditional, bourgeois family prevents
the maid from leaving the house
because she is the only friend she
has while her parents fight about
the father's gambling addiction.

AL AGLABIAY AL SAMITA
(The Silent Majority)
[Drama, 2004] Script and Dir:
Mahmoud Hojeij. Phot: Jocelyne
Abou Jebrayel. Players: Fadi Abi
Samra, Carmen Loubos, Assil
Hobbala, Carole Abboud. Prod:
Hojeij, CKP Managment.

WASAT ALZILAL
(Among Shadows)
[Drama, 2005] Script and Dir:
Ghassan Salhab. Phot: Jacques
Bonquin. Players: Carlos Chahine.
Prod: Agat Films.

ebanese cinema enjoyed a very active year in 2004, producing six feature films (four fiction and two documentaries), three of which were co-productions with Egypt. The annual Beirut Days for Cinema, organised by the private Beirut Development & Cinema foundation, enjoyed above-average attendance and the recently established Ministry of Culture organised in September the first ever round table debate between local officials and film-makers. This three-day meeting, geared towards generating a policy for the promotion of local cinema, was a goodwill gesture by the government, but the ministry has no power to provide direct financial aid to film-makers as its budget is controlled by the Ministry of Finance. Understandably, some within the industry remain somewhat pessimistic about the government's commitment to cinema.

More films are being produced as joint ventures between local film-makers and European, mainly French companies, but the theatrical market for Lebanese movies remains weak. The award won by director Randa Shahal Sabbag at Venice in 2003 for her third feature, *The Kite* (*Ta'ira min warak*; see *IFG 2004*), failed to translate into success at the box-office. The public virtually ignored the film, which focused on the Druze population, and the same fate befell Bahij Hojeij's Lebanese–French co-production, **Girdle of Fire** (*Zinnar el-nar*). This excellent character study examines a tense Lebanese high school teacher in civil war-ridden Beirut as he is gradually driven crazy by the horrific atmosphere of the war.

As Bahij Hojeij showed, the Lebanese civil war remains high on the agenda of film-makers, including some who were still very young when the conflict finally ended in 1986. One such is first-time director Daniel Arbied, who in **In the Battlefields** (*Maaraik hobb*) explores this painful memory indirectly. We hear bombs and shells falling. We see some evidence of the war, but the drama concentrates on the effects of the war within a divided Christian family, in particular a little girl (the director's alter ego) who tries to understand love in hate-filled times. The film is a modest achievement but audiences welcomed its message in Cannes and Paris.

His life as a dog

Scheduled for release in early 2005, Mahmoud Hojeij's **The Silent Majority** (*Al aglabiay al samita*) is a Kafkaesque black comedy

**HONA WA ROBAMA HONAK
(Here and Perhaps Elsewhere)**
*[Documentary, 2004] Dir, Phot
and Prod: Lamia Joreige.*
Joreige, who left Lebanon during
the war and attended a fine arts
school in New York, comes home
to make a film about people who
were kidnapped during the civil
war and were never found.

**SAYIDI AL RAIYIS AL KAIED
(Sir Mr Leader/President)**
*[Documentary, 2004] Script and
Dir: Jad Abi Khalil. Phot: Bassem
Fayad. Prod: 3 Productions.*
The first Lebanese (and the first
non-Iraqi Arab) documentary
about Iraq looks at the media
under Saddam Hussein and also
after the fall of the dictator.

about a man who one day turns into a dog and starts fresh
relationships with his family and neighbours. Borhan Alawiya's
Love Passed from Here (*Min hona marra alhob*), originally
scheduled for release in 2004, was delayed when its French
financing ran out just as the director was about to enter post-
production. He found alternative funding for editing but had to go
to Morocco for the sound mix and other final touches, after
securing backing from the Moroccan Cinema Centre.

This past year has witnessed an increasing number of
Egyptian–Lebanese co-productions, including Egyptian director
Yousri Nasrallah's **Sun's Gate** (*Bab el shams*; see also Egypt
section), which tells a largely Lebanese story using local writers,
actors and locations. The great Egyptian director Youssef Chahine's
company, Misr Al Alamiah, and Lebanese distributor Fatthalla Films
collaborated on two feature documentaries shot in Lebanon by
Lebanese directors.

The first of these is Samir Habshi's historical **The Lady of the
Palace** (*Sayidat al qassr*) and the second is Jan Shamoun's **The
Land of Women** (*Ard al nissaa*), an investigation into an Israeli
prison built on Lebanese soil during the Israeli occupation years.
The investigator is a former inmate who spent years in the gaol and
reveals the pain of her horrific experiences. Projects in the pipeline
for 2005 include Ghassan Salhab's third feature *Among Shadows*
(*Wasat alzilal*), likely to be released in the summer, and *Falafil*, the
first fiction feature by prolific documentary film-maker Michael Kammon.

MOHAMMED ROUDA (merci4404@earthlink.net) is a Lebanese-
born film critic who first wrote for *IFG* in the 1970s. He is the author
of several books, including *Hollywood and the Arabs* (2001) and the
four-part *Book of Cinema* (1984-1994).

A young girl tries to understand love in **In the Battlefields**

Lithuania Dr. Grazina Arlickaite

The Year's Best Films

Grazina Arlickaite's selection:

Easily and Sweetly
(Docu short. Ignas Miskinis)
Sunday As It Is
(Short. Ignas Jonynas)
The Diary (Oksana Buraja)
Short Circuit (Animation.
Antanas Janauskas)

Bartas Plausinaitis in **Sunday As It Is**

Recent and Forthcoming Filims

NIUJORKAS – MANO SUO
(New York Is My Dog)
*[Documentary, 2004] Script and
Dir: Vytautas V. Landsbergis.
Phot: Landsbergis. Prod:
Jonas Mekas Film Centre.*
Conversations with the great avant-
garde film artist Jonas Mekas.

KOMPLIKUOTAS REIKALAS
(A Complicated Matter)
*[Documentary, 2004] Script and
Dir: Arturas Jevdokimovas. Phot:
Giedrius Guntorius. Featuring:
Jonas Mekas. Prod: Jonas Mekas
Film Centre.*
Mekas' thoughts on cinema.

TRUMPAS SUJUNGIMAS
(Short Circuit)
*[Animation, 2003] Script and Dir:
Antanas Janauskas. Prod: Studio AJ.*
An accidental collision between a
man and a woman.

ike most Eastern European countries, Lithuania struggles to sustain regular feature film production because funding is so scarce, and only a handful of projects are completed each year. Kristijonas Vildziunas made a successful debut with *The Lease Agreement* (2002), which was screened in Venice and several other festivals. Then, after a long break, a feature for children, Vytautas V. Landsbergis' *John and Greta* (2002) and Jonas Vaitkus' *Utterly Alone* (2003), which dramatised the life of legendary Lithuanian partisan Juozas Luksa, both found audiences in local cinemas.

However, audiences were still waiting in autumn 2004 for the two most interesting feature films in the pipeline. Sarunas Bartas, the most famous Lithuanian director, was finishing *Seven Invisible Men (Septyni nematomi vyrai)*, which follows a group of hostile fugitives from Lithuania via Poland to the southern parts of the former Soviet Republic. One of them is running from the law, another from himself. Audrius Juzenas' *Ghetto (Getas)*, already mentioned in *IFG 2004*, was still in post-production at press time. The film tells the tragic story of the Jewish ghetto in Vilnius in 1942-43 and is adapted by Joshua Sobol from his celebrated stage play.

At press time, Janina Lapinskaite, acclaimed for her documentaries, was completing her first fiction feature, *Land of Glass (Stiklo salis)*, in which the birth and sickness of their second child bring unease and, ultimately, tragedy to a married couple and their seven-year-old daughter. The film will explore the complicated inner world of the mother's crisis.

The most popular short films were both directed by members of the younger generation and both, in different ways, reflected the concerns of contemporary Lithuanian youths. Ignas Miskinis' *Easily and Sweetly* is a documentary short about ordinary young guys who, like so many others, just want to be cool, to love, to survive and to fulfil their ambitions. But will the night streets grant them the opportunities they crave?

In Ignas Jonynas' fictional short, *Sunday As It Is*, the hero, Tomas, is a gang member who is arrested after helping his friends to escape from a burglary in which he has taken part. In jail, Tomas, who was raised in an orphanage, is visited by his mother, whom he has not seen since his birth. Eager to make him feel something for her, she

IS DANGAUS (From the Sky)
[Documentary, 2004] Script and Dir: Giedre Zickyte. Phot: Kastytis Maciunas, Robertas Zamaris. Prod: Vytautas V. Landsbergis. Examination of a nineteenth-century Lithuanian poem, *Anykschiai boscage.*

VERDEN (Whirlpool)
[Documentary, 2004] Script and Dir: Vytautas V. Landsbergis. Phot: Tomas Andrijauskas. Prod: A Propos. Portrait of Nijole Miliauskaite, the late Lithuanian Poet Laureate.

GETAS (Ghetto)
[Historical drama, forthcoming] Script: Joshua Sobol, based on his play. Dir: Audrius Juzenas. Players: Sebastian Hülk, Heino Ferch, Jork Lamprecht, Erica Moraszan. Prod: Juzenas, Almone Cepiene, Film Studio Seansas/Big Mother Pictures/Dragon Cine (Germany)/New Transit Entertainment (Germany).

STIKLO SALIS (Land of Glass)
[Drama, forthcoming] Script: Vanda Juknaite, Janina Lapinskaite. Dir: Lapinskaite. Players: Jurga Kalvaityte, Povilas Budrys, Urte Sejunaite. Prod: Kestutis Petrulis, Studio 2000.

SEPTYNI NEMATOMI VYRAI (Seven Invisible Men*)***
[Road movie, forthcoming] Script and Dir: Sarunas Bartas. Players: Bartas, Viktorija Kuodyte, Aleksandr Esaulov, Aleksandr Bashirov, Axel Neumann, Marina Makshina, Anatolij Gorin, Lina Drugaleva, Denis Kirilov. Prod: Bartas, Kinema.

Jorune Greiciute in **White on Blue**

Students on the street in **Easily and Sweetly**

tells him the story of their family and tries also to persuade him to betray his gang, in return for which the police would free him and give him a new life in Paris.

The works of young women are making an impact on the predominantly male Lithuanian film industry. Oksana Buraj's *Vapna* (2002) and *The Diary* (2003) and Giedre Beinoriute's *Trolleybus Town* (2002) and *Existence* (2004) were all original pieces, as was Inesa Kurklietyte's short, *Mild Witchcraft* (2004), about a clever and ambitious midwife.

Several local festivals are thriving. The International Film Festival "Vilnius Spring", which had its ninth edition in 2003, has become the biggest forum for European cinema in Lithuania (it screened 64 features from 14 countries). The Nordic Film Forum SCANORAMA takes place annually in Lithuania's three biggest cities – Vilnius, Kaunas and Klaipeda – screening films and welcoming directors from Sweden, Finland, Denmark, Norway and Iceland. The event also hosts co-production meetings. Finally, the seven-day International Short Film Festival "Tinklai" (meaning "nets") holds screenings, workshops and seminars in the port town of Klaipeda and also in Vilnius.

Dr. GRAZINA ARLICKAITE is artistic director of the International Film Festival "Vilnius Spring" and head of the International Relations department at Lithuanian Film Studio.

WHITE ON BLUE
[Short drama, 2004] Script, Dir and Phot: Ramuna Greicius. Players: Jorune Greiciute, Bartas Plausinaitis. Prod: Kestutis Drazdauskas.

In a seaside resort, a sensitive teenager (Jorune Greiciute) enters a strange world of happiness on the island where the town ornithologist traps birds.

Luxembourg Jean-Pierre Thilges

The Year's Best Films

Jean-Pierre Thilges' selection:

La Femme de Gilles
(Frédéric Fonteyne)
The Whore's Son
(Michael Sturminger)
Mister Why
(Docu. Andy Bausch)
George and the Dragon
(Tom Reeve)

Recent and Forthcoming Films

Al Pacino as The Merchant of Venice

THE MERCHANT OF VENICE
[Drama, 2004] Script: Michael
Radford, based on the play
by William Shakespeare.
Dir: Radford. Phot: Benoît
Delhomme. Players: Al Pacino,
Jeremy Irons, Joseph Fiennes,
Lynn Collins. Prod: Spice
Factory/Shylock Films/Delux.

LA FEMME DE GILLES
(literally, Gilles' Wife*)*
[Drama, 2004] Script: Philippe
Blasband, Frédéric Fonteyne,
based on the novel by Madeleine
Bourdouzhe. Dir: Fonteyne.
Phot: Virginie Saint Martin.
Players: Emmanuelle Devos,
Clovis Cornillac, Laura Smet.
Prod: Artemis/Liaison
cinématographique/Samsa Film.

The two most prestigious productions to go before the cameras in Luxembourg in 2003-04 were Michael Radford's *The Merchant of Venice*, co-produced by Delux and starring Al Pacino, which premiered at Venice 2004, and Irwin Winkler's rather clunky Cole Porter bio-musical, *De-Lovely*, the closing-night attraction at Cannes. Large chunks of the Shakespeare were shot on the lavish Venice film set erected in Esch-sur-Alzette by Delux several years ago, as were the Venice sequences for Winkler's film, and both took full advantage of Luxembourg's ever-popular tax incentives for visiting productions. The same set had earlier doubled for Delft in Peter Webber's *Girl with a Pearl Earring*.

Outfits such as Delux or The Carousel Picture Company, whose crazy adventure yarn **George and the Dragon** finally hit the screens (thus putting an end to a very convoluted production history), try to cater for the English-speaking market by participating in prestigious international co-productions. The other local powerhouse, Samsa Film, keeps carving its niche mainly in French-speaking co-ventures with neighbouring Belgium and France. After premiering the disappointing **Madame Edouard**, an over-the-top mystery-comedy-thriller starring French actors Michel Blanc, Didier Bourdon and Josiane Balasko, Samsa came up with the beautifully crafted and superbly acted period drama **La femme de Gilles** (literally, *Gilles' Wife*), from Belgian film-maker Frédéric Fonteyne, which had its world premiere in Venice.

Emmanuelle Devos and Clovis Cornillac play a 1930s couple in **La femme de Gille**

Artémis Productions

LA REVANCHE (The Revenge)
[Comedy, 2004] Script: Andy Bausch, Jean-Louis Schlesser, Nicolas Steil. Dir: Bausch. Phot: Klaus Peter Weber. Players: Thierry Van Werveke, André Jung, Cartouche, Sascha Ley, Fani Kolarova, Fernand Fox. Prod: Steil/Iris Productions/Paul Thiltges Distributions.

VICTOIRE (literally, **Victory**)
[Comedy-drama, 2005] Script: Stéphanie Murat, Gilles Laurent. Dir: Murat. Phot: Thomas Bataille. Players: Sylvie Testud, Mylène Demongeot, Pierre Arditi, Aurore Clément. Prod: A.D.R. Productions/Samsa Film.

MADAME EDOUARD
[Comedy, 2004] Script: Patrick Ligardes, Nadine Monfils, based on Monfils' novels, Les enquêtes du commissaire Léon. *Dir: Monfils. Phot: Luc Drion. Players: Michel Lang, Didier Bourdon, Josiane Balasko, Dominique Lavanant, Annie Cordy. Prod: Noé Productions/Samsa Film/Artémis Productions.*

Chulpan Khamatova in
The Whore's Son

HURENSOHN (The Whore's Son)
[Drama, 2003] Script: Michael Sturminger, Michael Glawogger, Gabriel Loidolt, based on Loidolt's novel. Dir: Sturminger. Phot: Jürgen Jürges. Players: Chulpan Khamatova, Miki Manojlovic, Stanislav Lisnic. Prod: A.I. Films/Tarantula. Ozren, 16, tells the story of life with his beautiful Croatian mother, a high-class call girl.

This intimate drama about a working-class family in the 1930s tells the story of Elisa (Emmanuelle Devos), the pregnant wife of blast-furnace worker Gilles (Clovis Cornillac), who takes loving care of her children and home, and spends all day waiting for her husband's return. Gilles often works long shifts at night, while Victorine (Laura Smet), Elisa's attractive sister, visits her to play with the children and help out. Strange ideas come to Elisa's jealous mind. Convinced that husband and sister are having an affair, she starts a strange interior combat, with courage, silence and self-sacrifice her only weapons. *La femme de Gilles* is definitely one of the most accomplished films ever shot in Luxembourg.

A sequel best served cold

Iris Productions' **The Revenge** (*La revanche*), finally released in October 2004, was the long-gestating sequel to Luxembourg's most successful film ever, *The Unemployment Club* (*Le club des chômeurs*), again directed by the country's senior film-maker, Andy Bausch. This was an idiosyncratic film which, like Luxembourg's population, speaks in (too) many tongues and somehow manages to miss out on all the funny and outrageous elements that made the first instalment such a huge crowd-pleaser. Shot on an incredibly tight budget, it has its moments, but at press time looked likely to attract at most 20,000 admissions, compared to the original's tally of more than 40,000. On the other hand, *The Revenge*'s incredible flow of Tower of Babel dialogue might help it to travel a bit further across the country's borders than its predecessor.

Bausch also weighed in with a funny documentary in 2004, **Mister Why** (*Monsieur Warum*), a whimsical and effective bit of nostalgia on the career of Luxembourg's most popular radio disc jockey, Camillo Felgen, now 80, who is also a regular actor in Bausch's movies. Feature documentaries could very well emerge as one of Luxembourg's strong points, as 2004 also saw the release of Claude Lahr's informative and well-researched Second World War study, **Deportation** (*Heim ins Reich*), about heroism and betrayal during the Nazi occupation between 1940 and 1945. At press time, Samsa Film, Paul Thiltges Distributions, Minotaurus and Tarantula were all putting the finishing touches to a series of documentaries bound for cinema release.

JEAN-PIERRE THILGES (jeanpierre@revue.lu) has written on film since 1970 and works as a critic for Luxembourg weekly magazines *REVUE* and *Télé-REVUE*.

Malaysia Baharudin A. Latif

Recent and Forthcoming Films

PONTIANAK HARUM SUNDAL MALAM
(Vampire Bitch of the Night)
[Horror, 2004] Script and Dir: Shuhaimi Baba. Phot: Filus Ghazali. Players: Maya Karin, Azri Iskandar, Rosyam Nor, Kavita Sidhu, Ida Nerina. Prod: Persona Pictures.

BULI (Bully)
[Comedy, 2004] Script: and Dir: Afdlin Shauki. Phot: Indra Che Muda. Players: Shauki, Nasha Aziz, Hans Isaac, Ako Mustapha, Hattan. Prod: Grand Brilliance.

GANGSTER
[Crime melodrama, 2004] Script and Dir: Bade Hj. Azmi. Phot: Raja Mukhriz. Players: Rosyam Nor, Siti Elizad, Hasnul Rahmat, Nana, Puspha Narayan. Prod: Tayangan Unggul.

BINTANG HATI
(Idol of My Heart)
[Musical romance, 2004] Script and Dir: Aziz M. Osman. Phot: Bade Hj. Azmi. Players: Amy Mastura, Anuar Zain, Fasha Sandha, Jaafar Onn, Umie Aida. Prod: Tayangan Unggul.

Fasha Sandha in **Race to the Sky**

BERLARI KE LANGIT
(Running to the Sky)
[Melodrama, 2004] Script and Dir: Bade Hj. Azmi. Phot: Azla Kamaruddin. Players: Rosyam

Winds of change have been sweeping across the Malaysian industry. The most notable innovation in 2004 was **Vampire Bitch of the Night** (*Pontianak harum sundal malam*), a rare foray into the long-neglected vampire genre, which did big business in the 1950s before falling foul of the draconian censorship that took such a heavy toll on Malaysian culture following independence in 1957. Horror films became taboo and producers shied away from resurrecting the dead.

Despite the quasi-intellectual pretensions of director Shuhaimi Baba, her film is nothing more than the cliché-ridden hokum that was once the domain of Hammer productions. Wronged gamelan dancer Merriam is killed and more than 50 years later her ever-youthful offspring Maria (Maya Karin) comes back thirsting for revenge. The acting by the beautiful Karin is minimal but the supporting performances by Rosyam Nor and Ida Nerriam are gems. Receipts touched the magic $1m mark and a sequel is promised.

A Legendary Love (*Puteri gunung ledang*) took three years to make and at $4m is the most expensive Malaysian film ever made. Chosen as the country's Oscar submission for 2004, it tells the story of a legendary fifteenth-century Malay warrior's romance with a Javanese princess and is a familiar tale of unrequited love. With even the biggest local hits struggling to take more than $1.5m, it will struggle to recoup its vast budget.

Female lyricist-turned-producer Habsah Hassan and American-trained director Raja Ahmad Alaudin have made the eagerly anticipated *Quisy and Laily*, a contemporary story of the Afghan refugee problem, seen through the involvement of a volunteer organisation, Malaysian Relief Team, and shot partly on location in Quetta, Afghanistan. It's refreshing to see a Malaysian film dealing with real life rather than presenting another puerile melodrama about youngsters making out.

The big two

Metrowealth Movies has been making more news and money. Since it re-emerged as a born-again company three years ago, all of its productions have done well and the latest is **Campus Love** (*Kuliah*

Nor, Fasha Sandha, Hasnul Rahmat, Siti Elizad. Prod: Tayangan Unggul.

AH LOKE CAFE
[Comedy, 2004] Script: Caroline Ho, based on the comic strip. Dir: Anwardi Jamil. Phot: Zainal Othman. Players: Leonard Tan, Othman Hafsham, Ida Nerina, Man Bai, Masnaida Samsudin. Prod: EnFiniTi Productions/Ah Lok Productions.

KULIAH CINTA (Campus Love)
[Youth romance, 2004] Script: Azahari Zaru. Dir: A. Razak Mohaideen. Phot: Zainal Othman. Players: Erra Fazira, Yusri, Saiful, Yasin, Farid Kamil. Prod: Metrowealth Movies.

HINGGA HUJUNG NYAWA (Till Life's End)
[Romantic melodrama, 2004] Script and Dir: A. Razak Mohaideen. Phot: Zainal Othman. Players: Erra Fazira, Yusri, Farid Kamil, Khatijah Tan, Abu Bakar Omar. Prod: Metrowealth Movies.

PUTERI GUNON LEDANG (A Legendary Love)
[Period romantic adventure, 2003] Script and Dir: Saw Tiong Hin. Phot: Teoh Gay Huan. Players: Tiara Jacqueline, M. Nasir, Sofea Jane, Rahim Razali, Rosyam Nor, Sabri Yunus, Christine Hakim. Prod: EnFiniTi Productions.

Unusual Love

CINTA LUAR BIASA (Unusual Love)
[Melodrama, 2004] Script and Dir: Rashid Sibir. Phot: Azla Kamaruddin. Players: Nasha Aziz, Hans Isaac, Saiful Aspek, Syanie, Erma Fatima, Ako Mustafa, Fauziah Nawi. Prod: Tayangan Unggul.

cinta). Another story of youthful romance, this time at a university, it grossed more than $1m. Highly bankable husband and wife Yusri and Erra Fazira dominate the plot and end the movie by getting hitched. Their pairing in the romantic comedy sequel **Cinderella 2** fared less well, taking only half as much as the original *Cinderella*.

Tayangan Unggul, just as prolific as Metrowealth, released **Race to the Sky** (*Berlari ke langit*), a sequel to the award-winning hit *KL Screams* (*KL menjerit*). Two country brothers who move to Kuala Lumpur face hard knocks adjusting to life in the big city. Another Tayangan title, **Trauma**, from talented young director Aziz M. Osman, is a suspense thriller about a young architect (Amy Mastura) whose life becomes a waking nightmare after a tragic road accident. The woman who offers to help her turns out to be the aide from hell.

Several films flopped, including **On the Edge of Mystery** (*Di ambang misteri*), a lacklustre thriller, **Ah Loke Cafe**, a sitcom adapted from a comic book, and **A Question of the Heart** (*Bicara hati*), an old-fashioned love story. The combined gross for all three was less than $150,000.

The problems of local censorship reached a ludicrous new low when the Film Censorship Board passed *The Passion of the Christ* – but only for Christians, who had to rely on the National Evangelical Christian Fellowship to vouch for the authenticity of their denomination before being allowed into cinemas. The ambitious E-Village project of the Multimedia Super Corridor – almost derailed by mismanagement and the Asian recession in 1997 – has been given a second lease of life. One of the companies involved in the project has bought an additional 142 acres to supplement the present 38-acre site and the industry is hopeful that the whole Media City scheme may now be back on track.

BAHARUDIN A. LATIF has written about Malaysian cinema for more than 37 years for publications such as *Variety*, *Asiaweek* and *Movie/TV Marketing*. He runs the Movie Magic Resource Centre & Facility in Petaling Jaya.

Rosyam Nor, centre, in crime melodrama **Gangster**

Mexico Carlos Bonfil

The Year's Best Films

Carlos Bonfil's selection:
Duck Season
(Fernando Eimbcke)
The Song of Pulque
(Docu. Everardo González)
Puños rosas (Beto Gómez)
The Sixth Section
(Docu. Alex Rivera)
XV in Zaachila
(Docu. Rigoberto Perezcano)

Puños rosas

Recent and Forthcoming Films

LADIES' NIGHT
[Comedy, 2003] Script: Issa López, Ignacio Darnaude. Dir: Gabriela Tagliavini. Phot: Javier Zarco. Players: Ana Claudia Talancón, Ana de la Reguera, Luis Roberto Guzmán, Fabián Corres. Prod: Argos Cine/Televisa Cine/Miravista Films/Epigmenio Ibarra/Carlos Payán.

PUÑOS ROSAS
[Drama, 2003] Script: Beto Gómez, Alfonso Suárez Romero. Dir: Gómez. Phot: Héctor Osuna. Players: Rodrigo Oviedo, José Yenque, Cecilia Suárez, Adal Ramones, Isela Vega. Prod: Videocine/Plural Entertainment/Fidecine.

Although film production rose from 14 features in 2002 to 29 in 2003, the increase had little effect in promoting a better image of Mexican cinema, either locally or abroad. There is a common assumption that increased production clearly indicates that a film industry enjoys good health. This is understandable when one considers Brazil or Argentina, where, after feature film-making almost disappeared one or two decades ago, annual production has reached an average of 30 and 50 films respectively. When Mexico produced only seven films in 1997, the lowest figure for 70 years, the situation was alarming because the country had for a long time been the most prolific in Latin America, producing an average of almost 100 films per year. Nowadays, there is little hope of a short-term recovery, thanks largely to the government's continuing indifference towards fostering a strong film industry.

Not only has President Vicente Fox failed to keep his campaign promise to defend national cinema and cultural identity, but in 2004 he proposed a bill to disband, as costly and inefficient ventures, the Mexican Film Institute (Imcine), the national film studios (Churubusco Azteca) and an important film school, the Centro de Capacitación Cinematográfica. Fortunately this bill was defeated in the National Assembly, but the presidential effort gave Mexican film-makers, producers and screenwriters a clear indication of what to expect from the conservative government.

There is no prospect of official incentives to revive the industry, like those offered by the state in Argentina and Brazil. Nor are there tax benefits encouraging private companies to invest in film production or legal obligations for local TV networks to co-produce new films. Many private producers are in any case reluctant to invest in films because of the inequitable system for profit recuperation. For each peso from the price of a cinema ticket, 15 cents goes on tax, 51 cents to the exhibitor and 21 cents to the distributor – leaving producers just 13 cents.

Copycat tactics

The 10 most successful films in Mexico in 2003 were all made in Hollywood, and American distributors and exhibitors are the main beneficiaries of film exhibition in Mexico. It is hardly surprising that in order to be relatively successful, a Mexican director feels obliged

NICOTINA
[Comedy, 2003] Script: Martín Salinas. Dir: Hugo Rodríguez. Phot: Marcelo Iaccarino. Players: Diego Luna, Rafael Inclán, Rosa María Bianchi, Daniel Jiménez Cacho. Prod: Altavista Films/Eckehardt Von Damm.

EL MISTERIO DEL TRINIDAD
[Drama, 2000] Script: José Luis García Agraz, Carlos Cuarón. Director: García Agraz. Phot: Pedro Juan López. Players: Eduardo Palomo, Rebecca Jones, Guillermo Gil, Alejandro Parodi. Prod: García Agraz y asociados/Videocine/Imcine.

UN DIA SIN MEXICANOS
(A Day without a Mexican)
[Comedy, 2003] Script: Yareli Arizmendi, Sergio Arau, Sergio Guerrero. Dir: Arau. Phot: Alan Caudillo. Players: Yareli Arizmendi, Eduardo Palomo, John Getz, Elpidia Carrillo. Prod: Videocine/Altavista Films/Cinépolis Producciones.

TEMPORADA DE PATOS
(Duck Season)
[Comedy, 2004] Script: Fernando Eimbcke, Paula Markovitch. Dir: Eimbcke. Phot: Alexis Zabé. Players: Enrique Arreola, Diego Cataño, Daniel Miranda, Danny Perea. Prod: Christian Valdelièvre, Jaime B. Ramos, Lulú Producciones, Cinepantera.

ZAPATA, EL SUEÑO DEL HÉROE
(Zapata – The Hero's Dream)
[Drama, 2003] Script and Dir: Alfonso Arau. Phot: Vittorio Storaro. Players: Alejandro Fernández, Jesús Ochoa, Angélica Aragón, Arturo Beristáin. Prod: Arau, Ricardo del Río, Pliny Porter.

ADAN Y EVA (TODAVÍA)
[Comedy-drama, 2004] Script and Dir: Iván Ávila Dueñas. Phot: Ciro Cabello, Alejandro Cantú. Players: Junior Paulino, Diana Lein, Raúl Adalid, Marta Riveros, Marta Aura. Prod: Iván Ávila Dueñas, Conaculta/Imcine.

to conform to Hollywood's current standards, both in looks and subjects. Romantic comedies and fast-paced thrillers, many bearing a Tarantino influence, have thus steadily replaced other cinematic genres, including melodrama (for decades a favourite of Mexican audiences).

Middle-class producers and film-makers show their pride each time their films are considered to be almost as effective and entertaining as their Hollywood counterparts, or each time a Mexican film-maker migrates to Hollywood and signs a hit (witness Guillermo Del Toro's *Hellboy* or Alfonso Cuaron's *Harry Potter and the Prisoner of Azkaban*). Profitable second-hand film-making and marketing have clearly become preferable to low-paying artistic novelty.

Comedies continuously blur the distinction between deliberate parody of and inevitable submission to the commercial formulas derived from American films. Recent examples of this syndrome include **Ladies' Night**, a thinly plotted but popular comedy in which a male stripper hired for a hen night makes the bride-to-be question her choice of groom. Rafael Montero's **Dame tu cuerpo** (literally, *Give Me Your Body*) was a trite imitation of American body-swap comedies, the victims this time a man and a woman who cannot stand each other. Luis Velez's **Corazón de melon** (literally, *Watermelon Heart*) was a simplistic rural fable about gastronomic pleasure and an obese woman's fight to overcome her low self-esteem. **A Day without a Mexican** (*Un día sin Mexicanos*) was another, more candid fable, in which Mexican workers suddenly disappear from California, leaving this rich state in total disarray and its citizens begging for their return.

Two other films mix their numerous parallel plots at frantic speed, hoping to outfox successful American screenwriters, dreaming of a local *Usual Suspects*. In **Nicotina**, a self-indulgent, cliché-laden film, cyber-piracy, Russian mafiosi and frustrated marriages all play a part as characters criss-cross relentlessly in a metaphor for hectic urban life. In **Matando cabos**, clumsy kidnappers abduct the wrong target and come across another gang caught up in similar misunderstandings.

When the government abandons high-quality film promotion, who can blame private investors for backing movies that maximise their chances of exploiting the market rather than risk-prone artistic innovation? Many film students in Mexico are increasingly aware that they have little chance of making independent films and reaching a significant audience. They get over-enthusiastic about the new technologies, particularly digital video, both as a means of original expression but more importantly as a strategy for low-cost production. Many interesting projects, mostly short films, animation and documentaries, do still receive some, albeit insufficient state support.

Duck shooting

Alongside the wannabe Hollywood titles, there were in 2003 several soap opera-inspired melodramas, such as Lorena Villarreal's **The Weeping Women** (*Las lloronas*), García Agraz's **El misterio del Trinidad** (literally, *The Mystery of the Trinity*) and Alfonso Aru's **Zapata – The Hero's Dream** (*Zapata, el sueño del héroe*). As a contrast, there were two promising film debuts: Avila Dueñas' **Adán y Eva (todavía)** (literally, *Adam and Eve (Still)*), an almost experimental exploration of changing sexual mores, and Fernando Eimbcke's **Duck Season** (*Temporada de patos*), a fresh, delightful comedy of teenage hopes and frustrations in urban middle-class Mexico. Beto Gomez's **Puños rosas** (literally, *Pink Fists*) cleverly blurs traditional genres as it probes into an erotically charged friendship between a lightweight boxer and a gangster. Film noir, melodrama and sexual incitement are equally intertwined in Jaime Humberto Hermosillo's new digital experience, **The Almond Tree Mystery** (*El misterio de los almendros*).

Optimum Releasing

Left to right: Enrique Arreola, Daniel Miranda and Diego Cataño in **Duck Season**

Once again, documentaries have this year shown their ability to offer strong alternatives to uninspired fiction. **The Song of Pulque** (*La canción del pulque*), **XV in Zaachila** (*XV en Zaachila*) and **The Sixth Section** (*La sexta sección*) are all lively and affectionate approaches to rural and urban realities, defending local traditions with popular humour. Until private investors and government officials decide to reinvigorate our nearly vanished film industry, alternative expressions such as low-budget documentaries, animation, short films and digital experiences will probably remain the best hope for artistic creation in Mexican cinema.

CARLOS BONFIL (bonfil@letraese.org.mx) has been a film critic since 1989 and contributes a weekly article on cinema to La Jornada, a leading Mexican newspaper. He is the author of *Through the Mirror: Mexican Cinema and its Audience* and a book on Cantinflas.

EL MISTERIO DE LOS ALMENDROS
(The Almond Tree Mystery)
[Drama, 2003] Script: Arturo Villaseñor. Dir: Jaime Humberto Hermosillo. Phot: Jorge Z. López. Players: María Rojo, Alejandro Tomassi, Juan José Meraz, Manuel Medina. Prod: Ramón Barba Loza, Producciones Alfa Audivisual.

LA SEXTA SECCION
(The Sixth Section)
[Documentary, 2003] Script, Dir and Phot: Alex Rivera. Prod: Rivera, Bernardo Ruiz, Second Generation Media.

XV EN ZAACHILA
(XV in Zaachila)
[Documentary, 2003] Script and Dir: Rigoberto Perezcano. Phot: Javier Zarco. Prod: 13 Lunas/ Conaculta/Imcine/Instituto de Culturas Oaxaqueñas.

MATANDO CABOS
[Comedy, 2002] Script: Tony Dalton, Kristoff, Alejandro Lozano. Dir: Lozano. Phot: Juan José Saravia. Players: Tony Dalton, Ana Claudia Talancón, Kristoff, Raúl Méndez. Prod: Bill Rovzar, Fernando Rovzar, Leslie Fastlicht.

LA CANCION DEL PULQUE
(The Song of Pulque)
[Documentary, 2002] Script, Dir and Phot: Everardo González. Prod: Ángeles Castro, Hugo Rodríguez, Centro de Capacitación Cinematográfica /Fonca/Padid.

ZURDO (*literally,* **Left-Handed**)
[Comedy-drama, 2003] Script: Blanca Montoya, Carlos Salces. Director: Salces. Phot: Chuy Chávez. Players: Alex Perea, Giovanni Florido, Arcelia Ramírez, Alejandro Camacho. Prod: Gustavo Montiel, Altavista Films.

Quote of the Year
"I raped official Mexican history, but I gave her a very pretty child."
ALFONSO ARUA, *director, on his* Zapata – The Hero's Dream.

Morocco Roy Armes

Recent Films

A CASABLANCA, LES ANGES NE VOLENT PAS
(In Casablanca, Angels Don't Fly)
[Drama, 2004] Script and Dir: Mohamed Asli. Phot: Mauro Lazzaro. Players: Abdessamad Miftahalkhair, Abderrazzak el Badaoui, Laila El Ahiani, Rachid El Hazmir. Prod: Dagham Films/Gam Film (Italy).

In Casablanca, Angels Don't Fly

CASABLANCA CASABLANCA
[Drama, 2003] Script: Farida Benlyazid based on the novel Les Puissants de Casablanca by Rida Lamrini. Dir: Benlyazid. Phot: Serge Palatci. Players: Younès Magri, Rachid El Ouali, Amal Ayouch, Ichrak Beraoui, Mohamed Razine, Mohamed Bastaoui. Prod: Tangitania Films/RTM/Waka Films.

FACE A FACE (Face to Face)
[Drama, 2003] Script: Nour Eddine Sail, Abdelkader Lagtaâ. Dir: Lagtaâ. Phot: Davi Nissen. Players: Sanaa Alaoui, Younès Mégri, Mohamed Merouazi, Laila Belarbi, Bouchra Ijouk, Houda Rihani. Prod: Cinétéléma/SMSoread/Ecrans du Maroc.

CASABLANCA LA NUIT
(Casablanca by Night)
[Drama, 2003] Script and Dir: Mostafa Derkaoui. Phot: Abdelkrim Derkaoui. Players: Samira Nour, Aziz El Hattab, Zakaria Atifi, Malika Hamoumi,

In quantitative terms, Moroccan cinema continues to flourish, the planned output of eight films a year – twice as many as 10 years ago – having been maintained, so that 16 new features could be shown at the seventh session of the biennial National Film Festival in Oudja in 2003. The state funding scheme continues to support established directors and encourages at least one newcomer a year. Yet the distinguished producer and screenwriter Nour Eddine Saïl recently noted that the principal characteristic of Moroccan cinema is "a lack of desire". There is undoubtedly a certain inward-looking quality about the older directors who continue to dominate Moroccan production but have made little foreign impact. And there is no independent cinema in Morocco: the only films that get made and shown are state-funded.

The work of the older generation offers few surprises, though several of its members have adopted new genres. Farida Benlyazid, for example, whose last film was the widely seen fairytale *Keid Ensa* has produced a thriller, **Casablanca Casablanca**, dealing with murder and corruption in contemporary Morocco. Mohamed Abderrahmane Tazi, well known for his studies of contemporary life, takes a historical subject for the first time in **Abou Moussa's Neighbours** (*Les voisines d'Abou Moussa*), the story of a fourteenth-century adviser to the sultan who acquires a beautiful new wife for his master.

After his commercially successful comedy *The Loves of Haj Moktar Soldi*, Mostafa Derkaoui offers a sombre tale of a 15-year-old girl who must confront **Casablanca by Night** (*Casablanca la nuit*) to pay for the medical care of her young sister. The strongest of the films by the veterans is Abdelkader Lagtaâ's **Face to Face** (*Face à face*). Since his debut in 1991, Lagtaâ has constantly confronted taboos in Moroccan society (his second feature, *The Closed Door*, was delayed for five years because of censorship problems), and now looks at the contradictions and frustrations of society in 1990s Morocco, through the misfortunes of a couple who separate and then try to get back together.

A journey of the *Soul*

Among the new generation, Hakim Belabbès, who lives and works in Chicago, made **Fibres of the Soul** (*Les fibres de l'âme*), which shows Morocco through the eyes of a girl brought up in the US. As she accompanies her father to Boujad, the small town where he grew up, Belabbès sketches the lives of a number of families, their dreams of escape and their ties to the past. Mohamed Asli, who trained in Italy and has set up a film school in Ouarzate in collaboration with CineCittà, directed his first feature after a long career in other capacities. **In Casablanca, Angels Don't Fly** (*A Casablanca, les anges ne volent pas*), which won the prize for first film at the Paris Biennale, deals with the harsh economic realities of rural life that lead a man to abandon his pregnant wife and seek his living in Casablanca.

Perhaps the biggest international impact has been made by the youngest members of the post-independence generation, Narjiss Nejjar (b. 1971) and Faouzi Bensaidi (b. 1967), both of whom had their two-hour-long first films shown at Cannes (Bensaidi also won the grand prix at the Milan African Film Festival). Nejjar's **Cry No More** (*Les yeux secs*), which ran into censorship problems at home, is a contemplative study of a village inhabited only by women who are driven to prostitution in order to survive, until a woman released after 25 years in prison arrives to give them hope of a fresh life.

Bensaidi, an actor as well as director, followed his three internationally acclaimed shorts (*The Cliff*, winner of a dozen prizes, *Journeys* and *The Wall*), with the meticulously shot **A Thousand Months** (*Mille mois*), the story of a small boy living in a remote village in the Atlas mountains whose father is a political prisoner. Though the film, which is set at Ramadan in 1981, concentrates on everyday life, the threat of violence is always in the background.

Faouzi Bensaidi's **A Thousand Months**

Optimum Releasing

Rajaa Moncif, Youssef Ez-zhar. Prod: Aflam.

LES VOISINES D'ABOU MOUSSA (Abou Moussa's Neighbours)
[Drama, 2003] Script: Amina Mouline, from the novel by Ahmed Taoufik. Dir: Mohamed Abderrahman Tazi. Phot: Federico Ribès. Players: Bouchra Charaf, Omar Chanbod, Mohamed Miftah, Taïb Laalej, Mohamed Nadif, Naima Lamcharki. Prod: Arts et Techniques Audiovisuels.

LES FIBRES DE L'AME (Fibres of the Soul)
[Drama, 2003] Script and Dir: Hakim Belabbès. Phot: Maida Sussman. Players: Azeddine Bouayad, Laura Marks, Souad Mellouk, Mohamed Zouheir, Ali Allali, Mostafa Salamat. Prod: La Cité en Fête/HAK Films/TVM-Télévision Marocaine.

MILLE MOIS (A Thousand Months)
[Drama, 2003] Script and Dir: Faouzi Bensaidi. Phot: Antoine Heberle. Players: Fouad Labied, Nezha Rahil, Mohamed Majd, Abdelati, Mohamed Bastaoui, Hajar Mazdouki, Faouzi Bensaidi. Prod: Gloria Films/Agora Films.

LES YEUX SECS (Cry No More)
[Drama, 2003] Script and Dir: Narjiss Nejjar. Phot: Denis Gravouil. Players: Siham Assif, Khalid Benchegra, Raouia, Rafika Belhaj. Prod: Jbila Mediterrané Production/Terre Sud Films.

Quote of the Year

"We learned how to make films abroad, but not what to say."
NARJISS NEJJAR, *Moroccan director.*

Netherlands Pieter van Lierop

The Year's Best Films

Pieter van Lierop's selection:
Simon (Eddy Terstall)
Cloaca (Willem van de
Sande Bakhuyzen)
Phileine Says Sorry
(Robert Jan Westdijk)
Passion Fruit
(Maarten Treurniet)
Hush Hush Baby
(Albert ter Heerdt)

Nadja Hüpscher and Cees Geel in Simon

Recent and Forthcoming Films

HOLLANDS LICHT
(Dutch Light)
[Documentary, 2003] Script:
Maarten de Kroon, Gerrit
Willems. Dir: Pieter-Rim de
Kroon. Phot: Paul van den Bos.
Prod: Pieter-Rim de Kroon,
Reinier Wissenraet.
Was the famous light in
seventeenth-century Dutch
landscape paintings real, a myth
or an artist's trick? Fascinating
investigation that won Best
Documentary at the Golden
Calves 2003.

CLOACA
[Black comedy, 2003] Script:
Maria Goos, based on her play.
Dir: Willem van de Sande
Bakhuyzen. Phot: Guido van
Gennep. Players: Pierre Bokma,

One singular and gruesome event overshadowed all others in the Dutch film community during 2004. On November 2, the controversial film-maker Theo van Gogh was murdered in Amsterdam, causing tremendous shock and sadness throughout Holland and a wave of violent reprisals. Van Gogh, 47, was shot off his bike and then stabbed with a knife that was left in his body, together with a written message in Arabic. A 26-year-old Muslim man was charged with the murder.

Theo, a direct descendant of Vincent van Gogh's brother, was the always provocative director of a loud, uneven but always interesting body of work, and also one of Holland's most prolific columnists and TV personalities, with a somewhat anarchic style and a pencil as sharp as his tongue, never politically correct but always forcing people to think – and rethink – social issues. In recent years, he had often turned his sarcastic attentions to what he saw as the growing menace of Muslim fundamentalism – just as he castigated intolerance from Christians, Jews or feminists. He loved to make enemies; yet he could surprise even his opponents with sudden gestures of kindness. Theo was, above all, a free spirit who championed the right not to keep silent. He died for it.

The most likely direct cause of his murder was a short film, *Submission*, which he made in 2004 in co-operation with a Dutch Liberal MP, Ayan Hirsi Ali. Exposing a half-naked, mistreated female body, the film is a lament for the systematic oppression of women in the name of Allah down the ages. Despite van Gogh's objections to Islam, he was no blind enemy to his country's Islamic immigrants. In August 2004 he had presented **Cool**, an almost tender film containing large quantities of humour, suspense and romance, about Moroccan teenagers who have lost their way in Dutch society and the efforts made by penitential institutions to help young offenders. On the day of his murder, he was in the last phase of editing a feature film, *06-05*, devoted to Pim Fortuyn, the Dutch politician shot dead in 2002. Van Gogh was a friend and kindred spirit of Fortuyn; how horrific that they died in identical fashion.

Two prominent film-makers involved in the birth of modern Dutch cinema 35 years ago hit the headlines in summer 2004. Wim Verstappen, who with his provocative *Blue Movie* (1971) was the first of his generation to attract an audience in excess of a million, died at the age of 67. He had been the country's most significant activist on matters such as copyright and support for the film industry.

Paul Verhoeven, the second *enfant terrible* to reach the masses, with *Turkish Delight* (1973), received the prestigious Bert Haanstra Award for his oeuvre and announced that he was to direct his first Dutch production for 20 years. *Black Book* will be set in the twighlight zone between resistance and collaboration in the Second World War. Shooting was set for completion by the end of 2004 but in October was postponed until April 2005 because of concerns over the director's health. The €9m budget is extremely low by Verhoeven's Hollywood standards, but vast for the Netherlands.

The tax incentives scheme that had prompted a five-year feature production boom was scheduled to terminate at the end of 2003, but the government made a one-off extension to January 1, 2005, after which point producers believed they would (as in the 1990s) be completely dependent for subsidy on the Netherlands Film Fund and its annual pot of around €12m. In September 2004, however, a group of MPs belonging to moderate left-wing party D'66 proposed a new incentive scheme that seemed likely to win a parliamentary majority. Details were sketchy at press time, but total production rebates would not exceed €20m a year.

Fruits of the boom

The recent surge in production greatly increased audience interest in domestic films, and the biggest draws were children's movies. Within a year of selling 900,000 tickets for *Peter Bell*, Maria Peters delivered **Peter Bell 2** (700,000 admissions). A similar (youthful) rogue's tale, **The Chameleon**, attracted 750,000 viewers, prompting director Steven de Jong to launch a sequel. Less successful (150,000 admissions) was **Pipo the Clown**, based on a TV series that has run for 35 years. TV spin-offs are becoming a trend. In the pipeline is *Floris,* a rousing story based on the 1960s, *Ivanhoe*-esque series that did well for Paul Verhoeven.

Yoram Lürsen's charming **In Orange** (*In oranje*) follows Remco, 11, a talented, fanatical soccer player who dreams of a place in the Dutch U12 team. He must confront a serious foot injury and the death of his father. The story was inspired by the early life of Johan Cruijff, about whom Ramón Gieling made an excellent documentary, **En un momento dado**, exploring what the Dutchman meant to the people of Catalonia as player and coach at F.C. Barcelona. Ineke Houtman's **Polleke** (100,000 admissions) was the year's best young people's film. Polleke, 11, falls in love with a Moroccan boy, Mimoen, whose parents oppose the cultural differences in this puppy love. Polleke's father ends up as a homeless junkie and her mother falls in love with one of her teachers. *Polleke* was part of a local trend

Peter Blok, Gijs Scholten van Aschat, Jaap Spijkers. Prod: IdtV Film BV.

GRIMM
[Black comedy, 2003] Script and Dir: Alex van Warmerdam. Phot: Tom Erisman. Players: Jacob Derwig, Halina Reijn, Carmelo Gomez, Elvira Minguez. Prod: Graniet Film BV.
Abandoned by their penniless Dutch father, Jacob and his sister travel to Spain to seek the uncle who could help them.

DE PASSIEVRUCHT (Passion Fruit, a.k.a A Father's Affair)
[Drama, 2003] Script: Kees van Beijnum. Dir: Maarten Treurniet. Phot: Wouter Suyderhoud. Players: Peter Paul Muller, Halina Reijn, Carice van Houten, Dai Carter, Jan Decleir, Frank Lammers. Prod: 24fps Features.

PHILEINE ZEGT SORRY (Phileine Says Sorry)
[Romantic comedy, 2003] Script: Robert Jan Westdijk, based on the novel by Ronald Giphart. Dir: Westdijk. Phot: Bert Pot. Players: Kim van Kooten, Michiel Huisman, Liesbeth Kamerling, Tara Elders, Hadewych Minis, Daan Schuurmans.

POLLEKE
[Youth film, 2003] Script: Rob Arends, Maarten Lebens. Dir: Ineke Houtman. Phot: Sander Snoep. Players: Liv Stig, Mamoun Elyounoussi, Daan Schuurmans, Halina Reijn. Prod: Egmond Film and Television.

SHOUF SHOUF HABIBI (Hush Hush Baby)
[Comedy, 2004] Script: Albert ter Heerdt, Mimoun Oaissa. Dir: ter Heerdt. Phot: Steve Walker. Players: Oaissa, Najib Amhali, Touriya Haoud, Bridget Maasland. Prod: Theorema Films.
A Dutch-born Moroccan kid makes some big mistakes as he tries to overcome cultural differences. Winner of the Dutch Critics' and Special Jury prizes at the Golden Calves 2004.

for increasing cultural interest in ethnic minorities, the most successful example of which was Albert ter Heerdt's **Hush Hush Baby** (*Shouf shouf habibi*), a comedy of manners about young Moroccans caught between liberal Western views and traditional family codes. The Moroccan community turned out in such numbers that the film took €2.3m, more than *The Passion of the Christ*.

Left to right: Mimoun Oaissa, Mimoun Ouled Radi and Mohammed Chaara in **Hush Hush Baby**

Television plays an increasingly prominent role in creating opportunities for young film-makers. Public broadcasters joined The Crossing, a scheme under which eight feature projects were selected by the Film Fund for further script development; four will be produced with the aid of €700,000 each. A similar project, One Night Stand, involves nine shorts, budgeted at up to €225,000 each, while the Telescope Project aims to produce two to four features a year, designed for theatrical release and then television, possibly as mini-series.

This co-operation between cinema and television recently produced Alex van Warmerdam's **Grimm**, a contemporary variation on *Hansel and Gretel*, with Freudian elements, whereby the story switches half way through from an absurdist Holland to an equally fictional Spain. Van Warmerdam's grim humour worked less well in the Spanish half.

The girlfriend, the gangster and the widower

Robert Jan Westdijk's **Phileine Says Sorry** (*Phileine Zegt Sorry*) had more success (almost 300,000 admissions). Phileine (Kim van Kooten; Golden Calf for Best Actress 2004) has a boyfriend who disappears off to New York for a theatre course. She follows him, suspects he's being unfaithful and behaves accordingly. Westdijk films the story playfully, with dreamt asides and sharp dialogue. Phileine learns to be less egocentric and to say sorry, just once.

Gerrard Verhage's **The Preacher** (*De Dominee*) deals with the rise and fall of Amsterdam gangster Klaas Bruinsma, who in the 1970s thought he could make a quick fortune from marijuana, which he expected to be legalised shortly. He was wrong, and was forced to adopt methods just as violent his rivals'. The criminal underworld is presented evocatively and the plot is exciting.

FIGHTING FISH
[Martial arts, 2004] Script: Kim Ho Kim, Jamel Attache. Dir: Attache. Phot: Peter-Jan van der Burgh. Players: Kim, Ron Smoorenburg, Chantal Janzen. Prod: Fighting Fish CV.

FEESTJE (The Best Man)
[Romantic comedy, 2004] Script: Mischa Alexander. Dir: Ruud van Hemert. Phot: Han Wennink. Players: Antonie Kamerling, Beau van Erven Dorens, Daphne Bunskoek, Chantal Janzen. Prod: PV Pictures.
Thijs and Ben are best buddies and believe in one-night-stands. Then Ben marries.

Yannick van de Velde dreams of football glory in **In Orange**

IN ORANJE (In Orange)
[Youth film, 2004] Script: Frank Ketelaar. Dir: Joram Lürsen. Phot: Remco Bakker. Players: Yannick van de Velde, Thomas Acda, Wendy van Dijk. Prod: Motel Films/Fu Works.

Frank Lammers in **The Preacher**

DE DOMINEE (The Preacher)
[Crime drama, 2004] Script and Dir: Gerrard Verhage. Phot: Theo Bierkens. Players: Peter Paul Muller, Frank Lammers, Chantal Janzen, Cas Jansen. Prod: Theorema Films.

SIMON
[Comedy-drama, 2004] Script and Dir: Eddy Terstall. Phot: Willem Nagtglass. Players: Cees Geel, Marcel Hensema, Rifka Lodeizen, Nadja Hüpscher. Prod: Spaghetti Film BV.

Winner of 2004 Golden Calves for Best Film, Direction and Actor (Geel) and the Public Award.

SNOWFEVER
[Romantic comedy, 2004] Script: Pieter Bart Korthuis. Dir: Pim van Hoeve. Phot: Maarten van Keller. Players: Hanna Verboom, Daan Schuurmans, Egbert Jan Weber, Eva van der Gucht. Prod: Nijenhuis en De Levita Film en TV BV.
Cinderella story about Dutch teenagers falling in love with Dutch ski instructors in the Austrian Alps.

Eva van der Gucht in **Snow Fever**

ELLIS IN GLAMOURLAND
[Romantic comedy, 2004] Script: Mischa Alexander. Dir: Pieter Kramer. Phot: Piotr Kukla. Players: Linda de Mol, Chris Tates, Joan Collins, Joan Nederloff. Prod: Nijenhuis en De Levita Film en TV BV.
A young woman joins a class to learn the skills needed to pick up a rich man. Won Best Script at Golden Calves 2004.

FLIRT
[Comedy of manners, 2004] Script: Eddy Terstall, Jaap van Eyck. Dir: van Eyck. Phot: Jasper Wolf. Players: Egbert Jan Weeber, Lidwij Mahler, Marcel Hensema, Rifka Lodeizen. Prod: Corrino Films BV.
An actor falls in love with a documentary-maker. He thinks he can have other girlfriends, she disagrees and makes him the subject of her new film.

ZWARTBOEK (Black Book)
[War drama, 2005] Script: Gerard Soeteman. Dir: Paul Verhoeven. Phot: Theo van de Sande. Players: Carice van Houten, Halina Reijn. Prod: San Fu Maltha, Fu Works.

Peter Paul Muller, rather too sphinx-like as Bruinsma, is more sympathetic in Maarten Treurniet's **Passion Fruit** (*De Passievrucht*), playing a widower who, despite having a 13-year-old son, is suddenly told that he is infertile. So who impregnated his late wife? His obsessive quest for the answer has disastrous results and the story has the drive of an unusual "whodunnit", believable, exciting and psychologically interesting. Excitement and credibility are lacking in Martin Koolhoven's **The South**, in which the owner of a laundry seduces one of her employees. When he is startled by touching the artificial breast she wears following a mastectomy she becomes unhinged and keeps him prisoner in a boiler room until he dies.

Life's a sewer and then...

The acting is sublime in Willem van de Sande Bakhuyzen's **Cloaca** (meaning 'sewer'), adapted by Maria Goos from her play. Four old friends from university meet again in the midst of mid-life crises: a lawyer, a theatre director, a politician and an art historian. The lame and the blind help the addicted and the deaf; Goos' sharp, intelligent dialogues are unparalleled in the Netherlands.

Left to right: Jaap Spijkers, Pierre Bokma and Peter Blok as close friends in **Cloaca**

Writer and director Eddy Terstall has distinguished himself with witty relationship comedies, usually set among thirtysomethings in Amsterdam. The hero of his latest film, **Simon**, chosen as the Netherlands' Oscar entry, is a homosexual dentistry student (Cees Geel) who accidentally becomes involved in the circle of Simon, a villainous hash dealer with a big mouth and a good heart. Everything seems on course for the hilarious chain reaction we expect from Terstall, when suddenly one of the central characters is diagnosed with a brain tumour and the mood darkens, addressing issues like homosexual marriage and euthanasia. Terstall's story is all about friendship and loyalty and his laconic sense of humour works wonders as a defence against false sentiment.

PIETER VAN LIEROP is film editor of the Netherlands Press Association (23 syndicated daily papers) and has been a correspondent for *IFG* since 1981.

New Zealand Peter Calder

The Year's Best Films

Peter Calder's Selection:

In My Father's Den
(Brad McGann)

Kaikohe Demolition
(Docu. Florian Habicht)

The Locals (Greg Page)

Christmas (Greg King)

Two Cars, One Night
(Short. Taika Waititi)

Rangi Ngamoki in **Two Cars One Night**

IN MY FATHER'S DEN
*[Thriller, 2004] Script: Brad
McGann, based on the novel by
Maurice Gee. Dir: McGann.
Phot: Stuart Dryburgh. Players:
Matthew MacFadyen, Miranda
Otto, Vicky Haughton, Colin
Moy, Jodie Rimmer, Emily
Barclay, Jimmy Keen. Prod:
Trevor Haysom, Dixie Linder.*

PERFECT STRANGERS
*[Drama, 2002] Script and Dir:
Gaylene Preston. Phot: Alun
Bollinger. Players: Sam Neill,
Rachael Blake, Joel Tobeck. Prod:
Robin Laing.*
A woman (Blake) agrees to go
home with a handsome man
(Neill) and finds she is the subject
of his romantic obsession.

THE LOCALS [Horror, 2003]
*Script and Dir: Greg Page. Phot:
Brett Nichols. Players: John Barker,
Dwayne Cameron, Kate Elliott,
Aidee Walker. Prod: Steve Sachs.*

I f there were any people who had not already come to regard New
Zealand as a film-making force, they were certainly brought up to
speed on Oscar night 2004, when *The Return of the King* became
the most successful film in Academy Awards history, winning all 11
categories in which it had been nominated. In a country whose
artists traditionally take a back seat to sporting heroes, it was a great
event. With a population that topped four million only in 2003, Kiwis
are always proud of their world-beaters. Almost everyone here
knows someone (or knows someone who knows someone) who
worked on the *Lord of the Rings* trilogy, a fact reflected in Oscars
host Billy Crystal's crack: "It's official: there is nobody in New Zealand
left to thank."

Even more gratifying to many was the spectacular success of
Whale Rider, since it was so conspicuously a New Zealand story.
It took more than $3.5m at home, making it the second biggest
local hit after *Once Were Warriors*, and more than $30m worldwide.
The Best Actress Oscar nomination for Keisha Castle-Hughes was
a bonus; everyone enjoyed the sight of a local contender not
connected with *Rings*.

Skeletons in the *Den*

After all that excitement, almost anything else was likely to seem
anti-climactic, but the period under review ended well with the
rapturously received festival screenings of Brad McGann's debut
feature, **In My Father's Den**, which took the FIPRESCI prize at
Toronto in September 2004. Based on a novel by well-regarded
local writer Maurice Gee, this New Zealand/UK co-production is the
first Kiwi film funded by the UK Film Council's New Cinema Fund.

Matthew MacFadyen uncovers family secrets in **In My Father's Den**

It's dark and gloomy, confirming Sam Neill's 1995 documentary observation that ours is a "cinema of unease", but also assured and accomplished, anchored by excellent performances by British star Matthew MacFadyen and local newcomer Emily Barclay. MacFadyen plays a celebrated war photographer who comes home for his father's funeral and unwittingly digs up a long-buried family secret. Moodily lensed by Stuart Dryburgh, who shot *The Piano*, it is an auspicious debut from a talented director.

Much less impressive was **Perfect Strangers**, by veteran Gaylene Preston (*War Stories, Bread and Roses*), which was billed as "a chilling romance". Preston is one of our most consistent and original talents but this film, Sam Neill's first local project since *The Piano*, was wilfully silly, full of plot holes and design-driven contrivances. Surprisingly well received by Australian critics, it was extraordinarily good-looking (cinematographer Alun Bollinger also shot *Heavenly Creatures*), but much of the credit must rest with its location, a remote bay on the rugged and beautiful west coast of the South Island.

Honourable mention goes to Greg Page's **The Locals**, which had a reasonable run at the local box-office. A snappy horror flick, it contained an extraordinary number of brilliantly lit scenes supposedly set in dark countryside, but had a cheeky sense of humour and showcased a bright new talent.

John Barker, second from right, in **The Locals**

Also of interest were two films that had good receptions at local festivals, even if their commercial prospects are limited. Gregory King's **Christmas** was a micro-budget digital black-and-white feature that anatomised a grotesquely dysfunctional family on the festive day when family dysfunction is at its most grotesque. It was grim but bleakly, absurdly comic. In **Kaikohe Demolition**, German-born Florian Habicht turned a foreigner's keen eye on a demolition derby in an economically depressed small town in the north of the country and gave us a down-to-earth yet distinctly surreal slice of Kiwiana. Taika Waititi's *Two Cars One Night*, named Best Short in the Panorama section at Berlin 2004, was a moving story of first love involving two youngsters in a car park, while their parents drink in a nearby bar.

Two best mates hit the road for a weekend of surfing and boozing and end up in the heartland of evil.

NEMESIS GAME
[Psychological thriller, 2003] Script and Dir: Jesse Warn. Phot: Aaron Mortin. Players: Ian McShane, Adrian Paul, Carly Pope, Rena Owen. Prod: Matthew Metcalfe.
A student is fascinated with riddles until her friends start dying.

SPOOKED
[Thriller, 2004] Script and Dir: Geoff Murphy. Phot: Rewa Harre. Players: Cliff Curtis, Chris Hobbs, Miriama Smith, John Leigh, Kelly Johnson. Prod: Don Reynolds, Merata Mita, Geoff Dixon, Murphy.

Jared Turner and Kate Elliott as brother and sister in **Fracture**

FRACTURE
[Psychological thriller, 2003] Script: Larry Parr, based on the novel by Maurice Gee. Dir: Parr. Phot: Fred Renata. Players: Kate Elliott, Jared Turner, Cliff Curtis, John Noble. Prod: Charlie McClellan.
A single mother (Elliott) is pushed to the brink when her brother (Turner) bungles a burglary.

FOR GOOD
[Psychological drama, 2003] Script and Dir: Stuart McKenzie. Players: Michelle Langstone, Adam Gardiner, Tim Gordon, Tim Balme, Miranda Harcourt. Phot: Duncan Cole. Prod: Neil Pardington, Larry Parr.
A young woman impersonates a journalist and enters a killer's world.

CHRISTMAS
[Drama, 2003] Dir and Script: Gregory King. Phot: Ginny Loane. Players: Darien Takle,

Tony Waerea, David Hornblow,
Helen Pearse Otene. Prod:
Leanne Saunders.

KAIKOHE DEMOLITION
[Documentary, 2004]
Dir and Prod: Florian Habicht.
Phot: Habicht, Christopher Pryor.

RIVER QUEEN *[Historical*
drama, 2004] Script: Vincent
Ward, Toa Fraser. Dir: Ward.
Phot: Alun Bollinger. Players:
Samantha Morton, Kiefer
Sutherland, Cliff Curtis, Temuera
Morrison. Prod: Don Reynolds,
Chris Auty.
1860s-set colonial drama about a
young woman caught between
Maori and *pakeha* (NZ
Europeans) cultures.

50 WAYS OF SAYING
FABULOUS
[Drama, 2004] Script: Stewart
Main, based on the novel by
Graeme Aitken. Dir: Main. Phot:
Simon Raby. Players: Andrew
Patterson, Harriet Beattie,
Georgia McNeil, Jay Collins,
Michael Dorman, Rima Te Wiata.
Prod: Michele Fantl.
Billy, a farmer's son, prefers
culture to cows and is out of step
with the knockabout farm boys.

PERFECT CREATURE
[Thriller, 2005] Script and Dir:
Glenn Standring. Phot: Leon
Narbey. Players: Dougray Scott,
Saffron Burrows, Stuart Wilson,
Scott Wills. Prod: Tim Sanders.
In a retro-futuristic world,
vampires are no longer mankind's
nemesis but its saviour, protecting
human life from viral and DNA
mutations.

Quote of the Year

"When they called Charlize
[Theron]'s name, it hit me.
Me, a kid from GI, had
been nominated for an
Academy Award."

KEISHA CASTLE-HUGHES
reacts to missing out on the Best
Actress Oscar. 'GI' is Glen Innes,
a poor suburb of Auckland.

At press time, the local release was imminent of Larry Parr's **Fracture**, also based on a Maurice Gee novel. The film, which had been tied up in the financial collapse of its production company, is most charitably described as frantic and incoherent and seems unlikely to make much of an impression.

Big names and financial carrots

Some big names from the past were working behind the camera this year. Geoff Murphy, whose anarchic road movie *Goodbye Pork Pie* was the first bona-fide local hit, was in post-production on *Spooked*, a contemporary conspiracy thriller based on the unsolved death of a computer dealer who unwittingly bought sensitive banking records as part of a second-hand deal. It stars Cliff Curtis, the most internationally successful Maori actor (*Three Kings*, *Blow*), as a hard-bitten television journalist, and was scheduled for an early 2005 release.

Shooting on Vincent Ward's *River Queen*, a historical drama, was interrupted in July 2004 by the illness of star Samantha Morton and the delay forced co-star Kiefer Sutherland to decamp temporarily to the US to shoot new episodes of *24*, but producer Don Reynolds said the footage already captured was sensational and the film would proceed. Finally, shooting wrapped in August on the futuristic vampire film *Perfect Creature*, another Kiwi/UK co-production, written and directed by Glenn Standring, whose *The Irrefutable Truth about Demons* performed well on video.

The Government dangled a cash-back carrot in front of producers considering filming in the land of the *Rings* when it unveiled a new funding regime that will reimburse big-budget productions one eighth of the money they spend here. The Big Budget Grant Scheme seeks to maintain the momentum generated by the *Rings* trilogy and *The Last Samurai*, which also shot here. Rebates are available only to film and television projects whose local spend is $30m or more, although spends over $10m may be eligible if that figure is more than 70% of the total budget.

The scheme was criticised by local film-makers excluded by the budget criteria, but expat Andrew (*Shrek*) Adamson said it was instrumental in persuading Walden Media to let him shoot *The Lion, the Witch and the Wardrobe* in New Zealand. The signs are that this will be the first of several films in a series. Meanwhile Peter Jackson was hard at work on his remake of *King Kong*.

PETER CALDER (peterc@ihug.co.nz), New Zealand correspondent for *Variety*, has been a film critic for the *New Zealand Herald*, the country's major daily newspaper, for 20 years.

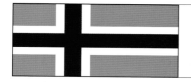

Norway Trond Olav Svendsen

The Year's Best Films

Trond Olav Svendsen's selection:

The Beautiful Country
(Hans Petter Moland)
Tradra
(Docu. Karoline Frogner)
The Beast of Beauty
(Hilde Heier)
Mother's Elling (Eva Isaksen)
The Woman of My Life
(Alexander Eik)

Virre Dahl/Maipo Film & TV

Per Christian Ellefsen in
Mother's Elling

Recent and Forthcoming Films

UNITED
[Comedy, 2003] Script and Dir:
Magnus Martens. Phot: Jakob
Ingimundarson. Players: Gjert
Haga, Vegar Hoel, Håvard
Lilleheie, Berte Rommetveit,
Ole-Jørgen Nilssen. Prod: Håkon
Øveraas/ Aagot Skjeldal/4.
Football fanatic Kåre dreams of
playing for Manchester United.

LILLE FRØKEN NORGE
(The Beast of Beauty)
[Children's film, 2003] Script:
Hilde Heier, Kjetil Indregård. Dir:
Heier. Phot: Philip Øgaard.
Players: Ingrid Lorentzen, Ida
Maria Dahr Nygaard, Amanda
Kvakland, Bård Tufte Johansen,

Cinema in Norway is very much alive and on the offensive. The country's Film Fund works from a broad perspective and supports many newcomers. More features are produced than ever before (about 20 per year) and the local film market share has on occasion been much bigger than usual. However, with 4.5 million people stretched thinly all the way to the Arctic, and with the capital Oslo as its only big city, Norway's cinema statistics can be shaken by the presence or absence of a single success. Each year's overall figures tend to depend on whether the industry produces one "locomotive" or not.

Optimism is very much in evidence among exhibitors. Exhibition in Norway has since the days of silent cinema been dominated by the municipal system, through which most cinemas have been owned and operated by the municipalities. This meant a monopoly in practically all cities and towns, including Oslo, but also nationwide co-operation between and support for local cinemas through the Association of Municipal Cinemas. This system has gradually lost favour.

In one sense this is a paradox, because the municipal cinemas have in general competed well against the plethora of other leisure activities offered to modern Norwegians. But anti-monopoly and pro-privatisation winds are blowing in most areas of Norwegian society. Oslo has surrendered one of its oldest and best-known suburban theatres, the two-screen Soria Moria, to a private company which is expanding into other areas of the city. SF Kino, owned by the Swedish conglomerate Bonnier, plans to build a multiplex beside the huge new opera house that has been emerging from the waters of the Oslo Fjord. There will also be a new multiplex at the former Oslo West railway station, downtown, and former film director Petter Vennerød has built a multiplex in Asker, outside Oslo.

Today's young film actors come from the theatre, as screen actors in Norway always have, but appear to take a stronger interest than previous generations in the particular challenges of film acting. For their portrayals of real-life characters, actors such as Kristoffer Joner, Aksel Hennie, Pia Tjelta and Laila Goody have earned the respect of audiences. Per Christian Ellefsen has in the popular *Elling* pictures given comedy performances that are more fleshed out than the over-the-top burlesque Norwegians are used to. This fine acting is perhaps the main reason for the successes of the last couple of years.

NORWEGIAN OSCAR® ENTRY
BEST FOREIGN LANGUAGE FILM

PARADOX

HAWAII, OSLO

A film by ERIK POPPE

A mother's obsession

Among the new films of the 2003-04 season **The Beast of Beauty** (*Lille frøken Norge*) certainly had good acting on its side, thanks to the performance of ballet dancer Ingrid Lorentzen as Kristin, wicked stepmother to nine-year-old Lotte who, with her widowed father, moves in to Kristin's home. Obsessed by how people look, Kristin is already grooming her 12-year-old daughter for Miss Universe, and her new marriage to Lotte's dad does nothing to alter her ambition. Lorentzen's character is cheerfully perverse in a way rarely seen in Norwegian films, but director Hilde Heier has some difficulty making the rest of the picture, which has elements of realism and fantasy, stick together.

Olav Dahl/Sandrew Metronome

Amanda Kvakland, Ingrid Lorentzen and Ida Maria Dahr Nygaard in **The Beast of Beauty**

Lars Göran Petterson's **Bázo** is a Sami feature, shot in Finland, Sweden and Norway. Sverre Porsanger plays Emil, a *bázo* (the Sami word for a slow if not quite retarded individual) who, after his smarter brother dies in an accident, sets out to discover the truth of what happened. The film never leaves the essentially melancholy mode established at the beginning. The northern landscapes, where most film-makers would go for the magnificent views, are here made to seem rather monotonous and limiting. There has been wide coverage in the local media of how the Sami people finally obtained their own parliament and flag, and what makes *Bazó* so interesting is that it is aware of the historic oppression of the Sami without expressing an idealised view of their struggle for independence.

Desperately seeking parents

Documentaries continue to form a vital part of Norwegian cinema and this year **Tradra** (*Tradra – i går ble jeg tater*) by Karoline Frogner aroused the most interest. Its protagonist, Bjørn, 45, is visited one day by a woman who claims to be his biological mother, and he suddenly learns that he was taken from his mother as a baby, with the blessing of the authorities, to be raised in a "normal" family. He sets out to find her among the travelling people of Norway (in

Marit Åslein. Prod: Finn Gjerdrum/Paradox.

Filmagoahti AS

Sverre Porsanger in **Bázo**

BÁZO
[Drama, 2003] Script and Dir: Lars Göran Pettersson. Phot: Svein Krøvel. Players: Göran Forsmark, Issáht Juakim Gaup, Sverre Porsanger, Anitta Suikkari, Nils Utsi. Prod: Nils Thomas Utsi, Filbmagoahti.

BUDDY
[Drama, 2003] Script: Lars Gudmestad. Dir: Morten Tyldum. Phot: John Andreas Andersen. Players: Nicolai Cleve Broch, Aksel Hennie, Anders Baasmo Christensen, Pia Tjelta, Janne Formoe. Prod: Gudny Hummelvoll, Knut Jensen, Happy Endings.
Three friends become the subject of a reality TV series.

KVINNEN I MITT LIV
(The Woman of My Life)
[Comedy, 2003] Script: Lars Espen Bakke. Dir: Alexander Eik. Phot: Jon Gaute Espevold. Players: Thomas Giertsen, Gard Eidsvold, Ane Dahl Torp, Pia Tjelta, Line Verndal, Kjersti Holmen, Eddie Skoller. Prod: John M. Jacobsen, Filmkameratene.
Lawyer Jacob has managed to stay out of long-term relationships, but then he meets Nina.

MORS ELLING (Mother's Elling)
[Drama, 2003] Script: Axel Hellstenius, based on a novel by Ingvar Ambjørnsen. Dir: Eva Isaksen. Phot: Rolv Håan. Players: Per Christian Ellefsen, Grete Nordrå, Helge Reiss. Prod: Dag Alveberg, Maipo.
Elling is a misfit who lives with his mother. She decides they are going on holiday to Mallorca.

GUNNAR GOES COMFORTABLE

[Documentary, 2003] Script, Dir, Phot and Featuring: Gunnar Hall-Jensen. Prod: Elin Sander, Agitator. The film-maker's uncensored self-portrait.

PÅ HAU' I HAVET
(Arctic Cabaret)

[Documentary, 2003] Dir: Knut Erik Jensen. Phot: Paal Bugge Haagenrud. Featuring: Finn A., Ole Anton, Randi. Prod: Jan-Erik Gammleng, Barentsfilm. A look at amateur vaudevillians.

TRADRA – I GÅR BLE JEG TATER (Tradra)

[Documentary, 2004] Script and Dir: Karoline Frogner. Phot: Halgrim Ødegård. Featuring: Bjørn Granum, Lasse Johansen. Prod: Frogner, Integritet.

THE BEAUTIFUL COUNTRY

[Drama, 2004] Script: Larry Gross, Terrence Malick. Dir: Hans Petter Moland. Phot: Stuart Dryburgh. Players: Damien Nguyen, Ling Bai, Tim Roth, Nick Nolte. Prod: Petter Borgli, Tomas Backström, Edward Pressman, Terrence Malick, Dinasun Productions.

SALTO, SALMIAKK OG KAFFE
(Chlorox, Ammonia and Coffee)

[Drama, 2004] Script and Dir: Mona J. Hoel. Phot: Hoyte van Hoytema. Players: Fares Fares, Benedicte Lindbeck, Dennis Storhøi, Kjersti Holmen. Prod: Malte Forsell, Freedom from Fear. A pregnant single woman robs a local shopkeeper.

ALT FOR EGIL
(This Is the Song You Need)

[Drama, 2004] Script: Tore Renberg, Tore Rygh. Dir: Rygh. Phot: Svein Krøvel. Players: Kristoffer Joner, Trond Høvik, Nina Ellen Ødegård, Morten Abel. Prod: Sigve Endresen/ Motlys. Egil is a pizza delivery boy with a mentally challenged friend and an obsession with real-life Norwegian pop star Morten Abel.

whose language *tradra* means travelling).The film tells of terrible injustices in twentieth-century Norwegian society, but sticks to a melancholy (and occasionally light) mood, more in tune with the travelling people themselves, who have a strong grasp of their modern history but refuse to drown it in tears.

With Terrence Malick among the producers and with no Norwegian-speaking characters, **The Beautiful Country**, directed by our leading film-maker, Hans Petter Moland, will perhaps not be perceived abroad as a Norwegian production. The film is also uneven, sometimes moving from unsatisfactory to profoundly satisfying in a matter of seconds. Binh (Damien Nguyen), the 20-year-old Vietnamese son of an American soldier, lives with a foster family but is actually an outcast. Though Nguyen is excellent, the early scenes do not seem fully realised emotionally, and episodes concerning Binh and his mother's work as servants in the house of a cruel woman are thinly drawn.

Damien Nguyen, standing centre (behind bottle), in **The Beautiful Country**

But when Binh begins his sea journey to America to search for his father, with his little brother and a young Chinese woman (Bai Ling) in tow, things improve. One harrowing event follows another. Tim Roth gives a subdued performance as the violent captain of the ship. *The Beautiful Country* grows on you, and the final scenes are the best. In an unpretentious performance, Nick Nolte plays the father, who turns out to be a blind loner. Moland is at his best here, showing how these two men slowly learn to know each other, and his bleak, but somehow positive view of America is refreshing because it occupies territory depicted differently by mainstream American directors.

TROND OLAV SVENDSEN (tos@kunnskapsforlaget.no) has worked as a researcher for the Norwegian Film Institute and as a newspaper film critic. Among his publications is a *Theatre and Film Encyclopedia*.

Pakistan Aijaz Gul

The Year's Best Films

Aijaz Gul's selection:
Honour (Rauf Khalid)
In Love (Fahim Burney)
Javaid Shampoo
(Short. Dir: Faisal Rahman)
Punjabi Girl (Syed Noor)
Just Talk (Short. Hasan Zaidi)

Saima and Shamyl Khan in **Punjabi Girl**

Recent and Forthcoming Films

SALAKHAIN (The Bars)
[Urdu. Action drama, 2004]
Script: Amjad Islam Amjad. Dir:
Shahzad Rafiq. Players: Ahmad,
Meera, Mansoor, Zara Shaikh.
Prod: Rashid Khawaja.
A young innocent joins the mafia,
with destructive consequences.

KEWOON TUM SEY ITNA
PYAR HAI (Why Do I Love You?)
[Urdu. Thriller, 2004] Script and
Dir: Ajab Gul. Players: Nadeem,
Ajab Gul, Veena Malik, Babrak,
Talat Hussain. Prod: Saqib Khan.
Two generations of superstars
feature in this tale of suspense.

SHAHID KARIM'S
CONSPIRACY
[Urdu. Short thriller, 2002]
Script and Dir: Farjad Nabi.
Prod: Matteela.

The wild piracy of films on cable television and through the sale of illicit VCDs and DVDs in markets nationwide continues unchecked and the knock-on effects for the film industry are obvious. Many cinemas in Karachi and other cities have closed because of high entertainment tax and piracy. Annual film production came down from 62 features in 2002 to 48 features in 2003. The first eight months of 2004 witnessed further decline; 15 new Urdu and Punjabi titles were made. Pushto-language films not available on cable TV have successfully withstood the pirates' onslaught.

Two of the major Urdu titles bombed because of their slow pacing and poor editing. Rauf Khalid's moderate **Honour** (*Laaj*) deals with a Pathan boy and a Hindu girl in 1932 against a British Raj backdrop; the love story ends with everyone blown up amid explosions and blazing guns. With **In Love** (*Pyar hi pyar mein*), Fahim Burny foolishly tried to defy the normal box-office formula that demands a virginal heroine. The married heroine loves the hero, a young man looking to move into the fast lane; then her husband conveniently dies, allowing the leads to get together. Audiences booed the film.

Syed Noor's **Punjabi Girl** (*Larki Punjaban*) was shot in picturesque Malaysia with newcomer Shamyl Khan as a Punjabi boy from Pakistan who falls for a Sikh girl from India (Saima). Together they must face the hostile world. The film played moderately well in Pakistan after a theatrical premiere in Britain. Jawed Sheikh's *This Heart Is Yours* (*Yeh dil aap ka huwa, 2002*) also had an impressive run in the UK. Superstar hero Shan worked overtime again, with 21 assignments in 2003 and 10 in the first seven months of 2004. Saima, the leading heroine, made 20 films in 2003 and nine in the first half of 2004. Her rival, Reema, is turning to modelling and direction.

A crop of digital shorts by young directors were the year's most impressive productions, shot in Lahore and Karachi on modest budgets and addressing socially meaningful themes. Faisal Rehman, Bilal Minto, Mehren Jabbar (*Office*), Hasan Zaidi (*Just Talk*), Farjad Nabi and Maheen Zia (*Hina* and *Multan – City of Living Crafts*) are now the torch-bearers for a new kind of Pakistani film-making, free of songs, dances and other hackneyed box-office gimmicks.

AIJAZ GUL (aijazgul2003@yahoo.com) has published numerous articles and three books on cinema. He lives in Islamabad.

Peru Isaac Léon Frías

Recent and Forthcoming Films

OJOS QUE NO VEN
(*literally,* **Eyes That Do Not See**)
[Drama, 2003] Script: Giovanna Pollarolo. Dir: Francisco Lombardi. Phot: Teo Delgado. Players: Paul Vega, Gustavo Bueno, Gianfranco Brero, Patricia Pereyra. Prod: Inca Cine.

BAÑO DE DAMAS
(**Ladies' Toilet**)
[Drama, 2003] Script and Dir: Michael Katz. Phot: Juan Durán. Players: Andrea Montenegro, Lorena Meritano, Coco Marusix, Sonia Oquendo. Prod: Iguana Films.

POLVO ENAMORADO
(**Lovesick Dust**)
[Drama, 2003] Script: Giovanna Pollarolo. Dir: Luis Barrios. Phot: Carlos de la Cadena. Players: Paul Vega, Gianella Neyra, Gustavo Bueno. Prod: Inca Cine.

UN MARCIANO LLAMADO DESEO (**A Martian Called Desire**)
[Comedy, 2003] Script and Dir: Antonio Fortunic. Phot: Micaela Cajahuaringa. Players: Christian Meier, Mónica Sánchez, Aristóteles Picho. Prod: Focus Producciones.

PALOMA DE PAPEL
(**Paper Dove**)
[Drama, 2003] Script and Dir: Fabrizio Aguilar. Phot: Micaela Cajahuaringa. Players: Antonio Callirgos, Aristóteles Picho, Sergio Galliani, Melania Urbina. Prod: Luna Llena Films.

DOBLE JUEGO (**Double Game**)
[Comedy, 2003] Script and Dir: Alberto Durant. Phot: Juan Durán. Players: Fabrizio Aguilar, Fernando Cayo, Maria Pili

Cinema attendance in Peru dropped in 2003 compared to 2002. Many local productions shot on video – shorts, feature documentaries and fiction features – failed to secure theatrical distribution. However, some young directors based in inland cities were able to reach a small audience at a very local level – a new development in a country whose film production has been concentrated historically in Lima. In all, six Peruvian features were released in 2003, the largest figure for many years. Three were reviewed in *IFG 2004*: *Eyes That Do Not See* (*Ojos que no ven*), *Lovesick Dust* (*Polvo enamorado*) and *Ladies' Toilet* (*Baño de damas*).

The other three were all feature debuts. Antonio Fortunic's **A Martian Called Desire** (*Un marciano llamado deseo*) was a "new age" comedy set in Cuzco, the old capital of the Inca empire. With a very weak script, this romance between a young woman from Lima and a blond American tourist lacked any humour or imagination and was a complete failure with local audiences and critics. A much better first impression was made by Fabrizio Aguilar with **Paper Dove** (*Paloma de papel*), a realistic drama about a country boy captured by the Sendero Luminoso (Shining Path) guerrillas and turned into an initially obedient militant who then perceives the cruelty of the guerrillas' methods. Aguilar achieves a fine balance between the political and personal elements of the story and drives it forward with fluent efficiency.

In **Destiny Has No Favourites** (*El destino no tiene favoritos*), Alvaro Velarde again demonstrated the familiarity with classic American film comedies that characterised his short films. In a grand house and garden, a lady and her two maids become entangled with a television crew shooting a soap opera. This is excellent genre film-making, examining class and the relationship between reality and fiction with an ironic eye.

Durante *Double* faults

Three Peruvian films were released in the first nine months of 2004. One was an unexpected change of direction from the experienced Alberto Durant. His previous films, *Dog Eyes* (*Ojos de perro*), *La Gringa* and *Courage* (*Coraje*) all had strong social or political themes. However, **Double Game** (*Doble juego*) was an unpretentious comedy with a routine plot about fraud and Durant was clearly uncomfortable with material that does not suit his sensibility.

Mother Coca (*Coca Mama*) was the fourth feature from Marianne Eyde, a Norwegian–Peruvian film-maker. Like her previous works, *The Patrolmen* (*Los ronderos*), *You Only Live Once* (*La vida es una sola*) and *The Bait* (*La carnada*), *Mother Coca* again shone a spotlight on society and revealed the contradictions between official image and reality. The action takes place within the Peruvian cocaine business and centres on a drug dealer, an ex-addict and a young woman from the coast. Unfortunately, the documentary-like presentation of the peasants extracting coca from leaves and the ancestral significance of the plant in their lives was undermined by the very weak depiction of the passionate love triangle involving the three principals.

Days of Santiago (*Días de Santiago*), a debut feature from Josué Méndez, tells the story of a demobbed soldier (Pietro Sibile) who comes back from fighting guerrillas in the Peruvian forests and finds that he is unable to readapt to family life. Sibile gives a remarkable performance that establishes the character's emotional instability and the film's tense climax expresses the confusion and lack of prospects for many Peruvian youngsters. *Days of Santiago* is the best Peruvian film of recent years.

Left to right: Ivy La Noire, Pietro Sibille and Marisela Puicón in **Days of Santiago**

Two documentaries screened in independent arthouse cinemas are worthy of mention. **Choropampa – The Price of Gold** (*Choropampa, el precio del oro*), produced and directed by Ernesto Cabellos and Stephanie Boyd, has as its point of departure a mercury leak from the gold mine in an Andean village. It then follows the villagers' fight to protect their health and critically exposes the gulf between the lives of the Andean people and those who run the prominent mining company. Also successful was Joel Calero's **Palpa and Guapido** (*Palpa y Guapido*), a look at a marriage celebration in an Andean village.

ISAAC LÉON FRÍAS (ileon@correo.ulima.edu.pe) has been a film critic since 1965 and is Professor of Language and Film History at the University of Lima. From 1965 to 1985 he was director of *Hablemos de Cine* magazine and from 1986 to 2001 he ran Filmoteca de Lima.

Barreda, Katia Condos, Gianfranco Brero. Prod: Agua Dulce Films.

COCA MAMA (Mother Coca)
[Drama, 2004] Script and Dir: Marianne Eyde. Phot: Mario Bassino. Players: Milagros del Carpio, Oscar Carrillo, Miguel Medina. Prod: Kusi Films.

DIAS DE SANTIAGO (Days of Santiago)
[Drama, 2004] Script and Dir: Josué Méndez. Phot: Juan Durán. Players: Pietro Sibile, Milagros Vidal, Marisela Puicón. Prod: Chullachaki.

CHOROPAMPA, EL PRECIO DEL ORO (Choropampa – The Price of Gold)
[Documentary, 2003] Script: Stephanie Boyd. Dir: Boyd, Ernesto Cabellos. Phot: Cabellos. Prod: Guarango Cine y Video.

PALPA Y GUAPIDO (Palpa and Guapido)
[Documentary, 2002] Script and Dir: Joel Calero. Phot: Mario Bassino. Prod: Guarango Cine y Video.

EL DESTINO NO TIENE FAVORITOS (Destiny Has No Favourites)
[Comedy, 2002] Script and Dir: Alvaro Velarde. Phot: Micaela Cajahuaringa. Players: Angie Cepeda, Elena Romero, Bernie Paz. Prod: Alvaro Velarde Producciones.

Philippines Tessa Jazmines

Recent and Forthcoming Films

IMELDA
[Documentary, 2004] Script and Dir: Ramona S. Diaz. Phot: Ferne Pearlstein. Prod: CineDiaz/Unitel.

The poster for **Imelda**

NAGLALAYAG (Silent Passage)
[Drama, 2004] Script and Dir: Irma Dimaranan, Maryo J. De Los Reyes. Phot: Odyssey Flores. Players: Nora Aunor, Yul Servo, Aleck Bovick. Prod: Angora Films.

MAGNIFICO
[Drama, 2004] Script and Dir: Michiko Yamamoto, Maryo J. De Los Reyes. Phot: Odyssey Flores. Players: Albert Martinez, Lorna Tolentino, Tonton Gutierrez, Jira Manio, Gloria Romero, Amy Austria, Celia Rodriguez. Prod: Violett Films Production.

BABAE SA BREAKWATER
(Woman in the Breakwater)
[Drama, 2004] Script and Dir: Mario O'Hara. Phot: Rey de

Reacting to media suggestions that Philippine cinema was dead, Tony Gloria, CEO of Unitel Pictures International, declared: "It is the best of times. It is the worst of times." It was easy to see what he meant. Movie production has been drastically reduced, thanks largely to piracy and the popularity of the TV soaps that, ironically, feature the same stars as local movies. Yet there are positive developments, too, and change is afoot.

A greater variety of creative projects, some with award-winning scripts, are making an impression at local and international festivals. The government of recently re-elected President Gloria Macapagal-Arroyo has thrown its support solidly behind the entertainment industry, passing an Optical Media Law designed to track down the illegal manufacture and sale of films, with seven-figure fines and jail terms of up to six years for convicted culprits.

The president is also putting her weight behind plans for a huge state-of-the-art studio facility at Subic Bay, which local independent producers could rent for a minimal fee. She sees this as one of the best ways to break the stranglehold of foreign movies at the box-office, create jobs and revive enthusiasm for the local movie industry. Her government has also introduced cash awards for non-commercial films and reduced amusement taxes. Both moves have encouraged film-makers to deviate from the formulaic movies of the early 1990s that earned fast bucks but lacked substance.

The proof came at the December 2003 Metro Manila Film Festival. Gone were the fantasy movies and scary flicks that have kept the popcorn crowd happy in recent years. In came artistically admirable productions that gained critical acclaim. **Crying Ladies**, a heartwarming comedy about three women who earn their living by crying at Chinese funerals, broke new ground and won Best Picture, Director and three other awards at the festival. It had a literate script by debutant director Mark Meily, a TV commercials whiz making a successful crossover into features. Unitel Pictures, the company behind the film, was making its festival debut. Manned by creative people from the advertising industry, it has introduced a new, inventive work ethic into the industry.

The festival also included **Mano Po 2**, an epic sequel about a Filipino–Chinese family, and **Filipinas**, an allegorical story of a Filipino family that seems to reflect the nation's own story. **Homecoming** was a realistic film about the SARS epidemic and **Mirage** (*Malikmata*) told a paranormal tale. For once, the perennial obsession with sex was toned down and respected critic Nestor Torre noted that the lone Manila entry in this genre, Jeffrey Jeturian and Chris Martinez's **Bridal Shower**, "brought wit and sophistication back to local sex comedies".

Mad about the boy

Directed by Maryo J. De Los Reyes, **Magnifico** was the runaway sensation of the Manila Film Festival in June 2004, taking Best Picture and nine other awards, including Director and Actor (it also won the Crystal Bear for Best Feature at the 2004 Kinderfilmfest in Berlin). It tells the amazing story of a young boy whose love, faith and courage shine through life's sadness and misfortunes. The prolific De Los Reyes scored more hits at Manila with **Silent Passage** (*Naglalayag*), a May–December romance between a retired judge and a young cab driver, and his first foray into horror, **Dark Shadows** (*Kulimlim*). However, both films suffered at the local box-office as the simultaneous release of *Spider-Man 2* blew away all other competition.

Magnifico *swept the board at the 2004 Manila Film Festival*

Local industry figures have now mounted a campaign to limit the screening of Hollywood films and give local productions a better chance at the tills. This is not really the solution, say pundits who believe the production of more high-quality local features is the long-term answer to this age-old problem. While major producers like Regal Films and Viva have drastically reduced their annual output, new, independent producers are coming up with interesting projects, however. "The industry is hanging on," says Tony Gloria, whose Unitel has also gone into international distribution via a sister company, Unico, based in New York. Don't cry for Filipino cinema just yet.

TESSA JAZMINES (tjazmines@yahoo.com) is *Variety* correspondent for the Philippines and Associate Professor of Journalism, University of the Philippines College of Mass Communication.

Leon. *Players: Katherine Luna, Kristoffer King, Gardo Verzosa. Prod: Arlene Aguas.*

CRYING LADIES
[Comedy-drama, 2003] Script and Dir: Mark Meily. Phot: Lee Meily. Players: Sharon Cuneta, Hilda Koronel, Angel Aquino, Ricky Davao, Julio Pacheco. Prod: Tony Gloria, Unitel Pictures.

Crying Ladies

KULIMLIM (Dark Shadows)
[Horror, 2004] Script and Dir: Roy Iglesias, Maryo J. De Los Reyes. Phot: Odyssey Flores. Players: Robin Padilla, Tanya Garcia. Prod: Viva Films.

MANO PO 3 (My Love)
[Drama, 2005] Script and Dir: Joel Lamangan. Players: Vilma Santos, Judy Ann Santos, Christopher De Leon. Prod: Lily Monteverde, Regal Films.

REPUBLIC OF PENITENCE
[Satirical drama, 2005] Script and Dir: Mark Meily. Phot: Lee Meily. Players: Robin Padilla, Ruffa Mae Quinto. Prod: Unitel Pictures.

BRIDAL SHOWER
[Sex comedy, 2003] Script and Dir: Chris Martinez, Jeffrey Jeturian. Phot: Nap Jamir. Players: Dina Bonnevie, Cherry Pie Picache, Francine Prieto. Prod: Robbie Tan, Seiko Films.

Quote of the Year

"I did [so much for the local film industry] because I have been a movie fan ever since I was small. But I'm still small, so I'm still a movie fan."
GLORIA MACAPAGAL-ARROYO, *diminutive President of the Philippines.*

Poland Barbara Hollender

The Year's Best Films

Barbara Hollender's selection:
The Welts
(Magdalena Piekorz)
Pornography
(Jan Jakub Kolski)
My Nikifor (Krzysztof Krauze)
Symmetry (Konrad Niewolski)
The Wedding
(Wojciech Smarzowski)

Recent and Forthcoming Films

CUD W KRAKOWIE
(Miracle in Cracow)
[Drama, 2004] Script: Diana
Groo. Dir: Groo, Andras Szeker.
Phot: Sandor Kardos. Players:
Maciej Adamczyk, Eszter Biro,
Itala Bekes, Bartlomiej Swiderski.
Prod: Studio Filmowe Tor/
Cinamea-Film/Katapult-Film.

DO POTOMNEGO
(To the Offspring)
[Documentary, 2004] Script and
Dir: Antoni Krauze. Phot: Jacek
Petrycki. Players: Dariusz Wnuk,
Janusz Radek, Marcin Przybylski,
Bartek Porczyk, Lukasz
Ploszajski. Prod: WFDiF/Agencja
Produkcji Filmowej/Fundacja
Filmowa Armii Krajowej.

LAWECZKA (The Bench)
[Drama, 2004] Script: Robert
Maka, Maciej Zak. Dir: Zak.
Phot: Grzegorz Kuczeriszka.
Players: Jolanta Fraszynska,
Artur Zmijewski, Artur Pontek.
Prod: Pleograf/Agencja
Produkcji Filmowej/Kino Swiat
International/TPS Studio Filmowe.

MOJ NIKIFOR (My Nikifor)
[Drama, 2004] Script: Joanna
Kos, Krzysztof Krauze. Dir:
Krauze. Phot: Krzysztof Ptak.

Polish cinema faced tough times in 2004. The Ministry of Culture earmarked just 22 million Zloty (around $5.3m) to production, while public broadcaster Polish Television – previously the largest domestic film producer – underwent a financial crisis. The switch to digital television reduced the revenue from the local branch of Canal Plus. Private terrestrial and cable TV stations are not legally obliged to support domestic movie production.

The banks, for whom recent big-budget productions such as *Quo vadis* and *Chopin. Desire of Love* remain bad debts, have largely withdrawn from film-making and private investors are reluctant to become involved in such a risky business when they are denied any tax incentives. The ministry limits state grants to a maximum of $200,000 per film when most feature budgets are in the region of $800,000 to $1.1m. Independent film-makers cannot therefore raise enough capital and summer 2004 was the first season since the Second World War when there was not a single Polish feature film crew in the field.

In this tough environment, the recent run of historical blockbusters adapted from Polish literary classics, with budgets of more than $5m (*Quo vadis* cost $18m), has ended and most films in 2003-04 were shot on video, quickly, cheaply and, unfortunately, with poor scripts. However, there are glimmers of hope, as some young directors turn away from politics and social issues, looking instead at the life of the average Pole and asking "how to live today".

The boy as father of the man

The largest surprise of the year, winner of the Golden Lion at the Polish Film Festival and chosen as the national entry for the Oscars, was Magdalena Piekorz's **The Welts** (*Pregi*), a story about childhood scars catching up with the victim in adult life. As a boy, Wojciech (Waclaw Adamczyk) had run away from his tyrannical father (Jan Frycz), a single parent. Now, in his thirties (Michal Zebrowski plays the adult Wojciech), he finds himself becoming more and more like his dad – incapable of showing love to anybody, intolerant, severe. But fatherhood forces him to change. *The Welts* reached number one in the box-office chart and had taken more than $650,000 after three weeks on release.

Parenthood also transforms the world-view of the leading character in Malgorzata Szumowska's **Stranger** (*Ono*). A pregnant girl who initially wants an abortion begins to love her unborn child. Told that foetuses can hear, she tries to explain to the little human inside her the world surrounding them. She tells "it" about feelings and they grow together.

Jan Hryniak's **The Third** (*Trzeci*), compared by critics to Polanski's *Knife in the Water*, presents two yuppies who on their upward path to wealth and success have lost sight of life's real values. Fate puts an old man in their path who, like an angel, forces them to stand still for a moment and consider what really matters.

Krystyna Feldman plays an elderly male painter in **My Nikifor**

Subtle, subdued storytelling is also apparent in the work of a "middle generation" director, Krzysztof Krauze, who in **My Nikifor** (*Moj Nikifor*) dramatises the last years of Nikifor (1895-1968), the painter from Krynica now regarded as one of the finest of naïve artists. Played by Krystyna Feldman, the 84-year-old actress who strongly resmbles Nikifor and won Best Actress at the annual Polish Film Festival in Gdynia in 2004, the artist is shown as an ill, half-incapacitated and mumbling beggar, who sold his pictures from a square by a spa.

Yet this wretched being was free, pursuing his interests unhindered by the opinions of others. Krauze's film is, above all, about friendship and sacrifice. When Nikifor had tuberculosis and the locals treated him as if he had the plague, only one man helped him, the painter Marian Wlosinski, who sacrificed his own career and jeopardised his family life to care for Nikifor in his final days.

An irresistible *Wedding* invitation

At the opposite end of the spectrum from the restrained films discussed above was **The Wedding** (*Wesele*), directed by Wojciech Smarzowski (another interesting representative of the young generation). This sharp social satire illustrates the sad state of contemporary Poland through the wedding of a rich man's daughter.

Players: Krystyna Feldman, Roman Gancarczyk, Lucyna Malec. Prod: Studio Filmowe Zebra/Telewizja Polska SA/Canal+ Polska.

NIGDY W ZYCIU (Never Ever)
[Comedy, 2004] Script: Ilona Lepkowska. Dir: Ryszard Zatorski. Phot: Tomasz Dobrowolski. Players: Danuta Stenka, Artur Zmijewski, Joanna Brodzik. Prod: TVN/ ITI Studio/Agencja Produkcji Filmowej/MTL Maxfilm.

OGROD ROKOSZY ZIEMSKICH (The Garden of Earthly Delights)
[Drama, 2004] Script, Dir and Phot: Lech Majewski. Players: Claudine Spiteri, Chris Nightingale, Barry Chipperfield. Prod: Mestiere Cinema/ Metaphysics Ltd./Angelus Silesius.

ONO (Stranger – Ono)
[Drama, 2004] Script: Malgorzata Szumowska, Przemyslaw Nowakowski. Dir: Szumowska. Phot: Michal Englert. Players: Malgorzata Bela, Teresa Budzisz-Krzyzanowska, Marek Walczewski. Prod: Pandora Film Produktion GmbH/Telewizja Polska SA/MG Bavaria/ STI Studio Filmowe/Eurimages/ Filmstiftung NRW.

PORNOGRAFIA (Pornography)
[Drama, 2003] Script: Jan Jakub Kolski, Luc Bondy, Gerard Brach, based on a novel by Wotold Gombrowicz. Dir: Kolski. Phot: Krzysztof Ptak. Players: Krzysztof Majchrzak, Krzysztof Globisz, Adam Ferency. Prod: Heritage Films/Telewizja Polska SA/ MACT P/Canal Plus Polska/ WFDiFroductions.

PREGI (The Welts)
[Drama, 2004] Script: Wojciech Kuczok. Dir: Magdalena Piekorz. Phot: Marcin Koszalka. Players: Jan Frycz, Michal Zebrowski, Agnieszka Grochowska. Prod: Studio Filmowe Tor/ Vision Film Production/ Non Stop Film Service.

Michal Zebrowski and Agnieszka Grochowska in **The Welts**

TULIPANY (Tulips)
[Drama, 2004] Script and Dir: Jacek Borcuch. Phot: Damian Pietrasik. Players: Jan Nowicki, Malgorzata Braunek, Zygmunt Malanowicz. Prod: RATS/Studio Filmowe Tor/ Film IT.

SYMETRIA (Symmetry)
[Drama, 2003] Script and Dir: Konrad Niewolski. Phot: Arkadiusz Tomiak. Players: Arek Detmer, Elzbieta Kijowska. Prod: EM/SPInka.

VINCI
[Thriller, 2003] Script and Dir: Juliusz Machulski. Phot: Edward Klosinski. Players: Robert Wieckiewicz, Borys Szyc, Kamila Baar. Prod: Studio Filmowe Zebra/TVN/ITI Film Studio/ CanalPlus Polska.

Kamila Baar and Borys Szyc in Vinci

WESELE (The Wedding)
[Drama, 2004] Script and Dir: Wojciech Smarzowski. Phot: Andrzej Szulkowski. Players: Marian Dziedziel, Iwona Bielska, Tamara Arciuch. Prod: Telewizja Polska SA/Film It/Agencja Produkcji Filmowej/WFDiF/ Grupa Filmowa/SPI International/ Non Stop Film Service.

Quote of the Year

"I dont like gloomy endings. I wish to leave viewers with at least one ray of sunshine."
MAGDALENA PIEKORZ,
director of The Welts.

The characters have only one God: money. Theirs is a world ruled by gangsters in which anybody can be bought, from priest to policeman. *The Wedding* was deservedly acclaimed by Polish critics.

Left to right: Bartlomiej Topa, Marian Dziedziel and Tamara Arciuch in **The Wedding**

Piekorz, Szumowska, Smarzowski and Hryniak are all names to be noted for the future – and they do not march alone. Recent years have seen other successful debuts from the likes of Piotr Trzaskalski, Iwona Siekierzynska, Lukasz Barczyk, Anna Jadowska, Ewa Stankiewicz, Slawomir Fabicki, Andrzej Jakimowski and Draiusz Gajewski (Barczyk has already made a second feature, *Changes*, and at press time Trzaskalski was working on his, *Champion*).

They are like a breath of fresh air in Polish cinema, but the older generation has certainly not retired. Among its representatives, Ryszard Zatorski made 2004's biggest local box-office hit (1.6 million admissions), **Never Ever** (*Nigdy w zyciu*), a romantic comedy promoted as Poland's answer to *Bridget Jones's Diary*, about a recently divorced woman in her forties who has to start a new life. Juliusz Machulski presented a very good thriller, **Vinci**, about an attempt to steal a Leonardo painting from a museum in Cracow. At press time, Krzysztof Zanussi was working on a crime drama, *Persona non grata*, and Robert Glinski on *The Call of the Toad* (*Wrozby kumaka*), adapted from a novel by Günter Grass.

The financial prospects for 2005 were healthier, as the Culture Ministry's film budget was set to rise from $5m to $8.4m and the bosses at Polish Television had signed a deal with Canal Plus that would see the French company investing around $1.5m a year in Polish films. Finally, the long-awaited new Cinematography Bill was due to be unveiled early in 2005.

BARBARA HOLLENDER (b.hollender@rp.pl) is a Warsaw-based journalist and film critic for the daily *Rzeczpospolita* and covers the Berlin, Cannes and Venice festivals. She has co-written, with Zofia Turowska, the books *Stars in Zoom* and *Studio Tor*.

Portugal Martin Dale

The Year's Best Films

Martin Dale's selection:
The Miracle According to Salomé (Mário Barroso)
The Immortals (António Pedro Vasconcelos)
The Fifth Empire (Manoel de Oliveira)
André Valente (Catarina Ruivo)
This is Our Faith (Docu. Edgar Pêra)

Football fans in **This Is Our Faith**

Recent and Forthcoming Films

ANDRÉ VALENTE
[Drama, 2003] Script and Dir: Catarina Ruivo. Phot: Rui Poças. Players: Leonardo Viveiros, Rita Durão, Pedro Lacerda. Prod: Madragoa Filmes.

A PASSAGEM DA NOITE
(Night Passage)
[Drama, 2003] Script and Dir: Luís Filipe Rocha. Phot: Edgar Moura. Players: Cristóvão Campos, João Ricardo, Leonor Seixas, Maria Rueff. Prod: Madragoa Filmes.

DAQUI P'RA ALEGRIA
(From Here to Joy)
[Drama, 2003] Script and Dir: Jeanne Waltz. Phot: Lisa Hagstrand. Players: Dinarte Branco, Raquel Cardoso, Anocas. Prod: Filmes do Tejo.

I n António Vasconcelos' **The Immortals** (*Os imortais*), Portugal's biggest local hit of 2003 (more than 55,000 admissions), police detective Malarranha Vasconcelos declares: "This humdrum country where nothing ever happens is enough to drive anyone crazy." Vasconcelos clearly identifies with the simmering rage of the five colonial war veterans featured in his film, feeling trapped inside a small, parochial and claustrophobic country. The director is also a vocal critic of national film policy, which underwent considerable turbulence in 2003-04.

At the end of 2003 the national film institute, ICAM, began to publish official box-office statistics for the first time in Portugal's history. The figures confirmed that more than 95% of the local box-office is occupied by English-language films and that Portuguese productions in 2003 claimed 0.7% of total box-office of $77m, from 20.5 million admissions at 565 screens. Portuguese films effectively occupy a ghetto on home turf, rarely breaking the 10,000 admissions barrier, and even *The Immortals* was well outside the year's top 50.

Portuguese cinema nonetheless has fervent supporters throughout the world, especially amongst specialist film critics, and when the centre-right government announced that it intended to create a new film investment fund with contributions from telecom operators and broadcasters and a permanent Selection Board focused on promoting mainstream "commercial" films, auteur directors such as Manoel de Oliveira, João Botelho and João Mário Grilo drew up a manifesto against what they described as "the beginning of the end of Portuguese cultural sovereignty". Signatures for the manifesto were gleaned from all parts of the world, including directors such as Jim Jarmusch, Jean-Jacques Beineix and even the Directors' Guild of America.

Despite this opposition, the new Film and Television Law establishing the fund came into force in September 2004, and major local media groups such as Portugal Telecom have announced that they will contribute. It is far too early to judge whether there will be quiet evolution or rapid revolution in the near future in Portuguese cinema. What is certain is that the dominant themes of national culture will continue to be the main well-spring of local creativity.

ÉS A NOSSA FÉ
(This Is Our Faith)
*[Documentary, 2004] Script, Dir
and Phot: Edgar Pêra. Prod:
Madragoa Filmes.*

LA FORA (Outside)
*[Drama, 2004] Script: João
Lopes. Dir: Fernando Lopes.
Phot: Edmundo Díaz. Players:
Alexandra Lencastre, Rogério
Samora, Joaquim Leitão. Prod:
Madragoa Filmes.*

MARIA E AS OUTRAS
(Maria and the Other Girls)
*[Comedy, 2003] Script: Rita
Benis, Possidónio Cachapa. Dir:
José de Sá Caetano. Phot: Rui
Poças. Players: Catarina Furtado,
Isabel Abreu, Ana Brito e Cunha.
Prod: Animatógrafo II.*

NOITE ESCURA
(In the Darkness of the Night)
*[Drama, 2004] Script and Dir:
João Canijo. Phot: Mário
Castanheira. Players: Rita Blanco,
Beatriz Batarda, Cleia Almeida.
Prod: Madragoa Filmes.*

NÓS (Us)
*[Drama, 2003] Script: Cláudia
Tomaz, João Pereira. Dir: Tomaz.
Phot: Lisa Hagstrand, Nuno
Ferreira. Players: João Pereira,
Alexandre Freudenthal, Susana
Vidal. Prod: Madragoa Filmes.*

O FASCÍNIO (Fascination)
*[Drama, 2003] Script: José
Fonseca e Costa, João
Constâncio. Dir: Fonseca e Costa.
Phot: Acácio de Almeida. Players:
Vítor Norte, Sylvie Rocha, José
Fidalgo. Prod: Madragoa Filmes.*

**O MILAGRE SEGUNDO
SALOMÉ (The Miracle
According to Salomé)**
*[Drama, 2004] Script: Carlos
Saboga. Dir: Mário Barroso. Phot:*

Ana Bandeira in **The Miracle
According to Salome**

Fado, football and Fatima

During the 50-year fascist regime in Portugal, Salazar liked to say that Portuguese culture revolved around the three Fs "fado, football and Fatima" – and three recent films seemed to pay tribute to this saying. The accomplished debut feature film by veteran cinematographer Mário Barroso, **The Miracle According to Salomé** (*O milagre segundo Salomé*), provides an interesting twist on the Fatima tale. According to the Catholic Church, the Virgin Mary appeared to three young shepherds in 1917, conveying a secret message for humanity. On this basis, a huge cathedral was built in the small village of Fatima and the three shepherds were proclaimed saints.

In Barroso's film, the angelic temptress Salomé (Ana Bandeira) leaves her sleepy country village for the bright lights of Lisbon. After a series of adventures – first as a prostitute, then as a chambermaid – she flees for home. On her way back she is sighted by three young shepherds in Fatima who believe she is the Madonna.

The nation's other two Fs were covered by **This Is Our Faith** (*És a nossa fé*), experimental director Edgar Pêra's fascinating documentary portrait of the fanatical world of Portuguese football fans. **All This Is Fado** (*Tudo isto é fado*) by Luís Galvão Teles is a comedy set in Portugal and Brazil that mixes the sounds of the samba and fado but inspires little laughter.

The godfathers (in several parts)

Manoel de Oliveira celebrated his ninety-sixth birthday in 2004 and completed two films in little more than 12 months, both produced by Paulo Branco. The latest, **The Fifth Empire** (*O quinto império*), revolves around the myth of Don Sebastian, Portugal's "lost king", who according to legend will one day ride through the mists on a white horse in order to usher in the "Fifth Empire" – enabling Portugal to fulfil her historical mission to enlighten the world.

Ricardo Trepa and Luís Miguel Cintra in **The Fifth Empire**

The title of De Oliveira's previous feature, **A Talking Picture** (*Um filme falado*), starring John Malkovich, Catherine Deneuve and Irene Pappas, was perhaps a fitting description for much of his recent work, full of slow-moving theatrical tableaux, where the narrative is principally dialogue-driven. De Oliveira and Branco are effectively the godfathers of Portuguese cinema. Branco secures around 40% of national production funding through his Madragoa Filmes company and his "stable" of directors encompasses the majority of established talent in the country.

Branco's other recent productions include *Outside* (*La fora*), *In the Darkness of the Night* (*Noite escura*) and *Fascination* (*O fascínio*). Fernando Lopes' **Outside** explores the claustrophobic atmosphere of a closed condominium and asks whether love is possible in the modern world – with Big Brother watching at every corner. First-time director Catarina Ruivo's **André Valente** tells the story of André, eight, who lives alone with his mother after the flight of his father and yearns for love, paternal guidance and happiness in a cold, wintry Lisbon.

João Canijo's **In the Darkness of the Night** explores the sad and sordid universe of a family-owned "girlie bar", where the father (Fernando Luís), under pressure from a Russian mafia boss who has lent him money, decides to hand over his virginal youngest daughter (Cicia Almeida) to repay the debt and ends up by destroying his family. Canijo asserts that the film is a parable of his country and claims that Portugal "has the highest number of girlie bars per square metre in Europe". José Fonseca e Costa's **Fascination** focuses on Lino (Vítor Norte), who inherits a huge estate in the sun-drenched Alentejo region only to discover that it is haunted by a deadly curse.

In the late 1990s, producer Tino Navarro enjoyed a series of popular hits but his luck seems to have run out more recently. His latest release is **Portugal S.A.** by Ruy Guerra, a vitriolic portrait of a country where everything is up for sale. However, both the narrative and characters lacked depth and the film was panned by the critics and attracted a meagre 15,000 admissions. Given present trends and expectations, Portuguese cinema is likely to be singing mournful *fado* for some while to come.

MARTIN DALE (formigueiro@mail.telepac.pt) has lived in Lisbon since 1994 and works as an independent media consultant. He has written several books on the film industry, including *The Movie Game* (Continuum, 1997).

Mário Barroso. Players: Nicolau Breyner, Ana Bandeira, Ricardo Pereira. Prod: Madragoa Filmes.

O QUINTO IMPÉRIO
(The Fifth Empire)
[Drama, 2004] Script and Dir: Manoel de Oliveira. Phot: Sabine Lancelin. Players: Ricardo Trepa, Luís Miguel Cintra, Glória De Matos. Prod: Madragoa Filmes.

OS IMORTAIS (The Immortals)
[Drama, 2003] Script and Dir: António Pedro Vasconcelos. Phot: Sabine Lancelin. Players: Nicolau Breyner, Joaquim de Almeida, Emmanuelle Seigner. Prod: Animatógrafo II.

PORTUGAL S.A.
[Drama, 2003] Script: Carlos Vale Ferraz, Alberto Fernandes. Dir: Ruy Guerra. Phot: Amílcar Carrajola. Players: Diogo Infante, Cristina Câmara. Prod: MGN Filmes.

PRETO E BRANCO
(Black and White)
[Drama, 2003] Script: Mário de Carvalho. Dir and Prod: José Carlos de Oliveira. Phot: Players: Cristina Homem de Mello, Luís Sarmento.

TUDO ISTO É FADO
(All This Is Fado)
[Comedy, 2004] Script: Suzanne Nagle, Gonçalo Galvão Teles. Dir: Luís Galvão Teles. Phot: Jako Raybaut. Players: Angelo Torres, Ana Cristina Oliveira, Danton Mello. Prod: Fado Filmes.

UM FILME FALADO
(A Talking Picture)
[Drama, 2003] Script and Dir: Manoel de Oliveira. Phot: Emmanuel Machuel. Players: Leonor Silveira, John Malkovich, Catherine Deneuve, Stefania Sandrelli. Prod: Madragoa Filmes.

Quote of the Year

"I like to dream and meditate and be in the hands of a master of this art."
JOHN MALKOVICH *on working with Manoel de Oliveira.*

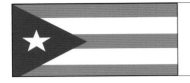

Puerto Rico José Artemio Torres

Recent and Forthcoming Films

CAYO
[Drama, 2004] Script: Pedro Muñiz, Ineabelle Colón. Dir: Vicente Juarbe. Phot: Milton Graña. Prod: Muñiz.

DESAMORES (Indifferences)
[Drama, 2004] Script: Gilberto Rodríguez, based on the novel by Wilfredo Matos. Dir: Edmundo Rodríguez. Phot: Demetrio Fernández. Prod: Luis Collazo, Propaganda Films.
A detective tries to solve the murder of a woman.

REVOLUCION EN EL INFIERNO (Revolution in Hell)
[Drama, 2004] Script: Roberto Ramos Perea, based on his play. Dir: Gilo Rivera Jr. Players: Ernesto Concepción, Cordelia González, Miguel Angel Suárez. Prod: Benito de Jesús, WIPR-TV Channel 6.
Ponce, 1936. A march organised by the Puerto Rico Nationalist Party is attacked by police.

SEXO Y GUAGUANCÓ
(Sex, Food and Guaguancó)
[Drama, 2004] Script and Dir: José Ramón Díaz. Phot: Frank Elías, P.J. López. Players: Yamaris Latorre, Teófilo Torres, Jaime Bello, Jerry Segarra, Rafi Torres.
A shy transvestite runs off with his idol, a female star of Guaguancó music.

Jerry Segarra in Sex, Food and Guaguancó

As anticipated, production picked up in 2003-04 after the Production Fund at the Puerto Rico Film Commission started its loans programme. A dramatic 35mm feature, *Cayo*, and a digital TV film, *Desamores*, went into production in 2004, and a documentary, *Carnivals of the Caribbean* directed by Sonia Fritz, was completed. However, these represent only a quarter of the 12 projects selected for funding. Another source of funding is the Lucy Boscana Dramatic Project, at public broadcaster Channel 6. In two years the project has produced three TV films and had another two in post-production at press time, when this correspondent was directing a mini-series, *The Last Case of Detective Prado* (*El ultimo caso del detective Prado*), about a soon-to-retire detective.

Commercial television, especially Channels 2 and 4, continues to produce TV movies, an area favoured by directors like Sonia Valentín and Vicente Castro. There is also a wave of low-budget and micro-budget features shot on DV, some by young people like Alex Matos (*Sabó*) or seasoned hands like copywriter José Ramón Díaz, who made *Sex and Guaguancó* (*Sexo y guaguancó*). The latest foreign production to shoot here was *Fascination*, an English-language thriller produced and directed by a German, Klaus Menzel, and starring Jacqueline Bisset. As with most visiting productions, the story was not set in Puerto Rico, but on this occasion in Florida.

If one asks crew members, not to mention some directors and producers, about the state of the industry, they tend to say it is in crisis. Traditionally, the film industry has been part of the larger, more lucrative advertising sector. However, because of globalisation and the constant movement of personnel within multi-national ad agencies, a large chunk of film and TV commercials production has gone to Uruguay and Argentina, a trend that local producers are trying to arrest by asking the government for trade protection.

In other areas, local distributor Premiere Films showed some growth after signing a deal to release Lions Gate titles and it is also buying features from Spain and Latin America. In exhibition, a new arthouse, Cines de Ballajá, opened in Old San Juan in May 2004, with three screens, one of which is equipped for digital projection.

JOSÉ ARTEMIO TORRES is a critic and film-maker.

Romania Cristina Corciovescu

The Year's Best Films

Cristina Corciovescu's selection:

Cigarettes and Coffee
(Short. Cristi Puiu)
A Trip to the City
(Short. Corneliu Porumboiu)
The Apartment
(Short. Constantin Popescu)
Exam (Titus Muntean)
Traffic (Short. Catalin Mitulescu)

Recent and Forthcoming Films

In Prod: credits, NCC indicates National Centre of Cinematography.

CAMERA ASCUNSA
(Never Enough)
[Romantic drama, 2004] Script: Lia Bugnar, Ana-Valentina Florescu. Dir: Bogdan Dumitrescu. Phot: Silviu Stavila. Players: Rutger Hauer, Maria Dinulescu, Oana Pellea. Prod: Titi Popescu, Filmex Romania/NCC/ Zutta Production (Germany).
Ileana, 27, is the hostess of a new *Candid Camera*-style TV show. Sebastian, 41, tries to profit from appearing on it.

FOTOGRAFII DE FAMILIE
(Family Album)
[Comedy-drama, 2004] Script: Bogdan Ficeag. Dir: Serban Marinescu. Phot: Dan Alexandru. Players: Dorel Visan, Coca Bloos, Manuela Harabor. Prod: MDV Film/NCC.
The boss of the biggest mass media corporation in Romania appears to be involved in corrupt political games. In the run-up to elections, his partners and old friends try to pull him down.

Romania now produces an average of eight feature films a year, but it has taken the country more than a decade to understand that cinema – part art, part industry – needs a lot of money and that it can no longer rely on the state for adequate production funding. The National Centre of Cinematography offers reimbursable funds (at most 49% of the projected budget) to films selected through competitions. The industry has also learned that the public no longer wants to see metaphorical or allegorical stories that are difficult to decode.

The creation of a stable industry is hampered by two major factors. The first is the lack of a regular flow of work at all levels, because of the shortage of production finance and the outsourcing of post-production to better equipped international facilities. Secondly local films are launched with virtually no publicity – again because of financial constraints – and the public shows minimal interest in them. With domestic productions generally securing less than 10% of the market, there is little to encourage potential investors.

If Romanian films often go unnoticed at home, they are increasingly prominent and successful at international festivals, and a new generation of young film-makers are demonstrating their interest in twenty-first century realities, which they approach with sincerity and without compromise. Calin Netzer's **Maria**, a drama about a woman forced to work as a prostitute to be able to feed her family, took three awards at Locarno 2003.

A mother turns to prostitution to feed her family in **Maria**

AZUCENA

[Drama, 2004] Script and Dir:
Mircea Muresan. Phot: Mihai
Sarbusca. Prod: Art
Production/NCC.
At the Romanian–Moldavian
border, a young officer falls in love
with a beautiful gypsy girl.

AVENTURILE UNEI ZILE

(*literally,* One-Day Adventures)
[Fantasy drama, 2004] Script:
Mihai Ispirescu. Dir: Petre
Nastase. Phot: Liviu Marghidan.
Players: Marcel Iures, Horatiu
Malaele, Mircea Diaconu. Prod:
Astra Entertainment/NCC.
An actor returns to his home
town to meet relatives and friends
and begin a new life. The people
he meets are the living dead.

ITALIENCELE (The Italian Girls)

[Comedy-drama, 2003] Script
and Dir: Napoleon Helmis. Phot:
Florin Mihailescu. Players: Mara
Nicolescu, Ana Ularu, Vlad
Zamfirescu, Emil Hostina. Prod:
Ro de Film/NCC.
Two young girls want to go to
Spain to work and become rich.
A man tricks them and sells them
as prostitutes in Kosovo.

LOTUS

[Drama, 2004] Script: Ioan
Carmazan, Constain Popescu.
Dir: Carmazan. Phot: Mihai
Malaimare Jr. Players: Mitica
Popescu, Radu Gheorghe, Imola
Kezdi, Nicodim Ungureanu,
Razvan Vasilescu. Prod:
Filmex/NCC.
In a seaside village a young man
saves a girl from being raped by
lowlifes. The pair fall in love, but
his past threatens their happiness.

ORIENT EXPRES

[Drama, 2004] Script: Sergiu
Nicolaescu, Ioan Carmazan,
based on a novel by Tudor
Teodorescu Braniste. Dir:
Nicolaescu. Phot: Dan
Alexandru. Players: Nicolaescu,
Gheorghe Dinica, Dan Bitman,
Maia Morgenstern, Daniela
Nane. Prod: Ro de Film/NCC.
In 1935 a Romanian prince looks
back to his tempestuous youth.

Cristi Puiu's *Cigarettes and Coffee* (*Un cartus de Kent si un pachet de cafea*), about the communication gulf between parents who find themselves disoriented in the "jungle of savage capitalism" and the children at home in this environment, won the Golden Bear and the Prix UIP for Best Short at Berlin 2004. The equivalent prize at Venice went to Constantin Popescu for his comical look at working-class life, *The Apartment* (*Apartamentul*), and Catalin Mitulescu triumphed at Cannes with *Traffic* (*Trafic*), which looked at the alienation of modern people who live with their hands stuck to the wheel of a car and their ears clamped to their mobile phones.

Alongside these names (all debutants, apart from Puiu), mention must also go to Titus Muntean, writer-director of **Exam** (*Examen*), a true-life drama set in the 1970s and representative of the judicial errors of the times, when Party guidelines ruled everything. Corneliu Porumboiu made two impressive shorts: *Liviu's Dream* (*Visul lui Liviu*), about the young members of a street gang, caught up in petty thefts and unavoidable betrayals, and *A Trip to the City* (*Calatorie la oras*; second prize at Cinéfondation, Cannes 2004), whose characters make comical attempts to learn new habits, according to the old saying: "Romanians can find solutions to any situation."

A double dose of psycho-drama

More established directors continue to work alongside the newcomers. Lucian Pintilie turned to a talented pair of young writers, Cristi Puiu and Razvan Radulescu, for his tenth movie, **Niki and Flo** (*Niki Ardelean colonel in rezerva*), a psychological drama about aggression and frustration, with sarcastic and grotesque moments. Flo constantly and deliberately humiliates her in-law Niki until the latter takes a hammer to Flo's head. After an 18-year absence, Dinu Tanase resumed his collaboration with writer Radu F. Alexandru on another psychological drama, **Damen Tango**. Unfortunately, the sub-soap opera story of a wife (Maia Morgenstern, now famous as Mary in *The Passion of the Christ*) who is abandoned by her husband in favour of her younger friend and gradually comes to want her replacement to pay with her life was not only incredible but sometimes laughable.

The 2004-05 season was scheduled to include the release of several promising films, some of which had been premiered in June 2004 at the third Transylvania International Film Festival (TIFF), in Cluj. In nine days, more than 80 features and shorts from 30 countries were screened for more than 15,000 spectators and 300 guests. There were also seminars, workshops, conferences and exhibitions. TIFF's young organisers' professionalism has made the festival worthy of international attention.

CRISTINA CORCIOVESCU is a film critic and the author of several film dictionaries.

Russia Kirill Razlogov

The Year's Best Films

Kirill Razlogov's selection:
Harvest Time
(Marina Razbezhkina)
Our Own (Dmitry Meskhiev)
Shiza (Guka Omarova)
Bright Is the Night
(Roman Balayan)
Russian (Alexander Veledinsky)

Recent and Forthcoming Films

72 METRA (72 Metres)
[Action drama, 2004] Script:
Valery Zalotukha, Vladimir
Khotinenko. Dir: Khotinenko.
Phot: Ilya Demin. Players: Sergey
Makovetsky, Andrey Krasko,
Marat Basharov, Dmitry
Ulyanov. Prod: Leonid
Vereschagin, TRITE.
The Slavianka submarine
faces catastrophe.

ANTIKILLER-2
[Action, 2003] Script: Youri
Petrov, Victor Shamirov, Fuad
Ibragimbekov, Egor
Konchalovsky, John Protass,
Yusup Bakhschiev. Dir:
Konchalovsky. Phot: Anton
Antonov. Players: Youri
Kutsenko, Alexey Serebryakov,
Lubov Tolkalina, Sergey Veksler.
Prod: Yousup Bachschiev,
Viktor Taknov, Vladimir Kilburg,
MB Productions/Golden
Key Entertainment.
"Diehard" Lis must thwart
terrorists' plans to destroy a
Russian city.

BOGINYA. KAK YA
POLYUBILA (The Goddess.
How I Fell in Love)
[Melodrama, 2004] Script and
Dir: Renata Litvinova. Phot:

The second half of 2004 was dominated by the tremendous commercial success of the first post-Soviet blockbuster, **Night Watch** (*Nochnoj dozor*), adapted from a series of popular fantasy novels by Sergey Lukianenko about magicians and wizards employed by Night Watch to protect present-day Moscow from invasion by dark forces.

This production by Russian television's Channel One premiered as closing film at the Moscow International Film Festival in June and was released after an unprecedented advertising campaign for a Russian film, including a spot almost every 15 minutes on Channel One (the country's most popular station) for a whole month. The result was a gross of more than $15m, the best result ever achieved in the post-Soviet period, beating the individual results for all parts of the *Matrix* and *Lord of the Rings* trilogies. Gemini Films, 20th Century Fox's representative in Russia and the CIS, distributed the film and Fox acquired worldwide rights.

Chosen as the national entry for the Oscars, *Night Watch* was attacked by leading critics, and dubbed *Night Disgrace*. They accused director and music video specialist Timur Bekmambetov of aping the worst Hollywood patterns. Two sequels, *Day Watch* and *Twilight Watch*, were on the way at press time, plus a Russian TV series and who knows how many American remakes.

Konstantin Khabensky, centre, in horror hit **Night Watch**

Vladislav Oppelyanz. *Players:*
Litvinova, Maxim Sukhanov,
Svetlana Svetlichnaya, Victor
Sukhorukov. Prod: Litvinova,
Elena Yatsura, Sergey Melkumov,
PK Bogwud Kino/PK Slovo.

VES'EGONSKAYA VOLCHITSA
(The Wolf of Ves'egon)
[Drama, 2004] Script: Eduard
Volodarsky, Nikolay Solovtsov.
Dir: Solovtsov. Phot: Elizbar
Karavaev. Players: Lev Durov,
Lev Borisov, Oleg Fomin,
Vladimir Gostyukhin. Prod:
Solovtsov, Aktualny Film/Ministry
of Culture of Russian Federation.
A huntsman cures and adopts a
wounded she-wolf, setting him at
odds with his family and the rest
of his village.

Lyudmila Motornaya in **Harvest Time**

VREMYA ZHATVY
(Harvest Time)
[Folk drama, 2004] Script and
Dir: Marina Razbezhkina. Phot:
Irina Ural'skaya. Players:
Lyudmila Motornaya, Vyacheslav
Batrakov, Dima Yakovlev, Dima
Ermakov. Prod: Tatiana Kanaeva,
Natalia Zheltukhina,
Risk/Ministry of Culture of
Russian Federation.

VSADNIK PO IMENI SMERT'
(The Rider Named Death)
[Historical action drama, 2004]
Script: Alexander Borodyansky,
Karen Shakhnazarov. Dir:
Shakhnazarov. Phot: Vladimir
Klimov. Players: Andrey Panin,
Ksenia Rappoport, Anastasia
Makeeva, Rostislav Bershauer.
Prod: Shakhnazarov, Galina
Shadur, Mosfilm.
The leader of a terrorist group,
Boris Savinkov, is obsessed with
killing Grand Prince Alexander.

Razbezhkina's bitter *Harvest*

At the opposite end of the aesthetic spectrum we find **Harvest Time** (*Vremya zhatvy*; FIPRESCI Prize at Moscow), a low-budget arthouse masterpiece by a documentary film-maker, Marina Razbezhkina. In her first fiction feature she constructs a fable about a combine operator (Lyudmila Motornaya) in a Soviet *kolkhoz* in the 1950s, who neglects her family because of the pressure to win the annual competition for harvesting the greatest quantity of crops.

Harvest Time was the best example of a retro wave that swept through the year's major productions. This was partly down to political timing: the 2004-05 season will be dominated by war films in preparation for the sixtieth anniversary of Russia's war victory (there are even plans for a new release of Yuri Ozerov's 1970s epic, *Liberation*). A good start to the year was made by **Our Own** (*Svoi*), a wartime drama by Dmitry Meskhiev that collected almost all the awards at Moscow, including Best Film, Director and Actor (for Ukraine's magnificent Bogdan Stupka). Well acted and not too controversial, the film combined Soviet traditions with Hollywood bravado à la *Saving Private Ryan*.

Mikail Evlanov, left, and Bogdan Stupka in **Our Own**

Covering a rather long period – from the early 1900s until the end of the Soviet era – the retro wave was well received by critics and audiences. It gave film-makers an opportunity to retreat from today's conflicts into a curious mixture of nostalgia and officially sanctioned criticism of the communist purges. At the same time the main TV channels presented a series of almost hagiographic documentary portraits of communist leaders (Andropov, Brezhnev, Suslov), directed by renowned names such as Vassily Pichul and Andrei Konchalovsky.

Theatrical fiction was more emotionally oriented. Pavel Chukhrai (*The Thief*) presented a melodramatic, 1960s-set love story, **A Driver for Vera** (see also Ukraine section), which ends in violent tragedy. Leading actor-director Vladimir Mashkov, who moves between Moscow and Los Angeles, adapted a stage play by Soviet era dissident Alexandre Galich. **Papa** tells the story of Abraham Schwarz (outrageously overacted by Mashkov himself), an elderly provincial Jew who sacrifices himself to promote the musical career of his son, a pupil at the Moscow Conservatory, only to be first rejected and in the end gratefully remembered after his death at the hands of the Nazis. Karen Shakhnazarov turns to the roots of Russian terrorism at the turn of the twentieth century in a psychological adventure story, **The Rider Named Death** (*Vsadnik po imeni smert'*).

The literary alibi

This retro wave follows the Russian tradition of literary adaptations. The idea that literature in Russia is more than just fiction, that it plays the role of teacher to the people, elaborating social rules, spiritual values and practical orientations is very much alive in artistic circles. Adapting new and, mostly, old classics gives film-makers, as in the past, a curious alibi: "It's not our fault, the writer said so." This ruse works even in deliberately provocative cases. Autobiographical youth stories by notorious writer and political activist Eduard Limonov were adapted for the screen by Alexander Veledinsky in a film with the symbolic (adjectival) title, **Russian** (*Russkoe*), which presents a rather sympathetic portrait of a young rebel in search of a cause.

Using black-and-white photography, Sergey Ursulyak tries to reconstruct the world of Yuri Trifonov in **The Long Farewell** (*Dolgoe proshchanie*). The writer – a cult figure during the last decades of the USSR – described in detail the way of life and contradictory feelings of those who accepted and then rejected communism (or were rejected by the Father of the Peoples). With more remote classics the ground is safer, but it does not guarantee success. Critics were harsh when Sergey Soloviev finally released his beautiful but empty combination of three Chekhov stories, **About Love** (*O ljubvi*). One story concerns a lovelorn 15-year-old boy.

Box-office gold or festival glory?

After the success of *Boomer* (see *IFG 2004*) had inspired new hopes of luring audiences back to domestic product and away from American imports, *Night Watch*, *Antikiller* and its sequel were evidently steps towards creating a local Hollywood. Vladimir Khotinenko's submarine drama, *72 Metres*, and *A Driver for Vera* successfully exploited local preferences and grossed more than $2m each, while Dmitry Astrakhan in his somewhat theatrical style

Andrey Panin in **The Rider Named Death**

DOLGOE PROSHCHANIE
(The Long Farewell)
[Drama, 2002] Script: Elga Lyndina, Sergey Ursulyak. Dir: Ursulyak. Phot: Mikhail Suslov. Players: Andrey Shchennikov, Polina Agureeva, Boris Kamorzin, Tatiana Lebed'kova. Prod: Evgeny Ulyushkin, Film-Pro.
Private relationships and reconsideration of values at the end of the Stalin era.

EGER' (Huntsman)
[Action drama, 2004] Script: Vladislav Romanov. Dir: Alexander Tsatsuev. Phot: Oleg Topoev. Players: Igor Lifanov, Andrey Fedortsov, Viktor Stepanov, Anna Bol'shova. Prod: Mikhail Churbanov, Dmitri Vorob'ev/Dea Torris.
A huntsman abandons the world and lives in the forest, but must still confront people and take sides.

IGRY MOTYLKOV
(Papillon's Playing)
[Youth drama, 2003] Script: Vladimir Zheleznikov, Galina Arbuzova, Andrey Proshkin, Vladimir Kozlov. Dir: Proshkin. Phot: Yuri Raisky. Players: Alexey Chadov, Oksana Akin'shina, Maria Zvonareva, Alexey Shevchenkov. Prod: Zheleznikov, Mikhail Litvak, Globus/Mosfilm/Ministry of Culture of Russian Federation.
A young rock musician from the Urals hijacks a car for fun but the joke ends in tragedy.

MOJ SVODNYJ BRAT FRANKENSTEIN
(My Stepbrother Frankenstein)
[Social-psychological drama, 2004] Script: Gennady Ostrovsky. Dir: Valery Todorovsky. Phot: Sergey

Mikhalchuk. Players: Daniil Spivakovsky, Leonid Yarmolnik, Elena Yakovleva, Sergey Garmash. Prod: Leonid Yarmolnik, Margarita Krzhizhevskaya, Prior-Premiere/Ministry of Culture of Russian Federation.
A long-lost elder brother brings conflict to a family's previously happy home.

NOCHNOJ DOZOR
(Night Watch)
[Mystical thriller, 2004] Script: Sergey Lukyanenko, Timur Bekmambetov. Dir: Bekmambetov. Phot: Sergey Trofimov. Players: Konstantin Khabensky, Vladimir Men'shov, Valery Zolotukhin, Maria Poroshina. Prod: Anatoly Maksimov, Konstantin Ernst, Tabbak/Bazelevs Production.

Vladimir Mashkov, top, in **Papa**

PAPA
[Melodrama, 2004] Script: Ilya Rubinstein, Vladimir Mashkov, based on a play by Alexander Galich. Dir: Mashkov. Phot: Oleg Dobronravov. Players: Vladimir Mashkov, Egor Beroev, Andrey Rosendent, Olga Kras'ko. Prod: Igor Tolstunov, Mikhail Silberman, Transmashholding/Rossijskie Kommunalnye Sistemy/Produserskaya Firma Igor Tolstunov/Ministry of Culture.

RUSSKOE (Russian)
[Drama, 2004] Script: Alexander Veledinsky, based on stories by Eduard Limonow. Dir: Veledinsky. Phot: Mikhail Ignatov. Players: Alexey Chadov, Olga Arntgoltz, Evdokia Germanova, Mikhail Efremov, Galina Polskih. Prod: Alexander

tried to capture young audiences with **Dark Night**, a love story involving a young, rich "new Russian" and a poor Cinderella girl. Combining just about every conceivable teen, emotional, social and sexual problem, director and writer tried to live up to their advertising slogan: "It's a film about YOU." Box-office results remained to be seen at press time.

On the international festival scene nothing much happened after the triumph of *The Return* at Venice in 2003 and hopes that this victory would start something big vanished very quickly. There were no Russian films in competition in Berlin and a marginal leftover of the rich New Russian cinema, **I Love You** (*Ya lyublyu tebya*), was in Panorama but brought disappointment. At Cannes, there was a single Kazakh–Russian co-production, **Shiza**, in *Un Certain Regard*. This first feature by a former Kazakh actress now living in the Netherlands, Guka (Gulshad) Omarova, was made under the obvious influence of her co-writer, Sergey Bodrov Sr., and was reminiscent of the Russian action series *The Brother* (which starred the late Bodrov Jr.). The film has the same type of superman hero, in this case a young Kazakh fighting the local mafia, falling in love and winning an impossible battle.

In Karlovy Vary, Valery Todorovsky's **My Stepbrother Frankenstein** (*Moj svodnyj brat Frankenstein*), a dramatic fable about a veteran of a war (perhaps Afghanistan or Chechnya), took the FIPRESCI Prize. In Venice, Svetlana Proskurina's **Remote Connection** (*Udalenny dostup*) and Kira Muratova's **Tuner** (see also Ukraine section) did not generate any buzz, but the young Ilya Khrzhanovsky (son of a famous animation master) made quite an impression with a drama, **4**, a successful screen version of Vladimir Sorokin prose. Two previous screenplays by this controversial writer had generated semi-successes (Alexander Zeldovich's *Moscow* and, in 2003, Ivan Dykhovichny's *The Kopeck*) and lots of polemics.

Justly ignored by all festival selectors was the most pretentious film of the year: **The Goddess. How I Fell in Love** (*Boginya. Kak ya polyubila*), by cult actress-scriptwriter-director Renata Litvinova, who plays a policewoman investigating a strange case and discovering her own mysterious capacities. Selectors also rejected its opposite: Roman Balayan's **Bright Is the Night**, whose lyrical love stories are set in and around a colony for deaf-mute children (see also Ukraine section).

The most celebrated names did not complete their ambitious projects. Alexander Sokurov was still working on his biography of the Emperor Hirohito (to follow his studies of Hitler and Lenin); Alexei German Sr. struggles with the screen adaptation of a fantastic novel by the Strugatsky Brothers, *It Is Difficult to Be God* (already filmed by Peter Fleischman in 1989). Nikita Mikhalkov was

Renata Litvinova: writer, director and star of **The Goddess. How I Fell in Love**

hoping to finish his sequel to the Oscar-winning *Burned by the Sun* in time for the sixtieth anniversary of the end of the war.

My optimistic prognosis in *IFG 2004* has been overshadowed recently by the announcement that public funding for film production is in danger again. The increase in state support that had (partly) generated the current domestic film production boom (up from 20 feature films in 1995 to almost 80 in 2004) might stop because of government reform. The Russian Ministry of Culture, which had assimilated the State Committee for Cinema, was reorganised and enlarged again as part of the Ministry of Culture and Mass Communication, incorporating TV and radio broadcasting, as well as archives, press and publishing. Within this mega-ministry several federal agencies were created, one of them for culture and cinema. As a result, the financing of film production in 2004 was delayed and some payments were still due for 2003, and the programme for 2005 might be extremely limited.

KIRILL RAZLOGOV (razlog@hotmail.com) is Director of the Russian Institute for Cultural Research and Programme Director of the Moscow International Film Festival. He has written 14 books on cinema and culture and hosts Kultura's weekly TV show, *Movie Cult*.

Correction: In Kirill Razlogov's Russia report for *IFG 2004* (p.252), an editing error created the impression that most Russian film critics had preferred *House of Fools* to the Russian Oscar committee's choice for the 2003 Foreign-Language Film category, *The Cuckoo*. In fact the committee was attacked by the media for nominating *House of Fools* ahead of *The Cuckoo*, which critics believed had a much better chance of an Academy nomination.

Robak, Maxim Lagashkin, Alexey Alyakin/Sinemafor. Kharkow, 1960s. A young poet, Eddy, faces his first success, love, betrayal and prison.

SVOI (Our Own)
[War drama, 2004] Script: Valentin Chernyh. Dir: Dmitry Meskhiev. Phot: Sergey Machilsky. Players: Konstantin Khabensky, Bogdan Stupka, Sergey Garmash, Mikhail Evlanov. Prod: Sergey Melkumov, Elena Yatsura, Viktor Glukhov, Slovo/Channel One/ Ministry of Culture of Russian Federation.
Soviet prisoners of war escape from the Germans in August 1941 and are forced to take refuge in a village already occupied by the enemy.

SEL' (Mudflow)
[Road movie melodrama, 2004] Script: Gennady Bokarev. Dir: Yaropolk Lapshin. Phot: Boris Shapiro, Anatoly Lesnikov. Players: Aslanbek Ganov, Anya Kuzminskaya, Nina Gogaeva, Lyudmila Zaitseva. Prod: Dmitry Vorobyev, Sverdlovsk Film Studio/Ministry of Culture of Russian Federation.
After losing relatives in a mudslide, Akhmet travels to Moscow to find his brother.

UDALENNY DOSTUP (Remote Connection)
[Melodrama, 2004] Script and Dir: Svetlana Proskurina. Phot: Alexander Burov, Sergey Yurizditsky. Players: Dana Agisheva, Alexander Plaxin, Elena Rufanova, Vladimir Il'in. Prod: Yuri Obukhov, Kinoproba/ Gorki Film Studio.
Years after a serious accident, a man's past interferes with his love life.

Quote of the Year

"*Our Own* is the best film I have seen in the last 20 years."

ALAN PARKER, *President of the International Jury, at the awards ceremony of the 26th Moscow International Film Festival.*

Rwanda Daddy Youssouf Ruhorahoza

Recent and Forthcoming Films

100 DAYS
[Drama, 2002] Script, Dir and Phot: Nick Hughes. Players: Cleophas Kabasita, Davis Kagenza, Mazimpaka Kennedy, Davis Kwizera, David Mulwa. Prod: Hughes, Eric Kabera, Vivid Features Production.

SOMETIMES IN APRIL
[Drama, 2004] Script and Dir: Raoul Peck. Players: Idriss Elba, Oris Erhuero, Debra Winger. Prod: Peck, Cinefacto/HBO.
The story of two Hutu brothers. One is in jail for war crimes and the other struggled during the war to save his Tutsi wife.

HOTEL RWANDA
[Drama, 2004] Script: Keir Pearson and Terry George. Dir: George. Phot: Robert Fraisse. Players: Don Cheadle, Desmond Dube, Mothusi Megano, Nick Nolte, Sophie Okonedo. Prod: George, Alex Ho, Miracle Pictures/Seamus Prods./ United Artists.
The true-life story of Paul Rusesabagina (Cheadle), manager of the Hotel Milles Collines in Kigali, who housed more than 1,000 Tutsi refugees during their struggle against the Hutu militia.

SHOOTING DOGS
[Drama, 2005] Script: David Wolstencroft. Dir: Michael Caton-Jones. Players: John Hurt, Hugh Dancy. Prod: David Belton, Pippa Cross, CrossDay Productions/Renaissance/BBC Films/UK Film Council.
Based on a true story. An exhausted Catholic priest (Hurt)

Rwanda's beautiful, mountainous landscapes have been featured in a number of high-profile films, including *King Solomon's Mines* and *Gorillas in the Mist*, but this small country's film industry benefited little from such Hollywood exposure. However, since the genocide of 1994, the country has been the subject of numerous documentaries and, more recently, drama-documentaries, too.

The first feature film to focus on the brutal conflict that claimed a million lives in 100 days emerged through the partnership of Nick Hughes, a freelance British news cameraman based in Nairobi, who had covered the Rwandan horrors for the BBC, CNN and others, and Eric Kabera, a Rwandan producer and director. They first teamed up in 1996 and the result was **100 Days** (2002), a story of love and brutality in which two Tutsi families try to survive the violent hatred of their Hutu neighbours. When young Josette's boyfriend comes back from the battle, he finds her pregnant by a Hutu priest who had saved her by obliging her to become his concubine. *100 Days* was described by *Variety* as "docu-drama at its finest" and screened at more than 40 international film festivals.

Hughes and Kabera's collaboration paved the way for a series of projects shot in Rwanda in 2003-04, as other film-makers sought to explore the genocide. The most notable of these are *Sometimes in April*, by Haitian film-maker Raoul Peck, *Hotel Rwanda*, by Irish writer-director Terry George, and *Shooting Dogs*, from *Scandal* and *Rob Roy* director Michael Caton-Jones.

Eric Kabera's documentary **Keepers of Memory** was shot in 2003 and screened around the world in 2004 to mark the tenth anniversary of the genocide. At the 2004 Toronto International Film Festival it was showcased alongside *Hotel Rwanda* (which took Toronto's audience award) and Canadian Peter Ramont's *Shake Hands with the Devil: The Journey of Romeo Dallaire*. Kabera also produced in 2004 another feature documentary which looks at Rwandan youth in the aftermath of the genocide, **Through My Eyes**, directed by Kenyan editor and director Kavial Matu.

Other local projects concerned with the genocide are *A Sunday at the Pool in Kigali*, adapted from Gil Courtemanche's novel of the same name, to be made by Montreal-based Lyla Films, with Lyse

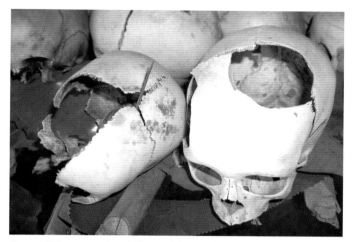

Keepers of Memory *examines the legacy of the Rwandan genocide*

Lafontaine as producer and Jacques Favreau as director, and *The Last Dog in Rwanda* (in pre-production at press time), a short comedy written and directed by Sweden's Jens Assur.

Taking the initiative

Rwanda currently has no cinema circuits to serve a population of 8.1 million. The only screening halls are in the French Cultural Centre and the National University of Rwanda amphitheatre, but these are for special screenings only. However, there are various video clubs in Kigali and other small cities, including Cine Elmay, Club Rafiki and Planet Cinema. Recently, Eric Kabera established the Rwanda Cinema Centre (RCC), a coalition of professionals, community-based organisations and private sector companies involved in the development and promotion of cinematography.

RCC has embarked on a project entitled Screen Rwanda, which aims to promote a filmgoing culture and generate interest in the movie industry among the country's young people by presenting to them films to which they can easily relate. At present, however, most of the films currently available in the video clubs and attracting young audiences are Hollywood productions. RCC has set out to share its vision with local communities, policy makers and various organisations, in the hope of implementing a structure that will promote local talents in Rwanda and around the world.

DADDY YOUSSOUF RUHORAHOZA is production manager at Eric Kabera's Kigali-based company, Link Media Production.

and an idealistic young English teacher (Dancy) find themselves caught up in the 1994 Rwandan genocide. They must choose whether to stay with the thousands of Tutsis about to be massacred, or flee to safety.

A SUNDAY AT THE POOL IN KIGALI

[Drama, 2005] Dir: Jacques Favreau. Prod: Lyse Lafontaine, Lyla Films Inc. (Canada).
Based on a true story. A Canadian journalist who tries to set up a TV station in Rwanda and falls in love with a waitress at a local hotel. It attacks western indifference to advance warnings of the impending genocide.

Quotes of the Year

"I hope this film will be a wake-up call."
TERRY GEORGE, *director, on his* Hotel Rwanda.

"Some people wanted me and [director] Nick Hughes to have a white hero in *100 Days*!"
ERIC KABERA, *producer, recalls unhelpful pre-production advice for his Rwandan genocide drama.*

Senegal Roy Armes

Recent Films

MADAME BROUETTE
[Comedy-thriller, 2002] Script:
Moussa Sene Absa and Gilles
Desjardins. Dir: Absa. Photo:
Jean-Jacques Bouhon. Players:
Ousseynou Diop, Rokhaya
Niang, Khadiatou Sy, Aboubacar
Sadikh Ba, Moustapha Niang,
Juliette Ba, Mody Fall. Prod:
Productions de la Lanterne/
Productions la Fête/MSA
Productions/Arte France Cinéma.

MOOLAADÉ
[Drama, 2004] Script and Dir:
Ousmane Sembène. Phot:
Dominique Gentil. Players:
Fatoumata Coulibaly, Maïmouna
Hélène, Salimata Traoré,
Dominique T Zeïda, Mah
Compaoré, Aminata Dao. Prod:
Filmi Doomireew (Dakar)/
Direction de la Cinématographie
Nationale (Burkina Faso)/Centre
Cinématographique Marocain
(Morocco)/ Les Films de la Terre
(Cameroon)/Cinésud
Productions (Paris).

NDOBINE
[Drama, 2003] Script and Dir:
Amadou Saalun Seck. Phot:
Moustapha Cissé. Players: Mass
Ndiaye, Aminata Ka. Prod:
Azanie Films.

REFERENCE SEMBENE
(Concerning Sembène)
[Documentary, 2003] Script:
Yacouba Traoré and Alfred
Nikiema. Dir: Traoré. Phot:
Désiré Zida. Prod: La
Médiathèque des Trois
Mondes (Paris).

Senegal makes up about a fifth of francophone West African cinema in terms of both films and directors, but it has never had a strong central state production organisation. Nine features had been produced before the Société Nationale de Productions Cinématographiques was set up in 1973 and, after producing just five features, it was dissolved in 1977. There was another attempt at state funding in the early 1980s, followed, as elsewhere, by a gap before the emergence of a new generation. With just 44 films made in 40 years of feature production, the difficulties faced by film-makers who want to follow up a full-length debut are evident. But recently two have managed to make second or third features.

Fifteen years after his debut in 1988, when he was the first of the younger generation to make the breakthrough, Amadou Saalum Seck (b. 1952) completed **Ndobine** (2003), the story of a couple whose son disappears and who have to face up to the prospect of his death. In 2002, the even younger Moussa Sene Absa (b. 1958), a versatile artist – painter, writer and musician as well as stage and screen actor and director – completed his third feature in 11 years, **Madame Brouette**, which has dialogue in French rather than the customary Wolof.

The structure is also complex and the levels of humour, dance and drama are constantly shifting. The film begins with the murder of Madame Brouette's husband while he's wearing grotesque drag for a local festival. Only at the end, when we have seen the wife's great strengths and learned of the husband's many deceits and the decline of the marriage, do we uncover the truth about the murder. A third feature, **A Child's Love** (*Un amour d'enfant*), Ben Diogaye Beye's first film for 22 years, was promised for screening at FESPACO in 2003, but did not appear.

Sembène offers sanctuary

The great event of 2004 for Senegalese cinema was the Cannes screening of **Moolaadé**, directed by 81-year-old Ousmane Sembène. This is Sembène's ninth feature in a 40-year film-making career which has run parallel to his equally prolific work as novelist and story-teller (10 volumes of fiction since 1957, including three novels subsequently brought to the screen: *The Money Order, Xala*

Ousmane Sembène's **Moolaadé** *offers a tale of village life*

and *Guelwaar*). *Moolaadé* is in every sense an African production, set in Senegal but shot in Burkina Faso, with additional production finance from Cameroon and post-production work undertaken in Morocco. Members of the crew came from Morocco, Ivory Coast, Benin, Mali, Burkina Faso and Senegal. The shooting of the film forms a key part of Tacouba Traoré's fascinating new documentary, **Concerning Sembène** (*Référence Sembène*).

Moolaadé is the second part of a planned trilogy that began with *Faat-Kine* in 2000. But whereas *Faat-Kine* was very much an urban story dealing with contemporary issues, *Moolaadé* is a tale of rural life, set in a village where traditional ways have stagnated. Like so many major African films, it is a study of the clash of tradition and modernity, though here the physical confrontation is between two aspects of tradition: on the one hand, the right to give and receive sanctuary (the meaning of the title) and, on the other, the age-old practice (still continued in 38 of the 54 states of the African Union) of female circumcision or, more precisely, female genital mutilation.

The action is triggered when a group of teenage girls decide to run away rather than face the ordeal, and four of them take refuge with an old woman, Colle Ardo Gallo Sy (Fatoumata Coulibaly), who has saved her own young daughter from this barbaric practice. Colle immediately finds herself confronted by the village elders and also by the girls' mothers, who unite in opposition to what they see as a break with sacred tradition. As so often in his work, Sembène celebrates both the forcefulness of his strong-willed female protagonist and the silent strength of the ordinary people.

Quotes of the Year

"I'm proud to say that *Moolaadé* was born on and of the [African] continent. Perhaps I'll be able to make other African film-makers, the younger ones, understand that we can create everything we need without leaving the continent."
OUSMANE SEMBENE, *director.*

"African intellectuals live a duality which they suppress most of the time. They speak French among themselves and, often, they live in France; but when they shoot a film, they shoot it in their own language!"
MOUSSA SENE ABSA *explains why he shot* Madame Brouette *in French rather than Wolof.*

Serbia & Montenegro Goran Gocic

The Year's Best Films

Goran Gocic's choice:
Life Is a Miracle
(Emir Kusturica)
Small World (Milos Radovic)
When I Grow Up I'll Be Kangaroo (Rasa Andric)
Run, Rabbit, Run
(Short. Pavle Vuckovic)

Recent and Forthcoming Films

BUDJENJE IZ MRTVIH (*literally, Awakening from the Dead*)
[Drama, forthcoming] Script and Dir: Milos Radivojevic. Phot: Radoslav Vladic. Players: Svetozar Cvetkovic, Ljuba Tadic. Prod: Testament Films/Prefiso/ Concept Films (Belgrade)/ Atalanta (Ljubljana).
A man dies during NATO bombing after a life of hesitation, then rises from the dead for 48 hours to put things straight.

DISI DUBOKO
(**Take a Deep Breath**)
[Drama, forthcoming] Script: Hajdana Baletic. Dir: Dragan Marinkovic. Phot: Boris Gortinski. Editing: Petar Markovic. Players: Ana Franic, Mira Furlan. Prod: Norga Investment, Inc./ Digital Video Solution (Belgrade).
In hospital after a traffic accident, a student becomes infatuated with her boyfriend's sister.

JUG JUGOISTOK
(**South by South-east**)
[Thriller, forthcoming] Script: Sasa Radojevic. Dir: Milutin Petrovic. Phot: Predrag Bambic. Players: Sonja Savic, Nesko Despotovic. Prod: Montage (Belgrade).

The most pleasant surprise of 2003 was an urban comedy, Milos Radovic's **Small World** (*Mali svet*). A former winner of the Palme d'Or for Best Short and a feature debutant at 48, after writing more than a dozen unproduced scripts, Radovic had to wait a long time for his chance and seized it with an unpretentious and original screenplay. Mostly set on a single day, it embellishes a simple theft with a hatful of crazy coincidences involving everyone from a suicidal doctor to a policeman struck by lightning. A first-rate cast of Belgrade actors rushed to appear in it and it drew more than 200,000 admissions.

Nothing inspires more than success, and Radovic managed to wrap another movie in the same season – an unprecedented achievement as far as this reviewer's memory reaches. Backed by a dozen domestic and international entities, including Eurimages (which has frequently supported the films of Goran Paskaljevic), **A Fall into Paradise** (*Pad u raj*) opened in April 2004, but Radovic's second comedy, another wartime story in which Serbs sleep with the enemy, was nowhere near as charming as his first. Something similar applies to a veteran director, Zdravko Sotra, who, flying high on the success of his local blockbuster *Zone* (see *IFG 2004*), over-hastily employed an almost identical cast for **Pljacka Treceg Rajha** (literally, *The Robbery of the Third Reich*) and produced average results.

Miki Manojlovic, Irena Micijevic, Branko Djuric and Milorad Mandic in **Small World**

Two films targeted the teenage and youth market. Directed by experienced Rasa Andric, **When I Grow Up I'll Be Kangaroo** (*Kad porastem bicu Kengur*) is somewhat dissipated but very entertaining. **An Almost Totally Ordinary Story** (*Skoro sasvim obicna prica*), directed by newcomer Milos Petricic, depicts a straightforward love affair, set among successful, self-assured and affluent Belgrade twentysomethings.

Laughs in all shapes and sizes

In the middle-aged generation Emir Kusturica, Srdjan Karanovic, Goran Markovic (all graduates of the Czech FAMU academy) and Slobodan Sijan all chose comedy for their latest features, from hilarious, romantic, bittersweet comedy, to period comedy, thriller-comedy, comedy-drama, as you like it. It was good news that talents such as Sijan and Karanovic, inactive for more than a decade, had woken up after a long hibernation, even if the results were below expectations.

Sijan's **Poor Little Hamsters** (*Siroti mali hrcki*) was an absurdist comedy, cryptic to anyone who did not live through the pits of the communist regime. The story had already been adapted for television, but Sijan relocated it to contemporary Serbia. Karanovic, who, like other artists, had made it a point of honour not to work during the war, offered **Loving Glances** (*Sjaj u ocima*), a bittersweet drama about the strife and loneliness of teenage refugees located against their will in Belgrade's slums. This was respectable festival fare (it was at Venice in 2003).

Markovic was quite active in public life during the Milosevic regime, so his second cinematic denunciation of it, **Cordon**, about public disobedience and police brutality in Belgrade, was more self-purge than worthwhile political stance. Still, *Cordon* achieved considerable success abroad (Best Film at Montreal) and in 2003 Markovic received a lifetime achievement award in Cleveland.

Zelimir Zilnik remains probably the country's most consistent film-maker. His latest, **Kennedy Comes Back Home** (*Kenedi se vraca kuci*), continues his recent series of docu-dramas about down-and-out European migrants, this time gypsy refugees suddenly returned to Serbia after a decade-long integration into German society. Like *Cordon* and *Hamsters*, *Kennedy* went straight from festivals to television without a local theatrical release.

Emir Kusturica's **Life Is a Miracle** (*Zivot je cudo*), opened in France immediately after its Cannes premiere in May 2004 (280,000 admissions in its first three weeks) and at home in October, where it quickly passed 150,000 admissions, the benchmark for a local blockbuster. Set in Bosnia in the thick of the recent war and shot

A Serbian actress appears after 12 years away in Slovenia and claims that her daughter is missing.

KAD PORASTEM BICU KENGUR (When I Grow up I'll Be Kangaroo)
[Teen comedy, 2004] Script: Miroslav Momcilovic. Dir: Rasa Andric. Phot: Dusan Joksimovic. Players: Sergej Trifunovic, Nebojsa Glogovac. Prod: Yodi Movie Craftsman (Belgrade).
A Belgrade goalkeeper, Kangaroo, starts playing in the UK's Premiership.

ZRTVE SU ZAHVALNE (Victims Are Thankful)
[Drama, forthcoming] Script: Feranc Deak. Dir: Karolj Vicek. Phot: Dusan Ninkov. Editing: Srdjan Arsenijevic. Players: Djerdj Feres, Gabriela Jonas. Prod: Digitel (Novi Sad).
Two families flee to a small village in Vojvodina, hiding from the recent war.

MEMO
[Drama, forthcoming] Script and Dir: Milos Jovanovic. Phot: Jovan Milinov. Players: Nemanja Jovanovic, Radoje Cupic. Prod: Hammer Communications (Novi Sad)/Rasta International (Belgrade).

MI NISMO ANDJELI II (We're No Angels II)
[Comedy, forthcoming] Script and Dir: Srdjan Dragojevic. Phot: Dusan Joksimovic. Players: Nikola Kojo, Srdjan Todorovic. Prod: Dragojevic, Delirium Film (Belgrade).
A jealous father tries to eliminate his daughter's potential suitors.

OPET PAKUJEMO MAJMUNE (literally, Packing the Monkeys, Again!)
[Comedy, forthcoming] Script: Milica Piletic. Dir: Marija Perovic. Phot: Dimitrije Jokovic. Players: Jelena Djokic, Andrija Milosevic. Prod: RTV of Montenegro (Podgorica).
A young couple face mounting problems when they rent an attic.

PAD U RAJ (A Fall into Paradise)
[Comedy, 2004] Script and Dir:
Milos Radovic. Phot: Piotr Kukla.
Players: Lazar Ristovski, Branka
Katic. Prod: Neue Impuls Film
(Hamburg)/MACT Productions
(Paris)/Rocketa Film (Amsterdam)/
Rotterdam Films (Rotterdam)/
Zillion Films (Belgrade).
Shot down by a Belgrade gang
lord, a US pilot parachutes on to
his balcony and falls for his
sister (Katic).

Branka Katic in **A Fall into Paradise**

PLJACKA TRECEG RAJHA
(*literally,* **The Robbery of the**
Third Reich)
[Comedy, 2003] Script: Miodrag
Andric. Dir: Zdravko Sotra. Phot:
Veselko Krcmar. Players: Nikola
Djuricko, Dragan Nikolic. Prod:
Dream Company (Nis)/Carudian
Filmproduktion (Austria).
Two Serbian thieves try to clear
out a Berlin bank.

SAN ZIMSKE NOCI
(**A Midwinter Night's Dream**)
[Drama, forthcoming] Script:
Goran Paskaljevic, Filip David.
Dir: Paskaljevic. Phot: Milan
Spasic. Players: Jovana Mitic,
Lazar Ristovski. Prod: Nova
Film, Zillion Films (Belgrade).
An autistic girl tries to survive in
contemporary Serbia.

Quote of the Year

"How else could I prove my
value? Today, even peasants
want a brand-name on their
jeans… It must have an
Armani or Ferre sticker, even if
it is a false one, made
somewhere in Serbia."

EMIR KUSTURICA *explains*
why he premiered Life Is a
Miracle *at Cannes.*

Emir Kusturica's **Life Is a Miracle** *was a hit at Serbian cinemas*

with a wholly Serbian cast and locations, it marks Kusturica's
homecoming and proves that there are still moulds to break:
contrary to the majority of films about the war it keeps optimism
and hope above all – even in the direst of circumstances. A love
story between a Serbian engineer dumped by his wife and a Muslim
nurse whom he hopes to exchange for his imprisoned son, it has all
the necessary ingredients for good entertainment.

The word "crisis" means "business as usual" here. The
assassination of the Serbian Prime Minister Zoran Djindjic in March
2003 emptied out cinemas for a few months as people lost their
appetite for entertainment. Thus admissions in 2003 fell by 27%
compared to 2002. All non-Hollywood films took 20% of the
market, with 17.9% for Serbian films (638,357 admissions), a
comparatively high figure, but only half the previous year's
whopping 34%, which was thanks to *Zone*, whose television
premiere in 2004 drew a record-breaking 2.9 million viewers. Finally,
three of the eight domestic films released in 2003 penetrated the
year's top ten, and another three (*I Think the World of you*, *An
Almost Totally Ordinary Story* and *Loving Glances*) had between
30,000 and 40,000 admissions each.

Although film piracy through street-level sales of illegal copies has
been reduced, the exhibition sector still leaves much to be desired,
as the number of screens has been stagnant for years, and only ten
cinemas have Dolby Stereo and air-conditioning. However, the
number of DVD players doubled, to an estimated 60,000.

GORAN GOCIC (gocic@hotmail.com) is a broadcast and print
journalist whose work has appeared in more than 30 media outlets
in seven languages. He is the author of monographs on Warhol and
Kusturica and chapters in 11 books on the mass media.

Singapore Yvonne Ng

The Year's Best Films

Yvonne Ng's selection:
The Twilight Kitchen
(Gerald Lee)
The Outsiders (Sam Loh)
3 Feet Apart (Animated
short. Jason Lai)
Lim Poh Huat
(Docu short. Lee Wong)
Cut (Short. Royston Tan)

3 Feet Apart

Recent and Forthcoming Films

15
[Drama, 2003] Script and Dir:
Royston Tan. Phot: Lim Ching
Leong. Players: Melvin Chen,
Erick Chun, Melvin Lee, Vynn
Soh, Shaun Tan. Prod: Zhao
Wei Films.

CITY SHARKS
[Road comedy, 2003] Script
and Dir: Esan Sivalingam.
Phot: Jamal J. Farley. Players:
Nicolas Lee, Sheikh Haikel, Hans
Isaac, Lim Kay Tong. Prod:
Hoods Inc. Productions.

CLOUDS IN MY COFFEE
[Drama, 2004] Script and Dir:
Gallen Mei. Phot: Fong Tong San.
Players: Ase Wang, Celeste Valdes
Lim, Cindy Ng. Prod: Under
Pressure Pictures.
Three young women trapped in
abusive relationships fantasise
about alternatives.

In early 2004, the talk of Singapore's film community revolved around Royston Tan's films. His debut feature, **15**, made headlines for its bold depiction of teen delinquents and their involvement with sex, drugs and secret societies. After almost five minutes' worth of cuts, *15* received for its theatrical release an R(A) – Restricted (Artistic) rating, limiting it to those aged 21 years and above. Tan promptly retaliated with *Cut* (2004), a provocative 12-minute musical satire on censorship, which premiered at the Singapore International Film Festival (SIFF) in April 2004.

In 2004, new censorship regulations were implemented, but the results were less groundbreaking than expected. An M18 (Mature 18) category was added and the R(A) changed to R21. However, films may still be cut prior to receiving the new ratings. More positively, movies can now be released theatrically under two ratings (but not at the same time), improving the chances that more films will be shown uncut.

Although artistically conservative, the government hopes to transform Singapore into a "Global Media City" by investing $60m over the next five years. This effort has been given a boost with the setting up of Lucasfilm Animation Singapore (LAS), a joint venture between Lucasfilm, the Economic Development Board and Sim Wong Hoo, the founder and CEO of Singapore's Creative Technology. LAS expected its digital animation studio to begin operations early in 2005.

To support its co-production policy, the Media Development Authority recently signed a $6m deal with Raintree Pictures to make at least 10 co-productions with international partners. Moreover, the Singapore Tourism Board announced the Film in Singapore! scheme in 2004. It will provide $5.8m over three years to lure international production to the city and, presumably, present Singapore in a good light.

Neo hits *Homerun*

The feature film harvest in 2003-04 was not as impressive as the previous year's. Raintree's major production in 2003 was Jack Neo's **Homerun**, a $900,000 remake of Iranian Majid Majidi's *Children of Heaven* (1997), which became the top-grossing Chinese title, securing a place in the top 10 for 2003. Set in 1965 (Singapore's independence year), *Homerun* transposes Majidi's story to a poor and

HAINAN JI FAN (Rice Rhapsody)
[Comedy drama, 2004] Script and Dir: Kenneth Bi. Players: Sylvia Chang, Martin Yan, Melanie Laurent. Prod: Kenbiroli Films/ JCE Movies/Ground Glass Images/ Singapore Film Commission.
Fearing her son may be gay, a single mother takes in a female French exchange student.

HOMERUN
[Drama, 2003] Script and Dir: Jack Neo. Phot: Kane Chen Kin Meng. Players: Huang Wen Yong, Xiang Yun, Shawn Lee, Chuang Rui, Megan Zheng, Zhi Yun. Prod: Raintree Pictures.

JIAN GUI 2 (The Eye 2)
[Horror, 2004] Script: Jojo Hui. Dir: Danny and Oxide Pang. Phot: Decha Srimantra. Players: Shu Qi, Yeung Lai Kai, Jessadaporn Pholdee. Prod: Applause Pictures/ Raintree Pictures.
A woman sees ghosts after attempting suicide.

NOTHING TO LOSE
[Action drama/black comedy, 2003] Script and Dir: Danny Pang. Players: Arisara Wongchalee, Pierre Png, Yvonne Lim. Prod: Raintree Pictures/ Golden Network Asia.
Two strangers attempting suicide become partners-in-crime.

OUTSIDERS
[Crime, 2004] Script and Dir: Sam Loh. Phot: Daniel Low. Players: Keagan Kang, Steph Song, Corinne Adrienne Tan. Prod: Sitting in Pictures.

PERTH
[Crime drama, 2004] Script and Dir: Djinn. Phot: Goh Meng Hing. Players: Lim Kay Tong, Liu Qiu Lian, Sunny Pang. Prod: Vacant Films/ Ground Glass Images.

SING TO THE DAWN
[Animation, 2005] Script and Dir: Frank Saperstein. Prod: Raintree Pictures/ Media Development Authority/ Silicon Illusions.
Thai girl fights sexist traditions.

undeveloped Singapore. Fine production values do little to enhance the credibility of the sanitised settings and Mandarin dialogues at a time when dialects ruled. A sentimental score and heavy-handed moralising further mar a film whose saving grace lies in the engaging performance of the children, particularly Megan Zheng.

Gerald Lee's Mandarin-language **Twilight Kitchen** (2003) was Singapore's first "community film". Jointly produced by government agencies and local company Gateway Entertainment for $150,000, it was made to help counter prejudices about employing former offenders. The realism of this sincere social drama about the lack of humanity in a materialistic society is supported by strong performances.

Local independents, however, are having a hard time finding screen space. Of the half dozen features made in 2004, only Jack Neo's **The Best Bet**, produced by Raintree, had been given a theatrical release by mid-year. Patterned after earlier successes such as *Money No Enough*, the comedy takes on Singaporeans' passion for lottery gambling, but its solid acting and intelligent blend of comic and serious elements are undermined by tiresome preachiness at the end. Nevertheless, the appeal of the lottery plot and Neo's popularity generated takings of $1.55m (S$2.7m).

Chen Liping and Richard Low in **The Best Bet**

Perth, directed by Djinn, which premiered at the 2004 SIFF, introduces the theme of the promised land (symbolised by Australia's Perth). This *Taxi Driver*-inspired story is about a jaded middle-aged taxi-driver, Harry Lee, who dreams of emigrating but gets involved with Singapore's underworld, leading him and several other characters to a gratuitously bloody denouement.

Toh Hai Leong's 60-minute **Zombie Dogs** is a "mockumentary", which reflects the film-maker's intense obsessions and eccentric personality. It presents a director (Toh) whose search for a suitable cast for his snuff movie leads to comical moments, personal revelations and satirical jabs against local politics and Singaporeans. Shot on DV for a three-figure sum, *Zombie Dogs* may have a chance with non-mainstream audiences abroad.

Sam Loh's debut feature **Outsiders** was supposed to premiere at the 2004 SIFF but was withdrawn by the festival when the censors demanded cuts. The film introduces a large cast of fringe characters, all linked to a serial killer. Shot on DV using jump cuts, sparse dialogue and noir photography, *Outsiders* feels close to experimental cinema.

Despite its modest production output, the awareness of Singapore cinema abroad is growing. In February 2004, a selection of Singapore films was featured at the Paris Asian Film Festival and in November 2004 Singapore was guest of honour at the Lyon Asian Film and Culture Festival. Even more than feature production, Singapore's shorts are gaining recognition at home and at festivals worldwide. This format has become a closely watched springboard for Singapore's aspiring film-makers, thanks to works such as Sherman Ong's documentary *The Ground I Stand* (*Di mana bumi dipijak;* 2002), Jason Lai's *3 Feet Apart* (2003) and Yong Mun Chee's *9:30* (2003).

YVONNE NG (kinema@watarts.uwaterloo.ca) has written on Asian cinema and is on the editorial board of *KINEMA* (published at the University of Waterloo, Ontario, Canada). She is the co-author of *Latent Images: Film in Singapore* (OUP, 2000; CD-Rom edition, Singapore, 2003).

TU RAN FA CAI (The Best Bet)
[Social comedy, 2004] Script and Dir: Jack Neo. Phot: Michael Chua. Players: Richard Low, Christopher Lee, Mark Lee, Chen Li Ping. Prod: Raintree Pictures.

TWILIGHT KITCHEN
[Drama, 2003] Script: Zhu Houren and Gerald Lee. Dir: Lee. Players: Moses Lim, Zhang Wenxiang. Prod: Gateway Entertainment.

ZOMBIE DOGS
[Mockumentary, 2004] Script: Hardly Annie Gore. Dir: Toh Hai Leong. Phot: Jimmy Tai. Players: Toh Hai Leong, Lim Poh Huat. Prod: Hardly Annie Gore.

Quote of the Year

"Basically, my movies have a very positive message, no matter what. At the end of the day, they're not meant to subvert the social order."
JACK NEO, *film-maker and actor, recipient of the Public Service Medal in 2004.*

CBC-TV/Kobal

JERRY GOLDSMITH, pictured at work in 1983, wrote the scores for almost 200 films, including Lonely Are the Brave, The Omen *(for which he won his only Oscar) and* Basic Instinct. *He died on July 21, 2004, aged 75, and Hollywood lost another of its greatest and most prolific composers on August 18, when ELMER BERNSTEIN died aged 82. As Philip Kemp wrote in November's* Sight & Sound, *Bernstein's "unforgettable march-theme for* The Magnificent Seven *(1960) stands as perhaps the archetypal Western score".*

Slovakia Hana Cielová

The Year's Best Films

Hana Cielová's choice:
Faithless Games
(Michaela Pavlátová)
Zelary (Ondrej Trojan)

Recent and Forthcoming Films

**JESENNÁ (ZATO)
SILNÁ LÁSKA**
(Autumn (yet) Strong Love)
*[Drama, 2003] Script: Zita
Furková, based on the story by
Rudolf Sloboda. Dir: Furková.
Phot: Dodo Simoncic. Players:
Ester Geislerová, Jozef Vajda.
Prod: Furková, Artkrea.*

Ester Geislerová in **Autumn (yet)
Strong Love**

NEVERNÉ HRY
(Faithless Games)
*[Drama, 2003] Script: Tina Diosi.
Dir: Michaela Pavlátová. Phot:
Martin Strba. Players: Zuzana
Stivínová, Peter Bebjak, Jana
Hubinská, Ady Hajdu, Kristína
Svarinská, Ivana Chylková. Prod:
Pavel Strnad, Negativ/Czech TV/
ARS MEDIA/Slovak TV.*

ZOSTANE TO MEDZI NAMI
(It Will Stay Between Us)
*[Drama, 2003] Script: Slavena
Pavlásková, Miro Sindelka. Dir:
Miro Sindelka. Phot: Ján Duris.
Players: Danica Jurcová, Michal
Dlouhy, Tomás Hanák. Prod:
Sindelka, Film Factory.*

T
wo weeks after joining the EU, in May 2004, Slovakia made its
first and quite symbolic appearance at the Cannes film market,
in a pavilion shared with the Czech Republic and Poland, an
initiative welcomed by the film industry and the foreign press. The bulk
of the work for Cannes was done by the Slovak Film Institute, which
provided information about old and recent Slovak films (see its
database at www.sfd.sfu.sk). There were fewer new films to promote
than Institute staff would have liked, although the situation is still better
than last year and may improve further when the government fulfils its
promises to pump more money into the industry.

For now, co-production is vitally important, as shown by Czech
director Ondrej Trojan's Oscar-nominated war drama Zelary (*Zelary*)
(Slovakia/ Czech Republic/Austria), which was shot in the breathtaking
mountain scenery of northern Slovakia with a partly Slovak cast and
crew, proving that the country has a lot to offer producers. Other co-
productions included **Faithless Games** (*Neverné hry*), the feature
debut of Czech animation director Michaela Pavlátová.

The drama takes places in southern Slovakia, near the Hungarian
border. The heroine is a Czech pianist who moves from Prague to a
sleepy Slovak village with her Slovak composer-husband and falls for
his best friend. This low-budget psychological drama was the nicest
surprise of the year – much more convincing than the second feature
from Miro Sindelka, **It Will Stay Between Us** (*Zostane to medzi nami*),
which involves another love triangle, this time in contemporary
Bratislava. Although formally very ambitious, its portrait of a modern,
detached world inhabited by equally detached people suffers from a
weak script and unconvincing characters.

Premiered at the 5th International Film Festival Bratislava, **Autumn
(yet) Strong Love** (*Jesenná (zato) silná láska*) is the directorial debut of
well-known Slovak actress Zita Furková and traces the passionate love
affair between an ageing, burnt-out composer (Jozef Vajda) and a
much younger, disturbed girl (Ester Geislerová). It wants to be *Last
Tango in Bratislava*, but Vajda is no Brando and the direction is old-
fashioned and better suited to TV. Geislerová, younger sister of the
Czech film star Ana Geislerová, is, however, a talent to watch.

HANA CIELOVÁ (Hana.Cielova@seznam.cz) is a freelance writer
and a programmer for the Karlovy Vary International Film Festival.

Slovenia Ziva Emersic

The Year's Best films

Ziva Emersic's selection:
Beneath Her Window
(Metod Pevec)
Heart Is But a Piece of Meat
(Short. Jan Cvitkovic)
Cheese & Jam
(Branko Djuric-Djuro)

*Polona Juh, left, and Sasa Tabakovic
in* **Beneath Her Window**

Recent and Forthcoming Films

PREDMESTJE (Suburbia)
*[Drama, 2003] Script: Vinko
Moederndorfer, based on his
novel. Dir: Moederndorfer. Phot:
Dusan Joksimovic. Players: Peter
Musevski, Jernej Sugman, Renato
Jencek, Silvo Bozic. Prod: Forum
Ljubljana/SFF.*

POD NJENIM OKNOM
(Beneath her Window)
*[Drama, 2003] Script and Dir:
Metod Pevec. Phot: Ziga
Koritnik. Players: Polona Juh,
Zlatko Sugman, Marjana Brecelj,
Sasa Tabakovic. Prod: TV
Slovenija/SFF/Emotion Film.*

OD GROBA DO GROBA
(From Grave to Grave)
*[Drama, 2004] Script and Dir:
Jan Cvitkovic. Phot: Simon
Tansek. Players: Gregor Bakovic,
Drago Milinovic, Natasa
Matjasec, Sonja Savic. Prod: Stara
gara/Propeler Film/TV
Slovenija/SFF.*

For Slovenian cinema, 2003-04 witnessed a revolution in the public's attitude to domestic film-making, brought about by **Cheese & Jam** (*Kajmak in marmelada*). Surprisingly backed by public broadcaster TV Slovenija, it became the biggest home-grown hit ever, selling 150,000 tickets in the latter half of 2003 and the first quarter of 2004.

Branko Djuric, the Bosnian scriptwriter, actor and director who made his name playing one of the stranded combatants in Danis Tanovic's Oscar-winning *No Man's Land*, exploited his status as a very successful kind of Bosnian *gastarbeiter* in Slovenia to mock the so-called "national character" of his adopted and home countries. He cast himself and his Slovenian actress wife (Tanja Ribic) in this bittersweet comedy about a loving couple of different ethnic backgrounds who must fight prejudices and clichés (Slovenian chauvinism, Bosnian laziness) to live together happily ever after.

His use of stereotypes and "street humour" was considered to be naughty, if not downright politically incorrect, and his success divided critics, who could not ignore the film's skilful crowd-pleasing but feared that this type of light entertainment could set a pattern that younger film-makers would seek to emulate.

One might have expected a flood of copycat productions to follow *Cheese & Jam* but it did not materialise. Independent producers had to look to other countries as co-producers because the Slovenian Film Fund's annual budget of €2.4m is far from satisfactory when average

Branko Djuric embodies stereotyped Bosnian laziness in **Cheese & Jam**

A gifted middle-aged writer who earns his living by writing funeral speeches but is terrified of death.

SRCE JE KOS MESA
(Heart Is But a Piece of Meat)
[Short drama, 2003] Script and Dir: Jan Cvitkovic. Phot: Simon Tansek. Players: Mojca Fatur, Primoz Petkovsek. Prod: Arkadena/SFF.
The butcher (Petkovsek) falls in love with the blonde of his dreams on a bus.

Primoz Petkovsek in **Heart Is But a Piece of Meat**

KAJMAK IN MARMELADA
(Cheese & Jam)
[Comedy, 2003] Script and Dir: Branko Djuric. Phot: Sven Pepeonik. Players: Djuric, Tanja Ribic, Dragan Bjelogrlic, Vlado Novak. Prod: TV Slovenija/ATA Production/SFF.

RDECA OBZORJA
(Red Horizons)
[Drama, 2004] Script and Dir: Igor Sterk. Phot: Simon Tansek. Players: Natasa Burger, Peter Musevski, Ana Kerin, Polona Juh, Tomi Janezic. Prod: A.A.C. Productions/TV Slovenija/SFF.

RUSEVINE (The Ruins)
[Drama, 2004] Script: Janez Burger, Ana Lasic. Dir: Burger. Phot: Simon Tansek. Players: Darko Rundek, Natasa Matjasec, Matjaz Tribuson. Prod: Vertigo/Emotion Film/TV Slovenija/SFF.

Quote of the Year

"I never think of people as Slovenians and Bosnians or blacks and whites. The only distinction I accept is the one between Beatles fans and Stones fans."
BRANKO DJURIC, *talking about* Cheese & Jam.

feature budgets are €800,000 and the state can only commit up to 60% of each project's production cost. There are no alternative sources of finance, such as a distribution tax (an idea rejected by parliament a few years ago). TV Slovenija does not offer consistent support and it's virtually impossible to recoup costs at home when the American majors claim 90% of the domestic theatrical market. However, the new Viba Studio in Ljubljana is now playing a crucial role in the ambitions of Slovenian Film Fund to support as many European co-productions as possible.

The ballerina and her stalker

Actor, writer and director Metod Pevec made **Beneath Her Window** (*Pod njenim oknom*), his second feature, a decade after his debut drama, *Carmen* (in the interval he made his name as a novelist, exploring female soul and destiny in different historical periods, including the Second World War). Originally made for television, this was a sweet love story about a former ballerina (Polona Juh) in her mid-thirties and her much younger "stalker" (Sasa Tabakovic) and it revealed Pevec's sophisticated feeling for human relationships and humour. It took awards for script, direction and lead actress (Juh) at the national film festival in Celje in 2003 and was loved by critics and audiences (70,000 admissions).

Vinko Moederndorfer, a well-established theatre director and novelist, shot his first feature film, *Suburbia* (*Predmestje*), based on his own bleak and violent novel. Like *Cheese & Jam*, it explores the clash of different ethnic groups in contemporary Slovenian society, but in far heavier style. A young Bosnian couple move into a quiet neighbourhood and are stalked by four men in their forties, including a closet homosexual and an alcoholic. The suburban setting plays the role of mental landscape, where weird characters dig deep into social pathology, revealing the unpleasant face of a country in which people want to see themselves as civilised Europeans. The film was accused of excessive violence and rejected by the domestic audience.

How to please fickle cinemagoers remains the crucial question for Slovenian film-makers, because public opinion and official cultural policy remain united on only one issue: that Slovenian cinema should be mercilessly tested on the domestic market. With only five local feature films produced annually, the success or failure of each one makes a huge impact.

ZIVA EMERSIC (Ziva.Mali@rtvslo.si) is a journalist and film critic and commissioning editor of the Documentary Programme at TV Slovenija. She was formerly programme director of the Slovenian National Film Festival.

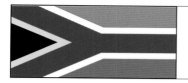

South Africa Martin Botha

The Year's Best Films

Martin Botha's choice:
Cosmic Africa (Docu. Craig and Damon Foster)
Yesterday
(Darrell James Roodt)
The Wooden Camera
(Ntshaveni Wa Luruli)
Proteus (John Greyson and Jack Lewis)
The Story of an African Farm (David Lister)

Cosmic Africa

Recent and Forthcoming Films

A FISHERMAN'S TALE
[Documentary, 2003] Script, Dir and Phot: Riaan Hendricks.

A CASE OF MURDER
[Thriller, 2003] Script and Dir: Clive Morris. Phot: Felix Meyburgh. Players: Steve Hofmeyr. Prod: Morris, Felix Meyburgh, Richard Nosworthy
.

CASA DE LA MUSICA
[Documentary, 2003] Dir: Jonathan de Vries. Phot: Guilio Biccari. Prod: Jack Lewis, Idol Pictures.

COMING TO SOUTH AFRICA
[Drama, 2004] Script: Chuks Obiora. Dir: Paul Louwrens. Phot: Ray Roberts. Players: Hakeem Kae-Kazim, Ramsey Nouah.

Ten years after South Africa became a democracy, its feature and documentary film industry is blossoming and in 2003-04 retrospectives on the first decade of post-apartheid cinema were held at numerous festivals, including FESPACO, Rotterdam, Berlin, Cannes and Zanzibar, plus a 40-year retrospective, on which this correspondent worked, at the 14th African, Asian and Latin American festival in Milan, which included the bold, sociocritical work of veterans such as Jans Rautenbach, Manie van Rensburg and Ross Devenish, landmark documentaries and recent works by Zola Maseko, Ramadan Suleman, Ntshaveni Wa Luruli and Teboho Mahlatsi.

Part of the excitement surrounding South African films derives from the support of the federal and local governments, particularly in Gauteng, KwaZulu Natal and the Western Cape, which have been quick to realise that the industry has huge earning and employment potential. The federal Industrial Development Corporation (IDC), which provides government loans, has an annual fund of $40m (R250m) earmarked for the film industry, while the Department of Arts and Culture and the National Film and Video Foundation (NFVF) have made grants worth $10m available to film-makers in recent years and has co-funded more than ten features.

Most significantly, on June 30, 2004, the government announced a new tax incentive scheme for foreign and local film-makers. Mandisi Mpahlwa, Trade and Industry Minister, said the Large Film and Television Production Rebate would offer around $40m worth of incentives to boost location filming over the next three years, with foreign companies earning a rebate of 15% and local companies 25% on production spending in South Africa, provided that at least 50% of the total budget is spent in the country. Feature films (excluding pornography) and TV films, drama series, mini-series and documentaries (excluding reality shows) are eligible.

Sound investments

Even before the rebate was announced, investor confidence in local productions had been demonstrated by the $15m budget for the crime drama **Stander**, the story of a disillusioned policeman who became a bank robber during the apartheid years. Another case is the lyrical period drama **The Story of an African Farm**, whose $3.1m budget came from multiple sources. Based on a classic

COSMIC AFRICA

[Documentary, 2003] Script: Hugh Brody. Dir and Phot: Craig and Damon Foster. Players: Thebe Medupe. Prod: Carina Rubin, Aland Pictures/Anne Rogers, Industrial Development Corporation of South Africa.

COUNTRY OF MY SKULL

[Drama, 2004] Script: Ann Peacock. Dir: John Boorman. Players: Samuel L. Jackson, Juliette Binoche. Prod: Boorman, Robert Chartoff, Lynn Hendee, Mike Medavoy, Kieran Corrigan, David Wicht (Film Africa) and Mfundi Vundla (Morula Pictures).

CRITICAL ASSIGNMENT

[Thriller, 2003] Script: Tunde Babalola. Dir: Jason Xenopoulos. Players: Michael Power, Nick Boraine, Richard Mofe-Damijo, Moshidi Motshepwa.

DRUM

[Historical drama, 2004] Script: Jason Filardi, Tim Grimes, Zola Maseko. Dir: Maseko. Phot: Lisa Rinzler. Players: Taye Diggs, Jason Flemyng. Prod: Dumisani Dlamini and Rudolf Wichmann (Nova Films)/Chris Sievernich and Matt Milich, Armada Pictures International)/Jason Filardi, Andreas Grosch, Andreas Schmid.

Jason Flemyng in **Drum**

FORGIVENESS

[Drama, 2004] Script: Greg Latter. Dir: Ian Gabriel. Phot: Giulio Biccari. Players: Arnold Vosloo, Quanita Adams, Zane Meas, Denis Newman, Christo Davids. Prod: Joel Phiri, Jeremy Nathan, DV8/National Film and Video Foundation.

novel by Olive Schreiner, this beautiful film shows the dramatic impact of an opportunistic and manipulative stranger (a splendid turn from Richard E. Grant) on the lives of three children and the rest of their remote farm community. Veteran director David Lister expertly combines serious drama with comedy and the film opened to strong local box-office results in September 2004.

The IDC contributed about a third of the €15m budget for John Boorman's **Country of My Skull**, adapted from Antjie Krog's account of the Truth and Reconciliation Commission hearings. The script, by South African-born Ann Peacock, follows a *Washington Post* journalist (Samuel L. Jackson) sent to cover the hearings and Juliette Binoche plays Anna Malan, an Afrikaaner poet covering the hearings for radio.

The IDC also contributed to the year's most outstanding production: Craig and Damon Foster's documentary feature **Cosmic Africa**. Shot on High Definition, this visual masterpiece uses oral storytelling to explore traditional African astronomy and follows the remarkable personal journey of African astronomer Thebe Medupe through the ancestral land of Namibia's hunter-gatherers, the Dogon country of Mali and the landscapes of the Egyptian Sahara. This seminal work won eight National Television and Video Association Stone Awards for 2003 and was ecstatically acclaimed at the Ten Years of Freedom festival in New York in 2004.

DV8 celebrates

The DV8 project, initiated by Ballistic Pictures' Kobus Botha, Joel Phiri of ICE Media and Avatar Digital's Jeremy Nathan, has received more than 300 submissions in response to its call for script proposals, eight of which were selected to be shot in South Africa on DV for an average of $250,000 each (initial funding from the Hubert Bals Fund has been supplemented by the NFVF). The first DV8 feature is Ian Gabriel's **Forgiveness**. Brilliantly shot by Guilio Biccari, it tells the story of an apartheid-era policeman (Arnold Vosloo) seeking redemption for the crimes he committed against a coloured family in the windswept landscape of the Atlantic West Coast.

Arnold Vosloo as a cop seeking redemption in **Forgiveness**

Biccari won the Best Cinematography award at the 25th Durban International Film festival and the film also picked up the Audience Choice Best Film Award and shared the Best South African Feature Film Award with Ntshaveni Wa Luruli's **The Wooden Camera**, a poetic account of the rites of passage of a young black boy, Sipho (Junior Singo), who finds a video camera and disguises it as a home-made wooden camera so that he can surreptitiously film life in Khayelitsha Township. It is one of the first films from South Africa to build a navigable road between the youth of the townships and upper-class society.

Leleti Khumalo as the HIV-positive mother of a young daughter (Lihle Mvelase) in **Yesterday**

The Wooden Camera vividly portrays marginalised communities, as does Darrell Roodt's **Yesterday** – a milestone in post-apartheid cinema. Arguably Roodt's best film since *Jobman*, *Yesterday* is the simple story of a young mother who lives in rural KwaZulu-Natal with her pre-school child, while her migrant labourer husband works on the mines in Johannesburg. The woman takes ill, and after many attempts to visit a local clinic, learns that she is HIV-positive. With masterful understatement Roodt and producer Anant Singh movingly highlight the difficulties encountered by impoverished rural people with Aids, and the devastating effects of social stigma. Shot on Super 35mm for $1.5m, *Yesterday* won the Eiuc Award at Venice and was chosen as the national entry for the 2004 Foreign-Language Oscar.

It is one of several films to have benefited from pay channel M-Net's "Movie of the Month" initiative. The broadcaster is putting around $200,000 into film to encourage additional investment from local producers (as happened with Singh's involvement in *Yesterday*).

GUMS AND NOSES
[Comedy, 2004] Script and Dir: Craig Freimond. Phot: Jon Kovel. Players: Antony Coleman, Lionel Newton, Tony Kgogore, Faye Peters, Sean Taylor. Prod: Robbie Thorpe, M-NET.

HOODLUM & SON
[Gangster drama, 2003] Script and Dir: Ashley Way. Phot: Buster Reynolds. Players: Ron Perlman, Robert Vaughn, Ian Roberts. Prod: Peakviewing Film Productions S.A.

IBALI (Myth)
[Short drama, 2003] Script and Dir: Harold Holscher. Phot: Catherine Hornby. Player: Chris April. Prod: CityVarsity Film and Television School.

THE LION'S TRAIL
[Documentary, 2003] Dir: Francois Verster.

PAVEMENT
[Thriller, 2003] Dir: Darrell Roodt. Phot: Giulio Biccarri. Players: Robert Patrick, Lauren Holly. Prod: Film Afrika for Apollo Media.

PROTEUS
[Drama, 2003] Script and Dir: John Greyson and Jack Lewis. Players: Neil Sandilands, Rouxnet Brown. Prod: Steven Markovitz, Anita Lee, Platon Trakoshis, Big World Cinema/Pluck Productions.

SKILPOPPE
[Drama, 2004] Script: Lizz Meiring. Dir: Andre Odendaal. Phot: Rene Smith. Players: Marius Weyers, Sandra Prinsloo, Kate Ascott-Evans, Therese Benade, Paul du Toit. Prod: Roberta Durrant, Penguin Films/M-NET.

STANDER
[Crime drama, 2003] Script: Bima Staff. Dir: Bronwyn Hughes. Player: Thomas Jane. Prod: The Imaginarium (South Africa)/Grosvenor Park (Canada)/Seven Arts (UK).

Richard E. Grant in **The Story of an African Farm**

THE STORY OF AN AFRICAN FARM
[Period drama, 2004] Script: Bonnie Rodini, Thandi Bewer, from the novel by Olive Schreiner. Dir: David Lister. Phot: Peter Tischhauser. Players: Richard E. Grant, Karin van der Laag, Kasha Kropinski, Elrisa Swanepoel, Anneke Weidemann, Luke Gallant. Prod: Rodini, Industrial Development Corporation of South Africa.

THE SUNFLOWER
[Musical drama, 2004] Script: Marc Wells. Dir: Lance Samuels. Phot: Buster Reynolds. Players: Hakeem Kae-Kazim, Bill Flynn, Mthobisi Joy Mwandla, Marc Wells. Prod: DuMarc cc.

THE WOODEN CAMERA
[Drama, 2003] Script: Yves Buclet and Peter Speyer. Dir: Ntshaveni Wa Luruli. Phot: Gorden Spooner. Players: Junior Singo, Dana de Agrella, Innocent Msimango, Lisa Petersen, Nicholas Jara, Andre Jacobs, Jean-Pierre Cassel. Prod: Richard Green Associates/ National Film and Video Foundation/Oliver Delahaye, Odelion/Ben Wolford, Paul Trijbits, UK Film Council.

YESTERDAY
[Drama, 2004] Script and Dir: Darrell James Roodt. Phot: Michael Brierly. Players: Leleti Khumalo, Lihle Mvelase, Kenneth Kambule. Prod: Anant Singh and Helena Spring, Videovision Entertainment/M-NET.

Another striking M-Net-backed feature is **Skilpoppe**, a moving drama about a family reeling from a devastating personal tragedy, as seen through the eyes of the teenage daughter. It powerfully taps the current mood of South African youth, for whom tragedy is a part of life and growing up can be brutal but beautiful.

The most outstanding short film of the past year is *iBali* (*Myth*) by Harold Holscher, a recent graduate of City Varsity Film, Television and Multimedia school. Winner of five Stone Awards in 2003, it magnificently blends magical realism and African mythology, with touches of the urban alienation of Antonioni (Holscher is an admirer of *Zabriskie Point*), the surrealism of Djibril Diop Mambety, Senegalese director of *Hyenas* and *Touki Bouki*, and the beautiful compositions of Kubrick. iBali shows how African heritage is passed from generation to generation through the art of story-telling, through the mythical tale of a boy discovering the essence of water.

Alongside *Cosmic Africa*, other outstanding documentaries included the poetic beauty of *A Fisherman's Tale* (26 mins), set in Kalkbay, Cape Town. It starts as the story of a young man who tells his mother how he took his father's fishing lines out to sea to find what the ocean means to fishermen, then seamlessly changes direction and becomes a moving reflection on the despair and hopelessness of these people's lives as globalisation devastates subsistence fishing communities. With funding from the NFVF, director Riaan Hendricks has realised this project after three hard years and, as with the Foster brothers' *Cosmic Africa* and *The Great Dance*, proves that non-fiction work can be personal and poetic. Finally, *Project 10*, a series of documentaries that looks back on individual experiences of the country's first 10 years of democray, was screened all over the world.

Dr MARTIN BOTHA (martin@cityvarsity.co.za) has published more than 200 articles and reviews and two books on South African and African cinema, including an in-depth study of the late Manie van Rensburg. He is working on a historical dictionary of African cinemas.

Junior Singo in **The Wooden Camera**

South Korea Stephen Cremin

The Year's Best Films

Stephen Cremin's selection:
Arahan (Ryu Seung-wan)
Old Boy (Park Chan-wook)
**Spirit of Jeet Kune Do:
Once upon a Time in High
School** (Yoo Ha)
**Spring, Summer, Autumn,
Winter... and Spring**
(Kim Ki-duk)
Untold Scandal (E J-yong)

Choi Min-shik in **Old Boy**

Recent and
Forthcoming Films
**BALRE KYOSEUBSO
(Flying Boys)**
*[Youth drama, 2004] Script: Shin
Hye-eun, Byun Young-joo. Dir:
Byun. Phot: Sung Seung-tae.
Players: Yoon Kye-sang, Kim
Min-jung, Do Ji-won, Jin Yu-
young, Eun Ju-wan. Prod: Kim
Mi-hee, Fun & Happiness Film.*

CHEUNG-YEON (Cheungyeon)
*[Biopic, 2004] Script: Lee In-hwa,
Yoon Jong-chan. Dir: Yoon. Phot:
Yoon Hong-shik. Players: Jang
Jin-young, Kim Ju-hyuk, Yu Min.
Prod: Benjamin Seok, Cineline II.*

**DALKOMHAN INSAENG
(A Bittersweet Life)**
*[Action noir, 2005] Script and
Dir: Kim Jee-hoon. Phot: Kim Ji-
yong. Players: Lee Byung-hun,*

Korean cinema has fortified its position as one of the most exciting film industries in Asia, both commercially and artistically. Korean films have never been more visible internationally, emerging as talking points at major festivals and finding new markets (export sales grew by two thirds in 2003). At home, admissions grew by 4.6% in 2003 and the market share of local films went beyond 50% nationwide.

Reaping the benefits at the box-office were distributors CJ Entertainment and Cinema Service, who enjoyed a combined market share of 40% in 2003, including 58% of local film releases. After buying out Cinema Service's parent company, Plenus Entertainment, in April 2004, CJ held 40% of its rival's stock. This dominance is offset somewhat by the entry into the market of new distributors with access to strong local titles, notably Chungeorahm Film, Showbox Inc., Show East and Lotte Cinema.

The biggest story of 2003-04 was the return of the local blockbuster in the form of **Silmido** (*Shilmido*) and **Taegukgi** (*Taegukgi hwinalrimyeo*). Both successively set new records for Korean cinema, drawing more than 10 million admissions each. Like *Shiri* (1999) and *Joint Security Area* (2000) before them, they have in common the theme of a divided Korea, which attracts an audience outside the typical moviegoing demographic. Competition between the two titles, directed by two of the most powerful figures in the local industry, boosted the grosses of both.

Won Bin, left, and Jang Dong-gun in **Taegukgi**

Shin Min-ah, Kim Young-chul.
Prod: Oh Jung-wan, b.o.m. Film.

HYEOL-UI NU (Blood Rain)
[Historical drama, 2004] Script:
Lee Won-jae, Kim Sung-je.
Dir: Kim Dae-seung. Phot:
Choi Young-hwan. Players:
Cha Seung-jae, Kim In-kwon,
Ji Sung. Prod: Kim Mi-hee, Fun
& Happiness Film.

JENI, JUNO (Jenny, Juno)
[Youth drama, 2004] Script and
Dir: Kim Ho-joon. Phot: Kim
Dong-chun. Players: Kim Hye-
sung, Park Min-ji. Prod: Kim
Dong-ju, Choi Sun-shik,
CultureCapMedia/Danal.

**JUHONGKEULSSI
(The Scarlet Letter)**
[Mystery, 2004] Script and Dir:
Daniel Byun. Phot: Choi Hyun-ki.
Players: Han Suk-kyu, Lee Eun-ju,
Sung Hyun-ha, Eom Ji-won. Prod:
Lee Seung-jae, LJ Film.

JUMEOKI UNDA (Crying Fist)
[Action, 2005] Script: Ryu Seung-
wan, Chun Chul-hong. Dir: Ryu.
Phot: Cho Yong-kyu. Players:
Choi Min-shik, Ryu Seung-bum.
Prod: Kim Dong-ju, SiO_t
film/Bravo Entertainment.

MALAHTON (Running Boy)
[Family drama, 2004] Script: Jung
Yoon-chul, Yoon Jin-ho. Dir:
Jung. Phot: Kwon Hyuk-joon.
Players: Cho Seung-woo, Kim
Mi-sook. Prod: Benjamin Seok,
Cineline II.

**MEON KIL
(Long and Winding Road)**
[Family drama, 2004] Script and
Dir: Koo Sung-jo. Phot: Choi
Chan-kyu. Players: Ko Do-shim,
Park Won-sang, Lee Hye-eun,
Son Byung-ho, Kim Ye-ryung,
Kim Yu-suk. Prod: Choi Yong-
bae, Chungeorahm.

**NAE MEORI SOK-UI
JIWOOGAE (A Moment
to Remember)**
[Romance, 2004] Script and Dir:
John H. Lee. Phot: Lee Yoon-kyu.
Players: Son Ye-jin, Chung
Woo-sung. Prod: Tcha Seung-jai,
Sidus Pictures.

Silmido, directed by Cinema Service president Kang Woo-suk, is based on the true story of 31 death row prisoners recruited on a covert mission to assassinate North Korean leader Kim Il-sung in 1968. They are taken to Shilmi Island for a punishing two-year training regime, at the end of which they discover that the mission has been cancelled. *Taegukgi*, Kang Jegyu's first film since *Shiri*, follows two brothers (played by two of Korea's hottest stars, Jang Dong-gun, as the elder, and Won Bin) who are caught up on opposing sides of the Korean War in the early 1950s.

A Kim for all seasons

The most exciting and prolific director of 2003-04 (profiled in depth at the front of this volume) was Kim Ki-duk, long considered an outsider in the industry. His Buddhist fable, **Spring, Summer, Autumn, Winter... and Spring** (Bom, yeoreum, kaeul, kyeul keurigo bom), traces the life of a monk through four seasons, representative of stages of his life. It ushers in a new maturity in Kim's self-taught aesthetic, opening new possibilities in his cinematic world that were explored in his next two features, recognised with Best Director honours at the 2004 Berlin and Venice film festivals respectively.

In **Samaritan Girl** (Samaria), after an under-age prostitute dies escaping from the police, her best friend attempts to redeem her sins by repaying her clients, sexually and financially, as her police detective father is one step behind, enacting his own lawless vengeance. In **3-iron** (Bin jib), a homeless man runs off with an abused housewife and they break into a new apartment each night. When the husband and police catch up, they lock up and abuse the outsider whose motivations are beyond their comprehension. *Samaritan Girl* asks the audience to transfer its empathy across three protagonists, only to find solace in the mind of a murderer; the almost silent *3-Iron* demands the suspension of our disbelief at characters who become effectively invisible. That he pulls off this feat is testament to Kim's growth as a film-maker.

The most controversial Korean film of the year, and winner of Cannes' Special Jury Prize, was Park Chan-wook's subversive **Old Boy** (Oldeu boi). Loosely adapted from a Japanese comic book, its hero (Choi Min-shik) finds himself locked in a motel room with only dumplings and a television for sustenance. Released after 15 years, he has just four days to discover the motive behind his imprisonment. Grossing $23m at the box-office, the dazzlingly cinematic *Old Boy* pushes the boundaries of commercial film-making in Korea with its radical "happy" ending.

Im Chan-sang's **The President's Barber** (Hyoja-dong ibalsa) explores one of the darkest periods of modern Korean history through the eyes of General Park Chung-hee's everyman barber, who becomes entangled in every significant political event of the 1960s and 1970s. Its genius lies in the way it confronts the real horrors of the times through absurdist humour and a lightness that belies the serious subject matter, even when the barber's son is tortured as a communist spy.

Moon So-ri, Lee Jae-eung and Song Kang-ho in **The President's Barber**

While the barber's ultimate goal is to be a good family man and keep his head firmly attached to his shoulders, the everyman protagonist of Ryu Seung-wan's **Arahan** (*Arahan: Jangpung dae jakjeon*) manages to find his inner superhero, get the girl and save the world. *Arahan* marks a turning point for Korean genre cinema, influenced by but not derivative of work by Hong Kong's Stephen Chow, Jackie Chan and Yuen Wo-ping. It is also an impressive showcase for action choreographer Jung Doo-hong, a key figure in the development of Korean genre cinema over the past decade.

The hero of Yoo Ha's **Spirit of Jeet Kune Do: Once upon a Time in High School** (*Maljukgeori janhoksa*) draws his inspiration from another Hong Kong legend, Bruce Lee. But until the bloody finale, this is a slow-burning coming-of-age tale that explores traditional elements: unrequited love, generational conflict and identity. Set in 1978-79, when Yoo himself was in high school, it also serves as an understated allegory for the violence at the end of the Park Chung-hee era.

Liaisons revisited

E J-yong's hit, **Untold Scandal** (*Seukaendeul: Joseon namnyeo sangyeol jisa*) brought life back to a long-dormant movie genre, the costume drama, with an adaptation of Choderlos de Laclos' eighteenth-century *Les liaisons dangereuses*, transposed to conservative eighteenth-century Korea. Sumptuously shot, with the costume budget alone reportedly more than $1m, it is an exciting packaging of eastern and western elements that suggests new possibilities for Korean cinema.

NAMGEUK ILGI
(Antarctic Journal)
[Mystery thriller, 2004] Script and Dir: Im Philsung. Phot: Jung Joon-hoon. Players: Song Kang-ho, Yu Ji-tae, Kang Hye-jung. Prod: Tcha Seung-jai, Sidus Pictures.

S DAIEORI (S Diary)
[Romantic comedy, 2004] Script: Park Sung-kyung, Kwon Jong-kwan. Dir: Kwon. Phot: Lim Chan. Players: Kim Sun-ah, Kim Su-ro, Lee Hyun-woo, Kong Yu. Prod: Jung Hoon-taek, I Film.

SHIN SEOK-KI BEURRUSEU
(Shin Suk-gi Blues)
[Youth drama, 2004] Script and Dir: Kim Do-hyuk. Phot: Moon Yong-shik. Players: Lee Seung-jae, Kim Hyun-ju, Lee Jong-hyuk, Kim Chang-won, Ok Ji-young. Prod: Kim Woo-taek, Popcorn Films.

SSEOM (Some)
[Thriller, 2004] Script: Kim Eun-jung. Dir: Chang Youn-hyun. Phot: Kim Sung-bok. Players: Ko Su, Song Ji-hyo, Lee Dong-kyu. Prod: Kang Woo-suk, Cinema Service.

TAEPUNG TAEYANG
(Born to Speed)
[Youth drama, 2005] Script and Dir: Jeong Jae-eun. Phot: Kim Byung-seo. Players: Kim Kang-woo, Chun Jung-myung, Lee Chun-hee, Cho Yi-jin. Prod: Kim Dong-ju, Film Mania Co. Ltd.

URI HYUNG (My Brother)
[Youth drama, 2004] Script and Dir: Ahn Kwon-tae. Phot: Hwang Ki-suk. Players: Won Bin, Shin Ha-kyun, Lee Bo-young. Prod: Park Dong-ho, Zininsa Films.

YEOSEONSAENG VS YEOJEJA
(Lovely Rivals)
[Comedy, 2004] Script: Jang Kyu-sung, Lee Won-jae. Dir: Jang. Phot: Lee Doo-man. Players: Yeom Jung-ah, Lee Se-young. Prod: Kim Ki-hee, Fun & Happiness Film.

YEOJA, JEONG-HYE
(This Charming Girl)
[Drama, 2004] Script and Dir: Lee Yoon-ki. Phot: Choi Jin-woong.

Players: *Kim Ji-su, Hwang Jung-min, Kim Hye-ok, Lee Dae-yeon, Lee Keum-ju, Kim Mi-sung. Prod: Lee Seung-jae, LJ Film.*

Quotes of the Year

"I don't really understand why Hollywood studios buy remake rights to Korean films. If they like the film in the first place, why don't they just distribute the Korean version?"
KIM KI-DUK, *director.*

"What Korean cinema needs now is not one movie that attracts 10 million viewers, but 10 movies that attract one million viewers."
ANONYMOUS *industry figure, quoted in* Variety.

41st Grand Bell Awards

Picture: *Spring, Summer, Autumn, Winter… and Spring* (Kim Ki-duk).
Special Jury Prize: *Silmido.*
Director: Park Chan-wook (*Old Boy*).
Screenplay: Choi Dong-hoon (*The Big Swindle*).
Adapted Screenplay: Kim Hee-jae (*Silmido*).
Actor: Choi Min-shik (*Old Boy*).
Actress: Moon So-ri (*A Good Lawyer's Wife*).
Supporting Actor: Heo Joon-ho (*Silmido*).
Supporting Actress: Kim Ka-yeon (*Mr. Handy*).
Cinematography: Hong Kyung-pyo (*Taegukgi*).
New Director: Choi Dong-hoon (*The Big Swindle*).
New Actress: Moon Keun-young (*My Little Bride*).
New Actor: Kim Rae-won (*My Little Bride*).
Musical Score: Cho Young-wook (*Old Boy*).
Costumes: Jung Ku-ho and Kim Hee-ju (*Untold Scandal*).
Special Effects: Moon Byung-yong et al (*Natural City*).
Executive Producing: Jonathan Kim (*Silmido*).

Lee Mi-suk, left, and Bae Yong-joon in **Untold Scandal**

Chang Hyun-soo's **Everybody Has Secrets** (*Nuguna bimil-eun issda*) was Korea's first official remake of a Western movie, Gerard Stembridge's Dublin-set *About Adam*, and was shot with all the hallmarks of a Hollywood romantic comedy. The plot sees a handsome lothario seduce three middle-class sisters – iconographic whore, virgin and mother figures – in three interwoven chapters. From a business point of view, *Secrets* is also significant for its record-breaking pre-sale to Japan (which now accounts for 70% of Korean film exports) on the back of only 30 minutes of footage and the promise of a star cast.

Korean cinema has maintained its hold on the local box-office by expanding creatively, taking inspiration from comic books, classical literature, national history and foreign sources to tell new, interesting stories. Early signs show 2004 box-office improving on the 2003 figures, but there is still room for improvement, especially in the home video market, which has yet to recover from its collapse in the 1990s; as a result, theatrical takings account for an unusually high 70% of total film revenues.

The industry's move towards vertical integration encourages blockbuster-scale distribution at the expense of limited releases that could potentially build given time (despite Korean features' success across Asia, few Asian films now get released in Korea). On average, local productions fail to recoup about 7% of their budget at home, so the industry is increasingly dependent on nascent international markets. Nevertheless, the miraculous rise of Korean cinema continues to defy expectations and the country appears to have the potent combination of creative talent and political will that can solve any problems that may lie ahead.

Spain Jonathan Holland

The Year's Best Films

Jonathan Holland's selection:
Astronauts (Santi Amodeo)
Hector (Gracia Querejeta)
The Sea Inside
(Alejandro Amenábar)
The Seventh Day
(Carlos Saura)
Take My Eyes (Iciar Bollaín)

Recent and Forthcoming Films

PARA QUE NO ME OLVIDES (LOS DIARIOS DE DAVID)
(*literally*, **So you Don't Forget me (David's Diaries)**)
[*Drama, 2004*] *Script: Patricia Ferreira, Virginia Yagüe. Dir: Ferreira. Phot: Marcelo Camorino. Players: Fernando Fernán Gómez, Emma Vilarasau, Marta Etura. Prod: Continental Producciones/TVG.*

ASOMBROSO MUNDO DE BORJAMARI Y POCHOLO
(*literally*, **Borjamari and Pocholo's Amazing World**)
[*Drama, 2004*] *Script and Dir: Enrique Lavigne, Juan Cavestany. Phot: Teo Delgado. Players: Santiago Segura, Javier Gutiérrez, Pilar Castro, Guillermo Toledo. Prod: Amiguetes Entertainment/Apache Films.*

ROTTWEILER
[*Drama, 2004*] *Script: Alberto Vázquez Figueroa. Dir: Brian Yuzna. Phot: Javier Salmones. Players: William Miller, Irene Montalà, Paulina Gálvez. Prod: Castelao Productions.*

LA FIESTA DEL CHIVO
(**The Feast of the Goat**)
[*Drama, 2005*] *Script: Luis Llosa, Augusto Cabada, Mario Vargas*

These are busy times for Spanish cinema financing. Broad industry smiles followed the victory of José Luis Rodríguez Zapatero's film-friendly Socialist Workers' Party in the March 2004 elections. Promises were made, some swiftly fulfilled, and the general tone is upbeat. In July, TV quotas requiring broadcasters to devote a percentage of annual revenue to European (generally Spanish-language) movies guaranteed that in 2005 around $160m from TV will go to local fare, a 40% improvement on 2004. In late September, it was confirmed that the central subsidy fund administered by national cinema institute ICAA would almost double to around €63.3m ($49.8m) in 2005, in line with what local producers had requested. This should guarantee subsidies of around $1m per qualifying film, a substantial rise compared to the previous Partido Popular government.

But the news is not all good: local distributors continue to be the poor man of the European independent sector. The number of screens rose by 13% in 2001-03 but admissions fell 6%. And although Spanish movies took a 16% domestic share in 2003, up by 2%, too often one or two big local hits make all the difference. This was again the case in 2004, as Alejandro Amenábar's *The Sea Inside* took more than €7m and Chema de la Peña's gross-out rock comedy *Isi/Disi: Love Like a Beast* more than €11.4m.

Film production dropped 20% to 110 films in 2003 and common consensus is that the market cannot handle this many titles when the majority make a negligible impression at the box-office. International sales on mid-price Spanish movies, meanwhile, have roughly halved compared with the mid-to-late 1990s.

Sogepaq

Javier Bardem and Bélen Rueda in **The Sea Inside**, *one of 2004's biggest local hits*

Llosa, based on the novel by
Vargas Llosa. Dir: Luis Llosa.
Phot: Javier Salmones. Players:
Isabella Rossellini, Thomas
Milian, Juan Diego Botto. Prod:
Lolafilms/Future Films.

AMOR IDIOTA (Idiot Love)
[Drama, 2005] Script: Ventura
Pons, Lluis-Antón Baulenas. Dir:
Pons. Phot: Mario Montero.
Players: Cayetana Guillén-Cuervo,
Santi Millán, Merce Pons. Prod:
Els Films de la Rambla.

HORMIGAS EN LA BOCA
(literally, **Ants in the Mouth**)
[Drama, 2005] Script: Mariano
Barroso, Alejandro Hernández,
based on a novel by Miguel
Barroso. Dir: Mariano Barroso.
Phot: Javier Aguirresarobe.
Players: Eduard Fernández,
Ariadne Gil, José Luis Gómez,
Jorge Perugorría. Prod: Cartel.

FRAGILE
[Thriller, 2005] Script: Jaume
Balaguero, Jordi Galcerán. Dir:
Balaguero. Phot: Xavi Giménez.
Players: Calista Flockhart,
Richard Roxburgh, Elena Anaya,
Gemma Jones. Prod: Filmax.

**SEMEN (UNA HISTORIA DE
AMOR) (Semen (A Love Story))**
[Comedy, 2005] Script and Dir:
Ines Paris, Daniela Fejerman.
Phot: Nestor Calvo. Players:
Hector Alterio, Ernesto Alterio,
Leticia Dolera. Prod: BocaBoca
Producciones/Future Films.

MORIR EN SAN HILARIO
(literally, **Dying in San Hilario**)
[Drama, 2004] Script and
Dir: Laura Maña. Players:
Ana Fernández, Lluis Homar,
Juan Echanove. Prod:
Castelao Producciones.

**EL PENALTI MAS LARGO DEL
MUNDO** (literally, **The Longest
Penalty in the World**)
[Drama, 2004] Script: Roberto
Santiago, Osvaldo Soriano. Dir:
Santiago. Phot: Juan Antonio
Castaño. Players: Fernando
Tejero, Marta Larralde, Maria
Botto, Carlos Kaniowsky. Prod:
Ensueño Films/Tornasol Films.

The politics of change

The arrival of the Socialists could also end a period during which
the industry has been treading water artistically. The social and
political urgency that dominated Spanish cinema 30 years ago
seems to have been under sedation, filtering through only
occasionally, almost as a thematic by-product. Politics and its
influence on characters' private lives remain ever-present themes in
the Spanish Civil War pictures that continue to emerge, and recent
examples include Salvador García Ruiz's **Voices in the Night**
(Voces en la noche), Jaime Chavarri's **The Year of the Flood** (El
año del diluvio) and Rosa Verges' **Iris**.

But contemporary social themes remain scarce. Only a handful of
recent features connect to present-day realities in any pressing way,
including Angeles González-Sinde's **Sleeping Luck** (La suerte
dormida) and Gerardo Herrero's **The Archimedes Principle** (El
principio de Arquímedes), each dealing with the trials of the Spanish
workplace. Achero Mañas' **November** (Noviembre) and Joaquín
Oristrell's **We the Undersigned** (Los abajo firmantes) tackle media
manipulation and Spain's involvement in the Iraq War respectively.
Iciar Bollaín's multiple award-winning **Take My Eyes** (Te doy mis
ojos) looked at domestic violence through the story of Pilar (Laia
Marull) and her abusive husband, Antonio (Luis Tosar).

Alta Producción

Laia Marull and Luis Tosar in **Take My Eyes**

The key exceptions to the no-politics rule were two controversial
documentaries that emerged from a diverse collection of high-
quality non-fiction work that also embraced **Eyengui, God of
Dreams** (Eyengui, el dios del sueño), José Manuel Novoa's lavish,
Pedro Almodóvar-produced examination of a pygmy tribe on the
verge of extinction. Julio Medem's polemical **The Basque Ball:
Skin Against Stone** (La pelota vasca: La piel contra la piedra),
consisting almost exclusively of interviews, lit a political fuse
following its San Sebastian 2003 premiere, polarised reactions with
its treatment of the issue of Basque Country violence and filled
acres of Spanish newsprint. For the first time in many years, a

Spanish film was at the centre of a nationwide political debate. In March 2004, 32 directors, many of them high-profile, realised that film can help shape public opinion and came together to produce the sequence of shorts **There's Good Cause** (*Hay motivo*), a dissection of what they perceived as the political abuses of the governing Popular Party. Unreleased in Madrid until October 2004, the film was screened at universities and cultural associations, twice on television and distributed via the internet. Its government-toppling efforts are now reaping the funding rewards mentioned above.

Have genres, will shoot

Those cinéastes not turning out political fare have tackled pretty much every other subject and style – and in industrial quantities. In the eclectic competition section of May 2004's Málaga festival (an increasingly influential showcase for the home industry), human relationships were analysed in depth in **The Violet Look** (*La mirada violeta*) by Nacho Pérez de la Paz, and Jesús Ruiz and Manuel Gómez Pereira's romantic comedy **Things That Make Living Worthwhile** (*Cosas que hacen que la vida valga la pena*). Genre fare was given an outing with Paco Plaza's **Romasanta**, a werewolf yarn from the prolific Filmax company, and with Miguel Bardem's twisting con-artist piece **The Swindled** (*Incautos*).

Only three women directors, including Gracia Querejeta, with the delicate, affecting family drama **Hector**, were on the 16-film slate at Málaga. However, a 20% female contribution is still far higher than normal in an industry that offers limited opportunities to women, who make the fewest films and some of the best. Following Isabel Coixet's success with *My Life without Me*, 2005 will see the release of her next English-language production, *The Secret Life of Words* (*La vida secreta de las palabras*), a drama set in Northern Ireland, starring Sarah Polley and Tim Robbins.

As ever, too few Spanish comedies make the grade either commercially or artistically. It's a sad fact that the biggest home-made hits are often clunky, unsubtle comedies conceived and made with lowest common denominator domestic audiences in mind, the latest example being **Isi-Disi, Love Like a Beast** (*Isi/Disi: amor a lo bestia*), which features Santiago Segura, Spain's most popular comic performer, as a heavy rocker who falls madly in love with the wrong girl.

There is a surfeit of flabby, youth-skewed genre pictures, such as David Serrano's recent **Football Days** (*Días de futbol*): it hired most of the cast of Emilio Martínez Lázaro's sexy romcom **The Other Side of the Bed** (*El otro lado de la cama*), which sold to the UK but was a critical flop at home. Two recent exceptions were the sprightly, subtle **Only Human** (*Seres queridos*), in which a Jew

HABANA BLUES
[Drama, 2005] Script: Benito Zambrano, Ernesto Chao. Dir: Zambrano. Phot: Jean-Claude Larrieu. Players: Alberto Yoel, Roger Pera, Marta Calvo. Prod: Maestranza Films.

HEROINA (Heroin)
[Drama, 2005] Script: Angeles González-Sinde. Dir: Gerardo Herrero. Players: Adriana Ozores, Javier Pereira, Carlos Blanco. Prod: Continental/Tornasol.

EL DESENLACE
(*literally,* **The Outcome**)
[Drama, 2005] Script and Dir: Juan Pinzas. Phot: Gerardo Moschini. Players: José Sancho, Beatriz Rico, Javier Gurruchaga, Carlos Bardem. Prod: Atlántico Films.

VOLANDO VOY
(*literally,* **I'm Flying**)
[Drama, 2005] Script: Miguel Albaladejo, Juan Carlos Delgado. Dir: Albaladejo. Players: Fernando Tejero, Mariola Fuentes. Prod: Mediapro/Sogecine

AUSENTES (*literally,* **Absent**)
[Thriller, 2005] Script: Daniel Calparsoro, Ray Loriga, Helio Quiroga. Dir: Calparsoro. Phot: Josep María Civit. Players: Ariadna Gil, Jordi Mollà, Omar Muñoz, Ignacio Pérez. Prod: Estudios Picasso/Fábrica de Ficción/Star Line.

REINAS (*literally,* **Queens**)
[Comedy, 2005] Script: Yolanda García Serrano, Joaquín Oristrell. Dir: Manuel Gómez Pereira. Phot: Juan Amoros. Players: Marisa Paredes, Carmen Maura, Veronica Forqué, Mercedes Sampietro. Prod: Warner Bros.

20 CENTÍMETROS
(*literally,* **20 Centimetres**)
[Comedy, 2005] Script and Dir: Ramón Salazar. Phot: Ricardo de Gracia. Players: Monica Cervera, Pablo Puyol, Rossy de Palma, Pilar Bardem. Prod: Aligator/ Estudios Picasso/Fabrica de Ficción.
Sex-change comedy with self-explanatory anatomical title.

EL VIENTO (*literally,* **The Wind**)
[Melodrama, 2005] Script:
Eduardo Mignogna, Graciela
Maglie. Dir: Mignogna. Phot:
Marcelo Camorino. Players:
Federico Luppi, Antonella Costa,
Pablo Cedrón, Mariana Briski.
Prod: Tesela.
Another heartstring-puller from the
Argentine master of melodrama.

GALATASARAY-DEPOR
[Drama, 2005] Script and Dir:
Hannes Stöhr. Phot: Florian
Hoffmeister. Players: Luis Tosar,
Miguel de Lisa, Florian Lukas.
Prod: Filmanova.

7 VIRGENES (*literally,* **7 Virgins**)
[Drama, 2005] Script: Alberto
Rodríguez, Rafael Cobos López.
Dir: Rodriguez. Phot: Alex
Catalán. Players: Juan José
Ballesta, Vicente Romero, Jesús
Carroza. Prod: La Zanfona/Tesela.

Lola Films

Victoria Abril in Carlos Saura's
The Seventh Day

takes her Palestinian boyfriend home, and Joaquín Oristrell's delightful period piece, **Unconscious** (*Inconscientes*), which deals with the birth of psychoanalysis. The dependable Alex de la Iglesia's **Ferpect Crime** (*Crimen ferpecto*) was a typically anarchic look at the horrors of department store life.

Does such eclecticism signal a playful willingness to experiment, or a lack of direction? As the auteur ethos fades, film-makers can be seen genre-hopping wildly. Take Gerardo Herrero, whose career takes in an adventure yarn, studies of thirtysomething angst and political thrillers; or Salvador García Ruiz, whose first film, *Mensaka*, looked at life on the teenage underbelly, but whose third, **Voices in the Night** (*Voces en la noche*), is a stately look at love under Franco. Happily, the lamentable tendency to try and ape Hollywood on Spanish budgets seems to be dwindling. Juan Martínez Moreno's debut, **Two Tough Guys** (*Dos tipos duros*), was a fine example of how US adventure movie motifs can be grafted onto specifically Spanish material to create an entertaining hybrid.

Spaced-out *Astronauts*

Production company caution meant first-time releases were thinner on the ground than a couple of years ago, with fewer companies willing to take risks on explicitly non-commercial fare. One exception is Santi Amodeo's memorably quirky solo debut, **Astronauts** (*Astronautas*), about a recovering junkie, produced by Tesela, which has a healthy commitment to the offbeat.

Other noteworthy debuts were Manuel Martín Cuenca's **The Weakness of the Bolshevik** (*La flaqueza del Bolchevique*), in which an older man dangerously romances a young woman, Xavier Ribera Perpiñá's super-stylish, low-content **A+** and **Out of Body** (*Fuera del cuerpo*) by Vicente Peñarrocha, a tricky, witty parallel-worlds drama. Pau Freixas's sea-based chiller, **Dark Chamber** (*Camera oscura*), and Pablo Malo's moody generation-gap drama, **Cold Winter Sun** (*Frio sol de invierno*), also suggested interesting futures for their directors. Meanwhile the grip of the veterans is as strong as ever, with Manuel Gutiérrez Aragón (**Your Next Life**/*La vida que te espera*), Vicente Aranda (*Carmen*) and Carlos Saura (**The Seventh Day**/*El séptimo día*) all turning in work that ranks with their finest.

A minor triumph has been the local success of two tentative attempts to break into new territory – big budget animation – with **El Cid: The Legend** (*El Cid: la leyenda*) and **The Three Kings** (*Los reyes magos*). Wresting power from the likes of *Finding Nemo* at the box-office was always going to be a challenge over Xmas 2003, but these two put the Pixar fish firmly back in the paella.

The A-Team

And then, of course, there is Spain's two-man A-Team: Pedro Almodóvar and Alejandro Amenábar. Almodóvar, of course, is now a figure so immense that he casts much of the rest of the Spanish industry into shadow – at least as far as the English-speaking world is concerned. **Bad Education** (*La mala educación*), his typically sumptuous take on the disastrous consequences of a Catholic education, opened Cannes and was better received abroad than at home.

Fele Martínez, left, and Gael García Bernal in **Bad Education**

In Spain, 2004 will be remembered as Amenábar's year. With **The Sea Inside** (*Mar adentro*), his potently emotional, universally praised exploration of the life and death of the real-life quadriplegic Ramón Sampedro, Amenábar, heretofore a fabricator of sophisticated genre pieces, revealed an unsuspected maturity and sensitivity. As Sampedro, Javier Bardem confirmed his reputation as one of Europe's finest actors and took Best Actor at Venice. A film that does many of the things to your heart and mind that films are supposed to, *The Sea Inside* represents an accomplishment to which much of the rest of the Spanish industry should aspire.

JONATHAN HOLLAND (jphollandjp@yahoo.es) is *Variety*'s film reviewer in Spain.

El Deseo

Quotes of the Year

"There are many directors who make two movies at the same time – their first, and their last."

JUANMA BAJO ULLOA, *director.*

"I want more Oscars. I need more Oscars!"

PEDRO ALMODÓVAR.

Spanish Film Academy Goya Awards 2004

Film: *Take My Eyes/ Te doy mis ojos* (Iciar Bollain).
Animated Film: *El Cid: the Legend/El Cid: la leyenda.*
Director: Iciar Bollain *(Take My Eyes).*
New Director: Angeles Gonzalez-Sinde *(Sleeping Luck/ La suerte dormida).*
Original Screenplay: *(Take My Eyes).*
Adapted Screenplay: Isabel Coixet *(My Life without Me/Mi vida sin mí).*
Actor: Luis Tosar *(Take My Eyes).*
Actress: Laia Marull *(Take My Eyes).*
Supporting Actor: Eduard Fernandez *(In the City/ En la ciudad).*
Supporting Actress: Candela Peña *(Take My Eyes).*
New Actor: Fernando Tejero *(Football Days/Días de futbol).*
New Actress: Maria Valverde *(The Weakness of the Bolshevik/ La flaqueza del Bolchevique).*
European Film: *Good-Bye, Lenin!* (Germany).
Foreign Spanish-Language Film: *Minimal Stories* (Argentina).

Sri Lanka Amarnath Jayatilaka

The Year's Best Films

Amarnath Jayatilaka's selection:

Forest Monastery
(Somaratna Disanayaka)

Mansion by the Lake
(Lester James Peries)

Wind Bird
(Inoka Sathyanganee)

The Garden (Sumitra Peries)

The Intruders
(Sudath Rohana)

Recent Films

WEKANDA WALAWWA
(Mansion by the Lake)
[Drama, 2003] Script: Somaweera
Senanayake, based on Chekhov's
The Cherry Orchard. Dir: Lester
James Peries. Phot: K. A.
Dharmasena. Players: Malini
Fonseka, Vasanthi Chathurani,
Ravindra Randeniya, Sanath
Gunathilaka. Prod: Chandran
Rutnam, Asoka Perrea,
Taprobane Pictures.

LE KIRI KANDULU
(Blood and Tears)
[Drama, 2003] Script and Dir:
Udayakantha Waranasuriya.
Phot: Jayanath Gunawardana.
Players: Nilmini Tennakoon,
Tony Ranasingha, Sanath
Gunatilaka, Sriyani Amarasena.
Prod: Film Vision.

YAKADA PIHATU
(Iron Feathers)
[Drama, 2003] Script and Dir:
Udayakantha Waranasuriya. Phot:
Jayanath Gunawardana. Players:
Ranjan Ramanayaka, Anoja
Weerasinghe, Dilhani Ekanayaka,
Semini Iddamalgoda. Prod: EAP
Films and Theatres Ltd.

Written and directed by Somaratna Disanayaka, **Forest Monastery** (*Suriya arana*) became one of Sri Lanka's biggest recent box-office hits in 2004. Set in the early 1920s, when Ceylon was under British rule, it is the story of a hunter (the versatile Jackson Anthony) who provides food for the people of a village in which he holds great authority. Then a novice Buddhist monk (a fine performance from child actor Dasun Madushanka) leaves the monastery of the title, enters the village and teaches loving kindness to all beings – including animals – and under his influence the villagers stop eating meat, threatening the hunter's dominance.

Meanwhile the novice and the hunter's son (played by Anthony's real-life child Sajitha Anuththara) become friends and release the animals that he traps. Ultimately the hunter is converted and allows his boy to become a novice. The film, well photographed by Channa Deshapriya, shows how goodness can change lives.

Lester James Peries achieved another first for Sri Lankan cinema when his loose adaptation of Chekhov's *The Cherry Orchard*, **Mansion by the Lake** (*Wekanda walawwa*) became the country's first film to have a commercial release in France. The widow Sujatha (veteran actress Malini Fonseka) rejoins her brother at the family's vast home, beside a lake in which years earlier her son had accidentally drowned. It is a location in which memories haunt a group of complex characters, including Sujatha's daughter, Aruni,

Jackson Anthony, left, and Sajitha Anuththara in **Forest Monastery**

hopelessly in love with her tutor, who is more interested in joining the revolutionaries. We also see the devotion of Sita, Sujatha's sister, who has sacrificed any hope of personal happiness by taking on responsibility for the estate.

Peries' wife, Sumitra, made her eighth film, **The Garden** (*Sakman maluwa*), after a break of eight years (half of which she spent in Paris as Sri Lanka's ambassador to France). *The Garden* is the story of middle-aged Tissa (Sanath Gunathilaka), who is obsessed by the produce in his garden. He is married to Prema (Kanchana Mendis), a woman half his age, but their relationship takes an irrevocable turn for the worse when one day a snake comes into the garden and corners Tissa. He asks his wife to kill it but she runs away.

When Tissa's younger brother, Ranjan (newcomer Dinidu Jagoda), a medical student, comes to stay on holiday, Tissa has no time for him but Ranjan confides in Prema and as their relationship develops so do Tissa's jealousy and suspicion, which ultimately reach boiling point. The garden of the title plays a major role in the drama, as does veteran Iranganie Serasingha as Tissa and Ranjan's mother. Her portrayal of this benevolent matriarch binds all the film's relationships together. *The Garden* was released by Ceylon Theatres, the country's oldest distributor, to celebrate its seventy-fifth anniversary.

Success at the first attempt

Several international festivals seleted the debut feature of Inoka Sathyangani, **Wind Bird** (*Sulang kirillie*), the story of a rustic young woman (Damitha Abeyarathna) living away from home and working in a garment factory. She falls pregnant by her lover, a soldier (Linton Semage), who turns out to be married with a pregnant wife. This brutish character somehow finds the money to procure an abortion for his lover, but after going through much anguish she decides that come hell or high water she will have the child.

Another debut was Sudath Rohana's **The Intruders** (*Sudi kaluwara*), another drama set in the days of British colonial rule, which boasted a starry cast. Wilson Harold, a British planter, transforms a natural forest into a coconut estate and falls in love with a local girl, Menike, whose father objects to their proposed inter-racial marriage. When Wilson and his friend, Banda, build the first tiled house in the area, they come into conflict with the immensely powerful village headman, who is dedicated to promoting British political interests.

AMARNATH JAYATILAKA is a writer and film-maker whose latest feature is the drama *A Drop in the Reign of Terror* (2003).

IRASMA
[Drama, 2003] Script, Dir and Prod: Ariyaratna Vithana. Phot: Suminda Weerasinghe. Players: Ama Wijesekara, Iranganie Serasinghe, Duleeka Marapana, Priyankara Ratnayaka.

THANI THATUWEN PIYABANNA
(Flying with One Wing)
[Drama, 2003] Script and Dir: Asoka Handagama. Phot: Channa Deshappriya. Players: Anoma Jinadari. Prod: Sanhinda Films.

DIYAYATA GINDARA
(Flames Beneath the Waves)
[Drama, 2003] Script and Dir: Udaya Kantha Warnasuriya. Phot: K. D. Dayananda. Players: Achala Alless, Amarasiri Kalansuriya, Sanath Gunatilaka, Tony Ranasinghe. Prod: Cine Entertainment Ltd.

Quote of the Year

"After 53 years in films, one begins to wonder how much one knows. And I can tell you one knows very little. I know what I don't know and I don't know what I know."
LESTER JAMES PERIES, *director, accepting an honorary doctorate from Peradeniya University.*

Sweden Gunnar Rehlin

Andreas Wilson in the Oscar-nominated **Evil**

The Year's Best Films

Gunnar Rehlin's selection:
As in Heaven (Kay Pollak)
Day and Night (Simon Staho)
Daybreak (Björn Runge)
A Hole in My Heart
(Lukas Moodysson)
Four Shades of Brown
(Tomas Alfredson)

Mikael Persbrandt and Maria Bonnevie in **Day and Night**

Recent and Forthcoming Films

ETT HÅL I MITT HJÄRTA
(A Hole in My Heart)
[Drama, 2004] Script: Lukas
Moodysson, in collaboration with
Björn Almroth, Sanna Brading,
Thorsten Flinck, Malin
Fornander, Jesper Kurlandsky,
Goran Marjanovic, Karl
Strandlind. Dir: Moodysson.
Players: Almroth, Brading, Flinck,
Marjanovic. Prod: Lars Jonsson,
Memfis Film.

The promising Björn Runge finally achieved a breakthrough. Kay Pollak returned in triumph after a prolonged absence and Lukas Moodysson directed his most relentlessly grim and provocative film to date. These were the three directors making waves in Swedish cinema in 2003-04. This survey begins, however, with the biggest hit of autumn 2003: Mikael Håfström's **Evil** (*Ondskan*), a very well-made adaptation of a bestseller about bullying at a boarding school. It was later named Best Film at the Golden Bugs and nominated for the Best Foreign-Language Film Oscar. Håfstrom was promptly signed up by Miramax to direct *Derailed*, starring Clive Owen and Jennifer Aniston.

Daniel Lind Lagerlöf's **Miffo** was also a big autumn hit. Its charming, comical story of a spoilt young man falling in love with a vulgar girl in a wheelchair was embraced by critics and audiences. Anders Nilsson's **The Third Wave** (*Den tredje vågen*), the final part in a trilogy about the escalating violence in Europe, was also a hit, though it proved less popular than the first two parts. The season's fourth biggest hit was **Slim Sussie** (*Smala Sussie*), a very funny and vulgar gangster comedy directed by Ulf Malmros and set in the rural region where he grew up.

The two big disasters of 2003 were Kjell Grede's **Make Believe** (*Kommer du med mig då*) and Christina Olofsson's **A Different Way** (*Hannah med H*). Veteran Grede's return to cinema, about a man and a woman who were friends as kids and meet again as adults, was booed by the critics and shunned by cinemagoers, as was Olofsson's account of a young girl's search for her identity. Results were better for Peter Dalle's innovative comedy, **Illusive Tracks** (*Skenbart*), which in glorious black-and-white followed an eventful journey between Stockholm and Berlin in 1945.

Daybreak is a breakthrough

Björn Runge's dark drama **Daybreak** (*Om jag vänder mig om*) opened in November 2003 and was generally praised by critics as his breakthrough film. A bleak but ultimately optimistic story of a handful of unhappy, desperate people in a small Swedish town, it went on to win four Golden Bugs, including Best Director and Actress (Ann Petrén) and at Berlin in 2004 took the Silver Bear for Best Acting Ensemble and The Blue Angel for Best European Film.

Several new Swedish films had their premieres at the Gothenburg Film Festival in January 2004. Richard Hobert's medieval drama, **Three Suns** (*Tre solar*), was venomously attacked, while Tomas Alfredson's dark comedy, **Four Shades of Brown** (*Fyra nyanser av brunt*), was justly praised. This three-hour epic tells four separate stories, all dealing with father-son relationships and featuring the Killinggänget comedy group, who have built up a cult following through a series of funny TV programmes.

Gothenburg also premiered Teresa Fabik's excellent **The Ketchup Effect** (*Hip hip hora*), a semi-autobiographical story about a young girl who is sexually assaulted and then labelled as the school slut. The film has travelled to several international festivals, and Fabik, still under 30, is a name to watch.

In August 2004, Simon Staho's **Day and Night** (*Dag och natt*) showed what you can do with artistic integrity, vision and a stellar cast. It depicts the last day of a man's life, from morning until his suicide at night, and takes place entirely within his car. Shot with just two fixed-camera set-ups it nevertheless feels faster and more alive than many movies that use elaborate camera moves. Mikael Persbrandt took the lead and gave what may well be a career-defining performance.

The same could be said for Mikael Nyqvist's leading portrayal in Kay Pollak's **As in Heaven** (*Såsom i himmelen*), his first film for 18 years. This deeply felt drama about a man who wants to move people's hearts with his music and finally succeeds after returning to his home village in northern Sweden was an instant critical and commercial hit, becoming, by November, the most popular Swedish release of the year. Its selection as national contender for the 2004 Oscars was a formality; of all the year's films, this was the one that seemed sure to find the warmest welcome in the US.

Anders Birkeland/Sonet

Villagers are inspired by music in **As in Heaven**

GITARRMONGOT
(The Guitar Mongoloid)
[Drama, 2004] Script and Dir: Ruben Ostlund. Phot: Tibor Gent. Players: Erik Rutstrom, Ola Sandstig, Britt-Marie Andersson, Julia Persdotter. Prod: Kalle Bohman, Anna Sohlman, Hinden Lanna.
Shot over several years, the film follows several non-conformist characters.

THE DROWNING GHOST
STRANDVASKAREN
(The Drowning Ghost)
[Horror, 2004] Script: Mikael Håfström, Vasa. Dir: Håfström. Phot: Peter Mokrosinski. Players: Rebecca Hemse, Kjell Bergqvist, Jesper Salén. Prod: Hans Lonnerheden, Greta Films.
Students are being murdered at a haunted boarding school.

BOMBAY DREAMS
[Youth drama, 2004] Script: Lena Koppel, Marten Skogman. Dir: Koppel. Phot: Kjell S. Koppel. Players: Gayathri Mudigonda, Nadine Kirschon, Sissela Kyle, Peter Dalle, Linn Staberg. Prod: Patrick Ryborn, SS Fladen.
A teenage girl adopted from India tries to arrange a meeting with her biological mother.

RANCID
[Thriller, 2004] Script: Jesper, Patrick and Jack Ersgard. Dir: Jack Ersgard. Phot: Kjell Lagerroos. Players: Matthew Settle, Fay Masterson, Currie Graham, Siena Goines. Prod: Peter Possne, Sonet Films.
An innocent man is hunted by the police and drawn into conspiracies.

THE QUEEN OF
SHEBA'S PEARLS
[Drama, 2004] Script and Dir: Colin Nutley. Phot: Jens Fischer. Players. Helena Bergstrom, Rolf Lassgard, Rollo Weeks, Peter Vaughn. Prod: Nutley, Sweetwater.
Semi-autobiographical story of a young boy growing up in post-war England.

Per-Anders Jörgensen/Memfis Film

Sofia Helin as Mia in **Masjävlar**

MASJÄVLAR
[Comedy-drama, 2004] Script and Dir: Maria Blom. Phot: Peter Mokrosinski. Players: Sofia Helin, Ann Petrén, Kajsa Ernst, Barbro Enberg, Joakim Lindblad. Prod: Lars Jönsson, Memfis Film.
Chaos ensues when three sisters are reunited for their father's seventieth birthday.

MACBETH
[Drama, 2004] Script: William Shakespeare. Dir: Bo Landin, Alex Scherpf. Players: Anitta Suikkari, Irene Lansman, Elisabeth H. Blind, Toivo Lukkari, Nils Henrik Buljo. Prod: Landin, Scandinature.
Macbeth relocated to Lapland. Partly shot at the Ice Hotel, Jukkasjarvi.

INNAN FROSTEN
(Before the Frost)
[Thriller, 2005] Dir: Kjell-Ake Andersson. Phot: Olof Johnson. Players: Krister Henriksson, Johanna Sallstrom, Ola Rapace. Prod: Lasse Bjorkmann, Ole Sondberg, Yellowbird Films.
Renowned police detective Kurt Wallander and his daughter hunt a brutal killer.

Reza Bagher's **Popular Music** (*Populärmusik från Vittula*) was a reasonably successful adaptation of the best-selling – and supposedly unfilmable – autobiographical novel by Mikael Niemi about growing up in the north of Sweden in the 1960s and discovering music through The Beatles. Still, it lacked many of the ingredients that had made the novel a raunchy must-read.

Heart of darkness

Lukas Moodysson alienated scores of his previously loyal audience with **A Hole in My Heart** (*Ett hål i mitt hjärta*). Set in a dingy apartment, it follows the shooting of an amateur porn film by director Rickard (Thorsten Flinck) and 'stars' Eric (Goran Marjanovic) and Tess (Sanna Brading). Rickard's introverted Goth son, Eric (Björn Almroth), watches as the trio drive each other to more and more outrageous extremes. Featuring realistic (but not explicit) sex scenes, full frontal nudity, sexually degrading behaviour and mutilation, it is not for the squeamish and will provoke heated debates in countries where it gets past the censors. Still, it confirms Moodysson as the most interesting young director working in Scandinavia today.

The big industry debate in autumn 2004 centred on the attempt by Svensk Filmindustri, Sweden's largest cinema owner, to acquire the cinemas of its principal but struggling competitor, Sandrew Metronome. In 2003, 56% of all paid admissions were at Svensk-owned screens, while Sandrew Metronome took 13% of the market and put its circuit up for sale. Svensk immediately stepped forward but the prospect that it might obtain an even greater hold on the exhibition market led the proposed takeover to be referred to the government. At press time, a decision was still pending, but Svensk had promised that if the deal went ahead, Sandrew's cinemas would be used to show arthouse fare rather than obvious blockbusters.

GUNNAR REHLIN (rehlin@pressart.se) is a Swedish film critic and journalist for newspapers, magazines and television and the author of a book about Stellan Skarsgård.

Gong by Bae Tae-Su

Per-Anders Jörgensen/Memfis Film

Björn Almroth as Eric in **A Hole in My Heart**

SANDOR SLASH IDA
*[Youth drama, 2005] Script:
Sara Kadefors. Dir: Henrik
Georgsson. Phot: Anders Bohman.
Players: Andrej Lunusjkin,
Aliette Opheim, Lia Boyssen.
Prod: Karl-Fredrik Ulfvung,
Breidablick Films.*
Two lonely teenagers get
connected via the internet.

VINNARE OCH FORLORARE
(Winners and Losers)
[Comedy, 2005] Script: Sara

*Heldt. Dir: Kjell Sundvall. Phot:
Goran Hallberg. Players: Frida
Hallgren, Daniel Gustavsson,
Mona Malm.*
Traditional comic love story set
at a racing track.

MINNA WAS HERE
*[Drama, 2005] Script and Dir:
Kristina Humle. Phot: Marek
Wieser. Player: Hanna Ohranen.
Prod: Lars Jonsson, Memfis Film.*
Minna, 19, tries to take control
of her life.

UNTITLED HAKAN NESSER PROJECT
*[Drama, 2005] Script: Martin
Asphaug, Hakan Nesser. Dir:
Asphaug. Phot: Philip Ogaard.
Players: Jonas Karlsson, Helena
af Sandeberg. Prod: Valdemar
Bergendahl, Svensk Filmindustri.*
Two brothers meet a beautiful
girl during a summer of sex
and murder.

SOM MAN BÄDDAR
(The Best Daddy in the World)
*[Comedy, 2005] Dir: Maria
Essén. Phot: P.-A. Svensson.
Players: Mikael Persbrandt,
Alexander Skarsgård. Prod:
Lennart Dunér, Omega Film.*
A married father tries to combine
full-time work and paternity leave.

Per-Anders Jörgensen/Memfis

Henna Ohranen as Minna in
Minna Was Here

Golden Bugs 2003
Presented in Göteborg on January 26, 2004.

Film: *Ondskan/Evil*
(Prod: Hans Lönnerheden, Ingemar Leijonborg).
Director: Björn Runge
(*Om jag vänder mig om/Daybreak*).
Actress: Ann Petrén (*Daybreak*).
Actor: Jonas Karlsson (*Detaljer/Details*)
Supporting Actress: Bibi Andersson
(*Elina – Som om jag inte fanns/Elina*)
Supporting Actor: Ingvar Hirdwall (*Daybreak*).
Screenplay: Björn Runge (*Daybreak*).
Cinematography: Peter Mokrosinski (*Evil*).
Foreign-Language Film: *The Hours*
(Stephen Daldry).
Short Film: *Min skäggiga mamma/My Bearded
Mother* (Maria Hedman).
Documentary: *Du ska nog se att det går
över/Don't You Worry, It Will Probably Pass*
(Cecilia Neant-Falk).

Svensk Filmindustri/Kobal

*Erland Josephson, winner of the Golden Bug for Lifetime
Achievement, in* **Faithless** *(2000)*

Production Design: Anna Asp (*Evil*).
Sound: Bo Persson, Stefan Ljungberg
(*Kommer du med mig då/Make Believe*).
Lifetime Achievement: Erland Josephson
(actor).
Ingmar Bergman Award: Klaus Härö (director).

Switzerland Michael Sennhauser

The Year's Best Films

Michael Sennhauser's
selection:

***Jagged Harmonies –
Bach vs. Frederick II***
(Dominique de Rivaz)

South of the Clouds
(J.F. Amiguet)

Strähl (Manuel Flurin Hendry)

***When the Right One Comes
Along*** (Oliver Paulus,
Stefan Hillebrand)

Trouble in Parliament
(Docu. Jean-Stéphane Bron)

Recent and Forthcoming Films

ABSOLUT
*[Drama, 2004] Script and Dir:
Romed Wyder. Phot: Denis
Jutzeler. Players: Vincent Bonillo,
Irene Godel, François Nadin,
Delphine Lanza, Ulysse Prévost,
Véronique Mermoud. Prod:
Wyder, Blow-up Film Production/
Télévision Suisse Romande/Almaz
Film Productions/Laïka Films*

Michael Koch in **Ready, Steady, Charlie!**

ACHTUNG, FERTIG, CHARLIE!
(Ready, Steady, Charlie!)
*[Comedy, 2003] Script: Michael
Sauter, David Keller. Dir: Mike
Eschmann. Phot: Roland Schmid.
Players: Michael Koch, Melanie
Winiger, Mia Aegerter, Marco
Rima, Martin Rapold. Prod:*

After years of battling its so-so reputation among the natives, Swiss fiction cinema is about to regain its domestic audience. Or so it seems. While the general European decline in attendance figures clearly hit Switzerland in 2003, one comedy broke records: **Ready, Steady, Charlie!** (*Achtung, fertig, Charlie!*) – the tailor-made product of a new generation of producers.

Young producer Lukas Hobi set out to make an *American Pie*-style comedy for teenagers and hired fledgling director Mike Eschmann and a cast led by Marco Rima, a renowned Swiss stand-up comedian, Melanie Winiger, a former Miss Switzerland, and several fresh young faces. The plot involved army boot-camp, a love triangle and some sex-starved potheads battling it out with the elite troops of an adjoining army camp. With the unwitting assistance of the Swiss Army, which loaned locations and equipment but ended up publicly denouncing the finished product as a base vilification of army morale and values, *Charlie!* took young audiences by storm and with 529,496 admissions reached third place in the year's top 10.

Because *Charlie!* was a blatantly commercial product rather than customary, auteur-driven fare, it caused quite a ruckus among the defendants of Swiss art cinema. This is mainly because this kind of crowd-pleaser thrives on *succès cinéma*, the firmly established box-office dependent subsidy system. That one movie should have attracted more than half the total audience for Swiss films in a year when no fewer than 180 (!) local releases clamoured for a share of the market is not really all that surprising, because in Switzerland, as in every other little film country, the hits are heavily outnumbered by the misses. That figure of 180 (including shorts, documentaries, old and new releases and limited screenings) is more notable.

Where does the financing come from for so many films, since they clearly cannot be sustained by the domestic market alone? The answer is subsidies and self-exploitation, which allowed for the production of 15 new fiction films in 2003, of which six were wholly Swiss-financed.

The success of *Charlie!* was not the only sign that there is more professional commercially savvy film-making going on than in previous decades. **When the Right One Comes Along** (*Wenn der Richtige kommt*), one of the more impressive fiction films, was made by two

Arcan Arican, left, and Isolde Fischer in **When the Right One Comes Along**

former film school trainees, Oliver Paulus and Stefan Hillebrand, who tell the story of a German cleaning woman who falls in love with a Turkish guardsman. While he is merely being polite, she is starting to dream and when she learns that he has left for Turkey, she undertakes the trip of her life. In their working lives, Paulus and Hillebrand move between Germany and Switzerland, using available funding with a mixture of the old auteur approach and professional panache.

Another fiction film in this mould is Manuel Flurin Hendry's **Strähl**. This fast-paced tale involves Strähl (Roeland Wiesnekker), a divorced, substance-abusing narcotics cop who falls madly in love with an energetic, foul-mouthed young junkie (Johanna Bantzer). While the plot is somewhat reminiscent of similar TV fare, the urban realism and the intensity of Wiesnekker and Bantzer hit all the right notes with urban audiences and critics and claimed 27,000 admissions in the German-speaking market.

Johanna Bantzer, left, and Roeland Wiesnekker in **Strähl**

Lukas Hobi, Zodiac Pictures/ Sabotage Films/Schweizer Fernsehen DRS/Impuls Home Entertainment/Teleclub/ Centauri Media.

AU LARGE DE BAD RAGAZ (Off Bad Ragaz)
[Romantic thriller, 2004] Script and Dir: François-Christophe Marzal. Phot: Séverine Barde. Players: Mathieu Amalric, Julia Batinova, Jean-Luc Bideau, Maria Schneider. Prod: Light Night Production/Gemini Films/ Télévision Suisse Romande.

DOWNTOWN SWITZERLAND
[Documentary, 2004] Dir: Christian Davi, Stefan Haupt, Kaspar Kasics, Fredi M. Murer. Phot: Pio Corradi, Jann Erne, Kasics, Pierre Mennel, Filip Zumbrunn. Prod: Fontana Film/Extra Film/ FMM Film/Hugofilm.

FERIEN IM DUETT (Holiday in Duo)
[Documentary, 2004] Script and Dir: Dieter Gränicher. Prod: momenta film/Schweizer Fernsehen DRS/Teleclub.

THE GIANT BUDDHAS
[Documentary, 2004] Dir: Christian Frei. Phot: Peter Indergand. Prod: PS Film/Christian Frei Filmproduktion.

IM NORDWIND (North Wind)
[Drama, 2004] Script and Dir: Bettina Oberli. Phot: Stéphane Kuthy. Players: André Jung, Judith Hofmann, Aiko Scheu, Corsin Gaudenz, Peter Arens, Jean-Pierre Cornu.

LOVE EXPRESS
[Comedy, 2004] Script: Elena Hazanov, Georges Gueirerro. Dir: Hazanov. Phot: Jean-Paul Cardinaux. Players: Mathilda May, Vincent Winterhalter. Prod: Navarro Films/Télévision Suisse Romande/Arte.

MAIS IM BUNDESHUUS
(Trouble in Parliament)
[Documentary, 2003] Script and Dir: Jean-Stéphane Bron. Phot: Eric Stitzel. Prod: Ciné Manufacture CMS/SRG SSR idée suisse.

MEIN NAME IST BACH
(Jagged Harmonies –
Bach vs. Frederick II)
[Drama, 2003] Script and Dir: Dominique de Rivaz. Phot: Ciro Cappellari. Players: Vadim Glowna, Jürgen Vogel, Karoline Herfurth, Anatole Taubman. Prod: CAB Productions/Pandora Filmproduktion/Twenty Twenty Vision/Télévision Suisse Romande/WDR – Westdeutscher Rundfunk Köln/Arte.

MONTE GRANDE
[Documentary, 2004] Dir: Franz Reichle. Phot: Reichle, Matthias Kälin. Prod: T&C Film.

NOTRE MUSIQUE (Our Music)
[Drama, 2004] Script and Dir: Jean-Luc Godard. Phot: Julien Hirsch. Players: Nade Dieu, Sarah Adler, Godard. Prod: Ruth Waldburger, Film/Avventura Films/Périphéria/JLG Films/Télévision Suisse Romande.

RICORDARE ANNA
(literally, **The Search for Anna)**
[Drama, 2004] Script: Walo Deuber, Josy Meier. Dir: Deuber. Phot: Stefan Runge, Knut Schmitz. Players: Mathias Gnädinger, Bibiana Beglau, Pippo Pollina, Suly Röthlisberger, Margareta von Kraus. Prod: Dschoint Ventschr Filmproduktion/MTM Medien & Television München/Dodici Dicembre.

SNOW WHITE
[Drama, 2005] Script: Michael Sauter, Samir. Dir: Samir. Phot:

Veteran French-speaking Swiss director Jean-François Amiguet's **South of the Clouds** (*Au sud des nuages*) is a poetic 'rail movie' that follows a stubborn old mountain man on his train journey to China and self-discovery. Amiguet is a slow worker and proud of it. In 20 years he has made only five very accomplished films and he considers his pace his personal rebellion against our speed-crazy times. The Swiss Film Prize 2004 for the best work of fiction went to Dominique de Rivaz's **Jagged Harmonies – Bach vs. Frederick II** (*Mein Name ist Bach*), a labour of love by an energetic director who has overcome career barriers (including linguistic ones). Her stylised (some thought stiff), very playful encounter between the old Johann Sebastian Bach and the young Frederick II of Prussia is a Western in classical surroundings, a unique and peculiar film.

A good form of box-office *Death*

The real winners, commercially at least, were once again documentaries. Jean-Stéphane Bron's **Trouble in Parliament** (*Mais im Bundeshuus*) was an intense and humorous journey with several politicians through their legislative debates, and unexpectedly reached more than 100,000 people (for once, a German-language film found audiences in both French- and German-speaking regions).

With more than 250,000 tickets sold at home and abroad by August 2004, Stefan Haupt's **Elisabeth Kübler-Ross – Facing Death** (*Elisabeth Kübler-Ross – Dem Tod ins Gesicht sehen*) set a new record for a Swiss documentary. The film follows the life story of Swiss-born MD Elisabeth Kübler, her pioneering work on death and dying in modern society, her almost guru-like status in the 1970s and finally her lonely days in the US and the paradox that she, who helped thousands accepting their own death, seemed unable to die for a very long time. She finally passed away in August 2004. In Germany it sold 140,000 tickets, and 40,000 people saw it in Austria.

A small but very peculiar documentary, premiered during the Locarno Critics' Week, was Dieter Gränicher's **Holiday in Duo**. He instructed four young couples on how to use a digital video camera and sent them off on their holidays. After their return he combined their video diaries with retrospective interviews and put together a delightful document on Swiss people abroad.

Finally, 2004 saw an important development in cultural politics. The two film promotion agencies of the Swiss Film Centre and the national culture foundation, Pro Helvetia, have combined their efforts and now operate nationally and internationally as Swiss Films.

MICHAEL SENNHAUSER (info@prevu.ch) is film editor at Swiss National Radio and joint head of Critics' Week at the Locarno International Film Festival.

Andreas Hutter. Players: Julie Fournier, Carlos Leal, Stefan Gubser, Stefan Kurt, Pascal Ulli, Patrick Rapold, Martin Rapold. Prod: Susann Rüdlinger, Samir, Dschoint Ventschr Filmproduktion/Filmhaus/ Schweizer Fernsehen DRS/ Praesens Film/Topic Film.

STRÄHL
[Drama, 2004] Script: Michael Sauter, David Keller. Dir: Manuel Flurin Hendry. Phot: Filip Zumbrunn. Players: Roeland Wiesnekker, Johanna Bantzer, Nderim Hajrullahu, Manuel Löwensberg, Mike Müller. Prod: Samir, Dschoint Ventschr Filmproduktion/ZDF.

TOUT UN HIVER SANS FEU (All Winter without Fire)
[Drama, 2004] Script: Pierre-Pascal Rossi. Dir: Greg Zglinski. Phot: Witold Plociennik. Players: Aurélien Recoing, Marie

Matheron, Gabriela Muskala, Blerim Gjoci, Nathalie Boulin, Antonio Buil, Michel Voïta. Prod: Gérard Ruey, Jean-Louis Porchet, CAB Productions/Mars Entertainment/Télévision Suisse Romande/RTBF/Arte/TVP Telewizja Polska.

ULTIMA THULE
[Docu-drama, 2005] Script and Dir: Hans-Ulrich Schlumpf. Phot: Pio Corradi. Players: Stefan Kurt, Barbara Auer, Patrick Frey. Prod: Ariane Film.

DIE VOGELPREDIGT ODER DAS SCHREIEN DER MÖNCHE (The Crying of the Friars, Preaching to the Birds)
[Tragi-comedy, 2004] Script, Dir and Phot: Clemens Klopfenstein. Players: Klopfenstein, Max Rüdlinger, Polo Hofer, Sabine Timoteo, Ursula Andress. Prod: Ombra Film/Pegasos Film.

WENN DER RICHTIGE KOMMT (When the Right One Comes Along)
[Comedy, 2003] Script and Dir: Oliver Paulus, Stefan Hillebrand. Phot: Mathias Schick. Players: Isolde Fischer, Helga Grimme, Can Sengül, Tülay Gönen, Arcan Arican. Prod: Oliver Paulus, Motorfilm Filmproduktionen/ Frischfilm Produktion/Schicke Bilder/Sprint Film, Far Horizons.

AU SUD DES NUAGES (South of the Clouds)
[Drama, 2003] Script: Anne Gonthier, Jean-François Amiguet. Dir: Amiguet. Phot: Hugues Ryffel. Players: Bernard Verley, François Morel, Maurice Aufair, Jean-Luc Borgeat. Prod: Langfilm/Zagora Films/Native/ Télévision Suisse Romande.

Elisabeth Kübler-Ross

ELISABETH KÜBLER-ROSS – DEM TOD INS GESICHT SEHEN (Elisabeth Kübler-Ross – Facing Death)
[Documentary, 2003] Script and Dir: Stefan Haupt. Phot: Jann Erne, Christian Davi, Patrick Lindenmaier. Prod: Haupt, Fontana Film/Schweizer Fernsehen DRS.

Vadim Glowna as Bach in **Jagged Harmonies**

Taiwan Stephen Cremin

The Year's Best Films

Stephen Cremin's selection:
20 30 40 (Sylvia Chang)
Formula 17 (D.J. Chen)
Gift of Life (Wu Yi-feng)
Goodbye, Dragon Inn
(Tsai Ming-liang)
Ocean Fever (Chen Lung-nan)

Recent and Forthcoming Films

**FU SHENG RUO MENG
(Free as Love)**
*[Drama, 2004] Script and Dir:
Alice Wang. Phot: Frank Kun.
Players: Kelly Huang, Alice Wang,
Ariel Lin, Duncan Chow, Tuan
Chun-hao, Ha Ri-su. Prod: Lin
Hsu, Core Image Production Co.*
Sequel to *Love Me If You Can*.
After the drowning of Ying, her
junior high school classmate Tai,
now a loveless police detective,
arrives in the harbour town to
investigate the murder and the
mystery of Ying's emotions for
cousin San.

KUANG FANG (Uninhibited)
*[Youth drama, 2004] Script and
Dir: Leste Chen. Phot: Yao Hung-
yi. Players: Huang Hung-sheng,
Han Yi-pang, Hsu An-an, Justine
Chi, Ke Huan-ju. Prod: Chen
Wei, 3X Films.*
Framed by a suicide and a
wedding, and divided into four
chapters – "Death", "Hair",
"Tattoos" and "Photos" – the
film charts three aimless high
school friends entering adulthood
in city of Taipei.

**MENG YOU XIA WEI YI
(Holiday Dreaming)**
*[Youth drama, 2004] Script and
Dir: Hsu Fu-chun. Phot: Ali
Chen. Players: Tony Yang, Huang*

The roller-coaster ride has continued for Taiwanese cinema. A new low for local films at the box-office in 2003 was followed by a period of potentially exciting change in 2004, which saw the emergence of film-makers in their twenties, several documentaries become hits and the industry acknowledge the validity of High-Definition (HD) as a medium for theatrical features.

The market share for local films in 2003 dropped from 2% in 2002 to less than 0.4%, mainly because of the dearth of new features in the first six months, as producers waited for the belated announcement of the annual round of government subsidies. By year's end, only 12 narrative features had been completed, only half of which were shot on film. Three were produced by Central Motion Picture Corporation (CMPC), Taiwan's only surviving film studio: Yin Chi's black comedy, **Comes the Black Dog** (*Hei gou lai liao*), about two brothers who stage a mock funeral, Alex Yang's relationship drama, **Taipei 21** (*Taibei er yi*), exploring a young couple's seven-year itch, and Tsai Min-chin's animated *Butterfly Lovers: Leon and Jo* (*Hu die meng: Liang Shanbo yu Zhu Yingtai*), which modernises a classic of Chinese literature.

All three had commercial ambitions, but failed at the box-office. **Butterfly Lovers**, CMPC's biggest project of the year, recouped just 1% of its reported $5m budget in Taipei, despite an extensive marketing campaign, a voice cast of popular singers and a coveted New Year release date. It fuses traditional 2D animation and Chinese painting, but the look was not visually stimulating enough for an audience accustomed to Pixar's 3D animation style. Tsai Ming-liang's meditation on the end of a cinematic era with the closing of Taiwan's oldest movie theatre, **Goodbye, Dragon Inn** (*Bu san*), is not an obvious commercial choice and yet became the highest-grossing local film of 2003 nationwide. It was initially conceived as an omnibus film incorporating actor Lee Kang-sheng's directorial debut, **The Missing** (*Bu jian*), whose aesthetics are clearly influenced by Tsai in the tale of an elderly woman desperately searching for her missing grandson, but both were released as separate features.

Entering 2004, the one sure bet was actor-director Sylvia Chang's romantic comedy **20 30 40** (picked up for international distribution by Columbia Pictures Film Production Asia). Despite high production values, an all-star cast and big-name cameos, the film grossed just $130,000 in Taipei. Releasing it close to Taiwan's presidential

Angelica Lee Sinje in 20 30 40

election did not help, but it also lacked the sassiness that might have attracted younger audiences. Two other highly anticipated projects that underperformed in 2004 were Hsu Hsiao-ming's **Love of May** (*Wu yue zhi lian*) and Yin Chi's **La Mélodie d'Hélène** (*Xin lian*), produced by Taiwan's leading producers, Peggy Chiao and Hsu Li-kong, respectively. Both employed foreign location shoots for romances that crossed international borders, but failed to attract young audiences who increasingly demand films with a local flavour.

7th Grade, and first-class

The hottest topic among local commentators in 2004 was the emergence of the so-called "7th Graders", directors born in or after 1980. Most notable among them are D.J. Chen (b. 1980), who directed surprise hit **Formula 17** (*Shi qi sui de tian kong*), and Leste Chen (b. 1981), whose **Uninhibited** (*Kuang fang*) competed in Venice's International Critics' Week. *Formula 17* became a talking point because of its young director, low budget ($150,000) and depiction of a homosexual utopia devoid of women or heterosexual men. An audience dominated by teenage girls embraced the film's simple and pure love story, making an overnight star of leading actor Tony Yang and catapulting the Taipei gross to $180,000. Yang has since appeared in two new features by first-time directors.

The success of these young directors has encouraged new investors to enter the industry, including electronics group BenQ, food conglomerate Uni-President Group and DVD distributor Film Mart Digital. In part this is thanks to the introduction of government tax incentives but it also reflects a renewed confidence in the profitability of local film.

One cannot talk about Taiwanese film without mentioning Alice Wang and Chu Yen-ping, currently responsible for 50% of local production.

Hung-sheng, Chang Chun-ning, Huang Tai-an. Prod: Liang Hung-chih, Good Film Co./Film Mart Digital Co. Ltd.
Ah-zhou and Hsiao-kuei are ordered to spend their five-day leave from military service tracking down Kuen-he, who has deserted with a loaded gun. Ah-zhou also has a personal mission: to find Chen Shin-shin, a girl who has suddenly reappeared in his dreams.

TIAN BIAN YI DUO YUN
(Wayward Wind)
[*Musical comedy, 2005*] Script and Dir: Tsai Ming-liang. Phot: Liao Pen-jung. Players: Lee Kang-sheng, Chen Shiang-chyi, Lu Yi-ching. Prod: Homegreen Films/ Arena Films/Arte France Cinema.
As Taipei suffers a serious water crisis, Shiang-chyi begins a romantic relationship with watch-seller Hsiao-kang, who keeps his new career as a porn actor secret even as he shoots a video in a neighbouring apartment.

WU YUE ZHI LIAN
(Love of May)
[*Romance, 2004*] Script: Huang Chih-hsiang. Dir: Hsu Hsiao-ming. Phot: Han Yun-chung. Players: Berlin Chen, Liu Yifei, Tin Fung, Mayday. Prod: Peggy Chiao, Arc Light Films Co.
Ah-lei is the younger brother of Shi-tou, guitarist of Taiwan's leading rock band Mayday. Answering an e-mail from a fan in Beijing, Xuan Xuan, he pretends to be lead singer Ah-hsing. A correspondence begins. But then Xuan Xuan arrives in Taipei for a Mayday concert.

XI HUAN NI XI HUAN WO
(I Love How You Love Me)
[*Drama, 2004*] Script: Lee Jia-ying, Yang Kun-jou. Dir: Chu Yen-ping. Players: Jimmy Lin, Ambrose Hsu, Kristy Yang, Liu Yifei. Prod: Chu Yen-ping, Yen Ping Films Production Pte. Ltd.
Han-wen, a teacher at a Buddhist monastery in the mountains, finds his inner peace disturbed by the arrival of sexy teacher Yue-shan.

XIN LIAN (La Mélodie d'Hélène)
[Romantic drama, 2004] Script: Hsu Li-kong, Yin Chi, Christin Huang, Wang Min-hsia. Dir: Yin. Phot: Shen Jui-yuan. Players: Tarcy Su, Chang Yung-chih, Niki Wu, Lin You-wei. Prod: Hsu Li-kong, Yeh Ju-feng, Zoom Hunt Intl. Prods. Co./Uni-President Dream Parks Corp.
Student Lo-ning discovers arrogant pianist Daniel, her music professor, drunk and unconscious and takes him back to his hotel. Despite his growing feelings for Lo-ning, he must go to Paris to finish a composition for former lover Hélène.

YAN GUANG SI SHE GE WU TUAN (Splendid Float)
[Musical drama, 2004] Script and Dir: Zero Chou. Phot: Hoho Liu. Players: James Chen, Chung Yi-ching, Ma Yu-hang, Lai Yu-chi, Wang Ming-chang, Wawa Wang. Prod: Li Chih-chiang, Cheng Hai-po/The 3rd Vision Films Ltd.
By day, Rose is a Taoist priest presiding over funerals. By night, he is drag queen "Rose". He falls in love with fisherman Sunny.

YONG BAO DA BAI XIONG (Bear Hug)
[Family drama, 2004] Script: Huang Li-ming, Wang Shaodi. Dir: Wang. Phot: Chin Ting-chang. Players: Chen Kuan-po, Hung Hao-hsuan, Wang Chien-min, Chou You-ting, Chen Shiang-chyi, Chen Chi-hsia. Prod: Huang Li-ming, Rice Film Intl. Co. Ltd.
Da-jun, nine, has yet to come to terms with his parents' divorce and takes out his unhappiness on 16-year-old babysitter Yi-fen, who is bullied at school for being overweight.

ZHONG JI XI MEN (West Town Girls)
[Action, 2004] Script: Alice Wang, Hsu Yu-hua. Dir: Wang. Phot: Lee Yi-hsu. Players: Annie Wu, Liliy Hsiao, Cherly Yang. Prod: Lin Hsu, Core Image Production Co.
Porsche returns to Tapei to take control of the weakening West Gate gang.

Tony Yang, left, and Duncan in **Formula 17**

Wang has directed six features in 18 months and Chu has directed or produced eight more. Wang's films are characterised by strong female characters, while Chu's run the gamut from military horror to children's action films. Both work predominantly on HD24p, have fresh casts and explore new genres for Taiwanese cinema.

The box-office success story of 2004 was local documentary cinema. The director of **Gift of Life** (*Sheng ming*), Wu Yi-feng, lived with the survivors of the country's devastating 1999 earthquake for four years. The film was endorsed by Taiwan's president, Chen Shui-bian, and grossed more than $300,000 in Taipei on just two screens. Other successes included **Viva Tonal: The Dance Age** (*Tiao wu shi dai*), Wayne Peng's **Burning Dreams** (*Ge wu zhong guo*) and Chen Lung-nan's **Ocean Fever** (*Hai yang re*), which share a focus on music and/or dance.

Approximately half of local features receive government grants ranging from $90,000 to $450,000. The latest round of subsidies announced in October 2004 prioritised commercial projects by younger directors, a marked departure from previous years. At press time, the most eagerly anticipated feature was Su Chao-pin's high-concept ghost movie, *Silk* (*Gui si*). Although 2003-04 did not fulfill the promises of 2002, the next two years will see the release of new films from internationally renowned masters Hou Hsiao-hsien, Tsai Ming-liang, Lin Cheng-sheng and Edward Yang and present new opportunities for the younger generation to establish themselves in the difficult and volatile Taiwanese market.

STEPHEN CREMIN (asianfilm@mac.com) has programmed Udine Far East Film Festival since 2002, edited the Asian Film Library industry newsletter (2000-01) and directed the London Pan-Asian Film Festival (1998-99).

Taiwan's Golden Horse Awards are listed on p.294.

Thailand Anchalee Chaiworaporn

The Year's Best Films

Anchalee Chaiworaporn's selection:

Last Life in the Universe
(Penek Rattanaruang)
Tropical Malady
(Apichatphong Weerasethakul)
My Girl
(Nithiwat Tharthorn et al.)
The Overture
(Itthisoonthorn Vichailak)
The Letter
(Phaoon Chandharasiri)

Sinitta Boonyasak in **Last Life in the Universe**

Recent and Forthcoming Films

INVISIBLE WAVE (working title)
[Film noir, 2005] Script: Prabda Yoon. Dir: Penek Rattanaruang. Phot: Christopher Doyle. Player: Asano Tadanubo. Prod: Five Stars Production/Fortissimo.
A sushi chef takes a slow journey to hell, full of sex, food and murder.

THE LETTER
[Romance, 2004] Script: Khongdej Jaturontrassamee. Dir: Phaoon Chandharasiri. Players: Atthaphorn Theemakorn, Ann Thongprason. Prod: Sahamongkol Film/Film Hansa.
Dew is in deep grief when she loses her husband, Ton. But she finds he has not totally departed.

Thai cinema has continued its period of rapid, record-breaking expansion. Production doubled from 25 films in 2002 to 48 titles in 2003 (a year in which Thai films claimed about 30% of total box-office of US$87.5m). Some 38 local titles secured theatrical release in the first eight months of 2004. Direct-to-disc movies are also booming (about 10 hit the shelves each month), thanks to the immense popularity of low-priced VCD players.

The most exciting news came when independent idol Apichatphong Weerasethakul had his third work, **Tropical Malady**, selected as the first Thai film ever to compete at Cannes, where it took the Special Jury Prize. Shot in the same jungle as Weerasethakul's previous film, *Blissfully Yours* (shown in Un Certain Regard in 2002), it satirises real-life prejudice against homosexuals, which makes them out to be monsters in Thai society. *Tropical Malady's* success inspired one of the local studios, GMM Pictures, to open a specialised operation for independent production, the Thailand Independent Film-makers' Alliance.

Another first for Thai film came at Venice 2003, which selected Penek Rattanaruang's **Last Life in the Universe**, which tells the unspoken love story between a Japanese librarian (cult star Asana Tadanobu) intent on suicide until a meeting with a Thai prostitute in Bangkok changes both their lives forever. Rattanaruang and Tadanobu teamed up again on their next project, *Invisible Wave* (working title), joined by cinematographer Christopher Doyle. In general, however, domestic audiences still preferred mainstream horror and comedy titles to internationally acclaimed films such as *Tropical Malady* and *Last Life in the Universe*.

Sakda Kaewbuadee, left, and Banlop Lomnoi in **Tropical Malady**

UKKABAT (Meteor)
[Action thriller, 2004] Script and Dir: Bandit Ritthakol. Phot: Theerawat Rujintham. Players: Supphakorn Kijsuwan, Phanu Suwanno. Prod: Five Stars Production.
A psychiatrist uses black magic to cure his patients and fight his own madness.

SHUTTER KOD TID WINYAN (The Shutter)
[Horror, 2004] Dir: Banjong Pisanthanakun, Pakpoom Wongpoom. Phot: Niramon Ross. Players: Ananda Everingham, Natthaveeranuj Thongmee. Prod: GMM Pictures/Phenomena Motion Pictures.

Natthaweeranuj Thongmee in **The Shutter**

TOM YUM KUNG
[Action, 2005] Script and Dir: Prachya Pinklaew. Players: Tony Jaa, Mam Jokmok. Prod: Sahamongkol Film/Baramyoo.
Kham (Jaa) rushes from Thailand to Australia to rescue his student sister from the clutches of Vietnamese gangsters.

ZEE-OUI
[Thriller, 2004] Script: Nida Sudasna, Buranee Rachaiboon, Parames Rachaibook, Deborag Kampeier. Dir: Rachaiboon, Sudasna. Phot: Thanisphong Sasinmanob. Players: Duan Long. Chatchai Plengpanich, Premsiri Rattanasopha. Prod: Matching Motion Pictures.

Duan Long as a serial killer in **Zee-oui**

Online ovation saves *Overture*

Audiences did not enjoy watching a woman travel to the court of King Rama V to meet her future husband before becoming involved in political conflict in **Siam Renaissance** and took matters into their own hands when **The Overture**, a mid-nineteenth-century tale of traditional Thai music, was unfairly pulled from theatres after its opening weekend and the movie flopped. So many viewers praised the film in messages posted on websites that it returned to cinemas and unexpectedly grossed $1m.

Stuntman-turned-actor Tony Jaa became Thailand's first international star with his kickboxing debut performance in **Ong Bak the Warrior**, which was picked up for European distribution by Luc Besson's Eurocorp. Jaa's credentials as Thailand's answer to Jackie Chan made a sequel – the $5m *Tom Yum Kung* – inevitable.

My Girl, a nostalgic picture in which a man looks back at his first love in a rural community in the 1980s, was made by six first-time directors: Nithiwat Tharthorn, Wicha Kojew, Songyos Sukmakanan, Khomkrit Treewimol, Witthaya Thongyooyong and Anusorn Treesirikasem. It unexpectedly took more than $3.3m, climbing into fourth place on Thailand's all-time top 10.

Two other twentysomething debutants, Banjong Pisanthanakul and Phakphoom Wongphoom, made another hit with **The Shutter**, a horror movie in which a photographer and his girlfriend find strange shadows and lights in his pictures after they kill a woman in a car crash. It grossed more than $2.5m in its first three weeks on release.

Female Thai directors have surprisingly been swarming into the industry after decades in which no woman film-maker had made an impact. After Pimpaka Tohveera's suspense drama, *One Night Husband* (2003), TV director Phaoon Chandharasiri delivered a remake of Korean romance **The Letter**. Other female directors include the sisters Nida Suthat Na Ayuthaya and Buranee Ratchaiboon with thriller **Zee-oui**, based on a true story of a Chinese child killer from the 1940s. At press time, actress-turned-director Mona Nahm was working on action-adventure *Khon Ra-luek Chat* (literally, *The Resurrection Man*), produced by Oxide Pang, about a couple who try to fight against a destiny determined by their previous lives.

ANCHALEE CHAIWORAPORN (anchalee_chai@yahoo.com) is a Thailand-based film critic who has been awarded grants from the Ford and Nippon foundations for research on Asian cinema.

Tunisia Roy Armes

Recent Films

LA VILLA (The Villa)
*[Drama, 2003] Script: Mohamed
Mahfoudh. Dir: Mohamed
Damak. Phot: Khaled Belkiria.
Players: Lotfi Abdelli, Mohamed
Jabali, Dorra Zarrouk, Lotfi
Dziri, Anissa Lotfi, Michket
Krifa. Prod: CTV Films.*

El-KOTBIA (The Bookstore)
*[Drama 2002] Script and Dir:
Nawfel Saheb-Ettaba. Phot:
Gilles Porte. Players: Hend Sabri,
Ahmed El Hafienne, Martine
Gafsi, Yadh Beji, Raouf Ben
Amor, Mustapha El Adouani.
Prod: Stratus Films/ANPA
(Tunisia)/YMC Productions
(France)/2M (Morocco).*

UNE ODYSSEE (An Odyssey)
*[Thriller, 2003] Script: Abdelaziz
Belkodja, Tahar Fazaa and Jean-
Marc Rudnicki, from an idea by
Brahim Babaï. Dir: Babaï. Phot:
Zbignew Rybcynski. Players:
Saba Moubareck, Jamel Madani,
Ezzedinne Gannoun, Noureddine
Souli. Prod: Rives Productions.*

SeptièmArt *magazine's 101st issue,
featuring* **The Odyssey**

**MITTERRAND EST MORT
(Mitterrand is Dead)**
*[Short, 2003] Script and Dir: Hedi
Sassi. Phot: Florence Levasseur.*

Tunisia offers a textbook example of the difficulties faced by African film-makers to the north and south of the Sahara because the tiny local market makes it extremely difficult to raise finance. Tunisian cinema seems at its richest in the year in which North Africa's leading film festival, the biennial Journées Cinématographiques de Carthage (JCC), takes place in Tunis and in 2002 (a festival year) Tunisian cinema reached an all-time peak, with six new releases.

In 2003, that number fell to two, which has been the annual average since Omar Khlifi directed the country's first (aptly named) feature, *The Dawn*, in 1966. Such a paucity of production means that Tunisian directors often have to wait 10 years or more between projects, the most extreme case being the 22-year gap (1980-2002) between Abdellatif Ben Ammar's third and fourth features.

The other problem is quality. As Ahmed Baha Eddine Attia, the leading Tunisian producer, has noted: "Tunisian cinema, after a magnificent decade, which was marked by diversified and high quality production, has, since 1995, had difficulty positioning itself in relation to its audience and in imposing itself on the international market." The two features released in 2003 reflect these factors.

Thirteen years after the second of his two realistic studies of Tunisian life, Brahim Babaï has made Tunisia's first thriller, **An Odyssey** (*Une Odyssée*), which deals with the efforts of police and archeologists to thwart thieves who have stolen a unique statue of Hannibal. Mohamed Damak's **The Villa** (*La villa*), made 18 years after his debut film, *The Cup* (a comedy about a fanatical football fan), treats a more serious contemporary subject: an adolescent's initial awareness of love and corruption while on holiday on the Côte d'Azur. It was shown at the Paris Biennale of Arab Cinemas, alongside Nawfel Saheb-Ettaba's 2002 release, *The Bookstore* (*El Kotbia*; see *IFG 2004*).

Working at the margins

Eight Tunisian directors, including three newcomers, have films in preparation, all with crucial funding from the French ADC Sud scheme. Unfortunately this was replaced in January 2004 by a new scheme, the Fonds Images Afrique, targeted principally at sub-Saharan Africa. As Moroccan director Abdelkader Lagtaâ observed: "We Maghrebians

Players: Sophie Quinton,
Mohamed Damraoui, Yann de
Monterno, Gilles Carbello. Prod:
Capharmaüm Production (France).

L'ESPRIT ET LE COEUR
(The Spirit and the Heart)
[Documentary short, 2003] Script
and Dir: Molka Mahdaoui. Phot:
Mahdaoui, Karine Haton. Prod:
Les Films du Village.

Musicians in **The Spirit and the Heart**

LE REFUGE (The Refuge)
[Documentary short, 2003]
Script, Dir and Phot: Nedia
Touijer. Prod: Atelier de
Production GSARA.

are becoming more and more marginalised." Two major Tunisian figures are among those currently working with French support. Nacer Khemir's *Bab Aziz* will be just his third film in 20 years; he made his debut with *The Searchers of the Desert* (1984). Taïeb Louhichi, Khemir's exact contemporary (they were both born in 1948), has been working on his fourth feature, *The Dance of the Wind*.

Just three Tunisian shorts were shown at major European festivals in 2004, all by young film-makers from the post-independence generation beginning to make its mark. Two were documentaries by graduates of European film schools and both competed at the African Film Festival in Milan. Molka Mahdaoui (b. 1975) showed her second film, *The Spirit and the Heart* (*L'esprit et le coeur*), a documentary following a group performing sacred songs as they journey across Tunisia. Nedia Touijer (b. 1976) screened *The Refuge* (*Le refuge*), the story of an unemployed man who moves into a Tunis cemetery and makes a living helping the families of the dead.

The third work, shown in competition at the Paris Biennale, was a fictional short, *Mitterrand is Dead* (*Mitterrand est mort*), by Hedi Sassi (b. 1971), which depicts the battle of wills between an irascible old man and the girl trying to help him. Finally, congratulations go to the Tunis-based film magazine *SeptièmArt*, which in 2004 marked 40 years of continuous publication (and 101 issues).

40th Golden Horse Awards (Taiwan)
Presented in Tainan on December 13, 2003.

Picture: *Infernal Affairs*.
Director: Andrew Lau, Alan Mak (*Infernal Affairs*).
Actor: Tony Leung Chiu-wai (*Infernal Affairs*).
Actress: Sandra Ng (*Golden Chicken*).
Supporting Actor: Anthony Wong (*Infernal Affairs*).
Supporting Actress: Lin Mei-hsiu
(*Black Dog Is Coming*).
New Actor: Wang Baoqiang (*Blind Shaft*),
Megan Zheng (*Homerun*).
Original Screenplay: Yau Nai-hoi, Au Kin-yee
(*Infernal Affairs*).
Adapted Screenplay: Li Yang (*Blind Shaft*).
Cinematography: Liao Pen-jung (*The Missing*).
Visual Effects: Eddy Wong (*The Twins Effect*).
Art Direction: Yee Chung-man, Pater Wong
(*Golden Chicken*).
Make-Up & Costume Design: Yee Chung-man,
Dora Ng (*Golden Chicken*).
Action Choreography: Donnie Yen
(*The Twins Effect*).

Original Score: Marco Wan (*Colour of the Truth*).
Original Song: Lam Yat-fung (*Turn Left, Turn Right*).
Editing: Chen Sheng-chang (*Goodbye, Dragon Inn*).
Sound Effects: Kinson Tsang (*Infernal Affairs*).
Documentary: *Viva Tonal: The Dance Age.*
(Chien Wei-ssu, Kuo Chen-ti).
Short Film: *Badu's Homework* (Cheng Wen-tang).
Lifetime Achievement: Yuan Tsung-mei.
Taiwanese Film: *Goodbye, Dragon Inn*
(Tsai Ming-liang).
Taiwanese Film Professional: Liao Pen-jung.
People's Choice: *Infernal Affairs*.

Andy Lau in **Infernal Affairs**, *winner of seven Golden Horse Awards*

Basic Pictures/Media Asia/Kobal

Turkey Atilla Dorsay

The Year's Best Films

Atilla Dorsay's selection:
Encounter (Ömer Kavur)
The Waiting Room
(Zeki Demirkubuz)
Where's Firuze? (Ezel Akay)
Tales of Intransigence
(Reis Çelik)
Under Construction
(Ömer Vargi)

Where's Firuze?

Recent and Forthcoming Films:

ASMALI KONAK
*[Romantic drama, 2003] Script:
Mahinur Ergun, Abdullah Oguz.
Dir: Oguz. Phot: Ken Lelsch.
Players: Özcan Deniz, Nurgül
Yesilcay. Prod: Ans Film.*

BEKLEME ODASI
(The Waiting Room)
*[Drama, 2003] Script, Dir and
Phot: Zeki Demirkubuz. Players:
Demirkubuz, Nurhayat Kιvrak,
Nilüfer Acikalin. Prod: Mavi Film.*

BULUTLARI BEKLERKEN
(Waiting for the Clouds)
*[Political drama, 2003] Script:
Yesim Ustaoglu, Petros
Markaris, based on Tamama by
George Andeadis. Dir: Ustaoglu.
Phot: Jacek Petrycki. Prod:
Ustaoglu Filmcilik.*

Although the overall economic crisis in Turkey continued in 2003-04, audiences were more attracted by local films than ever and the new right-wing government of Tayyip Erdogan seemed more willing to support cinema, passing with unheard-of speed a new film law whose impact should soon be felt.

As in 2002, 17 new films were released in 2003, among them some respectable commercial successes and a few interesting personal films. In the latter category, Zeki Demirkubuz, the country's main auteur alongside Nuri Bilge Ceylan, presented **The Waiting Room** (*Bekleme odasi*), about the creative travails of a young director (Demirkubuz, taking a leading role in one of his films for the first time) who wants to adapt *Crime and Punishment*. It had the sombre atmosphere that so often attaches to films dealing with artistic creation, but Demirkubuz's performance sincerely expressed his own problems. There was also some mildly entertaining humour, as when the hero, desperate to find an actor, finally decides to entrust the role to the young thief who's tried to rob him.

Reis Celik's **Tales of Intransigence** (*Inat Hikayeleri*) is best described as a semi-documentary. It visualises three popular myths of deepest Anatolia, through the popular story-tellers who still ply their ancient trade in the eastern part of the region. Celik, already responsible for several impressive political films, chose a daring method, shooting with a two-man crew: himself and his main actor, Tuncel Kurtiz (the film's only professional performer). Kurtiz sat with the local people, encouraging them to 'act' and talk and tell stories passed down from generation to generation for centuries. The result was unique, in both cinematic and ethnic terms.

Equally personal was **Mud** (*Camur*), the third film of Dervis Zaim, already well known to international festival followers for his debut, *Somersault in a Coffin*. *Mud* was a more serious and sombre effort, depicting the complex relations between the Turks and Greeks of Cyprus (where Zaim comes from) through a very allegorical story. But the allegories were too heavy and meandering.

Ömer Kavur, a prominent auteur, made an impressive comeback with **Encounter** (*Karsilasma*), the story of a man who, after losing his son in an accident, falls into a psychological crisis. In therapy, he meets another man with personal problems, who later on is

CAMUR (Mud)
[Political drama, 2003] Script and
Dir: Dervis Zaim. Phot: Feza
Caldiran. Players: Mustafa
Ugurlu, Yelda Reynaud, Taner
Birsel. Prod: Downtown
Pictures/Marathon Filmcilik.

ESKI ACIK SARI DESENE
[Documentary, 2003] Script and
Dir: Ömer Ali Kazma. Phot:
Tolga Yüceil. Prod: NuaCo.
Portrait of the famous
Galatasaray soccer team.

FIRSAT (Crude)
[Comedy-drama, 2003] Script:
Paxton Winters, Keriman
Güleryüz. Dir and Phot:
Winters. Players: Paul
Schneider, David Connolly,
Yigit Özsener, Ipek Deger.

HABABAM SINIFI MERHABA
(literally, Hello, Lazy Class)
[Comedy, 2003] Script: K. Kenan
Ergen. Dir: Kartal Tibet. Phot:
Ertunc Senkay. Players: Mehmet
Ali Erbil, Hülya Kocyigit, Halit
Akcatepe, Zeki Alasya. Prod:
Arzu Film/Fida Film.

INAT HIKAYELERI
(Tales of Intransigence)
[Ethnic semi-documentary, 2003]
Script, Dir and Phot: Reis Çelik.
Players: Tuncel Kurtiz and
local people. Prod: RH
Politic International.

INSAAT (Under Construction)
[Black comedy, 2003] Script:
Ömer Vargi, Serdar Tantekin.
Dir: Vargi. Phot: Ferenc Pap.
Players: Sevket Coruh, Emre
Kinay, Suna Pekuysal, Yesim
Büber. Prod: Filma-Cass.

INSAN NEDIR KI...
(What's a Human Anyway?)
[Comedy, 2004] Script: Reha
Erdem, Nilüfer Güngörmüs. Dir:
Erdem. Phot: Florent Herry.
Players: Ali Düserkalkar, Isil
Yücesoy, Köksal Engür. Prod:
Atlantik Film Ltd.

**KARPUZ KABUGUNDAN
GEMILER YAPMAK**
(Boats Out of Watermelon Rinds)
[Comedy-drama, 2004] Script
and Dir: Ahmet Ulucay. Phot:

announced to have died on an Aegean island. Intrigued, our hero comes to the island and finds that he is deeply bound to the mysterious man who may be more alive than dead. It has the psychological tension and visual maturity that are the hallmarks of this prestigious director and was good enough to win all the major awards of 2004 in festivals from Antalya to Istanbul.

Behind the *Green* door

Amongst more commercially oriented titles, Abdullah Oguz, the successful producer of, among others, an extremely popular TV serial, **The Green Mansion** (*Asmali konak*), decided to direct the big-screen version. The result – a complex love story set against the thrilling scenery of Cappadocia – was a big commercial success, but held virtually no appeal to anyone but addicts of the TV version. The passed-over director of the TV serial, Cagan Irmak, took 'revenge' by making a much more personal film, **Everything about Mustafa** (*Mustafa hakkinda hersey*), a psychological thriller about a sick man and the deep secret hidden in his childhood.

Another first feature came from Ezel Akay, who in **Where's Firuze?** (*Neredesin Firuze?*) successfully told the story of close friends working in the pop music industry in Istanbul. Akay not only cast an unprecedented number of real-life music and TV celebrities but almost succeeded in realising the crazy world of the Turkish record business, using a fresh comic style that owed much to absurdism.

Yilmaz Erdogan, the extremely popular actor and TV personality, followed up his box-office champion of 2002, *Vizontele*, with **Vizontele-Tuuba**, depicting this time the days of the military intervention of 1980 (the last time, let us hope, that the Turkish army took power from the civil government) and its effects on different kinds of people. Again, this was a film that shone more for its heartfelt sincerity than pure cinematic values.

Yilmaz Erdogan in **Vizontele-Tuuba**

Ömer Vargi, the successful producer and director of the popular *Everything's Gonna Be Great* (1998) gave us **Under Construction** (*Insaat*), a bizarre comedy about two naïve workers who find their construction site being used as an unofficial graveyard by the local mafia. Funny at times, but not often enough.

From street to classroom

Ümit Cin Güven, co-director of last year's *Children of Secret*, returned to the street kids of Istanbul with **Nightmare in the Metropolis** (*Metropol Kabusu*), a not very convincing film, despite its documentary style and sincerity. Veteran Kartal Tibet offered nothing new, but still had a big hit with **Hababam Sinifi, Merhaba** (literally, *Hello, Lazy Class*), which focused on the conflict between old-fashioned education and today's students. In their debut feature, **The School** (*Okul*), brothers Durul and Yagmur Taylan offered a novelty in Turkish cinema: a supernatural horror story. They could not bring off the mix of comedy and horror. Paxton Winters, a young American living in Turkey, made the unique and curious **Crude** (*Firsat*), where an artificially mysterious story presents a foreigner's perspective on Turkey.

With more than 40 films shooting or in preparation in August 2004, the next season should be a boom time, and three features seen at the last Istanbul festival (but not released by press time) are good enough to tour the festival circuit. In **Waiting for the Clouds** (*Bulutlari beklerken*), Yesim Ustaoglu, the successful woman director of *Journey to the Sun*, depicts the complex relations of the one-time Turks and Greeks of northern Turkey. The main protagonist changed her name from Eleni to Ayse when the Greeks of the Black Sea were deported in a period of hostility and lived as a Turkish Muslim – only to discover that identities are not easily changed, nor pasts easily forgotten.

Following his prestigious *Aaaay* and *Run Money Run*, Reha Erdem's **What's a Human Anyway?** (*Insan nedir ki …*) tells the strange story of a man who, after an accident, loses his memory and has to regain the acquaintance of everyone in his life. This bittersweet film uses Istanbul as an impressive backdrop. Finally, a unique personality, Ahmet Uluçay. A native of a village in Anatolia, this director, who refuses to come to Istanbul, has at last, after many shorts and documentaries, made a fiction feature. **Boats Out of Watermelon Rinds** (*Karpuz kabugundan gemiler yapmak*) is a kind of Turkish *Cinema Paradiso*, an autobiographical story of a passion for cinema born in a small village, it is so sincere and beautifully told that it won many hearts and took first prize in the national competition at Istanbul in 2004.

ATILLA DORSAY has been a film critic since 1966, and is the author of 30 books, including a trilogy of *100 Films*, *100 Directors* and *100 Actors* and biographies of Yilmaz Güney and Türkan Soray. He is founder and president of SIYAD, the Association of Turkish Critics.

Ilker Berke. *Players: Ismail Hakki Taslak, Kadir Kaymaz. Prod: IFR.*

KARSILASMA (Encounter)
[Drama, 2003] Script: Ömer Kavur, Macit Koper. Dir: Kavur. Phot: Ali Utku. Players: Ugur Polat, Lale Mansur. Prod: Alfa Film/Objective Film Studio.

METROPOL KABUSU (Nightmare in the Metropolis)
[Drama, 2003] Script and Dir: Ümit Cin Güven. Phot: Bahadir Eren. Players: Mine Cayiroglu, Timur Ölkebas, Murat Baran. Prod: MGD Filmcilik.

MUSTAFA HAKKINDA HERSEY (Everything about Mustafa)
[Drama, 2003] Script and Dir: Cagan Irmak. Phot: Salahattin Sancakli. Players: Fikret Kuskan, Nejat Isler, Basak Köklükaya. Prod: ANS International.

NEREDESIN FIRUZE? (Where's Firuze?)
[Comedy, 2003] Script: Levent Kazak. Dir: Ezel Akay. Phot: Haik Kirakosian. Players: Haluk Bilginer, Özcan Deniz, Cem Özer. Prod: IFR/Cinemedya AS.

OKUL (The School)
[Comedy-horror, 2003] Script: Dogu Yücel. Dir: Yagmur and Durul Taylan. Phot: Soykut Turan. Players: Burak Altay, Nehir Erdogan, Sinem Kobal, Melissa Sözen. Prod: Plato Film.

VIZONTELE TUUBA
[Comedy, 2003] Script and Dir: Yilmaz Erdogan. Phot: Ugur Icbak. Players: Erdogan, Demet Akbag, Altan Erkekli, Tarik Akan, Tuba Ünsal. Prod: BKM Film.

Quote of the Year

"The director I would like to work with most is Nuri Bilge Ceylan. But unfortunately he either works with amateurs or members of his family. And for me, it's too late to be in both categories."

YELDA REYNAUD,
Turkish actress.

Ukraine Goga Lomidze

Recent and Forthcoming Films

VODITEL DLA VERY
(Driver for Vera)
[Drama, 2003] Script and Dir:
Pavel Chukhrai. Phot: Igor
Klebanov. Players: Igor Petrenko,
Alena Babenko, Bogdan Stupka,
Andrei Panin, Ekaterina Yudina.
Prod: Igor Tolstunov,
PROFIT/"1+1".

NASTROISHIK (Tuner)
[Melodrama, 2003] Script: Sergei
Chetvertkov, Evgeny Golubenko,
Kira Muratova. Dir: Muratova.
Phot: Genady Kariuk. Players:
Georgii Deliev, Renata Litvinova,
Alla Demidova, Nina Ruslanova,
Alexei Pavlovski. Prod: Sergei
Chliants, Pygmalion Production/
Odessa Film Studio.

Nina Ruslanova and Alexei Pavlovski
in **Tuner**

C o-operation with Russia plays an increasingly important role in Ukraine's film industry, with the majority of the annual feature output financed partly with Russian money. Among Ukraininan companies, the biggest producers are the Odessa and Dovzhenko film studios, followed by the smaller Yalta studio. The independent company "1+1" is also successfully consolidating an important position in the national film and television industry.

Hollywood films dominate the box-office, with the rare exception of some Russian and French and (even less often) Ukrainian ones. More positively, this vast country has an increasing number of festivals, led by Molodist, Brigantina and Kino-Yalta. Ukrainian films appeared at several international festivals, notably the Ukrainian–Russian co-production **Driver for Vera** (*Voditel dla Very*) by Pavel Chukhrai, which took the Grand Prix and the Best Director and Script awards at Russia's Kinotavr festival.

In Chukhrai's film, when a general (Bogdan Stupka) comes back to his summer residence with his young driver, Viktor (Igor Petrenko), everything starts to change in his life. His handicapped daughter, Vera (Alena Babenko), falls for Viktor, who starts a complicated romance with Lida, the general's housemaid. The drama takes place in the 1960s and is filmed in exotic locations on the Crimean peninsula, which in the days of the USSR was the Soviet Riviera, filled with luxury villas and members of a jet-setting 'golden generation'.
Also competing at Kinotavr was Roman Balayan's **Bright is the Night** (*Noch svetla*), his first film for 10 years. When pretty Lika

Igor Petrenko and Alena Babenko in **Driver for Vera**

arrives in a special boarding school to prepare her college thesis, her sexual advances towards Aleksei, a young teacher, cause moral upheaval. Balayan follows an idealistic, romantic path and makes *Bright Is the Night* a tender film with some unforgettable moments. A co-production with American and Slovakian involvement, Oleg Harncar's **Bloodlines** (*Krovnye Uzy*) is a drama about a young man who finds out that his real mother was a Slovakian woman. It was shown at the Moscow International Film Festival in 2004.

Kira Muratova, who first came to prominence in the Soviet period, made her new film, **Tuner** (*Nastroishik*) at Odessa Film Studio. Andrei, a poor, young ex-piano player, is in love with Lina (popular Renata Litvinova), a spoiled high-society girl. He cannot give her the life she wants, and instead plans to fleece two elderly women (prominent Russian theatre actresses Alla Demidova and Nina Ruslanova). Muratova as usual turns her attention without prejudice to small personal dramas. Screened out of competition at Venice, this is a genuine tragicomedy with sweet and bitter scenes.

Bright Is the Night

**NOCH SVETLA
(Bright Is the Night)**
[Drama, 2004] Script: Rustam Ibragimbekov, Roman Balayan. Dir: Balayan. Phot: Bogdan Verzhbitsky. Players: Andrei Kuzichev, Alexei Panin, Olga Sutulova, Irina Kupchenko, Bogdan Khizhnyak. Prod: Production MakDos/ Ilyuzion Filmz.

Caretaker Films/Kobal

ALAN BATES, right, with Donald Pleasence in The Caretaker *(1964), one of Bates' earliest and most forceful screen appearances in a film, television and theatre career that lasted more than 45 years. He died on December 27, 2003, aged 69.*

United Kingdom Philip Kemp

The Year's Best Films

Philip Kemp's selection:
Vera Drake (Mike Leigh)
Dead Man's Shoes
(Shane Meadows)
My Summer of Love
(Pawel Pawlikowski)
Touching the Void
(Docu. Kevin Macdonald)
Shaun of the Dead
(Edgar Wright)

Recent and Forthcoming Films

AE FOND KISS
[Drama, 2004] Script: Paul Laverty. Dir: Ken Loach. Phot: Barry Ackroyd. Players: Atta Yaqub, Eva Birthistle, Shamshad Akhtar, Gizala Avan. Prod: Sixteen/Bianca/EMC/Tornasol.

Atta Yaqub and Eva Birthistle in
Ae Fond Kiss

BLIND FLIGHT
[Drama-documentary, 2003] Script: John Furse, Brian Keenan. Dir: Furse. Phot: Ian Wilson. Players: Ian Hart, Linus Roache. Prod: UK Film Council/Scottish Screen/Moviehouse.

BRIDE & PREJUDICE
[Musical comedy, 2004] Script: Paul Mayeda Burges, Gurinder Chadha. Dir: Chadha. Phot: Santosh Sivan. Players: Aishwarya Rai, Martin Henderson, Naveen

By now, you might think the British film industry would be used to having the rug whisked from under it by the government. After all, it has happened often enough over the years. But that did not prevent the usual howls of outrage and anguish in February 2004, when the Treasury abruptly pulled the plug on the system of accountancy-based tax funding that had recently become one of the most popular devices for financing movies in the UK.

Schemes such as Ingenious Media's "Inside Track" or Grosvenor Park's "First Choice" exploited a loophole in the tax laws by using generally accepted accountancy principles – GAAP for short – to raise up to 35% of a production's budget. They also made generous wads of money for the suited middlemen operating these schemes. Hardly surprising, then, that the Chancellor made sternly clear that, though such "principles" might be "generally accepted" by accountants, he would no longer tolerate them.

For some time prior to Tuesday February 10 (promptly dubbed "Black Tuesday" by the industry), warning growls had been emanating from the Inland Revenue that such abuse (as films minister Estelle Morris openly termed it) of the tax laws would not be allowed to continue and that the cash cow was overdue for the abattoir. But when the blow fell, several prestigious productions were caught with their budgets down.

The most notable casualty was DreamWorks' $45m costume drama *Tulip Fever*, adapted from Deborah Moggach's best-selling novel and scheduled to star Jude Law and Keira Knightley, but some 20 other films in various stages of pre-production or production also had to scramble for replacement funding. Some found it in unexpected places. *The Libertine*, with Johnny Depp playing notorious seventeenth-century rake the Earl of Rochester, swung a providential deal with the Isle of Man Film Commision, thanks in part to some shrewd lobbying by Depp's co-star John Malkovich.

Two months later, another door was slammed shut by the Treasury. Under the rules of tax law Section 48, UK co-productions could claim sizeable tax subsidies on their whole budget – not just on what was spent in the UK. This was an obvious invitation to sharp practice, creating what *Screen International* called "a sub-industry of UK co-producers and tax financiers… doing little more than providing international productions with access to UK tax funds". In April 2004 the rules were tightened, making it far harder to claim co-production status. Myriad Pictures' *The River King*, a supernatural murder-mystery with Edward Burns and Jennifer Ehle, was unlucky enough to get hit by the double whammy. Having just managed to replace the third of their budget lost on Black Tuesday, the producers were then refused UK status as a UK–Canadian co-production.

The overall disruption was compounded by the imminent demise of Section 48, which the government had always made clear would be phased out in 2004, to be replaced after consultation with the industry by a new tax support system. Anxious professionals had to wait until September to find out what "Son of Section 48" would look like and when it was finally unveiled industry response was (predictably) mixed. In theory, the new rules would provide 20% of a production's budget right across the board – more generous terms than the old Section 48. But as financial experts soon pointed out, things were not that clear-cut. Factors such as pre-sales, they warned, could bring the amount of subsidy available down to 15% or less. Investors hung fire, preferring to wait until the full implications of the new legislation had been worked out.

Back from the dead (fact and fiction)

Ironically, all this coincided with British cinema making its strongest creative showing for years in 2004, after the second half of 2003 had offered dispiritingly slim pickings. Among the few movies that stood out in the latter period was Kevin Macdonald's breathtaking dramatised documentary, **Touching the Void**, about the ordeal suffered by young British climbers Simon Yates and Joe Simpson on an Andean peak in 1985. Macdonald combines stunningly recreated mountain sequences, in which actors play Yates and Simpson, with present-day interviews with the two men. This knuckle-chewingly vivid account of survival against the odds leaves most fictional mountain movies on the nursery slopes.

Unexpectedly excellent – and extremely funny – was Edgar Wright's **Shaun of the Dead**, billed as "the first rom-zom-com", in which a group of slackers only gradually wake up to the fact that their nondescript corner of north London and, indeed, the whole world, are being taken over by flesh-eating zombies. Simon Pegg as reluctant hero Shaun heads an accomplished cast, most of whom were known principally for their television sitcom work, and the ever-wonderful Bill Nighy contributes a sardonic cameo. The lovingly quotidian tone is encapsulated by Penelope Wilton as Shaun's haplessly apologetic mum; fatally bitten by a zombie, she explains that she kept quiet about her predicament because "I didn't want to make a fuss".

Andrews, Namrata Shirodka, Nitin Ganatra. Prod: Pathé/UK Film Council/Kintop/Bend It.

Pathé

Nitin Ganatra in **Bride and Prejudice**

BRIDGET JONES: THE EDGE OF REASON
[Comedy, 2004]] Script: Andrew Davies, Helen Fielding, Richard Curtis, Adam Brooks, based on Fielding's novel. Dir: Beeban Kidron. Phot: Adrian Biddle. Players: Renée Zellweger, Colin Firth, Hugh Grant, Jim Broadbent. Prod: Working Title.

Laurie Sparham/Working Title

Renée Zellweger returns as **Bridget Jones**

BULLET BOY
[Social drama, 2004] Script: Saul Dibb, Catherine Johnson. Dir: Dibb. Phot: Marcel Zyskind. Players: Ashley Walters, Luke Fraser, Claire Perkins, Leon Black. Prod: BBC Films/UK Film Council/Shine.

CODE 46
[Science-fiction, 2003] Script: Frank Cottrell Boyce. Dir: Michael Winterbottom. Phot: Alwin Küchler, Marcel Zyskind. Players: Tim Robbins, Samantha Morton, Jeanne Balibar, Essie Davis. Prod: UK Film Council/BBC Films/ UA/Revolution.

DEAD MAN'S SHOES
[Thriller, 2004] Script: Paddy Considine, Shane Meadows. Dir:

Meadows. *Phot: Danny Cohen.
Players: Paddy Considine, Gary
Stretch, Toby Kebbell, Stuart
Wolfenden. Prod: FilmFour/
EMMI/Warp/Big Arty.*

ENDURING LOVE
*[Drama, 2004] Script: Joe
Penhall, based on the novel by
Ian McEwan. Dir: Roger Michell.
Phot: Haris Zambarloukos.
Players: Daniel Craig, Rhys Ifans,
Samantha Morton, Alexandra
Aitken. Prod: Free Range/
Pathé/Ridgeway.*

Rhys Ifans in **Enduring Love**

FROZEN
*[Thriller, 2004] Script: Juliet
McKoen, Jayne Steel. Dir:
McKoen. Phot: Hugh Fairs,
Philip Robertson. Players:
Shirley Henderson, Roshan Seth,
Ger Ryan. Prod: Liminal/
Shoreline/Freedonia/RS.*

GIRL WITH A PEARL EARRING
*[Period drama, 2003] Script:
Olivia Hetreed, based on the novel
by Tracey Chevalier. Dir: Peter
Webber. Phot: Eduardo Serra.
Players: Colin Firth, Scarlett
Johansson, Tom Wilkinson, Judy
Parfitt. Prod: Pathé/UK Film
Council/Archer Street/DeLux.*

I'LL SLEEP WHEN I'M DEAD
*[Thriller, 2003] Script: Trevor
Preston. Dir: Mike Hodges. Phot:
Mike Garfath. Players: Clive
Owen, Charlotte Rampling,
Jonathan Rhys Meyers, Sylvia
Syms, Malcolm McDowell. Prod:
Revere/Seven Arts/Will & Co.*

THE JACKET
*[Thriller, 2005] Script: Marc
Rocco, Massy Tadjedin. Dir: John
Maybury. Phot: Peter Deming.
Players: Adrien Brody, Keira
Knightley, Jennifer Jason Leigh,
Kris Kristofferson. Prod:*

Dylan Moran, Kate Ashfield, Simon Pegg and Lucy Davis in **Shaun of the Dead**

Three low-budget independent features deserved greater
exposure than they received. As so often, their lack of promotional
muscle resulted in insultingly brief, limited releases; they had
vanished from cinemas almost before the favourable reviews were
published. **One for the Road**, an assured first feature from writer-
director Chris Cooke, offers a painfully accurate portrayal of boozy
male self-delusion. Four convicted drink-drivers on a rehabilitation
scheme share beer-sodden lunches, blustering and boasting, and
foster each other's foolishly grandiose schemes of success. The
grainy digital visuals make a perfect vehicle for Cooke's edgy,
pitch-black comedy.

Another first-time director, ex-punk singer Richard Jobson, draws
on his own background in the mean backstreets of Edinburgh for
16 Years of Alcohol. The film works a doomy, poetic-realist riff on
Kubrick's *A Clockwork Orange*, as Jobson's young protagonist
comes to realise – too late – the fatal limitations of his chosen
lifestyle of macho thuggishness.

Kevin McKidd, Laura Fraser and Ewen Bremner in **16 Years of Alcohol**

Bille Eltringham's **This Is Not a Love Song**, shot on DV in just two weeks, nods towards *Of Mice and Men* with its tale of two ill-fated loners on the run, the smaller and brighter vainly trying to protect his impulsive, child-like companion. The script by Simon Beaufoy is more abrasive and less upbeat than one might expect from the writer of *The Full Monty*. Shot in 2002 and winner of an award at Rotterdam, *Love Song* was premiered simultaneously in a handful of cinemas and – a first for a British feature – on the internet.

Mike Hodges' noirish thriller, **I'll Sleep When I'm Dead**, looks like a slightly too calculated bid to repeat the unexpected success of his sleeper hit, *Croupier*. The new film again stars Clive Owen, this time playing a former hitman trying to go straight but pulled back into the London underworld by the rape and death of his younger brother. Owen broods effectively, Hodges ladles on the atmosphere and there's a bluesy, sax-laden score from Simon Fisher-Turner, but it's all a little slow and self-conscious, and inevitably revives memories of a much more accomplished Hodges movie, the iconic *Get Carter*, with Michael Caine at his most icily inexorable.

Stephen Fry's first directorial outing, **Bright Young Things**, adapted from Evelyn Waugh's *Vile Bodies*, only reaffirmed what other directors have found: that Waugh's brittle, mocking tone is damnably difficult to capture on the big screen. Cinematographer Eduardo Serra made **Girl with a Pearl Earring** look exquisite, as befits a film about Vermeer, and, as the artist's model and love-object, Scarlett Johansson gives a performance of quiet intensity. But for all its beauty and its scrupulous recreation of seventeenth-century Delft, the film felt cold, uninvolving. These apart, there seemed to be little on offer in 2003 except bland, crowd-pleasing fare like Nigel Cole's *Monty*-lite **Calendar Girls**, or Richard Curtis' terminally saccharine **Love Actually**, which slung together an ill-structured, opportunistic grab-bag of all the tried-and-tested elements that make up a hit Brit rom-com. The latter's makers, Working Title, were to storm the box-office yet again with **Bridget Jones: The Edge of Reason** in November 2004.

Flood follows drought

The impression that British cinema was passing through one of its sojourns in the doldrums seemed confirmed when not a single UK film was considered worthy of inclusion at the 2004 Cannes Festival. But one of those rejected – quite inexplicably – was Mike Leigh's masterly 1950s-set social drama, **Vera Drake**, which went on to vindicate itself by winning the Golden Lion and Best Actress at Venice. The triumph of Leigh's film – considered in more detail in the Director of the Year profile at the front of this volume – coincided with the appearance of a whole raft of movies that more than redeemed the preceding fallow period.

Mandalay/Warner/Section Eight.

LADIES IN LAVENDER
[Period drama, 2004] Script and Dir: Charles Dance. Phot: Peter Biziou. Players: Judi Dench, Maggie Smith, Daniel Brühl, Natascha McElhone, David Warner. Prod: UK Film Council/Baker Street/Future/Paradigm.

LAYER CAKE
[Thriller, 2004] Script: J.J. Connolly, based on his novel. Dir: Matthew Vaughn. Phot: Ben Davis. Players: Daniel Craig, Colm Meaney, Kenneth Cranham, Jamie Foreman, Michael Gambon. Prod: Columbia/MARV.

THE LIBERTINE
[Costume drama, 2004] Script: Stephen Jeffreys, based on his play. Dir: Laurence Dunmore. Phot: Alexander Melman. Players: Johnny Depp, John Malkovich, Samantha Morton, Tom Hollander. Prod: Mr. Mudd/Isle of Man Film/First Choice.

MRS. HENDERSON PRESENTS
[Comedy-drama, 2005] Script: Martin Sherman. Dir: Stephen Frears. Phot: Andrew Dunn. Players: Bob Hoskins, Judi Dench, Christopher Guest. Prod: BBC Films.

MY SUMMER OF LOVE
[Drama, 2004] Script: Pawel Pawlikowski, Michael Wynne, based on the novel by Helen Cross. Dir: Pawlikowski. Phot: Ryszard Lenczewski. Players: Natalie Press, Emily Blunt, Paddy Considine. Prod: BBC Films/Film Consortium/Take Partnerships.

9 SONGS
[Sex drama/concert film, 2004] Script and Dir: Michael Winterbottom. Phot: Marcel Zyskind. Players: Kieran O'Brien, Margot Stilley. Prod: Revolution.

ONE FOR THE ROAD
[Dark comedy, 2003] Script and Dir: Chris Cooke. Phot: N.G. Smith. Players: Rupert Proctor, Greg Chisholm, Mark Devenport, Hywel Bennett. Prod: EMMI/UK

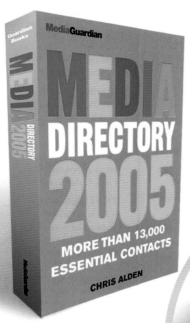

Optimum Releasing

Toby Kebbell, left, and Paddy Considine play brothers in **Dead Man's Shoes**

Dead Man's Shoes was the film that admirers of Shane Meadows' freewheeling Nottingham-based talent have long been waiting for. After the disappointment of *Once Upon a Time in the Midlands*, *Shoes* packs the ruthless punch that its predecessor so disappointingly pulled. The plot is not dissimilar to that of *I'll Sleep When I'm Dead*: a man comes back to avenge the mistreatment of his younger brother. The avenging angel this time is Paddy Considine (who also co-wrote the script), confirming his growing reputation as one of the finest British actors of his generation. Making masterly use of its Derbyshire locations, from the austere beauty of the Peak District to the drab streets of provincial housing estates, Meadows' film plays out its stripped-down drama with a compelling blend of grim humour and deglamorised violence. Once again, comparisons are invited with *Get Carter* and, indeed, with John Boorman's *Point Blank*, but *Shoes* can sustain them.

Considine turns up again, saturnine and unnerving as ever, in Pawel Pawlikowski's **My Summer of Love**. He plays an ex-con-turned-born-again Christian, pouring away the alcohol in his small-town Yorkshire pub and banishing the regulars in favour of religious gatherings. Meanwhile his teenage sister (Natalie Press), alienated and bored by

Content Film

Natalie Press, left, and Emily Blunt in **My Summer of Love**

Film Council/FilmFour.

PICCADILLY JIM
[Period comedy, 2004] Script: Julian Fellowes. Dir: John McKay. Phot: Andrew Dunn. Players: Sam Rockwell, Lucy Brown, Frances O'Connor, Tom Wilkinson. Prod: Myriad/Isle of Man/Mission.

THE PURIFIERS
[Martial arts thriller, 2004] Script and Dir: Richard Jobson. Phot: John Rhodes. Players: Kevin McKidd, Gordon Alexander, Rachel Grant, Dominic Monaghan, Amber Sainsbury. Prod: Bill Kenwright/ S2S Post/Vestry.

THE RECKONING
[Period drama, 2001; released 2004] Script: Mark Mills. Dir: Paul McGuigan. Phot: Peter Sova. Players: Willem Dafoe, Paul Bettany, Brian Cox, Gina McKee. Prod: Renaissance/ KanZaman/MDA.

SHAUN OF THE DEAD
[Zombie romantic comedy, 2004] Script: Simon Pegg, Edgar Wright. Dir: Wright. Phot: David M. Dunlap. Players: Pegg, Kate Ashfield, Lucy Davis, Nick Frost, Bill Nighy. Prod: Universal/ StudioCanal/Working Title 2.

16 YEARS OF ALCOHOL
[Drama, 2003] Script and Dir: Richard Jobson. Phot: John Rhodes. Players: Kevin McKidd, Laura Fraser, Susan Lynch, Jim Carter, Ewen Bremner. Prod: Scottish Screen/ Metro Tartan/ Fortissimo.

STAGE BEAUTY
[Period comedy-drama, 2004] Script: Jeffrey Hatcher, based on his play Compleat Female Stage Beauty. *Dir: Richard Eyre. Phot: Andrew Dunn. Players: Billy Crudup, Claire Danes, Rupert Everett, Tom Wilkinson. Prod: Momentum/BBC Films/Qwerty.*

TOUCHING THE VOID
[Documentary, 2003] Script: Based on the book by Joe Simpson. Dir: Kevin Macdonald. Phot: Mike Eley. Players/Featuring: Brendan

her brother's new obsession, makes friends with a posh girl her own age (Emily Blunt) – a friendship that takes on increasingly erotic overtones. As he did in his feature debut *Last Resort* (which also starred Considine), the Polish-born Pawlikowski brings a shrewd, outsider's perspective to his material, subverting the very English matter of a rural idyll, while drawing astonishingly natural and convincing performances from newcomers Press and Blunt.

The prospect of yet another British gangster movie hardly quickens the pulse, especially when it's revealed that **Layer Cake** was turned down by Guy Ritchie, perpetrator of the meretricious and much-imitated *Lock, Stock and Two Smoking Barrels* and then taken up by that film's producer, Matthew Vaughn, for his directorial debut. But *Layer Cake* proved unpredictably stylish and involving (and did very well at the box-office), with a compelling central performance from Daniel Craig as the nameless drug dealer hoping to go straight and cash in his profits. True, the set-up is nothing new, but as scripted from his own novel by crime-writer J.J. Connolly, and directed with wit, pace and a keen eye for non-touristy London locations, the film exerts a formidably intelligent grip. The main weakness is an excess of exposition-laden dialogue, but Vaughn and Connolly's vision of the underworld as a class-ridden, hierarchical mirror image of 'respectable' society – a layer cake – rings horribly true.

Dan Smith/Columbia TriStar Films

Colm Meaney, left, and Daniel Craig as partners in crime in **Layer Cake**

A mellower Loach

After *My Name Is Joe* and *Sweet Sixteen*, Ken Loach rounds off his informal Scottish trilogy in uncharacteristically optimistic mode with **Ae Fond Kiss**. An inter-racial *Romeo and Juliet*, it traces the fraught affair between two attractive young Glaswegians, a club DJ from a Muslim Asian family (Atta Yaqub) and an Irish Catholic music teacher (Eva Birthistle). Predictably enough, bigotry on both sides stands in their way, and some of the plotting is over-schematic. But the film is imbued with Loach's generous humanism – besides including his first real sex scene – and it's not hard to warm to Birthistle and Yaqub.

Mackey, Nicholas Aaron/Joe
Simpson, Simon Yates. Prod:
FilmFour/UK Film Council/
Darlow Smithson.

VANITY FAIR
[Costume drama, 2004] Script:
Matthew Faulk, Mark Skeet,
Julian Fellowes, based on
Thackeray's novel. Dir: Mira
Nair. Phot: Declan Quinn.
Players: Reese Witherspoon,
James Purefoy, Jim Broadbent,
Bob Hoskins, Eileen Atkins.
Prod: Focus/Granada/Tempesta.

VERA DRAKE
[Period drama, 2004] Script and
Dir: Mike Leigh. Phot: Dick
Pope. Players: Imelda Staunton,
Philip Davis, Eddie Marsan, Alex
Kelly. Prod: UK Film Council/
StudioCanal/Inside Track/
Thin Man Films.

A WAY OF LIFE
[Social drama, 2004] Script and
Dir: Amma Asante. Phot: Ian
Wilson. Players: Leigh-Anne
Williams, Nathan Jones, Gary
Sheppeard, Dean Wong. Prod:
UK Film Council/Arts Council of
Wales/ITV Wales/Portman.

WIMBLEDON
[Romantic comedy, 2004] Script:
Adam Brooks, Jennifer Flackett,
Mark Levin. Dir: Richard
Loncraine. Phot: Darius Khondji.
Players: Paul Bettany, Kirsten
Dunst, Sam Neill, Jon Favreau,
Bernard Hill. Prod: Universal/
StudioCanal/Working Title.

YASMIN
[Social drama, 2004] Script:
Simon Beaufoy. Dir: Kenny
Glenaan. Phot: Tony Slater-Ling.
Players: Archie Panjabi, Renu
Setna, Steve Jackson. Prod:
Parallax/EuroArts Medien.

Quotes of the Year

"There's a self mockery that's very strong in English culture, the ability of the English person to be an idiot, to be embarrassed about being an idiot, and then be quite intelligent about it, in terms of mocking oneself."
COLIN FIRTH, *actor.*

"Don't take any notice of good criticism or bad criticism. You've got to face the canvas, stare at it and think, well, I think it's purple. And start to paint purple."
RIDLEY SCOTT *on directing.*

"The only reason I get work is that all the others have had plastic surgery and I haven't."
EILEEN ATKINS *on acting at 70.*

"He says 'To Hell with you all.' He takes on the world like Coriolanus. That's been the story of my life as well."
ANTHONY HOPKINS *on his role in* The Human Stain.

"The one thing we hardly ever do is comedies. They're so sort of pastel."
HAMISH McALPINE, *boss of Tartan Films, UK distributors of* Bad Guy, Anatomy of Hell *and other 'extreme' titles.*

The British Academy Film Awards 2003

Film: *The Lord of the Rings: The Return of the King.*
British Film: *Touching the Void* (John Smithson/Kevin Macdonald).
Direction: Peter Weir (*Master and Commander: The Far Side of the World*).
Actor: Bill Murray (*Lost in Translation*).

Restlessly prolific, Michael Winterbottom directs with exceptional frequency and rarely visits the same genre twice. **Code 46** is his first venture into science-fiction, with Tim Robbins as a psychically endowed fraud investigator and Samantha Morton as his quarry (with whom, inevitably, he falls in love) in an environmentally wrecked future where the underprivileged live in the desert wastes beyond heavily fortified cities. Shooting in Shanghai, Dubai and Jaipur, Winterbottom effectively creates a disorienting future out of existing locations (not unlike the way Godard used Paris in *Alphaville*).

There is little chemistry between Robbins and Morton, though; much of the time feels it as if they're acting in different movies, an impression enhanced by their startling difference in height. And as so often with Winterbottom's films, *Code 46* is easier to admire than to engage with, which may explain its relatively unimpressive box-office showing.

Verve Pictures

Michael Winterbottom, centre, directs Tim Robbins and Samantha Morton in **Code 46**

By the time of *Code 46*'s release, Winterbottom had completed **9 Songs**, the most sexually explicit UK mainstream movie yet made, featuring prolonged scenes of penetration, oral sex and mild bondage. The minimal plot traces the year-long affair between a young Englishman, Matt (Kieran O'Brien), and a visiting American student, Lisa (newcomer Margo Stilley), in London, interspersed with footage of the rock concerts they attend. The sex scenes, shot in available light on hand-held DV, are attractively intimate. But the concert footage is routine and Matt's retrospective voice-over narration (while on a research trip to the Antarctic) is a pretentious irrelevance. Still, Winterbottom deserves credit for pushing the envelope of what's acceptable onscreen. Predictably, the film began generating "Ban This Filth" tabloid headlines immediately after its Cannes premiere, but was passed uncut as an '18' and scheduled for March 2005 release.

Still banking on the Yanks

So for the moment, at least, the British film industry seems to be going through one of its healthier patches. As far as the studios are concerned, the weak dollar and government clampdowns on co-production rules seem to have done little damage. In 2003, total UK-based production hit a record-breaking $2.13 billion, and 2004 looked like coming close to that figure. Heavyweight productions like Ridley Scott's Crusades epic, *Kingdom of Heaven*, the first in the revitalised Batman franchise, *Batman Begins*, and Tim Burton's eagerly awaited *Charlie and the Chocolate Factory* all spent much or all of their budgets in the UK.

Even Woody Allen, a notoriously reluctant traveller, chose to shoot his latest project in Britain. Most lumbering of them all was Joel Schumacher's $80m-plus production of Andrew Lloyd Webber's *Phantom of the Opera*, said to be the biggest musical ever filmed, which took up eight sound stages at Pinewood for several months.

Hoping to mop up spare capacity, several new studios are in the offing. Wales' first studio complex, benignly presided over by Richard Attenborough, is nearing completion at a projected cost of $225m. Cornwall, too, may soon have its own production facility, South-West Film Studios, in St Agnes. Its $10m cost may be more modest, but the claims in its promotional material are not: "the most advanced film, television and multi-media facility in the world". Elsewhere on the Celtic fringe, talks of a Scottish studio were once again being revamped, this time for a site near Inverness.

On the exhibition front, the much-sold Odeon chain yet again changed hands. Bought at what many thought was an inflated price in 2003 by German bank West LB and leading UK independent distributors Entertainment Film, the troubled chain was resold in September 2004 to investment group Terra Firma Capital Partners for $54m less than the previous price. Simultaneously, Terra Firma also snapped up the UCI chain, giving them 35% of the UK exhibition market and leaving some observers to predict rumbles from the Monopolies and Mergers Commission.■

Corrections: The screens in the UK Film Council's (UKFC) planned digital cinema network will not, as incorrectly stated in *IFG 2004* (p.299), be hired. UKFC will contribute to the cost of installing digital equipment on what is intended to be a permanent basis.

The report stated (p.300) that the British Film Institute (BFI) had cut its support for small independent cinemas by $263,000. The responsibility for supporting local cinemas has in fact moved from the BFI, which only supported Regional Film Theatres (RSAs), to the new Regional Screen Agencies. Services previously provided to the RFTs through the BFI are still provided, on an enlarged basis, through the Independent Cinema Office, which is funded through the RSAs, which are partially funded by UKFC.

UKFC's running costs represent 15% of its turnover, not 20% (p.300).

Actress: Scarlett Johansson (*Lost in Translation*).
Supporting Actor: Bill Nighy (*Love Actually*).
Supporting Actress: Renée Zellweger (*Cold Mountain*).
Original Screenplay: Tom McCarthy (*The Station Agent*).
Adapted Screenplay: Fran Walsh, Philippa Boyens, Peter Jackson (*The Return of the King*).
Film Music: Gabriel Yared (*Cold Mountain*).
Cinematography: Andrew Lesnie (*The Return of the King*).
Production Design: William Sandell (*Master and Commander*).
Costume Design: Wendy Stites (*Master and Commander*).
Editing: Sarah Flack (*Lost in Translation*).
Sound: Richard King, Doug Hemphill, Paul Massey, Art Rochester (*Master and Commander*).
Visual Effects: Joe Letteri, Jim Rygiel, Randall William Cook, Alex Funke (*The Return of the King*).
Make-Up & Hair: Ve Neill, Martin Samuel (*Pirates of the Caribbean*).
Best Foreign-Language Film: *In this World* (Andrew Eaton, Anita Overland, Michael Winterbottom).
Short Film: *Brown Paper Bag* (Natasha Carlish, Mark Leveson, Michael Baig Clifford, Geoff Thompson).
Short Animation: *Jojo in the Sky* (Sue Goffe, Marc Craste).
Carl Foreman Award: Emily Young, writer-director (*Kiss of Life*).
Audience Award: *The Return of the King*.
Fellowship: John Boorman.
Michael Balcon Award: Working Title Films.

United States Eddie Cockrell

The Year's Best Films

Eddie Cockrell's selection:

Open Range (Kevin Costner)

The Station Agent
(Tom McCarthy)

**Eternal Sunshine of the
Spotless Mind**
(Michel Gondry)

I ♥ Huckabees
(David O. Russell)

Sideways (Alexander Payne)

Recent and Forthcoming Films

BATMAN BEGINS
*[Adventure, 2005] Script: David
Goyer, Christopher Nolan. Dir:
Nolan. Phot: Wally Pfister.
Players: Christian Bale, Michael
Caine, Katie Holmes, Ken
Watanabe, Liam Neeson, Morgan
Freeman, Gary Oldman, Cillian
Murphy, Rutger Hauer, Tom
Wilkinson. Prod: Emma Thomas,
Charles Roven, Larry Franco,
Warner Bros.*

BE COOL
*[Comedy-thriller, 2005] Script:
Peter Steinfeld, from the novel by
Elmore Leonard. Dir: F. Gary
Gray. Phot: Jeffrey Kimball.
Players: John Travolta, Uma
Thurman, Harvey Keitel, Vince
Vaughn, Dwayne "The Rock"
Johnson, Cedric the Entertainer,
Danny DeVito. Prod: DeVito,
Michael Shamberg, Stacey Sher,
David Nicksay, Jersey Films/
Double Feature Films.*

BEE SEASON
*[Family, 2005] Script: Naomi
Foner Gyllenhaal. Dir: Scott
McGehee, David Siegel. Phot:
Giles Nuttgens. Players: Richard
Gere, Juliette Binoche, Max*

I t should come as no surprise that the polarisation prevalent in American politics had seeped so thoroughly into the country's movie culture by the time of George W. Bush's re-election: not when the third highest-grossing film of 2004 was *The Passion of the Christ* (behind only the *Shrek* and *Spider-Man* sequels) and Michael Moore, that portly polemicist, had parlayed a wearying blitzkrieg of media-hogging into a record documentary box-office haul – a breathtaking $119m – for *Fahrenheit 9/11*.

The divisive and uncertain atmosphere in the worlds of politics and movies ran at approximately the same fever pitch. "Where, Oh Where, Are the Oscar Contenders?" asked the *New York Times* – a headline on a fearsome par with the Associated Press' "Do Film Critics Still Matter?" (the latter provokes an admittedly more personal terror). At press time the legacy of 2004 looked to be Jesus and Peter Parker, George W. Bush and Donkey: the age of the Event Picture was upon us.

Let us return for a moment to a simpler time, 2003 B.E. (that's Before Events), when, during the early days of the divisive Gulf War, the gulf between "big" and "little" pictures was not nearly as pronounced. Domestic box-office revenue for 2003 was actually down 0.3%, from $9.52 billion to $9.49 billion, even though six more films (473 in total) were released and the average ticket price jumped 3.8%, to $6.03. Though the number of theatrical screens swelled to 35,786 (up 1.4%, the first increase since 2000), total admissions, after increasing 10.2% in 2002, dropped 4%; at 1.57 billion, the total was still the second highest ever.

Philippe Antonello/Icon

The Passion of the Christ *grabbed headlines and a $370m gross*

Though it was once again the fourth quarter that brought the 2003 tally out of the doldrums, yielding 26% of the year's total to compensate for a dreadful first quarter, the number of movies earning more than $200m – traditionally the big-budget, lowest common denominator summer escapes – dropped from seven in 2002 to only four. And while no fewer than 29 films passed the formerly magical $100m mark, such noble earners as the third *Lord of the Rings* entry (a rare instance of the box-office champ also taking the Best Picture Oscar) and *Seabiscuit* were in the minority alongside vacuous popcorn pictures like *The Cat in the Hat*, *Bad Boys II* and *Cheaper by the Dozen*.

Let's look at this another way. In 2003, *The Return of the King* led the gross list at $377m, followed by *Finding Nemo* ($340m) and *Pirates of the Caribbean: The Curse of the Black Pearl* ($305m). By November 2004, *Shrek 2* topped the year's chart with $440m, followed by *Spider-Man 2* ($373m) and *The Passion of the Christ* ($370m) – significantly higher numbers. Yet alongside the trio entering the $300m-plus club, only 14 other movies had passed $100m (remember, 29 did so in 2003), and in that list there was, not surprisingly, less wheat (*Harry Potter and the Prisoner of Azkaban*, *The Bourne Supremacy*, *Fahrenheit 9/11*, *Dodgeball*, *Collateral*, *The Incredibles*) than chaff (*The Day After Tomorrow*, *I, Robot*, *Shark Tale*, *Troy*, *50 First Dates*, *The Grudge*, *The Village* and *Van Helsing*).

Frank Connor/Dream Works/Paramount

Tom Cruise, Jamie Foxx and Barry Shabaka Henley in **Collateral,** *one of the best films to gross $100m in 2004*

What does it all mean? Fewer people paid more money at more theatres to see a growing number of pre-sold blockbusters, lowbrow entertainments and flashpoints of political and/or religious controversy. Hollywood, it may be said, continues to put larger eggs in smaller baskets, where the economics of the Event Picture could eventually rule the roost.

Minghella, Flora Cross, Kate Bosworth. Prod: Peggy Rajski, Mark Romanek, Bee Season Productions.

BEWITCHED
[Comedy, 2005] Script: Nora Ephron, Delia Ephron, Adam McKay. Dir: Nora Ephron. Phot: John Lindley. Players: Nicole Kidman, Will Ferrell, Shirley MacLaine, Michael Caine, Jason Schwartzman, Joan Plowright. Prod: Doug Wick, Lucy Fisher, Penny Marshall, Bewitched/Columbia.

BROKEBACK MOUNTAIN
[Drama, 2005] Script: Larry McMurtry, Diana Ossana. Dir: Ang Lee. Phot: Rodrigo Prieto. Players: Jake Gyllenhaal, Heath Ledger, Michelle Williams, Anne Hathaway, Randy Quaid. Prod: Diana Ossana, James Schamus, Focus Features/Paramount.

CHARLIE AND THE CHOCOLATE FACTORY
[Fantasy, 2005] Script: John August, from the novel by Roald Dahl. Dir: Tim Burton. Phot: Philippe Rousselot. Players: Johnny Depp, Freddie Highmore, David Kelly, Helena Bonham Carter, Noah Taylor, Christopher Lee. Prod: Brad Grey, Richard D. Zanuck, Zanuck Co./ Plan B Entertainment.

THE CHRONICLES OF NARNIA: THE LION, THE WITCH AND THE WARDROBE
[Fantasy, 2005] Script: Ann Peacock, Christopher Markus, Stephen McFeely, Andrew Adamson, from the books by C.S. Lewis. Dir: Adamson. Phot: Don McAlpine. Players: Jim Broadbent, Elizabeth Hawthorne, Georgie Henley, Patrick Kake, Skandar Keynes, James McAvoy, Tilda Swinton. Prod: Mark Johnson, Lamp Post Productions.

CINDERELLA MAN
[Sports drama, 2005] Script: Cliff Hollingsworth, Charlie Mitchell, Akiva Goldsman. Dir: Ron Howard. Players: Russell Crowe, Renée Zellweger, Paddy

Considine, Paul Giamatti, Craig
Bierko. Prod: Brian Grazer,
Imagine Entertainment.

DON'T COME KNOCKING
[Drama, 2005] Script: Sam
Shepard. Dir: Wim Wenders.
Players: Shepard, Jessica Lange,
Jean Reno, Tim Roth, Sarah
Polley, Eva Marie Saint, Fairuza
Balk. Prod: Peter Schwartzkopff,
Road Movies.

THE DUKES OF HAZZARD
[Action comedy, 2005] Script:
Jonathan Davis, John O'Brien.
Dir: Jay Chandrasekhar. Phot:
Larry Sher. Players: Johnny
Knoxville, Sean William Scott,
Jessica Simpson, Burt Reynolds,
Willie Nelson. Prod: Billy Gerber,
Village Roadshow/Warner Bros.

ELIZABETHTOWN
[Romantic comedy, 2005] Script
and Dir: Cameron Crowe. Phot:
John Toll. Players: Orlando
Bloom, Kirsten Dunst, Susan
Sarandon, Judy Greer, Jessica
Biel, Paul Schneider, Gaillard
Sartain, Bruce McGill, Loudon
Wainwright III. Prod: Tom
Cruise, Paula Wagner, Cameron
Crowe for Cruise-Wagner
Productions/Vinyl Films.

FANTASTIC FOUR
[Action, 2005] Script: Simon
Kinberg, from the Marvel comics.
Dir: Tim Story. Players: Ioan
Gruffudd, Michael Chiklis, Chris
Evans, Jessica Alba, Julian
McMahon, Kerry Washington.
Prod: Avi Arad, Michael
Barnathan, Chris Columbus,
Stan Lee, Ralph Winter,
1492 Productions.

THE FOUNTAIN
[Sci-fi drama, 2005] Script:
Darren Aronofsky, Ari Handel.
Dir: Aronofsky. Phot: Matthew
Libatique. Players: Hugh
Jackman, Rachel Weisz, Ellen
Burstyn, Sean Gullette. Prod:
Gilbert Adler, Eric Watson,
Warner Bros./New Regency.

**THE HITCHHIKER'S GUIDE
TO THE GALAXY**
[Adventure, 2005] Script:

But despite the mainstream media's fixation on box-office performance, for most of the American movie going public films are not numbers, they're experiences. Week-to-week moviegoing in the United States has devolved into the navigation of a series of 'googolplex' mazes, containing featureless boxes sporting plush seats from which one can observe a bewildering array of interchangeable young stars in instantly forgettable films. No wonder the vast majority of contemporary films live or die by their opening weekend.

The Mel and Michael show

It is precisely this all-or-nothing atmosphere that breeds the Event Picture, and led to the controversy -– and success – of **The Passion of the Christ** and **Fahrenheit 9/11**. On the surface, they were improbable hits: the former spoken in Aramaic and Latin, with English subtitles, the latter (gasp!) a documentary. That both were conceived as modest pictures but were subsequently co-opted as tools for the various agendas of political and religious groups says far more about the contemporary marketplace than film as art. Seen at some remove from the events that swirled around their theatrical releases, each has strengths and weaknesses. Both are strident and manipulative, to be sure: Mel Gibson really likes Jesus Christ and Michael Moore really dislikes George W. Bush. Both have gripping, propulsive narratives, yet, in the end, are ultimately sabotaged by their directors' blinkered fervour.

Other releases bore the stamps of their creators, with varying degrees of success. The intense angularity and taut delivery of the average Clint Eastwood performance is reflected in his directorial efforts, and in this light **Mystic River** can be seen as a natural new addition to his œuvre. Superbly acted and cleanly shot, this morality tale involving the tangled fates of three south Boston chums in the wake of a murder earned Oscars for lead actor Sean Penn and supporting actor Tim Robbins.

Returning to the Western genre that Eastwood has largely vacated, Kevin Costner reclaimed the compassionate film-making authority that won Dances with Wolves the Best Picture Oscar with the elegiac and altogether magnificent **Open Range**. A character study of two proud but weary cattlemen (Costner and Robert Duvall) on the cusp of change, the film features a mischievous and enthralling performance by Duvall that some say should have won the Oscar that went to Robbins (the veteran was not even nominated). Perhaps because the genre itself has receded even further from the collective consciousness since Eastwood's Unforgiven surprised everyone by winning Best Picture for 1992, Open Range moseyed all too quietly into the sunset.

Quentin's kung-fu paradise

Though embraced with the requisite fervour by his fan base and admired with critical respect that often seemed to verge on wariness, Quentin Tarantino's **Kill Bill: Volume 1** and **Volume 2** remain guilty pleasures writ large. Stuffed to the gills with references to obscure martial arts movies and Westerns, this revenge opus in which wronged assassin Beatrix Kiddo (the smashing Uma Thurman) methodically hunts down and maybe kills her mentor/lover Bill (David Carradine) is, in the end, much smaller than the sum of its vivid parts. Split in two on the pretext of length, it could just as easily have been a serial in a dozen chapters, so jarring are the moods and styles of each sequence. It will be interesting to see if *Kill Bill* ages poorly like *Pulp Fiction*, which looks dangerously mannered only a decade after it was made, or as gracefully as the masterful and criminally unsung *Jackie Brown*.

A Band Apart/Miramax/Kobal

Chia Hui Liu and Uma Thurman in **Kill Bill: Volume 2**

David Mamet's largely unseen **Spartan** is a far less showy genre exercise from a director who prizes economy and gamesmanship above all. In a career-best turn, Val Kilmer plays Scott, a Special Ops veteran summoned from the training field to the urban battleground when the president's daughter is kidnapped. Or is she? Among the most individualistic and uncompromising film-makers currently at work, Mamet gives us a widescreen thriller that lives up to the spirit of its terse title.

The moviegoing public also found it difficult to cosy up to new films from Tim Burton (the ambitious but distancing **Big Fish**), the Coen Brothers (the laboured Ealing remake **The Ladykillers**) and Steven Spielberg (the sincerely saccharine **The Terminal**). That two of these three titles toplined Tom Hanks doing odd accents was lost on few critics, the general consensus being that the closer he stayed to his American everyman persona the more satisfying his high-profile vehicles would be.

Douglas Adams. Dir: Garth Jennings. Phot: Igor Jadue-Lillo. Players: Martin Freeman, Zooey Deschanel, Mos Def, Sam Rockwell, Bill Nighy, John Malkovich, Steve Pemberton. Prod: Roger Birnbaum, Gary Barber, Jonathan Glickman, Jay Roach, Nick Goldsmith, Walt Disney Pictures/Spyglass Entertainment/Hammer & Tongs.

HOSTAGE
[Crime thriller, 2005] Script: Robert Crais, Doug Richardson, from Crais' novel. Dir: Florent Emilio Siri. Phot: Giovanni Fiore Coltellacci. Players: Bruce Willis, Jonathan Tucker, Serena Scott Thomas, Michelle Horn, Rumer Willis. Prod: Bob Yari, Mark Gordon, Arnold Rifkin, Stratus Films/Cheyenne Enterprises.

THE INTERPRETER
[Thriller, 2005] Script: Charles Randolph, Scott Frank, Steven Zaillian. Dir: Sydney Pollack. Phot: Darius Khondji. Players: Nicole Kidman, Sean Penn, Catherine Keener, Jesper Christensen. Prod: Tim Bevan, Eric Fellner, Kevin Misher, Interpreter Productions.

THE JACKET
[Drama, 2005] Script: Marc Rocco, Massey Tadjedin. Dir: John Maybury. Phot: Peter Deming. Players: Adrien Brody, Keira Knightley, Jennifer Jason Leigh, Kelly Lynch, Kris Kristofferson, Daniel Craig. Prod: Steven Soderbergh, George Clooney, Peter Guber, Mandalay Pictures/Section Eight.

KICKING AND SCREAMING
[Sports comedy, 2005] Script: Leo Benvenuti, Steve Rudnick. Dir: Jesse Dylan. Phot: Lloyd Ahern. Players: Will Ferrell, Robert Duvall, Mike Ditka, Kate Walsh, Musetta Vander. Prod: Jimmy Miller, Charles Roven.

KINGDOM OF HEAVEN
[Historical drama, 2005] Script: William Monahan. Dir and Prod: Ridley Scott. Phot: John Mathieson. Players: Orlando

Bloom, Liam Neeson, Eva Green, Marton Csokas, Jeremy Irons, David Thewlis, Brendan Gleeson, Jon Finch.

KING KONG
[Action, 2005] Script: Fran Walsh, Philippa Boyens, Peter Jackson. Dir: Jackson. Phot: Andrew Lesnie. Players: Naomi Watts, Adrien Brody, Jack Black, Thomas Kretschmann, Colin Hanks, Andy Serkis. Prod: Jan Blenkin, Carolynne Cunningham, Walsh, Jackson, Big Primate Pictures.

LAND OF THE DEAD
[Horror, 2005] Script and Dir: George A. Romero. Phot: Miroslaw Baszak. Players: Simon Baker, Dennis Hopper, Asia Argento, Robert Joy, John Leguizamo. Prod: Mark Canton, Bernie Goldmann, Peter Grunwald, Dead Land North.

LAST DAYS
[Drama, 2005] Script and Dir: Gus Van Sant. Phot: Harris Savides. Players: Michael Pitt, Lukas Haas, Asia Argento. Prod: Van Sant, Dany Wolf, HBO Films.

THE LONGEST YARD
[Sports comedy, 2005] Script: Sheldon Turner. Dir: Peter Segal. Phot: Dean Semler. Players: Adam Sandler, Chris Rock, James Cromwell, Burt Reynolds, Nelly, Nick Turturro, Cloris Leachman, William Fichtner. Prod: Sandler, Jack Giarraputo, Van Toffler, David Gale for Happy Madison Productions/MTV Films.

THE LORDS OF DOGTOWN
[Sports drama, 2005] Script: Stacy Peralta. Dir: Catherine Hardwicke. Phot: Elliot Davis. Players: Heath Ledger, Victor Rasuk, Emile Hirsch, John Robinson, Michael Angarano, Nikki Reed, Jeremy Renner, Johnny Knoxville. Prod: Art Linson, John Linson.

THE MATADOR
[Thriller, 2005] Script and Dir: Richard Shepard. Phot: David Tattersall. Players: Pierce Brosnan, Hope Davis, Greg Kinnear, Philip Baker Hall, Dylan Baker, Adam

They'll always have Paris

Among the more pleasant surprises from newer talents were Sofia Coppola's **Lost in Translation** and Tom McCarthy's **The Station Agent**, each of which boasted a palpable sense of place and a firm, mature storytelling voice. Richard Linklater coasted from the joyous high of 2003's **School of Rock** to 2004's most serendipitous sequel, **Before Sunset**. Based in large part on the e-mails and improvs of *Before Sunrise* stars Ethan Hawke and Julie Delpy, the film gracefully revisits the star-crossed lovers nearly a decade after their impromptu amble through nocturnal Vienna. As they wander once again, this time through Paris, their chemistry – both poignant and pungent – speaks to anybody who has let that one special love slip away. Among its many strengths, *Before Sunset* features the year's most emotionally resonant final line.

Julie Delpy and Ethan Hawke in **Before Sunset**

There were riches to be found further from the star-driven spotlight as well. While some believe the professed altruism of the Sundance festival has never quite meshed with the event's cut-throat competitive nature at ground level, its 2004 slate was particularly strong, resonating well into the fourth quarter thanks to several satisfying and modestly successful titles.

The Dramatic Grand Jury winner, Shane Carruth's **Primer**, is an ultra-low-budget time-travel movie that substitutes mood and words for razzle-dazzle special effects, while Ondi Timoner's **Dig!** earned the Documentary Grand Jury prize for its decade-long exposé of the volatile competition between indie rock bands The Dandy Warhols and the Brian Jonestown Massacre. Debuting writer-director Joshua Marston almost transcends a movie-of-the-week vibe in the Spanish-language Dramatic Audience Award-winning **Maria Full of Grace** (see also Colombia section), via his shrewd direction of luminous young actress Catalino Sandino Moreno as a drug mule who survives her disastrous first and only job through a combination of luck and guile.

If Werner Herzog had conceived and directed the cheesy, 'gotta dance!' 1980s musical *Footloose*, the results might have looked something like first-time director Jared Hess' Sundance competition entry, **Napoleon Dynamite**, in which the eponymous übergeek (played by newcomer Jon Heder with the somnambulistic intensity of Herzog's Bruno S.) finds himself home alone in socially retarded Preston, Idaho, with his dorky, net-surfing brother Kip (Aaron Ruell) and Uncle Rico (Jon Gries), an inept schemer. Sighing sarcastically all the while, Napoleon gets involved with the political ambitions of his new friend Pedro (Efren Ramirez), as well as a cloddish mating dance with the alluring Deb (Tina Majorino). A one-of-a-kind movie that kept quietly drawing crowds long after its modest opening, *Napoleon Dynamite* flags Hess as a talent to watch – provided he can move beyond a one-joke premise in his subsequent work.

Other films of note from Sundance 2004 that subsequently acquitted themselves well on the arthouse circuit included Jonathan Caouette's self-absorbed but startling **Tarnation**, Chris Kentis' high-concept two-hander, **Open Water**, actor-film-maker Zach Braff's self-conscious but sincere **Garden State** and Brad Anderson's chilling **The Machinist**, which features a fearless leading performance from the next Batman, Christian Bale.

Re-entering the *Mind* of Charlie Kaufman

Kate Winslet was fond of telling interviewers that she had the Jim Carrey part in Michel Gondry's **Eternal Sunshine of the Spotless Mind** and such mischievous role reversal is at the heart of the director's second collaboration with screenwriter Charlie Kaufman (the first, *Human Nature*, was Kaufman's weakest script to date). Carrey is fine as Joel, a shy and brooding man determined to have the same memory-erasing procedure as his ex-girlfriend, Clementine (Winslet), to end his post-break-up anguish once and for all. With its intricate, time-shifting narrative callisthenics and seemingly effortless technical fluidity, the film was an early-year critical success that was expected to make an impact come the awards season.

Jim Carrey and Kate Winslet in **Eternal Sunshine of the Spotless Mind**

David Lee/Focus Features/Kobal

Scott, Roberto Sosa. Prod: Brosnan, Beau St. Clair, Sean Furst, Bryan Furst, Stratus Films.

MEMOIRS OF A GEISHA
[Drama, 2005] Script: Ron Bass, Akiva Goldsman, Robin Swicord, Doug Wright, from the novel by Arthur Golden. Dir: Rob Marshall. Phot: Dion Beebe. Players: Zhang Ziyi, Ken Watanabe, Michelle Yeoh, Gong Li, Koji Yakusho, Youki Kudoh, Cary Tagawa. Prod: Douglas Wick, Lucy Fisher, Steven Spielberg, Columbia/ DreamWorks/Spyglass.

THE MOGULS
[Comedy, 2005] Script and Dir: Michael Traeger. Phot: Denis Maloney. Players: Jeff Bridges, Jeanne Tripplehorn, Patrick Fugit, Tim Blake Nelson, Jennifer Coolidge, Isaiah Washington, William Fichtner, Gleanne Headly, Joe Pantoliano. Prod: Aaron Rider, Qwerty Films.

MONSTER-IN-LAW
[Comedy, 2005] Script: Anya Kochoff, Richard LaGravenese. Dir: Robert Luketic. Phot: Russell Carpenter. Players: Jennifer Lopez, Jane Fonda, Michael Vartan, Wanda Sykes. Prod: Paula Weinstein, Chris Bender, J.C. Spink, Julio Caro, Avery Productions.

THE NEW WORLD
[Historical drama, 2005] Script and Dir: Terrence Malick. Phot: Emmanuel Lubezki. Players: Colin Farrell, Q'orianka Kilcher, Christopher Plummer, Christian Bale, August Schellenberg, Wes Studi, David Thewlis, John Savage, Noah Taylor. Prod: Sarah Green, The Virginia Company.

THE PRODUCERS: THE MOVIE MUSICAL
[Musical comedy, 2005] Script: Mel Brooks, Thomas Meehan. Dir: Susan Stroman. Phot: John Bailey. Players: Nathan Lane, Matthew Broderick, Nicole Kidman, Will Ferrell, Roger Bart, Gary Beach. Prod: Brooks, Jonathan Sanger, Brooksfilms.

SHADOWBOXER
[Crime thriller, 2005] Script:
Will Rokos. Dir: Lee Daniels.
Phot: M. David Mullen. Players:
Cuba Gooding Jr., Helen Mirren,
Vanessa Ferlito, Mo'Nique. Prod:
Brook Lenfest, Lisa Cortes, Dave
Robinson, Shadowboxer.

SHOPGIRL
[Romantic comedy, 2005] Script:
Steve Martin, from his novella.
Dir: Anand Tucker. Phot: Peter
Suschitzky. Players: Martin, Claire
Danes, Jason Schwartzman,
Frances Conroy, Sam Bottoms,
Rebecca Pidgeon. Prod: Ashok
Amritraj, Jon Jashni, Martin, Hyde
Park Entertainment/Shopgirl.

SIN CITY
[Crime action, 2005] Script: Frank
Miller. Dir and Phot: Robert
Rodriguez. Players: Bruce Willis,
Benicio Del Toro, Clive Owen,
Mickey Rourke, Elijah Wood,
Nick Stahl, Carla Gugino, Brittany
Murphy, Michael Clarke Duncan,
Josh Hartnett. Prod: Rodriguez,
Elizabeth Avellan, Frank Miller,
Dimension Films.

TISHOMINGO BLUES
[Historical thriller, 2005] Script:
John Richards, from the novel by
Elmore Leonard. Dir: Don
Cheadle. Players: Matthew
McConaughey, Cheadle. Prod:
Cathy Schulman, Rebecca
Yeldham, Bull's Eye Entertainment.

WALK THE LINE
[Biographical musical-drama,
2005] Script: James Mangold,
Gill Dennis. Dir: Mangold. Phot:
Phedon Papamichael. Players:
Joaquin Phoenix, Reese
Witherspoon, Shelby Lynn,
Robert Patrick, Ginnifer
Goodwin. Prod: Cathy Konrad,
James Keach, Fox 2000 Films.

THE WEATHER MAN
[Drama, 2005] Script: Steve
Conrad. Dir: Gore Verbinski.
Phot: Phedon Papamichael.
Players: Nicolas Cage, Hope
Davis, Michael Caine. Prod:
Todd Black, Steve Tisch, Jason
Blumenthal, David Alper,
Escape Artists.

In the US, the popularity of documentary cinema discussed in the dossier at the front of this volume went beyond *Fahrenheit 9/11*. Among the most notable non-fiction releases was Brit Kevin Macdonald's *Touching the Void*, a gripping true-life tale of mountain-climbing heroism that pulls off the rare triumph of leaning on staged sequences without their distracting from the story.

A more high-profile success also sprang from personal risk. To make **Super Size me**, Morgan Spurlock ate nothing but McDonald's fast food for 30 days – a diet that had disastrous effects on his health. Displaying a cocky, gung-ho spirit, Spurlock's fearlessness results in a film sure to make even the most inattentive eater take stock of his or her diet. As *Super Size me* and *Fahrenheit 9/11* vied for attention in the entertainment press, humour magazine *The Onion* summarised their startling success: "Michael Moore Kicking Self for Not Filming Last 600 Trips to McDonald's".

Raising the *Dead*

Remake fever continues unabated, the surprising success of Zack Snyder's retooled **Dawn of the Dead** being emblematic of this dismaying trend. Speeded up and dumbed down, it displays flashes of creepiness and genuine wit without ever establishing the connection between zombies and consumerism that made George A. Romero's 1978 original the acknowledged king of the genre. Thankfully, Romero's fourth chapter in the saga, *Land of the Dead*, is on the way. Future retreads run the gamut from Peter Jackson's take on *King Kong* to the Adam Sandler starrer *The Longest Yard*, inspired by Robert Aldrich's 1974 gridiron comedy (at least Sandler has had the wit to get original star Burt Reynolds involved). Some remakes are so successful they spawn sequels of their own: if all goes to plan, the second *Italian Job* will hit theatres in November 2005.

While the 2004 kudos sweepstakes remained wide open at press time, some fourth quarter releases had already distinguished themselves. Alexander Payne's magnificent **Sideways**, discussed in his *IFG* Director of the Year profile, was not the only autumn opener that dared to be unabashedly humanist. Quite rightly compared to the heyday of satirist Preston Sturges, David O. Russell's **I♥ Huckabees** is a breathless, wide-eyed existential comedy that manages to stuff meditations on September 11, personal responsibility and the importance of family into a fast-paced farce about an idealistic environmentalist (Jason Schwartzman) who proudly bucks the system. Encouragingly, the film's limited opening weekend in New York and Los Angeles in October garnered the highest per-screen average of the year.

There were many other prominent stories during 2003-04, including the piracy-fuelled battle over distribution of industry screener tapes and DVDs of films clamouring for awards, the struggle between the Weinstein brothers and Disney over the fate of Miramax, and the future of animation powerhouse Pixar. Yet these and other industry sub-plots only enhanced the peculiar and often contrary business of moviemaking. From great uncertainty comes solid art.

20th Century Fox

Jude Law, Naomi Watts, Dustin Hoffman and Lily Tomlin in I ♥ Huckabees

Quotes of the Year

"We see January as an opportunity for carefully selected product. It's for people who've gotten tired of seeing really good movies."
ANONYMOUS *studio source explains Hollywood release patterns, reported by* Newsweek, *January 2004.*

"I think there will be a lot of powerful people in Hollywood saying, 'Somebody get me a Jesus picture.'"
PAUL LAUER, *Mel Gibson's publicist, anticipates studio executives' response to* The Passion of the Christ.

"I encourage all teenagers to see my movie, by any means necessary. If you need me to sneak you in, let me know."
MICHAEL MOORE *reacts to the MPAA's 'R' rating for* Fahrenheit 9/11.

Correction: Eddie Cockrell's selection of the Year's Best Films was inadvertently omitted from his US report in *IFG* 2004. They were: *Far from Heaven* (Todd Haynes), *Antwone Fisher* (Denzel Washington), *Punch-Drunk Love* (Paul Thomas Anderson), *About Schmidt* (Alexander Payne), *Capturing the Friedmans* (Docu. Andrew Jarecki).

The 76th Academy Awards (2003)

Film: *The Lord of the Rings: The Return of the King.*
Animated Feature Film: *Finding Nemo* (Andrew Stanton).
Direction: Peter Jackson (*The Return of the King*).
Actor: Sean Penn (*Mystic River*).
Actress: Charlize Theron (*Monster*).
Supporting Actor: Tim Robbins (*Mystic River*).
Supporting Actress: Renée Zellweger (*Cold Mountain*).
Original Screenplay: Sofia Coppola (*Lost in Translation*).
Adapted Screenplay: Fran Walsh, Philippa Boyens and Peter Jackson (*The Return of the King*).
Cinematography: Russell Boyd (*Master and Commander: The Far Side of the World*).
Film Editing: Jamie Selkirk (*The Return of the King*).
Sound Mixing: Christopher Boyes, Michael Semanick, Michael Hedges and Hammond Peek (*The Return of the King*).
Sound Editing: Richard King (*Master and Commander*).
Visual Effects: Jim Rygiel, Joe Letteri, Randall William Cook, Alex Funke (*Return of the King*).
Costume Design: Ngila Dickson, Richard Taylor (*Return of the King*).
Art Direction/Set Decoration: Grant Major/Dan Hennah and Alan Lee (*The Return of the King*).
Make-Up: Richard Taylor and Peter King (*Return of the King*).
Original Score: Howard Shore (*The Return of the King*).
Original Song: "Into the West" from *The Return of the King*. Music and Lyrics by Fran Walsh, Howard Shore and Annie Lennox.
Foreign-Language Film: *The Barbarian Invasions* (Canada).
Documentary Feature: *The Fog of War* (Errol Morris).
Documentary Short: *Chernobyl Heart* (Maryann DeLeo).
Short Film (Animated): *Harvie Krumpet* (Adam Elliot).
Short film (Live Action): *Two Soldiers* (Aaron Schneider and Andrew J. Sacks).
Honorary Award: Blake Edwards.

Uruguay Jorge Jellinek

The Year's Best Films

Jorge Jellinek's selection:
Whisky (Juan Pablo Rebella,
Pablo Stoll)
Seawards Journey
(Guillermo Casanova)
Palabras Verdaderas
(Ricardo Casas)

Recent and Forthcoming Films

WHISKY

*[Comedy-drama, 2003] Script:
Juan Pablo Rebella, Pablo Stoll,
Gonzalo Delgado. Dir: Stoll,
Rebella. Phot: Bárbara Alvarez.
Players: Jorge Bolani, Mirella
Pascual, Andrés Pazos, Daniel
Hendler. Prod: CTRL-Z Films.*

Werner Schünemann in **Alma Mater**

ALMA MATER

*[Drama, 2004] Script and Dir:
Alvaro Buela. Players: Roxana
Blanco, Nicolás Becerra, Walter
Reyno, Werner Schünemann.
Prod: José Pedro Charlo,
Austero Producciones.*
A shy thirtysomething virgin who
works in a supermarket has her
routine life transformed by mystic
signs and the influence of a
Brazilian evangelical preacher
(Schünemann), who convinces her
she has been chosen as mother of
the new Messiah.

ruguayan cinema experienced mixed emotions in 2003-04.
Good news came from abroad, with an exceptional harvest
of more than 60 international prizes for Uruguayan film-
makers, but at one point the financial woes affecting the whole
country threatened to paralyse movie production.

There was public success and international recognition for Guillermo
Casanova's *Seawards Journey*, which became one of the biggest hits
of the year and won top prize at the Huelva festival, and the
controversy surrounding *Aside* (*Aparte*; see *IFG 2004*), Mario Handler's
powerful and gritty documentary about youths living in poverty in the
Montevideo suburbs, helped it sell 60,000 tickets. The greatest impact
was made by *Whisky*, the brilliant comedy-drama by Juan Pablo
Rebella and Pablo Stoll, the successful team behind *25 watts*. Their
ironic, melancholy portrait of their parents' generation won two awards
in Un Certain Regard at Cannes 2004 (the FIPRESCI prize and the
jury's Regard Original) and nine other international prizes.

Whisky features a funny performance from Daniel Hendler, who won
the Silver Bear for Best Actor at Berlin for the Argentinean drama
A Lost Embrace (*El abrazo partido*; see Argentina section),
confirming the increasing international recognition for young
Uruguayan talents. Another Uruguayan who works in Argentina is
director Adrián Caetano, best known for *The Red Bear*, who
returned home to make a high-rating mini-series, *Uruguayos
campeones* (literally, *Uruguayan Champions*), about a popular but
impoverished football team's struggle for survival.

Jorge Bolani in **Whisky**, *winner of two awards at Cannes*

A time of crisis

These international awards arrived as the country experienced one of the most severe economic crises in recent history. Somehow, film production continued at normal speed despite the absence of state support, even when banks were collapsing and unemployment soaring. The Ministry of Culture stopped contributing to the Municipality of Montevideo's Fondo Nacional del Audiovisual (FONA). FONA, established in 1995, is co-financed by cable TV operators who are supposed to put in around $70,000 each annually, enabling it to hold an open competition that gives prizes of around $70,000 to fiction and documentary features (including *Whisky* and *Seawards Journey*). However, in the absence of state and cable contributions, FONA was forced to suspend its call for entries for 2003 (its competition resumed in 2004).

In November 2003, the ministry also seemed likely to default on its annual $100,000 contribution to the international fund Ibermedia, which is essential to many Uruguayan projects. This prompted several directors, including Walter Tournier, Luis Nieto and Ricardo Casas, to go on hunger strike, a protest that eventually persuaded the ministry to resume its Ibermedia payments (at press time it looked as though financial arrangements for 2005 would not be finalised until the new left-wing government took office in March). The protest also revealed the determination of a cinematic movement that is developing into a mature expression of Uruguayan cultural identity.

With its deadpan humour and minimalist style, **Whisky** (the title refers to the word used to get people to smile when photographed), reflects the contradictions of a society divided between the need for change and the paralysing fear this need can induce. Two middle-aged brothers are reunited after many years. Jacobo Koller (Andrés Pazos) is the tall, reserved Jewish owner of a failing sock factory, who is jealous of his livelier, successful brother, Herman (Jorge Bolani), who has returned from Brazil. Jacobo's decision to pretend that he is married to one of his workers, Marta (Mirella Pascual), a solitary, unattractive and romantic daydreamer, sparks a series of passionate deceptions.

All three actors are superb (especially Pascual) and *Whisky*'s hapless, stagnating characters reflect the predicament of younger people, many of whom are forced to emigrate in search of brighter horizons. The austere visual style bears the influence of Jim Jarmusch and Aki Kaurismäki, and *Whisky* is a major step forward for Rebella and Stoll.

To see the sea

A more optimistic image was presented by Guillermo Casanova's colourful **Seawards Journey** (*El viaje hacia el mar*), which with

RUIDO (*literally,* **Noise**)
[*Comedy, 2004*] *Script and Dir:* Marcelo Bertalmío. *Phot: Daniel Machado. Players: Lucía Carlevari, Jorge Bazzano, Mariana Olazabal, Jorge Visca. Prod: Lavorágine Films/Jorge Rocca (Argentina)/ Zeppelin Films (Spain).*
Basilio is an unhappy man with a golden heart and a tendency to get involved in other people's problems. Depressed and on the brink of suicide, he is rescued by a 12-year-old girl who asks for his help.

FAN (working title)
[*Comedy-drama, 2004*] *Script and Dir: Gabriela Guillermo. Players: Gabriela Iribarren, María Mendive, Eduardo Méndez. Prod: BFS Producciones/Truque (Brazil)/Joel Films (Venezuela)/ Cinema Public Film (France).*
A middle-aged woman returns to her home country in search of a new meaning to life. Her obsession with a peculiar Brazilian musician leads to a dangerous mixture of fantasy with reality.

PALABRAS VERDADERAS (*literally,* **True Words**)
[*Documentary, 2004*] *Script and Dir: Ricardo Casas. Phot: Daniel Rodríguez, Pedro Luque. Prod: Yvonne Roucco, Guazú Media/Zeppelin Films (Spain).*
Portrait of Mario Benedetti, the politically active Uruguayan novelist and poet who lived long years in exile during the military regime. Fellow writers, including José Saramago, Manuel Vázquez Montalbán, Juan Gelman and Eduardo Galeano, and singer Joan Manuel Serrat discuss his work.

EL BAÑO DEL PAPA (**The Pope's Toilet**)
[*Comedy, forthcoming*] *Script and Dir: Enrique Fernández. Prod: Elena Roux.*
In 1988, during the Pope's visit to Uruguay, the news that he will visit the little town of Melo inspires an ambitious local smuggler to build a public toilet and make money from the thousands of visitors expected.

LA PERRERA (Dog Pound)
[Comedy-drama, forthcoming]
Script and Dir: Manuel Nieto.
Prod: CTRL-Z Films.
After losing his scholarship,
David, a failed student, must
return to the house in a small,
isolated beach town, where his
authoritarian father spends the
weekends. Taking care of dogs
becomes an important part of the
his life as he starts building his
own home on an abandoned lot.

TOKYO BOOGIE
*[Comedy, forthcoming] Script
Pablo Casacuberta, Yukihiko
Goto, Viki Anderson, Inés
Bortagaray. Dir: Casacuberta,
Goto. Prod: Casacuberta.*
In the 1950s, a Japanese film crew
arrives by mistake in a small town
in Uruguay, looking for locations
to make a Western. The film shoot
stalls as confusion grows.

EL VIAJE HACIA EL MAR
(Seawards Journey)
*[Comedy, 2003] Script: Guillermo
Casanova and Julio César Castro,
based on the short story by Juan
José Morosoli. Dir: Casanova.
Phot: Bárbara Alvarez, Daniel
Rodríguez. Players: Hugo Arana,
César Troncoso, Diego Delgrossi,
Julio Calcagno, Héctor Guido,
Bruno Musitelli, Julio César
Castro. Prod: Lavorágine
Films/Jorge Rocca (Argentina).*

Quotes of the Year

"It does not matter if the
government cuts its support
for film production. We're
here to stay and they can't
stop us."
GUILLERMO CASANOVA,
director of Seawards Journey,
*filmed in the middle of a national
economic crisis.*

"It was a weird experience.
We felt like we had won the
football World Cup."
PABLO STOLL, *co-director of*
Whisky, *after winning two
awards at Cannes.*

lighthearted humour and lyricism presents an idealised image of the
1950s. Adapted from a short story by popular writer Juan José
Morosoli (1899-1957), this subtle, sensitive road movie aims to
recover the essence of national identity through the adventure of a
group of country folk who on a hot summer's day travel in an old red
truck from the hills to the coast, to contemplate the sea for the first
time. It contains inspired moments and a talented cast, including
Julio César Castro (also known as "Juceca"), who sadly died a few
months after the film opened, and Argentina's Hugo Arana.

*Left to right: Aquino the dog, Julio César Castro, Hugo Arana, Julio Calcagno, Héctor
Guido and Diego Delgrossi in* Seawards Journey

Riding the waves made by Handler's *Aside*, documentary
production is on the rise. In **Palabras verdaderas** (literally, *True
Words*), Ricardo Casas delivers a revealing, warm portrait of Mario
Benedetti, the internationally celebrated Uruguayan writer. The life of
musician Gerardo Mattos Rodríguez is assessed in **La Cumparsita,
el tango uruguayo** (literally, *La Cumparsita, the Uruguayan Tango*),
a serious biography by Darío Medina that proves the true authorship
of arguably the world's most famous tango, written in 1917.

More releases are expected for 2005, including the surrealist
comedy **Ruido** (literally, *Noise*) by Marcelo Bertalmío, an exploration
of popular mysticism in Alvaro Buela's **Alma Mater**, presented at
San Sebastian, and the film noir **Orlando Vargas**, a co-production
with France, directed by debutant Juan Pittaluga, which features
France's Aurelien Recoing and Romania's Elina Löwensohn. Polish
master Krzysztof Zanussi has chosen Uruguayan locations for his
forthcoming *Persona non grata*, his morality tale about the intriguing
world of diplomats. All this intense activity in late 2004 comes in the
context of slow economic recovery and the election of a new
government more inclined to support film production, so the
prospects seem brighter than ever for the audiovisual industry.

JORGE JELLINEK (jorjelli@adinet.com.uy) has been a film critic and
journalist for 20 years, contributing to newspapers, magazines and
radio. He writes for the Pan-American weekly *Tiempos del Mundo*
and is vice-president of the Uruguayan Critics' Association.

Zimbabwe Martin Botha

Recent and Forthcoming Films

THE BIG TIME
[Romantic drama, 2004]
Script and Dir: Olley Maruma.
Players: Karen Stally, Herbert
Shwarmborn, Erica Glyn Jones,
Desdemona Kinnards. Prod:
Moonlight Productions.

MY LAND MY LIFE
[Documentary, 2002] Dir: Rehad
Desai. Prod: Dan Jawitz, Desai.

SECRETS
[Drama, 2004] Dir: Ngugi wa
Mirii. Players: Fortune Rego,
Margaret Wairimu Ngugi. Prod:
wa Mirii, Visions of Africa.

THE LEGEND OF THE
SKY KINGDOM
[Animated drama, 2003]
Dir: Roger Hawkins.
Prod: Phil Cunningham,
Sunrise Productions.

The Legend of the Sky Kingdom

ZIMBABWE COUNTDOWN
[Documentary, 2002] Script and
Dir: Michael Raeburn. Phot:
Raeburn, Ed Maplanga. Prod:
Arte France/T.A.C.T. Production.

ZIMBABWE 2002
[Documentary, 2002]
Dir: Farai Sevenzo.

Since the last *IFG* report on Zimbabwe, in the 2003 edition, the crisis in the country has deepened. With an economy that has left 70% of the population in poverty, the local film industry is inevitably languishing – and yet an oppositional cinema has emerged, thanks to expatriate Zimbabwean film-makers. Three personal documentaries by progressive directors who reflect with sadness on the present crisis stand out.

With **My Land My Life**, Rehad Desai takes the viewer into the heart of the crisis, following a farmer, a 'war veteran' and a farm worker in the run-up to the 2002 presidential elections. All three are caught up in the land crisis and have very different hopes and expectations for the future.

Winner of the Best Documentary award at the 13th African Film Festival in Milan in 2003, **Zimbabwe Countdown** is a very personal and political film by Michael Raeburn. The title refers to Raeburn's 1970 documentary, *Rhodesia Countdown*, an exposé of the regime of Ian Smith, which led to Raeburn's expulsion from his home country.

His latest film examines the background to the hardships and harassment endured daily by Zimbabweans under Mugabe. Through interviews with high-level contacts and ordinary citizens Raeburn exposes the ruling ethos of the ZANU-PF party and reflects on the betrayal of the ideals that initially convinced people to elect Mugabe. After this film, Raeburn again finds himself unwelcome in his home country.

For **Zimbabwe 2002**, Farai Sevenzo returned to the country during the elections to observe first-hand how the voting process would affect people and charts the manner in which ordinary families persevere at a time of political conflict.

Some critics also read an oppositional viewpoint into the animated feature **The Legend of the Sky Kingdom**, shot between 1999 and 2002. On the surface, this fable comes across as an exciting tale of four friends battling evil on their journey to freedom. In the context of current affairs, the story articulates a sincere wish to be freed from an oppressive regime.

Rest of the World

BAHRAIN

Bassam Al-Thawadi made **The Visitor** (*Al za'ir*), his second feature film, in 2004. It is a drama that borders on the paranormal, twisting back and forth between reality and fantasy, and represents a major change of direction for Al-Thawadi, who in 1990 made the first Bahrainian feature, *The Fence* (*Al hajis*). Though *The Visitor* is a lesser artistic achievement, its very existence is remarkable in a country without a film industry – or even the seeds of one.

Al-Thawadi, whose day job is as a producer and director with Bahrain Television (he also runs the Bahrain Film Festival), was so keen to direct another fiction feature that he convinced local distributors to make *The Visitor* with him for less than $200,000. On local release it recouped its money and made some profit, which should help the director make his third picture (already written) within a year or two. It was also well received in other Gulf states, at a time when the whole area is witnessing its first major wave of film-making since the 1970s. – *Mohammed Rouda*

BANGLADESH

After a bright start, the film industry in Bangladesh started to decline in the late 1970s and the downward trend has continued ever since. The industry is now a hostage to an antiquated censorship policy and rampant over-commercialisation. Appointments to the Censorship Board are politically motivated, often with seemingly little regard for a candidate's film industry experience. In the marketplace there is a vicious cycle: an all-pervasive atmosphere of unhealthy vulgarity in an industry serving audiences interested only in raw entertainment. Most Bangladeshi films today are a slapdash mixture of elements from two or three Bollywood or Hollywood movies, or are outright remakes.

It is high time for opinion formers and civilised society as a whole to demand better films and to support a group of promising alternative film-makers, who are currently shunned by mainstream cinemas. The impact of Tareque Masud's *The Clay Bird* (*Matir moina*, 2002) has at least encouraged new directors such as Morshedul Islam, Tanvir Mokammel, Abu Sayeed and Humayun Ahmed, who have started making films that are once again drawing middle-class viewers to cinemas. Encouragingly, in 2003 almost all of the National Film Awards went to these young enthusiasts, who have been influenced by the local Film Societies movement. Quite a revolution!

Among the features from 2003, four are worthy of mention. Chashi Nazrul Islam's **Hason Raja** was a historical drama about a descendent of Raja Birendra Singhdev, the Hindu king who became Muslim. Hason was a fascinating character – he lost his elder brother at an early age, and became Zeminder, as cruel as he was affectionate – but Islam, despite his wealth of directing experience (more than 20 films), could not bring life to the story. Most of his actors appeared stiff, and everything from the make-up to the dialogue seemed artificial.

Humayun Ahmed's **The Tale of the Moon** (*Chandrakatha*) and Moushumi's **Sometimes Clouds, Sometimes Rain** (*Kakhono megh kakhonob brishti*) were both given warm receptions by audiences and critics, but the best film of 2003 was probably Saidul Anam Tutul's **The Battle of the Sharecroppers** (*Adhiar*), which dramatises the Bengal Association of Provincial Peasants' great movement to secure its members a two-thirds share of their crops. For this feature debut, Tutul took a major commercial risk by casting unknown actors from television and theatre instead of established local cinema stars.

Three notable films appeared in 2004. Mostafa Sarwar Farooki's **Bachelor** is the commercially successful tale of six bachelors, aged 22 to 44, who share a rented flat in Dhaka: Fahim, a producer at Radio Bangladesh, Rumel, who works for an NGO, Maruf, a computer accessories supplier, Hasan Mahmud, a retired army officer, Marzuk, an architect, poet and lyricist and Shohag, a university student.

Arman Parvez Murad as Maruf in **Bachelor**

In Morshedul Islam's **The Distance** (*Duratta*), an 11-year old boy runs away from the impersonal atmosphere of his wealthy family home and encounters a new life in the outside world. He feels guilty for being so rich, and in a biting winter dawn confronts a puzzling question to which he has no answer. Finally, **Clouds After Clouds** (*Megher pore megh*), directed by Chashi Nazrul Islam, is a story of love, patriotism and Bangladesh's Liberation War. Human weakness and capacity for greatness are explored in a most efficient manner.

By **AHMED MUZTABA ZAMAL**
(amzamal@bdcom.com), Secretary General of FIPRESCI Bangladesh and Festival Director of the Dhaka International Film Festival.

BENIN

Before looking at Benin and other francophone West African countries individually, it's important to note the common factor uniting virtually all film-making in this region: its reliance on French government initiatives. In the mid-1960s, it was the French who established a 16mm production system in Africa, through the funding decisions of the French Ministry of Co-operation, which was set up specifically to sustain economic and cultural links between France and its former African colonies. As a result, African film-makers were cut off from the commercial 35mm distribution systems in their own countries. Another move by the French government, in the mid-1980s, led to the shift to 35mm filming which characterises African film production today.

The current French government aim seems to be to sponsor "prestige" African productions that can get European screenings, ideally at Cannes. There is also a very conscious effort to make French aid all-embracing, and during the four years' existence of the funding body ADCSud (2000-2003), funding was given to at least one film-maker from each of the 12 independent states created by the break-up of the former giant French colonies (French West Africa and French Equatorial Africa), as well one apiece from the Democratic Republic of Congo (ex-Zaire) and the former Portuguese colonies of Angola, Mozambique and Guinea-Bissau. The new French funding body, the Fonds Images Afrique, set up on January 1, 2004, appears likely to adopt a similar policy.

Given the extent of French dominance and the paucity of African film production infrastructure, the "nationality" of an African film often reflects little more than its director's place of birth, seldom his place of residence. Half the West African film-makers considered on these pages have their homes, production base and sources of funding in Paris.

Two of these Parisian "exiles" were originally from Benin (formerly Dahomey), where there was an embryonic "national" cinema in the 1970s. A state film organisation was established and a couple of features made, but only one more film followed in the next 24 years. One of the two film-makers involved in the renewal in 1999 was the Paris-based actor Jean Odoutan (b. 1965 in Cotonou) who, with four films in five years, has became the most prolific of the new young African directors.

A man of immense vitality, he made his first film, *Barbeque Pejo* (1999), in Benin, and quickly followed it with two others, both set in the immigrant districts of Paris: *Djib* (2000) and *Mama Aloko* (2001). He founded his own company in Paris and the only production company in Benin, Tabou-Tabac Films. Working with minuscule budgets, Odoutan is a complete auteur, not only producer, scriptwriter and director, but also composer and lead actor.

His latest feature, **The Waltz of the Fat Bottoms** (*La valse des gros derrières*, 2003), again set in Paris, is a typically lively comedy, described on the poster as "a caramelised tidbit". It deals with the attempts of a voluptuous 28-year-old hairdresser, Akwélé, proud of her nickname, "Incommensurable Antelope", to achieve her life's ambition and become a top model. – *Roy Armes*

A poster for **The Waltz of the Fat Bottoms**

BURKINA FASO

Three currently active West African cinemas – Burkina Faso, Ivory Coast and Mali (as well as Senegal; see p.254) – have production bases which keep their film-makers on home soil,

though French funding is still indispensible. Burkina Faso occupies a paradoxical position. Though it possessed only six cinemas at the time of independence and was slow to develop feature film production, it became the centre of African film-making and is currently home to Black Africa's leading biennial film festival, FESPACO, the African Film-makers' Association (FEPACI) and the African film library (the Cinémathèque Africaine). However, with 17 feature directors and an output of just 36 films in 35 years, opportunities for individuals in the country are limited.

Fire (*Tasuma*, 2002) was Daniel Sanou Kollo's first feature for 20 years (spent mostly on television work). Celebrating the strengths of village life, it tells of the struggle of a former soldier in the French army to get his pension paid. Despite the difficulties of obtaining production finance, newcomers still break through, as Hébié Missa did with **Diarabi** (2003).

The three key figures in Burkinan cinema, responsible for almost half the national output, were all born in the 1950s, studied film-making in Paris and began their careers in the 1980s. Gaston Kabore's last film dates from 1996, but Idrissa Ouedraogo and Pierre Yaméogo are still active. Since his debut with three internationally acclaimed village films (*Yam daabo*, *Yaaba* and *Tilaï*) in the late 1980s, Ouedraogo has tackled a wide variety of subjects, both traditional and modern.

His eighth feature, **The Gods' Anger** (*La colère des dieux*, 2002), is a return to traditional Africa. Originally planned as an epic of African struggle against the French, along the lines of Med Hondo's *Sarraounia* (co-produced by Burkina Faso), the film for which Ouedraogo found funding is a more inward-looking piece, probing the reasons for African defeat and examining how this might be the result of African society's complex relationship with its gods.

Pierre Yaméogo's fifth film, by contrast, is a thoroughly modern piece in his customary direct realist style. **Me and My White Guy** (*Moi et mon* blanc, 2002) is the story of a student who faces a squalid world of vice and corruption when he is forced to take a job as a car park attendant. When he and his white colleagues discover the loot from a robbery, they are pursued by drug dealers and must flee to Burkina Faso. Underpinning the action is a vigorous denunciation of French racism and African corruption. – *Roy Armes*

Pierre Yaméogo's **Me and My White Guy**

CENTRAL AFRICAN REPUBLIC

In 2003, the Central African Republic (Centrafrique) became the twelfth and final French West African ex-colony to have a film funded by Paris. The French-trained Didier Ouenangaré's first feature, **The Silence of the Forest** (*Le silence de la forêt*), co-directed with the experienced Cameroonian director Bassek Ba Kobhio, tells of a school inspector who is disillusioned when he returns from France to Africa. Frustrated, he turns his attention to the fate of the pygmies, and his subsequent misadventures are told with verve and humour. – *Roy Armes*

CHAD

As with Benin, the cinema of Chad exists essentially in Paris. The country is the birthplace of two Paris-trained and French-based film-makers. Mahamat-Saleh Haroun (b. 1961 in

Ambéche) worked for several years in France as a journalist before turning to film-making. His first feature, *Bye Bye Africa* (1999), was shot on video and transferred to 35mm. Essentially it is the story of the director's return to his origins, using a dazzling mixture of documentary and fiction, colour and black-and-white, observation and meditation.

Abouna (2002), shot on 35mm, is a more sober and conventionally structured work. Impeccably framed and shot, it focuses on the lives of two small boys abandoned by their father. It shows the details of their daily lives and dreams, the weight of the past and their desire for the future. – *Roy Armes*

Mahamat Saleh Haroun's **Abouna**

DEMOCRATIC REPUBLIC OF CONGO

The turbulent and chaotic history of Zaire, now the Democratic Republic of Congo, under President Mobuto meant that no film production structures developed there and most of the country's film-makers live in exile. José Zéka Laplaine (b. 1960) came to Europe aged 18 and studied theatre in Brussels and Paris, where he now lives. He began his career as an actor and when he turned to film-making (without formal training), his first feature, *Macadam Tribu* (1996), became an international success.

Daddy's Garden (*Le jardin de papa*, 2003), his third feature, tells of a French couple, Jean and Marie, who go on honeymoon to Dakar, where the husband grew up, only to find themselves plunged into chaos because of the country's approaching elections, a road accident and a hostage situation. – *Roy Armes*

A couple are caught up in chaos in **Daddy's Garden**

GUINEA

Since its first feature was produced in 1966, the cinema of Guinea comprises essentially three stages: a trio of films by Dansogho Mohamed Camara and a dance film by Moussa Kemoko Diakite, made between 1977 and 1990; three films directed between 1991 and 2002 by Cheik Doukouré (b. 1943), who has lived in France for 40 years; and debut films by three younger directors since 1997.

Doukouré's third film, the low-budget **Paris According to Moussa** (*Paris selon Moussa*, 2002), is the story of a farmer who comes to Paris to buy a water pump for his village but is immediately robbed. While he stays on for the month allowed by his visa, to try to earn the money he needs, he gets involved in a church protest by illegal immigrants. Based on a true incident, the film is told with warmth and humour and Doukouré's performance as the farmer won him the top acting award at FESPACO 2003.

Mama Keïta (b. 1956) is a Paris-based member of the younger generation. His second film, **The River** (*Le fleuve*, 2003), tells of Alfa, who kills a drug dealer and flees to stay with family relatives he does not know in Senegal. The immediate impact of Africa is brutal, but eventually he rediscovers both himself and his roots. – *Roy Armes*

IVORY COAST

The country's two, very different major film-makers are both 1970s pioneers: Henri Duparc, who has made six features, most of them exuberant comedies, and Roger Gnoan Mbala, who has made five, specialising of late in village dramas treating themes of power and religion. Though Ivory Coast is the fourth-largest West African cinema in terms of volume, none of the other dozen or so directors has made more than a couple of films, so it is difficult to give a focus to Ivory Coast cinema, beyond noting that nine of the 13 feature directors born there are graduates of one or other of the Paris film schools.

Among those not trained in Paris are the authors of the two latest Ivory Coast features, both made in 2002 and shown at FESPACO 2003. Didier Aufort (b. 1951, Djibouti) has dual French–Ivory Coast nationality and a background in television commercials and institutional documentaries. His **Betting on Love** (*Le pari de l'amour*), is the romantic tale of an Abidjan hairdresser who wins the lottery and thinks, wrongly, that she has met the love of her life.

By contrast, Sidiki Siriji Bakaba (b. 1949) is one of Africa's most distinguished theatre actor-directors and has appeared in more than a dozen French and African films. His second feature, **Freewheeling** (*Roues libres*), made 14 years after his first, is again an urban tale set in the mythical African capital of Katakata.

This time the story concerns two crippled men who compel a taxi driver to become their accomplice in a series of robberies and murders. But they are pursued by the implacable Commissioner Blazo (Bakaba himself) and their killing spree leads inevitably to death, on the waterfront at dawn. Despite the violence perpetrated by his protagonists, Bakaba's press release described the film as "a cry of hope, because the life of a handicapped person is a daily lesson in courage, intelligence and resourcefulness". – *Roy Armes*

KUWAIT

Kuwait is the only one of the Gulf states to have seen any kind of a film-making "wave" in the past 35 years, thanks largely to Khalid Al-Siddiq, who in 1969 gained international fame as he wrote, directed and produced his first film, *Hush, Sea* (*Bass ya bahir*). He followed it with *The Wedding of Zein* (*Ors al zein*, 1976), a Kuwaiti–Sudanese film based on a internationally acclaimed novel by (Sudanese) writer Al Taib Saleh. Siddik managed to find backing from Kuwait, Italy and India for his third project, *Shahin* (1980), named after a type of eagle found only in the Gulf region.

After that, Siddik and Kuwaiti cinema were dormant – not helped by the crash of the Kuwati trade market and the first Gulf War. Then suddenly, in 2004, out of nowhere, two films were made. Abdullah Al Salman financed **Midnight** (*Mintasaf ellayl*) from his own pocket, in order, he has said "to make sure that I take the full responsibility and risk". Another newcomer, Mohammed Daham, made **Young and Cool** (*Shabab Kool*), and both films did well in Kuwiat, despite the limited size of the local market.

A major player in Kuwaiti production is Hashim Mohammed, who in 1981 made *The Silence* (*Al samt*) and now heads the governmental Joint Programme Production Institution, which is financed and managed by Gulf Corporation Council. Mohammed reports that since the end of the war in 1991, the firm has produced documentaries, educational films and animation. At press time he was readying the organisation for its first pan-Gulf feature in 2006.
– *Mohammed Rouda*

MACEDONIA

Despite Macedonia's ongoing political and economic problems, its film industry remains active and in 2003-04 six feature films were produced, five with substantial co-production finance from Italy and France. One of the Macedonian–Italian joint ventures was Darko Mitrevski's **Bal-Can-Can**, in which an Italian

criminal makes a deathbed request to his son to go and find the friend he betrayed years earlier. This story of friendship and moral conformism is fleshed out in fine Balkan style.

In Svetozar Ristovski's feature debut, **Mirage** (*Ilusija*), a student, Marko, tries to make sense of his life. A very interesting short, *Bugs* (*Bubachki*) by Igor Ivanov Izy, about an autistic man, Petar, who must confront the outside word, competed at Berlin in 2004. – *Goga Lomidze*

Darko Mitrevski's **Bal-Can-Can**

MALI

The pattern for cinema in Mali was set in the early 1960s when the then Marxist government set up the first national film centre, began to accept technical assistance from Yugoslavia and sent a number of budding film-makers for training in the USSR and the German Democratic Republic. The five sent for training in the communist system, including the great pioneer Souleymene Cisse, returned with a real sense of social commitment, though not, happily, a preoccupation with simple social realism.

Cisse's output – like that of his contemporary, Cheikh Omar Sissoko – contains socially committed features with present-day settings as well as powerful evocations of the African past (the most famous of which is *Yeelen*). Sissoko was director of the Mali Film Centre (the only such organisation in sub-Saharan Africa to continue operating into the 2000s) when it was reorganised to become the CNPA in 1977, and recently went on to become Mali's Minister of Culture.

This is the context in which the Moscow-trained Assane Kouyaté won the Special Jury Prize at FESPACO 2003, in Burkina Faso, with **Kabala** (2002). Focusing on a drought-stricken village, the film deals with a number of issues that continue to be relevant to rural Africa today, such as ways of confronting the rigidities of traditional thinking and of adopting fruitful ways of entering the modern world. – *Roy Armes*

Assane Kouyaté's **Kabala**

MALTA

Since the simultaneous production of *Gladiator* and *U–571* on Malta in 1999, Malta and neighbouring Gozo and Comino have been consistently popular film and television locations, almost invariably doubling for other cities or towns, often parts of the ancient world. However, indigenous film-making has yet to take flight.

The biggest recent production to use the islands was Wolfgang Petersen's *Troy*, which shot in Malta for 10 weeks between May and July 2003, following seven months of pre-production, and injected around $28m into the local economy. The huge set for the fortified city of Troy was built at Fort Riccasoli, on the Malta coast, and several scenes were shot at other locations, which doubled for Sparta, Greece and Troy.

For *Alexander*, Oliver Stone shot footage of Valletta's Grand Harbour, which stood in for the ancient port of Alexandria in digitally enhanced shots. Marek Kanievska's *A Different Loyalty* (UK/Canada, 2004), a $15m romantic thriller based on the life of notorious British spy Kim Philby (Rupert Everett) and his wife, Eleanor (Sharon Stone), used parts of Valletta to stand in for Beirut in the early 1960s.

One of the few features both filmed and set on

Warner Bros. Pictures

This scene from **Troy** *was filmed on the Maltese island of Comino*

the island was *Clarion's Call* (Canada/Malta/UK, 2004; scheduled for release in 2005), a low-budget romantic comedy directed by Joan Carr-Wiggin and starring Juliet Stevenson, Daniel Stern and Tchéky Karyo.

At press time, Malta-born director Mario Azzopardi, whose CV includes hundreds of hours of American television and a Canadian guild Best Diretor nomination for the low-budget feature *Savage Messiah* (Canada, 2002), was attached to direct *Flight to Oblivion* (working title only), a political thriller based on the true story of the 1985 hijacking of an Egyptair flight at Malta Airport. More than 50 passengers died when Egyptian commandos stormed a Boeing 737 on the runway in November 1985.

The Maltese government's plans for its 2005 Budget, announced in late November 2004, included new incentives for the local film industry and visiting productions. In addition to existing VAT refunds, the additional measures include the refunding of social security contributions paid by international producers to local employess, and a cash rebate on expenditure in Malta.
– *Daniel Rosenthal*

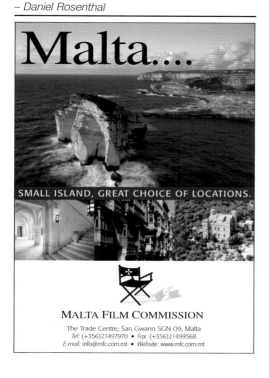

MAURITANIA

Feature film-making in Mauritania is represented by just two directors living in Paris, Med Hondo and Abderrahmane Sissako. Both are major figures in African cinema, but the gulf between them is enormous. Hondo (b. 1936) is one of the great veterans of African cinema, having produced six politically committed features and a number of long documentaries, from *Soleil O* (1970), through *Sarraounia* (1986) to *Watani* (1997).

His latest, **Fatima: The Algerian Woman in Dakar** (*Fatima, l'Algérienne de Dakar*, 2004), examines questions of violence, religion and family. During the Algerian war, a Senegalese officer (Aboubacar Sadikh Ba) in the French Army rapes and impregnates an Algerian girl, Fatima (Amel Djemal). Years later, the officer's father, a devout Muslim, makes him seek out Fatima and their son, and bring her back to Dakar to marry her in expiation.

Fatima (Amel Djemal) is reunited with her rapist (Aboubacar Sadikh Ba) in **Fatima: The Algerian Woman in Dakar**

Though Sissako (b. 1961) trained at the Moscow Film School, his work is never explicitly political, but totally personal and full of ambiguities. He established himself as one of the great hopes of the new African cinema with his first feature, *Life on Earth* (1998), shot in the village where his father grew up. **Waiting for Happiness** (*Heremakono*, 2002), which won the top prize, the Etalon de Yennenga, at FESPACO 2003, is another semi-autobiographical narrative, this time concerning a man visiting his mother before setting off for exile in Europe. While he waits, he

observes in fragmented fashion the life around him in the little Mauritanian port of Nouadhidou.
– *Roy Armes*

NAMIBIA

In April 2000, Namibia's National Assembly passed a bill designed to provide Namibians with the opportunity to gain film-making experience, through the establishment of the Namibian Film Commission. The commission has three full-time employees and a board consisting of five government-appointed commissioners from various ministries and two professional film-makers, all appointed for a three-year term. Their goal is to promote Namibia as a film location to international producers and encourage the use of Namibian crews when incoming productions are on location in the country.

Namibia has long been a favourite location for South African commercial producers and their overseas clients because of its brilliant light, spectacular sand dunes and deserted beaches, and, recently, a very favourable exchange rate. Early in 2004, Namibia hosted the 20th Century Fox remake of the classic desert drama *The Flight of the Phoenix*, directed by John Moore (*Behind Enemy Lines*) and starring Dennis Quaid, Giovanni Ribisi and Miranda Otto as survivors of a C-119 cargo plane crash. Namibia doubled for Mongolia's Gobi Desert and around 130 Namibian personnel were among the 280-strong crew.

Also shot in Namibia in 2004 was *The Trail*, co-written and directed by Eric Valli (*Himalaya*). The plot deals with a geologist (Julian Sands) whose plane crashes during a storm in the Namibian desert, where he is captured by a gang of desperados, survivors of the Angolan civil war. His survival depends on his geological knowledge and his desire to see his daughter, Grace, who in her desperate search for her father connects with Kadjiro (Eriq Ebouaney), the Himba guide who was her childhood companion.

Namibian directors include Bridget Pickering,

who in 1999 was one of six female African film-makers asked to direct a short story for the *Mama Africa* series; her episode was *Uno's World*. She also produced *Kauna's Way* (1999), the debut of writer-director Vickson Hangula, which won rave reviews at numerous festivals and was named Best Film Shot on Video at the M-Net All Africa Film Awards 2000. Hangula's other films, also shot on video, include *Okapana* (documentary), *Picture This* (short fiction) and *The Worrier*, a 75-minute drama on HIV–Aids.
– *Martin P. Botha*

NEPAL

The Nepali cinema industry, which enjoyed a golden period in the late 1990s, continues to be shrouded in dark clouds. The political unrest and, in particular, regular bomb threats from Maoist rebels have led to widespread cinema closures, while some theatres are being converted into nightclubs. Producers and directors are increasingly involved in TV soap operas and other series for local commercial channels, rather than cinema films of potentially high quality. The dearth of new films means that many actors and actresses are obliged to seek alternative employment.

Arjun Shrestha, left, and Bimla Giri in **Lifeline**

Among the very small number of notable new films is Shiva Regmi's family drama **Lifeline** (*Jeewan rekha*), about a billionaire industrialist

(Neer Shah) with three sons. The youngest brother (Shree Krishna Shrestha) meets and falls in love at first sight with an actress (Bipana Thapa), but must also fulfil his obligations to his parents, because his elder brothers (Arjun Shrestha, Simanta Udas) have very selfish wives who keep their husbands to themselves. One of the most realistic scenes shows Shrestha's character back in Nepal after seven years of study in the United States but able to find work only as a parking warden.

By **UZZWAL BHANDARY**, who appears as a comedian and satirist on Nepal TV.

SAUDI ARABIA

Saudi Arabia is becoming more open to film-making and film culture than ever before. This is a very conservative country in which cinemas have traditionally not been permitted. However, Saudi newspapers are devoting more space to features about movies, and DVD and video distribution is open, because of firmly enforced freedom of trade and copyright laws. Film fans who do not want to wait for the latest releases on home video often drive to cinemas in Bahrain and the United Arab Emirates, where films generally open at the same time as in the US and Europe.

The most important development is the emergence of the first Saudi female director, Hafa'a Al Mansour, a graduate of the Cairo Film Academy, who made two short films in 2003: the energetic *Who* (*Men*) and *Me and the Other* (*Ana wa al ahkaroon*). At press time she was in pre-production on her first fiction feature, which she will direct from her original screenplay.

Abdulla Moheissin has since the early 1980s made several short and long documentaries and animations and has recently been working on a fiction feature, *City of Silence* (*Madinat al samt*). It will be interesting to see whether Moheissin or Al Mansour wins the race to complete the first Saudi fiction feature for many years.
– *Mohammed Rouda*

SYRIA

Syrian cinema experienced a dull period in 2003-04, because the positive initiatives launched by the new president of the General Foundation for Cinema, Mohammed Al Ahmad, still require time and steady funding in order to give the local industry the desired boost. However, 2005 should witness the release of two new features by established Syrian figures. Mohamad Malas has finished **The Door of the Highness** (*Bab el maqam*), a Syrian–French co-production, which he showed as a rough cut in Tunis, where he led the jury of the Carthage Film Festival in October.

Samir Zikra was at press time putting the finishing touches to his fourth feature in 12 years, **Public Affairs** (*Alakat amma*), which looks at a love triangle involving a Muslim woman and two men, one Muslim the other Christian. It's a departure for Zikra and a subject rarely dealt with in Arab cinema. This film was fully funded by the General Foundation For Cinema.

Omar Amiralay's *The Deluge* (*Al tawafan*), a hard-hitting and controversial documentary on the Al Baath Party (the ruling party in Syria for the last 30 years), has divided Arab audiences everywhere. The film examines the Euphrates Dam 30 years after its construction, re-evaluating its role in the modernisation of Syrian agriculture and its effect on the environment. The 46-minute film also finds time to criticise the Al Baath Party's school education system, which Amiralay suggests has brainwashed successive generations. Produced by AMIP and Arte, both based in Paris, this is an extremely effective and clever film, designed to stimulate debate about environmental and educational issues in Syria.
– *Mohammed Rouda*

UNITED ARAB EMIRATES

In 2004, the fourth Films from Emirates Film Festival was held in Abu Dhabi, screening 72 films, of which 65 were made in UAE and by local film-makers. They were a mixture of short and feature documentaries and short and medium-length fiction works, mostly shot on digital video, with a few on 16mm or 35mm. The results, artistically speaking, varied a great deal, the majority of works relying heavily on a very direct approach, sustained by loud music and marked by the makers' inexperience. But a few showed that their directors have bright futures awaiting them if they can find the money they need for more ambitious projects.

Dubai, the financial centre of the country, held the first Dubai International Film Festival in early December 2004 – a huge gathering of more than 75 films (including more than 50 features), in themed sections such as "Cinema from the Subcontinent", "Bollywood Meets Hollywood" and "Arabian Shorts". It enabled local film-makers and audiences to see many international productions that would not otherwise have been screened in UAE.

With a budget of $6m, the festival is organised by Dubai Media City (DMC), which was established as a free-trade zone in January 2001 by the Crown Prince, Sheik Mohammed bin Rashid Al Maktoum, and is headed by CEO Abdul Hamid Juma.

It is a very ambitious project and has already registered positive results. Located close to Dubai, the city is now a base for CNN, Reuters, Al Arabia, Middle Eastern Broadcasting and more than 500 other media companies. DMC has plans for a film school and a film commission and already offers production facilities and services to international projects. Michael Winterbottom shot desert scenes for *Code 46* (see UK section) in Dubai and in November 2004 Warner Brothers' political thriller *Syriana*, starring Matt Damon and George Clooney, began a scheduled four-week shoot there.
– *Mohammed Rouda*

Pirates of the Caribbean: Curse of the Black Pearl *was a massive global hit in 2003. See World Box-Office Survey, opposite.*

Elliott Marks/Walt Disney Pictures/Kobal

World Box-Office Survey 2003

ARGENTINA

	Admissions
1. Finding Nemo	2,125,000
2. The Matrix Reloaded	2,048,000
3. The Two Towers	1,676,000
4. Bruce Almighty	1,459,000
5. Pirates of the Caribbean	1,418,000
6. Terminator 3	1,300,000
7. The Matrix Revolutions	1,062,000
8. Trying to Live (Argentina)	1,013,000
9. X2: X-Men United	862,000
10. Hulk	730,000

Population:	37.5 million
Admissions:	33.4 million
Total box-office:	$50m
Screens:	1,000
Avge. ticket price:	$1.90

$1 = ARS 2.97. Source: INCAA/SICA.

ARMENIA

1. Die Another Day
2. The Matrix Reloaded
3. The Two Towers
4. The Chamber of Secrets
5. Terminator 3
6. The Matrix Revolutions
7. Bruce Almighty
8. Aram (France)
9. Pirates of the Caribbean
10. Charlie's Angels: Full Throttle

Population:	3.7 million
Admissions:	N/A
Total box-office:	N/A
Local films' market share:	N/A
Sites/screens:	N/A
Avge. ticket price:	$2

$1 = Drams 530. Source: Ministry of Culture.

AUSTRALIA

	$m
1. Finding Nemo	27.85
2. The Matrix Reloaded	25.21
3. The Two Towers	21.05
4. Pirates of the Caribbean	18.84
5. Bruce Almighty	15.35
6. Terminator 3	14.32
7. Chicago	14.25
8. Return of the King	14.23
9. Charlie's Angels: Full Throttle	14.17
10. The Matrix Revolutions	13.46

Population	19.94 million
Admissions:	90 million
Total box-office:	$649.35m
Local films' market share:	3.5%
Screens:	1,907

*$1 = A$1.28. Sources: Motion Pic. Distributors' Assoc./
Australian Film Commission.*

AUSTRIA

	Admissions
1. The Two Towers	1,006,449
2. Finding Nemo	972,164
3. The Chamber of Secrets	794,321
4. Pirates of the Caribbean	666,123
5. The Return of the King	632,825
6. The Matrix Reloaded	569,556
7. Die Another Day	500,246
8. Terminator 3	463,853
9. Johnny English (US/Fr./UK)	428,394
10. Bruce Almighty	422,803

Population:	8 million
Admissions:	17.71 million
Total box-office:	$137m
Sites/screens:	176/553
Avge. ticket price:	$7.74

$1 = €0.74

Source: Association of the Audiovisual & Film Industry.

BELARUS

1. The Matrix Revolutions
2. Taxi 3 (France)
3. Terminator 3
4. Pirates of the Caribbean
5. Bruce Almighty
6. The Matrix Reloaded
7. The League of Extraordinary Gentlemen
8. The Chamber of Secrets
9. The Two Towers
10. Die Another Day

Population:	10.5 million
Admissions:	11.5 million
Total box-office:	$32.3m
Screens:	148
Avge. ticket price:	$3

$1 = Roubles 216.1
Source: Department Filmvideoart (Ministry of Culture).

BELGIUM

	Admissions
1. Finding Nemo	922,938
2. The Return of the King	749,345
3. The Matrix Reloaded	677,169
4. Pirates of the Caribbean	672,831
5. The Alzheimer Case (Belgium)	576,855
6. Bruce Almighty	568,521
7. Johnny English (US/Fr./UK)	443,391
8. Bad Boys II	429,901
9. Catch Me If You Can	390,900
10. Gangs of New York	379,079

Population:	10.36 million
Admissions:	22.9 million
Sites/screens:	126/525
Avge. ticket price:	$4.82

$1 = €1.20
Source: Federation of Belgian Cinemas.

BRAZIL

	Admissions
1. Bruce Almighty	5,453,916
2. The Matrix Reloaded	5,124,947
3. Finding Nemo	4,946,650
4. Carandiru (Brazil)	4,693,853
5. The Two Towers	4,133,452
6. X2: X-Men United	3,567,223
7. Lisbela and the Prisoner (Brazil)	3,152,713
8. Os Normais (Brazil)	2,957,556
9. The Matrix Revolutions	2,927,174
10. Terminator 3	2,517,040

Population:	170 million
Admissions:	102.96 million
Total box office:	$647.59m
Local films' market share:	21.4%
Screens:	1,817
Avge. ticket price:	$2.18

$1 = R$2.89. Source: Filme B.

BULGARIA

	Admissions
1. The Matrix Reloaded	212,909
2. The Two Towers	172,198
3. The Matrix Revolutions	142,966
4. Bad Boys 2	134,135
5. Terminator 3	93,387
6. S.W.A.T.	77,405
7. Pirates of the Caribbean	70,831
8. Master and Commander	65,629
9. The League of Extraordinary Gentlemen	69,428
10. Ice Age	72,560

Population:	7.8 million
Admissions:	3.53 million
Total box-office:	$7.9m
Local films' market share:	0.22%
Sites/screens:	149/200
Avge. ticket price:	$2.24

$1 = BGN 1.73. Source: National Statistical Institute/Geopoly Ltd.

CANADA

	$m
1. The Return of the King	28.5
2. The Two Towers	27.6
3. The Matrix Reloaded	26.2
4. Pirates of the Caribbean	24.9
5. Finding Nemo	20.4
6. X2: X-Men United	18.6
7. Bruce Almighty	16.7
8. Chicago	15.0
9. The Matrix Revolutions	14.1
10. Catch Me If You Can	13.5

Population:	31.4 million
Admissions:	125.7 million
Total box-office:	$758.3m
Local films' market share:	3%
Sites/screens:	645/2,974
Avge. ticket price:	$5.78

$1 = C$1.25. Source: Motion Pic. Theatre Assocs.

CHILE

	Admissions
1. Sex with Love (Chile)	990,696
2. Finding Nemo	838,757
3. The Return of the King	852,196
4. The Two Towers	763,919
5. The Matrix Reloaded	682,280
6. Sub-Terra (Chile)	470,343
7. Terminator 3	384,098
8. The Matrix Revolutions	362,096
9. The Ring	333,770
10. Brother Bear	310,540

Population:	15.12 million
Admissions:	11.44 million
Total box-office:	$39.1m
Local films' market share:	15%
Screens:	260
Avge. ticket price:	$3.4

$1 = Ch$632. Source: Cámara Chilena de Comercio Cinematográfico.

CHINA

1. Cell Phone (China)
2. Warriors of Heaven and Earth (China)
3. Infernal Affairs III (HK/China)
4. Cat and Mouse (HK/China)
5. Zhou Yu's Train (China)
6. Nuan Chun (China)
7. Heroic Duo (HK/China)
8. Deng Xiaoping (China)
9. Love for All Seasons (HK/China)
10. Sound of Colours (HK/China)

Screens:	2,000 (est.)

No official figures are issued.

COLOMBIA

	Admissions
1. The Passion of the Christ	1,359,830
2. The Return of the King	937,597
3. Brother Bear	470,234
4. The Last Samurai	451,411
5. The Car (Colombia)	430,394
6. Something's Gotta Give	306,535
7. Spy Kids 3D: Game Over	252,134
8. Scooby Doo 2	220,680
9. Peter Pan	129,940
10. Maria Full of Grace (US/Colombia)	119,987

December 2003 to March 2004.

Population:	42 million
Admissions:	18 million
Total box-office:	$74.01m
Local films' market share:	2% (est.)
Screens:	300
Avge. ticket price:	$2.30

$1 = COP 2,468. Source: Cine Colombia.

CROATIA

	Admissions
1. The Two Towers	265,176
2. The Matrix Reloaded	103,549
3. Terminator 3	82,402
4. Finding Nemo	75,689
5. Pirates of the Caribbean	75,476
6. The Matrix Revolutions	71,915
7. The Chamber of Secrets	67,877
8. Johnny English (US/Fr./UK)	64,351
9. Charlie's Angels: Full Throttle	60,633
10. American Pie: The Wedding	58,263

Population:	4.38 million
Admissions:	2.2 million
Local films' market share:	2%
Screens:	64
Avge. ticket price:	$3.50

$1 = Kunas 5.94. Source: Central Bureau of Statistics/ Hollywood magazine.

CYPRUS

	Admissions
1. Bruce Almighty	58,000
2. The Return of the King	43,000
3. The Matrix Reloaded	40,200
4. 2 Fast 2 Furious	36,300
5. Johnny English (US/Fr./UK)	35,000
6. The Two Towers	33,200
7. Two Weeks Notice	31,300
8. American Pie: The Wedding	26,100
9. The Ring	22,400
10. 8 Mile	21,800

Population:	700,000
Admissions:	1 million
Sites/screens:	12/35
Avge. ticket price:	$8

$1 = CY£0.47. Source: Prooptiki.

CZECH REPUBLIC

	Admissions
1. Pupendo (Czech)	958,327
2. The Two Towers	718,061
3. The Matrix Reloaded	497,715
4. The Chamber of Secrets	475,086
5. One Hand Can't Clap (Czech)	457,505
6. Kamenak (Czech)	417,669
7. Zelary (Czech)	386,810
8. Finding Nemo	324,917
9. Terminator 3	320,264
10. Pirates of the Caribbean	313,254

Population:	10.2 million
Admissions:	12.14 million
Total box-office:	$40.15m
Local films' market share:	23.7%
Screens:	758
Avge. ticket price:	$3.30

$1 = CZK 25.65. Source: Czech Film Centre.

DENMARK

	Admissions
1. The Return of the King	620,000
2. The Two Towers	600,000
3. Die Another Day	458,000
4. The Matrix Reloaded	406,000
5. Inheritance (Denmark)	374,000
6. Anja After Viktor (Denmark)	346,000
7. Finding Nemo	318,000
8. Pirates of the Caribbean	311,000
9. Bruce Almighty	309,000
10. Nasty Brats (Denmark)	298,000

Population:	5.4 million
Admissions:	12.3 million
Total box-office:	€97.7m
Local films' market share:	26%
Sites/screens:	166/379
Avge. ticket price:	€7.94

€1 = DKK 7.43. Source: Danish Film Institute.

EGYPT

	Admissions
1. Lemby 2	19,692,565
2. The Danish Experiment	13,287,906
3. Sleepless Nights	11,172,820
4. Meedo Troubles	10,864,309
5. Askar in the Camp	10,047,797
6. Speak to Mum	7,476,405
7. Thieves in Thailand	5,786,307
8. I Love You Too	4,492,368
9. How to Make Girls Love You	3,722,329
10. I Want My Right	3,586,313

All films are Egyptian.

Population:	71 million
Admissions:	16.75 million
Total box-office:	$22.03m
Local films' market share:	73.64%
Sites/screens:	162/220
Avge. ticket price:	$2.55

$1 = LE 6.50. Source: United Motion Pictures.

ESTONIA

	Admissions
1. Made in Estonia (Estonia)	81,921
2. The Two Towers	71,231
3. The Matrix Reloaded	71,046
4. Terminator 3	44,939
5. Pirates of the Caribbean	43,430
6. Johnny English (US/Fr./UK)	42,819
7. The Matrix Revolutions	39,459
8. Bruce Almighty	24,582
9. Bad Boys 2	22,672
10. 2 Fast 2 Furious	22,573

Population:	1.36 million
Admissions:	1.27 million
Total box-office:	$5.89m
Local films' market share:	7.5 %
Sites/screens:	12/81
Avge. ticket price:	$4.64

$1 = EEK 13.56. Source: Estonian Film Foundation.

FINLAND

	Admissions
1. Bad Boys – A True Story (Finland)	614,757
2. The Two Towers	466,154
3. The Return of the King	355,728
4. The Matrix Reloaded	333,929
5. Bruce Almighty	279,105
6. Johnny English (US/Fr./UK)	260,978
7. Sibelius (Finland)	257,060
8. Pirates of the Caribbean	244,919
9. Piglet's Big Movie	225,945
10. Pearls and Pigs (Finland)	213,385

Population:	5.2 million
Admissions:	7.9 million
Total box-office:	$71.34m
Local films' market share:	21%
Sites/screens:	340
Avge. ticket price:	$8.97

Source: Finnish Film Foundation.

FRANCE

	Admissions (millions)
1. Finding Nemo	7.46
2. Taxi 3 (France)	6.06
3. The Matrix Reloaded	5.60
4. The Return of the King	4.76
5. Chouchou (France)	3.80
6. Pirates of the Caribbean	3.61
7. Catch Me If You Can	3.57
8. The Jungle Book 2	3.28
9. The Matrix Revolutions	3.20
10. Terminator 3	3.03

Population:	59 million
Admissions:	174.15 million
Total box-office:	€1 billion
Local films' market share:	35%
Sites/screens:	2,128/5,295
Avge. ticket price:	€5.74

Source: Centre National du Cinéma.

GERMANY

	Admissions
1. Finding Nemo	7,656,947
2. The Return of the King	6,594,748
3. Good Bye, Lenin! (Germany)	6,439,777
4. Pirates of the Caribbean	5,897,793
5. The Two Towers	4,989,928
6. The Matrix Reloaded	4,773,455
7. Catch Me If You Can	3,473,003
8. Johnny English (US/Fr./UK)	3,460,394
9. Bruce Almighty	3,450,067
10. The Miracle of Bern (Germany)	3,253,216

Population:	82.52 million
Admissions:	149 million
Total box-office:	$961.5m
Local films' market share:	17.5%
Sites/screens:	1,831/4,868
Avge. ticket price:	$6.45

$1 = €0.88. Source: Federal Film Board.

GREECE

	Admissions
1. A Touch of Spice (Greece)	1,300,000
2. The Return of the King	950,000
3. Troy	800,000
4. Pirates of the Caribbean	580,000
5. Bruce Almighty	510,000
6. The Last Samurai	500,000
7. The Passion of the Christ	430,000
8. Finding Nemo	360,000
9. The Day After Tomorrow	310,000
10. Mystic River	300,000

July 2003 to June 2004. Figures unconfirmed officially.

Population:	10.9 million
Admissions:	14.7 million
Screens:	460
Avge. ticket price:	$6.80

Source: Cinema Department, Ministry of Culture.

HONG KONG

		$m
1.	The Return of the King	4.83
2.	Finding Nemo	4.10
3.	Infernal Affairs III (HK/China)	3.89
4.	The Twins Effect (HK)	3.65
5.	The Matrix Reloaded	3.44
6.	The Two Towers	3.41
7.	Running on Karma (HK)	3.39
8.	My Lucky Star (HK)	3.21
9.	Infernal Affairs II (HK/China)	3.20
10.	Love for All Seasons (HK)	3.18

Population:	6.8 million
Total box-office:	$116m
Local market share:	47% (est.)
Sites/screens:	58/195
Avge. ticket price:	$5.40

$1 = HK$7.8. Sources: HK Theatres Assoc./City Ent./ S. China Morning Post.

HUNGARY

		Admissions
1.	The Return of the King	727,956
2.	Shrek 2	721,384
3.	The Prisoner of Azkaban	515,777
4.	Troy	509,351
5.	The Passion of the Christ	496,813
6.	The Day After Tomorrow	474,758
7.	Terminator 3	453,210
8.	Hungarian Vagabond (Hungary)	453,063
9.	Finding Nemo	401,547
10.	American Pie: The Wedding	399,649

Population:	10.1 million
Admissions:	15.15 million
Total box-office:	$59.71m
Local films' market share:	6.96%
Screens:	580
Avge. ticket price:	$4

$1 = Forints 200. All figs. for Aug. 2003 to Aug. 2004. Sources: Assoc. of Hungarian Film Distribs./ Magyar Filmunio.

ICELAND

		$
1.	The Return of the King	579,572
2.	Pirates of the Caribbean	478,671
3.	The Matrix Reloaded	438,534
4.	Bruce Almighty	396,634
5.	Love Actually (UK/US/Fr.)	330,092
6.	Charlie's Angels: Full Throttle	313,919
7.	Matrix Revolutions	282,378
8.	Kill Bill: Volume 1	270,210
9.	Johnny English (US/Fr./UK)	260,873
10.	Terminator 3	256,859

Population:	290,570
Admissions:	1.46 million
Total box-office:	$13.56m
Local films' market share:	3%
Sites/screens:	23/46
Avge. cinema ticket price:	$9.38

$1 = ISK 71.85. Source: Statistics Iceland.

IRAN

		$
1.	The Lizard	877,241
2.	Coma	669,744
3.	Tokyo Non-Stop	491,592
4.	The Lucky Bride	408,617
5.	Donya	406,799
6.	The Iranian Girl	392,311
7.	Mama's Guest*	384,418
8.	Honey Poison	232,954
9.	Fifth Reaction	214,866
10.	The Equation*	190,511

*Still on release in 2004. All films are Iranian.

Population:	70 million
Admissions:	4.11 million
Total box-office:	$4.11m
Screens:	75
Avge. ticket price:	$1

$1 = Rials 8,800. Source: Farabi Cinema Foundation.

IRELAND

		$m
1.	Veronica Guerin (US/Ireland)	5.0
2.	Finding Nemo	4.5
3.	The Matrix Reloaded	3.9
4.	American Pie: The Wedding	3.8
5.	The Return of the King	3.4
6.	Intermission (Ireland)	3.4
7.	Bruce Almighty	3.4
8.	Gangs of New York	3.3
9.	Love Actually (UK/US/Fr.)	3.1
10.	The Two Towers	3.0

Population:	3.91 million
Admissions:	17.4 million
Total box-office:	$119.92m
Local films' market share:	11%
Screens:	329
Avge. ticket price:	$6.75

$1 = €0.82. Source: AC Nielsen EDI/ Carlton Screen Advertising.

ITALY

		$m
1.	Unexpected Paradise (Italy)	30.1
2.	The Return of the King	27.6
3.	Finding Nemo	26.4
4.	The Passion of the Christ	24.1
5.	Christmas in India (Italy)	23.2
6.	The Last Samurai	21.9
7.	The Prisoner of Azkaban	18.4
8.	Troy	18.2
9.	Master and Commander	14.5
10.	The Day After Tomorrow	12.1

Aug. 2003 to June 2004 (approx. 65% of annual gross).

Population:	57.8 million
Admissions:	71 million
Total box-office:	$515.37m
Local films' market share:	25.3%
Screens:	3,628
Avge. ticket price:	$7

$1= €0.82. Sources: Cinetel/Agis.

JAPAN

		$m
1.	Bayside Shakedown 2 (Japan)	159.17
2.	The Chamber of Secrets	158.72
3.	The Matrix Reloaded	100.91
4.	Terminator 3	75.23
5.	The Two Towers	72.48
6.	Pirates of the Caribbean	62.39
7.	The Matrix Revolutions	61.47
8.	Minority Report	49.91
9.	Hero (China)	47.16
10.	Pokemon 6: Advanced (Japan)	41.28

Population:	127.6 million
Admissions:	162.2 million
Total box-office:	$1.86 billion
Local films' market share:	33%
Screens:	2,681
Avge. ticket price:	$11.48

$1 = Yen 109. Source: Japan Motion Picture Producers' Association.

KENYA

		Admissions
1.	The Return of the King	25,580
2.	The Matrix Reloaded	20,752
3.	Johnny English (US/Fr./UK)	18,206
4.	Charlie's Angels: Full Throttle	16,928
5.	Bad Boys 2	16,530
6.	The Matrix Revolutions	13,148
7.	Terminator 3	12,508
8.	Catch Me If You Can	11,658
9.	National Security	11,552
10.	The Tuxedo	11,295

Population:	34 million
Sites/Screens:	10/17
Local films' market share:	less than 1%
Avge. ticket price:	$3.5

$1 = KES 8.2. Sources: ComMattersKenya Ltd./ ArtMatters.Info/African Cine Week.

LATVIA

		Admissions
1.	The Matrix Reloaded	63,680
2.	The Matrix Revolutions	51,011
3.	The Two Towers	50,062
4.	Terminator 3	34,561
5.	Johnny English (US/Fr./UK)	30,388
6.	Bruce Almighty	28,029
7.	The Chamber of Secrets	27,000
8.	Pirates of the Caribbean	26,629
9.	Catch Me If You Can	23,950
10.	Chicago	23,879

Population:	2.31 million
Admissions:	1.07 million
Total box-office:	$3.34m
Local films' market share:	2.2%
Sites/screens:	25/37 (full-time cinemas)
Avge. ticket price:	$3.48

$1 = LVL 0.57. Source: Film Registry of the National Film Centre.

LITHUANIA

		Admissions
1.	Troy	34,443
2.	The Return of the King	33,397
3.	The Day After Tomorrow	28,926
4.	Bruce Almighty	27,814
5.	The Last Samurai	25,129
6.	The Matrix Revolutions	25,018
7.	Ghosts of the Abyss	19,501
8.	The Passion of the Christ	18,564
9.	Pirates of Caribbean	18,008
10.	Finding Nemo	17,336

July 2003 to July 2004.

Population:	3.44 million
Admissions:	827,000
Screens:	346
Avge. ticket price:	$4.13

$1 = LT 2.81. Source: Forum Cinemas Vingis.

LUXEMBOURG

		Admissions
1.	Finding Nemo	56,000
2.	The Two Towers	50,200
3.	Pirates of the Caribbean	39,200
4.	The Matrix Reloaded	37,200
5.	Catch Me If You Can	31,000
6.	The Return of the King	30,900
7.	Johnny English (US/Fr./UK)	30,200
8.	Bruce Almighty	26,400
9.	Taxi 3 (France)	25,200
10.	Terminator 3	22,600

Population:	451,600
Admissions:	1.2 million
Screens:	24
Avge. ticket price:	$8.5

Source: Utopia/Centre national de l'audiovisuel/Statec.

MEXICO

		$m
1.	Finding Nemo	17.1
2.	X2: X-Men United	16.1
3.	Bruce Almighty	13.9
4.	The Matrix Reloaded	13.1
5.	Hulk	9.9
6.	Pirates of the Caribbean	9.6
7.	The Return of the King	9.2
8.	Terminator 3	9.2
9.	Spy Kids 3D: Game Over	9.0
10.	The Matrix Revolutions	8.5

Population:	105 million
Admissions:	137 million
Total box-office:	$392m
Local films' market share:	5.5%
Sites/screens:	493/3,054
Avge. ticket price:	$2.85

$1 = M$11.60. Sources: Instituto Mexicano de Cinematografía/Cineteca Nacional.

NETHERLANDS

		Admissions
1.	The Two Towers	1,013,000
2.	The Matrix Reloaded	996,000
3.	Pirates of the Caribbean	991,000
4.	Die Another Day	966,000
5.	Finding Nemo	937,000
6.	Bruce Almighty	906,000
7.	Schippers of the Chameleon (Netherlands)	744,000
8.	The Return of the King	724,000
9.	Johnny English (US/Fr./UK)	583,000
10.	The Matrix Revolutions	528,000

Population:	16.2 million
Admissions:	26 million
Total box-office:	$204m
Local films' market share:	12.4%
Screens:	602
Avge. ticket price:	$7.85

Source: Netherlands Cinematographic Federation.

NEW ZEALAND

		$m
1.	The Return of the King	5.4
2.	The Matrix Reloaded	4.2
3.	Whale Rider (New Zealand)	4.2
4.	Finding Nemo	4.1
5.	Pirates of the Caribbean	3.1
6.	Terminator 3	2.7
7.	X2: X-Men United	2.4
8.	Charlie's Angels: Full Throttle	2.3
9.	The Matrix Revolutions	2.3
10.	Die Another Day	2.2

Population:	4 million
Admissions:	18.37 million
Total box-office:	$103m
Local films' market share:	5%
Screens:	337
Avge. ticket price:	$5.75

$1 = NZ$1.3. Source: Motion Picture Distributors' Association of New Zealand.

NORWAY

		Admissions
1.	Finding Nemo	556,648
2.	The Return of the King	521,775
3.	The Two Towers	512,014
4.	Die Another Day	475,543
5.	Pirates of the Caribbean	442,526
6.	The Matrix Reloaded	408,448
7.	Mother's Elling (Norway)	367,062
8.	Junior Olsen Gang Goes Submarine (Norway)	366,263
9.	Bruce Almighty	351,126
10.	Kops (Sweden)	293,740

Population:	4.5 million
Admissions:	13.05 million
Total box-office:	$120.25m
Local films' market share:	16.4%
Screens:	601
Avge. ticket price:	$9.2

$1 = NOK 6.78
Source: National Association of Municipal Cinemas.

PAKISTAN

1.	Commando
2.	Punjabi Girl
3.	Blessing
4.	The Boy
5.	Remand
6.	Rascal
7.	Soldier
8.	Scoundrel
9.	Warlord
10.	Sacrifice

All films are Pakistani. Individual figures N/A.

Population:	140 million
Admissions:	20 million
Total box-office:	$10m
Local films' market share:	80%
Screens:	300
Avge. ticket price:	$1

$1 = Rs. 60.

PERU

		Admissions
1.	The Two Towers	560,665
2.	The Matrix Reloaded	478,971
3.	Finding Nemo	456,992
4.	Terminator 3	379,582
5.	The Return of the King	376,868
6.	Bruce Almighty	336,570
7.	Hulk	308,513
8.	Pirates of the Caribbean	307,871
9.	X2: X-Men United	298,095
10.	The Matrix Revolutions	294,835

Population:	28 million
Admissions:	14 million
Screens:	176 (Lima only)
Avge. ticket price:	$2.50

$1 = PEN 3.29.

PHILIPPINES

1.	The Two Towers
2.	The Matrix Revolutions
3.	The Matrix Reloaded
4.	X2: X-Men United
5.	Finding Nemo
6.	Crying Ladies (Philippines)
7.	Lastikman (Philippines)
8.	Pirates of the Caribbean
9.	Catch Me If You Can
10.	Bruce Almighty

Population:	27.4 million
Total box-office:	$20.81m
Avge. ticket price:	$2.75

Individual films' figures not available.
$1 = PHP 56.05.

POLAND

	Admissions
1. The Two Towers	1,788,281
2. The Chamber of Secrets	1,690,834
3. The Matrix Reloaded	1,637,033
4. Finding Nemo	1,291,142
5. The Matrix Revolutions	931,123
6. When the Sun Was God (Poland)	900,550
7. Bruce Almighty	619,522
8. Chicago	509,368
9. Pirates of the Caribbean	493,940
10. Terminator 3	420,757

Population:	38.23 million
Admissions:	23.77 million
Total box-office:	$22.83m
Local films' market share:	9.5%
Sites/screens:	310/589
Avge. ticket price:	$0.96

$1 = Zloty 14.2.

ROMANIA

	Admissions
1. The Matrix Reloaded	229,867
2. The Matrix Revolutions	161,951
3. Pirates of the Caribbean	118,139
4. Bad Boys II	114,641
5. The Two Towers	110,880
6. Terminator 3	109,038
7. Bruce Almighty	108,537
8. American Pie: The Wedding	96,560
9. 2 Fast 2 Furious	83,748
10. Die Another Day	76,629

Population:	21.73 million
Admissions:	4.53 million
Total box-office:	$6.6m
Local films' market share:	0.5%
Screens:	213
Avge. ticket price:	$1.5

$1 = ROL 28,249. Source: Statistical Report of Romanian Cinematography.

RUSSIA

	$m
1. Terminator 3	12.82
2. The Matrix Reloaded	11.62
3. The Matrix Revolutions	11.18
4. The Two Towers	9.37
5. Pirates of the Caribbean	9.05
6. The Chamber of Secrets	8.09
7. Spy Kids 3D: Game Over	5.96
8. Die Another Day	4.60
9. Bruce Almighty	3.90
10. X2: X-Men United	3.73

Population:	150 million
Admissions:	160 million
Total box-office:	$175m
Local films' market share:	8%
Sites/screens:	1,300 urban sites/ 17,000 provincial screens
Avge. ticket price:	$3 (in modernised cinemas)

$1 = Rubles 29.2. Source: Rossiiskaya Kinematografia 2003.

SERBIA & MONTENEGRO

	Admissions
1. The Two Towers	242,594
2. Small World (Serbia)	224,885
3. The Professional (Serbia)	214,378
4. The Return of the King	193,475
5. The Matrix Reloaded	132,631
6. Terminator 3	107,497
7. The Matrix Revolutions	90,415
8. Jagoda in the Supermarket (Serbia)	74,506
9. Daddy Day-Care	73,351
10. Fuse (Bosnia)	60,550

Population:	8.5 million
Admissions:	3.57 million
Total box-office:	$7.41m
Local films' market share:	17.88%
Sites/screens:	180/200
Avge. ticket price:	$2.08

$1 = Dinars 60.09. Source: Film Distribs.' Assoc. of Serbia.

SINGAPORE

	$m
1. The Return of the King	2.60
2. Finding Nemo	2.45
3. X2: X-Men United	2.22
4. The Matrix Reloaded	2.21
5. Shanghai Knights	1.75
6. The Matrix Revolutions	1.75
7. Bruce Almighty	1.70
8. Charlie's Angels: Full Throttle	1.39
9. Terminator 3	1.38
10. Homerun (Singapore)	1.36

Population:	4.19 million
Admissions:	14.7 million
Total box-office:	$64m
Local films' market share:	3.25%
Screens:	150
Avge. ticket price:	$4.37

$1 = SG$1.71. Sources: S'pore Film Soc./ Film Exhibs.' Assoc./S'pore Film Commission.

SLOVAKIA

	Admissions
1. The Matrix Reloaded	177,189
2. The Chamber of Secrets	155,580
3. The Two Towers	155,580
4. Finding Nemo	145,273
5. The Matrix Revolutions	102,480
6. Pirates of the Caribbean	88,492
7. Bruce Almighty	73,206
8. Terminator 3	72,175
9. American Pie: The Wedding	63,867
10. Die Another Day	63,297

Population:	5.4 million
Admissions:	2.97 million
Total box-office:	$7.76m
Local films' market share:	0.93%
Sites/screens:	265/283
Avge. ticket price:	$2.70

$1 = Crowns 33. Source: Slovak Distributors' Association.

SLOVENIA

	Admissions
1. The Two Towers	122,609
2. Johnny English (US/Fr./UK)	105,433
3. Cheese & Jam (Slovenia)	102,499
4. Bruce Almighty	101,547
5. Pirates of the Caribbean	90,745
6. American Pie: The Wedding	71,871
7. The Matrix Reloaded	71,024
8. Catch Me if You Can	67,308
9. Bad Boys 2	62,978
10. The Matrix Revolutions	60,215

Population:	1.98 million
Admissions:	3 million
Total box office:	$12.5m
Screens:	104
Avge. ticket price:	$4

$1 = SIT 195. Source: Slovenian Film Fund.

SOUTH AFRICA

	$m
1. The Return of the King	3.63
2. Finding Nemo	3.34
3. The Matrix Reloaded	3.06
4. Johnny English (US/Fr./UK)	2.60
5. Bad Boys 2	2.33
6. Charlie's Angels: Full Throttle	2.27
7. Two Weeks Notice	2.14
8. The Matrix Revolutions	1.74
9. Pirates of the Caribbean	1.73
10. Maid in Manhattan	1.71

Population:	45 million
Total box-office:	$25m
Local films' market share:	less than 1%
Sites:	70/562 (excluding independents)
Avge. ticket price:	$5.38

$1 = R 6.5. Source: National Film and Video Foundation/ Ster-Kinekor.

SOUTH KOREA

	Admissions
1. Silmido (South Korea)	11,074,000
2. The Return of the King	5,960,000
3. Memories of Murder (South Korea)	5,101,645
4. My Tutor Friend (South Korea)	4,809,871
5. The Matrix Reloaded	3,600,000
6. Untold Scandal (South Korea)	3,345,268
7. Old Boy (South Korea)	3,260,000
8. Oh! Brothers (South Korea)	3,125,256
9. A Tale of Two Sisters (South Korea)	3,110,000
10. Once Upon a Time in HS (South Korea)	2,835,000

Population:	48.3 million
Admissions:	119 million
Total box-office:	$602m
Local films' market share:	53.5%
Sites/screens:	280/1,132
Avge. ticket price:	$5

$1 = Won 1,107. Source: Korean Film Council.

SPAIN

	$m
1. Mortadelo and Filemon's Big... (Spain)	28.99m
2. Pirates of the Caribbean	28.16
3. The Return of the King	25.50
4. Finding Nemo	25.49
5. Bruce Almighty	21.94
6. The Matrix Reloaded	21.12
7. The Two Towers	16.49
8. Football Days (Spain)	14.75
9. Terminator 3	14.58
10. The Matrix Revolutions	13.82

Population:	40.21 million
Admissions:	61.14 million
Total box-office:	$770.4m
Local films' market share:	15.8%
Sites/screens:	938/3,980
Avge. ticket price:	$6.50

$1 = €0.82. Source: Instituto de la Cinematografía y de las Artes Audiovisuales.

SWEDEN

	Admissions
1. The Return of the King	934,532
2. The Two Towers	914,441
3. Finding Nemo	868,670
4. Pirates of the Caribbean	865,766
5. Evil (Sweden)	856,839
6. Kops (Sweden)	770,207
7. The Matrix Reloaded	634,894
8. The Jungle Book 2	523,730
9. Bruce Almighty	478,979
10. Miffo (Sweden)	439,831

Population:	8.97 million
Admissions:	18.17 million
Local films' market share:	20%
Sites/screens:	817/1,170
Avge. ticket price:	$10.22

$1 = SEK 7.37. Source: Swedish Film Institute.

SWITZERLAND

	Admissions
1. Finding Nemo	898,686
2. The Matrix Reloaded	532,646
3. Ready, Steady, Charlie! (Switzerland)	529,496
4. The Return of the King	526,527
5. Catch Me If You Can	513,489
6. Pirates of the Caribbean	495,067
7. Johnny English (US/Fr./UK)	459,748
8. The Two Towers	428,006
9. The Matrix Revolutions	287,609
10. 8 Mile	284,942

Population:	7.32 million
Admissions:	16.96 million
Total box-office:	$187.65m
Local films' market share:	5.95%
Sites/screens:	335/528
Avge. ticket price:	$11

$1 = CHF 1.28

Source: Pro Cinema/Federal Office of Culture/Swiss Films.

TAIWAN

	$m
1. The Return of the King	5.92
2. The Matrix Reloaded	2.40
3. Hero (China)	2.20
4. Finding Nemo	2.10
5. Catch Me If You Can	2.00
6. Pirates of the Caribbean	1.96
7. Die Another Day	1.92
8. The Matrix Revolutions	1.91
9. Bruce Almighty	1.87
10. Hulk	1.70

Population:	2.6 million
Admissions:	8.48 million
Total box-office:	$59.68m
Local films' market share:	0.36%
Sites/screens:	21/129
Avge. ticket price:	$7.03

$1 = NT$32.15. All figures for Taipei only.
Source: Government Information Office.

TURKEY

	Admissions
1. The Green Mansion (Turkey)	1,776,335
2. He's in the Army Now (Turkey)	1,657,051*
3. The Matrix Reloaded	1,470,316
4. The Matrix Revolutions	903,041
5. The Return of the King	815,671
6. The Russian Bride (Turkey)	657,546*
7. Bruce Almighty	622,327
8. Ghost Ship	607,463
9. Catch Me If You Can	606,286
10. The Ring	550,372

Excludes 2002 admissions.

Population:	70 million
Admissions:	22.15 million
Total box-office:	$84.3m
Local films' market share:	27%
Sites/screens:	446/995
Avge. ticket price:	$3.50

$1 = TRL 1,406,000. Source: Antrakt-Sinema magazine.

UNITED KINGDOM

	$m
1. Finding Nemo	67.51
2. The Return of the King	63.96
3. The Matrix Reloaded	60.25
4. Love Actually (UK/US/Fr.)	54.80
5. Pirates of the Caribbean	50.98
6. The Two Towers	45.19
7. Bruce Almighty	42.78
8. X2: X-Men United	37.28
9. Calendar Girls (UK/US)	36.79
10. Johnny English (US/Fr./UK)	35.53

January 3, 2003 to January 1, 2004.

Population:	59.6 million
Admissions:	167.3 million
Total box-office:	$1.343 billion
Local films' market share:	16%
Sites/screens:	687/3,318
Avge. ticket price:	$8.02

$1 = £0.51. Sources: Film Distribs.' Assoc./UK Film Council.

UNITED STATES

	$m
1. Finding Nemo	340
2. Pirates of the Caribbean	305
3. The Return of the King	290
4. The Matrix Reloaded	282
5. Bruce Almighty	243
6. X2: X-Men United	215
7. Elf	171
8. Chicago	161
9. Terminator 3	150
10. The Matrix Revolutions	138

Population:	293.8 million
Admissions:	1.574 billion
Total box-office:	$9.488 billion
Sites/screens:	6,066/35,786
Avge. ticket price:	$6.03

Sources: Motion Picture Association of America/Variety.

URUGUAY

	Admissions
1. Finding Nemo	200,300
2. The Return of the King	103,083
3. The Matrix Reloaded	88,179
4. Bruce Almighty	84,184
5. The Two Towers	80,221
6. Seawards Journey (Uruguay)	72,841
7. Terminator 3	63,970
8. Chicago	63,638
9. Mystic River	58,000
10. The Matrix Revolutions	54,556

Population:	3.24 million
Admissions:	2.21 million
Total box-office:	$5.53m
Local films' market share:	4.5%
Screens:	52
Avge. ticket price:	$2.50

$1 = UYU 26.64. Source: RBS Distribution Company.

WORLDWIDE

	$m
1. Finding Nemo	766
2. The Matrix Reloaded	739
3. Pirates of the Caribbean	653
4. The Return of the King	607
5. Bruce Almighty	482
6. Terminator 3	427
7. The Two Towers	423
8. The Matrix Revolutions	417
9. X2: X-Men United	407
10. Chicago	297

Source: Variety.

Unless otherwise indicated all titles are US productions and all figures are for January to December 2003. The Lord of the Rings: The Return of the King (US/New Zealand) was still in worldwide release in 2004. Harry Potter and the Chamber of Secrets and Harry Potter and the Prisoner of Azkaban both (US/UK).

Guide to Film Festivals

In May, which film will succeed 2004's **Look at Me** *as winner of Best Screenplay at Cannes?*

Pathé

Leading Festivals

American Film Market
November 2-9, 2005

Founded in 1981, AFM has become the world's largest movie industry event. The Loews Santa Monica Beach Hotel hosts the international market and all 23 screens on the Promenade are used to present more than 400 features for more than 7,000 delegates. Hundreds of films are financed, packaged and licensed. *Inquiries to:* 10850 Wilshire Blvd, 9th Floor, Los Angeles, CA 90024-4311, USA. Tel: (1 310) 446 1000. Fax: 446 1600. e: info@ifta-online.org. Web: www.americanfilmmarket.com.

Amiens
November 10-20, 2005

Discovery of new talents, new cinematography and reassessment of film masters. A competitive festival in northern France for shorts, features, animation and documentaries. Also retrospectives, tributes and works from Africa, Latin America and Asia. "Europe, Europes" presents new works from Young European Talents (Shorts, Documentaries and Animation). *Inquiries to:* Amiens International Film Festival, MCA, Place Léon Gontier, 80000 Amiens, France. Tel: (33 3) 2271 3570. Fax: 2292 5304. e: contact@filmfestamiens.org. Web: www.filmfestamiens.org.

AWARDS 2003
Golden Unicorn (Feature): **Song for a Raggy Boy** (Ireland), Aisling Walsh.
Special Prize: **The Missing Half** (Belgium), Benoît Mariage.
Golden Unicorn (Short): **Clandestin** (France), Philippe Larve.
Best Actor: Bogdan Diklic, **Fuse** (Bosnia), Pjer Zalica.
Best Actress: Yvonne Fourney, **Blood** (Argentina), Pablo Cesar.
Audience Prize: **Song for a Raggy Boy**.

AWARDS 2004
Golden Unicorn (Feature): **The Buffalo Boy** (France/Belgium/Vietnam), Minh Nguyen-Vô.
Special Prize: **Tenja** (Morocco), Hassan Legzouli.
Golden Unicorn (Short): **Two Cars One Night** (New Zealand), Taika Waititi.
Best Actor: Sid Ali Kouiret, **The Suspects** (Belgium), Kamal Dehane.
Best Actress: Shaghayeh Farahani, **A Butterfly in the Wind** (Iran), Abbas Rafeï.
Audience Prize: **Next Exit** (Argentina), Nicolas Tuozzo.

Amsterdam – International Documentary Film Festival (IDFA)
November 17-27, 2005

The world's largest documentary festival, IDFA screens 200 films – all premieres – and sells more than 100,000 tickets. The programme offers creative documentaries, includes numerous awards and a special "Kids & Docs" section. Also the Forum, a market for international co-financing. *Inquiries to:* International Documentary Film Festival – Amsterdam, Kleine-Gartmanplantsoen 10, 1017 RR Amsterdam, Netherlands. Tel: (31 20) 627 3329. Fax: 638 5388. e: info@idfa.nl. Web: www.idfa.nl.

Austin Film Festival
October 20-27, 2005

Celebrating its eleventh year, a nationally recognised Film Festival and Screenwriters' Conference – one of the select few in the US accredited by AMPAS. It brings together established and up-and-coming directors, writers and industry professionals for screenings, panels and networking. In 2004, panelists included Garry Shandling and Barry Levinson. *Inquiries to:* Austin Film Festival, 1604 Nueces, TX 78701, USA. Tel: (1 512) 478 4795. Fax: 478 6205. e: info@austinfilm.com. Web: www.austinfilmfestival.com.

Bergen
October 2005

Norway's beautiful capital of the fjords launches the sixth BIFF in 2005. The festival has a main International Competition of about 15 films, as well as an International Documentary Competition. The festival has sidebars with international arthouse films, Norwegian shorts, gay and lesbian shorts, videorama, as well as premieres of the upcoming Christmas theatrical releases, through extensive collaboration with Norway's distributors. Also hosts seminars and other events.
Inquiries to: Bergen International Film Festival, Georgernes verft 12, NO-5011 Bergen, Norway. Tel: (47) 5532 2590. Fax: 5532 3740. e: biff@biff.no. Web: www.filmweb.no/biff.

Report 2003 and 2004
The opening film in 2003 was *Facing Window*, directed by Ferzan Ozpetek, and Takeshi Kitano's bloody tale of *Zatoichi* the blind swordsman closed the festival. The Competition Programme consisted of 16 films, and the Jury Award went to Li Yang's *Blind Shaft* (China); the Critics' Award to Sang-soo Im's *A Good Lawyer's Wife* (South Korea); the Audience Award to Quentin Tarantino's *Kill Bill: Volume 1* (US). In 2004, the festival moved to Bergen Kino's new Magnus Barfot multiplex in the centre of Bergen. The Jury Award went to Gregg Araki's *Mysterious Skin* (US), while audiences chose Park Chan-wook's *Old Boy* (South Korea).
– **Tor Fosse**, Festival Director.

Berlin – Internationale Filmfestspiele
February 2006

Situated at the Potsdamer Platz, the Berlinale has increased its popularity with the public and film professionals. In 2004, it had 16,146 accredited guests and sold a remarkable 390,000 tickets for 1,152 screenings in 12 cinemas. The website registered 37.8 million hits between December 15, 2003 and February 15, 2004. Some 3,696 journalists from 106 countries reported on the programme and visits by the likes of Diane Keaton, Renée Zellweger, Jack Nicholson, Peter Fonda, Jude Law and Harvey Weinstein. The European Film Market recorded another increase in participants (up to 2,472, from 62 countries), screenings and turnover. The second Berlinale Talent Campus offered panels and workshops on film-making, theory and marketing, with a special focus on "The Sound and Music", and involved 520 young film-makers from 84 countries (see www.berlinale-talentcampus.de). The first Berlinale Co-Production Market was a great success and was expanded for 2005. Inquiries to: Internationale Filmfestspiele Berlin, Potsdamer Str 5, D-10785 Berlin, Germany. Tel: (49 30) 259 200. Fax: 2592 0299. e: info@berlinale.de. Web: www.berlinale.de.

AWARDS 2004
Golden Bear: **Head-On** (Germany), Fatih Akin.
Jury Grand Prix: **A Lost Embrace** (Argentina/France/Italy/Spain), Daniel Burman.
Best Director: Kim Ki-Duk, **Samaritan Girl** (South Korea).
Best Actor: Daniel Hendler, **A Lost Embrace**.
Best Actress (ex aequo): Catalina Sandino Moreno, **Maria Full of Grace** (US/Colombia) and Charlize Theron, **Monster** (US).
Best Short: **Coffee and Cigarettes** (Romania), Cristi Puiu.

Bermuda International Film Festival
March 18-28, 2005

Features the best of independent film from around the world in three competition categories: features, documentaries and shorts. Q&A sessions with directors, and the festival's popular lunchtime "Chats with…" sessions give filmgoers and film-makers a chance to mix. A competition victory earns each film's director an invitation to sit on the festival jury the following year. AMPAS recognises the festival as a qualifying event for the Short Films Oscars. Submission deadline: October 1, 2005. *Inquiries to:* Bermuda International Film Festival, PO Box 2963, Hamilton HM MX, Bermuda. Tel: (441) 293 3456. Fax: 293 7769. e: bdafilm@ibl.bm. Web: www.bermudafilmfest.com.

AWARDS 2004

Feature: **Summer in the Golden Valley** (Bosnia and Herzegovina), Srdjan Vuletic.
Documentary: **Born into Brothels** (US), Zana Briski and Ross Kauffman.
Short: **Wasp** (UK), Andrea Arnold.
Audience Choice: **Born into Brothels**.
Special Jury Mention: **Dad's Dead** (Short, UK), Chris Shepherd.

Report 2004

The seventh festival featured record attendance, and visits by 27 film-makers. Hollywood film journalist David Poland conducted an entertaining one-on-one discussion with Jim Sheridan. The festival jury was chaired by Willem Dafoe and included screenwriters Guillermo Arriaga and Carlos Cuarón, film-makers Patricia Flynn and Helen Lee, artistic director Shane Smith (Worldwide Short Film Festival) and journalist Mark Salisbury (*Premiere* magazine).

Brisbane International Film Festival

Late July – early August 2005

The BIFF is in its fourteenth year and is Queensland's leading film event. Presented annually by the Pacific Film and Television Commission, it provides a focus for film culture in Queensland by showcasing the best and most interesting world cinema. Screening more than 200 films, the diverse non-competitive programme includes features, documentaries, shorts, experimental work, animation and some video. *Inquiries to:* Brisbane International Film Festival, GPO Box 909, Brisbane, QLD, 4001, Australia. Tel: (61 7) 3007 3003. Fax: 3007 3030. e: publicist@biff.com.au. Web: www.biff.com.au.

Buenos Aires International Independent Film Festival (BAFICI)

April 12-24, 2005

The Buenos Aires International Independent Film Festival was created in 1999. Sections include the two Official Competitions, for features and shorts. "Argentina – Brand-New Novelties" has, since 2001, highlighted the increasing production of independent films in Argentina, complemented by the "Work in Progress" section. BAFICI also programmes sections dedicated to outstanding directors. *Inquiries to:* Buenos Aires Festival Internacional de Cine Independiente, Av Corrientes 1530, Piso 8, Oficina 7, 1042 Buenos Aires, Argentina. Tel: (54 11) 4373 8930. Fax: 4374 0320. e: produccion@bafilmfest.com. Web: www.bafilmfest.com

Cannes

May 11-22, 2005

Cannes remains the world's top festival, attracting key films, personalities and industry personnel. The official selection includes the Competition, films out of competition, "Un Certain Regard", Cinéfondation and Cannes Classics (created 2004). The Marché du Film, with facilities improved and extended since 2000 (Riviera–Producers network, Short Film Corner) is part of the official organisation. There are also the Directors' Fortnight, the Critics' Week and other useful screenings (e.g. Australian, New Zealand and Scandinavian films). The 2004 festival jury, presided over by Quentin Tarantino, included Emmanuelle Béart, Tilda Swinton, Kathleen Turner, Tsui Hark and Jerry Schatzberg. *Inquiries to:* Festival de Cannes, 3, rue Amélie 75007 Paris, France. Tel: (33 1) 5359 6100. Fax: 5359 6110. e: festival@festival-cannes.fr. Web: www.festival-cannes.org.

AWARDS 2004

Palme d'Or: **Fahrenheit 911** (US), Michael Moore.
Grand Prix: **Old Boy** (South Korea), Park Chan-Wook.
Best Actor: Yagira Yuuya, **Nobody Knows** (Japan).

Best Actress: Maggie Cheung, **Clean** (France).
Best Screenplay: **Look at Me** (Agnès Jaoui,
Jean-Pierre Bacri)
Jury Prize: **The Ladykillers** (US), Irma P. Hall.

Cartagena
Feb/March 2005

Ibero-Latin American films, including features,
shorts, documentaries, tributes to Latin
American directors and a film and TV market. A
competitive section for Colombian films was
added in 2000. *Inquiries to:* Victor Nieto Nuñez,
Director, Cartagena International Film Festival,
Centro, Calle San Juan de Dios, Baluarte San
Francisco Javier, Cartagena, Colombia.
Tel: (57 5) 664 2345.
e: info@festicinecartagena.com.
Web: www.festicinecartagena.com.

Chicago
October 13-27, 2005

Having celebrated its fortieth birthday in 2004,
the Chicago International Film Festival is among
the oldest competitive events in North America.
It spotlights the latest work by established
international directors and newcomers. It
bestows its highest honour, the Gold Hugo, on
the best feature in the International Competition,
with separate prizes for documentaries, student
films and shorts. Chicago is one of two US sites
to award the FIPRESCI prize for first- and
second-time directors, judged by top
international critics. *Inquiries to:* Philip Bajorat
(Entries and Awards Co-ordinator), Chicago
International Film Festival, 32 W Randolph St,
Suite 600, Chicago, IL 60601, USA.
Tel: (1 312) 425 9400. Fax: 425 0944.
e: info@chicagofilmfestival.com.
Web: www.chicagofilmfestival.com.

Cinéma Tout Ecran
November 2005

For its tenth anniversary, Cinéma Tout Ecran
maintains more than ever its unique approach.
With its selection orientated towards the artistic
quality and the talent of the filmmaker, the
festival despises the artificial frontier between
cinema and television and makes a point of
letting the public discover the best of series –
this year *The L-Word* or *The 4400*, produced by
Francis Ford Coppola. International Seminar:
The film-maker: cinema and television, in
partnership with *Variety*; Tribute to the Stephen
Frears, presenting his work for television and
cinema. *Inquiries to:* Sandra Mudronja:
Communication & PR; Eileen Hofer: Press,
Cinéma Tout Ecran, International Cinema &
Television Festival, Maison des Arts du Grütli, 16
rue Général Dufour, CP 5759 CH-1211 Geneva
11, Switzerland.
Tel: (41 22) 800 1554. Fax: 329 3747.
e: presse@cinema-tout-ecran.ch.
Web: www.cinema-tout-ecran.ch.

Clermont-Ferrand Short Film Festival
Late January – early February 2006

International, National and "Lab" competitions
for 16mm, 35mm films and digital works on
DigiBeta, all completed after January 1, 2005, of
40 minutes or less. All the entries will be listed in
the Market catalogue. Many other side
programmes (retrospectives and panoramas).
Inquiries to: Clermont-Ferrand Short Film
Festival, La Jetée, 6 place Michel-de L'Hospital
63058 Clermont-Ferrand Cedex 1, France.
Tel: (33 473) 916 573. Fax: 921 193.
e: info@clermont-filmfest.com.
Web: www.clermont-filmfest.com.

AWARDS 2004
Grand Prix: **Natan** (Sweden), Jonas Holmström
and Jonas Bergergård; **Diary** (Lithuania),
Oksana Buraja.
Audience Prizes: **My Parents** (Germany), Neele
Vollmar; **L'Aîné de mes soucis** (France), Carine
Tardieu; **We Have Decided Not to Die** (Australia),
Daniel Askill; **Non-Fat** (UK), Oliver Manzi.

Denver
November 10-20, 2005

The Starz Denver International Film Festival
presents approximately 200 films from around the
world and plays host to more than 100 film-
makers. Includes new international features,
cutting-edge independent fiction and non-fiction

works, shorts and a variety of special programmes. Also pays tribute to established film artists with retrospective screenings of their works. Entry fee: $40 ($20 for students). The Denver Film Society also programmes the Starz FilmCenter, Colorado's only cinematheque, daily throughout the year, and produces the Denver Pan African Film Festival in April and the Aurora Asian Film Festival in June. *Inquiries to:* Denver Film Society, 1725 Blake St, Denver, Colorado 80202, USA. Tel: (1 303) 595 3456. Fax: 595 0956. e: dfs@denverfilm.org. Web: www.denverfilm.org.

AWARDS 2004

Mayor's Lifetime Achievement Award: Morgan Freeman.
John Cassavetes Award: Kevin Bacon.
Krystof Kieslowski Award: **Python** (Latvia), Laila Pakalnina; **Here** (Croatia), Zrinko Ogresta.
Emerging Film-maker Award: Rich Devaney, **Brooklyn Bound** (US).
The Maysles Brothers Documentary Award: Danny Schechter, **WMD: Weapons of Mass Deception** (US).
Stan Brakhage Vision Award: Ken Jacobs.
Starz People's Choice Award (Feature):

STARZ DENVER
INTERNATIONAL
FILM FESTIVAL

Celebrating 28 years
November 10-20, 2005

Inquiries to:
303.595.3456
www.denverfilm.org
dfs@denverfilm.org

Denver Film Society • Starz FilmCenter

Tomorrow's Weather (Poland), Jerzy Stuhr.
Starz People's Choice Award (Documentary):
A Touch of Greatness (US), Leslie Sullivan.

Larry Laszlo

John Cassavetes Award recipient Kevin Bacon and wife Kyra Sedgwick at Denver in 2004

Edinburgh International Film Festival
August 17-28, 2005

The world's longest continually running film festival, Edinburgh is also one of the most accessible. The emphasis is on new films, innovation and excellence worldwide, UK films and young directors, retrospectives and seminars. There's an offbeat sparkle to the mix of local audiences and visitors. Edinburgh also encapsulates Film UK, a focus for all matters concerning UK Film. FilmFour is the principal sponsor. *Inquiries to:* Edinburgh International Film Festival, 88 Lothian Rd, Edinburgh EH3 9BZ, Scotland. Tel: (44 131) 228 4051. Fax: 229 5501. e: info@edfilmfest.org.uk. Web: www.edfilmfest.org.uk.

AWARDS 2004
Michael Powell Award: **My Summer of Love** (UK), Pawel Pawlikowski.
Guardian *New Director's Award:* **Super Size Me** (US), Morgan Spurlock.
Standard Life Audience Award: **Inside I'm Dancing** (Ireland/UK), Damien O'Donnell.
Kodak/UK Film Council Short Film Award: **Billy's Day Out**, Iain B. MacDonald; **Who Killed Brown Owl**, Christine Molloy and Joe Lawlor.
McLaren Animation Award: **Good Song**, Shynola for Blur; **Brand Spanking**, John-Paul Harney.
European Short Film Award: **Cleopatra's Nose**, Richard Jordan.

Saltire Society Grierson Award for Short Documentary: **And So Goodbye**, Jim Hickey.

Report 2004

At our fifty-eighth festival, an audience of 54,000 enjoyed 415 films from 48 countries. After opening with the UK Premiere of *The Motorcycle Diaries*, the festival offered a line-up of UK premieres, including *Hero*, *Ae Fond Kiss*, *Coffee and Cigarettes*, *Dear Frankie*, *Dead Man's Shoes*, *The Green Hat*, *Old Boy*, *My Summer of Love*, *Somersault* and *Untold Scandal*. Notable live events featuring luminaries such as Malcolm McDowell, Christopher Doyle, Zbignew Preisner, Sir Richard Eyre and Ken Loach. Guests who walked up the red carpet included Paul Laverty, Colin Firth, Catherine Breillat, Antonia Bird, Marc Evans, Romola Garai, Andrew Davies, Damien O'Donnell, Richard Jobson, Paddy Considine, James McAvoy, Shane Meadows, Peter Mullan and Sylvia Chang.
– **Sadie McKinlay**, Head of Development.

Espoo Ciné International Film Festival
August 23-28, 2005

Espoo Ciné has established itself as the annual showcase of contemporary European, primarily long feature, cinema in Finland. The traditional section should appeal to every movie buff in Finland, and the growing fantasy selection should attract those hungry for stimulation of the imagination. It is a member of the European Fantastic Film Festivals Federation and organises every year a Méliès d'Argent fantastic film competition. Also US indies, new films from other continents, the best of contemporary Finnish cinema, outdoor screenings, retrospectives, sneak previews, seminars and distinguished guests.

Inquiries to: Espoo Ciné, PO Box 95, FIN-02101 Espoo, Finland. Tel: (358 9) 466 599. Fax: 466 458. e: office@espoocine.org. Web: www.espoocine.org.

Fajr International Film Festival
February 1-11, 2006

Apart from the International Competition, the programmes include "Festival of Festivals" (a selection of outstanding films presented at other international festivals), "Special Screenings" (films of documentary or narrative content which introduce cinema or cultural developments in certain geographical regions) and retrospectives. The newly-created Competition of Spiritual Cinema emphasises cinema's role as a rich medium for the expression of the essence of religious faith. Another new addition is the Competition of Asian Cinema, organised with the aim of promoting film art and industry in Asian countries. Festival Director: Alireza Rezadad. *Inquiries to:* Fajr International Film Festival, 2nd Fl., No. 19, Delbar Alley, Toos St. Valiye Asr Ave., Tehran 19617, Iran.
Tel: (98 21) 273 4801/273 5090/271 1958.
Fax: 273 4801. e: fcf2@dpi.net.ir.
Web: www.icff-ir.com.

AWARDS 2004

Special Prize of the Jury: **Gavkhuni** (Iran), Behruz Afkhami.
Direction: Kurosawa Kiyoshi, **Bright Future** (Japan).
Script: Christopher Hampton and Robert Shenkan, **The Quiet American** (US/Australia/Germany).
Performance: Ezzatollah Entezami, **Gavkhuni**.
Technical and Artistic Achievement: Shibanushi Takahide (cinematographer, **Bright Future**).

Fantasporto
February 21 – March 7, 2005

To commemorate its twenty-fifth anniversary in 2005, the festival was preparing to bring to Oporto some previous winners and well-known faces, including Guillermo del Toro, who won Fantasporto in 1994 with *Cronos* and who recently directed *Hellboy*, Vincenzo Natali, the Canadian director who was behind *Cube* (Best

Film at Fantasporto 1999). Other plans for 2005 included a Bollywood Retrospective. All major Portuguese print and broadcast media cover the festival (yielding some 5,000 cuttings) and average public attendance is around 114,000 (140,000 in 2003). Director: Mário Dorminsky. *Inquiries to:* Fantasporto, Rua Anibal Cunha 84, Sala 1.6, 4050-048 Porto, Portugal.
Tel: (35 1) 222 076 050 Fax: 222 076 059.
e: info@fantasporto.online.pt.
Web: www.fantasporto.com.

AWARDS 2004
Fantasy Section
Film: **A Tale of Two Sisters** (South Korea), Kim Jee-woon.
Special Jury Award: **Killing Words** (Spain), Laura Maña.
Special Mention: **The End of Our Love** (Belgium), Heléne Cattet and Bruno Forzani.
Director: Kim Jee-Woon, **A Tale of Two Sisters**.
Actor: Dario Grandinetti, **Killing Words** (Spain).
Actress: Im Soo-Jung, **A Tale of Two Sisters**.
Screenplay (ex-aequo): Fernando de Felipe and Jordi Galcerán, **Killing Words**; Hubert Selby Jr. and Nicholas Winding Refn, **Fear X** (Denmark).
Best Visual Effects: Michael O'Brien and Wayne

Toth, **House of 1,000 Corpses** (US).
Short Film: **I'll See You in My Dreams** (Portugal), Miguel Angel Vivas.
Directors' Week
Film: **The Green Butchers** (Denmark), Anders Thomas Jensen.
Director: Anders Thomas Jensen, **The Green Butchers**.
Special Jury Award: **The Other Side of the Bed** (Spain), Emilio Martinez Lazaro.
Actor: Mads Mikkelsen, **The Green Butchers**.
Actress: Rachael Blake, **Perfect Strangers** (New Zealand).
Screenplay: David Serrano, **The Other Side of the Bed**.

Far East Film Festival
April 22-29, 2005

Annual themed event which, since 1998, has focused on Eastern Asian cinema. *Inquiries to:* Centro Espressioni Cinematografiche, Via Villalta 24, 33100 Udine, Italy. Tel: (39 04) 3229 9545. Fax: 3222 9815. e: fareastfilm@cecudine.org, Web: www.fareastfilm.com.

Report 2004
Attendance at Teatro Nuovo reached around 50,000 during eight days of non-stop screenings. Three international festival premieres – *Dance with the Wind*, *Turn Left Turn Right* and *Taegukgi* – were among the 56 features presented, alongside an important focus on director Zhang Yuan and a retrospective on Hong Kong master Chor Yuen. The Audience Award went to Yoji Yamada's *The Twilight Samurai* (Japan).
– **Paolo Neri**.

Festival Des 3 Continents
November 22-29, 2005

The only annual competitive festival in the world for films originating solely from Africa, Asia and Latin and Black America. It's one of the few festivals where genuine discoveries may still be made. From Hou Hsiao-hsien or Abbas Kiarostami in the 1980s, to Darejan Omirbaev or Jia zang Ke more recently, unknown great authors have been shown and acknowledged in Nantes. For 26 years, F3C has also charted the film history of the southern countries through retrospectives (genres, countries, actors and actresses), showing more than 1,200 films and bringing to light large pieces of an unrecognised part of the world's cinematographic heritage. *Inquiries to:* Alain and Philippe Jalladeau, Directors, Festival des 3 Continents, BP 43302, 44033 Nantes Cedex 1, France.
Tel: (33 2) 4069 7414. Fax: 4073 5522.
e: festival@3continents.com.

AWARDS 2003
Fiction
Golden Montgolfier: **Seven Days, Seven Nights** (Cuba), Joel Cano.
Silver Montgolfier: **Silent Waters** (Pakistan), Sabiha Sumar.
Special Jury Award: **Min** (Malaysia), Ho Yuhang.
Direction (Tribute to Jacques Demy): **Goodbye Dragon Inn** (Taiwan), Tsaï Ming-liang.
Actress: Shinobu Terashima, **Vibrator** (Japan).
Actor: Erjan Bekmuratov, **Small People** (Kazakhstan).
Young Audience Award: **Goodbye Dragon Inn**.
Audience Award: **Silent Waters** (Pakistan), Sabiha Sumar.
Documentary
Golden Montgolfier: **West of the Tracks-1/Rust** (China), Wang Bing.
Audience Award: **Gift of Life** (Taiwan), Wu Yii-Feng.

AWARDS 2004
Fiction
Golden Montgolfier: **Day and Night** (China), Wang Chao.
Silver Montgolfier: **Bombon the Dog** (Argentina), Carlos Sorin.
Special Jury Award: **One Out of Two** (Argentina), Alejo Taube.
Direction (Tribute to Jacques Demy): Wang Chao, **Day and Night**.
Actress: Golshifteh Farahani, **Boutique** (Iran), Hamid Nematollah.
Actor: Juan Villegas, **Bombon the Dog**.
Young Audience Award: **Day and Night**.
Audience Award: **A Hero** (Angola), Zézé Gamboa.
Documentary
Golden Mongolfier: **Final Solution** (India), Rakesh Sharma.
Audience Award: **Final Solution**.

Filmfest Hamburg
September 22-29, 2005

Filmfest Hamburg is Germany's premiere springboard for independent productions. It focuses on young cinema from around the world, screening 80–100 features in five theatres along the Filmfest Mile in the city centre. It previews some Hollywood productions and also shows TV movies. The Douglas Sirk Prize honours outstanding contributions to film culture and business. There are more than 30,000 admissions and about 1,000 industry professionals attend. *Inquiries to:* Filmfest

Eduardo Ponti with his mother, Sophia Loren, at the Filmfest Hamburg 2003 premiere of Ponti's **Between Strangers**

Hamburg, Steintorweg 4, D-20099 Hamburg, Germany. Tel: (49 40) 3991 9000. Fax: 3991 90010. e: info@filmfesthamburg.de. Web: www.filmfesthamburg.de.

Report 2003 and 2004

The eleventh edition time introduced new director Albert Wiederspiel. Some 30,000 spectators watched 90 movies from all over the world. A warm welcome was given to Sophia Loren, promoting the movie directed by her son, Eduardo Ponti, *Between Strangers*. Highlights included the nightly 'Hyatt Film Talk', hosted by BBC Journalist Phillip Bergson. The Douglas Sirk Award was presented to Isabelle Huppert. In 2004, guests included directors Fatih Akin, Susanne Bier and François Ozon and actors Katja Riemann, Hanna Schygulla and Marielou Berry.
– **Sven Schwarz**, Press and Communication.

Flanders International Film Festival (Ghent)
October 11-22, 2005

Belgium's most prominent annual film event, which celebrated its thirtieth anniversary in 2003, attracts attendance of 100,000-plus. Principally focused on "The Impact of Music on Film", this competitive festival awards grants worth up to $90,000 and screens around 150 features and 80 shorts, most without a Benelux distributor. Other sections include the World Cinema spectrum (world, European, Benelux or Belgian premieres), film music concerts, retrospectives, seminars and a tribute to an important film-maker. The festival's Joseph Plateau Awards are the highest film honours in Benelux. Presented for the first time in 2001, the World Soundtrack Awards, judged by 180 international composers, celebrate excellence in film scoring. *Inquiries to:* Flanders International Film Festival-Ghent, 40B Leeuwstraat, B-9000 Ghent, Belgium. Tel: (32 9) 242 8060. Fax: 221 9074. e: info@filmfestival.be. Web: www.filmfestival.be.

AWARDS 2003

Film: **In America** (Ireland/US), Jim Sheridan.
Music: Zygmunt Konieczny, **Pornography** (Poland/France), Jan Jacob Kolski.
Screenplay: Bent Hamer and Jörgen Bergmark, **Kitchen Stories** (Norway).
Director: Im Songsoo, **A Good Lawyer's Wife** (South Korea).
FNAC Audience Award: **The Alzheimer Case** (Belgium), Eric Van Looy.
Prix UIP/Ghent 2003: **J'attendrai le suivant** (France), Philippe Orreindy.

AWARDS 2004

Film: **Nobody Knows** (Japan), Fore-Eda Hirokazu.
Music: Miguel Angel Miranda, José Miguel Tobar, **Machucha** (Chile/Spain/France), Andres Wood.
Screenplay: Suha Arraf and Eran Riklis, **The Syrian Bride** (Israel).
Director: Atiq Rahimi, **Earth and Ashes** (Afghanistan).
Audience Award: **Facing Window** (Italy), Ferzan Ozpetek.
Prix UIP/Ghent: **Little Terrorist** (India/UK), Ashvin Kumar.

Fort Lauderdale International Film Festival
October 14 – November 13, 2005

FLIFF features more than 150 films from 40 countries during the world's longest film event, with screenings in Miami, Palm Beach and Fort

Bruce Birmelin/DreamWorks/Kobal

Ben Kingsley was at Fort Lauderdale in 2003 with
House of Sand and Fog

Lauderdale. Awards include Best Film, Best Foreign-Language Film, Best American Indie, Best Director, Actor, Screenplay, Best Florida Film and Kodak Student prizes for Narrative (over 25 minutes), Short Narrative (25 minutes or under), Documentary and Experimental. The Festival has a fun party side, too, with a Beach Party, Sunday Brunch Cruise, Champagne Starlight Sail, a Fashion show aboard a 300-passenger luxury barge, and a gala featuring 25 of South Florida's top restaurants. The Sundance Channel Festival Cafe has daily and nightly parties. Attendance topped 58,000 in 2003. The deadlines for entries are as follows: July 1 (Professional Early Deadline 1st Call), August 15 (Final Professional Deadline), Sept 15 (Student Deadline for catalogue) and Sept 30 (Final Deadline). *Inquiries to:* The Fort Lauderdale International Film Festival, 1314 East Las Olas Blvd. Suite 007, Fort Lauderdale, FL 33301, USA. Tel: (1 954) 760 9898 ext 101. Fax: 760 9099. e: brofilm@aol.com. Web: www.fliff.com.

Freedom Film Festival
Late January 2006

Founded in 1997 by the American Cinema Foundation, this showcase of films from Eastern and Central Europe is dedicated to illuminating Europe's recent history and creating opportunities for its film-makers. The films relate to the struggle for personal, political, economic and artistic freedom during Stalin's times and in the wake of the Cold War. It has activities at Karlovy Vary and Moscow. *Inquiries to:* American

Cinema Foundation, 9911 W Pico Blvd, Suite 1060, Los Angeles, CA 90035, USA. Tel: (1 310) 286 9420. Fax: 286 7914. e: acinema@cinemafoundation.com. Web: www.cinemafoundation.com.

Fribourg
March 2006

Features, shorts and documentaries from Asia, Africa and Latin America unspool at this Swiss event, with a competitive section. *Inquiries to:* Fribourg Film Festival, Rue Nicolas-de-Praroman 2, Case Postale 550, 1701 Fribourg, Switzerland. Tel: (41 26) 347 4200. Fax: 347 4201. e: films@fiff.ch. Web: www.fiff.ch.

AWARDS 2004
Le Regard d'Or: **Days of Santiago** (Peru), Josué Méndez.
Special Mention: **August Sun** (Sri Lanka), Prasanna Vithanage.
Special Jury Award: **The Wick** (Argentina), Raul Perrone.
Ecumenical Jury Award: **Days of Santiago**.
E-changer Award: **Days of Santiago**.
FICC Award: **A Thousand Months** (Morocco/France/Belgium), Faouzi Bensaïdi.
FIPRESCI Award: **Days of Santiago** (Peru).
General Public Award: **Cuentos de la Guerra Saharaui** (Spain), Pedro Pérez Rosado.

Giffoni
July 16-23, 2005

Located in Giffoni Valle Piana, a small town about 40 minutes from Naples, the Giffoni International Film Festival for Children and Young People was founded in 1971 by Claudio Gubitosi to promote films for youthful audiences and families. Now includes four competitive sections: Kidz (animated and fiction shorts that tell fantastic stories, juried by 70 children aged six to nine); First Screens (fiction features and animated shorts, mainly fantasy and adventure, juried by 400 children aged nine to 11); Free 2 Fly sees 350 teenagers (aged 12 to 14) assessing features and shorts about the pre-adolescent world; Y GEN has 250 jurors (aged 15 to 19) and takes a curious look at cinema for

young people. *Inquiries to:* Giffoni Film Festival, Cittadella del Cinema, Via Aldo Moro 4, 84095 Giffoni Valle Piana, Salerno, Italy. Tel: (39 089) 802 3001. Fax: 802 3210. e: info@giffoniff.it. Web: www.giffoniff.it.

AWARDS 2003
Free 2 Fly – Golden Gryphon: **Wondrous Oblivion** (UK), Paul Morrison.
Y Gen – Golden Gryphon: **One Way Ticket to Mombassa** (Finland), Hannu Tuomainen.
First Screens – Golden Gryphon: **AAA Achille** (Italy), Giovanni Albanese.

AWARDS 2004
Free 2 Fly – Golden Gryphon: **4th Floor** (Spain), Antonio Mercero.
Y Gen – Golden Gryphon: **Bonjour M. Shlomi** (Israel), Shemi Zarhin.
First Screens – Golden Gryphon: **Daniel & the Superdogs** (Canada/UK), André Melançon.

Gijón International Film Festival
November 24 – December 2, 2005

One of Spain's oldest festivals (forty-second edition in 2004), Gijón is now at the peak of its popularity. Having firmly established itself as a barometer of new film trends worldwide, it draws a large and enthusiastic public. Gijón has built on its niche as a festival for young people, programming innovative and independent films made by and for the young, including retrospectives, panoramas, exhibitions and concerts. Alongside the lively Official Section, sidebars celebrate directors who have forged new paths in film-making. *Inquiries to:* Gijón International Film Festival, Paseo de Begona, 24-Ent, 33201 Gijon, Spain. Tel: (34 98) 518 2940. Fax: 518 2944. e: festivalgijon@telecable.es. Web: www.gijonfilmfestival.com.

AWARDS 2003
International Jury
Best Feature: **Schultze Gets the Blues** (Germany), Michael Schorr.
Best Short: **7:35 in the Morning** (Spain), Nacho Vigalondo.
Young Jury

Best Feature Film: **Children's Games** (France), Yann Samuell.
Best Short Film: **The Man without a Head** (France), Juan Solanas.

AWARDS 2004

International Jury
Best Feature: **Vento di terra** (Italy), Vincenzo Marra.
Best Short: **Bregman, el siguiente** (Uruguay/Spain), Federico Veiroj; **Heart Is But a Piece of Meat** (Slovenia/Czech Republic), Jan Cvitkovic.
Young Jury
Best Feature Film: **Lila Says So** (France), Ziad Doueiri.
Best Shortfilm: **Flatlife** (Belgium), Jonas Geinaert.

Göteborg

Late January – early February 2006

Now in its twenty-eighth year, Göteborg Film Festival is one of Europe's key film events. Large international programme and a special focus on Nordic films, including the Nordic Competition. In 2004, 369 short and feature films were screened. International seminars and the marketplace Nordic Event attract buyers and festival programmers to the newest Scandinavian films. Some 1,500 professionals attend and more than 110,000 tickets are sold. *Inquiries to:* Göteborg Film Festival, Olof Palmes Plats, S- 413 04 Göteborg, Sweden.
Tel: (46 31) 339 3000. Fax: 410 063.
e: goteborg@filmfestival.org.
Web: www.filmfestival.org.

Report 2004

During the festival, Carl Johan De Geer won the Nordic Film Award for his autobiographical werewolf-movie *Hiding Behind the Camera, Part 2* (Sweden) and Niklas Rådström was awarded with the new Swedish short film prize for his directorial debut, *The Eiffel Tower*. Other highlights included Teresa Fabik's *The Ketchup Effect*, Errol Morris' Oscar-winning documentary *The Fog of War* and Andrej Zvjagintsev's *The Return*. We had a special focus on Soviet director Mikheil Kalatozov and screened Marco Tullio Giordana's six hour-epic The Best of Youth. Directors Christoffer Boe (*Reconstruction*) and Roger Michell (*The Mother*) shared their experiences around script work in well-attended masterclasses, in collaboration with The Script Factory.
– **Sara Hultman,** Programme Co-Ordinator.

Haugesund – Norwegian International Film Festival

August 19-26, 2005

Held in Haugesund, on the west coast of Norway, the festival has become the country's major film event, attended by many international visitors and more than 1,000 representatives from the Norwegian and Scandinavian industries. Award-winning films receive Amanda Statuettes, and the New Nordic Film market runs for three days at the beginning of the festival. Festival Director: Gunnar Johan Løvvik. Programme Director: Håkon Skogrand. Honorary President: Liv Ullmann. *Inquiries to:* PO Box 145, N-5501 Haugesund, Norway.
Tel: (47 52) 743 370. Fax: 743 371.
e: info@filmfestivalen.no.
Web: www.filmfestivalen.no.

Report 2004

Our thirty-second festival celebrated Haugesund's 150th anniversary with the King and Queen present, and the national Amanda film awards' twentieth anniversary. More than 400 professionals attended the Nordic programme and market New Nordic Films, this year in its tenth consecutive year and containing 30 new features. The festival also presented its Main Programme with international highlights for the coming season in the cinemas, the Children's Film Fest, and, amongst other sidebars, the special report: Cinema Italia.
– **Håkon Skogrand**, Programme Director.

Helsinki Film Festival - Love & Anarchy
September 15-25, 2005

An important festival for current cinema in Finland, now in its eighteenth year, Helsinki promotes high-quality international film-making to Finnish audiences and distributors. True to its subtitle, "Love and Anarchy", the event uncompromisingly challenges limits of cinematic expression and experience. Non-competitive. Submission deadline: June 30. *Inquiries to:* Helsinki Film Festival, Mannerheimintie 22-24, PO Box 889, 00101 Helsinki, Finland. Tel: (358 9) 6843 5230. Fax: 6843 5232. e:office@hiff.fi. Web: www.hiff.fi.

Hong Kong
March 22 – April 6, 2005

The Hong Kong International Film Festival (HKIFF), entering its twenty-ninth year in 2005, is one of Asia's most reputable platforms for film-makers, professionals and filmgoers from all over the world to launch new works and experience outstanding cinema. The 16-day event, which encompasses the Easter holidays, showcases more than 200 new features and several retrospective programmes (Shimizu Hiroshi and Ernst Lubitsch in 2004) and special focuses (Stan Brakhage and William Chang in 2004). The open competitions, with cash prizes, were established in 2003. Attendance topped 230,000 in 2004. *Inquiries to:* Hong Kong International Film Festival, 22/F, 181 Queens Rd Central, Hong Kong. Tel: (852) 2970 3300. Fax: 2970 3011. e: hkiff@hkiff.org.hk. Web: www.hkiff.org.hk.

AWARDS 2004
Golden Firebird Award: **South of the Clouds** (China), Zhu wen.
Silver Firebird Award: **Up Against Them All** (Brazil), Roberto Moreira.
Golden DV Award: **Incense** (China), Ning Hao.
Silver DV Award: **ASTIGmatism** (Philippines), Jon Red.
Humanitarian Award for Best Documentary: **S21, The Khmer Rouge Killing Machine** (Cambodia/France), Rithy Panh.
Humanitarian Award for Outstanding Documentary: **Final Solution** (India), Rakesh Sharma.
SIGNIS Award: **Since Otar Left** (France/Belgium), Julie Bertuccelli.
FIPRESCI Award: **South of the Clouds**.
People's Choice: **Pieces of April** (US), Peter Hedges.

Huelva
November 2005

The main aim of Huelva Latin American Film Festival is to show and promote films of artistic

quality which contribute to a better knowledge of Latin American production, including works from the Hispanic US. Huelva has become a key rendezvous, enabling European buyers and film buffs to catch up with the latest developments. It includes a competition for films from Latin America and the Hispanic US, tributes and round-table discussions. *Inquiries to:* Casa Colon, Plaza del Punto s/n, 21003 Huelva, Spain. Tel: (34 95) 921 0170/0171/0299. Fax: 921 0173. e: prensa@festicinehuelva.com. Web: www.festicinehuelva.com.

IFP Market
September 2005

IFP/New York is a 25-year-old, not-for-profit membership and advocacy organisation that supports and serves the independent film community by connecting creative talent and the industry. Wide-reaching programmes provide invaluable information, resources, networking and support to film-makers while promoting film as a vital and influential public art form. IFP Market & Conference is the only film market in the US showcasing narrative and documentary works-in-progress. The Market gives more than $200,000 in grants and services to emerging talent and is divided into four sections: Emerging Narrative, Spotlight on Documentaries, No Borders International Co-Production Market and Film Conference & Expo. Comprised of dozens of panels and workshops, four days of screenings, special events and more than 1,000 scheduled meetings between industry reps and film-makers, the IFP Market & Conference provides connections for film-makers and a place of discovery for funders, programmers and other professionals. *Inquiries to:* Michelle Byrd, Executive Director, IFP/New York, 104 West 29th St, 12th Floor, New York, NY 10001, USA. Tel: (1 212) 465 8200. Fax: 465 8525. e: ifpny@ifp.org. Web: www.ifp.org.

India
October 2005

Annual, government-funded event recognised by FIAPF and held in Goa under the aegis of India's Ministry of Information and Broadcasting. Comprehensive "Cinema of the World" section, foreign and Indian retrospectives and a film

market, plus a valuable panorama of the year's best Indian films, subtitled in English. *Inquiries to:* The Director, Directorate of Film Festival, Siri Fort Auditorium 1, August Kranti Marg, Khel Gaon, New Delhi 110049, India.
Tel: (91 11) 649 9371/9357. Fax: 649 7214/0457).
e: dffiffi@bol.net.in. Web: www.mib.nic/dff.

Internationale Hofer Filmtage / Hof International Film Festival

October 26-30, 2005

Dubbed "Home of Film" (HOF) by Wim Wenders, Hof is famous for its thoughtful selection of some 50 features. Founded by the directors of the New German Cinema, Hof enjoys a high reputation among German film-makers and international luminaries such as Peter Jackson, Mike Leigh and Atom Egoyan. Directed by one of the most respected German film enthusiasts, Heinz Badewitz, Hof has enjoyed a rising reputation these past 38 years. A screening here often results in a distribution deal. *Inquiries to:* Postfach 1146, D-95010 Hof, Germany or Heinz Badewitz, Lothstr 28, D-80335 Munich, Germany.
Tel: (49 89) 129 7422. Fax: 123 6868.
e: info@hofer-filmtage.de.
Web: www.hofer-filmtage.de.

Report 2003 and 2004

Some 59 features and documentaries and 29 shorts celebrated their German premiere at the thirty-seventh Hof in 2003. An audience of more than 29,000 visited 165 screenings showing films from Afghanistan, Australia, Austria, Belgium, Canada, Denmark, El Salvador, France, Great Britain, Ireland, Italy, Japan, Croatia, New Zealand, Sweden, Switzerland, Spain, the US and Germany. The retrospective was dedicated

to Ulli Lommel, who personally presented his own choice of films. The directors' soccer team, 1. FC Hofer Filmtage, played a select Hof Team and the thrilling match ended 2–3. In 2004, attendance exceeded 28,000 for 62 features and 36 shorts. The retrospective was dedicated to US director John McNaughton and 1. FC Hofer Filmtage won the annual soccer clash 3–2.
– **Heinz Badewitz**, Festival Director.

Werner Herzog at the annual Hof International Film Festival football match in 2003

Istanbul

April 2-17, 2005

The only film festival which takes place in a city where two continents meet, the Istanbul International Film Festival, recognised as a specialised competitive event by FIAPF, acts as a valuable showcase for distributors internationally. Attendance exceeds 100,000. Now in its twenty-fourth edition, this dynamic event focuses on features dealing with the arts, with other thematic sections such as tributes, selections from World Festivals, "A Country – A Cinema", and a panorama of Turkish cinema. *Inquiries to:* Ms. Hulya Ucansu, Istanbul Foundation for Culture and Arts, Istiklal Caddesi Luvr Apt 146, Beyoglu 34435, Istanbul, Turkey.

Tel: (90 212) 334 0700 exts. 720 & 721.
Fax: 334 0702. e: film.fest@istfest.org.
Web: www.istfest.org.

AWARDS 2004
Golden Tulip: **Goodbye Dragon Inn** (Taiwan),
Tsaï Ming-Liang.
Special Prize of the Jury: **The Professional**
(Serbia & Montenegro), Dusan Kovacevic;
L'Esquive (France), Abdellatif Kehiche
(International Competition); **Waiting for the
Clouds**, Yesim Ustaoglu (National Competition).
FIPRESCI Awards: **L'Esquive** (International
Competition); **What's Human Anyway**, Reha
Erdem (National Competition).
Turkish Film of the Year: **Boats Out of
Watermelon Rinds**, Ahmet Uluçay.
Turkish Director of the Year: Zeki Demirkubuz,
The Waiting Room.
Turkish Actor: Emre Kinay and Sevket Coruh,
Under Construction, Ömer Vargi.
Turkish Actress: Rüçhan Çaliskur, **Waiting for
the Clouds**.
Peoples Choice Awards: **Reconstruction**
(Denmark), Christoffer Boe (International
Competition); **A Little Bit of Freedom**
(Germany/Turkey), Yüksel Yavuz
(National Competition).

Jerusalem International Film Festival
July 7-16, 2005

Israel's most prestigious cinematic event
showcases more than 180 films: Best of
International Cinema, Documentaries, Israeli
Cinema, Animation, Short Films, American
Independents, Avant Garde, New Directors,
Jewish Themes, Classics, Restorations and
Special Tributes. Prize categories include the

Wolgin Awards for Israeli Cinema, Lipper Award
for Best Israeli Screenplay, international awards
like the Wim van Leer "In the Spirit of Freedom",
for films focusing on human rights, and the Films
on Jewish Themes Award. *Inquiries to:* Jerusalem
Film Festival, PO Box 8561, Jerusalem 91083,
Israel. Tel: (972 2) 565 4333. Fax: 565 4334.
e: festival@jer-cin.org.il. Web: www.jff.org.il.

Karlovy Vary International Film Festival
July 1-9, 2005

Founded in 1946, Karlovy Vary is one of the
most important film events in Central and
Eastern Europe. It includes international
competitions for features and documentaries
and every year foreign visitors welcome the
chance to see new productions from former
Eastern Bloc countries. *Inquiries to:* Film Servis
Festival Karlovy Vary, Panská 1, CZ 110 00
Prague 1, Czech Republic.
Tel: (420 2) 2141 1011. Fax: 2141 1033.
e: festival@kviff.com. Web: www.kviff.com.

Report 2004
At our thirty-ninth festival, 123,700 spectators
enjoyed 235 new and classic films. The jury,
presided over by American producer Al Ruban,
awarded the Grand Prix, the Crystal Globe, to *The
Children's Story* (Italy), Andrea and Antonio Frazzi.
Further awards were given to *Here* (Croatia),
Zrinko Ogresta, *León and Olvido* (Spain), Xavier
Bermudez, *Napola* (Germany), Dennis Gansel. The
Audience Prize went to *The Story of the Weeping
Camel* (Germany/Mongolia), Byambasuren Davaa
and Luigi Falorni. Highlights included tributes to
John Cassavetes and Sergio Leone, a
retrospective, 10 Best Turkish Films, and Focus on
Catalan Cinema. Special Crystal Globes were
awarded to Harvey Keitel, Roman Polanski and
Miroslav Ondrícek.
– **Eva Zaoralová**, Artistic Director.

La Rochelle
July 1-11, 2005

In a friendly atmosphere, this non-competitive
festival showed 150 films to audiences of
69,182 in 2004. Five films are screened a day in
each of the twelve theatres situated around the

old port. There is a daily 4pm meeting for public and press with a different film-maker. The festival includes Retrospectives for directors or actors and tributes to important but unjustly neglected directors or actors. Films for children are shown every morning. Special Events, such as film previews, silent films with piano accompaniment, are open to all. The festival ends with an all-night programme of five films, followed by breakfast in cafés overlooking the old port. *Inquiries to:* La Rochelle International Film Festival, 16 rue Saint Sabin, 75011 Paris, France.
Tel: (33 1) 4806 1666. Fax: 4806 1540.
e: info@festival-larochelle.org.
Web: www.festival-larochelle.org. Director: Mrs. Prune Engler; Artistic Director: Mrs. Sylvie Pras.

Le Giornate del Cinema Muto
October 8-15, 2005

The world's first and largest festival dedicated to silent cinema. Officially based in Pordenone, for the past six years it has taken place in the nearby historic town of Sacile. It is invaded by international archivists, historians, scholars, collectors and enthusiasts, along with cinema students chosen to attend the internationally recognised "Collegium". An innovation is the annual music school, with masterclasses for budding silent film accompanists. The Film Fair, which features books, CD-ROMs and DVDs, continues to provide a valued meeting place for authors and publishers. Festival director: David Robinson. *Inquiries to:* Le Giornate del Cinema Muto, c/o La Cineteca del Friuli, Palazzo Gurisatti, Via Bini 50, 33013 Gemona (UD), Italy. Tel: (39 04) 3298 0458. Fax: 3297 0542. e: info.gcm@cinetecadelfriuli.org.
Web: www.cinetecadelfriuli.org/gcm/.

Report 2004
Principal offerings were the most complete retrospective ever of the early Soviet genius Dziga Vertov, the rediscovery of Britain's lively commercial cinema of the 1920s and a celebration of the centenary of America's first film capital, Fort Lee, New Jersey. Orchestral events in Pordenone's first Forum of Live Film Music included the premiere of Neil Brand's score for Paul Leni's brilliant horror-comic

The Cat and the Canary.

Leeds
October/November 2005

The UK's largest regional film festival, based in the country's fastest-growing city. Competitive for debut/sophomore features, short films and animation. Leeds is buzzing with more than a number of unique, including Fanomenon, the 'cult-ural' heart of the festival (a feast of fantasy film); 'Fringe', a focus on experimental and underground work; and a major spotlight on new and archive European cinema. Attendance exceeds 20,000. *Inquiries to:* Leeds International Film Festival, The Town Hall, The Headrow, Leeds, LS1 3AD, UK. Tel: (44 113) 247 8398. Fax: 247 8494. e: filmfestival@leeds.gov.uk. Web: www.leedsfilm.com.

AWARDS 2003
Audience Award for Best Feature: **The Revolution Will Not Be Televised** (Ireland/US), Kim Bartley.
Louis Le Prince for Fiction Short: **Other People's Kisses** (France), Carine Tardieu.
Louis Le Prince Award for Animated Short: **Harvie Krumpet** (Australia), Adam Elliot.

AWARDS 2004
Audience Award for Best Feature: **Evil** (Sweden), Mikael Hafström.
Louis Le Prince for Fiction Short: **Doing Mikles Well** (Italy), Christian Angeli.
World Animation Award: **Ryan** (Canada), Chris Landreth.

Locarno
August 3-13, 2005

2005 will see the fifty-eighth birthday of a festival which made a name for itself through the careful attention paid by its directors to film-making both young and eccentric, in all senses of the term. Under its current director, Irene Bignardi, the Locarno Film Festival keeps alive this tradition of experimentation, discovery, eclecticism and passion for auteur cinema. It also provides an international showcase for major new films from around the world and

maintains the magical atmosphere of an artistic event that knows how to be convivial – never more so than when 7,000–8,000 (sometimes even more) moviegoers and professionals of all ages, nationalities and backgrounds gather under the stars in Piazza Grande, to watch a movie on one of the world's biggest screens (26m x 14m). *Inquiries to:* Festival Internazionale del Film Locarno, Via Ciseri 23, CH-6601 Locarno, Switzerland.
Tel: (41 91) 756 2121. Fax: 756 2149.
e: info@pardo.ch. Web: www.pardo.ch.

AWARDS 2004
International Competition
Golden Leopard: **Private** (Italy), Saverio Costanzo.
Special Jury Prize: **Tony Takitani** (Japan), Jun Ichikawa.
Silver Leopards: **En Garde** (Germany), Ayse Polat; **Story Undone** (Iran/Ireland/Singapore), Hassan Yektapanah.
Actress Leopard: Maria Kwiatkowsky and Pinar Erincin, **En Garde**.
Actor Leopard: Mukhammad Bakri, **Private**.

Video Competition
Golden Leopard: Conversations de Salon 1-2-3 (France), Danielle Arbid.
Public Choice Award: **The Syrian Bride** (Israel), Eran Riklis.

London
Late October – early November 2005

The UK's largest, most prestigious festival, sponsored by the *Times* and presented at the National Film Theatre and at cinemas throughout the capital. The programme comprises around 200 features and documentaries, as well as shorts. There is a British section and a strong selection from Asia, Africa, Europe, Latin America, US independents and experimental work. More than 1,200 UK and international press and industry representatives attend. *Inquiries to:* Sarah Lutton, London Film Festival, National Film Theatre, South Bank, London SE1 8XT, UK. Tel: (44 20) 7815 1322.
Fax: 7633 0786. e: sarah.lutton@bfi.org.uk.
Web: www.lff.org.uk.

Málaga
April 22-30, 2005

The Festival of Málaga is firmly established as the key national showcase for Spanish cinema. Málaga enjoys large turnouts from local audiences and Spanish actors and directors. Besides a competition for features, shorts and documentaries, it has retrospectives, exhibits and the Market of European and Latin American Documentaries (MERCADOC), and Market Screenings for Spanish films. *Inquiries to:* Salomón Castiel, Director, Málaga Festival–Spanish Cinema, Ramos Marín 2, 1ºC, 29012, Málaga, Spain. Tel: (34 95) 222 8242. Fax: 222 7760. e: info@festivaldemalaga.com. Web: www.festivaldemalaga.com.

Mannheim-Heidelberg
November 2005

The Newcomers' Festival: for young independent film-makers from all over the world. Presents around 35 new features and around 10 shorts in two main sections, International Competition and International Discoveries (entry deadline: August 6). The Newcomers' Market & Industry Screenings: reserved for international buyers and distributors. The Mannheim Meetings: Part 1 is one of only four worldwide co-production meetings for producers (alongside Rotterdam, New York and Pusan) and runs in parallel to the main event (entry deadline: July 31). Part 2 is the unique European Sales & Distribution Meetings for theatrical distributors and sales agents. The Distribution Market will take place during the festival. More than 60,000 filmgoers and 1,000 film professionals attend. *Inquiries to:* Dr. Michael Koetz, International Filmfestival Mannheim-Heidelberg, Collini-Center, Galerie, D-68161 Mannheim, Germany. Tel: (49 621) 102 943. Fax: 291 564. e: ifmh@mannheim-filmfestival.com. Web: www.mannheim-filmfestival.com.

AWARDS 2003
Best Fiction Film: **Plastic Tree** (South Korea), Eo Il-seon.
Best Short Film: **Perebisnes** (Estonia), Andres Tuisk.
Rainer Werner Fassbinder Prize: **Saturday**

(Chile), Matias Bize.
Special Award of the Jury: **Miffo** (Sweden), Daniel Lind-Lagerlöf.
Audience Award: **Donau, Dunaj, Duna, Dunav, Dunarea** (Austria), Goran Rebic.

AWARDS 2004
Best Fiction Film: **Chlorox, Ammonia and Coffee** (Norway), Mona J. Hoel.
Best Short Film: **Like Twenty Impossibles** (Palestine), Annemarie Jacir.
Rainer Werner Fassbinder Prize: **Mila from Mars** (Bulgaria) Zornitsa Sophia.
Special Award of the Jury: **Doo Wop** (France), David Lanzmann; **My Jealous Barber** (Norway), Annette Sjursen; **On the Corner** (Canada), Nathaniel Geary.
Audience Award: **Follow the Feather** (Germany), Nuray Sahin; **Red Coloured Grey Truck** (Serbia & Montenegro), Srdjan Kolevic.

Mar del Plata International Film Festival
March 10-20, 2005

The festival was first held in 1954, but because of a 26-year hiatus is only celebrating its twentieth edition in 2005. Held annually since 1996. The festival's President is acclaimed film-maker Miguel Pereira. It is the only A-grade film festival in Latin America with an Official Competition, usually comprising around 15 movies, generally two from Argentina. Key sections include "Latin American Films" and "Women and Film". Also important is the Mercosur Film Market (MFM; Director: Gabriel Giandinoto). Inquiries to: Mar Del Plata International Film Festival, Av de Mayo 1222, 3er, (1085) Cap Fed, Argentina. Tel: (54 11) 4383 5115. e: gabriel.giandinoto@mardelplatafilmfest.com. Web: www.mardelplatafilmfest.com,

Melbourne International Film Festival
Late July – early August 2005

The longest-running festival in the southern hemisphere will present its fifty-fourth edition in 2005, with more than 400 features, shorts, documentaries and new media works,

presented in five venues. *Inquiries to:* PO Box 2206, Fitzroy Mail Centre 3065, Melbourne, Victoria, Australia.
Tel: (61 3) 9417 2011. Fax: 9417 3804.
e: miff@melbournefilmfestival.com.au.
Web: www.melbournefilmfestival.com.au.

MIFED (Milan)
November 2005

Established market held in the expansive Milan Fair, particularly well attended by international buyers and sellers. Third on the annual calendar after the American Film Market and Cannes, MIFED's atmosphere is considered by many to be more sober and business-like. MIFED is unique because its exhibition and screening facilities are all under one roof. Its 28 screening rooms have Dolby stereo, and it continues to invest substantially in technological and logistical improvements. *Inquiries to:* Audiovisual Industry Promotion Spa, c/o Fiera Milano, Piazzale Giulio Cesare, 1 Palazzo Cisi, 20145 Milan, Italy. Tel: (39 02) 4855 0279. Fax: 4855 0420.
e: mifed@aip-mifed.com. Web: www.mifed.com.

Mill Valley
October 6-16, 2005

The Mill Valley Film Festival presents a wide variety of international programming, shaped by a commitment to cultural and artistic excellence. This intimate, welcoming event of unusually high calibre and dedication is set in a beautiful small town just north of San Francisco. The non-competitive festival includes the innovative VFest, as well as the Children's Film Fest, tributes, seminars and special events. *Inquiries to:* Mill Valley Film Festival, 38 Miller Ave, Suite 6, Mill Valley, CA 94941, USA.
Tel: (1 415) 383 5256. Fax: 383 8606.
e: info@cafilm.org. Web: www.mvff.com.

Montreal World Film Festival
August 25 – September 5, 2005

Films from more than 70 countries are selected and attendance increases each year. Apart from the "Official Competition" and the "First Films Competition", the festival presents "Hors Concours" (World Greats), a "Focus on World

Cinema" and "Documentaries of the World", plus tributes to established film-makers and a section dedicated to Canadian student films. All the theatres are within walking distance of one another and this contributes to the relaxed atmosphere. Festival guests have included Jane Fonda, Clint Eastwood, Gérard Depardieu, Jackie Chan, Gong Li, Jeanne Moreau, Liv Ullmann and many others. *Inquiries to:* Montreal World Film Festival 1432 de Bleury St, Montreal, Quebec, Canada H3A 2J1. Tel: (1 514) 848 3883 Fax: 848 3886. e: info@ffm-montreal.org. Web: www.ffm-montreal.org.

AWARDS 2004
Grand Prix of the Americas (Best Film):
The Syrian Bride (Israel), Eran Riklis.
Jury Awards: **The Parking Attendant in July** (China), An Zhanjun; **Around the Bend** (US), Jordan Roberts.
Director: Carlos Saura, **The 7th Day** (Spain).
Artistic Contribution: Ghyslaine Côté, director, **The Five of Us** (Canada).
Actress: Karin Viard, **The Role of Her Life** (France).
Actors: Fan Wei, **The Parking Attendant in July**; Christopher Walken, **Around the Bend** (US).
Best Screenplay: François Favrat, Julie Lopes-Curval, Jérôme Beauséjour and Roger Bohbot, **The Role of Her Life**.
Innovation Award: **The Crying Wind** (Japan), Yoichi Higashi.
Air Canada People's Choice Award:
The Syrian Bride.
Award for the Most Popular Canadian Film:
The Five of Us.
FIPRESCI Prize: **The Syrian Bride**.
Ecumenical Prize: **The Syrian Bride**.
Special Grand Prix of the Americas for Exceptional Contribution to the Cinematographic Art: Isabelle Adjani, Theo Angelopoulos, Krsto Papic.

Moscow International Film Festival
June 17-26, 2005

Biannual from 1959-98, the festival provided an open window on world cinema, with an international competition for domestic productions and many from Eastern Europe and developing countries, and a non-competitive

panorama of commercial hits absent from regular local distribution. Since going annual in 1999, the programme has become more arthouse-oriented (Hollywood now dominates mainstream cinemas) and there are visits by A-list stars and directors (Jack Nicholson, Meryl Streep, Fanny Ardant, Quentin Tarantino, William Friedkin, Emir Kusturica) attracted by the Life Achievement and Stanislavsky acting awards. The large competition remains international in scope and genres, covering Europe and the CIS, South East Asia, Latin and North America. A new competitive section, Perspectives, started in 2004. The Media-Forum (panorama and competition) is devoted to experimental films and video art.
Inquiries to: Moscow International Film Festival, 10/1 Khokhlovsky Per, Moscow 109028, Russia. Tel: (7 095) 917 2486. Fax: 916 0107. e: info@miff.ru. Web: www.miff.ru.

AWARDS 2004
Saint George
Film: **Our Own** (Russia), Dmitry Meskhiev.
Director: Dmitry Meskhiev, **Our Own**.
Actor: Bogdan Stupka, **Our Own**.
Actress: China Zorilla, **Conversations with Mother** (Argentina).
Special Jury Prize: **Revolution of Pigs** (Estonia), Rene Reinumagi and Jaak Kilmi.
Perspectives Award: **The Hotel Venus** (Japan), Hideta Takahata.
Life Achievement: Emir Kusturica.
Stanislavsky Award: Meryl Streep.

Netherlands Film Festival, Utrecht
September 21-30, 2005

Since 1981, Holland's only event presenting an overview of the year's entire output of Dutch film-making. The festival opens the new cultural season with Dutch retrospectives, seminars, talk shows and premieres of many new Dutch films. Dutch features, shorts, documentaries and TV dramas compete for local cinema's grands prix, the Golden Calf, in 18 categories. The Holland Film Meeting, the sidebar for international and national film professionals, includes a Market Programme and the Netherlands Production Platform for Dutch and European producers.
Inquiries to: Nederlands Film Festival, PO Box

1581, 3500 BN Utrecht, Netherlands.
Tel: (31 30) 230 3800 Fax: 230 3801.
e: info@filmfestival.nl. Web: www.filmfestival.nl.

New York
September 23 – October 9, 2005

Highlights the best of American and international
cinema. Deadline around July. Application forms
and details available from May. No entry fee.
Non-competitive. All categories and lengths
accepted. Formats accepted: VHS (NTSC or
PAL), u-matic, 16mm, 35mm. For acceptance,
you must have a 16mm or 35mm print available.
Works must be New York City premieres.
Inquiries to: Sara Bensman, Film Society of
Lincoln Center, 70 Lincoln Center Plaza, New
York, NY 10023-6595, USA.
Tel: (1 212) 875 5638. Fax: 875 5636.
e: festival@filmlinc.com. Web: www.filmlinc.com.

Nordische Filmtage Lubeck
November 3-6, 2005

Held in the charming medieval town of Lubeck,
north of Hamburg, the festival spotlights
Scandinavian and Baltic cinema, enabling
members of the trade, critics and other
filmgoers to see the best new productions. Also
features a large documentary section.
Attendance exceeds 18,000 for more than 130
screenings. *Inquiries to:* Janina Prossek,
Nordische Filmtage Lubeck, Schildstrasse 12,
D-23539 Lubeck, Germany.
Tel: (49 451) 122 1742. Fax: 122 1799.
e: info@filmtage.luebeck.de.
Web: http://filmtage.luebeck.de.

AWARDS 2003
NDR Promotion Prize: **Inheritance** (Denmark),
Per Fly.
Baltic Film: **Kitchen Stories** (Norway),
Bent Hamer.
Audience Prize: **Falling Sky** (Norway),
Gunnar Vikene.
Children's Film: **Wolf Summer** (Norway),
Peder Nordlund.
Documentary Film: **Only a German** (Denmark),
Soren Lindbjerg.
Children's Jury: **FIA!**.

AWARDS 2004

NDR Promotion Prize: **Illusive Tracks** (Sweden), Peter Dalle.
Baltic Film: **Aftermath** (Denmark), Paprika Steen.
Audience Prize: **Illusive Tracks**.
Children's Film: **The Colour of Milk** (Norway), Torun Lian.
Documentary Film: **Red Wine Skirt and Lambskin Coat – A Documentary About a Laundry** (Germany), Hannah Metten and Jan Gabbert.
Children's Jury: **Nasty Brats** (Denmark), Giacomo Campeotto.

Nyon
April 18-24, 2005

Visions du Réel, the International Film Festival of Nyon, aims to promote independent films and audiovisual productions classified as creative documentaries. These 'films du réel' are treated as a specific and committed form of cinema. The works (irrespective of length or format) are divided into six sections: International Competition; Regards Neufs (international competition for first films); Tendances; Investigations; Helvétiques (Swiss selection); Ateliers, Séances spéciales. Deadline: mid-January (regulations and entry form available each autumn on festival website). *Inquiries to:* Visions du Réel, 18, rue Juste Olivier, PO Box 593, CH-1260 Nyon 1, Switzerland.
Tel: (41 22) 365 4455. Fax: 365 4450.
e: docnyon@visionsdureel.ch.
Web: www.visionsdureel.ch.

Oberhausen
May 5-10, 2005

The world's oldest short film festival celebrated an extremely successful fiftieth anniversary in 2004. A retrospective programme presented 50 years of short film history, while the traditional competitions – International, German, children's shorts and music video – once again provided an overview of current international short film and video production, and three special programmes presented alternative versions of "The Next 50 Years?". Closing date for entries: mid-January. *Inquiries to:* Oberhausen

International Short Film Festival, Grillostrasse 34, D-46045 Oberhausen, Germany.
Tel: (49 208) 825 2652. Fax: 825 5413.
e: info@kurzfilmtage.de.
Web: www.kurzfilmtage.de.

AWARDS 2004

International Competition
Grand Prize (ex aequo): **Od-El Camino** (Colombia), Martin Mejía; **La tresse de ma mère** (France), Iris Sara Schiller.
Two Principal Prizes: **WASP** (UK), Andrea Arnold; **Fabulous Creatures** (US), Eunjung Hwang.
German Competition
Prize for the Best Contribution: **Living a Beautiful Life**, Corinna Schnitt.

The international jury in front of the festival cinema at Oberhausen 2004 (left to right): Robert Cahen (France), Jayne Parker (UK), Piotr Krajewski (Poland), Catrin Lundqvist (Sweden) and Abraham Ravett (US)

Odense
August 15-20, 2005

Denmark's only international short film festival invites unusual films with original, surprising and imaginative content. All 16mm, 35mm and Beta SP can participate. Maximum length: 60 mins. At the nineteenth festival, 200 films were screened and there were numerous 'Meet the Audience' sessions, three seminars, several film professional get-togethers and open-air screenings. The 2005 festival is part of the Hans Christian Andersen 2005 worldwide celebration and includes a special competition for Hans Christian Andersen films. *Inquiries to:* Odense

20th INTERNATIONAL ODENSE FILM FESTIVAL

[AUGUST 15-20, 2005]

Imaginative and surprising shorts
All 16 mm, 35 mm and BetaSP can compete.

Entry deadline April 1st 2005.

Download entryform at www.filmfestival.dk

20th INTERNATIONAL ODENSE FILM FESTIVAL

[August 2005]

Celebrates the 200 anniversary of the famous Danish writer Hans Christian Andersen. All shorts based on his fairytales or in his spirit are invited to a special Hans Christian Andersen programme.

---

www.filmfestival.dk

Vindegade 18 · DK-5000 Odense C · Denmark
Tel: + 45 6613 1372 / +45 6551 4044
Fax: +45 6591 4318
E-mail: off.ksf@odense.dk

Film Festival, Vindegade 18, DK-5000 Odense C, Denmark. Tel: (45) 6613 1372, ext 4044. Fax: 6591 4318. e: off.ksf@odense.dk. Web: www.filmfestival.dk.

AWARDS 2004
International Grand Prix: **Fragile** (Sweden), Jens Jonsson.
Special Prize: **The Hole** (Iran), Vahid Nasirian.
Special Prize: **At 7:35AM** (Spain), Nacho Vigalondo.
Special Prize: **Goodbye Cruel World** (UK), Vito Rocco.
Special Mention: **Scattered in the Wind** (Finland), Raimo O. Niemi.
Special Mention: **The Man without a Head** (France), Juan Solanas.
Press Jury Prize: **Passing Hearts** (Sweden), Johan Brisinger.
Prize of the Juvenile Jury: **Love Tricycle** (Australia), Andrew Goode.
The Humanist Award: **Passing Hearts**.
Jameson Short Film Award: **Land in the Mist** (Denmark), Suvi Andrea Helminen.

Oulu International Children's Film Festival
November 14-20, 2005

Annual festival with competition for full-length feature films for children, it screens recent titles and retrospectives. Oulu is set in northern Finland, on the coast of the Gulf of Bothnia.
Inquiries to: Oulu International Children's Film Festival, Torikatu 8, 90100 Oulu, Finland. Tel: (358 8) 881 1293/94. Fax: 881 1290. e: oek@oufilmcenter.inet.fi. Web: www.ouka.fi/lef.

Youngsters dressed up in honour of the festival's Star Boy Award at Oulu in 2004

Palm Springs
January 2006

Each year Palm Springs honours individuals with awards, including the Charles A. Crain Desert Palm Achievement, International Film-maker, Director's Lifetime Achievement, Frederick Loewe Achievement and the Outstanding Achievement in Craft. The festival has more than 600 entries and 75,000 attendees. *Inquiries to:* Darryl MacDonald, 1700 E. Tahquitz Canyon Way, Suite 3, Palm Springs, CA 92262, USA. Tel: (1 760) 322 2930. Fax: 322 4087. e: info@psfilmfest.org. Web: www.psfilmfest.org.

Pesaro
June 24 – July 2, 2005

The Mostra Internazionale del Nuovo Cinema Focuses on new directors and emerging, innovative cinemas, including non-fiction, animation, shorts and videos. For the past 40 years, the Mediterranean resort of Pesaro has hosted lively screenings and debates. In recent seasons, the programme has been devoted in part to a specific country or culture. The main festival (in the summer) is coupled each autumn with a six-day themed retrospective of Italian cinema. *Inquiries to:* Mostra Internazionale del Nuovo Cinema (Pesaro Film Festival), Via Villafranca 20, 00185 Rome, Italy. Tel: (39 06) 445 6643/491 156. Fax: 191 163. e: pesarofilmfest@mclink.it. Web: www.pesarofilmfest.it.

Report 2004
At our fortieth festival, more than 10,000 spectators enjoyed 258 new and classic films. Highlights included retrospectives on Lucian Pintilie, Mexican Cinema of the 1990s and the Taviani Brothers, all of which featured lively panel discussions and open-air screenings. The Public Award went to Tom McCarthy's *The Station*

Agent (US).
– **Pedro Armocida,** General Manager.

Portland
February 12-27, 2006

The twenty-ninth Portland International Film Festival will be an invitational event presenting more than 100 films from 30-plus countries to 35,000 people from throughout the Northwest. Along with new international features, documentaries and shorts, the 2006 festival will feature showcases surveying Hispanic film and literature, Pacific Rim cinema and many of the year's foreign-language Oscar submissions. The 2004 Audience Award winners were Yoji Yamada's *The Twilight Samurai* (Japan), Byambassuren Davaa and Luisi Falormi's *The Story of the Weeping Camel* (Mongolia/Germany) and Martin Strange-Hansen's *This Charming Man* (Denmark). *Inquiries to:* Northwest Film Center, 1219 SW Park Ave, Portland, OR 97205, USA. Tel: (1 503) 221 1156. Fax: 294 0874. e: info@nwfilm.org. Web: www.nwfilm.org.

Pusan International Film Festival (PIFF)
Mid-October 2005

Established in 1996 in Busan, Korea. Known as the most energetic film festival in Asia, Pusan has been promoting Asian and Korean cinema for a decade, as well as introducing high-quality films from all corners of the world. Also retrospectives, special programmes, seminars and other related events. Celebrating its eighth edition, the Pusan Promotion Plan (PPP) market has been a platform for moving Asian projects forward in the marketplace worldwide. *Inquiries to:* Annex 2-1, 1393, Woo 1-Dong Yachting Center, Haeundae-Gu, Busan, Korea. Tel: (82 51) 747 3010. Fax: 747 3012. e: publicity@piff.org. Web: www.piff.org.

AWARDS 2004
New Currents: **This Charming Girl** (South Korea), Lee Yun-ki.
Netpac Award: **3-iron** (South Korea), Kim Ki-duk.
FIPRESCI Award: **Soap Opera** (China), Wu Ershan.
Woonpa Award (Korean Docu.): **What Do**

People Live For?, Lee Kyung-soon.
Sunjae Fund Award (Korean Short): **Punk Eek**,
Son Kwang-ju.
Audience Award: **Survive Style 5+** (Japan),
Gen Sekiguchi.

Raindance
October 2005

Raindance is the largest independent film festival
in the UK and aims to reflect the cultural, visual
and narrative diversity of international
independent film-making by screening features
and shorts. It screens more than 100 features
and 200 shorts from 40-plus countries and has
premiered and showcased films as diverse as
Pulp Fiction, *The Blair Witch Project*, *Chuck and
Buck*, *Audition*, *101 Reykjavik* and *Memento*.
Inquiries to: Oli Harbottle, Festival Producer,
Raindance Film Festival, 81 Berwick St, London,
W1F 8TW, UK. Tel: (44 20) 7287 3833.
Fax: 7439 2243. e: festival@raindance.co.uk.
Web: www.raindance.co.uk/festival.

AWARDS 2003
Official Selection Feature: **Fuse** (Bosnia &
Herzgovina), Pjer Zalica.
Official Selection Short: **Salaryman 6** (UK),
Jake Knight.
UK Feature: **The Last Horror Movie** (UK),
Julian Richards.
UK Short: **One Small Leap** (UK), Ed Boase and
James Walker.
Debut Feature: **Nate Dogg** (US), Thomas Farone.
Documentary: **And Along Came a Spider** (Iran),
Maziar Bahari.

AWARDS 2004
Official Selection Feature: **Marebito** (Japan),
Takashi Shimizu.
Official Selection Short: **Arthur 'Killer' Kane:
1949–2004** (US), Greg Whiteley.
UK Feature: **EMR** (UK), James Erskine and
Danny McCullough.
UK Short: **You Are My Favourite Chair** (UK),
Rob Hardy.
Debut Feature: **End of the Century** (US),
Jim Fields and Michael Gramaglia.
Documentary: **Jandek on Corwood** (US),
Chad Friedrichs.

Diesel Film of the Festival (US): **American
Fame Pt. 1: Drowning River Phoenix** (US),
Cam Archer.

International Film Festival Rotterdam
Late January – early February, 2006

For 34 years, Rotterdam has showcased the
best of contemporary independent and
experimental film. With more than 200 features,
including 60 world or European premieres, it
supports diversity, discoveries and film talent
worldwide. It also hosts the leading co-
production market, the CineMart. Rotterdam's
Hubert Bals Fund (HBF) supports film-makers
from non-Western countries. Recently acclaimed
HBF-backed films include Nuri Bilge Ceylan's
Distant (Turkey), *Osama* by Siddiq Barmak (Iran)
and *Silent Waters* by Sabiha Sumar (Pakistan).
Inquiries to: International Film Festival Rotterdam,
PO Box 21696, 3001 AR Rotterdam, Netherlands.
Tel: (31 10) 890 9090. Fax: 890 9091.
e: tiger@filmfestivalrotterdam.com.
Web: www.filmfestivalrotterdam.com.

Report 2004
In 2004, returning sidebars like the VPRO Tiger
Awards Competition for first and second
features, Film-makers in Focus (honouring the
works of Raul Ruiz, Isaac Julien, Tunde Kelani
and Ken Jacobs) and Exploding Cinema were
complemented by themed programmes like
'Homefront USA' and 'Romani Cinema',
exhibitions and public debates. The festival drew
350,000 spectators and 2,500 professionals.
Tiger Awards in 2004 went to: Jan Krueger's *En
Route* (Germany); Sdrjan Vuletic's *Summer in the
Golden Valley* (Bosnia & Herzegovina) and Lee
Kang-sheng's *The Missing* (Taiwan).

San Francisco International Film Festival
April 21 – May 5, 2005

The oldest film festival in the Americas, in its
forty-eighth year, San Francisco continues to
grow in importance and popularity. It presents
more than 175 international features and shorts.
Special awards include the Skyy Prize ($10,000
cash for an emerging director), The Golden Gate

Awards and the FIPRESCI Prize. *Inquiries to:* San Francisco International Film Festival, San Francisco Film Society, 39 Mesa St, Suite 110, The Presidio, San Francisco, CA 94129, USA. Tel: (1 415) 561 5000. Fax: 561 5099. e: publicity@sffs.org. Web: www.sffs.org.

AWARDS 2004
Skyy Prize: **Squint Your Eyes** (Poland), Andrezej Jakimowski.
FIPRESCI Prize: **The Story of the Weeping Camel** (Germany/Mongolia), Byambasuren Davaa and Luigi Falorni.
Golden Gate Awards
Best Short: **A Life to Live** (Poland), Maciej Adamek.
Best Documentary: **Checkpoint** (Israel), Yoav Shamir.
Best Bay Area Short: **Crystal Harvest** (US), Annelise Wunderlich.
Best Bay Area Documentary: **Girl Trouble** (US), Lexi Leban and Lidia Szajko.
New Visions: **Papillon d'amour** (Belgium), Nicolas Provost.
Best Narrative Short: **Chinese Dream** (US), Victor Quinaz.
Best Bay Area Non-Documentary Short: **The Greater Vehicle** (UA), Robert Fox.
Best Animated Short: **The Way** (South Korea), Jung Min-young.
Audience Award Narrative: **The Miracle of Bern** (Germany), Sönke Wortmann.
Audience Award Documentary: **Double Dare** (US), Amanda Micheli.

Report 2004
Some 175 films from 52 countries drew more than 73,000 spectators to the San Francisco area. Highlights included tributes to Milos Forman and Chris Cooper, with captivating on-stage interviews, and appearances by special guests Danny DeVito, Gary Ross and Treat Williams.
– **Hilary Hart,** Director of Publicity.

San Sebastian
September 2005

Held in an elegant Basque seaside city known for its superb gastronomy and beautiful beaches, the Donostia–San Sebastian Festival remains Spain's

most important event in terms of glamour, competition, facilities, partying, number of films and attendance (more than 550 production and distribution firms, government agencies and festival representatives from 40 countries, and some 1,000 accredited professionals). Events include the Official Competitive section, Zabaltegi, Horizontes Latinos and meticulous retrospectives. In partnership with the Rencontres Cinémas Amérique Latine in Toulouse, the Films in Progress industry platform aims to aid the completion of six Latin American and two Spanish projects. *Inquiries to:* San Sebastian International Film Festival, Apartado de Correos 397, 20080 Donostia, San Sebastian 20080, Spain. Tel: (34 943) 481 212. Fax: 481 218. e: ssiff@sansebastianfestival.com. Web: www.sansebastianfestival.com.

AWARDS 2004
Golden Shell for Best Film: **Turtles Can Fly** (Iran/Iraq), Bahman Ghobadi.
Special Jury Award: **A Midwinter Night's Dream** (Serbia & Montenegro), Goran Paskaljevic.
Silver Shell for Best Director: Xu Junglei, **Letter from An Unknown Woman** (China).
Silver Shell for Best Actress: Connie Nielsen, **Brothers** (Denmark).
Silver Shell for Best Actor: Ulrich Thomsen, **Brothers**.
Jury Award for Best Photography: Marcel Zyskind, **9 Songs** (UK).
Jury Award for Best Screenplay: Guy Hibbert and Paul Greengrass, **Omagh** (UK/Ireland).

Santa Barbara
Late January – early February 2006

Established in 1986 in the glamorous seaside resort 90 minutes north of LA, Santa Barbara International Film Festival has received worldwide recognition for its diverse programming. A jury of industry professionals selects winners in several categories, including Best US Feature, Best Foreign Feature, Best Director, Best Documentary Feature and Best Short. *Inquiries to:* SBIFF, 2064 Alameda Padre Serra, Suite 120 Santa Barbara, CA 93103, USA. Tel: (1 805) 963 0023. Fax: 962 2524. e:info@sbfilmfestival.org. Web: www.sbfilmfestival.org.

Sarasota

Late January – early February 2006

Ten days of independent film, symposiums and events in a beautiful location; hospitable, inquisitive audiences plus a well-organised and publicised programme. Past guests include Todd Haynes, Sydney Pollack, Gena Rowlands, Ismail Merchant and William H. Macy. Executive Director: Mr. Jody Kielbasa (jody@sarasotafilmfestival.com). Programme Director: Tom Hall (tom@sarasotafilmfestival.com). *Inquiries to:* Cemantha Crain, Marketing Director, Sarasota Film Festival, 635 S Orange Ave, Suite 10B, Sarasota, Florida 34236, USA.
Tel: (1 941) 364 9514. Fax: 364 8411.
e: info@sarasotafilmfestival.com.
Web: www.sarasotafilmfestival.com.

AWARDS 2004

Audience Award (Comedy): **A Tale of Two Pizzas** (US), Vincent Sassone.
Audience Award (Documentary): **My Uncle Berns** (US), Lindsay Crystal.
Audience Award (Drama): **Off the Map** (US), Campbell Scott.

Audience Award (Foreign Film): **Buddy** (Norway), Morten Tyldum.
Audience Award Best Short: **Chicken Party** (US), Tate Taylor.
Emerging Film-maker: **Mimmo and Paulie** (US), Domenic Silipo.
Festival Programmer's Choice: **Eternal Gaze** (US), Sam Chen.

Report 2004

Our sixth festival opened to a sold-out audience of 1,700 for *If Only*, with director Gil Junger and producer/star Jennifer Love Hewitt attending. More than 80 features and 70 shorts screened for record-breaking attendance of 40,000 (up 60% on 2003). Sam Elliott, Valentina de Angelis, Patrick Stewart and Woody Harrelson joined more than 130 film-makers.
– **Cemantha Crain,** Marketing Director.

Seattle International Film Festival

May 19 – June 12, 2005

One of the largest festivals in the US, Seattle presents more than 220 features and 100 shorts. There are cash prizes for the juried New Directors Competition, New American Cinema Competition and Documentary Competition. Also: Contemporary World Cinema, Emerging Masters, Asian Tradewinds, Women in Cinema, Tributes and an archive section. *Inquiries to:* Seattle International Film Festival, 400 Ninth Avenue North, Seattle, WA 98109, USA.
Tel: (1 206) 464 5830. Fax: 264 7919.
e: info@seattlefilm.com.
Web: www.seattlefilm.com.

Report 2004

At our thirtieth festival, more than 175,000 filmgoers enjoyed 224 features from more than 60 countries. Highlights included the world premieres of *Donnie Darko – The Director's Cut*, *Criminal* and *Incident at Loch Ness*; a Tribute to Patrice Leconte; an evening with Stephen Fry; Cinematography Masterclass with Christopher Doyle; and a strong focus on contemporary French cinema. The juried awards went to Zak Penn's *Incident at Loch Ness*, Lisa Cholodenko for *Cavedweller*, Sebastien Lifshitz's *Wild Side* and Ross Kauffmann and Zana Briski for *Born*

into Brothels. The 2004 juries included David Ansen (Newsweek), Peggy Chiao (ArcLight Films, Taiwan), Kelly Devine (IFC Films) and Simon de Santiago (Sogepaq, Spain).
– **Helen Loveridge**, Festival Director.

Singapore International Film Festival
April 15-30, 2005

Founded in 1987, SIFF is one of the leading festivals in Southeast Asia. Some 300 films from more than 40 countries are shown to 50,000 viewers through the main, fringe and special programmes and retrospectives. Fringe screenings are free and begin a week before the main programme. The festival's Asian focus and film selection attract programmers from all over the world. The Silver Screen Awards honour the best in Asian cinema, including the unique, combined NETPAC–FIPRESCI prize, co-ordinated by the Network for Promotion of Asian Cinema and the International Federation of Film Critics. Highlights in 2004 included retrospectives for Filipino film-maker and actress Laurice Guillen and Italian film-maker Paolo Virzi. Special programmes included Hong Kong Shaw Studios' erotic cinema of the 1960s and 1970s and Martin Scorsese's *The Blues* television series. *Inquiries to:* Singapore International Film Festival, 45A Keong Saik Rd, Singapore 089136, Singapore. Tel: (65) 738 7567. Fax: 738 7578. e: filmfest@pacific.net.sg. Web: www.filmfest.org.sg

Sitges International Film Festival of Catalonia
Late November – early December 2005

Now preparing for its thirty-ninth edition in a pleasant town on the Catalan coast, 30 kilometres from Barcelona, Sitges focuses on fantasy films and is considered one of Europe's leading specialised festivals, but is also open to new trends. The one official category, "Fantàstic", brings together the year's best genre productions. Other wide-reaching categories include Gran Angular (contemporary cinema with a language of its own), Orient Express (Asian genre films), Anima't (animation), Seven Chances (seven discoveries made by film critics), Audiovisual Català (Catalan productions) and

Retrospectives. *Inquiries to:* Sitges Festival Internacional de Cinema de Catalunya, Avenida Josep Tarradellas, 135 Esc A 3r 2a, 08029 Barcelona, Spain. Tel: (34 93) 419 3635. Fax: 439 7380. e: info@cinema.sitges.com. Web: www.sitges.com/cinema.

Sithengi, The Southern African International Film & TV Market / Cape Town World Cinema Festival
November 2005

Sithengi marks its tenth year in 2005 and has become Africa's leading media event, attended by many international broadcasters, directors and producers. It features a Film & TV Market and trade expo, a Pitching Forum, Conferences and Training Workshops. Business conducted at Sithengi exceeds $75m. The Cape Town World Cinema Festival has grown into one of South Africa's largest cinema events, with 15,000 admissions in 2004 and 19 feature films in competition. Award-winers included Siddiq Barmak's *Osama* (Afghanistan, Best Film and Best Director), Gael García Bernal (Best Actor for *Bad Education*) and Ian Gabriel's *Forgiveness* (Best African Feature). *Inquiries to:* Sithengi, PO Box 52120, Waterfront 8002, Cape Town, South Africa. Tel: (27 21) 430 8160. Fax: 430 8186. e: info@sithengi.co.za. Web: www.sithengi.co.za.

41ˢᵗ Solothurn Film Festival
January 16 – 22 2006   www.solothurnfilmfestival.ch

Solothurn Film Festival
January 2006

The most important forum for Swiss film-making, Solothurn is popular with media and public. For 38 years it has been the place to see new Swiss films, make discoveries and form opinions. There are Swiss retrospectives, a film school section, an annual focus on a guest country, international shorts and discussions and seminars. The annual Swiss Film Prizes (for feature, documentary, short film, actor and actress) guarantee suspense and the appearance of well-known faces. *Inquiries to:* Solothurn Film Festival, Postfach 1564, CH-4502 Solothurn, Switzerland. Tel: (41 32) 625 8080. Fax: 623 6410. e: info@solothurnerfilmtage.ch. Web: www.solothurnerfilmtage.ch.

Stockholm
November 10-20, 2005

The Stockholm International Film Festival is in its sixteenth year as one of Europe's leading cinema events. Recognised by FIAPF, it hosts a FIPRESCI jury and is a member of European Coordination of Film Festivals. In 2003, the festival scored an all-time high with 85,000 visitors, 500 accredited media and business representatives and more than 85 international guests. Some 160 features from 40 different countries were presented. David Lynch, Ang Lee, Joel and Ethan Coen, Quentin Tarantino, Lauren Bacall, Gaspar Noé and Dennis Hopper have all enjoyed the festival. It heads regional film fund, Film Stockholm, which has produced Swedish shorts and documentaries since 2001. Some 190 films have gained distribution in connection with the festival, which launched distribution company Edge Entertainment in 2000. Inquiries to: Stockholm International Film Festival, PO Box 3136, S-103 62 Stockholm, Sweden. Tel: (46 8) 677 5000. Fax: (46 8) 200 590. e: info@filmfestivalen.se. Web: www.filmfestivalen.se.

AWARDS 2003
Film and First Feature: **Schultze Gets the Blues** (Germany), Michael Schorr.
Short Film: **Wasp** (UK), Andrea Arnold.
Actress: So-ri Moon, **A Good Lawyer's Wife** (South Korea).
Actor: Horst Krause, **Schultze Gets the Blues**.
Screenplay: Michael Schorr, **Schultze Gets the Blues**.
Cinematography: Woo-hyeong Kim, **A Good Lawyer's Wife**.
Lifetime Achievement: David Lynch.
Audience Award: **The Station Agent** (US), Tom McCarthy.
FIPRESCI Award: **Elle est es notres** (France), Siegrid Alnoy.

AWARDS 2004
Film: **Innocence** (France), Lucile Hadzihalilovic.
First Feature: **Mean Creek** (US), Jacob Aaron Estes.
Short Film: **Gospel of the Creole Pig** (Haiti), Goran Kapetanovic.
Actress: Lisa Blount, **Chrystal** (US).
Actor: Peter Sarsgård, **Garden State** (US).
Screenplay: Jean-Pierre Bacri and Agnès Jaoui, **Look at Me** (France).
Cinematography: Benoït Cebie, **Innocence**.
Lifetime Achievement: Oliver Stone.
Audience Award: **Old Boy** (South Korea), Park Chan-wook.
FIPRESCI Award: **Producing Adults** (Finland), Aleksi Salmenperä.

Tartan Films

Old Boy *won the Audience Award at Stockholm 2004*

Sundance Film Festival
January 19-29, 2006

Sundance is the premiere showcase for American and international independent films. The Dramatic and Documentary Feature Film Competitions are the highlights, open to independently produced features (dramatic features must be 70 minutes-plus; documentary features 50 minutes-plus), which must be US premieres, have at least 50% US financing and have been completed after October 2004. All films submitted for the Competition are also considered for American Spectrum, Showcase, Frontier, Native Forum and Park City at Midnight programmes. International films are considered for World Cinema, World Cinema-Documentary, Frontier and Park City at Midnight. *Inquiries to:* Geoffrey Gilmore, Director, Festival Programming Department, Sundance Institute, 8857 West Olympic Blvd, Beverly Hills, CA 90211, USA. Tel: (1 310) 360 1981.

Fax: 360 1969. e: institute@sundance.org.
Web: www.sundance.org.

AWARDS 2004
Grand Jury Prize (Documentary): **DIG!** (US),
Ondi Timoner.
Grand Jury Prize (Dramatic): **Primer** (US),
Shane Carruth.
Audience Award (Documentary): **Born into
Brothels** (US), Ross Kauffman and Zana Briski.
Audience Award (Dramatic): **Maria Full of
Grace** (US/Colombia), Joshua Marston.

Tampere
March 9-13, 2005

This is the thirty-fifth year of one of the world's
leading short film festivals. Famous for its
international sauna party, it attracts entries from
more than 60 countries. The 700 professionals
and nearly 30,000 spectators can see 400-plus
shorts in some 100 screenings: international
competition (with a Grand Prix and other
awards); international retrospectives and
tributes; training seminars for professionals. The
market includes shorts and documentaries from
northern and eastern Europe. *Inquiries to:*
Tampere Film Festival, PO Box 305, 33101
Tampere, Finland. Tel: (358 3) 213 0034.
Fax: 223 0121. e: office@tamperefilmfestival.fi.
Web: www.tamperefilmfestival.fi.

AWARDS 2004
Grand Prix International: **Headway** (Sweden),
Jens Jonsson.
Documentary: **The Transformer** (Russia),
Pavel Kostomarov and Anton Cattin.
Fiction: **Flat Point** (Mexico), Carolina Rivas.
Animation: **The Tram No 9 Goes** (Belarus),
Viktor Asliuk.
Prix UIP Tampere: **Fender Bender** (Estonia),
Daniel Elliot.
Finnish Short: **Rhythm**, Sami Hyrynkangas.
Jameson Short Film Award: **Hankerchiefs for
Sale** (Finland), Jan Andersson.

Telluride
September 2-5, 2005

Each Labor Day weekend, Telluride triples in

size. More than 5,000 passionate film
enthusiasts flood the town for four days of total
cinematic immersion. This is a unique, friendly
gathering in a historic mining town, spectacularly
located in the mountains of Colorado. Telluride
remains one of the world's most influential
festivals, as famous directors, players and critics
descend on the Sheridan Opera House and
other theatres. The dedication of organisers and
participants to cinema gives Telluride a sincere,
authentic feel – not forgetting the "surprise"
element: the programme is only announced on
the first day. There are several tributes each year
(Peter Brook, Krzysztof Zanussi and Toni Collette
in 2003; Laura Linney, Theo Angelopoulos and
Jean-Claude Carrière in 2004). The festival
promotes discussions with a film's creator or a
historian who champions it; in 2003, Guest
Director Stephen Sondheim curated a
retrospective of the films of France's Julien
Duvivier. Guest Director for 2004 was writer,
director and actor Buck Henry. *Inquiries to:* The
Telluride Film Festival, 379 State St, Portsmouth,
NH 03801, USA. Tel: (1 603) 433 9202.
Fax: 433 9206. e: mail@telluridefilmfestival.org.
Web: www.telluridefilmfestival.org.

Thessaloniki International Film Festival
November 18-27, 2005
Thessaloniki Documentary Festival
April 1-10, 2005

In its forty-sixth year, the oldest and one of the
most important film events in southeastern
Europe targets a new generation of film-makers
as well as independent films by established
directors. The International Competition (for first
or second features) awards the Golden
Alexander (€37,000), won in 2003 by Alexei
German Jr.'s *The Last Train* (Russia) and the
Silver Alexander (€22,000), won in 2003 by
Michelangelo Frammartino's *The Gift* (Italy).
Other sections include Greek Film Panorama,
retrospectives, Balkan Survey, New Horizons
information section, plus galas and exhibitions.
The Documentary Festival is Greece's major
annual non-fiction film event. Its sections include
"Views of the World" (subjects of social interest),
"Portraits – Human Journeys" (highlighting the
human contribution to cultural, social and

7th
Thessaloniki
Documentary
Festival

1-10
April
2005

Doc Market
2-8 April

9, Alexandras Ave., GR-114 73
Athens, Greece

tel: +302108706000
newhorιzons@filmfestival.gr
www.filmfestival.gr

IMAGES
OF THE 21st
CENTURY

46th Thessaloniki
International
Film Festival
November 18-27, 2005

9, Alexandras Avenue, 114 73 Athens, Greece, Tel: +30210 8706000
Fax: +30210 6448143, e-mail: info@filmfestival.gr - www.filmfestival.gr

historical developments) and "Recording of Memory" (facts and testimony of social and historic origin). The festival also hosts the International Documentary Market. *Inquiries to:* Thessaloniki International Film Festival, 9 Alexandras Ave, 114 73 Athens, Greece. Tel: (30 210) 870 6000. Fax: 644 8143. e: info@filmfestival.gr. Web: www.filmfestival.gr. *Inquiries to:* Thessaloniki Documentary Festival (address and Tel/Fax numbers as above). Director: Dimitri Eipides. e: eipides-newhorizons@filmfestival.gr.

AWARDS 2004
Golden Alexander: **Bitter Dream** (Iran), Mohsen Amiryousefi.
Silver Alexander: **Harvest Time** (Russia), Marina Razbezkhina; **One or the Other** (Argentina), Alejo Taube.
Director: Fernando Eimbcke, **Duck Season** (Mexico).
Screenplay: Juan Pablo Rebella and Pablo Stoll, **Whisky** (Uruguay).
Actress: Mirella Pascual, **Whisky**.
Actor: Simon Abkarian, **To Take a Wife** (Israel).
Artistic Achievement: **Harvest Time**.

Tokyo International Film Festival
October 2005

Major competitive international event; cash prize of $100,000 awarded for the Tokyo Grand Prix (won in 2004 by Juan Pablo Rebella and Pablo Stoll's *Whisky*, Uruguay) and $20,000 for the Special Jury Prize. Other sections include: Special Screenings, Winds of Asia and Japanese Eyes. *Inquiries to:* Tokyo International Film Festival, 5F Tsukiji Yasuda Building, 2-15-14 Tsukiji Chuo-ku, Tokyo 104-0045, Japan. Tel: (81 3) 5148 3861. Fax: 3524 1087. e: info@tiff-jp.net. Web: www.tiff-jp.net. Director: Tsuguhiko Kadokawa.

Torino Film Festival
November 11-19, 2005

Dubbed second only to Venice on the crowded Italian festival circuit, and known for its discoveries as well as for its unique retrospectives, Torino constitutes a meeting point for contemporary international cinema. The festival pays particular attention to emerging cinemas and film-makers and promotes awareness of new directors whose work is marked by strong formal and stylistic research. Its programme includes competitive sections for international features, Italian documentaries and Italian shorts, as well as spotlights and premieres. *Inquiries to:* Torino Film Festival, Via Monte di Pietà 1, 10121 Torino, Italy. Tel: (39 011) 562 3309 Fax: 562 9796. e: info@torinofilmfest.org. Web: www.torinofilmfest.org.

Toronto International Film Festival
September 8-17, 2005

A rich diversity of world cinema is featured, offering more than 300 films in 10 days in several programmes: Galas, Special Presentations, Contemporary World Cinema, Planet Africa, Dialogues, Talking with Pictures, Reel to Reel, Directors Spotlight, Midnight Madness, Canada First!, Shortcuts Canada and Masters. The Rogers Industry Centre includes a Sales Office and industry programming and services. *Inquiries to:* Toronto International Film Festival, 2 Carlton St, 16th Floor, Toronto, Ontario, M5B 1J3, Canada. Tel: (1 416) 967 7371. Fax: 967 9477. e: tiffg@torfilmfest.ca. Web: www.bell.ca/filmfest.

Tribeca Film Festival
April 21 – May 1, 2005

Founded by Robert De Niro, Jane Rosenthal and Craig Hatkoff and now in its fourth year, Tribeca's stated goals are "to inspire film-makers and artists" and "revitalise lower Manhattan and support the charitable and cultural activities of the Tribeca Film Institute". The programme includes international juried competitions for Narrative Features (won in 2004 by Liu Fen Dou's *Green Hat*, China), Feature Documentaries and Short Films. *Inquiries to:* Peter Scarlet, Executive Director, 375 Greenwich St, New York, NY 10013, USA. Tel: (1 212) 941 2400. Fax: 941 3939. e: festival@tribecafilmfestival.org. Web: www.tribecafilmfestival.org.

Welcome to Tromsø International Film Festival, Norway

January 17th – 22nd 2006

The world's northernmost film festival invites you to an exotic week in the polar night and a cutting edge selection of fresh quality feature films.

Tromsø International Film Festival
January 17-22, 2006

The world's northernmost film festival is also Norway's best-attended, with more than 40,000 admissions. Tromsø International Film Festival is known for presenting the best of current international art cinema, screening more than 150 titles, including a feature competition and several exciting sidebars. "Films from the North" presents new shorts and docs from arctic Scandinavia and Russia. *Inquiries to:* Tromsø International Film Festival, PO Box 285, N-9253 Tromsø, Norway. Tel: (47) 7775 3090. Fax: 7775 3099. e: filmfestival@tiff.no. Web: www.tiff.no.

AWARDS 2004
Norwegian Peace Film: **In this World** (UK), Michael Winterbottom.
Aurora Prize: **Since Otar Left** (Georgia/France), Julie Bertuccelli.
FIPRESCI Prize: **The Silence Between Two Thoughts** (Iran), Babak Payami.

Umeå
September 15-21, 2005

Umeå International Film Festival, now in its twentieth year, is a competitive event screening around 100 features and 100 shorts. It has considerable standing as a gateway for distribution in Sweden and the Nordic countries and is the largest film festival in northern Scandinavia. The lively programme includes an international competitive panorama, innovative shorts, Swedish and Nordic documentaries, seminars, workshops and special guests. The popular "Camera Obscura" section includes obscure films and restored or neglected classics. Artistic Director: Thom Palmen. *Inquiries to:* Umeå International Film Festival, Box 43, S-901 02 Umeå, Sweden. Tel: (46 90) 133 388. Fax: 777 961. e: info@ff.umea.com. Web: www.ff.umea.com.

Valencia International Film Festival – Mediterranean Cinema
October 2005

Launched in 1980 and organised by the Valencia Municipal Film Foundation, the Valencia

20th Umeå International Film Festival
15 - 21 September 2005
Umeå, Sweden

www.filmfest.se

Mostra/Cinema del Mediterrani aims to promote greater understanding among people and culture in the Mediterranean area, stressing its historical roots by showing high-quality films which contribute to a better critical awareness of each country's film industry and art. *Inquiries to:* Valencia Mostra/Cinema del Mediterrani, Plaza de Arzobispo 2, 46003 Valencia, Spain. Tel: (34 96) 392 1506. Fax: 391 5156. e: festival@mostravalencia.com. Web: www.mostravalencia.org.

Valladolid
October 21-29, 2005

This year Valladolid International Film Festival celebrates its fiftieth anniversary. Firmly established as one of Spain's key events, it focuses on arthouse films as well as the latest work of established international directors and has introduced the cinema of many newcomers to Spain. Valladolid is famous for its organisation and hospitality, hosts a FIPRESCI jury and is competitive for features, shorts and documentaries. Also offers retrospectives, focus

on a film school, a selection of recent Spanish productions, an exhibition and a congress of new directors. Sidebars in 2004 were dedicated to Amos Gitai, Imanol Uribe, Focus on Switzerland, Chinese Cinema: The 6th Generation, Docs in Europe (3) and VGIK Film School, Moscow. *Inquiries to:* Fernando Lara, Director, Teatro Calderón, Calle Leopoldo Cano, s/n 4 planta, 47003 Valladolid, Spain. Tel: (34 983) 305 700/77/88. Fax: 309 835. e:festvalladolid@seminci.com. Web: www.seminci.com.

AWARDS 2003
Golden Spike: **Osama** (Afghanistan/Japan/Ireland), Siddiq Barmak; **Crimson Gold** (Iran), Jafar Panahi.
Silver Spike: **Kitchen Stories** (Norway/Sweden), Bent Hamer.
Special Jury Prize: **Good Bye, Lenin!** (Germany), Wolfgang Becker.
Pilar Miró Prize for Best New Director: Sofia Coppola **Lost in Translation** (US).
Actor: Jamie Sives, **Wilbur Wants to Kill Himself** (Denmark/UK), Lone Scherfig.

Actress: Helen Buday, **Alexandra's Project** (Australia), Rolf de Heer.

Lost in Translation *earned Sofia Coppola the Best New Director prize at Valladolid 2003*

AWARDS 2004
Golden Spike: **3-iron** (South Korea), Kim Ki-duk.
Silver Spike: **Private** (Italy), Saverio Costanzo.
Special Jury Prize: **In Your Hands** (Denmark), Annette K. Olesen.
Pilar Miró Prize for Best New Director: Leonardo di Cesare, **Good Life Delivery** (Argentina/France).
Actor: Ricardo Darín, **Avellaneda's Moon** (Argentina/Spain), Juan José Campanella.
Actress: Pilar Bardem, **My Dear Maria** (Spain), José García Sánchez.

Vancouver
September 29 – October 14, 2005

Now in its twenty-fourth year, this festival has grown into an event of considerable stature. Approximately 150,000 people attend more than 300 international films. Vancouver also hosts an Annual Film & Television Trade Forum. *Inquiries to:* Alan Franey, 1181 Seymour St, Vancouver, British Columbia, Canada V6B 3M7.
Tel: (1 604) 685 0260. Fax: 688 8221.
e: viff@viff.org. Web: www.viff.org.

Venice
Early September 2005

Under Marco Müller's trendy regime, the 62-year-old Mostra del Cinema is trying to overcome problems such as its old-fashioned facilities on expensive Lido Island, a weak market and heavy political interference. Retrospectives, tributes and parties galore, plus prime art exhibitions around downtown Venice,

make a visit here essential, especially if you need to meet Italian business partners. John Boorman was president of the 2004 jury, alongside Spike Lee, Scarlett Johansson and others. The opening film was Spielberg's *The Terminal* and Quentin Tarantino and Joe Dante hosted panels on Italian B-movies to accompany the retrospective "Italian Kings of the B's: The Secret History of Italian cinema". *Inquiries to:* La Biennale di Venezia, San Marco, 1364, Cà Giustinian, 30124 Venezia, Italy.
Tel (39 041) 521 8711. Fax: 522 7539.
e: cinema@labiennale.org.
Web: www.labiennale.org/en/cinema.

Imelda Staunton: Best Actress at Venice for **Vera Drake**

AWARDS 2004
Golden Lion for Best Film: **Vera Drake** (UK/France), Mike Leigh.
Grand Jury Prize: **The Sea Inside** (Spain), Alejandro Amenábar.
Best Direction: Kim Ki-duk, **3-iron** (South Korea).
Coppa Volpi for Best Actor: Javier Bardem, **The Sea Inside**.
Coppa Volpi for Best Actress: Imelda Staunton, **Vera Drake**.

Victoria Independent Film & Video Festival
Late January – early February 2006

From the mainstream to the original, the festival offers up the finest contemporary international independent cinema. It has a strong interest in putting programmers, media and industry professionals together with emerging film-makers and is dedicated to raising awareness of film and its artistic insights. Set in beautiful Victoria, it includes a film forum, new media event, discussions, family day, lectures and a film-related art exhibition. *Inquiries to:* Victoria Independent Film & Video Festival, 808 View St, Victoria, British Columbia, V8W 1K2, Canada. Tel: (1 250) 389 0444. Fax: 389 0406. e: festival@vifvf.com. Web: www.vifvf.com.

AWARDS 2004

Star!TV Award for Best Feature: **Wilbur Wants To Kill Himself** (Denmark/UK), Lone Scherfig.
Famous Players Award for Best Canadian Feature: **Love, Sex and Eating the Bones**, David "Sudz" Sutherland.
Times Colonist Award for Best Short: **Fast Film** (Austria), Virgil Widrich.
Government of Canada Award for Best Short Animation: **More Sensitive**.
Audience Favourite: **Seducing Dr. Lewis** (Canada).

Wellington International Film Festival
July 15-31, 2005

The Wellington International Film Festival launched its thirty-third annual programme of 140 feature programmes from over 30 countries in 2004 with Walter Salles' *The Motorcycle Diaries*. The festival provides a non-competitive New Zealand premiere showcase and welcomes many international film-makers, restorers and musicians. Brimming with animation, arthouse, documentaries and a screening of silent classic *Steamboat Bill Jr.*, enriched by live orchestral music, this year's festival and its 36-year-old Auckland sibling set new records for attendance. *Inquiries to:* Wellington Film Festival, Box 9544, Marion Square, Wellington 6037, New Zealand. Tel: (64 4) 385 0162. Fax: 801 7304. e: festival@nzff.co.nz. Web: www.nzff.co.nz.

Wine Country Film Festival
July 21 – August 7, 2005

World cinema, culture and conscience converge in the heart of Northern California's premium wine region, Napa and Sonoma Valleys. The festival is gently paced, mainly non-competitive and accepts features, documentaries, shorts, and animation. All genres are welcome. Programme sections are: World Cinema, American Independents, EcoCinema (environment), Food on Food, Music and Film, Arts in Film and Cinema of Conscience (social issues). Many of the films are shown outdoors. In 2004, the eighteenth edition screened 124 films from 32 countries with more than 75 film-makers in attendance. Award-winners included Best of the Fest (Patrice Leconte's *Intimate Strangers*; France), World Cinema: Best First Feature International (Dino Mustafic's *Remake*; Bosnia). *Inquiries to:* PO Box 303, Glen Ellen, CA 95442, USA. Tel: (1 707) 996 2536. e: wcfilmfest@aol.com. Web: www.wcff.us.

WorldFest–Houston
April 22-May 1, 2005

Celebrating its thirty-eighth year, the festival offers competition for independent features, shorts, documentaries, student films, TV productions, commercials and screenplays. WorldFest is the largest competition in the world in terms of number of entries received. There will be 60 indie features premiering, 104 award-winning shorts and nine professional production seminars. It is the only truly independent festival in North America, as it does not accept major studio films. Festival Founding Director J. Hunter Todd operates a Discovery Festival programme,

NORTH AMERICA'S PREMIER INDEPENDENT FILM FESTIVAL!

THE HOUSTON INTERNATIONAL FILM FESTIVAL

THE 38TH ANNUAL

WORLDFEST HOUSTON

APRIL 22-MAY 1, 2005

Deadlines for 2006 Entries:
Earlybird: November 15, 2005
Regular: December 15, 2005
Late Deadline: January 15, 2006

For Poster, Entry Kit, and Information contact:

J. Hunter Todd
P.O. Box 56566
Houston, TX USA 77256-6566
713-965-9955 (USA)
FAX 713-965-9960
mail@worldfest.org

Enter On-line:
www.worldfest.org

"FIERCELY INDEPENDENT"

THE ONLY TOTALLY DEDICATED INDIE FILM FESTIVAL IN NORTH AMERICA!

which automatically notifies the leading 200 international film festivals of the WorldFest winners. Co-ordinators also submit all student, short and screenplay winners to the top US talent agencies. WorldFest offers more than $25,000 in cash grants and film and equipment awards, including the $2,500 Eastman Kodak Student Award and the HP Awards. Attendance consistently exceeds 25,000. Deadline: mid-December. *Inquiries to:* WorldFest–Houston, PO Box 56566, Houston, TX 77256, USA. Tel: (1 713) 965 9955. Fax: 965 9960. e: mail@worldfest.org. Web: www.worldfest.org.

AWARDS 2004
Best Theatrical Feature: **Love's Brother** (Australia), Jan Sardi.
Best Film & Video: **In the Shadow of the Blade** (US), Patrick and Cheryl Fries.
Best TV & Cable Production: **The Blues** (US), Clint Eastwood.
Best New Media: **Clariant AG** (Germany), DMS Partnership.
Best Experimental Film & Video: **Fastener** (Japan), Kouki Tange.
Best Unproduced Screenplay: **Divided Highways** (US), Phillip Boland & Jim Engelhard.
Best Music Video: **To the Mountains – An Argentinean Story** (Argentina), Marcelo Mitnik.
Best Short Subject: **In the Arms of Angels** (US), T.C. Christensen.
Best TV Commercial: **AOL's Sting** (US), Quiet Man.
Kodak Cinematography Crystal Vision: **To the Mountains – An Argentinean Story**.
Hewlett Packard Crystal Vision: **Interruption**, Brian Lovell; **Break a Leg**, Monika Mitchell.

Other Festivals and Markets of Note

AFI FEST, 2021 N Western Ave, Los Angeles, CA 90027-1625, USA. Tel: (1 323) 856 7896. Fax: 462 4049. e: afifest@afi.com. Web: www.afifest.com. (*One of North America's fastest growing film events and the leading international festival in LA - Nov.*)

Alcalá de Henares/Comunidad de Madrid Film Festival, Plaza del Empecinado 1, 28801 Alcalá de Henares, Madrid, Spain. Tel: (34 91) 879 7380. Fax: 879 7381. e: festival@alcine.org. Web: www.alcine.org. (*Competition for Spanish shorts, new directors and Madrid-made videos, plus international shorts and Spanish director sidebars - Nov.*)

Alexandria International Film Festival, 9 Orabi St, Cairo 1111, Egypt. Tel: (20 2) 574 1112. Fax: 576 8727. e: info@alexandriafilmfestival.com. Web: www.alexandriafilmfestival.com. (*Competitive for Mediterranean countries and internationally for first films - Sept.*)

Almería International Short Film Festival, Diputación de Almería, Departamento de Cultura y Juventud, Calle Navarro Rodrigo 17, 04071 Almeria, Spain. Tel: (34 950) 211 100 Fax: 269 785. e: coordinador@almeriaencorto.net. Web: www.almeriaencorto.net. (*Competition for international shorts - May/June.*)

Ann Arbor Film Festival, PO Box 8232, Ann Arbor, MI 48107, USA. Tel: (1 734) 995 5356. Fax: 995 5396. e: info@aafilmfest.org. Web: www.aafilmfest.org. (*Experimental films from all over the world - March.*)

Angelus Awards Student Film Festival, 7201 Sunset Blvd., Hollywood, CA 90046, USA. Tel: (800) 874 0999. Fax: 874 1168. e: info@angelus.org. Web: www.angelusawards.org. (*International competition honouring college level student films that demonstrate respect for the human condition. Drama, comedy, animation, documentary and narrative. Call for entries is July 1. Screening and awards ceremony held at the Directors Guild of America, Hollywood - late Oct/early Nov.*)

Annecy/International Animated Film Festival and International Animated Film Market (MIFA), Centre International du Cinéma d'Animation, 18 Avenue du Trésum, BP 399, 74013 Annecy Cedex, France. Tel: (33 4) 5010 0900. Fax: 5010 0970. e: info@annecy.org. Web: www.annecy.org. (*Long established international and competitive festival with a useful sales/distribution market (MIFA) - Festival: June 6-11, 2005; MIFA: June 8-10, 2005.*)

Animerte Dager, Fredrikstad Animation Festival, Kasernen Gamlebyen, Box 1405, N-1602 Fredrikstad, Norway. Tel: (47) 6932 0075. Fax: 6932 0077. e: ad@animertedager.no. Web: www.animertedager.no. (*Nordic, Baltic and international animation, with retrospectives and student films. Competitive - Nov.*)

Aspen Shortsfest & Filmfest, 110 E Hallam, Ste 102, Aspen, CO 81611, USA. Tel: (1 970) 925 6882. Fax: 925 1967. e: filmfest@aspenfilm.org. Web: www.aspenfilm.org. (*Shortsfest: Short subject competition - April 6-10, 2005; Filmfest: Feature-length invitational - Sept/Oct.*)

Atlantic Film Festival, PO Box 36139, Suite 220, 5600 Sackville St, Halifax, NS, B3J 1L2, Canada. Tel: (1 902) 422 3456. Fax: 422 4006. e: festival@atlanticfilm.com. Web: www.atlanticfilm.com. (*Film and video features, shorts, documentaries and animation; also includes industry workshops and panels - Sept.*)

Auckland International Film Festival, PO Box 9544, Marion Sq, Wellington 6001, New Zealand. Tel: (64 4) 385 0162. Fax: 801 7304. e: festival@nzff.co.nz. Web: www.nzff.co.nz. (*Leading showcase for more than 110 features and 50 shorts. Twinned with the Wellington Film Festival - July.*)

Augsburg Children's Film Festival, Filmbüro Augsburg, Schroeckstrasse 8, 86152 Augsburg, Germany. Tel: (49 821) 349 1060. Fax: 155 518. e: filmbuero@t-online.de. Web: www.lechfremmem.de. (*International features for children - March.*)

Banff Mountain Film Festival, The Banff Centre for Mountain Culture, Box 1020, Station 38,

Banff, AB, T1L 1H5, Canada. Tel: (1 403) 762
6675.Fax: 762 6277. e: cmc@banffcentre.ca.
Web: www.banffmountainfestivals.ca. *(Nov.)*
**Belgrade International Festival of
Documentary & Short Films**, Majke Jevrosime
20, 11000 Belgrade. Tel/Fax: (381 11) 334 6837.
e: festivalkmd@fest.org.yu. Web:
www.kratikimetar.org.yu. *(March/April)*.
**Bilbao International Documentary and Short
Film Festival**, Calle Colón de Laurreategui,
37-4 Derecha, 48009 Bilbao, Spain. Tel: (34 94)
424 8698. Fax: 424 5624. e: info@zinebi.com.
Web: www.zinebi.com. *(Long-running
competitive festival for shorts and documentaries
- Nov; Deadline: mid-Sept.)*
Birmingham Screen Festival, 9 Margaret St,
Birmingham B3 3BS, UK. Tel: (44 121) 643
0631. e: info@film-tv-festival.org.uk. Web:
www.film-tv-festival.org.uk. *(International event.
Respected South Asian film focus - March.)*
Bite the Mango Film Festival, National
Museum of Photography, Film & TV, Bradford,
BD1 1NQ, UK. Tel: (44 1274) 203 311.
Fax: 394 540. e: irfan.ajeeb@nmsi.ac.uk.
Web: www.bitethemango.org.uk. *(A celebration
of cultural cinema from Asia - Sept 30-Oct 6, 2005.)*
Bogotá Film Festival, Residencias
Tequendama, Centro Internacional Tequendama,

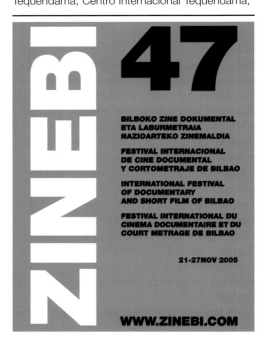

Bogotá, Colombia. Tel: (57 1) 341 7562
Web: www.bogocine.com. *(Colombian films - Oct.)*
Boston Film Festival, Loews Copley Place
Theatre, 100 Huntington Avenue, Boston,
MA 02116, USA. Tel: (1 617) 331 9460.
e: gemsad@aol.com. Web:
www.bostonfilmfestival.org. *(Studio releases,
American independents, documentaries and
shorts - Sept 9-18, 2005.)*
Bradford Animation Festival, National Museum
of Photography, Film & Television, Bradford, BD1
1NQ, UK. Tel: (44 1274) 203 308. Fax: 394 540.
e: adam.pugh@nmsi.ac.uk. Web:
www.baf.org.uk. *(Industry-based animation
festival; Home to the BAF Awards - Nov
16-19, 2005.)*
Bradford Film Festival, [contacts as for
Animation, above].
Web: www.bradfordfilmfestival.org.uk. *(Includes
the BFF Lifetime Achievement Award,
masterclasses, retrospectives - March.)*
British Silent Cinema, Broadway, 14-18
Broad St, Nottingham, NG1 3AL, UK.
Tel: (44 115) 952 6600. Fax: 952 6622.
Web: www.broadway.org.uk. *(April 7-10, 2005.)*
Brussels Animation Film Festival, Folioscope,
Avenue de Stalingrad 52, B-1000 Brussels,
Belgium. Tel: (32 2) 534 4125. Fax: 534 2279.
e: info@folioscope.be. Web:
www.awn.com/folioscope. *(Feb.)*
**Brussels International Festival of Fantastic
Film**, 8 Rue de la Comtesse de Flandre 1020
Brussels, Belgium. Tel: (32 2) 201 1713. Fax:
201 1469. e: info@bifff.org. Web: www.bifff.org.
*(Competitive international and European selection
for shorts and features - March 11-26, 2005.)*
**Cph:Dox – Copenhagen International
Documentary Festival**, Store Kannikestraede 6,
1169 Copenhagen K, Denmark. Tel: (45) 3312
0005. Fax: 3312 7505. e: info@cphdox.dk. Web:
www.cphdox.dk. *(Nov 4-13, 2005.)*
Cairo International Film Festival, 17 Kasr el
Nile St, Cairo, Egypt. Tel: (20 2) 392 3562. Fax:
393 8979. Web: www.cairofilmfest.com.
(Competitive - March.)
Camerimage, Rynek Nowomiejski 28, 87-100
Torun, Poland. Tel/Fax: (48 56) 621 0019.
e: office@camerimage.pl. Web:
www.camerimage.pl. *(Competition, Special*

Screenings, William Fraker's Retrospective, Student Festival, World Panorama Retrospective, seminars, workshops, press conferences, exhibitions - Nov 26-Dec 3, 2005.)

Cartoons on the Bay, Rai Trade, Via Umberto Novaro 18, 00195 Rome, Italy. Tel: (39 06) 3749 8315. Fax: 3751 5631.
e: cartoonsbay@raitrade.it.
Web: www.cartoonsbay.com. (International Festival and Conference on television animation, organised by RAI Trade - April 27-30, 2005; Deadline: Jan 21.)

Chicago International Children's Film Festival, Facets Mulimedia, 1517 W Fullerton, Chicago, IL 60614, USA. Tel: (1 773) 281 9075. Fax: 929 0266. e: kidsfest@facets.org. Web: www.cicff.org. (Largest and oldest festival of children's films in the US - Oct 20-30, 2005.)

Chicago Latino Film Festival, International Latino Cultural Center of Chicago, c/o Columbia College Chicago, 600 S Michigan Ave, Chicago, IL 60605-1996, USA. Tel: (1 312) 431 1330. Fax: 344 8030. e: info@latinoculturalcenter.org. Web: www.latinoculturalcenter.org. (ILCC promotes awareness of Latino culture through the arts, including this festival - April 8-20, 2005.)

Cinekid, Korte Leidsedwarstraat 12, 1017 RC Amsterdam, Netherlands. Tel: (31 20) 531 7890. Fax: 531 7899. e: info@cinekid.nl. Web: www.cinekid.nl. (International film, TV and new media festival for children and young people - Oct 22-30, 2005.)

Cinema Jove International Film Festival, Calle La Safor 10, Despacho 5, 46015 Valencia, Spain. Tel: (34 96) 331 1047. Fax: 331 0805. e: cinemajove@gva.es Web: www.gva.es/cinemajove. (Low-glam, high-fun foray into state-of-the-art youth cinema - June 18-25, 2005.)

Cinéma Mediterranéen Montpellier, 78 Avenue du Pirée, 34000 Montpellier, France. Tel: (33 4) 9913 7373. Fax: 9913 7374.
e:info@cinemed.tm.fr. Web: www.cinemed.tm.fr. (Competitive festival for fiction works by directors from the Mediterranean Basin, the Black Sea states, Portugal or Armenia. Categories: Feature, Short, Documentary. Formats: 16mm, 35mm. Preview on VHS and DVD - Oct.)

Cinéma Italien Rencontres D'Annecy, Bonlieu Scène Nationale, 1 rue Jean Jaures, BP 294, 74007 Annecy Cedex, France. Tel: (33 450) 334 400. Fax: 518 209.
e: com@annecycinemaitalien.com.
Web: www.annecycinemaitalien.com. (Feature films from Italy, with tributes and retrospectives. Competitive - early Oct.)

Cinemagic World Screen Festival for Young People, 49 Botanic Avenue, Belfast, BT7 1JL, Northern Ireland. Tel: (44 28) 9031 1900. Fax: 9031 9709. e: info@cinemagic.org.uk. Web: www.cinemagic.org.uk. (Children's films in competition - end Nov/beg Dec, 2005.)

Cinemayaat (Arab Film Festival), 2 Plaza Ave, San Francisco, CA 94116, USA. Tel (1 415) 564 1100. Fax: 564 2203. e: info@aff.org. Web: www.aff.org. (Arab films – Oct.)

Cinequest, PO Box 720040, San Jose, CA 95172-0040, USA. Tel: (1 408) 995 5033. Fax: 995 5713. e: info@cinequest.org. Web: www.cinequest.org. (Maverick films, film-makers and technologies. Competition for features, documentaries and shorts, plus tributes, seminars, entertainment - March 2-13, 2005.)

Cleveland International Film Festival, 2510 Market Ave, Cleveland, OH 44113-3434, USA. Tel: (1 216) 623 3456. Fax: 623 0103. e: cfs@clevelandfilm.org.
Web: www.clevelandfilm.org. (International "World Tour" progamme with specials such as family films, American independents and lesbian and gay films - March)

Cognac International Thriller Film Festival, Le Public Système Cinéma, 40, rue Anatole France, 92594 Levallois-Perret Cedex, France. Tel: (33 1) 4134 2033. Fax: 4134 2077. e-mail: fbataille@le-public-systeme.fr. Web: www.festival.cognac.fr. (International thrillers and "films noir"; competitive for features and French-speaking shorts - April.)

Cork Film Festival, 10 Washington St, Cork, Republic of Ireland. Tel: (353 21) 427 1711 Fax: 427 5945. e: info@corkfilmfest.org. Web: www.corkfilmfest.org. (Features, documentaries, competitive shorts, animation - Oct 2005; Deadline: July. 2005 is the festival's fiftieth anniversary and we will host a major international Short Film Symposium.)

Cottbus Film Festival – Festival of East European Cinema, Werner-Seelenbinder-Ring

44/45, D-03048 Cottbus, Germany. Tel: (49 355) 431 070. Fax: 4310 720. e: info@filmfestivalcottbus.de. Web: www.filmfestivalcottbus. (*International festival of East European films: competitive for features and shorts; plus children's and youth film, spectrum, national hits, focus - late Oct/early Nov.*)

Deauville Festival of American Film, Le Public Système Cinéma, 40, rue Anatole France, 92594 Levallois-Perret Cedex, France. Tel: (33 1) 4134 2033. Fax: 4134 2077. e: fbataille@le-public-systeme.fr. Web: www.festival-deauville.com. (*Showcase for US features and independent films - Sept.*)

Dhaka International Film Festival, 75 Science Laboratory Road, Dhanmondi, Dhaka-1205, Bangladesh. Tel: (880 2) 862 1062. e: amzamal@bdcom.com. Web: www.dhakafilmfest.org. (*Competitive section for Asian cinema. Also non-competitive sections, including 'Retrospective', 'Cinema of the World', 'Children's Film' and 'Bangladesh Panorama'. Festival Director: Ahmed Muztaba Zamal. Submission deadline: Oct 15, 2005 - January 17-25, 2006*).

Divercine, Calle Lorenzo Carnelli 1311, 11200 Montevideo, Uruguay. Tel: (59 82) 418 2460/5795. Fax: 419 4572. e: cinemuy@chasque.apc.org. Web: www.cinemateca.org.uy. (*July.*)

Dubai International Film Festival, Dubai Media City, PO Box 53777, Dubai, United Arab Emirates. Tel: (971 4) 391 3378. Fax: 391 4589. e: louise.saade@dubaimediacity.ae. Web: www.dubaifilmfest.com. (*Seeks to celebrate true excellence in Arab cinema while screening films which reflect Dubai's cosmopolitan and multi-cultural character. Five full days, consisting of 11 programmes, featuring a total of approximately 80 films – Dec.*)

Dublin International Film Festival, 13 Merrion Sq, Dublin 2, Ireland. Tel: (353 1) 661 6216. Fax: 661 4418. e: info@dubliniff.com. Web: www.dubliniff.com. (*Founded in 2002 and aimed squarely at the cinema-going public. Non-competitive, largely composed of new international feature films (92 in 2004, including 11 Irish productions or co-productions). Daily*

Talking Pictures events offer lunchtime panel discussions on a variety of film-making topics - Feb 10-19, 2006.)

Duisburg Film Week, Am König Heinrich Platz, D-47049 Duisburg, Germany. Tel: (49 203) 283 4187. Fax: 283 4130. e: stoehr@duisburger-filmwoche.de. Web: www.duisburger-filmwoche.de. (*German-language documentaries from Germany, Switzerland and Austria - Nov.*)

Durban International Film Festival, University of KwaZulu-Natal, Centre for Creative Arts, Durban 4001, South Africa. Contact: Nashen Moodley. Tel: (27 31) 260 1145. Fax: 260 1055. e: diff@ukzn.ac.za. moodleyn@ukzn.ac.za. Web: www.cca.ukzn.ac.za. (*An important forum for South African and international cinema. Most of the 250-plus screenings are national or African premieres - June 15-26, 2005.*)

Edmonton International Film Festival, Edmonton International Film Society, 006-11523 100 Avenue NW, Edmonton, Alberta, T5K 0J8, Canada. Tel: (1 780) 423 0844. Fax: 447 5242. e: mailbox@edmontonfilm.com. Web: www.edmontonfilm.com. (*Oct.*)

Emden International Film Festival, An der Berufschule 3, 26721 Emden, Germany. Tel: (49 49) 219 155-0. Fax: 915 599. e: filmfest@vhs-emden.de. Web: www.filmfestemden.de. (*Focus on films from northwest Europe, particularly Germany and UK - June 1-8, 2005.*)

L'Etrange Festival, 81 Boulevard de Clichy, 75009 Paris, France. Tel (33 1) 5320 4860. Fax: 5320 4869. e: gilles@etrangefestival.com. (*Created in 1993 and dedicated to international features, documentaries and shorts by maverick directors - Aug 31-Sept 13, 2005.*)

European First Film Festival (Premiers Plans), Festival d'Angers, 54 rue Beaubourg, 75003 Paris, France. Tel: (33 1) 4271 5370. Fax: 4271 0111. e: paris@premiersplans.org. Web: www.premiersplans.org. (*Competitive festival for European debut features, shorts and student works - Jan.*)

Femme Totale International Women's Film Festival, Dortmund, c/o Kulturbüro Stadt Dortmund, Küpferstrasse 3, D-44122 Dortmund, Germany. Tel: (49 231) 502 5162. Fax: 502 5734. e: info@femmetotale.de. Web: www.femmetotale.de. (*Biennial festival with* changing themes, highlighting films made by women. International feature film competition for women directors: €25,000; Advancement Camera Award for German women cinematographers: €5,000 - April 12-17, 2005.)

Festival International du Film Francophone de Namur, 175, Rue des Brasseurs, 5000 Namur, Belgium Tel: (32 81) 241 236. Fax: 224 384. e: info@fiff.be. Web: www.fiff.be. (End Sept/early Oct.)

Festival Dei Popoli, Borgo Pinti 82 Rosso, 50121 Firenze, Italy. Tel: (39 055) 244 778. Fax: 241 364. e: fespopol@dada.it. Web: www.festivaldeipopoli.org. (Partly competitive and open to documentaries on social, anthropological, historical and political issues - Nov 26-Dec 2, 2005.)

Festival du Cinema International en Abitibi-Temscamingue, 215 Mercier Avenue, Rouyn-Noranda, Quebec J9X 5WB, Canada. Tel: (1 819) 762 6212. Fax: 762 6762. e: festivalcinema@telebecinternet.com. Web: www.lino.com/festivalcinema. (International shorts, medium and full-length features; animation, documentary and fiction - end Oct/early Nov.)

Festroia, Forum Luisa Dodi, 2900-461 Setúbal Codex, Portugal. Tel: (351 265) 525 908. Fax: 525 681. e: geral@festroia.pt. Web: www.festroia.pt. (Held in Setúbal, near Lisbon. Official section for countries producing fewer than 25 features per year - June.)

Film & Literature Week, 667 Ponce de León Ave, Box 367, San Juan 00907, Puerto Rico. Tel: (787) 723 2362. Fax: 723 6412. e: llmagica@tld.net. President: José Artemio Torres. (International films based on literary works - April 1-7, 2005).

Filmfest München, Sonnenstr 21, D-80331, Munich, Germany. Tel: (49 89) 381 9040. Fax: 381 90426. e: info@filmfest-muenchen.de. Web: www.filmfest-muenchen.de. (International screenings, TV movies and retrospectives - June 25-July 2, 2005.)

Filmfestival Max Ophüls Prize, Mainzerstrasse 8, 66111 Saarbruecken, Germany. Tel: (49 681) 906 8910. e: cruth@max-ophuels-preis.de. Web: www.filmfestival-max-ophüls.de. (Competitive event for young directors from German-speaking countries - Jan.)

Florida Film Festival, Enzian Theatre, 1300 South Orlando Ave, Maitland, Florida 32751, USA. Tel: (1 407) 629 1088. Fax: 629 6870. e: filmfest@gate.net. Web: www.floridafilmfestival.com. (Specialises in independent American films: features, shorts, documentaries and non-competitive spotlight films - April 8-17, 2005.)

Focus on Asia Fukuoka International Film Festival, c/o Fukuoka City Hall, 1-8-1, Tenjin, Chuo-ku, Fukuoka 810 8620, Japan. Tel: (81 92) 733 5170. Fax: 733 5595. e: info@focus-on-asia.com. Web: www.focus-on-asia.com. (Dedicated to promoting Asian film. Non-competitive - Sept.)

Future Film Festival, Via del Pratello 21/2, 40122 Bologna, Italy. Tel: (39 051) 296 0664. Fax: 656 7133. e: future@futurefilmfestival.org. Web: www.futurefilmfestival.org. (Jan.)

Galway Film Fleadh, Cluain Mhuire, Monivea Road, Galway, Ireland. Tel: (353 91) 751 655. Fax: 735 831. e: gafleadh@iol.ie. Web: www.galwayfilmfleadh.com. (Irish and international features. Accompanied by the Galway Film Fair, Ireland's only film market - July 5-10, 2005.)

Gerardmer International Fantasy Film Festival, Le Public Système Cinéma, 40, rue Anatole France, 92594 Levallois-Perret Cedex, France. Tel: (33 1) 4134 2033. Fax: 4134 2077. e-mail : fbataille@le-public-systeme.fr. Web: www.gerardmer-fantasticart.com. (International fantasy, sci-fi, psychological thriller and horror films, with competition for features and French-speaking shorts - late Jan-early Feb.)

Go East Festival of Central and Eastern European Film in Wiesbaden, Deutsches Filminstitut, Schaumainkai 4, 60596 Frankfurt. Tel: (49 69) 9612 2025. Fax: 6637 2947. e: kopf@filmfestival-goeast.de. Web: www.filmfestival-goeast.de. (Established in 2001

for audiences interested in Eastern European film, with a mix of current productions and historical series, an academic symposium, student competition and related events. Member of FIAPF and European Coordination of Film Festivals, hosts FIPRESCI jury. Deadline: mid-Jan. April 6-12, 2005.)

Haifa International Film Festival, 142 Hanassi Ave, Haifa 34 633, Israel. Tel: (972 4) 8353 521/4. Fax: 8384 327. e: film@haifaff.co.il. Web: www.haifaff.co.il. (Broad spectrum of new international films, special tributes and retrospectives - end Sept/early Oct.)

Hawaii International Film Festival, 1001 Bishop St, Honolulu, Hawaii 96813, USA. Tel: (1 808) 528 3456. Fax: 528 1410. e: info@hiff.org. Web: www.hiff.org. (Seeks to promote cultural understanding between East and West through film - Oct 20-30, 2005.)

Heartland Film Festival, 200 S Meridian, Suite 220, Indianapolis, Indiana 46225-0176, USA. Tel: (1 317) 464 9405. Fax: 464 9409. e: info@heartlandfilmfestival.org. Web: www.heartlandfilmfestival.org. (Established in 1991 to honour film-makers whose work expresses hope and respect for positive values - Oct 13-21, 2005.)

Holland Animation Film Festival, Hoogt 4, 3512 GW Utrecht, Netherlands. Tel: (31 30) 233 1733. Fax: 233 1079. e: info@haff.nl. Web: www.haff.nl. (International competitions for independent and applied animation; special programmes, retrospectives, student films, exhibitions. Biennial – Nov 2006.)

Hometown Video Festival, Alliance for Community Media, 666 11th Street NW, Suite 740, Washington, DC 20001, USA. Tel: (1 202) 393 2650. Fax: 393 2653. e: acm@alliancecm.org. Web: www.alliancecm.org. (US and international community productions - July.)

Huesca Film Festival, Avenida del Parque 1,2, 22002 Huesca, Spain. Tel: (34 974) 212 582. Fax: 210 065. e: huescafest@tsai.es. Web: www.huesca-filmfestival.com. (Well-established competitive shorts festival in country town, with features sidebars - June.)

Hungarian Film Week, Magyar Filmunió, Városligeti, Fasor 38, 1068 Budapest, Hungary.

Tel: (36 1) 351 7760. Fax: 352 6734. e: filmunio@filmunnio.hu. Web: www.filmunio.hu. (Competitive national festival showcasing Hungarian production from the previous year - Feb.)

Il Cinema Ritrovato, Mostra Internazionale del Cinema Libero, Cineteca del Comune di Bologna, Via Riva di Reno 72, 40122 Bologna, Italy. Tel: (39 051) 219 4814. Fax: 219 4821. e: cinetecamanifestazioni1@comune.bologna.it. Web: www.cinetecadibologna.it. (A selection of the best film restorations from all over the world. Four theatres and open-air screenings - July.)

Imago – International Young Film & Video Festival, Apartado 324 Avenida Eugénio de Andrade, Bloco D, 3° Drt-Trás, 6230-909 Fundão, Portugal. Tel/Fax: (00351) 275 771 607. e: info@imagofilmfest.com. Web: www.imagofilmfest.com. (Oct).

Independent Film Days, Filmbüro Augsburg, Schroeckstrasse 8, 86152 Augsburg, Germany. Tel: (49 821) 153 078. Fax: 155 518. e: filmbuero@t-online.de. Web: www.filmfest-augsburg.de. (International event for documentary and independent features, with retrospectives, national focus and student symposium - Nov.)

International Documentary Festival of Marseille (FID Marseille), 14 Allée Léon Gambetta, 13001 Marseille, France. Tel/Fax: (33 4) 9504 4490/91. e: welcome@fidmarseille.org. Web: www.fidmarseille.org. (July).

International Film Camera Festival "Manaki Brothers", Ul 8 Mart #4, 1000 Skopje, Republic of Macedonia. Tel/Fax: (389 2) 211 811. e: ffmanaki@mt.net.mk. Web: www.manaki.com.mk. (Held in remembrance of Yanaki and Milton Manaki, the first cameramen of the Balkans – end Sept/early Oct.)

International Film Festival Innsbruck, Museumstrasse 31, A-6020 Innsbruck, Austria. Tel: (43 512) 5785 0014. Fax: 5785 0013. e: info@iffi.at. Web: www.iffi.at. (Films about Africa, Latin America and Asia, Austrian premieres - June 1-5, 2005.)

International Film Festival of Uruguay, Lorenzo Carnelli 1311, 11200 Montevideo, Uruguay. Tel: (59 82) 418 2460/5795. Fax: 419 4572. e: cinemuy@chasque.net. Web: www.cinemateca.org.uy. (Presents independent and documentary films - March 19-3 April, 2005.)

International Film Forum "Arsenals", Marstalu 14, Riga, LV-1050, Latvia Tel: (371) 7221 620. Fax: 7820 445. e: programm@arsenals.lv. Web: www.arsenals.lv. (*Biannual competitive festival with $10,000 international competition and latest releases from Latvia, Lithuania and Estonia in features, documentary, shorts and animation - Sept 2006.*)

International Women's Film Festival, Maison des Arts, Palace Salvador Allende, 94000 Créteil, France. Tel: (33 1) 4980 3898. Fax: 4399 0410. e: filmsfemmes@wanadoo.fr. Web: www.filmdefemmes.com. (*Features, shorts and animation made by women - March.*)

Israel Film Festival, Israfest Foundation, 6404 Wilshire Blvd, Suite 1240, Los Angeles, CA 90048, USA. Tel: (1 323) 966 4166. Fax: 658 6346. e: info@israelfilmfestival.com. fest@earthlink.net. Web: www.israelfilmfestival.com. (*US showcase for Israeli features, shorts, documentaries and TV dramas - late April/early May in LA; June/July in NY; Nov in Chicago; Dec in Miami.*)

Kidfilm/USA Film Festival, 6116 N Central Expressway, Suite 105, Dallas, Texas 75206, USA. Tel: (1 214) 821 6300. Fax: 821 6364. e: usafilmfestival@aol.com. Web: www.usafilmfestival.com. (*Non-competitive; accepts US and international shorts and features - Jan.*)

Kracow Film Festival, Ul Pychowicka 7, 30-364 Krakow, Poland. Tel: (48 12) 427 1355. Fax: 267 2340/1060. e: festiwal@apollofilm.pl. Web: www.cracowfilmfestival.pl. (*Poland's oldest international film festival and respected short film showcase - end May/early June.*)

Las Palmas de Gran Canaria International Film Festival, C/ León y Castillo 322, 4ª Planta, 35007 Las Palmas de Gran Canaria. Tel: (34 928) 446 623/446 619. Fax: 446 651. e: laspalmascine@hotmail.com. Web: www.festivalcinelaspalmas.com. (*The Festival Internacional de Cine de Las Palmas de Gran Canaria is the Canary Islands' first forum for independent productions that would not otherwise be picked up by the mainstream distribution circuit. Sixth edition in 2005. Competitive Official Selection in which feature films, mainly from Europe and Latin*

America, compete for the top prize, the Golden Lady Harimaguada, and other awards – March.*)

London Lesbian & Gay Film Festival, National Film Theatre, South Bank, London SE1 8XT, UK. Tel: (44 20) 7815 1323. Fax: 7633 0786. e: anna.dunwoodie@bfi.org.uk. Web: www.llgff.org.uk. (*Films of special interest to lesbian and gay audiences. Selected highlights tour regional film theatres April to September - March 30-April 13, 2005.*)

Lucas International Children's Film Festival, c/o Deutsches Filmmuseum, Schaumainkai 41, 60596 Frankfurt/Main, Germany. Tel: (49 69) 9637 6380/81. Fax: 9637 6382. e: lucas@deutsches-filmmuseum.de. Web: www.lucasfilmfestival.de. (*Germany's oldest children's film festival, it has FIAPF's A-grade. In competition, Lucas presents selected new international productions for children aged from five to 12 - Sept 18-25, 2005.*)

Margaret Mead Film & Video Festival, American Museum of Natural History, 79th St at Central Park W, New York, NY 10024, USA. Tel: (1 212) 769 5305. Fax: 769 5329. e: meadfest@amnh.org. Web: www.amnh.org/mead. (*International*

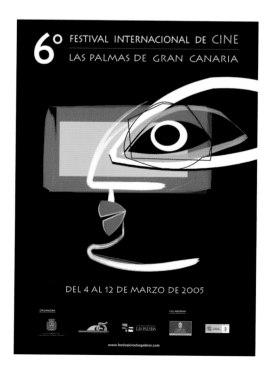

documentaries, shorts and animation - Nov.)

Marseilles Documentary Film Festival,
14 Allée Léon Gambetta, 13001 Marseilles,
France. Tel: (33 4) 9504 4490. Fax: 9504 4491.
e: welcome@fidmarseille.org. Web:
www.fidmarseille.org. (*The best international
documentaries - July 1-6, 2005.*)

**"Message to Man" International
Documentary, Short and Animated Film
Festival**, Karavannaya 12, 191011, St
Petersburg, Russia. Tel: (7 812) 235 2660/230
2200. Fax: 235 3995. e: info@message-to-
man.spb.ru. Web: www.message-to-man.spb.ru.
(*International competition, international debut
competition, national documentary competition
and special programmes - June.*)

Miami International Film Festival, Miami Dade
College, 300 NE 2nd Avenue, Miami, Florida
33132-2204, USA. Tel: (1 305) 237 3456.
(1 305) 237 7344. e: info@miamifilmfestival.com.
Web: www.miamifilmfestival.com. (*The best of
world cinema; special focus on Ibero-American
films - Feb.*)

Midnight Sun Film Festival, Lapintie 16 As 2,
99600 Sodankylä, Finland. Tel: (358 16) 614 525.
Fax: 618 646. e: office@msfilmfestival.fi. Web:
www.msfilmfestival.fi. (*International and silent
films, plus award-winners from Cannes, Berlin,
Locarno and Stockholm - June.*)

**Minneapolis/St Paul International Film
Festival**, Minnesota Film Arts, 309 Oak St
Ave SE, Minneapolis, MN 55414, USA.
Tel: (1 612) 331 7563. Fax: 378 7750.
e: info@mnfilmarts.org. Web:
www.mnfilmarts.org. (*Built up over 20 years by
the reliable Al Milgrom. Screens scores of foreign
films, especially Scandinavian - April 1-16, 2005.*)

**Montreal International Festival of New
Cinema**, 3530 Boulevard St-Laurent, Bureau
304 Montreal, Quebec, Canada H2X 2V1.
Tel: (1 514) 847 9272. Fax: 847 0732.
e: info@fcmm.com. Web: www.fcmm.com.
(*Seeks to explore high-quality experimental films
as an alternative to conventional commercial
cinema - Oct 13-23, 2005. Deadline: June 1.*)

Mumbai International Film Festival, Rajkamal
Studio, S S Rao Road, Parel, Mumbai 400 012,
India. Tel: (91 22) 2413 6571/72. Fax: 2412
5268. e-mail: iffmumbai@yahoo.com. Web:

www.iffmumbai.com. (*Established in 1997, the
only independent film festival in India, organised
by Mumbai Academy of the Moving Image. Full-
length feature films only. Sections include World
Cinema, Retro, Tribute, Focus on Film-maker and
Focus on One Country. Competition for Indian
Films, judged by an international jury. Jan.*)

Munich International Festival of Film Schools,
Sonnenstrasse 21, D-80331 Munich, Germany.
Tel: (49 89) 3819 040. Fax: 3819 0426.
e: info@filmfest-muenchen.de.
Web: www.filmfest-muenchen.de. (*Competition
for student productions from about 30 film
schools - Nov 19-26, 2005.*)

NatFilm Festival, Store Kannikestraede 6, 1169
Copenhagen, Denmark. Tel: (45) 3312 0005.
Fax: 3312 7505. e: info@natfilm.dk. Web:
www.natfilm.dk. Producer: Andreas Steinmann.
Programmer: Kim Foss. (*Offbeat international
retrospectives and tributes - April 1-17, 2005.*)

New Directors/New Films, Film Society of
Lincoln Center, 70 Lincoln Center Plaza, New
York, NY 10023, USA. Tel: (1 212) 875 5638.
Fax: 875 5636. e: sbensman@filmlinc.com.
Web: www.filmlinc.com. (*Works by new
directors; co-sponsored by the Film Society and
MOMA - March 23-April 7, 2005.*)

New Orleans Film Festival, 843 Carondelet St,
New Orleans, LA 70130, USA. Tel: (1 504) 523
3818. Fax: 975 3478. e:
admin@neworleansfilmfest.com. Web:
www.neworleansfilmfest.com. (*Competition
for all lengths, genres and formats and a non-
competitive programme that includes remastered classics and cutting-edge new
releases - Oct.*)

New York EXPO of Short Film and Video,
224 Centre St, New York, NY 10013, USA.
Tel: (1 212) 505 7742. e: nyexpo@aol.com.
Web: www.nyexpo.org. (*America's longest-
running shorts festival seeks fiction, animation,
documentary and experimental works under
60 minutes and completed in the previous
two years. Student and international entries
welcome - Dec.*)

Nordic Film Festival, 75 rue General le Clerc,
76000 Rouen, France. Tel: (33 232) 767 322.
Fax: 767 323. e: festival-cinema-
nordique@festival-cinema-nordique.asso.fr.

Web: www.festival-cinema-nordique.asso.fr. (*Competitive festival of Nordic cinema, including retrospectives - March.*)

Northwest Film and Video Festival, Northwest Film Center, 1219 SW Park Ave, Portland, Oregon 97205, USA. Tel: (1 503) 221 1156. Fax: 294 0874. e: info@nwfilm.org. Web: www.nwfilm.org. (*Annual survey of new moving-image art produced in the Northwest US and British Columbia; features, shorts and documentaries - Nov.*)

OFFICINEMA, Cineteca del Comune di Bologna, Via Riva di Reno 72, 40122 Bologna, Italy. Tel/Fax: (39) 051 204 820. e: cinetecamanifestazioni1@comune.bologna.it. Web: www.cinetecadibologna.it. (*Competition for final projects from European schools. Deadline: July. Visioni Italiane competition for Italian shorts and first features: 8,000 spectators, 200 films, 150 guests, 10 awards. Deadline: Sept. - Nov.*)

OKOMEDIA – International Environmental Film Festival, Oekomedia Institute Nussmannstr 14, D-79098 Freiburg, Germany. Tel: (49 761) 52 024. Fax: 555 724. e: info@oekomedia-institut.de. Web: www.oekomedia-institut.de. (*International film and TV productions about contemporary ecological/environmental issues - late Oct.*)

Open Air Filmfest Weiterstadt, Kommunales Kino Im Buergerzentrum, Carl-Ulrich-Strasse 9-11, D-64331 Weiterstadt, Germany. Tel: (49 61) 501 2185. Fax: 501 4073. e: filmfest@weiterstadt.de. Web: www.filmfest-weiterstadt.de. (*Aug 11-15, 2005; Deadline: May 15.*)

Palm Beach International Film Festival, 289 Via Naranjas, Royal Palm Plaza, Suite 48, Boca Raton, Florida 33432, USA. Tel: (1 561) 362 0003. Fax: 362 0035. e: info@pbifilmfest.org. Web: www.pbifilmfest.org. (*More than 80 films: American and international features, shorts, documentaries and large format. Competitive - April 14-21, 2005.*)

Palm Springs International Festival of Short Films, 1700 E Tahquitz Canyon Way, Suite 3, Palm Springs, CA 92262, USA. Tel: (1 760) 322 2930. Fax: 322 4087. e: info@psfilmfest.org. Web: www.psfilmfest.org. Contact: Rhea Lewis-Woodson. (*Largest competitive shorts festival in US. Student, animation, documentary and international competition with Audience and Juried Awards. Seminars and workshops - Sept 20-26, 2005.*)

Peñíscola International Comedy Film Festival, Patronato Municipal de Turismo, Festival de Cine, Plaza Constitución, s/n, 12598 Peñíscola, Castellón, Spain. Tel: (34 964) 480 483. Fax: 481 079. e: info@festivalpeniscola.com. Web: www.festivalpeniscola.com. (*Enjoyable festival in spectacular Mediterranean resort - June.*)

Philadelphia International Film Festival, Philadelphia Film Society, 4th Floor, 234 Market St, Philadelphia, PA 19106, USA. Tel: (1 215) 733 0608. Fax: 733 0668. e: festival@phillyfests.com. Web: www.phillyfests.com. (*International features, documentaries and shorts - April 7-20, 2005.*)

Prix Italia, Via Monte Santo 52, 00195 Rome, Italy. Tel: (39 06) 372 8708. Fax: (39 06) 372 3966. e: prixitalia@rai.it. Web: www.prixitalia.rai.it. (*International competition for radio, TV programmes and multi-media; open only to 75 member organisations - Sept.*)

RAI Trade Screenings, Rai Trade, Via Umberto Novaro 18, 00195 Rome, Italy. Tel: (39 06) 3749 8257. Fax: 3701 343. e: eleuteri@raitrade.it. Web: www.raitrade.rai.it. (*International programming buyers view RAI productions for broadcast, video and other rights - April 6-8, 2005.*)

Saint Louis International Film Festival, 394A Euclid Ave, St Louis, MO 63108, USA. Tel: (1 314) 454 0042. Fax: 454 0540. e: chris@cinemastlouis.org. Web: www.cinemastlouis.org. (*Showcases approximately 180 US and international independent films, documentaries and shorts. Competitive, with awards in 15 categories - Nov 10-20, 2005.*)

St Petersburg Festival of Festivals, 10 Kamennostrovsky Ave, St Petersburg 197101, Russia. Tel: (7 812) 237 0072. Fax: 237 0304. e: info@filmfest.ru. Web: www.filmfest.ru. (*International and local productions - June 23-29, 2005; Deadline: June 1.*)

San Francisco International Asian American Film Festival, c/o NAATA, 145 9th Street, Suite 350, San Francisco, CA 94103, USA. Tel: (1 415) 863 0814. Fax: 863 7428. e: festival@naatanet.

Web: www.naatanet.org. (*Film and video works by Asian-American and Asian artists - March.*)

San Francisco International Lesbian and Gay Film Festival, Frameline, 145 9th St, Suite 300, San Francisco, CA 94103, USA. Tel: (1 415) 703 8650. Fax: 861 1404. e: info@frameline.org. Web: www.frameline.org. (*Focus on gay, lesbian, bisexual and transgender themes - June 16-26, 2005.*)

San Juan Cinemafest of Puerto Rico, PO Box, San Juan 00902-0079, Puerto Rico. Tel: (787) 723 5015. Fax: 724 4333. President: Mario L Paniagua. (*International features, Caribbean features and shorts - November*).

San Sebastian Horror and Fantasy Film Festival, Donostia Kultura, Plaza de la Constitucion 1, 20003 Donostia-San Sebastian, Spain. Tel: (34 943) 481 197/53/57. Fax: 430 621. e: cinema_cinema@donostia.org. Web: www.donostiakultura.com/terror. (*Cult, cutting-edge horror fantasy festival; short film and feature competition - Oct 30-Nov 5, 2005.*)

San Sebastian Human Rights Film Festival, [contacts as for Horror and Fantasy Festival, above] Web: www.donostiakultura.com. (*Short films and features about human rights - March.*)

Sao Paulo International Film Festival, Rua Antonio Carlos, 288 2° Andar, 01309-010 Sao Paulo, Brazil. Tel: (55 11) 3141 1068/2548. Fax: 3266 7066. e: info@mostra.org. Web: www.mostra.org. (*Competitive event for new film-makers and international panorama - late Oct/early Nov.*)

Sevilla International Film Festival, Pabellón de Portugal, Avda. De Cid1, 41004 Seville, Spain. Tel: (34 954) 297 833. Fax: 297 844. e: info@festivaldesevilla.com. Web: www.festivaldesevilla.com (*European cinema. Competition for European features and documentaries. Plus panorama of films produced with Eurimages support and a non-competitive section for European shorts. Fifth edition in 2005. Director: Manuel Grosso. Registration deadline: mid-Sept. - Nov.*)

Siberian International Festival – Spirit of Fire, Festival Committee, 1 Mosfilmovskaya St, Moscow, 119992 Russia. Tel: (7 095) 143 9484. Fax: 938 2312. e: festival@spiritoffire.ru. Web: www.spiritoffire.ru. (*Showcases 15 films directed* by young talents; all formats eligible. Numerous debates - March).

Sydney Film Festival, PO Box 96, Strawberry Hills, NSW 2012, Australia. Tel: (61 2) 9280 0511. Fax: 9280 1520. e: info@sydneyfilmfestival.org. (Broad-based, non-competitive event screening new Australian and international features and shorts - June.)

Taormina International Film Festival, Corso Umberto 19, 98039 Taormina Messina, Italy. Tel: (39 094) 221 142. Fax: 223 348. e: info@taormina-arte.com. Web: www. taormina-arte.com. (Films by English-language directors. Restorations. Silver Ribbons awarded by Italian film critics - June 11-18, 2005.)

Tel-Aviv International Student Film Festival, Cinema & Television Dept, The Yolanda & David Katz Faculty of the Arts, Tel Aviv University, Ramat Aviv 69978, Israel. Tel: (972 3) 640 9936. Fax: 640 9935. e: naomim@tauex.tau.ac.il. Web: www.taufilmfest.com. (Workshops, retrospectives, tributes, premieres - June.)

Tudela First Film Festival, Centro Cultural Castel Ruiz, Plaza Mercadal, 7, 31500, Tudela, Navarra, Spain. Tel: (34 948) 825 868. Fax: 412 003. e: jasone.cr@tudela.com. Web: www.geocities.com/operaprimafestival. (Late Oct-early Nov.)

Uppsala International Short Film Festival, PO Box 1746, SE-751 47 Uppsala, Sweden. Tel: (46 18) 120 025. Fax: 121 350. e: info@shortfilmfestival.com. Web: www.shortfilmfestival.com. (Sweden's only international shorts festival. Competitive. Deadline: June - Oct.)

USA Film Festival, 6116 N Central Expressway, Suite 105, Dallas, Texas 75206, USA. Tel: (1 214) 821 6300. Fax: 821 6364. e: usafilmfestival@aol.com. Web: www.usafilmfestival.com. (Non-competitive for US and international features. Academy-qualifying National Short Film/Video competition with cash awards - April 21-28, 2005.)

Valdivia International Film Festival, Cine Club, Universidad Austral de Chile, Campus Isla Teja s/n, Valdivia, Chile. Tel: (56 63) 215 622/221 961. Fax: 221 209. e: cineclub@uach.cl. Web: www.festivalcinevaldivia.com. (International feature contest, plus Chilean and international

shorts, documentaries and animation - Sept/Oct.)

Valley International Film Festival, PO Box 3609, Chatsworth, CA 91313, USA. Tel: (1 818) 968 0052. Fax: 709 8597. e: info@viffi.org. Web: www.viffi.org. (Competition for films and screenplays; showcase for film-makers and writers who believe in entertainment that should not contain gratuitous violence or profanity - April 8-17, 2005.)

VIENNALE Vienna International Film Festival, Siebensterngasse 2, 1070 Vienna, Austria. Tel: (43 1) 526 5947. Fax: 523 4172. e: office@viennale.at. Web: www.viennale.at. (New international films, creative documentaries, shorts and tributes - Oct 14-26, 2005.)

Viewfinders International Film Festival for Youth, PO Box 36139, 220-5600 Sackville St, Halifax, NS, B3J 3S9, Canada. Tel: (1 902) 4 22 3456. Fax: 422 4006. e: festival@atlanticfilm.com. Web: www.atlanticfilm.com. (April.)

Vila do Conde, Festival Internacional de Curtas Metragens Auditório Municipal, Praa da República, 4480-715 Vila do Conde, Portugal. Tel: (351 252) 248 469/646 516. Fax: 248 416. e: festival@curtasmetragens.pt Web: www.curtasmetragens.pt. (National and international shorts competitions. Special programme and retrospectives - July.)

Warsaw International Film Festival, PO Box 816, 00-950 Warsaw 1, Poland. Tel: (48 22) 621 4647. Fax: 621 6268. e: festiv@wff.pl. Web: www.wff.pl. (Key event in Poland. Fiction and documentary features. New Films and New Directors competition - Oct 6-17, 2005.)

Washington, DC International Film Festival (Filmfest DC), PO Box 21396, Washington, DC 20009, USA. Tel: (1 202) 628 3456. Fax: 724 6578. e: filmfestdc@filmfestdc.org. Web: www.filmfestdc.org. (Celebrates the best in world cinema - April 20-May 1, 2005.)

Back Copies

International Film Guide

2004

the definitive annual review of world cinema

Re-live the year of *City of God*, *Good Bye, Lenin!*, *Hero* and *Lilya 4-ever*

To order *IFG 2004* for £18.99/€ 29.99/$34.99 per copy (including postage & packing), send a cheque, payable to Button Group plc, and your name and address, to:

"IFG Orders"
Button Group plc
246 Westminster Bridge Road
London SE1 7PD, England

Credit Card orders – Tel: +44 (0) 20 7401 0400

"*IFG* is like a set of tidal tables for the arthouse film world."
– *The Times*

"The best annual guide to world cinema"
– *The Observer*

BUTTON
live communications

London   Los Angeles   Cannes

The Global Directory

ALGERIA

Useful Address

Cinémathèque Algérienne,
49 rue Larbi Ben M'Hidi, Algiers.
Tel: (213 2) 737 548/50. Fax: 738
246. www.cinematheque.art.dz/.

ARGENTINA

All Tel/Fax numbers begin (54 11)

Archive

**Pablo Hicken Museum and
Library**, Defensa 1220, 1143
Buenos Aires. Tel: 4300 5967.
Fax: 4307 3839.
museodelcinedb@yahoo.com.ar.

Film School

Film University, Pasaje Giufra 330,
1064 Buenos Aires. Fax: 4300 1413.
Fax: 4300 1581. fuc@ucine.edu.ar.
www.ucine.edu.ar.

Useful Addresses

Critics Association of Argentina,
Maipu 621 Planta Baja, 1006
Buenos Aires. Tel/Fax: 4322 6625.
cinecronistas@yahoo.com.
**Directors Association of
Argentina (DAC)**, Lavalle 1444,
7° Y, 1048 Buenos Aires. Tel/Fax:
4372 9822. dac1@infovia.com.ar.
www.dacdirectoresdecine.com.ar.
**Directors of Photography
Association**, San Lorenzo 3845,
Olivos, 1636 Buenos Aires.
Tel/Fax: 4790 2633. adf@ba.net.
www.adfcine.com.ar.
**Exhibitors Federation of
Argentina**, Ayacucho 457, 1° 13,

Buenos Aires. Tel/Fax: 4953 1234.
empcinemato@infovia.com.ar.
General Producers Association,
Lavalle 1860, 1051 Buenos Aires.
Tel/Fax: 4371 3430.
argentinasonofilm@impsat1.com.ar.
**National Cinema Organisation
(INCAA)**, Lima 319, 1073 Buenos
Aires. Tel: 6779 0900. Fax: 4383
0029. info@incaa.gov.ar.
**Producers Guild of Argentina
(FAPCA)**, Godoy Cruz 1540, 1414
Buenos Aires. Tel: 4777 7200.
Fax: 4778 0046.
recepcion@patagonik.com.ar.
**Sindicato de la Industria
Cinematográfia de Argentina
(SICA)**, Juncal 2029, 1116 Buenos
Aires. Tel: 4806 0208. Fax: 4806
7544. sica@sicacine.com.ar.
www.sicacine.com.ar.

ARMENIA

All Tel/Fax numbers begin (374 1)

Useful Addresses

**Armenian National
Cinematheque**, 25A Tbilisyan
Highway, 375052 Yerevan. Tel: 285
406. filmadaran@yahoo.com.
Armenian Union of Filmmakers,
18 Vardanants, Yerevan. Tel: 540
528. Fax: 540 136.
**Association of Film Critics &
Cinema Journalists**, 5 Byron Str,
374009 Yerevan. Tel/Fax: 564 484.
aafccj@arminco.com. www.arm-
cinema.am. www.arvest.am.
Hayfilm Studio, 50 Gevork
Chaush, 375088 Yerevan.
Tel: 343 000. Fax: 393 538.

hayfilm@arminco.com.
Hayk Documentary Studio,
50 Gevork Chaush, 375088
Yerevan. Tel: 357 032.
Paradise Ltd, [Production &
Distribution], 18 Abovyan Str,
375010 Yerevan. Tel: 521 271.
Fax: 521 302. paradi@arminco.com.
Yerevan Studio, 26 Hovsepyan Str,
47 Nork, 375047 Yerevan.
Tel: 558 022. tx-yes@media.am.
http://home.media.am/yestudio.

AUSTRALIA

Archive

Screensound Australia,
The National Screen and Sound
Archive, GPO Box 2002, Canberra
ACT 2601. Tel: (61 2) 6248 2000.
Fax: 6248 2222.
enquiries@screensound.gov.au.
Stock: 3,800 Western Australian titles.

Bookshop

Electric Shadows Bookshop, City
Walk, Akuna St, Canberra ACT
2601. Tel: (61 2) 6248 8352.
Fax: 6247 1230.
esb@electricshadowsbookshop.com.au.
www.electricshadowsbookshop.com.au.
Free quarterly Film/Media
catalogue available by e-mail
which lists new film books, DVDs,
videos & soundtracks. Australian
material highlighted.

Film School

**Australian Film Television &
Radio School (AFTRS)**, Postal
address: PO Box 126, North Ryde
NSW 2113. Tel: (61 2) 9805 6611.

Fax: 9887 1030.
direct.sales@syd.aftrs.edu.au.

Magazine
AFC News, GPO Box 3984,
Sydney NSW 2001. Tel: (61 2)
9321 6444. Fax: 9357 3737.
info@afc.gov.au.
www.afc.gov.au/newsandevents.
Monthly, with regular production
and multimedia reports, industry
statistics, funding approvals and
news of Australian films at
international markets and festivals.

Useful Addresses
**Australian Entertainment Industry
Association (AEIA)**, 8th Floor,
West Tower, 608 St Kilda Rd,
Melbourne VIC 3004. Tel: (61 3)
9521 1900. Fax: 9521 2285.
aeia@aeia.org.au.
Australian Film Commission (AFC),
150 William St, Woolloomooloo
NSW 2011. Postal address: GPO
Box 3984, Sydney NSW 2001. Tel:
(61 2) 9321 6444. Fax: 9357 3737.
info@afc.gov.au. www.afc.gov.au.
**Australian Film Finance
Corporation (AFFC)**, 130 Elizabeth
St, Sydney NSW 2000. Postal
address: GPO Box 3886, Sydney
NSW 2001. Tel: (61 2) 9268 2555.
Fax: 9264 8551. www.ffc.gov.au.
**Australian Screen Directors
Association (ASDA)**, Postal
address: PO Box 211, Rozelle
NSW 2039. Tel: (61 2) 9555 7045.
Fax: 9555 7086.
www.asdafilm.org.au.
Film Australia, 101 Eton Rd,
Lindfield NSW 2070.
Tel: (61 2) 9413 8777. Fax: 9416
9401. www.filmaust.com.au.
**Office of Film & Literature
Classification (OFLC)**,
23 Mary St, Surry Hills NSW 2010.
Tel: (61 2) 9289 7100. Fax: 9289
7101. oflcswitch@oflc.gov.au.

**Screen Producers Association of
Australia (SPAA)**, Level 7, 235
Pyrmont St, Pyrmont NSW 2009.
Tel: (61 2) 9518 6366.
Fax: 9518 6311. www.spaa.org.au.

More information can be found via
the web on www.nla.gov.au/oz/gov/.
Also www.sna.net.au for Screen
Network Australia, which is a
gateway to more than 250 film and
television sites.

AUSTRIA
All Tel/Fax numbers begin (43 1)

Archives
Austrian Film Museum,
Augustinerstr 1, A-1010 Vienna,
Tel: 533 7054-0. Fax: 533 7054-25.
office@filmmuseum.at.
www.filmmuseum.at.
Director: Alexander Horwath. Stock:
approx 17,000 film titles and an
extensive library and large collection
of stills and photographs.
Filmarchiv Austria,
Obere Augartenstr 1, A-1020
Vienna. Tel: 216 1300. Fax: 216
1300-100. augarten@filmarchiv.at.
www.filmarchiv.at. Director:
Ernst Kieninger.

Film School
**University of Music & Performing
Arts**, Dept of Film & TV,
Anton-von-Webern-Platz 1,
A-1030 Vienna.
Tel: 7115 5290. Fax: 7115 5299.
filmakademie@mdw.ac.at.
www.mdw.ac.at. Director:
Peter Mayer.

Magazine
RAY Kinomagazin,
c/o PVS Verleger, Friedmanngasse
44, A-1160 Vienna. Tel: 407 2497.
Fax: 407 4389. www.ray-
kinomagazin.at. Austria's leading
international movie magazine.

Useful Addresses
**Association of Austrian Film
Directors**, c/o checkpointmedia
Multimediaproduktionen AG,
Seilerstätte 30, A-1010 Vienna.
Tel/Fax: 513 0000-0.
Fax: 513 0000-11.
www.austrian-directors.com.
**Association of Austrian Film
Producers**, Speisingerstrasse 121,
A-1230 Vienna. Tel/Fax: 888 9622.
aafp@austrian-film.com.
www.austrian-film.com.
**Association of the Audiovisual
& Film Industry**,
Wiedner Hauptstrasse 53, PO Box
327, A-1045 Vienna. Tel: 5010
53010. Fax: 5010 5276.
film@fafo.at. www.fafo.at.
Austrian Film Commission,
Stiftgasse 6, A-1070 Vienna.
Tel: 526 33 23-0. Fax: 526 6801.
office@afc.at. www.afc.at.
Austrian Film Institute (OFI),
Spittelberggasse 3, A-1070 Vienna.
Tel: 526 9730-400. Fax: 526 9730-
440. office@filminstitut.at.
www.filminstitut.at.
Location Austria, Opernring 3,
A-1010 Vienna. Tel: 588 5836.
Fax: 586 8659. office@location-
austria.at. www.location-austria.at.
ORF, Austrian Broadcasting
Corporation, Würzburggasse 30,
A-1136 Vienna. Tel: 878 780.
www.orf.at.
Vienna Film Fund,
Stiftgasse 6, A-1070 Vienna.
Tel: 526 5088. Fax: 526 5088 20.
office@filmfonds-wien.at.
www.filmfonds-wien.at.

AZERBAIJAN
All Tel/Fax numbers begin (994 12)

Useful Addresses
Azerbaijan Film Fond & Museum,
69 H Zardabi St, 370122 Baku.
Tel: 328 975.

Azerbaijanfilm J Jabbarly,
1 Tbilisi Avenue, 370012 Baku.
Tel: 312 960.
Filmmakers Union,
The Government House,
16 U Hajybayov St, Baku.
Tel: 932 727. Fax: 939 620.

BELARUS

Useful Addresses
All Tel/Fax numbers begin (375 17)

Belarusfilm, Scaryna Prospect 98,
220023 Minsk. Tel: 233 8820.
Ministry of Culture,
Film & Video Department,
Masherov Avenue 11, 220004
Minsk. Tel: 223 7114.
Fax: 223 9045.

BELGIUM

Archive
Royal Film Archive, 23 Rue
Ravenstein, B-1000 Brussels.
Tel: (32 2) 507 8370.
Fax: 513 1272.
cinematheque@ledoux.be.
www.ledoux.be. Founded 1938.

Film School
Institut National des Arts du
Spectacle et Techniques de
Diffusion (INSAS),
8 Rue Thérésienne, B-1000
Brussels. Tel (32 2) 511 9286.
Fax: 511 0279. sec@insas.be
www.insas.be

Magazines
FilmMagie, Cellebroerstraat 16
Bus 2, B-1000 Brussels.
Tel: (32 2) 546 0810.
Fax: 546 0819. info@filmmagie.be.
www.filmmagie.be. Extensive
treatises on important films,
cinematic themes, aspects and
trends in film history, TV, music
videos, profiles.

Signis Media, Rue du Saphir 15,
B-1030 Brussels. Tel (32 2) 734
9708. Fax: 734 7018.
sg@signis.org. www.signis.net.
Trilingual (English, French and
Spanish) bi-monthly published by
Signis, the World Catholic
Association for Communication,
covering cinema information in
more than 140 countries and
giving specialised information
about Signis and the Ecumenical
awards worldwide.

Useful Addresses
A Private View, Vaderlandstraat 47,
B-9000 Ghent. Tel: (32 9) 240 1000.
Fax: 240 1009.
Artémis Productions, [Producer],
50 Ave Dailly, B-1030 Brussels.
Tel: (32 2) 216 2324.
Fax: 216 2013.
contacts@artemisproductions.com.
Communauté Française de
Belgique, Centre du Cinéma et de
l'Audiovisuel, Bld Léopold II, 44,
B-1080 Brussels. Tel: (32 2) 413
2519. Fax: 413 2415.
Corridor, Handelskaai 40/4,
B-1000 Brussels. Tel: (32 2) 219
6076. Fax: 219 6595.
silentface@planetinternet.be.
Corsan, Verversrui 17-19,
B-2000 Antwerp.
Tel: (32 3) 234 2518. Fax: 226 2158.
severinewillems_corsan@belgacom.net.
De Filmfabriek, Hoogstraat 33,
B-3360 Bierbeek.
Tel: (32 16) 460 100. Fax: 461 276.
areyouvital@filmfabriek.com.
Entre Chien et Loup, [Producer],
28 Rue de l'Amblève, B-1160
Brussels. Tel: (32 2) 736 4813.
Fax: 732 3383.
dianna.elbaum@brutele.be.
Era Films, Werfstraat 2, B-1000
Brussels. Tel: (32 2) 229 3780.
Fax: 219 6686. erafilms@online.be.
Favourite Films, [Producer],
Vandenbusschestraat 3, B-1030

Brussels. Tel: (32 2) 242 4510. Fax:
242 1408. info@favouritefilms.be.
Flanders Image, Handelskaai
18/3, B-1000 Brussels.
Tel: (32 2) 226 0630. Fax: 219 1936.
flandersimage@vaf.be.
Contact: Christian De Schutter.
cdeschutter@vaf.be.
Flemish Audiovisual Fund (VAF),
Handelskaai 18/3, B-1000
Brussels. Tel: (32 2) 226 0630.
Fax: 219 1936. info@vaf.be.
www.vaf.be.
Fobic Films, Nieuwe Vaart 118,
Bus 48, B-9000 Ghent.
Tel: (32 9) 329 0052. Fax: 329
0052. info@fobicfilms.com.
Help Desk for the Audiovisual Arts
in Flanders (IAK), Bijlokekaai 7E,
9000 Ghent. Tel: (32 9) 235 2260.
Fax: 233 0709. info@iak.be.
K2 /Dominique Janne, [Producer],
81/3 Ave Franklin Roosevelt, B-1050
Brussels. Tel: (32 2) 646 7270.
Fax: 646 9145. k.2@skynet.be.
Kinepolis Film Production,
Eeuwfeestlaan 20, B-1020
Brussels. Tel: (32 2) 474 2720. Fax:
474 2726. ecaroen@kinepolis.com.
Les Films de l'Etang, 12 avenue
des Klauwaerts, B-1050 Brussels.
Tel: (32 2) 219 2842. Fax: 218 5936.
Les Films du Fleuve, [Producer],
13 Quai de Gaulle, B-4020 Liège.
Tel: (32 4) 342 9939.
Fax: 342 6698. derives@skynet.be.
MMG, Nieuwstraat 99, 1730 Asse.
Tel: (32 2) 453 0304. Fax: 453
0920. info@mmg.be.
Man's Films, [Producer],
65 Ave Mostinck, B-1150 Brussels.
Tel: (32 2) 771 7137. Fax: 771 9612.
e-mail manfilms@skynet.be.
Ministry of the Flemish
Community, Dept of Media & Film,
North Plaza B, 3rd Floor, Koning
Albert II-Laan 7, B-1210 Brussels.
Tel: (32 2) 553 4650. Fax: 553 4672.
media@vlaanderen.be or
film@vlaanderen.be.

Prime Time/Ciné 3, Antonino
Lombardo, Potaerdegatstraat 18A,
B-1080 Brussels. Tel: (32 2) 469
1700. Fax: 469 1426.
primetime@planetinternet.be.
Radowsky Films, [Producer], 13
Rue de Belgrade, B-1190 Brussels.
Tel: (32 2) 534 5261. Fax: 538 5571.
radowsky.films@online.be.
Wallonie Bruxelles Image (WBI),
Place Flagey 18, B-1050 Brussels.
Tel: (32 2) 223 2304. Fax: 218 3424.
wbimages@skynet.be.
www.cfwb.be.

BOSNIA & HERZEGOVINA
All Tel/Fax numbers begin (387 33)

Useful Addresses
Academy for Performing Arts,
Obala, Sarajevo. Tel/Fax: 665 304.
Association of Filmmakers,
Strosmajerova 1, Sarajevo.
Tel: 667 452.
Cinemateque of Bosnia & Herzegovina, Alipasina 19,
Sarajevo. Tel/Fax: 668 678.
kinoteka@bih.net.ba.
Deblokada Production, Sarajevo.
Tel: 668 559. deblok@bih.net.ba.
Forum Production, Mis Irbina 2,
Sarajevo. forum@bih.net.ba.
Refresh Production, Sarajevo.
Tel: 211 093. fresh@bih.net.ba.
Sarajevo Film Festival, Sarajevo.
Tel: 209 411. programmes@sff.ba.
www.sff.ba.

BRAZIL

Archives
Cinemateca Brasileira, Largo
Senador Raul Cardoso, Vila
Clementino 207, 04021-070 São
Paulo. Tel: (55 11) 5084 2318
Fax: 5575 9264.
info@cinemateca.com.br.
www.cinemateca.com.br.

Cinemateca do Museu de Arte Moderna, Ave Infante Dom
Henrique 85, Parque do Flengo,
20021-140 Rio de Janeiro.
Tel: (55 21) 2240 4913.
cinemateca@mamrio.com.br.

Useful Addresses
ANCINE (National Agency for Cinema), Praça Pio X, 54, 10th
Floor, 22091-040 Rio de Janeiro.
Tel: (55 21) 3849 1339.
www.ancine.gov.br.
Brazilian Cinema Congress (CBC), (Federation of Cinema
Unions/Associations), Rua Cerro
Cora 550, Sala 19, 05061-100 São
Paulo. Tel/Fax: (55 11) 3021 8505.
congressocinema@hotmail.comww
w.congressocinema.com.br.
Grupo Novo de Cinema,
[Distributor], Rua Capitao Salomao
42, 22271-040 Rio de Janeiro.
Tel: (55 21) 2539 1538.
braziliancinema@braziliancinema.co
m. www.gnctv.com.br.
Ministry of Culture,
Films & Festivals Dept, Esplanada
dos Ministerios, Bloco B, 3rd Floor,
70068-900 Brasilia.
www.cultura.gov.br.

BULGARIA
All Tel/Fax numbers begin (359 2)

Archive
Bulgarian National Film Library,
36 Gurko St, 1000 Sofia.
Tel: 987 0296. Fax: 987 6004.
bmateeva@bnf.bg.

Useful Addresses
Alexandra Film, [Distributor],
17 Naycho Tzanov St, 1000 Sofia.
Tel: 980 6070. Fax: 981 0715.
Borough Film Ltd, [Producer],
3A Murgash St, 1000 Sofia.
Tel: 445 880. Fax: 943 4787.
borough@mbox.cit.bg.

Bulgarian Film Producers Association, 19 Skobelev,
[Distributor],
17A Tzar Osvoboditel Blvd,
1000 Sofia. Tel: 943 4849.
Fax: 943 3703.
Bulgarian National Television,
29 San Stefano St, 1000 Sofia.
Tel: 985 591. Fax: 987 1871.
www.bnt.bg/.
Gala Film Ltd, [Producer],
3 Uzundjovska St, 1000 Sofia.
Tel: 981 4209. Fax: 981 2971.
gala@techno-link.com.
Geopoly Ltd, [Producer],
16 Kapitan Andreev St, 1421 Sofia.
Tel/Fax: 963 0661.
geopoly@mail.techno-link.com.
Klas Film, [Producer],
156 Kniaz Boris I St, 1000 Sofia.
Tel/Fax: 526 868.
klasfilm@fofianet.net.
Ministry of Culture,
17 Stamboliiski St, 1000 Sofia.
Tel: 980 6191. Fax: 981 8559.
www.culture.government.bg/.
National Film Centre,
2A Dondukov Blvd, 1000 Sofia.
Tel: 987 4096. Fax: 987 3626.
nfc@mail.bol.bg.
Paralax Ltd, [Producer],
67 Dondukov Blvd, 1504 Sofia.
Tel: 447 326. Fax: 463 676.
dimo@omega.bg.
Sofia Film, [Distributor],
26 Maria Luiza Blvd, 1000 Sofia.
Tel: 983 5584. Fax: 983 3707.
Sunny Films, [Distributor],
17A Tzar Osvoboditel Blvd, 1000
Sofia. Tel: 943 4849. Fax: 943 3703.
Union of Bulgarian Film Makers,
67 Dondukov Blvd, 1504 Sofia.
Tel: 946 1068. Fax: 946 1069.
sbfd@bitex.com.

BURKINA FASO

Magazine
Fespaco News,
01 BP 2524 Ouagadougou 01.

www.fespaco.bf/news.
Monthly newsletter of the Pan-
African Federation of film-makers.

CANADA

Archives

La Cinémathèque Québécoise,
335 Blvd de Maisonneuve E,
Montréal, Quebec, H2X 1K1.
Tel: (1 514) 842 9763. Fax: 842
1816. info@cinematheque.qc.ca.
www.cinematheque.qc.ca.
National Archives of Canada,
Visual & Sound Archives, 344
Wellington St, Ottawa, Ontario,
K1A 0N3. Tel: (1 613) 995 5138.
Fax: 995 6274. www.archive.ca.

Bookshop

Theatrebooks, 11 St Thomas St,
Toronto, Ontario, M5S 2B7.
Tel: (1 416) 922 7175. Fax: 922
0739. action@theatrebooks.com.
www.theatrebooks.com.
Founded in 1975 first as a source
of theatre, opera and dance books,
Theatrebooks has also been
developing a first-class film book
collection since 1980. Worldwide
mail order handled.

Film Schools

Queen's University, 160 Stuart St,
Kingston, Ontario, K7L 3N6.
Tel: (1 613) 533 2178. Fax: 533
2063. film@post.queensu.ca.
www.film.queensu.ca. In its four-
year BA (Honours) degree
programme and three-year BA
degree programme, the Dept of
Film Studies provides an integrated
approach to film criticism, history
and production.
Sheridan College, School of
Animation, Arts & Design, 1430
Trafalgar Rd, Oakville, Ontario, L6H
2L1. Tel: (1 905) 845 9430.
infosheridan@sheridanc.on.cawww.
sheridanc.on.ca. Intensive and

award-winning diploma and applied
degree programmes in: Classical
Animation, International Summer
School of Animation, Computer
Animation, Computer Graphics and
Media Arts.
Simon Fraser University,
School for the Contemporary Arts,
8888 University Drive, Burnaby,
British Columbia, V5A 1S6.
Tel: (1 604) 291 3363.
Fax: 291 5907.
ca@sfu.ca. www.sfu.ca/sca.
University of Manitoba,
Film Studies Program, 367 University
College, Winnipeg, Manitoba, R3T
2N2. Tel: (1 204) 474 9581.
Fax: 474 7684. film@umanitoba.ca.
www.umanitoba.ca.
Basic and advanced film-making and
screenwriting courses.
University of Windsor,
401 Sunset Ave, Windsor, Ontario,
N9B 3P4. Tel: (1 519) 253 3000.
Fax: 973 7050. register@uwindsor.ca.
www.uwindsor.ca. Film, radio, TV.
Vancouver Film School,
198 West Hastings St, Suite 200,
Vancouver, British Columbia, V6B
1H2. Tel: (1 604) 685 5808.
Fax: 685 5830.
admissions@vfs.com. www.vfs.com.
A unique training centre that offers
programmes in communication
production: Film Production,
Interactive Media, 2D Animation,
3D Animation, Writing and Acting
for Film and Television. All
programmes have been designed
with industry consultation and are
taught by industry professionals.
York University,
Film & Video Dept, 4700 Keele St,
Toronto, Ontario, M3J 1P3.
Tel: (1 416) 736 5149.
Fax: 736 5710. www.yorku.ca.

Magazines

Ciné-Bulles, 4545 Ave Pierre-de-
Coubertin, CP 1000, Succursale M,

Montréal, Quebec, H1V 3R2.
cinebulle@loisirquebec.qc.ca.
www.cinemasparalleles.qc.ca.
Remarkable and informative
Québécois quarterly, possibly the
best in Canada.
Film Canada Yearbook,
Moving Pictures Media, Box 720,
Port Perry, Ontario, L9L 1A6.
Tel (1 905) 986 0050.
Fax: 986 1113.
deborah@filmcanadayearbook.com.
www.filmcanadayearbook.com.
Completely updated annually;
a comprehensive national
overview of the Canadian film and
television industry.
Kinema, Fine Arts & Film Studies,
University of Waterloo, 200
University Ave, Waterloo, Ontario,
N2L 3G1. Tel: (1 519) 888 4567
ext. 3709. Fax: 746 4982.
kinema@watarts.uwaterloo.ca.
www.kinema.uwaterloo.ca.
A journal of history, theory and
aesthetics of world film and audio-
visual media. Twice yearly.
Séquences, 1850 rue Joliette,
Montréal, Quebec, H1W 3G3.
Tel: (1 514) 598 9573.
Fax: 598 1789. cast49@hotmail.ca.

Useful Addresses

**Academy of Canadian Cinema &
Television**, 172 King St E, Toronto,
Ontario, M5A 1J3.
Tel: (1 416) 366 2227. Fax: 366
8454. www.academy.ca.
**Canadian Association of Film
Distributors & Exporters**, 30
Chemin des Trilles, Laval, Quebec,
H7Y 1K2. Tel: (1 450) 689 9950.
Fax: 689 9822. cic@total.net.
**Canadian Film & Television
Production Association**,
151 Slater St, Suite 605, Ottawa,
Ontario, K1P 5H3.
Tel: (1 613) 233 1444.
Fax: 233 0073. ottawa@cftpa.ca.
Canadian Motion Picture

Distributors Association (CMPDA), 22 St Clair Ave E, Suite 1603, Toronto, Ontario, M4T 2S4. Tel: (1 416) 961 1888. Fax: 968 1016.

Directors Guild of Canada, 1 Eglinton Ave E, Suite 604, Toronto, Ontario, M4P 3A1. Tel: (1 416) 482 6640. Fax: 486 6639. www.dgc.ca.

Motion Picture Theatre Associations of Canada, [Exhibitors], 146 Bloor St W, 2nd Floor, Toronto, Ontario, M5S 1P3. Tel: (1 416) 969 7057. Fax: 969 9852. www.mptac.ca.

National Film Board of Canada, PO Box 6100, Station Centre-Ville, Montréal, Quebec, H3C 3H5. Tel: (1 514) 283 9246. Fax: 283 8971. www.nfb.ca.

Telefilm Canada, 360 St Jacques St W, Suite 700, Montréal, Quebec, H2Y 4A9. Tel: (1 514) 283 6363. Fax: 283 8212. www.telefilm.gc.ca.

CHILE

All Tel/Fax numbers begin (56 2)

Useful Addresses

Arauco Films, Silvina Hurtado 1789, Providencia, Santiago. Tel: 209 2091. Fax: 204 5096. araucofi@entelchile.net.

Departamento de Creación y Difusión Artística, Consejo Nacional de la Cultura y las Artes, Edificio Centenario, Piso 20, Bellavista 168, Valparaíso. Tel: 326 612. cgutierrez.cultura@mineduc.clwww. consejodelacultura.cl.

Chilefilms, La Capitanía 1200, Las Condes, Santiago. Tel: 220 3086. Fax: 229 6406/212 9053. info@chilefilms.cl. www.chilefilms.cl.

Corporación de Fomento de la Producción (CORFO), Moneda 921, Santiago. Tel: 631 8597. Fax: 671 7735. lordonez@corfo.cl. www.corfo.cl.

Filmosonido, Rodolfo Lenz 3399, Ñuñoa, Santiago. Tel: 341 2110. Fax: 204 2054. marcos@filmosonido.cl. www.filmosonido.cl.

PWI, Cruz del Sur 133, Of. 403-404, Las Condes, Santiago. Tel: 207 2883/2760. Fax: 207 2963. marketing@pwimedia.com. www.pwimedia.com.

CHINA

Archive

China Film Archive, 3 Wenhuiyuan Lu, Xiao Xiao Xitian, Haidian District, Beijing 100088. Tel: (86 10) 6225 4422. chinafilm@cbn.com.cn.

Magazines

Film Art, (Dianying yishou), 77 Beisanhuan Zhonglu, Beijing 100088. Quarterly, leading mainland academic film journal.

Popular Cinema, (Dazhong dianying), 22 Beisanhuan Donglu, Beijing. Official popular film magazine published fortnightly.

New Cinema Magazine, (Xin dianying), 55 Xingfu Yi Cun, Chaoyang District, Beijing 100027. Tel: (86 10) 6417 6943. http://www.wfj.cc/magazine/20030 3/index.htm. Leading mainland popular international film magazine.

Useful Addresses

August First Film Studio, A1, Beili, Liuliqiao, Guang'anmenwai, Beijing 100073. Tel: (86 10) 6681 2329. Fax: 6326 7324.

Beijing Film Academy, 4 Xitucheng Rd, Haidian District, Beijing 100088. Tel: (86 10) 8204 8899. http://www.bfa.edu.cn.

Beijing Film Studio, 77 Beisanhuan Central Rd, Haidan District, Beijing 100088. Tel: (86 10) 6200 3191. Fax: 6201 2059.

Beijing Forbidden City Film Company, 67 Beichizi Street, Dongcheng District, Beijing 100006. Tel: (86 10) 6513 1275. Fax: 6513 1275.

China Film Group Corp, 25 Xinjiekouwai St, Beijing 100088. Tel: (86 10) 6225 4488. Fax: 6225 0652. cfgc@chinafilm.com. www.chinafilm.com.

China Film Co-Production Corp, 5 Xinyuan South Rd, Chaoyang District, Beijing 100027. Tel: (86 10) 6466 3330. Fax: 6466 3983. www.cfcc-film.com.cn.

Hengdian TV & Movie City, Zhejiang Province, 1 Wansheng South Street, Hengdian, Zhejiang. Tel: (86 579) 655 5668. Fax: 655 5885.

Huayi Brothers & Taihe Film Investment, Wenyuhe Loutaiduan, Tianzhu Shunyi District, Beijing 101312. Tel : (86 10) 6457 9338. Fax : 6457 1299. www.huayifilm.com/.

Meishi Film Academy of Chongqing University, Chongqing 400044. Tel: (86 23) 6510 6258/6511 1919. Fax: 6510 5671. meishi@public.cta.cq.c. www.msfilm.cqu.edu.cn/eng/index.aspx.

Poly-Asian Union Film, Building B, 5 Shuguang Tower, Jingshun Road, Chaoyang District, Beijing 100028. Tel : (86 10) 8440 9919. Fax: 8440 9918. service@asian-union.com.

Shanghai Film Studio/Shanghai Film Group, 595 Caoxi Beilu, Shanghai 200030. Tel: (86 21) 6438 7100. www.sfs-cn.com/.

COLOMBIA

Archive

Colombian Film Archives, Carrera 13, No 13-24, Piso 9, Bogotá. Tel: (57 1) 281 5241. Fax: 342 1485.

patfilm@colnodo.apc.org.
www.patrimoniofilmico.org.co.
Director: Myriam Garzón de García.

Magazine
Kinetoscopio, Carrera 45, No 53-
24, Apartado 8734, Medellin. Tel:
(57 4) 513 4444, ext 178. Fax: 513
2666. kineto@colomboworld.com.
www.colomboworld.com/kinetoscopio.
Quarterly covering international and
Latin American cinema, Colombian
directors and festival news.

Useful Addresses
**Association of Film & Video
Producers & Directors**,
Calle 97, No 10-28, Bogotá.
Tel: (57 1) 218 2455. Fax: 610 8524.
gustavo@centauro.com.
**Colombian Association of
Cinemas**, Calle 23, No 5-85, Int
202, Bogotá. Tel: (57 1) 284 5752.
Fax: 334 0809. e-mail:
acocine@hotmail.com.
**Colombian Association of
Documentary Film Directors**,
Calle 35, No 4-89, Bogotá.
Tel: (57 1) 245 9961.
aladoscolombia@netscape.net.
www.enmente.com/alados.
**Colombian Association of Film
Directors,** Carrera 6, No 55-10,
Apartado 202, Bogotá.
Tel: (57 1) 235 9798. Fax: 212
2586. lisandro@inter.net.co.
**Colombian Association of Film
Distributors**, Carrera 11,
No 93A-22, Bogotá.
Tel: (57 1) 610 6695. Fax: 618
5417. fabogado@impsat.net.co.
Film Promotion Fund, Calle 35,
No 4-89, Bogotá. Tel: (57 1) 287
0103. Fax: 288 4828.
claudiatriana@proimagenescolombia.
com.
www.proimagenescolombia.com.
Ministry of Culture, Censorship
Committee, Calle 35, No 4-89,
Bogotá. Tel: (57 1) 287 0203.

Fax: 285 5690.
mcortes@mincultura.gov.co.
www.mincultura.gov.co.
Ministry of Culture, Film Division,
Calle 35, No 4-89, Bogotá.
Tel: (57 1) 288 2995. Fax: 285
5690. cine@mincultura.gov.co.
www.mincultura.gov.co.
National Film Council,
Calle 35, No 4-89, Bogotá.
Tel: (57 1) 288 4712. Fax: 285
5690. cine@mincultura.gov.co.
www.mincultura.gov.co.
Director: Claudia Aguilera.

CROATIA
All Tel/Fax numbers begin (385 1)

Useful Addresses
Alka Film, 10000 Zagreb,
Dedici 12. Tel: 467 4187.
Croatia Film d.o.o, Katanciceva 3,
10000 Zagreb. Tel: 481 3711.
Fax: 492 2568.
Croatian Film Directors Guild,
Britanski Trg 12, 10000 Zagreb.
Tel: 484 7026. info@dhfr.hr.
www.dhfr.hr.
Croatian Film Clubs' Association,
Dalmatinska 12, 10000 Zagreb.
Tel: 484 8764. vera@hfs.hr.
www.hfs.hr.
DA Film d.o.o, Juriciceva 16A.,
10000 Zagreb. Tel: 954 3362.
Druzba d.o.o, B Magovca 147,
10000 Zagreb. Tel/Fax: 668 1261.
Gama studio d.o.o, Tuckanac 63,
10000 Zagreb. Tel: 483 4168.
Fax: 299 3545.
Gral Film, Ilica 42, 10000 Zagreb.
Tel: 484 7575.
HRT (Croatian Television),
Prisavlje 3, 10000 Zagreb.
Tel: 634 3683. Fax: 634 3692.
Interfilm Produkcija, Nova Ves 45,
10000 Zagreb. Tel: 466 7296.
Fax: 466 7291.
Jadran Film, Oporovecka I2, Dugi
dol 13, 10000 Zagreb.
Tel: 298 7222. Fax: 285 1394.

Maxima Film d.o.o, Belostenceva
6, 10000 Zagreb. Tel: 618 4731.
M.B.M. d.o.o, 10000 Zagreb.
Tel: 487 3292.
Zagreb Film, Vlacka 72, 10000
Zagreb. Tel: 455 0489.

CUBA

Archives
Archivo Fílmico,
Calle 23 No 1109, Entre 8 & 10,
Vedado, Havana. Tel: (53 7) 833
6321. archivo@icaic.inf.cu.
Cinemateca de Cuba,
Calle 23 No 1155, Entre 10 & 12,
Vedado, Havana. Tel: (53 7)
552 844. cinemateca@icaic.inf.cu.

Film Schools
**Escuela Internacional de Cine y
TV**, Finca San Tranquilino, Carretera
Vereda Nueva, KM 4.5, San Antonio
de Los Baños, Havana.
Tel: (53 650) 383 152. Fax: 382 366.
eictv@eictv.org.cu. www.eictv.org.
Instituto Superior de Arte,
Facultad de Comunicación
Audiovisual, 5ta, Avenida Esq A20,
Miramar, Playa, Havana. Tel: (53 7)
209 1302. isafaud@cubarte.cult.cu.

Magazines
Cine Cubano, Calle 23 No 1115,
El Vedado, Havana. Tel: (53 7) 552
865. publicaciones@icaic.inf.cu.
ECOS, Arzobispado de La Habana,
Calle Habana No 152,
Esq Chacón, La Habana Vieja.
Tel: (53 7) 862 4009. Fax: 338 109.
signis@cocc.co.cu.

Useful Addresses
Cinematografía Educativa,
Calle 7MA 2802, Entre 28 & 30,
Miramar, Playa, Havana. Tel: (53 7)
202 6971. cined@ceniai.inf.cu.
National Film Institute (ICAIC),
Calle 23, No 1155, Entre 8 & 10,
Vedado, Havana.

Tel: (53 7) 552 859. Fax: 833 3281.
omar@icaic.inf.cu.
www.cubacine.cu.
Televisión Serrana,
San Pablo de Yao, Buey Arriba,
Granma. Tel: (53 23) 23548.
cip214@enet.cu.

CYPRUS
All Tel/Fax numbers begin (357 22)

Cyprus Cinema Advisory Committee, Cultural Services,
Ministry of Education & Culture,
Kimonos & Thoukididou Street,
1434 Nicosia. Tel: 809 507. Fax:
809 506. echristo@cytanet.com.cy.
Directors Union, 11 Pente
Pygadion Street, Flat 4, Ayioi
Omologites, 1076 Nicosia.
Tel: 458 717. Fax: 458 718.
artvision@cytanet.com.cy.

CZECH REPUBLIC
All Tel/Fax numbers begin (420 2)

Archive
National Film Archive, Malesická
12, 130 00 Prague 3.
Tel: 7177 0509. Fax: 7177 0501.
nfa@nfa.cz. www.nfa.cz.

Film School
FAMU, Film & Television Faculty,
Academy of Performing Arts,
Smetanovo 2, 116 65 Prague 1.
Tel: 2422 9176. Fax: 2423 0285.
kamera@f.amu.cz.
Dean: Karel Kochman.

Useful Addresses
**Association of Czech Filmmakers
(FITES),** Pod Nuselskymi Schody
3, 120 00 Prague 2.
Tel: 691 0310. Fax: 691 1375.
Association of Producers,
Národní 28, 110 00 Prague 1.
Tel: 2110 5321. Fax: 2110 5303.
www.apa.iol.cz.
Czech Film & Television

Academy, Na Îertvách 40, 180 00
Prague 8. Tel: 8482 1356.
Fax: 8482 1341.
Czech Film Centre, Národní 28,
110 00 Prague 1.
Tel: 2110 5302. Fax: 2110 5303.
www.filmcenter.cz.
Ministry of Culture,
Audiovisual Dept, Milady Horákové
139, 160 00 Prague 6.
Tel: 5708 5310. Fax: 2431 8155.
Union of Czech Film Distributors,
Národní 28, 110 00 Prague 1.
Tel: 2494 5220. Fax: 2110 5220.

DENMARK
All Tel/Fax numbers begin (45)

Archive
**Danish Film Institute/Archive &
Cinemateque (DFI),** Gothersgade
55, DK-1123 Copenhagen K.
Tel: 3374 3400. Fax: 3374 3401.
dfi@dfi.dk. www.dfi.dk. Also
publishes the film magazine, *Film*.

Film Schools
European Film College,
Carl Th Dreyers Vej 1, DK-8400
Ebeltoft. Tel: 8634 0055.
Fax: 8634 0535.
administration@efc.dk. www.efc.dk.
National Film School of Denmark,
Theodor Christensens Plads 1,
DK-1437 Copenhagen K.
Tel: 3268 6400. Fax: 3268 6410.
info@filmskolen.dk.
www.filmskolen.dk.

Magazine
FILM, Gothersgade 55, DK-1123
Copenhagen K. Tel: 3374 3400.
susannan@dfi.dk and
agnetes@dfi.dk. Published by the
Danish Film Institute. Eight issues
per year (some two to three in
English). A selection of articles is
released on www.dfi.dk.
Subscriptions: ninac@dfi.dk.

Useful Addresses
**Danish Actors' Association
(DSF),** Sankt Knuds Vej 26, DK-
1903 Frederiksberg C.
Tel: 3324 2200. Fax: 3324 8159.
dsf@skuespillerforbundet.dk.
www.skuespillerforbundet.dk.
Danish Film Directors (DF),
Vermundsgade 19, 2nd Floor,
DK-2100 Copenhagen Ø.
Tel: 3583 8005. Fax: 3583 8006.
mail@filmdir.dk. www.filmdir.dk.
**Danish Film Distributors'
Association (FAFID),**
Sundkrogsgade 9, DK-2100
Copenhagen Ø. Tel: 3363 9684.
Fax: 3363 9660. www.fafid.dk.
Danish Film Institute,
Gothersgade 55, DK-1123
Copenhagen K. Tel: 3374 3400.
Fax: 3374 3401. dfi@dfi.dk.
Danish Film Studios,
Blomstervaenget 52, DK-2800
Lyngby. Tel: 4587 2700.
Fax: 4587 2705. ddf@filmstudie.dk.
www.filmstudie.dk.
Danish Producers' Association,
Bernhard Bangs Allé 25, DK-2000
Frederiksberg. Tel: 3386 2880.
Fax: 3386 2888. info@pro-f.dk.
www.producentforeningen.dk.

ECUADOR
All Tel/Fax numbers begin (59 32)

Film School
**Universidad San Francisco de
Quito,** Contemporary Arts
Department, Film and TV,
Via Interoceánica & Jardines del
Este, Cumbayá. Tel: 289 5723.
hburgos@usfq.edu.ec.
www.usfq.edu.ec.

Useful Addresses
Cabeza Hueca Producciones,
Foch 265 & Plaza Edif.
Sonelsa 1er piso, Quito. Tel: 223
9090. cabezahueca@hoy.net.
Cine Ocho y Medio,
Valladolid N24 353 & Vizcaya,

Quito. Tel: 290 4720. Fax: 256 5524. rbarriga@ochoymedio.net. www.ochoymedio.net.
Corporación Cine Memoria, Venezuela N6-09 & Mejía–Of A1, Quito. Tel: 295 9132. cinememoria@andinanet.net. www.cinememoria.com.
Sapo Inc, juan@sapoinc.com. www.sapoinc.com.

EGYPT
All Tel/Fax numbers begin (20 2)

Archive
National Egyptian Film Archive, c/o Egyptian Film Centre, City of Arts, Al Ahram Rd, Guiza. Tel: 585 4801. Fax: 585 4701. President: Dr Mohamed Kamel El Kalyobi.

Film School
Higher Film Institute, Pyramids Rd, Gamal El-Din El-Afaghani St, Guiza. Tel: 537 703. Fax: 561 1034. aoarts@idsc.gov.eg.

Useful Addresses
Al-Adl Group, [Producer/Distributor], 10 Geziret El Arab St, Mohandessin, Cairo. Tel: 761 6934. Fax: 767 6945.
Al-Sobki, [Producer/Distributor], 103 Tahrir St, Dokki, Cairo. Tel: 749 9525. Fax: 335 3348.
El-Arabia Cinema, [Producer/Distributor], 21Ahmed Orabi St, Mohanesseen, Cairo. Tel: 344 4788. Fax: 344 5040.
Central Audio-Visual Censorship Authority, Opera Ground, Gezira, Cairo. Tel: 738 1674. Fax: 736 9479.
Chamber of Film Industry, 1195 Kornish El Nil, Industries Union Bldg, Cairo. Tel: 578 5111. Fax: 575 1583.
Egyptian Radio & TV Union, Kornish El Nil, Maspero St, Cairo. Tel: 576 0014. Fax: 579 9316.

Media City, [Producer/Distributor], Al Haram Ave, City of Cinema, Giza. Tel: 584 4217. Fax: 584 4219.
Misr International, [Producer/Distributor], 35 Champolion St, Cairo. Tel: 574 0020. Fax: 574 8878.
National Film Center, Al-Ahram Ave, Giza. Tel: 585 4801. Fax: 585 4701.
Oscar for Distribution & Theatres, Ramsis Hilton, Cairo. Tel: 574 7436. Fax: 574 7437.
Shoa's Cultural Media Arab Co, [Producer/Distributor], Marwa St, Dokki, Cairo. Tel: 336 9510. Fax: 336 9511.

ESTONIA

Archive
Estonian National Archive, Ristiku 84, 10318 Tallinn. Tel: (372 6) 938 613. Fax: 938 611. filmiarhiiv@ra.ee. www.filmi.arhiiv.ee.

Film School
Department of Audiovisual Arts, Faculty of Fine Arts, Tallinn Pedagogical University, Lai 13, 10133 Tallinn. Tel: (372 6) 411 627. Fax: 412 525. kultuur@tpu.ee. www.tpu.ee.

Useful Addresses
Association of Professional Actors of Estonia, Uus 5, 10111 Tallinn. Tel: (372 6) 464 512. Fax: 464 516. enliit@delfi.ee. www.enliit.ee.
Estonian Association of Film Journalists, Narva Mnt 11E, 10151 Tallinn. Tel: (372 5) 533 894. Fax: 698 154. jaan@ekspress.ee.
Estonian Film Foundation, Vana-Viru 3, 10111 Tallinn. Tel: (372 6) 276 060. Fax: 276 061. film@efsa.ee. www.efsa.ee.
Estonian Film Producers Association, Rävala pst 11-12,

10143 Tallinn. Tel: (372 6) 67 8 270. Fax: 67 8 721. produtsendid@rudolf.ee.
Estonian Filmmakers Union, Uus 3, 10111 Tallinn. Tel/Fax: (372 6) 464 068. kinoliit@online.ee.
Union of Estonian Cameramen, Faehlmanni 12, 15029 Tallinn. Tel: (372 5) 662 3069. Fax: 568 401. bogavideo@infonet.ee.

FINLAND

Archive
Finnish Film Archive, Pursimiehenkatu 29-31A, PO Box 177, FIN-00151, Helsinki. Tel: (358 9) 615 400.

Film School
University of Art & Design Helsinki (UIAH), Dept of Film, Hämeentie 135 C, FIN-00560, Helsinki. Tel: (358 9) 756 31.

Magazines
Filmihullu, Malminkatu 36, FIN-00100, Helsinki. Tel: (358 9) 685 2242.
Filmjournalen, Finlandssvenskt Filmcentrum, Nylandsgatan 1, FIN-20500, Åbo. Tel: (358 2) 250 0431. www.fsfilmcentrum.fi/fj/.

Useful Addresses
Artista Filmi Oy, [Producer], Post Box 69, FIN-28401, Ulvila. Tel: (338 2) 647 7441. timo.koivusalo@ artistafilmi.com.
Blind Spot Pictures Oy, [Producer], Kalliolanrinne 4, FIN-00510, Helsinki. Tel: (358 9) 7742 8360.
Dada Filmi Oy, 3 Linja 5, FIN-00530 Helsinki. Tel: (358 9) 774 4780. fennada@dada.pp.fi.
Kinotar Oy, [Producer], Meritullinkatu 33E, FIN-00170, Helsinki. Tel: (358 9) 135 1864. kinotar@kinotar.com.

MRP Matila & Röhr Productions, [Producer], Tallbrginkatu 1A 141, FIN-00180, Helsinki. Tel: (358 9) 540 7820. Fax: 685 2229. mrp@matilarohr.com.

Solar Films Oy, [Producer], Kiviaidankatu 1, FIN-00210, Helsinki. Tel: (358 9) 417 4700.

FRANCE

Archives

Archives du Film, 7 bis rue Alexandre Turpault, 78395 Bois d'Arcy. Tel: (33 1) 3014 8000. Fax: 3460 5225.

Cinémathèque de Toulouse, BP 824, 31080 Toulouse Cedex 6. Tel: (33 5) 6230 3010. Fax: 6230 3012. contact@lacinemathequedetoulouse.com. www.lacinemathequedetoulouse.com. President: Martine Offroy.

Cinémathèque Française, 4 rue de Longchamp, 75116 Paris. Tel: (33 1) 5365 7474. Fax: 5365 7465. contact@cinemathequefrancaise.com. www.cinemathequefrancaise.com. Founded in 1936 by Henri Langlois. Stock: 23,000 film titles from around the world.

Institut Lumière, 25 rue du Premier-Film, BP 8051, 69352 Lyon Cedex 8. Tel: (33 4) 7878 1895. Fax: 7878 3656. contact@institut-lumiere.org. www.institut-lumiere.org. President: Bertrand Tavernier.

Bookshops

Atmosphère, Librairie du Cinema, 10 rue Broca, 75005 Paris. Tel: (33 1) 4331 0271. Fax: 4331 0369. librairie.atmosphere@frisbee.fr. Atmosphère offers a wide range of film publications, with a large stock of stills, postcards, posters of new and old movies of all origins and sizes. Also stocks back issues of magazines.

Gilda, 36 rue de Boudonnais, 75001 Paris. Tel: (33 1) 4233 6000. Videos, books, film magazines, compact disc videos, CDs, CD Roms.

Librairie Contacts, 24 rue du Colisée, 75008 Paris. Tel: (33 1) 4359 1771. Fax: 4289 2765. librariecontacts@wanadoo.fr. www.medialibrarie.com. Cinema bookshop established 46 years ago in the Champs-Elysées area, close to the film production companies. Amply stocked with French and foreign-language books on technique, theory, history and director monographs. Also magazines. Reliable mail order service. Free "new acquisitions" list.

Film Schools

Conservatoire Libre du Cinéma Français, 9 quai de l'Oise, 75019 Paris. Tel: (33 1) 4036 1919. Fax: 4036 0102. info@clcf.com. www.clcf.com.

ESEC (Ecole Superieure d'Etudes Libres Cinematographique), 21 rue de Citeaux, 75012 Paris. Tel: (33 1) 4342 4322. Fax: 4341 9521. esec@esec.edu. www.esec.edu.

Femis (École Nationale Supérieure des Métiers de L'Image et du Son), 6 rue Francoeur, 75018 Paris. Tel: (33 1) 5341 2100. Fax: 5341 0280. femis@femis.fr. www.femis.fr.

Magazines

Cahiers du Cinema, 9 passage de la Boule Blanche, 75012 Paris. Tel: (33 1) 5344 7575. Fax: 4343 9504. cducinema@lemonde.fr. Celebrated French monthly journal.

Le Film Français, 150 rue Gallieni, 92514 Boulogne Cedex. Tel: (33 1) 4186 1600. Fax: 4186 1691. lefilmfrancais@emapfrance.com. www.lefilmfrancais.com. Lightweight weekly, with news, reviews, box-

office and production schedules.

Positif, 3 rue Lhomond, 75005 Paris. Tel: (33 1) 4432 0590. Fax: 4432 0591. www.johnmichelplace.com.fr In-depth interviews, articles, all immaculately researched and highly intelligent. By a clear margin, this is Europe's best film magazine.

Premiere, 151 rue Anatole France, 92534 Levallois-Perret. Tel: (33 1) 4134 9111. Fax: 4134 9119. www.premiere.fr. France's familiar movie monthly, packed with information, reviews and filmographies.

Useful Addresses

Centre National de la Cinématographie, 12 rue de Lubeck, Paris 75016. Tel: (33 1) 4434 3440. Fax: 4755 0491. webmaster@cnc.fr. www.cnc.fr.

Ile de France Film Commission, 11, rue du Colisée, Paris 75008. Tel: (33 1) 5688 1280. Fax: 5688 1219. idf-film@idf-film.com. www.iledefrance-film.com.

Michael Raeburn, 20 Rue de Clignancourt, Paris. Tel: (33 1) 6203 33740. mraeburn@compuserve.com. www.michaelraeburn.com.

Unifrance, 4 Villa Bosquet, Paris 75007. Tel: (33 1) 4753 9580. Fax: 4705 9655. info@unifrance.org. www.unifrance.org.

GEORGIA

All Tel/Fax numbers begin (995 32)

Archive

Central Film Photo Archive, Vaja-Pshavelas Gamziri 1, Tbilisi. Tel: 386 529.

Film School

Georgian State Institute of Theatre & Film,

Rustavelis Gamziri 37, 380004
Tbilisi. Tel: 997 588. Fax: 991 153.

Useful Addresses

National Film Centre,
Rustavelis Gamziri 37, 380008
Tbilisi. Tel: 984 201. Fax: 999 037.
www.kinocentre.myweb.ge.
**Society of Audiovisual Authors &
Producers**, Dzmebi Kakabadzeebis
Qucha 2, 380008 Tbilisi.
Tel: 998 995. Fax: 932 820.
www.itic.org.ge.

GERMANY

Archives

Deutsches Filminstitut-DIF,
Schaumainkai 41, 60596 Frankfurt
am Main. Tel: (49 69) 961 2200.
Fax: 620 060.
info@deutsches-filminstitut.de.
www.deutsches-filminstitut.de.
Stock: 10,000 film titles, 70,000
books, 260 periodicals, 140,000
programmes, 16,000 dialogue lists,
5,000 scripts, circa 1.8 million stills,
850,000 clippings files on
international film production,
advertising material.
**Deutsches Filmmuseum
Frankfurt am Main**,
Schaumainkai 41, 60596 Frankfurt
am Main. Tel: (49 69) 2123 8830.
Fax: 2123 7881.
info@deutsches-filmmuseum.de.
www.deutsches-filmmuseum.de.
Assistant Director:
Hans-Peter Reichmann.
**Filmmuseum Berlin-Deutsche
Kinemathek**, Potsdamer Str 2,
10785 Berlin. Tel: (49 30) 300
9030. Fax: 3009 0313.
info@filmmuseum-berlin.de.
www.filmmuseum-berlin.de.
Director: Hans Helmut Prinzler.
Stock: 10,000 film titles, 2,000,000
film stills, 20,000 posters, 15,000
set and costume designs, 60,000
film programmes, 30,000 scripts

etc. The library contains about
50,000 books and periodicals.
**Kino Arsenal/Home of
Independent Cinema**,
Potsdamer Str 2, 10785 Berlin.
Tel: (49 30) 2695 5100. Fax: 2695
5111. fdk@fdk-berlin.de. www.fdk-
berlin.de. The nearest equivalent to
Britain's NFT. The Freunde also
runs a non-commercial distribution
of about 800 films, most of them
from the International Forum, the
independent programme of the
Berlin Film Festival, organised by
the Freunde.
**Münchner Stadtmuseum/
Filmmuseum**, St Jakobsplatz 1,
80331 Munich. Tel: (49 89) 2332
2348. Fax: 2332 3931.
filmmuseum@muenchen.de.
www.stadtmuseum-
online.de/filmmu.htm.
Founded in 1963, this municipal film
archive runs a daily cinema
programme. Film archive holds
approx. 5,000 titles, including many
restored silent German film classics,
New German cinema, and the Orson
Welles Collection. Estate holdings
from GW Pabst, Arnold Fanck etc.
Library holds over 6,000 film books,
10,000 film periodicals.

Bookshops

Buchhandlung Langenkamp,
Beckergrube 19, 23552 Lübeck.
Tel: (49 451) 76479. Fax: 72645.
Buchhandlung Walther König,
Ehrenstr 4, 50672, Cologne.
Tel: (49 221) 205 9625.
Fax: 205 9625.
order@buchhandlung-walther-
koenig.de. www.buchhandlung-
walther-koenig.de. Offers a
comprehensive catalogue of
international titles in the film
department, also useful small
antiquarian department.
H Lindemann's Bookshop,
Nadlerstr 4 & 10, 70173 Stuttgart 1.

Tel: (49 711) 2489 9977.
Fax: 236 9672.
fotobuecher@lindemanns.de.
www.lindemanns.de.
Photography and film literature.
Catalogue covering cinema/film and
photography published twice yearly.
Sautter & Lackmann,
Filmbuchhandlung, Admiralitädstr
71/72, 20459 Hamburg.
Tel: (49 40) 373 196. Fax: 365 479.
info@sautter-lackmann.de. Mainly
books, but also videos etc.
Marga Schoeller Buecherstube,
Knesebeckstr 33, 10623 Berlin.
Tel: (49 30) 881 1122. Fax: 881
8479. schoeller.buecher@gmx.net.
One of the fabled literary haunts of
western Europe, Marga Schoeller's
shop is justly proud of its film
book selection.
**Verlag fur Filmschriften Christian
Unucka**, Postfach 63, 85239
Hebertshausen.
Tel: (49 8131) 13922. Fax: 10075.
order@unucka.de. www.unucka.de.
Books, posters, programmes, stills,
postcards, videos, rare items etc.

Film Schools

**Deutsche Film und
Fernsehakademie Berlin**,
Potsdamer Str 2, 10785 Berlin.
Tel: (49 30) 257 590. Fax: 257
59161. info@dffb.de. www.dffb.de.
Four-year course deals with
theories of film-making, film history
and all aspects of practical film and
TV production, scriptwriting,
direction, camerawork, and editing
(Media Lab).
Filmakademie Baden-Würtenberg,
Mathildenstr 20, 71638
Ludwigsburg. Tel: (49 7141) 969
108. Fax: 969 292.
info@filmakademie.de.
www.filmakademie.de.
**Hochschule für Fernsehen und
Film**, Frankenthaler Str 23, 81539
Munich. Tel: (49 89) 689 570.

Fax: 689 57189. Info@hff-muc.de
www.hff-muc.de.
Approx. 300 students and 80 staff.
Four-year course provides instruction
in the theory and practice of film and
TV. Facilities provide for work in
16mm and 35mm and video.
Two-stage admission process takes
place Nov each year.

Magazines

Blickpunkt Film, Einsteinring 24,
85609 Dornach. Tel: (49 89) 4511
4124. Fax: 4511 4451.
hspoerl@e-media.de.
www.blickpunktfilm.de.
Strong on box-office returns and
marketing, this German weekly also
covers the video and TV markets.
EPD Medien, Postfach 50 05 50,
60439 Frankfurt am Main.
Tel: (49 69) 5809 8141.
Fax: 5809 8261. medien@epd.de.
www.epd.de/medien. Highbrow
publication covering radio, TV and
the press. Twice weekly.
Entertainment Markt, Einsteinring
24, 85609 Dornach.
Tel: (49 89) 451 140.
Fax: 4511 4444. emv@e-media.de.
www.e-mediabiz.de.
Bi-weekly business magazine that
covers German video, CD-ROM and
computer games, from multimedia to
business news. The trade magazine
for innovative dealers, distributors
and decision-makers.
Film-Echo/Filmwoche,
Marktplatz 13, 65183 Wiesbaden.
Tel: (49 611) 360 980.
Fax: 372 878. info@filmecho.de.
www.filmecho.de. Doyen of the
German trade. Weekly.
Kino, Export-Union des Deutschen
Films GmbH, Sonnenstr 21, 80331
Munich. Tel: (49 89) 599 7870.
Fax: 5997 8730.
export-union@german-cinema.de.
www.german-cinema.de.
Information on new German features

(in production and on release), and
selected German film personalities.
Published four times a year in
English; yearbook also available.
**Kino German Film & Intl.
Reports**, Helgoländer Ufer 6,
10557 Berlin. Tel: (49 30) 391
6167. Fax: 391 2424.
ronaldholloway@aol.com. Excellent
magazine published twice a year,
also includes special issues devoted
to both German cinema and
international festival reports. Features,
reviews, interviews and credits.

Useful Addresses

Association of Distributors,
Kreuzberger Ring 56, 65205
Wiesbaden. Tel: (49 611) 778 920.
Fax: 778 9212. vdfkino@aol.com.
Association of Exhibitors, Grosse
Praesidentenstr 9, 10178 Berlin.
Tel: (49 30) 2300 4041. Fax: 2300
4026. info@kino-hdf.de.
**Association of German Film
Exporters**, Tegernseer Landstr 75,
81539 Munich. Tel: (49 89) 692
0660. Fax: 692 0910.
vdfe@kanziel-wedel.de.
Export Union, Sonnenstr 21,
80331 Munich. Tel: (49 89) 599
7870. Fax: 5997 8730.
export-union@german-cinema.de.
www.german-cinema.de.
Federal Film Board (FFA), Grosse
Praesidentenstr 9, 10178 Berlin.
Tel: (49 30) 275 770.
Fax: 2757 7111. www.ffa.de.
**New German Film Producers
Association**, Agnesstr 14, 80798
Munich. Tel: (49 89) 271 7430. Fax:
271 9728. ag-spielfilm@t-online.de.
**Umbrella Organisation of the
Film Industry**, Kreuzberger Ring
56, 65205 Wiesbaden.
Tel: (49 611) 778 9114. Fax: 778
9169. statistik@spio-fsk.de.

GREECE
All Tel/Fax numbers begin (30 210)

Useful Addresses
AMA Films, 54 Themistokleous,
106 81 Athens. Tel: 383 3118/381
2640. Fax: 384 2559.
amafilms@amafilms.gr.
**Association of Independent
Producers of Audiovisual Works
(SAPOE)**, 30 Aegialias, 151 25
Maroussi. Tel: 683 3212. Fax: 683
3606. sapoe-gr@otenet.gr.
Cinema Department,
5 Metsovou, 106 82 Athens. Tel:
825 0767/0720. Fax: 825 3604.
Film Trade, 130A Kifissias,
115 26 Athens. Tel: 698 1083. Fax:
698 3430. vassilis@filmtrade.gr.
Greek Film Centre, President &
Managing Director: Diagoras
Chronopoulos, 10 Panepistimou,
106 71 Athens. Tel: 367 8500. Fax:
364 8269. info@gfc.gr. www.gfc.gr.
Greek Film, Theatre & Television
Directors Guild, 11 Tossitsa, 106 83
Athens. Tel: 822 8936/3205.
Fax: 821 1390. ees@ath.forthnet.gr.
Hellas Film, 10 Panepistimiou, 106
71 Athens. Tel: 367 8500. Fax: 361
4336. info@gfc.gr. www.gfc.gr.
Hellenic Ministry of Culture, 20
Bouboulinas, 106 82 Athens.
Tel: 820 1100. w3admin@culture.gr.
http://culture.gr.
Odeon SA, (Public Performance
Enterprise for the Production &
Exploitation of Audiovisual Works),
275 Mesogion, 152 31 Halandri.
Tel: 678 6511/6600. Fax: 672
8927. distribution@hvh.com.gr.
Play Time, 11 Mitropoleos, 2nd
Floor, 105 56 Athens.
Tel: 331 5175. Fax: 331 1309.
theoni@infoplaytime.com.gr.
Prooptiki SA, 40-42 Koleti, 106 82
Athens. Tel: 330 7700. Fax: 330
7798. prooptiki@prooptiki.gr.
**Rosebud SA Motion Picture
Enterprises**, 275 Mesogion,

152 31 Halandri. Tel: 678 6511.
Fax: 672 8927.

Spentzos Films, 9-13 Gravias,
106 78 Athens. Tel: 382 5953.
Fax: 380 9314. festival@otenet.gr.

UIP, 4 Gamveta, 106 78 Athens.
Tel: 380 7430. Fax: 383 5396.
uipgreece@uip.com.

**Union of Greek Film Directors
and Producers**, 33 Methonis,
106 83 Athens. Tel: 825 3065.
Fax: 825 3065.

**Union of Greek Film, TV &
Audiovisual Sector Technicians
(ETEKT-OT)**, 25 Valtetsiou,
106 80 Athens. Tel: 360 2379/361
5675. Fax: 361 6442.
etekt-ot@ath.forthnet.gr.

Village Roadshow Greece,
47 Marinou Antipa, 14121 Neo
Hrakleio. Tel: 270 4809.
Fax: 271 0009.
eleni_voultepsis@village.com.gr.

HONG KONG

All Tel/Fax numbers begin (852)

Archive

Hong Kong Film Archive,
50 Lei King Rd, Sai Wan Ho.
Tel: 2739 2139. Fax: 2311 5229.
www.filmarchive.gov.hk.

Film School

**Hong Kong Academy for
Performing Arts**, School of Film
& Television, 1 Gloucester Rd,
Wan Chai. Tel: 2584 8500.
Fax: 2802 4372. www.hkapa.edu.

Magazine

City Entertainment, Flat B2, 17/F,
Fortune Factory Bldg, 40 Lee
Chung Rd, Chai Wan.
Tel: 2892 0155. Fax: 2838 4930.
www.cityentertainment.com.hk.
Indispensable Hong Kong bi-
weekly in Chinese for anyone
interested in Chinese cinema.

Useful Addresses

Film Services Office, 40/F, Revenue
Tower, 5 Gloucester Rd, Wan Chai.
Tel: 2594 5745. Fax: 2824 0595.
www.fso-tela.gov.hk.

Hong Kong Film Academy,
Room 906 Sunbeam Commercial
Building, 469-471 Nathan Road,
Kowloon. Tel: 2786 9349.
Fax: 2742 7017.
www.filmacademy.com.hk.

**Hong Kong Film Awards
Association**, Room 1601-2 Austin
Tower, 22-26A Austin Ave, Tsim
Sha Tsui, Kowloon. Tel: 2367 7892.
Fax: 2723 9597. ww.hkfaa.com.

**Hong Kong Film Critics
Association**, 4G, Hoi To Court,
275 Gloucester Rd, Causeway Bay,
Tel: 2573 7498. Fax: 2574 6726.
www.hkfca.org.

Hong Kong Film Critics Society,
Unit 104, 1/F, Corn Yan Centre, 3
Jupiter St, Tin Hau.
Tel: 2575 5149. Fax: 2891 2048.
www.filmcritics.org.hk.

Hong Kong Film Directors Guild,
2/F, 35 Ho Man Tin St, Kowloon.
Tel: 2760 0331. Fax: 2713 2373.
www.hkfdg.com.

Hong Kong Film Institute, 6/F,
Pak Cheung Building, 295 Lai Chi
Kok Rd, Kowloon. Tel: 2728 2690.
Fax: 2728 5743. www.hkfilm.com.

**Hong Kong, Kowloon and New
Territories Motion Picture
Industry Association**, 13/F, Tung
Wui Commercial Bldg, 27 Prat Ave,
Tsim Sha Tsui, Kowloon.
Tel: 2311 2692. Fax: 2311 1178.
www.mpia.org.hk.

**Hong Kong Theatres
Association**, 21/F, Hong Kong
Chinese Bank, 42 Yee Woo St,
Causeway Bay.
Tel: 2576 3833. Fax: 2576 1833.

HUNGARY

All Tel/Fax numbers begin (36 1)

Archive

Hungarian National Film Archive,
Budakeszi Ut 51B, H-1021
Budapest. Tel: 200 8739.
Fax: 398 0781. filmintezet@ella.hu.
www.filmintezet.hu.
Stock: 7,022 feature titles, 8,713
short films, 3,756 newsreels,
13,224 books, 3,710 periodicals,
2,708 scripts, 5,381 manuscripts,
143,159 stills, 15,365 posters. In
addition to housing the archive,
the institute does research into
the history of cinema, particularly
Hungarian cinema, and
encourages the development of
film culture in Hungary.

Film School

Academy of Drama & Film,
Szentkiralyi Utca 32A, H-1088,
Budapest. Tel: 338 4855.

Magazine

Filmvilag, Hollan Ernö Utca 38A,
H-1137 Budapest.
filmvilag@chello.hu.
www.filmvilag.hu. Monthly with
reviews and interviews.

Useful Addresses

**Association of Hungarian Film
Artists**, Városligeti Fasor 38,
H-1068 Budapest. Tel/Fax: 342
4760. filmszovetseg@axelero.hu.

**Association of Hungarian
Producers**, Szinhaz Utca 5-9,
H-1014 Budapest. Tel: 355 7049.
Fax: 355 7639.
producer@mpsz.axelerol.net.

Hungarian Film Union, Városligeti
Fasor 38, H-1068 Budapest.
Tel: 351 7760/1. Fax: 352 6734.
filmunio@filmunio.hu.
www.filmunio.hu.

**Hungarian Motion Picture
Foundation**, Városligeti Fasor 38,

H-1068 Budapest. Tel: 351 7696. Fax: 352 8789. www.mma.hu.

Hungarian Independent Producers Assocation, Róna Utca 174, H-1145 Budapest. Tel: 220 5421. Fax: 220 5420. eurofilm@axelero.hu.

National Film Office, Wesselenyi Utca 16, H-1075 Budapest. Tel: 327 7070. Fax: 321 9224. info@filmoffice.hu.

ICELAND
All Tel/Fax numbers begin (354)

Archive
National Film Archive, Hvaleyrarbraut 13, 220 Hafnarfjordur. Tel: 565 5993. Fax: 565 5994. kvikmyndasafn@kvikmyndasafn.is. www.kvikmyndasafn.is. Nearly 400 titles in the collection, the majority documentaries. Numerous sources of information regarding Icelandic films and the national film history.

Film Schools
Icelandic Film & Television Academy, Túngata 14, 101 Reykjavík. Tel: 861 9126/562 6660. Fax: 562 6665. kristinatla@simnet.is. bjorn@hugsjon.is. www.spark.is.

Icelandic Film School, Laugarvegur 176, 105 Reykjavík. Tel: 533 3309 Fax: 533 3308. kvikmyndaskoli@kvikmyndaskoli.is. www.kvikmyndaskoli.is.

Useful Addresses
Association of Icelandic Film Directors, Leifsgata 25, 101 Reykjavík. Tel: 588 6003/898 0209. ho@ismennt.is.

Association of Icelandic Film Distributors, SAM-Bíóin, Álfabakka 8, 109 Reykjavík. Tel: 575 8900. Fax: 587 8910. thorvaldur@sambio.is.

Association of Icelandic Film Producers, Túngötu 14, PO Box 5367, 125 Reykjavík. Tel: 863 3057. Fax: 555 3065. sik@producers.is. www.producers.is.

Film Censor, Túngötu 14, 101 Reykjavík. Tel: 562 8020. kvikmynd@mmedia.is. www.mmedia.is/~kvikmynd/.

Icelandic Film Centre, Túngötu 14, 101 Reykjavík. Tel: 562 3580. Fax: 562 7171. info@icelandicfilmcentre.is. www.icelandicfilmcentre.is.

Icelandic Film Makers Association, PO Box 5162, 128 Reykjavík. Tel: 562 6660. Fax: 562 6665. bjorn@spark.is.

Icelandic Film & Television Academy/EDDA Awards, Túngötu 14, 101 Reykjavík. Tel: 562 3580. Fax: 562 7171. bjorn@ spark.is.

INDIA

Archive
National Film Archive of India, Law College Rd, Pune 411 004. Tel: (91 020) 565 8049. Fax: 567 0027. nfai@vsnl.net. Its objective is to acquire, preserve and restore the rich heritage of national cinema, and the cream of international cinema.

Film School
Film & Television Institute of India, Law College Rd, Pune 411 004. Tel: (91 020) 543 1817/3016/0017. www.ftiindia.com.

Magazine
Film India Worldwide, Confederation of Indian Industry, 105 Kakad Chambers, 132 Dr Annie Besant Rd, Worli, Mumbai 400 018. Tel: (91 22) 2493 1790. Fax: 2493 9463. www.ciionline.org. www.ciiwest.org. In addition to

news, views and reviews, *FIWW* offers an interactive databank service that covers: new Indian cinema, film based material referenced for teaching purposes, casting service for actors of Indian origin criss-crossing the globe, news and programming of Indian films for film festivals, etc.

Useful Addresses
Film Federation of India, B/3 Everest Bldg, Tardeo, Bombay 400 034. Tel/Fax: (91 22) 2351 5531. Fax: 2352 2062. supransen22@hotmail.com.

Film Producers Guild of India, G-1, Morya House, Veera Industrial Estate, OShiwara Link Road, Andheri (W), Mumbai 400 053. Tel: (91 22) 5691 0662/2673 3065. Fax: 5691 0661. tfpgoli1@vsnl.net. www.filmguildindia.com.

Mukta Arts, 6 Bashiron, 28th Rd, Bandra (W), Mumbai 400 050. Tel: (91 22) 2642 1332. Fax: 2640 5727. muktaarts@vsnl.com. www.muktaarts.com.

National Film Development Corporation Ltd, Discovery of India Bldg, Nehru Centre, Dr Annie Besant Rd, Worli, Bombay 400 018. Tel: (91 22) 2492 6410. www.nfdcindia.com.

INDONESIA
All Tel/Fax numbers begin (62 21)

Archive
Pusat Perfilman H Usmar Ismail, Jalan H.R. Rasuna Said Kav C-22, Kuningan, Jakarta 12940. Tel: 526 8458. Fax: 526 8456. www.pphui.or.id/.

Film Schools
Jakarta Institute of The Arts, Faculty of Film & TV, Jalan Cikini Raya 73, Jakarta 10001. Tel/Fax: 392 4018.

Science, Aesthetics and

Technology Foundation (SET), Jalan Bacang III No 5, Gandaria Mayestik, Jakarta Selatan 12130. Tel: 725 1095. Fax: 722 9638. set@indo.net.id.

Useful Addresses
Boemboe, [Distributor], Jalan Mampang Prapatan XVI No 28, Jakarta 12760. Tel/Fax: 7919 8858. boemboeforum@yahoo.com.
Kalyana Shira Film, [Producer], Jalan Bunga Mawar No 9, Cilandak, Jakarta 12410. Tel: 750 3225. Fax: 769 4318. kalyana@kalyanashira.com.
Minikino, [Producer & Distributor], Jalan Diponegoro 114, Denpasar 80113, Bali. www.minikino.org.
Miles Productions, Jalan Angeran Antasari 17, Arteri Cipete, Jakarta 12410. Tel: 750 0503/ 571 7755/6186 2587.
Ministry of Information for Film & Video, Departemen Penerangan RI, Jalan Merdeka Barat 9, Gedung Belakang, Jakarta Pusat. Tel: 384 1260. Fax: 386 0830.
Ministry of Tourism, Art and Culture, Jalan Medan Merdeka Barat 17, Jakarta 10110. Tel: 383 8000/381 0123. Fax: 386 0210. http://gateway.deparsenibud.go.id.
Offstream Production, Jalan Kelud No 23, Guntur, Setiabudi, Jakarta 12980. Tel/Fax: 829 6185. email@offstream.net. www.offstream.net.
PT Multi Inter Media, [Multivision Plus Production], Komplek Perkantoran Roxi Mas, Jalan KH Hasyim Ashari Blok C2 No 40, Jakarta 12140. Tel: 633 5103. redaksi@multivisionplus.com.
PT Soraya Intercine Films, Jalan Pintu Air Raya 20, Jakarta 10710. Tel: 380 9126/384 2371. Fax: 384 7538.
Rexinema, [Producer], Jalan Pangeran Antasari No 20,

Jakarta 12410. Tel: 769 6071. Fax: 766 1267. www.rexinema.com.
Tit's Film Workshop, [Producer & Distributor], Jalan Jatipadang-Kebagusan Raya Gg, Damai No 61C, Pasar Minggu, Jakarta 12520. Tel./Fax: 7884 3307.

IRAN
All Tel/Fax numbers begin (98 21)

Archive
National Film Archive of Iran, Baharestan Sq, Tehran 11365. Tel: 3851 2583. Fax: 3851 2710. crb@kanoon.net. Director: Mohammad Hassan Koshneviss.

Film Schools
Institute for Intellectual Development of Children & Young Adults. Tel: 871 0661. Fax: 872 9290. Info@kanoonparvaresh.com.
Sahra Film Cultural Institute, 39 Corner of 6th Alley, Eshqyar St, Khorramshahr Ave, Tehran. Tel: 876 5392/6110. Fax: 876 0488. modarresi@dpir.com.
Tamasha Cultural Institute, 124 Khorramshahr Ave, Tehran 15537. Tel: 873 3844/876 9146. Fax: 873 3844/9146. info@tamasha.net.

Useful Addresses
Behnegar, [Producer/Distributor], 3rd Floor, 9 Bahman 22nd Alley, Yakhchal St, Shariatie Ave, Tehran. info@behnegar.com.
Cima Film, [Producer/Distributor], 53 Kuhyar Alley, Fereshte St, Tehran. Tel: 221 8116/7. Fax: 221 5889.
Farabi Cinema Foundation, [Producer/Distributor], 1st Floor, No.19, Delbar Alley, Toos St, Valise-Asr Avr, Tehran 19617. Tel: 273 4939/4891. Fax: 273 4953. fcf1@dpi.net.ir. www.fcf-ir.com.

Fardis Co, [Producer/Distributor], 113 Shahid Malayeri Pour St, Fath Ave, Haftetir Sq, Tehran. Tel: 830 7732. Fax: 882 5522.
Hedayat Film, [Producer/Distributor], 15 7th St, Khaled Estamboli Ave, Tehran 15137. Tel: 872 7188/89. Fax: 871 4220. info@hedayatfilm.net.
Jozan Film, 20 Razmandegan Alley, Fajr St, Motahhari Ave, Tehran. Tel: 883 7271/83 02704. Fax: 882 6876.
Sureh Cinema Development Organisation, [Producer/ Distributor], 213 Somayeh Ave, Tehran 15998-19613. Tel: 880 5294/6682. Fax: 880 5998. international@surehcinema.com.

IRELAND

Film Schools
Ballyfermot College of Further Education, Ballyfermot Rd, Dublin 10. Tel: (353 1) 626 9421. Fax: 626 6754. info@bcfe.cdvec.ie. www.bcfe.ie.
National Film School/Institute of Art, Design & Technology, Kill Ave, Dun Laoghaire, Co Dublin. Tel: (353 1) 214 4600. Fax: 214 4700. donald.taylorblack@iadt.ie. www.iadt.ie. Head of Dept of Film & Media: Donald Taylor Black. Courses offered: Film/Television Production (Honours Degree); Direction (Add-on Degree); Animation (Honours Degree); Modelmaking/SFX (Degree); Radio Broadcasting (Higher Certificate); Make-up (Higher Certificate) and MA in Screenwriting. Full member of CILECT.

Useful Addresses
Abbey Films, [Distributor], 29 Lower Georges St, Dun Laoghaire, Co Dublin. Tel: (353 1) 236 6686. Fax: 236 6668. www.abbeyfilms@eircom.net.

Eclipse Pictures, [Distributor], 6 Eustace St, Dublin 2. Tel: (353 1) 633 6002. Fax: 633 6000. www.eclipsepictures.ie.

Film Censor's Office, 16 Harcourt Terrace, Dublin 2. Tel: (353 1) 799 6100. Fax: 676 1898. info@ifco.gov.ie.

Film Institute of Ireland, 6 Eustace St, Dublin 2. Tel: (353 1) 679 5744. Fax: 679 9657. www.fii.ie.

Irish Film Board, Rockfort House, St Augustine St, Galway, Co Galway. Tel: (353 91) 561 398. Fax: 561 405. www.filmboard.ie.

Screen Directors Guild of Ireland, 18 Eustace St, Temple Bar, Dublin 2. Tel: (353 1) 633 7433. Fax: 478 4807. info@sdgi.ie.

Screen Producers Ireland, The Studio Bldg, Meeting House Sq, Temple Bar, Dublin 2. Tel: (353 1) 671 3525. Fax: 671 4292. www.screenproducersireland.com.

ISRAEL

Archive

Israel Film Archive, Jerusalem Film Centre, Derech Hebron, PO Box 8561, Jerusalem 91083. Tel: (972 2) 565 4333. Fax: 565 4335. jer-cin@jer-cin.org.il. www.jer-cin.org.il. Director: Lia van Leer. Stock: 20,000 prints: international, Israeli, Jewish film collections. Books, periodicals, stills, posters and scripts. Film documentation and educational programme for school children and adults. Permanent exhibition of early cinema apparatus and cinema memorabilia. 6,000 members. Screening five films every day in two auditoriums. Organisers of the Jerusalem Film Festival.

Film School

Department of Cinema &

Television, David & Yoland Katz Faculty of the Arts, Tel Aviv University, Mexico Bldg, Tel Aviv. Tel: (972 3) 640 9483. Fax: 640 9935. www.tau.ac.il/arts.

Useful Addresses

Israel Film Fund, 12 Yehudith Blvd, Tel Aviv 67016. Tel: (972 2) 562 8180. Fax: 562 5992. info@filmfund.org.il. www.filmfund.org.il.

Israeli Film Council, 14 Hamasger St, PO Box 57577, Tel Aviv 61575. Tel: (972 3) 636 7288. Fax: 639 0098. etic@most.gov.il.

ITALY

Archives

Cineteca del Comune, Via Riva di Reno, 40122 Bologna. Tel: (39 051) 204 820. www.cinetecadibologna.it.

Cineteca del Friuli, Via Bini 50, Palazzo Gurisatti, 33013 Gemona del Friuli, Udine. Tel: (39 04) 3298 0458. Fax: 3297 0542. cdf@cinetecadelfriuli.org. http://cinetecadelfriuli.org. Established in 1977, this excellent Italian archive conceived the idea for the Pordenone Silent Film Festival, and organises regular screenings. Stock: 3,000 film titles, 3,300 newsreels, 18,000 books. Director: Livio Jacob; Deputy Director: Lorenzo Codelli; Librarian: Piera Patat.

Cineteca Nazionale, Via Tuscolana 1524, 00173 Rome. Tel: (39 06) 722 941. Fax: 721 1619. www.snc.it. Stock: 45,000 films, 600,000 black-and-white stills and transparencies, 50,000 posters. Viewing service for students and researchers.

Fondazione Cineteca Italiana, Villa Reale, Via Palestro 16, 20121 Milan.

Tel: (39 02) 799 224. Fax: 798 289. info@cinetecamilano.it. www.cinetecamilano.it/. President: Gianni Comencini.

Fondazione Federico Fellini, Via Oberdan 1, 47900 Rimini. Tel (39 0541) 50085. Fax: 57378. fondazione@federicofellini.it. www.federicofellini.it/.

Museo Nazionale del Cinema, Via Montebello 15, 10124 Turin. Tel: (39 011) 812 2814. www.museonazionaledelcinema.org.

Bookshop

Libreria Il Leuto, Via Di Monte Brianzo 86, 00186 Rome. Tel: (39 06) 686 9269.

Film Schools

Magica (Master Europeo in Gestione di Impresa Cinematografica e Audiovisiva), Via Lucullo 7 Int 8, 00187 Rome. Tel: (39 06) 420 0651. Fax: 4201 0898. magica@mediamaster.org. www.mediamaster.org. An international organisation offering online and in-class audiovisual and multimedia management and creative training for professionals and graduates. Specialisations include: audiovisual law and economics, multimedia studies, co-production, management in all areas of production and distribution. All the programmes are designed and taught by European and US industry professionals.

Scuola Nazionale di Cinema, Via Tuscolana 1524, 00173 Rome. Tel: (39 06) 722 941. Fax: 721 1619. snccn@tin.it. www.snc.it.

Magazines

Box Office, Via Donatello 5/B, 20131 Milan. Tel: (39 06) 277 7961. Fax: 2779 6300. www.e-duesse.it. Bi-monthly.

Cineforum, Via G. Reich 49,

24020 Torre Boldone, Bergamo.
Tel: (39 035) 361 361. Fax: 341
255. www.cineforum.it. Monthly.
Griffithiana, Cineteca del Friuli,
Via Bini 50, Palazzo Gurisatti,
33013 Gemona, Udine.
Tel: (39 04) 3298 0458. Fax: 3297
0542. cdf@cinetecadelfriuli.org.
www.cinetecadelfriuli.org.
Distribution agent in North America:
Bilingual Review Press, Hispanic
Research Center, Arizona State
University, PO BOX 872702,
Tempe, AZ 85287-2702, USA.
gary.keller@asu.edu.
Quarterly devoted exclusively to
silent cinema and animation –
in English and Italian.
Nocturno, Via Trieste 42, 20064
Gorgonzola, Milan. Tel: (39 02)
9534 0057. www.nocturno.it.
Rivista del Cinematografo,
Via Giuseppe Palombini 6, 00165
Rome. Tel: (39 06) 663 7514.
Fax: 663 7321.
ariccobene@cinematografo.it.
www.cinematografo.it.

Useful Addresses

Anica, Viale Regina Margherita
286, 00198 Rome. Tel: (39 06) 442
5961. Fax: 440 4128.
anica@anica.it. www.anica.it.
**Associazione Generale Italiana
Dello Spettacollo (AGIS)**, Via di
Villa Patrizi 10, 00161 Rome. Tel:
(39 06) 884 731. Fax: 4423 1838.
www.agisweb.it.
**Audiovisual Industry Promotion-
Filmitalia**, Via Aureliana 63, 00187
Rome. Tel: (39 06) 4201 2539. Fax:
4200 3530. www.aip-filmitalia.com.
Bianca Film, via Lampertico 7,
00191 Rome. Tel: (39 06) 329
6791. Fax: 329 6790.
biancafilm@flashnet.it.
Cattleya, Via della Frezza 59,
00186 Rome. Tel: (39 06) 367 201.
Fax: 367 2050. www.cattleya.it.
Cinecittà Holding Spa, Via

Tuscolana 1055, 00173 Rome.
Tel: (39 06) 722 861. Fax: 722 1883.
direzione@cinecitta.it.
www.cinecitta.com.
Duea Film,
Piazza Cola di Rienzo 69, 00192
Rome. Tel: (39 06) 321 4851.
Fax: 321 5108. www.dueafilm.it.
Fandango, Via Ajaccio 20, 00198
Rome. Tel (39 06) 8535 4026.
Fax: 8535 3790. www.fandango.it.
Filmauro, Via XXIV Maggio 14,
00187 Rome. Tel: (39 06) 699 581.
Fax: 6995 8410. www.filmauro.it.
Istituto Luce, Via Tuscolana 1055,
00173 Rome. Tel: (39 06) 729 921.
Fax: 722 1127. luce@luce.it.
www.luce.it.
Medusa Film, Via Aurelia Antrica
422/424, 00165 Rome.
Tel: (39 06) 663 901. Fax: 6639
0450. www.medusa.it.
Mikado Film, Via Vittor Pisani 12,
20124 Milan. Tel: (39 02) 6707
0665. Fax: 6671 1488.
www.mikado.it.
Rai Cinema, Piazza Adriana 12,
00193 Rome. Tel: (39 06) 684 701.
Fax: 687 2141. info@01distribution.it.
www.raicinema.it.
Sacher Film, Viale Piramide Cestia
1, 00153 Rome.
Tel: (39 06) 574 5353. Fax: 574
0483. sacher.film@flashnet.it.

JAPAN
All Tel/Fax numbers begin (81 3)

Archives
Kawakita Memorial Film Institute,
Kawakita Memorial Bldg,
18 Ichiban-cho, Chiyoda-ku, Tokyo
102-0082. Tel: 3265 3281.
Fax: 3265 3276. info@kawakita-
film.or.jp. www.kawakita-film.or.jp.
National Film Center,
3-7-6 Kyobashi, Chuo-ku, Tokyo
104-0031. Tel: 5777 8600.
www.momat.go.jp.

Film School
Nihon University College of Art,
4-8-24 Kudanminami, Chiyoda-ku,
Tokyo 102. Tel: 5275 8110. Fax:
5275 8310. adm@cin.nihon-u.ac.jp.
www.nihon-u.ac.jp.

Useful Addresses
Gaga Communications,
East Roppongi Bldg, 16-35
Roppongi 3-Chome, Minato-ku,
Tokyo 106-0032. Tel: 3589 1026.
Fax: 3589 1043.
fujimura@gaga.co.jp.
**Motion Picture Producers
Association of Japan**,
Tokyu Ginza Bldg 3F, 2-15-2 Ginza,
Chuo-ku, Tokyo 104-0061.
Tel: 3547 1800. Fax: 3547 0909.
eiren@mc.neweb.ne.jp.
Shochiku Co Ltd, Intl Business
Division, Togeki Bldg, 1-1 Tsukiji,
4-Chome, Chuo-ku, Tokyo 104-
8422. Tel: 5550 1623. Fax: 5550
1654. ibd@shochiku.co.jp.
**Studio Ghibli International
Distribution**, 1-4-25 Kajino-cho,
Koganei-shi, Tokyo 184-0002.
Tel: 4225 35674. Fax: 4225 35721.
mikko@tintl.co.jp.
Toei Co Ltd, Intl Dept, 2-17 Ginza,
3 Chome, Chuo-ku, Tokyo 104-
8108. Tel: 3535 7621. Fax: 3535
7622. international@toei.co.jp.
www.international@toei.co.jp.
Toho International Co Ltd,
15th Floor, Yurakucho Denki Bldg,
1-7-1 Yurakucho, Chiyoda-ku, Tokyo
100-0006. Tel: 3213 6821.
Fax: 3213 6825. tohointl@toho.co.jp.
www.toho.co.jp.
Tokyo International Anime Fair,
29F No 1 Bldg, 2-8-1 Nishi-
Shinjuku, Shinjuku-ku, Tokyo 163-
8001. Tel: 5320 4786. Fax: 5388
1463. tokyo-anime-fair@nifty.com.
UniJapan Film, 11-6 Ginza,
2-Chome, Chuo-ku, Tokyo 104-
0061. Tel: 5565 7511. Fax: 5565
7531. office@unijapan.org.

KENYA

All Tel/Fax numbers begin (254 2)

Useful Addresses
Alliance Francaise.
Tel: 336 263/4/5. Fax: 336 253.
visualfr@accesskenya.com.
ArtMatters Info, PO Box 842,
00208 Nairobi.Tel: 021 3318/733
703 374. sayit@artmatters.info.
www.artmatters.info/.
Baraka Films Ltd, [Producer],
PO Box 40158, 00100 Nairobi.
Tel: 0 2730388. Fax: 027 30388.
baraka@mitsuminet.com.
**Broadcast Automation
Technologies Limited (BATL)**, PO
Box 25639, Nairobi. Tel: 057 3571.
kenny@batl.net.
ComMatters Kenya Ltd,
PO Box 842, 00208 Nairobi.
Tel: 021 3318/733 703 374.
commatters@artmatters.info.
www.artmatters.info/.
Development Through Media,
PO Box 34696, 00100 Nairobi.
Tel: 022 8459. Fax: 022 8464.
dtm@nbnet.co.ke.
Film Production Department,
PO Box 74934, 00200 Nairobi.
Tel: 065 0120. Fax: 055 3003.
fpd@skyweb.co.ke.
Fox Theatres (EA) Ltd,
[Distributor], PO Box 40067,
Nairobi. Tel: 022 6981-4. Fax: 022
7957. trushna@foxtheatres.co.ke.
**Kenya Film & Television
Professional Association**,
PO Box 315, 00600 Nairobi.
Tel/Fax: 027 30388.
kftvpa@hotmail.com.
ShoCo_The Show Company Ltd,
PO Box 25639, Nairobi.
Tel: 057 3571. Fax: 057 5360.
kenny@batl.net.
**Themescape Movies EPZ
Limited/Themescape Media Ltd**,
PO Box 10078, 00100 Nairobi.
Tel: 057 7121.
themescape@wananchi.com.

Viewfinders Ltd, Nairobi.
Tel: 058 3582/580 869.
Fax: 058 0424.
viewfinders@africaonline.co.ke.

LATVIA

All Tel/Fax numbers begin (371 7)

Archive
Riga Film Museum,
3 Smerla St, Riga LV-1006.
Tel: 755 4190. Fax: 754 5099.
kinomuz @com.latnet.lv.

Useful Addresses
FA-Filma, Kalku 6-4a, Riga,
LV-1006. Tel: 944 3254.
fafilm@re-lab.com.
www.re-lab.lv/fafilma.
Hargla, Valtaiku 19, Riga, LV-1029.
Tel: 923 5618. Fax: 577 686.
laila_pakalnina@diena.lv.
Kaupo Filma, Stabu 17, Riga,
LV-1011. Tel: 291 720.
Fax: 270 542. kaupo@latnet.lv.
Media Desk. Tel: 505 079.
Ielda.ozola@nfc.gov.lv.
www.mediadesk.lv.
National Film Centre of Latvia,
Elizabetes 49, Riga, LV-1010.
Tel: 505 074. Fax: 505 077.
nfc@nfc.gov.lv. www.nfc.lv.
Platforma Filma,
Dzintaru Prospekts 19,
Jurmala LV-2015. Tel: 754 647.
Fax: 811 308. alina@lnt.lv.
Subjektiv Filma, Kurzemes
Prospekts 2-6, Riga, LV-1067.
Tel: 929 9564. Fax: 843 072.
subjektivfilma@inbox.lv.
Vides Filmu Studija, Pils 17,
Riga, LV-1050. Tel: 503 588.
Fax: 508 589. vfs@apollo.lv.

LEBANON

All Tel/Fax numbers begin (961 1)

Useful Addresses
Crystal Films
[Producer & Distributor],

PO Box 113-5646, Hamra, Beirut.
Tel/Fax: 567 419.
crystalff@cyberia.net.lb.
**La Office de George Haddad &
Co**, Sodiko Sq, Bloc A, 3rd Floor,
PO Box 4680, Damascus St,
Beirut. Tel: 616 600. Fax: 616 700.
info@circuitempire.com.lb.
Mideast Film Foundation,
PO Box 175088, Beirut.
Tel: 202 411. Fax: 585 693.
info@mefilmfestival.org.
National Film Centre, Ministry of
Culture, Unisco Palace, Beirut.
Tel: 807 181. Fax: 807 206.
Beirut Development & Cinema,
PO Box 116-5118, Beirut.
Tel/Fax: 293 212.
beirutdc@inco.com.
www.beirutdc.org.

LITHUANIA

All Tel/Fax numbers begin (370 5)

Archive
**Lithuanian State Archive of
Vision & Sound**, O Milasiaus G 19,
10102 Vilnius.
Tel: 247 7819. lvga@takas.lt.

Film School
**Centre of Cinema & Theatre
Information & Education**,
Bernandine G 10, 01124 Vilnius.
Tel: 262 6502. audral@theater.it.

Useful Addresses
Lithuanian Filmmakers Union,
Birutes G 18, 08117 Vilnius.
Tel/Fax: 212 0759.
lks1@auste.elnet.lt.
Ministry of Culture,
J Basanaviciaus G 5, 01118 Vilnius.
Tel: 261 2932. culture@muza.lt.
www.muza.lt.
Media Desk, J Basanaviciaus G 5,
01118 Vilnius. Tel: 212 7187.
info@mediadesk.lt.

LUXEMBOURG

All Tel/Fax numbers begin (352)

Archive

Cinémathèque Municipale de la Ville de Luxembourg,
10 Rue Eugene Ruppert,
L-2453 Luxembourg.
Tel: 4796 2644. Fax: 407 519.
cinematheque@vdl.lu.
Contains more than 16,000 films of all genres.

Useful Addresses

Association des Techniciens et des Acteurs du Cinema (ATAC),
57 Rue de l'Hippodrome,
L-1730 Luxembourg.
Tel: 483 823. Fax: 490 605.

Association Luxemboureoise des Realisateurs et Scenaristes,
102 Rue Ermesinde, L-1469
Luxembourg. Tel/Fax: 227 681.
pkmw@pt.lu

Broadcasting Centre Europe,
Centre de Television 45, Blvd Pierre
Frieden, L-1543 Luxembourg.
Tel: 4214 2700. Fax: 4214 27009.
bce@atelgroup.com.

Film Fund Luxembourg,
5 Rue Large, L-1917 Luxembourg.
Tel: 478 2165. Fax: 220 963.
info@filmfund.etat.lu.
www.filmfund.lu.

Media Desk Luxembourg,
5 Rue Large, L-1917 Luxembourg.
romain.kohn@mediadesk.etat.lu.
www.mediadesk.lu.

MALAYSIA

Useful Addresses

Film Directors Assocation of Malaysia (FDAM), Studio Merdeka
Complex, Jalan Hulu Kelang,
68000 Ampang, Kuala Lumpur.
Tel/Fax: 4107 4525.

Film Workers Assocation of Malaysia, Studio Merdeka
Complex, Jalan Hulu Kelang,
68000 Ampang, Kuala Lumpur.
Tel: 4106 0116. Fax: 4108 0008.

National Film Development Corporation (FINAS), Studio
Merdeka Complex, Jalan Hulu
Kelang, 68000 Ampang, Kuala
Lumpur. Tel: (603) 4108 5722.
Fax: 4107 5216.

MEXICO

All Tel/Fax numbers begin (52 5)

Archive

Cineteca Nacional, Avenida
México-Coyoacán 389, Col Xoco,
México DF. Tel: 1253 9314.
www.cinetecanacional.net.

Useful Addresses

Alameda Films [Distributor].
Tel: 5688 7318. Fax: 5605 8911.
Contact: Daniel Birman.
alamedafilms@iserve.net.mx.

Altavista Films [Distributor],
Insurgentes Sur 1898, Piso 12,
Col Florida, CP 03900, México DF.
Tel: 5322 3358. Contact: Francisco
González Compéan.
frago@altavista films.com.mx.

Artecinema de México
[Distributor], Gobernador Ignacio
Esteve 70, Col San Miguel
Chapultepec, CP 11850, México DF.
Tel: 5277 8999.

Arthaus Films [Distributor],
Alfonso Esparza Oteo 144-702,
Col Guadalupe Inn, CP 01020,
México DF. Tel: 5661 1430/0709.

Association of Mexican Film Producers & Distributors, Avenida
División del Norte 2462, Piso 8,
Colonia Portales, México DF.
Tel: 5688 0705. Fax: 5688 7251.

Cinema Production Workers Syndicate (STPC),
Plateros 109 Col San José
Insurgentes, México DF.
Tel: 5680 6292.
cctpc@terra.com.mx.

Dirección General de Radio,
Televisión y Cinematografía (RTC),
Roma 41, Col Juárez, México DF.
Tel: 5140 8010.
ecardenas@segob.gob.mx.

Instituto Mexicano de Cinematografía (IMCINE),
Insurgentes Sur 674 Col del Valle,
CP 03100, México DF. Tel: 5448
5300. Contact: Susana López
Aranda: suslopez@hotmail.com or
Miguel Ángel Ortega:
mercaint@institutomexicanodecine
matografía.gob.mx.

Latina [Distributor], Atletas 2, Piso
2, Col Country Club, CP 04220,
México DF. Tel: 6689.3850. Fax:
6549 1820.

Nuvisión [Distributor], Paseo de las
Lomas 1005, Lomas de
Chapultepec, CP 11000, México
DF. Tel: 5201 9102/9332.

Videocine [Distributor], Benito
Juárez 7, Col Del Carmen,
Coyoacán, CP 04100, México DF.
Tel: 5659 5929/5224 5487.

MOROCCO

Useful Address

Moroccan Cinematographic Centre, Quartier Industriel,
Ave Al Majd, BP 421, Rabat.
Tel: (212 7) 798 110. Fax: 798 105.
www.mincom.gov.ma/cinemaroc/ccm.

NETHERLANDS

Archives

Filmmuseum, Rien Hagen,
Vondelpark 3, PO Box 74782,
1070 BT Amsterdam.
Tel: (31 20) 589 1400. Fax: 683
3401. info@filmmuseum.nl.
www.filmmuseum.nl.

Netherlands Institut voor Beeld en Geluid, PO Box 1060, 1200 BB
Hilversum. Tel: (31 35) 677 2672/7.
Fax: 677 2835.
klantenservice@naa.nl. www.naa.nl.

Bookshop

Ciné-Qua-Non, Staalstraat 14, 1011 JL Amsterdam. Tel: (31 20) 625 5588. Books about film; specialty vintage posters.

Film Schools

Maurits Binger Film Institute, Nieuwezijds Voorburgwal 4-10, 1012 RZ Amsterdam. Tel: (31 20) 530 9630. Fax: 530 9631. binger@binger.ahk.nl. www.binger.ahk.nl. Contact: Dick Willemsen. International centre for film and television opened in 1996, devoted to developing skills for working professionals. The Institute provides talented screenwriters, script editors, directors and producers with the opportunity to improve their skills under the guidance of prominent filmmakers and experienced coaches from around the world.

Netherlands Film & Television Academy (NFTA), Markenplein 1, 1011 MV Amsterdam. Tel: (31 20) 527 7333. Fax: 527 7344. info@nfta.ahk.nl. www.nfta.ahk.nl. Contact: Marieke Schoenmakers.

Magazines

Holland Animation Newsbrief, Hoogt 4, 3512 GW Utrecht. Tel/Fax: (31 30) 240 0768. info@holland-animation.nl. www.holland-animation.nl. Newsletter from the Holland Animation Foundation, published twice yearly.

Skrien, Vondelpark 3, 1071 AA Amsterdam. Tel: (31 20) 689 3831. skrien@xs4all.nl. An excellent, enthusiastic monthly.

Useful Addresses

Circle of Dutch Film Critics (KNF), PO Box 10650, 1011 ER Amsterdam. Tel: (31 6) 2550 0668. Fax: 627 5923. knfilm@xs4all.nl.

Cobo Fund, PO Box 26444, Postvak M54, 1202 JJ Hilversum. Tel: (31 35) 677 5348. Fax: 677 1995. cobo@nos.nl. Contact: Jeanine Hage.

Dutch Film Fund, Jan Luykenstraat 2, 1071 CM Amsterdam. Tel: (31 20) 570 7676. Fax: 570 7689. info@filmfund.nl. Contact: Toine Berbers.

Holland Film, Jan Luykenstraat 2, 1071 CM Amsterdam. Tel: (31 20) 570 4700. Fax: 570 7570. hf@hollandfilm.nl. www.hollandfilm.nl.

Ministry of Education, Culture & Science, Arts Dept, Sector Film, Europaweg 4, PO Box 25000, 2700 LZ Zoetermeer. Tel: (31 79) 323 4321. Fax: 323 4959. j.j.cassidy@minocw.nl.

Netherlands Cinematographic Federation (NFC), Jan Luykenstraat 2, PO Box 75048, 1070 AA Amsterdam. Tel: (31 20) 679 9261. Fax: 675 0398. info@nfc.org. Contact: Wilco Wolfers.

Netherlands Institute For Animation Film, PO Box 9358, 5000 HJ Tilburg. Tel: (31 13) 535 4555. Fax: 580 0057. niaf@niaf.nl. Contact: Ton Crone.

Rotterdam Film Fund, Rochussenstraat 3C, 3015 EA Rotterdam. Tel: (31 10) 436 0747. Fax: 436 0553. info@rff.rotterdam.nl. Contact: Jacques van Heijnigen.

More information can be found on www.hollandfilm.nl (click on Who's Where).

NEW ZEALAND

Archive

New Zealand Film Archive, PO Box 11449, Wellington. Tel: (64 4) 384 7647. Fax: 382 9595. nzfa@actrix.gen.nz. www.filmarchive.org.nz.

Magazine

Onfilm, PO Box 5544, Wellesley St, Auckland. Tel: (64 9) 630 8940. Fax: 630 1046. nick@onfilm.co.nz. www.profile.co.nz. Film, television and video magazine for New Zealand, with location reports and a production survey.

Useful Addresses

Film New Zealand, PO Box 24142, Wellington. Tel: (64 4) 385 0766. Fax: 384 5840. info@filmnz.org.nz. www.filmnz.com.

New Zealand Film Commission, PO Box 11546, Wellington. Tel: (64 4) 382 7680. Fax: 384 9719. marketing@nzfilm.co.nz.

Ministry of Economic Development, 33 Bowen St, PO Box 1473, Wellington. Tel: (64 4) 472 0030. Fax: 473 4638. www.med.govt.nz. Chief Executive: Geoff Dangerfield.

Office of Film & Literature Classification, PO Box 1999, Wellington. Tel: (64 4) 471 6770. Fax: 471 6781. information@censorship.govt.nz.

Screen Production & Development Association (SPADA), PO Box 9567, Wellington. Tel: (64 4) 939 6934. Fax: 939 6935. info@spada.co.nz.

NORWAY
All Tel/Fax numbers begin (47)

Archive

Henie-Onstad Art Centre, Sonja Henie Vei 31, 1311 Høvikodden. Tel: 6780 4880. post@hok.no. www.hok.no.

Magazine

Film & Kino, PO Box 446 Sentrum, 0104 Oslo. Tel: 2247 4628. Fax: 2247 4698. www.filmweb.no/filmogkino/tidsskriftet.

Editor: Kalle Løchen. Wide-ranging with expressive layout; covers new releases as well as national and international trade news and festival reports. The best film magazine in Scandinavia.

Useful Addresses
National Association of Municipal Cinemas (Film & Kino), PO Box 446 Sentrum, 0104 Oslo. Tel: 2247 4500. Fax: 2247 4699. Contact: Lene Løken. www.filmweb.no/filmogkino.
Norwegian Film & TV Producers Association, Dronningens Gt 16, 0152 Oslo. Tel: 2311 9313. Fax: 2311 9316. produsentforeningen@produsentforeningen.no. Contact: Tom G Eilertsen.
Norwegian Board of Film Classification, PO Box 371 Sentrum, 0102 Oslo. Tel: 2247 4660. Fax: 2247 4694. post@filmtilsynet.no. Contact: Tom Løland.
Norwegian Film Development, PO Box 904 Sentrum, 0104 Oslo. Tel: 2282 2400. Fax: 2282 2422. mail@norskfilmutvikling.no. Contact: Kirsen Bryhni.
Norwegian Film Fund, PO Box 752 Sentrum, 0106 Oslo. Tel: 2247 8040. Fax: 2247 8041. post@filmfondet.no. Contact: Stein Slyngstad.
Norwegian Film Institute, Dept of International Relations, PO Box 482 Sentrum, 0105 Oslo. Tel: 2247 4500. Fax: 2247 4597. int@nfi.no.
Norwegian Film Workers Association, Dronningens Gt 16, 0152 Oslo. Tel: 2247 4640. Fax: 2247 4689. nff@filmenshus.no. Contact: Kjetil Hervig.

PAKISTAN

Useful Addresses
Ministry of Culture, Block D, Pak Secretariat, Islamabad. Tel: (92 51) 921 3121. Fax: 922 1863.
Pakistan Film Producers Association, Regal Cinema Bldg, Sharah-e-Quaid-e-Azam, Lahore. Tel: (92 42) 732 2904. Fax: 724 1264.

PERU

All Tel/Fax numbers begin (51 1)

Useful Addresses
Asociación de Cineastas del Peru, Calle Manco Capac 236, Lima-18. Tel: 446 1829. cineperu@chavin.rcp.net.pe.
Cine Arte del Centro Cultural de San Marcos, cinearte.ccsm@unmsm.edu.pe.
Consejo Nacional de Cinematografía (Conacine), Museo de la Nación, Avenida Javier Prado 2465, Lima. Tel/Fax: 225 6479.
Encuentro Latinoamericano de Cine, Centro Cultural de la Universidad Católica, Avenida Camino Real 1075, Lima-27. Tel/Fax: 616 1616. elcine@pucp.edu.pe.

POLAND

Archives
Muzeum Kinematografi, Pl Zwyciestwa 1, 90 312 Lódz. Tel: (48 42) 674 0957. Fax: 674 9006.
National Film Library, Ul Pulawska 61, 00 975 Warsaw. Tel: (48 22) 845 5074. filmoteka@filmoteka.pl. www.fn.org.pl.

Film Schools

National Film, Television & Theatre School, 63 Targowa Str, 90 323 Lódz. Tel: (48 42) 634 5800. info@film.lodz.pl. www.filmschool.lodz.pl.
Silesian University Radio & Television Faculty, 40-955 Katowice, Ul Bytkowska 1B. Tel/Fax: (48 32) 258 7070. doktorow@us.edu.pl.

Magazines
Film, Ul Pruszkowska 17, 02 119 Warsaw. Tel: (48 22) 668 9083. Fax: 668 9183. film@film.com.pl. www.film.com.pl. Popular monthly with international slant.
Kino, Ul Chelmska 21, 00 724 Warsaw. Tel: (48 22) 841 6843. Fax: 841 9057. http//.kino.onet.pl. Culturally inclined monthly designed to promote European cinema, with interviews, reviews and essays.

Useful Addresses
Association of Polish Filmmakers, Ul Pulawska 61, 02-595 Warsaw. Tel: (48 22) 845 5132. Fax: 845 3908. biuro@sfp.org.pl. www.sfp.org.pl.
Film Polski, Ul Mazowiecki 6/8, 00 048 Warsaw. Tel: (48 22) 826 0849. Fax: 826 8455. info@filmpolski.com.pl. www.filmpolski.com.pl.
Film Production Agency, Ul Pulawska 61, 02-595 Warsaw. Tel: (48 22) 845 5324. info@pakietyfilmowe.waw.pl. www.pakietyfilmowe.waw.pl.
National Board of Radio and Television (KRRIT), Skwerks Wyszynskiego 9, 01-015 Warsaw. Tel: (48 22) 635 9925. Fax: 838 3501. krrit@krrit.gov.pl. www.krrit.gov.pl.
National Chamber of Audiovisual Producers, Ul Pulawska 61, 02-595 Warsaw. Tel: (48 22 845 6570. Fax: 845 5001. kipa@org.pl.

Polish TV Film Agency (TVP), Ul JP Woronicza 17, 00-999 Warsaw. Tel: (48 22) 547 9167. Fax: 547 4225. www.tvp.pl.

WFDIF Film Studio, Ul Chelmska 21, 00-724 Warsaw. Tel: (48 22) 841 1210-19. Fax: 841 5891. wfdif@wfdif.com.pl. www.wfdif.com.pl.

PORTUGAL

Archive

Cinemateca Portuguesa, Rua Barata Salgueiro 63, 1269-059 Lisbon. Tel: (351 21) 359 6200. Fax: 352 3180. www.cinemateca.pt.

Magazine

Estreia, Rua de Anibal Cunha 84, Sala 1.6, 4050-846 Porto. Tel: (351 22) 207 6050. Fax: 207 6059. www.estreia.online.pt. Bi-monthly magazine dealing with international and Portuguese topics.

Useful Addresses

Animatógrafo, Rua da Rosa 252, 2°, 1200-391 Lisbon. Tel: (351 21) 347 5372. Fax: 347 3252. animatografo@mail.telepac.pt.

Costa de Castelo, Avenida Engenheiro Arantes e Oliveira 11A, 1°, 1900-221 Lisbon. Tel: (351 21) 843 8020. info@costacastelo.pt. www.costacastelo.pt.

Filmes Castelo Lopes, Rua Castilho 90, 1250-071 Lisbon. Tel: (351 21) 381 2600. Fax: 386 2076. www.castelolopes.com.

Institute of Cinema, Audiovisual & Multimedia (ICAM), Rua de S Pedro de Alcântara 45, 1°, 1250 Lisbon. Tel: (351 21) 323 0800. Fax: 343 1952. mail@icam.pt. www.icam.pt.

Lusomundo Audiovisuais, Avenida da Liberdade 266, 3°, 1250 Lisbon. Tel: (351 21) 318

7300. Fax: 352 3568. www.lusomundo.pt.

MGN Filmes, Rua de S Bento 644, 4° Esq, 1250-223 Lisbon. Tel: (351 21) 388 7497. Fax: 388 7281. mgnfilmes@mail.telepac.pt.

Madragoa Filmes/Atalanta Filmes, Rua da Palmeira 6, 1200-313 Lisbon. Tel: (351 21) 325 5800. Fax: 342 8730. geral.madragoa@madragoafilmes.com. www.madragoafilmes.pt or www.atalantafilmes.pt.

Rosa Filmes, Largo Maria Isabel Aboim Inglês 2B, 1400-244 Lisbon. Tel: (351 21) 303 1810. Fax: 303 1819. rosafilmes@vianw.pt. www.rosafilmes.pt.

Short Film Agency, Apartado 214, 4481-911 Vila do Conde. Tel: (351 25) 264 6683. Fax: 263 8027. agencia@curtasmetragens.pt. www.curtasmetragens.pt.

PUERTO RICO

All Tel/Fax numbers begin (1 787)

Useful Addresses

Corporation for Public Broadcasting of Puerto Rico (Channel 6), Sonya Canetti, Director, PO Box, San Juan 00919. Tel: 766 0505. Fax: 753 9846. Contact: Lucy Boscana, Dramatic Project.

Film & Audiovisual Producers Association, PO Box 190399, San Juan 00919-0399. Tel: 725 3565. Fax: 724 4333. tvegsjpr@prtc.net. Contact: Ramón Almodóvar, President.

Puerto Rico Film Commission, PO Box 2350, San Juan 00936-2360. Tel: 754 7110. Fax: 756 5706. lavelez@pridco.com. Contact: Laura A. Vélez, Executive Director.

ROMANIA

All Tel/Fax numbers begin (40 1)

Archive

Arhiva Nationala de Filma, 4-6 Dem I Dobrescu Str, Sector 1, Bucharest. Tel: 313 4904. Fax: 313 4904. anf@xnet.ro.

Film School

Universitatea de Arta Teatrala si Cinematografica, Str Matei Voievod 75-77, Bucharest. Tel: 252 8001. www.edu.ro/uatcb.htm.

Useful Addresses

National Centre of Cinematography, Str Dem I Dobrescu 4-6, Bucharest. Tel: 310 4301. Fax: 310 4300. cncin@pcnet.ro.

Romania Film, Str Henri Coanda 27, Bucharest . Tel: 310 4499. Fax: 310 4498. coresfilm@hotmail.com.

Uniunea Cineatilor, Str Mendeleev 28-30, Sector 1, Bucharest 70169. Tel: 650 4265. Fax: 311 1246. czucin@rnc.ro.

RUSSIA

All Tel/Fax numbers begin (7 095)

Archive

Gosfilmofond of Russia, Belye Stolby, Moskovskaya Oblast 142050. Tel: 546 0520. Fax: 548 0512. General Director: Nicolai Borodatchov. gff@t50.ru. www.gosfilmofond.ru. Holds more than 55,000 motion pictures.

Magazine

Iskusstvo Kino, 9 Ul Usievich, Moscow 125319. Tel: 151 5651. Fax: 151 0272. filmfilm@mtu-net.ru. www.kinoart.ru. Chunky, theoretical; the most authoritative Russian monthly.

Useful Addresses

Alliance of Independent Distribution Companies.
Tel: 243 4741. Fax: 243 5582.
felix_rosental@yahoo.com. Contact:
Felix Rosental, Executive Director.

Double D Research & Information Group, 13
Vassilyevskaya St, Moscow
123825/Postal address: 28-2-16
Bol Polyanka St, Moscow 119180.
Tel/Fax: 238 2984. vengern@df.ru.
Contact: Daniil Dondurei,
Head of Research.

Empire Cinema,
(Major Cinema Chain),
Komsomolsky Ave 21-10,
Moscow 119146.
Tel: 241 4626. Fax: 241 4104.
general@formulakino.ru. Contact:
Marala Charyeva, President.

Federal Agency of Culture & Cinema of the Russian Federation, Film Service, 7 Maly
Gnezdnikovsky Lane, Moscow
103877. Tel: 923 8677/229 7055.
Fax: 299 9666. Contact: Alexandre
Golutva, First Deputy Minister of
Culture. Dept of International
Relations Contact: Konstantin
Borisovich Gavrushin. Tel: (7 095)
229 1096. gavrushin@kino.mkrf.ru.

Karo Premier Film Co,
Pushkin Sq, Moscow 103006.
Tel: 209 4585. Fax: 209 3812.
bessedin@karo.ru.
Contact: Irina Ussacheva, Director
of Intl. Relations.

Ministry of Culture & Mass Communication of the Russian Federation, 7 Kitaisky Proezd,
Moscow. Tel: 975 2420.
Fax: 975 2420/928 1791.

National Academy of Cinema Arts & Sciences,
13 Vassilyevskaya St, Moscow
123825. Tel: 200 4284.
Fax: 251 5370. unikino@aha.ru.
Contact: Vladimir Naumov,
President.

Russian Guild of Film Directors,
13 Vassilyevskaya St, Moscow
123825. Tel: 251 5889. Fax: 254
2100. stalkerfest@mtu-net.ru.
Contact: Marlen Khutsiev, President.

Russian Guild of Producers,
1 Mosfilmovskaya St, Moscow
119858. Tel: 745 5635/143 9028.
plechev@mtu-net/ru.
Contact: Vladimir Dostal.

Union of Filmmakers of Russia,
13 Vassilyevskaya St, Moscow
123825. Tel: 250 4114. Fax: 250
5370. unikino@aha.ru. Contact:
Nikita Mikhalkov, Chairman.

RWANDA

Useful Addresses

Future Production (Music4Films),
BP 2401, Kigali. Tel 0864 8562.
bizab@hotmail.com.

Image Media, KBC Building, BP
4556, Kigali. Tel: 517 978.
imagesmedia@rwanda1.com.

Kemit, BP 1936. Tel: 502 468.
kemit01@yahoo.fr.

Link Media Production, BP 4065,
Kigali. erickabera@yahoo.com.
admilink@yahoo.co.
www.linkmedia.co.rw. Tel: 0830
6480/0883 1324.

Nord Sud International, Avenue
de la Paix, BP183. Tel: 575 810.
iraja99@yahoo.com.

Rwanda Cinema Centre, BP
4065, Kigali. ccr_rwanda@yahoo.fr.
erickabera@yahoo.com. Tel: 0830
6480/0883 1324.

SERBIA & MONTENEGRO
All Tel/Fax numbers begin (381 11)

Archive

Yugoslav Film Archive,
Knez Mihailova 19, 11000
Belgrade. Tel/Fax: 622 555.
kinoteka@eunet.yu.
www.kinoteka.org.yu. Open to all
researchers and scientists who deal

with the history and theory of film.
Through lectures, exhibitions and
book promotions the archive takes
an active part in the education and
broadening of film culture.

Film School

Faculty of Dramatic Arts, Bulevar
Umetnosti 20, 11070 Belgrade.
Tel: 214 0419. Fax: 213 0862.
fduinfo@eunet.yu.

Useful Addresses

Association of Film Producers,
Kneza Viseslava 88, 11000
Belgrade. Tel: 323 1943. Fax: 324
6413. info@afp.yu. www.afp.co.yu.

Avala Film International,
[Production Facilities], Kneza
Viseslava 88, 11000 Belgrade.
Tel: 354 8284. Fax: 354 8410.
office@avalafilm.com.
www.avalafilm.com.

Beograd Film, [Chain of Theatres],
Terazije 40, 11040 Belgrade.
Tel: 688 940. Fax: 687 952.
www.beogradfilm.com.

Yugoslav Film Institute, Cika
Ljubina 15/II, 11000 Belgrade.
Tel: 625 131. Fax: 634 253.
ifulm@eunet.yu.

SINGAPORE
All Tel/Fax numbers begin (65)

Film School

School for Film & Media Studies,
Ngee Ann Polytechnic, Block 52,
535 Clementi Rd, Singapore
599489. Tel: 6460 6992.
Fax: 6462 5617. vtv@np.edu.sg.
www.np.edu.sg.

Useful Addresses

Cathay Organisation,
[Distributor & Exhibitor],
#02-04, 11 Unity St, Robertson
Walk, Singapore 237995.
Tel: 6337 8181. Fax: 6334 3373.
www.cathay.com.sg.

Cinematograph Film Exhibitors Association, 13th & 14th Storey, Shaw Centre, 1 Scotts Rd, Singapore 228208. Tel: 6235 2077. Fax: 6235 2860.

Eng Wah Organisation, [Distributor & Exhibitor], 400 Orchard Rd, #16-06 Orchard Towers, Singapore 238875. Tel: 6734 0028. Fax: 6235 4897. www.ewcinemas.com.sg.

Golden Village Multiplex Pte Ltd, [Distributor & Exhibitor], 68 Orchard Rd, #07-10/14 Plaza Singapura, Singapore 238839. Tel: 6334 3766. Fax: 6334 8397. www.goldenvillage.com.sg.

Mega Media, [Producer], 32 Maxwell Rd, 01-05, Whitehouse, Singapore 069115. Tel: 6536 9140. Fax: 6536 9154.

Raintree Pictures, [Producer], Caldecott Broadcast Centre, Andrew Rd, Singapore 299939. Tel: 6350 3759. Fax: 6251 1916. puiyin@raintree.com.sg. www.raintree.com.sg.

Shaw Organisation, [Distributor & Exhibitor], 1 Scotts Rd, #14-01 Shaw Centre, Singapore 228208. Tel: 6235 2077. Fax: 6235 2860. www.shaw.com.sg.

Singapore Film Commission, 140 Hill St, Mita Bldg #04-01, Singapore 179369. Tel: 6837 9943. Fax: 6336 1170. www.sfc.org.sg.

Singapore Film Society, Golden Village Marina, 5A Raffles Ave, #03-01 Marina Leisureplex, Singapore 039801. Fax: 6250 6167. ktan@sfs.org.sg. www.sfs.org.sg.

Substation, 45 Armenian St, Singapore 179936. Tel: 6337 7535. Fax: 6337 2729. wenjie@substation.org. www.substation.org.

Zhao Wei Films, [Producer], 22 Scotts Rd, Unit 01-28, Singapore 228221.

Tel: 6735 7053. Fax: 6735 7124. zhaowei@pacific.net.sg. www.zhaowei.com.

SLOVAKIA
All Tel/Fax numbers begin (421 2)

Film School
Academy of Music & Dramatic Art (V_MU), Ventúrska 3, 813 01 Bratislava. Tel: 5443 2306. www.vsmu.sk.

Useful Addresses
Association of Slovak Film & TV Directors, Konventná 8, 811 03 Bratislava. Tel: 5441 9479. artfilm@artfilm.sk.

Association of Slovak Film Distributors, Senická 17, 811 04 Bratislava. Tel: 5479 1936. Fax: 5479 1939. dusan.hajek@saturn.sk.

Association of Slovak Film Producers, Grösslingova 32, 811 09 Bratislava. Tel: 5556 5643. Fax: 5296 1939. sapa@webdesign.sk.

Slovak Film Institute, Grösslingova 32, 811 09 Bratislava. Tel: 5710 1501/27. Fax: 5296 3461. sfu@sfu.sk. www.sfu.sk.

SLOVENIA
All Tel/Fax numbers begin (386 1)

Useful Addresses
Association of Slovenian Film Makers, Miklosiceva 26, Ljubljana. e-mail. dsfu@guest.arnes.si.

Association of Slovenian Film Producers, Brodisce 23, Trzin, 1234 Menges. dunja.klemenc@guest.arnes.si

Film Studio Viba, Stegne 5, 1000 Ljubljana. Tel: 513 2402. viba.film@siol.net.

Slovenian Cinematheque, Miklosiceva 38, Ljubljana. Tel: 434 2520. silvan.furlan@kinoteka.si.

Slovenian Film Fund, Miklosiceva

38, 1000 Ljubljana. Tel: 431 3175. info@film-sklad.si.

SOUTH AFRICA

Film School
Cityvarsity Film, Television & Multimedia School, 32 Kloof St, Cape Town 8000. Tel: (27 21) 423 3366. Fax: 423 6300. amanda@cityvarsity.co.za. www.cityvarsity.co.za. Contact: Amanda Solomon. Modelled on the Vancouver International Film School, with eight departments including film, animation, acting, multimedia and sound under one roof.

Useful Addresses
Aland Pictures, 155 Buitenkant St, Gardens 8001. Contact: Carina Rubin. Tel: (27 21) 462 3306. Fax: 462 3308. carina@gem.co.za. www.fosterbrothers.co.za.

Big World Cinema, PO Box 2228, Cape Town 8000. Tel: (27 21) 488 0608. Fax: 448 1065. steven@bigworld.co.za. Contact: Steven Markovitz or Trakoshis Platon.

Cape Film Commission, 6th Floor, NBS Waldorf Bldg, 80 St George's Mall, Cape Town 8001. Tel: (27 21) 483 9070. Fax: 483 9071. martin.cuff@capetown.gov.za. Contact: Martin Cuff, CEO.

Film Afrika, PO Box 12202, Mill St, Cape Town 8010. Tel: (27 21) 461 7950. Fax: 461 7951. info@filmafrika.com. www.filmafrika.com. Contact: David Wicht.

Gauteng Film Office, 88 Fox St, Johannesburg/ PO Box 61840, Marshalltown 2107. Tel: (27 11) 833 8750. Fax: 834 6157. themba@gfo.co.za. Contact: Themba Sibeko, CEO.

Independent Producers Organisation,
PO Box 2631, Saxonwold 2132.
Tel: (27 11) 726 1189.
Fax: 482 4621. info@ipo.org.za.
www.ipo.org.za.

M-Net Local Productions,
PO Box 2963, Randburyg 2123.
Tel: (27 11) 686 6123. Fax: 686 6643. cfischer@mnet.co.za.
www.mnet.co.za.
Contact: Carl Fischer.

National Film & Video Foundation, 87 Central St, Houghton, Private Bag x04, Northlands 2116.
Tel: (27 11) 483 0880.
Fax: 483 0881. info@nfvf.co.za.
www.nvfv.co.za.
Contact: Eddie Mbalo, CEO.

Nu Metro, [Distributor],
Gallo House, 6 Hood Ave,
Rosebank, Johannesburg 2196.
Tel: (27 11) 340 9300.
Fax: 442 7030.

South African Broadcasting Co (SABC), Private Bag 1,
Auckland Park, Johannesburg 2006. Tel: (27 11) 714 9797.
Fax: 714 3106. www.sabc.co.za.

Ster-Kinekor, [Distributor],
2nd Floor, Fountainview House,
Constantia Park, Corner Hendrik
Potgieter & 14th Ave, Weltevreden
Park, Johannesburg 1715.
Tel: (27 11) 475 5699. Fax: 475 2840. www.sterkinekor.com.

Videovision Entertainment,
134 Essenwood Rd, Berea, Durban
4001. Contact: Anant Singh. Tel:
(27 31) 204 6000. Fax: 202 5000.
nilesh@videovision.co.za.
www.videovision.co.za.

SOUTH KOREA
All Tel/Fax numbers begin (82 2)

Archive
Korean Film Archive,
700 Seocho-dong, Seocho-gu,
Seoul 137-718. Tel: 521 3147.
Fax: 582 6213. www.koreafilm.or.kr.

Useful Addresses
CJ Entertainment,
[Producer/Distributor], 26th Floor,
Star Tower, 737 Yeoksam-dong,
Kangnam-gu, Seoul 100-802.
Tel: 2112 6559. Fax: 2112 6549.
www.cjentertainment.co.kr.

Cineclick Asia,
[Producer/Distributor], Incline Bldg,
3rd Floor, 891-37 Daechi-Dong,
Kangnam-gu, Seoul 135-280.
Tel: 538 0211 ext 212. Fax: 538 0479. www.cineclickasia.com.

Cinema Service,
[Producer/Distributor], 5th Floor,
Heungkuk Bldg, 43-1 Juja-dong,
Jung-gu, Seoul 100-240.
Tel: 2192 8734. Fax: 2192 8790.
www.cinemaservice.com.

Korea Pictures, 5th Floor,
Isoni Plaza, 609 Shinsa-dong,
Kangnam-gu, Seoul 135-120.
Tel: 544 4312. Fax: 3444 9831.
www.koreapictures.com.

Korean Film Council (KOFIC),
206-46, Cheongnyangni-dong,
Tongdaemun-gu, Seoul 130-010.
Tel/Fax: 958 7582. www.kofic.or.kr.

MK Buffalo, 6th Floor,
Cowell Bldg, 66-1 Banpo-dong,
Seocho-gu, Seoul 137-804.
Tel: 2193 2050. Fax: 2193 2197.
www.mkbuffalo.com.

Mirovision, [Producer/Distributor],
1-151 Shinmunro, 2 Ga,
Jongno-gu, Seoul 110-062.
Tel: 737 1185. Fax: 737 1184.
www.mirovision.com.

Show East,
10th Floor, New Seoul Bldg,
618-3 Shinsa-dong, Kangnam-gu,
Seoul 135-894.
Tel: 3445 9688. Fax: 3446 9620.
www.showeast.co.kr.

Showbox/Mediaplex,
16th Floor, Hansol Bldg,
736-1 Yeoksam-dong,
Kangnam-gu, Seoul 135-983.
Tel: 3218 5639. Fax: 3444 6688.
www.showbox.co.kr.

Tube Entertainment,
[Producer/Distributor],
664-21 Shinsa-dong, Kangnam-ku,
Seoul 135-897.
Tel: 547 8435. Fax: 547 3279.
www.tube-entertainment.co.kr.

SPAIN

Archives
Filmoteca de la Generalitat de Catalunya, Carrer del Portal de
Santa Madrona 6-8, Barcelona
08001. Tel: (34 93) 316 2780.
Fax: 316 2783.
filmoteca.cultura@gencat.net.

Filmoteca Espanola,
Calle Magdalena 10, 28012
Madrid. Tel: (34 91) 467 2600.
Fax: 467 2611.
www.cultura.mecd.es/cine/film/
filmoteca.isp.

Filmoteca Vasca,
Avenida Sancho el Sabio,
17 Trasera, Donostia,
20010 San Sebastian.
Tel: (34 943) 468 484. Fax: 469 998.
www.filmotecavasca.com.
andaluciafilmcom@fundacionava.org.

Bookshop
Ocho y Medio,
Martin de los Heros 23, 28008
Madrid. Tel: (34 91) 559 0628.
Fax: 540 0672.
libros@ochoymedio.com.
www.ochoymedio.com.
Friendly bookstore with a wide
range of Spanish and foreign
language books.

Film Schools
Academia de las Artes y las Ciencias Cinematograficas de Espana, Sagasta 20, 3º Derecha,
28004 Madrid. Tel: (34 91) 593 4648. Fax: 593 1492.
inforaca@infonegocio.com.

**Centre d'Estudis
Cinematogràfics de Catalunya,**
Casp 33 Pral, 08010 Barcelona.
Tel: (34 93) 412 0484.
Fax: 450 4283. info@cecc.es.
www.cecc.es. Three-year course.
**Escola Superior de Cinema
Audiovisuals de Catalunya
(ESCAC),** Inmaculada 25-35,
08017 Barcelona.
Tel: (34 93) 212 1562.
www.escac.es. Four-year course.
**Escuela de Cinematografía y de
la Audiovisual de la Comunidad
de Madrid (ECAM),**
Centra de Madrid a Boadilla,
Km 2200, 28223 Madrid.
Tel: (34 91) 411 0497.
escuelacine@ecam.es.
www.ecam.es.
Director: C de la Imagen.
Popular three-year course.
**Instituto de la Cinematografía y
de las Artes Audiovisuales
(ICAA),** Plaza del Rey S/N, 28070
Madrid. Tel: (34 91) 701 7000.
www.cultura.mecd.es/cine.
Media Business School,
Velazquez 14, 28001 Madrid,
Spain. Tel: (34 91) 575 9583.
Fax: 431 3303.
fcm@mediaschool.org.
www.mediaschool.org.
One of the biggest industry
training programmes.

Magazines
Academia & Boletín, Sagasta 20,
3° Derecha, 28004 Madrid.
Tel: (34 91) 593 4648/448 2321.
Fax: 593 1492.
www.sie.es/acacine/boletin.
Excellent twice yearly.
Cine & Tele Informe, Gran Via 64,
4° Derecha, 28013 Madrid.
Tel: (34 91) 541 2129.
Fax: 559 4282.
cineinforme@cineytele.com.
www.cineytele.com.
Monthly covering Spanish and

international film, video and TV.
Cinevideo 20, Calle Pantoja,
10 - 4ª Planta, 28002 Madrid.
Tel: (34 91) 519 6586. Fax: 519
5119. cinevideo@cinevideo20.es.
www.cinevideo20.es.
Fotogramas, Gran Via de les Corts
Catalanes 133, 08014 Barcelona.
Tel: (34 93) 223 2790. Fax: 432
2907. fotogramas@hachette.es.
www.fotogramas.es.
A glossy monthly with authoritative
film reviews, news, location reports
and features.
Nickelodeon, Bárbara de
Braganza 12, 28004 Madrid.
Tel: (34 91) 308 5238. Fax: 308
5885. revista@nickel-odeon.com.
www.nickel-odeon.com.
Quarterly; very well illustrated
and researched.

Useful Addresses
Andalucia Film Commission,
Avenida Matemáticos Rey Pastor
y Castro s/n, 41092 Seville.
Tel: (34 95) 446 7310/3.
Fax: 446 1516.
andaluciafilmcom@fundacionava.org.
www.andaluciafc.org/afc.
Catalan Films & TV, Portal Santa
Madrona 6-8, 08001 Barcelona.
Tel: (34 93) 316 2780.
Fax: 316 2781.
**Federación de Entidades de
Empresarios de Cine de España,**
Alberto Aguilera, 10 7° Derecha,
28003 Madrid.
Tel/Fax: (34 91) 448 8211.
feece@feece.com. www.feece.com.
**Federation of Associations of
Spanish Audiovisual Producers
(FAPAE),** Calle Luis Bunuel 2-2°
Izquierda, Ciudad de la Imagen,
Pozuelo de Alarcón, 28223 Madrid.
Tel: (34 91) 512 1660.
Fax: 512 0148. web@fapae.es.
www.fapae.es.
**Federation of Cinema
Distributors (FEDICINE),**

Orense 33, 3°B, 28020 Madrid.
Tel: (34 91) 556 9755. Fax: 555
6697. www.fedicine.com.

SRI LANKA
All Tel/Fax numbers begin (94 1)

Magazine
Cinesith, Asian Film Centre,
118 Dehiwala Rd, Boralesgamuwa.
Fax: 509 553. afc@sri.lanka.net.
www.lanka.net/asianfilm/.
Sri Lanka's only serious film
magazine focuses on national and
international cinema with special
reference to Asia. Recognised as
a reference journal in Sri Lankan
universities and libraries.
Published quarterly.

Useful Addresses
Ceylon Theatres Ltd,
[Producer, Exhibitor & Importer],
8 Sir C Gardiner Mawatha,
Colombo 02. Tel: 431 242/109.
Eap Film & Theaters (PVT) Ltd,
[Producer, Distributor, Exhibitor &
Importer], Savoy Bldg, 12 Galle Rd,
Wellawatta, Colombo 06.
Tel: 552 877. Fax: 552 878.
eapfilms@sltnet.lk.
National Film Corporation,
[Distributor & Importer], 303
Bauddhaloka Mawatha,
Colombo 07. Tel: 580 247.
Fax: 585 526. filmcorp@sltnet.lk.
Winson Films,
[Producer & Importer], 215/2 Park
Rd, Colombo 05. Tel: 503 451.
Fax: 588 213. winfilms@dynanet.lk.
Contact: Ranjith Perera, Chairman.

SWEDEN

Archives
Cinemateket, Swedish Film
Institute, Box 27126, SE-102 52
Stockholm. Tel: (46 8) 665 1100.
Fax: 666 3698. info@sfi.se.
www.sfi.se. Stock: 19,000 film

titles, 42,000 books, 250 subscriptions to periodicals, 1,500,000 film stills, 31,000 posters, and unpublished script material on 7,650 foreign films and 1,950 Swedish films. The collection of microfilmed clippings holds 53,500 jackets on individual films, 17,000 jackets on film personalities and jackets on general subjects classified by the FIAF scheme. Cinemateket has four daily screenings at two theatres in Stockholm. A selection of the programme is also shown in Göteborg and Malmö.

Swedish National Archive for Recorded Sound & Moving Images, Box 24124, SE-10451 Stockholm. Tel: (46 8) 783 3700. Fax: 663 1811. info@ljudochbildarkivet.se.

Bookshop

Movie Art Gallery, Sodra Hamngatan 2, SE-411 06 Goteborg. Tel/Fax: (46 31) 151 412. www.movieartofsweden.com. New and vintage film posters, stills, postcards, props, T-shirts. Mail order available.

Film Schools

University College of Film, Radio, Television & Theatre, Box 27090, SE-102 51 Stockholm. Tel: (46 8) 665 1300. Fax: 662 1484. kansli@draminst.se. www.draminst.se. University Diploma in Performing Arts & Media.

University of Stockholm, Department of Cinema Studies, Borgvägen 1-5, Box 27062, SE-102 51 Stockholm. Tel: (46 8) 674 7000.

Magazines

Film International, Lilla Fiskaregatan 10, SE-222 22 Lund. Tel/Fax: (46 46) 137 914. michael.tapper@filmint.nu. www.filmint.nu.

Ingmar, Hantverkargatan 88, SE-112 38 Stockholm. Tel: (46 8) 652 4806. redrum@ingmar.se.

Stardust Magazine, Holländargatan 22, 113 59 Stockholm. Tel: (46 8) 690 0580. seo@stardustmagazine.se. www.stardustmagazine.se. Eleven issues per year.

Teknik & Mnniska (TM), Borgvgen 1-5, PO Box 27126, SE-102 52 Stockholm. Tel: (46 8) 665 1100. Fax: 662 2684. tm@sfi.se. www.sfi.se/tm. Six issues per year. News of Swedish production from the Swedish Film Institute.

Useful Addresses

Swedish Film Distributors Association, Box 23021, SE-10435 Stockholm. Tel: (46 8) 441 5570. Fax: 343 810.

Swedish Film Institute, Box 27126, SE-10252 Stockholm. Tel: (46 8) 665 1100. Fax: 666 3698. info@sfi.se.

Swedish Film Producers Association, Box 27298, SE-102 53 Stockholm. Tel: (46 8) 665 1255. Fax: 666 3748. info@frf.net.

SWITZERLAND

Archives

Cinémathèque Suisse, Casino de Montbenon, 3 Allée Ernest Ansermet, CP 2512, 1002 Lausanne. Tel: (41 21) 331 0101. Fax: 320 4888. lausanne@cinematheque.ch. www.cinematheque.ch. Stock: 60,000 titles (1,500,000 reels), 600 apparati, 40,000 posters, 5,000,000 prints, 19,000 books, and 1,500,000 stills. Three screenings each day.

Cinémathèque Suisse, Dokumentationsstelle Zürich, Neugasse 10, Postfach, CH-8031 Zürich. Tel: (41 43) 818 2465. www.cinematheque.ch.

Bookshops

Filmbuchhandlung Rohr, Oberdorfstr 3, CH-8024, Bern. Tel: (41 1) 251 3639. Fax: 251 8922. For many years, Hans Rohr has offered an efficient and reliable mail order service for any book or magazine in print.

Librairie du Cinema, 9 rue de la Terrassiere, CH-1207, Geneva. Tel: (41 22) 736 8888. Fax: 736 6616. www.librairieducinema.ch. Immaculate display of posters, books, stills, postcards, photos, soundtrack CDs and videos. A veritable treasure trove for the movie buff.

Film Schools

Hochschule Für Gestaltung Und Kunst, Studienbereich Film/Video, Limmatstrasse 65, CH-8031 Zürich. Tel: (41 43) 446 3112. Fax: 446 2355. www.hgkz.ch.

Hochschule Für Gestaltung Und Kunst Luzern, Rössligasse 12, CH-6003 Lucerne. Tel: (41 41) 228 5460. Fax: 410 8084. www.hgk.fhz.ch.

Ecole Cantonale d'Art de Lausanne, Département Cinéma, 46 Rue de l'Industrie, CH-1030 Bussigny-Lausanne. Tel: (41 21) 316 9223. Fax: 316 9266. www.ecal.ch.

Ecole Supérieure des Beaux Arts, Section Cinéma/Vidéo, 2 Rue Général Dufour, CH-1204 Geneva. Tel: (41 22) 317 7820. Fax: 310 4636. www.hesge.ch/esba.

Magazines

Ciné-Bulletin, Rue du Maupas 10, CP 271, CH-1000 Lausanne. Tel: (41 21) 642 0303. Fax: 642 033. www.cine-bulletin.ch. Serious Swiss monthly in French and German with box-office news and films in production.

Film Bulletin, Hard 4, Postfach 68, CH-8408 Winterthur. Tel: (41 52) 226 0555. Fax: 226 0556. www.filmbulletin.ch. Informative, straightforward look at international cinema, with useful Swiss material. Bi-monthly. Strong in film history, essays on the work of famous directors, plus varied interviews.

Hors-Champ, Revue de cinéma, Rue de la Vigie 3, CH-1003 Lausanne. Tel: (41 24) 441 0870. Fax: 323 9253. Twice-yearly.

Swiss Audiovisual Guide, c/o Avant Première, Rédaction 35, Rue des Bains, CH-1205 Geneva. Tel: (41 22) 809 9494. Annual publication.

Useful Addresses

Federal Office of Culture & Film, Hallwylstrasse 15, CH-3003 Bern. Tel: (41 31) 322 9271. Fax: 322 5771. www.kultur-schweiz.admin.ch.

Film Location Switzerland, Place de la Gare 3, CH-1800 Vevey. Tel: (41 21) 648 0380. Fax: 648 0381. info@filmlocation.ch. www.filmlocation.ch.

Gruppe Autoren, Regisseure, Produzenten (GARP), Postfach 1211, CH-8034 Zürich. Tel/Fax: (41 43) 344 5945. info@garp-cinema.ch. www.garp-cinema.ch.

ProCinema, Schweizerischer Verband Für Kino Und Filmverleih, Schwarztorstrasse 56, CH-3000 Berne 14. Tel: (41 31) 387 3700. Fax: 387 3707. www.procinema.ch.

Swiss Film Assocation, Theaterstrasse 4, CH-8001 Zürich. Tel: (41 1) 258 4110. Fax: 258 4111. info@swissfilm.org. www.swissfilm.org.

Swiss Film Producers Association (SFP), Zinggstrasse 16, CH-3007 Bern. Tel: (41 31) 370 1060. Fax: 372 4053. info@swissfilmproducers.ch. www.swissfilmproducers.ch.

Swiss Filmmakers Association, Clausiusstrasse 68, Postfach, CH-8033 Zürich. Tel: (41 1) 253 1988. Fax: 253 1948. www.realisateurs.ch.

Swiss Films, Neugasse 6, Postfach, CH-8031 Zürich. Tel: (41 43) 211 4050. Fax: 211 4060. info@swissfilms.ch. www.swissfilms.ch.

SYRIA

All Tel/Fax numbers begin (963 11)

Magazine

Al Haya Al Cinemaia, Rawda 26 Takritt, Damascus. Tel: 333 1884. Fax: 332 3556. cinema@mail.sy. A quarterly film magazine published by the National Film Organization devoted to local and (translated) film studies.

Useful Address

National Film Organisation, Rawda 26 Takritt, Damascus. Tel: 333 1884. Fax: 332 3556. cinema@mail.sy.

TAIWAN

All Tel/Fax numbers begin (886 2)

Archive

Chinese Taipei Film Archive, 4F, 7 Chingtao East Rd, Taipei. Tel: 2392 4243. Fax: 2392 6359. www.ctfa.org.tw.

Useful Addresses

3H Productions Ltd, 2F, 5, Lane 23, Wanning St, Taipei 116. Tel: 2239 5822. Fax: 2230 3963.

Arc Light Films, 1F, 19 Lane 2, Wanli St, Taipei 116. Tel: 2230 7639. Fax: 2230 7454. www.arclightfilms.com.tw.

CMC Magnetics Corp, 15F, 53 Mingchuan West Rd, Taipei 104. Tel: 2598 9890. Fax: 2597 3047. www.cmcnet.com.tw.

Central Motion Picture Corp, 6/F, 116 Hanchung St, Taipei 108. Tel: 2371 5191. Fax: 2331 9241. www.movie.com.tw.

Chang Tso-chi Film Studio, 2F, 1 Yuying St, Taipei. Tel: 8663 5179. Fax: 8663 5182. www.changfilm.com.tw.

Core Image Production Co, 1F, 2 Wusheng St, Lane 449, Alley 2, Taipei 110. Tel: 2345 5245. Fax: 2723 3763. www.coremovies.com.

Digital Content Industry Promotion Office, Suite 1105, 18 Chang'an E Rd, Sec 1, Taipei 104. Tel: 2536 1226. Fax: 2536 2100. www.digitalcontent.org.tw.

Flash Forward Entertainment, 6 Henyang Rd, #807, Taipei 100. Tel: 2311 7275. Fax: 2311 7276. www.ffe.com.tw.

Good Film Co, 3A, 9 Sanmin Rd, Taipei 105. Tel: 2753 4055. Fax: 2760 5188.

Government Information Office, Department of Motion Picture Affairs, 2 Tientsin St Taipei 100. Tel: 3356 7870. Fax: 2341 0360. www.gio.gov.tw.

Homegreen Films, 27 Shuanghe St, Yung Ho, Taipei. Tel: 2920 8422. Fax: 2920 8421.

Motion Picture Association of Taipei, 5F, 196 Chunghwa Rd, Sec 1, Taipei. Tel: 2331 4672. Fax: 2381 4341.

Nan Fang Film Productions, 2F, No 33, 290 Lane, Kuangfu

South Rd, Taipei.
Tel: 2771 1622. Fax: 2731 9983.
Pandasia Entertainment Corp,
No 24, Lane 50, Nankang Rd,
Sec 3, Taipei 115.
Tel: 2785 9010. Fax: 2785 2944.
www.pandasia.com.tw.
**Public Television Service
Foundation**, No 70, Lane 75,
Kangning Rd, Sec 3, Taipei.
Tel: 2630 1892. Fax: 2633 8050.
www.pts.org.tw.
Rice Film International Co Ltd,
1F, 346-1 Fujin St, Taipei 105.
Tel: 8787 1060. Fax: 8787 1061.
www.ricefilm.com.tw.
Sinomovie Co Ltd,
5F, 67-4 Chunghsiao East Rd,
Taipei. Tel: 8771 9392.
Fax: 8771 9391.
www.sinomovie.com.
Three Dots Entertainment, 3F,
189 Minsheng West Rd, Taipei 103.
Tel: 2557 5157. Fax: 2557 5094.
www.3dots-entertainment.com.
**Yen Ping Films Production
Pte Ltd**, 1F, 178-1 Sungteh Rd,
Taipei 110. Tel: 8780 6086.
Fax: 8780 6040.
**Zoom Hunt International
Production Co**, 12F-1, 140 Sec 2,
Roosevelt Rd, Taipei 100.
Tel: 2364 2020. Fax: 2367 0627.
www.zoomhunt.com.tw.

THAILAND

All Tel/Fax numbers begin (66 2)

Archive
National Film Archive,
93 Moo 3, Phutthamonton 5 Rd,
Salaya, Nakorn Prathom 73170.
Tel: 441 0263/4 ext 116.

Useful Addresses
Cinemasia,
73/5 Ladprao 23, Ladyao, Jatujak,
Bangkok 10900.
Tel: 939 0693-4.
office@cinemasia.co.th.

Film Board Secretariat, 7th Floor,
Public Relations Dept, Soi Aree
Samphan, Rama VI Rd, Bangkok
10400. Fax: 618 2364/72.
thaifilmboard@hotmail.com.
Five Star Production Co Ltd,
[Producer/Distributor],
61/1 Soi Thaweemit 2, Rama 9 Rd,
Huaykwang, Bangkok 10310.
Tel: 246 9025-9.
info@fivestarent.com.
www.fivestarent.com.
GMM Tai Hub Co Ltd,
[Producer/Distributor], 92/11 Soi
Taweesuk Sukhumvit 31, Klongton
Nua Wattana, Bangkok 10110. Tel:
662 6223. www.gmmtaihub.com.
Matching Motion Pictures,
16th Sriayudthaya Bldg, 487/1
Sriayudthya Rd, Rajchathewi,
Bangkok10400. Tel: 248 8071-6.
chalermkiat_mmp@matchinggroup.com.
www.matchinggroup.com.
RS Film International,
[Producer/Distributor], 419/1
Ladphrao 15, Jatujak, Bangkok
10900. Tel: 511 0555 ext 85.
pornrudee@rs-film.com.www.rs-film.com.
Sahamongkol Film, SP (IBM) Bldg,
338 Room 3B, Phaholyothin Rd,
Phyathai, Bangkok 10400.
Tel: 273 0930-9.
www.sahamongkolfilm.com.

TURKEY

All Tel/Fax numbers begin (90 212)

Archive
Turkish Film & Television Institute,
80700 Kislaönü-Besiktas, Istanbul.
Tel: 266 1096. Fax: 211 6599.
sinematv@msu.edu.tr.
The Institute is a science and art
centre engaged in cinema and
television education, research and
archiving. Stock: 6,000 film titles,
3,500 video titles. Library of books,
periodicals, newspaper clippings and
photos available to researchers.

Useful Addresses
Association of Actors (CASOD),
Istiklal Caddesi, Atlas Sinemasi,
Pasaj-C Blok 53/3, Beyoglu,
Istanbul. Tel: 251 9775.
Fax: 251 9779. casod@casod.org.
**Association of Directors (FILM-
YON)**, Ayhan Isik Sokak 28/1,
Beyoglu, Istanbul. Tel: 293 9001.
**Association of Film Critics
(SIYAD)**, Hakki Sehithan Sokak-
Barlas Apt 33/13, Ulus, Istanbul.
Tel: 279 5998. Fax: 269 8284.
al.dorsay@superonline.com.
Contact: Atilla Dorsay.
**Istanbul Culture & Arts
Foundation (IKSV)**,
Istiklal Caddesi, Louvre Apt 146,
800070 Beyoglu, Istanbul.
Tel: 334 0700. Fax: 334 0702.
film.fest@istfest-tr.org.
Özen Film,
[Producer/Distributor], Sakizaggaci
Caddesi, 21 Beyoglu, Istanbul.
Tel: 293 7070/1. Fax: 244 5851.
ozenfilm@superonline.com.
**Turkish Cinema & Audiovisual
Culture Foundation (TÜRSAK)**,
Gazeteci Erol Dernek Sokak,
11/ 2 Hanif Han, Beyoglu, Istanbul.
Tel: 244 5251. Fax: 251 6770.
tursak@superonline.com.
UIP, [Producer/Distributor],
Spor Caddesi, Acisu Sokak,
Tahsin Bey Apt 1- D 7-8,
90690 Macka, Istanbul.
Tel: 227 8205. Fax: 227 8207.
www.uip.com.
Umut Sanat,
[Producer/Distributor], Akasyali
Sokak 18, 4 Levent, Istanbul.
Tel: 325 8888. Fax: 278 3282.
info.umut@umutsanat.com.tr.
Warner Bros,
[Producer/Distributor],
Topcu Caddessi, Uygun Is Merkezi
2/6, 80090 Taksim, Istanbul.
Tel: 219 2030. Fax: 219 2035.
haluk.kaplanoglu@warnerbros.com.

UKRAINE

All Tel/Fax numbers begin (380 44)

Archive

Central State Archives of Film,
Photo & Sound Documents,
24 Solomyanska St, Kiev 252601.
Tel: 277 3777. Fax: 277 3655.

Useful Addresses

Dovzhenko National Film Studio,
Prospekt Peremogy 44,
Kiev 252057.
Tel: 446 9231. Fax: 446 4044.
**Karpenko-Kary Kiev State
Institute of the Theatre Arts,**
40 Yaroslaviv St, Kiev 252034.
Tel: 212 1142. Fax: 212 1003.
Ministry of Culture & Art,
19 Franka St, Kiev 252030.
Tel: 226 2645. Fax: 225 3257.
Odessa Film Studio,
Frantsuzky Bulvar 33, Odessa
270044. Tel: 260 0355.
Fax: 260 0355.
Studio 1+1,
14/1 Mechnikova St,
1st Entrance, 5th Floor, Kiev
252023. Tel: 246 4600.
Fax: 246 4518.
Ukrainian Filmmakers Union,
6 Saksaganskogo St, Kiev 252033.
Tel: 227 7557. Fax: 227 3130.

UNITED ARAB EMIRATES

Dubai Media City, PO Box 53777,
Dubai, UAE. Tel: (971 4) 391 4555.
Fax: 391 4657.
www.dubaimediacity.com

UNITED KINGDOM

Archives

Imperial War Museum,
Lambeth Rd, London SE1 6HZ.
Tel: (44 20) 7416 5320. Fax: 7416
5374. filmcommercial@iwm.org.uk.
www.iwmcollections.org.uk.
Stock: over 120 million feet of

actuality film relating to conflict in
the twentieth Century, from Britain
and other countries. Viewing
facilities for students and
researchers, by appointment only;
public film screenings.
**National Film & Television
Archive,** British Film Institute,
21 Stephen St, London W1P 1LN.
Tel: (44 20) 7255 1444.
Fax: 7436 0439.
cataloguing.films@bfi.org.uk.
www.bfi.org.uk.
Stock: 275,000 film and television
titles, over 5,000,000 black-and-
white stills, 700,000 colour
transparencies, 18,000 posters,
2,500 set-designs. Viewing service
for students and researchers.
Scottish Screen Archive,
1 Bowmont Gardens, Glasgow
G12 9LR. Tel: (44 141) 337 7400.
Fax: 337 7413.
archive@scottishscreen.com.
www.scottishscreen.com.
The archive was established in
1976 to locate, preserve and
provide access to moving images
reflecting Scottish history. The
collection dates from 1896 and
concerns aspects of Scottish
industrial, agricultural, social and
cultural history.

Bookshops

Cinema Bookshop,
13-14 Great Russell St, London
WC1B 3NH. Tel: (44 20) 7637 0206.
Fax: 7436 9979.
Fred Zentner's film bookshop close
to the British Museum has
succeeded by virtue of prompt and
friendly service and an eye for rare
items. Books in print, out of print,
stills and posters.
Cinema Store, Unit 4B/C,
Orion House, Upper Saint Martin's
Lane, London WC2H 9NY.
Tel: (44 20) 7379 7838. Fax: 7240
7689. cinemastor@aol.com.

www.thecinemastore.com.
Fine selection of magazines, toys and
models, laser discs, DVDs, posters
etc. in friendly and recently expanded
store; now stocking rare/new VHS,
soundtracks and trading cards.
Mail order catalogue £1.
Flashbacks, 6 Silver Place,
Beak St, London, W1F 0JS.
Tel/Fax: (44 20) 7437 8562.
shop@flashbacks.freeserve.co.uk
www.dacre.org/.
Most impressively stocked
establishment in London's West
End that caters for those interested
in movie ephemera – posters, stills,
press books – from many countries
and every period of cinema history.
Also extensive mail order service.
No catalogues issued, but
individual requests answered.
Mon to Sat, 10:30am to 7pm.
Greenroom Books, 9 St James Rd,
Ilkley, West Yorkshire LS29 9PY.
Tel: (44 1943) 607 662.
greenroombooks@blueyonder.co.uk.
Mail order service for second-hand
books on the performing arts.
Ed Mason, Room 301,
Riverbank House, 1 Putney Bridge
Approach, London, SW6 3JD.
Tel: (44 20) 7736 8511.
Organises the Collector's Film
Convention. Held six times a year at
Westminster Central Hall, London.
Movie Boulevard,
3 Cherry Tree Walk, Leeds LS2
7EB. Tel: (44 113) 242 2888.
Fax: 243 8840.
rick@movieboulevard.co.uk.
www.movieboulevard.co.uk.
Welcome north of England
addition to the ranks of shops
specialising in soundtracks,
DVDs and memorabilia.
**Offstage Film & Theatre
Bookshop,** 37 Chalk Farm Rd,
London, NW1 8AJ. Tel: (44 20)
7485 4996. Fax: 7916 8046.
offstagebookshop@aol.com.

Bright square space crammed with play and film scripts and books on all aspects of theatrical, broadcast and cinematic media, including criticism, stagecraft, comedy, writing and education.

Rare Discs, 18 Bloomsbury St, London WC1B 3QA.
Tel: (44 20) 7580 3516.
masheter@softhome.net.
Specialists in film soundtracks and vinyl and film memorabilia.

Reel Poster Gallery,
72 Westbourne Grove, London W2 5SH. Tel: (44 20) 7727 4488.
Fax: 7727 4499.
info@reelposter.com.
www.reelposter.com.
London's first gallery dedicated to original vintage film posters.
An extensive yet selective stock includes posters of all genres, from Westerns to science fiction, and Hollywood classics to cult titles, seen through the eyes of artists from various countries.

Shipley Media, 80 Charing Cross Rd, London WC2H 0BB.
Tel: (44 20) 7240 4157. Fax: 7240 4186. www.artbooks.co.uk.
Selection of new and out-of-print film books, mainly American, British and World cinema, film theory and a directors section. Mail order inquiries welcome.

Film Schools

London International Film School,
24 Shelton St, London WC2H 9UB.
Tel: (44 20) 7836 9642.
Fax: 7497 3718. info@lfs.org.uk.
www.lfs.org.uk.
Principal: Ben Gibson.
Offers a practical, two-year MA course to professional levels. About half of each term is devoted to film production and the other half to practical and theoretical tuition.
All students work on one or more films each term and are encouraged

to experience different skill areas. Facilities include two cinemas, shooting stages, rehearsal stages, and 15 cutting rooms. Equipment includes 16mm and 35mm Panavision, ArriFlex and rostrum cameras, Nagra recorders, Steenbeck editing machines and U-matic video. Faculty made up of permanent and visiting professionals. Entrance requirements: a degree or art or technical diploma, with exceptions for special ability or experience. Applicants must submit samples of their work and be proficient in English. New courses commence each Jan, April and Sept.

Middlesex University, School of Arts, Cat Hill, Barnet, Herts EN4 8HT. Tel: (44 20) 8411 5066.
Fax: 8411 5013. www.mdx.ac.uk.

National Film & Television School,
Station Rd, Beaconsfield, Bucks, HP9 1LG. Tel: (44 1494) 671 234.
Fax: 674 042. admin@nftsfilm-tv.ac.uk. www.nftsfilm-tv.ac.uk.
MA Courses in: Directing (Animation, Documentary or Fiction); Cinematography; Editing; Post-production Sound; Producing; Production Design; Composing for Film & TV; Screenwriting. Diploma in Sound Recording. Project Development Labs for experienced professionals. Short courses for freelancers. Short courses in digital post-production.

School of Art, Media & Design,
University of Wales College, Newport, Caerleon Campus, PO Box 179, NP18 3YG. Tel: (44 1633) 432 643. Fax: 432610.
florenceayisi@newport.ac.uk.
www.newport.ac.uk.
BA (Hons) Film and Video, Animation, and Media and Visual Culture. MA Film.

Surrey Institute of Art & Design,
Farnham Campus, Falkner Rd, Farnham, Surrey GU9 7DS.

Tel: (44 1252) 722441.
Fax: 892616. bfoulk@surrart.ac.uk.
www.surrart.ac.uk.

University of Bristol,
Dept of Drama, Film & Television Studies, Cantocks Close, Woodland Rd, Bristol BS8 1UP.
Tel: (44 117) 928 7838. Fax: 928 7832. kate.withers@bristol.ac.uk.
www.bris.ac.uk.

University of Derby, School of Arts, Design & Technology, Kedleston Rdk Derby DE22 1GB. Tel: (44 1332) 591736. Fax: 597739.
artdesign@derby.ac.uk.
www.derby.ac.uk.

University of Stirling,
Dept of Film & Media Studies, Stirling FK9 4LA. Tel: (44 1786) 467520. Fax: 466855.
stirling.media@stir.ac.uk.
www.fms.stir.ac.uk.

University of Westminster,
Media Art & Design, Watford Rd, Northwick Park, Harrow, HA1 3TP.
Tel: (44 20) 7911 5903. Fax: 7911 5955. hunninj@wmin.ac.uk.
www.wmin.ac.uk.

Magazines

Empire, 4th Floor, Mappin House, 4 Winsley St, London W1W 8HF.
Tel: (44 20) 7436 1515.
Fax: 7343 8703.
empire@emap.com.
www.empireonline.co.uk.
Supercharged monthly with profiles, reviews and behind-the-scenes reports. Often far ahead of its rivals in breaking news and interviews.

Image Technology – Journal of the BKSTS, Pinewood Studios, Iver Heath, Buckinghamshire, SL0 0NH. Tel: (44 1753) 656656.
Fax: 657016. info@bksts.com.
www.bksts.com.
Covers technologies of motion picture film, multimedia, television and sound at professional level.
Ten times yearly.

Screen International,
33-39 Bowling Green Lane,
London, EC1R 0DA. Tel: (44 20)
7505 8080/8099. Fax: 7505 8117.
www.screendaily.com. International
film trade magazine; weekly.
Sight & Sound, British Film
Institute, 21 Stephen St, London
W1T 1LN. Tel: (44 20) 7255 1444.
Fax: 7436 2327. s&s@bfi.org.uk.
www.bfi.org.uk/sightandsound.
Established in 1932, the UK's
leading film journal. Publishes
complete cast and crew listings for
all films released in the UK.
Total Film, Future Publishing,
99 Baker St, London W1U 6FP.
Tel: (44 20) 7317 2600. Fax: 7486
5678. totalfilm@futurenet.co.uk.
The UK's fastest growing monthly
mainstream movie magazine,
covering everything from Hollywood
blockbusters to European arthouse
cinema. Editor: Matt Mueller.

Useful Addresses
**British Academy of Film &
Television Arts (BAFTA)**,
195 Piccadilly, London, W1V 0LN.
Tel: (44 20) 7734 0022.
Fax: 7734 1792. www.bafta.org.
**British Actors Equity Association,
Guild House**,
Upper St Martins Lane, London,
WC2H 9EG. Tel: (44 20) 7379 6000.
Fax: 7379 7001. info@equity.org.uk.
www.equity.org.uk.
**British Board of Film
Classification (BBFC)**,
3 Soho Sq, London, W1D 3HD.
Tel: (44 20) 7440 1570.
Fax: 7287 0141.
webmaster@bbfc.co.uk.
www.bbfc.co.uk.
British Council, Films & Literature
Dept, 10 Spring Gardens, London,
SW1A 2BN. Tel: (44 20) 7389
3051. Fax: 7389 3175.
filmandliterature@britishcouncil.org.
www.britishcouncil.org.

British Film Institute, 21 Stephen
St, London, W1T 1LN. Tel: (44 20)
7255 1444. Fax: 7436 7950.
sales.films@bfi.org.uk.
www.bfi.org.uk.
Cinema Exhibitors Association,
22 Golden Sq, London, W1F 9JW.
Tel: (44 20) 7734 9551. Fax: 7734
6147. cea@cinemauk.ftech.co.uk.
**Directors Guild of Great Britain
(DGGB)**, Acorn House, 314-320
Grays Inn Rd, London, WC1X 8DP.
Tel: (44 20) 7278 4343.
Fax: 7278 4742. guild@dggb.org.
www.dggb.org.
Film Distributors' Association,
22 Golden Square, London, W1F
9JW. Tel: (44 20) 7437 4383.
Fax: 7734 0912. info@fda.uk.net.
www.launchingfilms.com
Film London, 20 Euston Centre,
Regent's Place, London, NW1 3JH.
Tel: (44 20) 7387 8787. Fax: 7387
8788. info@filmlondon.org.uk.
www.filmlondon.org.uk.
PACT, 45 Mortimer St, London,
W1W 8HJ. Tel: (44 20) 7331 6000.
Fax: 7331 6700.
enquiries@pact.co.uk.
www.pact.co.uk.
Scottish Screen, 249 West
George St, 2nd Floor, Glasgow,
G2 4QE. Tel: (44 141) 302 1700.
Fax: 302 1711.
info@scottishscreen.com.
www.scottishscreen.com.
The Script Factory, 66–67 Wells
Str, London W1T 3PY. Tel: (44 20)
7323 1414. Fax: 7323 9463.
general@scriptfactory.co.uk.
www.scriptfactory.co.uk.
Film-makers' organisation. Runs UK
and international screenwriting,
production and development
training, in partnership with the UK
Film Council and MEDIA.
UK Film Council, 10 Little Portland
St, London, W1W 7JG. Tel: (44 20)
7861 7861. Fax: 7861 7862.
info@ukfilmcouncil.org.uk.

www.ukfilmcouncil.org.uk.
UK Film Council International,
10 Little Portland St, London, W1W
7JG. Tel: (44 20) 7861 7860.
Fax: 7861 7864.
internationalinfo@ukfilmcouncil.org.uk.
www.ukfilmcouncil.org.uk.

UNITED STATES

Archives
**Academy of Motion Picture Arts
& Sciences**, Margaret Herrick
Library, Fairbanks Center for Motion
Picture Study, 333 S. La Cienega
Boulevard, Beverly Hills, CA 90211.
Tel: (1 310) 247 3000.
Fax: 657 5431. mpogo@oscars.org.
www.oscars.org.
**American Film Institute/
National Center for Film & Video
Preservation**, 2021 North Western
Ave, Los Angeles, CA 90027.
Tel: (1 323) 856 7600. Fax: 467
4578. info@afi.com. www.afi.com.
**George Eastman House/
International Museum of
Photography & Film**,
900 East Ave, Rochester, NY
14607. Tel: (1 585) 271 3361
Fax: 271 3970. film@geh.org.
www.eastman.org.
Getty Images Motion Collections,
75 Varick St, 5th Floor, New York,
NY 10013. Tel: (1 646) 613 4100.
Fax: 613 3601.
www.gettyimages.com.
The Archive Film collection
comprises a historical footage library
with more than 40,000 hours of
stock footage, including Hollywood
feature films, newsreels, TV news,
silent films, documentaries and
vintage industrial and educational
films, and many special collections.
Also 20 million photographs,
engravings and drawings spanning
3,000 years of world history.
Harvard Film Archive,
Carpenter Center for the Visual Arts,

Harvard University, 24 Quincy St, Cambridge, MA 02138. Tel: (1 617) 496 6046. Fax: 496 6750. info@harvardfilmarchive.org. www.harvardfilmarchive.org. Films (16mm, 35mm, video); 9,000 titles.

Library of Congress, Motion Picture, Broadcasting and Recorded Sound Division, Washington, DC 20540-4690. Tel: (1 202) 707 8572. Fax: 707 2371. mpref@loc.gov. www.loc.gov/rr/mopic. The nation's largest public research collection and preservation archive for motion pictures, videos, TV and radio broadcast and sound recordings. Available to qualified researchers, 8:30 am to 5:00 pm, Monday through Friday, through the facilities of the Motion Picture and Television Reading Room in the James Madison building.

Museum of Modern Art, Dept of Film and Video, 11 West 53rd St, New York, NY 10019. Tel: (1 212) 708 9400. Fax: 333 1145. info@moma.org. www.moma.org. Stock: 17,500 film titles, 2,500 books, 250 periodicals, 4,000,000 film stills. The excellent research and screening facilities of the department are available to serious students only by appointment; thousands of its films are available for rental, sale and lease. Stills Archive open by appointment.

Human Studies Film Archives, National Museum of Natural History, Room MSC G1300, 4210 Silver Hill Rd, Suitland, MD 207460-0534.

Tel: (1 301) 238 2875. Fax: 238 2880. hsfa@nmnh.si.edu. www.nmnh.si.edu/naa. Open by appointment only.

Pacific Film Archive, University of California and Berkeley Art Museum, 2625 Durant Ave, Berkeley, CA 94720-2250. Tel: (1 510) 642 1412. Fax: 642 4889. bampfa@uclink.berkeley.edu. www.bampfa.berkeley.edu.

UCLA Film & Television Archive, Commercial Services Division, 1015 North Cahuenga Blvd, Hollywood, CA 90038. Tel: (1 323) 466 8559. Fax: 461 6317. footage@ucla.edu. www.cinema.edu. One of the world's largest libraries of historical footage documenting the people, places, events and lifestyles of the twentieth Century.

Wisconsin Center for Film & Theater Research, 816 State St, Madison, WI 53706. Tel: (1 608) 264 6466. Fax: 264 6472. wcftrref@whs.wisc.edu. www.wisconsinhistory.org/wcftr.

Bookshops

Applause, 211 West 71st St, New York, NY 10023. Tel: (1 212) 496 7511. Fax: 721 2856. www.applausebooks.com. Now one of the few – and certainly the only uptown – film and showbiz bookstores in Manhattan.

Cinema Books, 4753 Roosevelt Way NE, Seattle, WA 98105. Tel: (1 206) 547 7667. stephanieogl@msn.com. www.cinemabooks.net.

Fine selection of film books and magazines, with space also devoted to TV and theatre. Mail order welcome.

Cinemonde, 478 Allied Drive, Suite 105, Nashville, TN 37211. Tel: (1 615) 832 1997. Fax: 832 2082. cinemonde@earthlink.net. www.cinemonde.com. Cinemonde is a poster store for movie buffs. Items are meticulously stored & displayed.

Déja Vu Enterprises Inc, 2934 Beverly Glen Circle, Suite 309, Los Angeles, CA 90077. Tel: (1 818) 996 6137. Fax: 996 6147. dejavugallery@socal.rr.com. www.dejavugallery.com. Collectors gallery. Thousands of autographed photos and original movie posters.

Dwight Cleveland, PO Box 10922, Chicago, IL 60610-0922. Tel: (1 773) 525 9152. Fax: 525 2969. posterboss@aol.com. www.movieposterbiz.com. Buys and sells movie posters.

Larry Edmund's Bookshop, 6644 Hollywood Blvd, Hollywood, CA 90028. Tel: (1 323) 463 3273. Fax: 463 4245. info@larryedmunds.com. www.larryedmunds.com. The stills collection alone is a goldmine for any film buff. Back numbers of movie annuals, posters, lobby cards and one of the largest collections of new and used books in the world.

Samuel French's Theatre & Film Bookshop, (2 Locations) 7623 Sunset Blvd, Hollywood, CA 90046. Tel: (1 323) 876 0570. Fax: 876 6822. Extended evening hours at 11963 Ventura Blvd, Studio City, CA 91604. Tel: (1 818) 762 0535. www.samuelfrench.com. The world's oldest and largest play publisher (est. 1830) operates a separate film and performing arts bookshop. Complete range of new movie and performing arts books available: directories, reference, writing, acting biography, screenplays etc. Worldwide mail-order service.

Gotham Book Mart, 16 East 46th St, New York, NY 10017. Tel: (1 212) 719 4448. Fax: 719 3481. This famous literary bookshop (Est. 1920) in mid-Manhattan, is the only New York City bookstore offering new, used and out-of-print film and theatre books. Also, an extensive stock of "quality" film magazines dating from the 1950s to the present.

Limelight Film & Theatre Bookstore, 1803 Market St, San Francisco, CA 94103. Tel: (1 415) 864 2265. limelightbooks@sbcglobal.net. www.limelightbooks.com. Collection includes plays, screenplays, biographies, history and criticism of films, film and television technique.

Movie Madness, 1083 Thomas Jefferson St, Washington, DC 20007. Tel: (1 202) 337 7064. Current, classic and campy movie posters available at this unique store in Georgetown.

Movie Star News, 134 West 18th St, New York, NY 10011. Tel: (1 212) 620 8160. Fax: 727 0634. www.moviestarnews.com. Features the largest stock of movie photos and posters in the world.

Jerry Ohlinger's Movie Material Store Inc, 253 West 35th St, New York, NY 10001. Tel: (1 212) 989 0869. Fax: 989 1660. jomms@aol.com. www.moviematerials.com. The shop stocks a wealth of stills from the 1930s through the 1990s, specialising in colour material. Posters are also plentiful, and there

are some magazines as well.

Film Schools

Information on the thousands of US film schools and courses available can be obtained in the American Film Institute's Guide to College Courses in Film and Television, which can be ordered from Publications, The American Film Institute, 2021 North Western Ave, Los Angeles, CA 90027. Tel: (1 323) 856 7600. Fax: 467 4578. www.afi.com.

Magazines

American Cinematographer, ASC Holding Corp, 1782 North Orange Drive, Hollywood, CA 90028. Tel: (1 323) 969 4333. Fax: 876 4973. customerservice@theasc.com. www.theasc.com. Glossy monthly on film and electronic production techniques.

Animation Journal, 108 Hedge Nettle, Crossing, Savannah, GA 31406-7220. Tel: (1 912) 352 9300. editor@animationjournal.com. www.animationjournal.com. Quarterly.

Animation Magazine, 30941 West Agoura Rd, Suite 102, Westlake Village, CA 91361. Tel: (1 818) 991 2884. Fax: 991 3773. info@animationmagazine.net. www.animationmagazine.net.

Box Office, 155 South El Molino Ave, Suite 100, Pasadena, California, 91101. Tel: (1 626) 396 0250. Fax: 396 0248. editorial@boxoffice.com; advertising@boxoffice.com. www.boxoffice.com. Business monthly for Hollywood and the movie theatre industry.

Cineaste, 304 Hudson St, 6th Floor, New York, NY 10013-1015. cineaste@cineaste.com.

www.cineaste.com. Perhaps the finest anti-establishment movie magazine. Quarterly.

Classic Images, 301 E 3rd St, Muscatine, IA 52761. Tel: (1 563) 263 2331. Fax: 262 8042. classicimages@classicimages.com. www.classicimages.com. A good source for film buffs eager to enlarge their library of movies. Monthly.

Film Comment, Film Society of Lincoln Center, 70 Lincoln Center Plaza, New York, NY 10023. Tel: (1 212) 875 5614. Fax: 875 5636. editor@filmlinc.com. Informative, feisty and usually uncompromising articles. Still the best US cinema bi-monthly.

Film Criticism, Allegheny College, Box D, Meadville, PA 16335. Tel: (1 814) 332 4333/43. Fax: 332 2981. lmichael@allegheny.edu. Scholarly essays on film history, theory and culture. Tri-quarterly.

Film Literature Index, Film & Television Documentation Centre, State University of New York, 1400 Washington Ave, Albany, NY 12222. Tel: (1 518) 442 5745. Fax: 442 5367. fatdoc@albany.edu. www.albany.edu/sisp/fatdoc/index.html.

Film Quarterly, University of California Press, 2000 Center St, Suite 303, Berkeley, CA 94704-1223. Tel: (1 510) 642 9740. Fax: 642 9917. ann.martin@ucpress.edu. www.filmquarterly.org. Publishes readable discussions of issues in contemporary, classical and silent film, as well as TV and video. Plus substantial film reviews and interviews, and analyses of independent, documentary, avant-garde and foreign films. Comprehensive book reviews.

Filmmaker Magazine, 501 5th Ave, Room 1714,

New York, NY 10017. Tel: (1 212) 983 3150. Fax: 973 0318. publisher@filmmakermagazine.com. www.filmmakermagazine.com. Aimed at independent film-makers, this quarterly offers interviews, news and sound advice.

Hollywood Reporter, 5055 Wilshire Blvd, Los Angeles, CA 90036-4396. Tel: (1 323) 525 2000. Fax: 525 2377. www.hollywoodreporter.com. Daily.

International Documentary Magazine, International Documentary Association, 1201 West 5th St, Suite M320, Los Angeles, CA 90017. Tel: (1 213) 534 3600. Fax: 534 3610. info@documentary.org. www. documentary.org. The only US publication to focus exclusively on non-fiction film and video. Informative articles, reviews and interviews. Published ten times a year.

Movieline's Hollywood Life, 10537 Santa Monica Blvd, Suite 250, Los Angeles, CA 90025. Tel: (1 310) 234 9501. Fax: 234 0332. andre@movieline.com. www.movieline.com. Intelligent, irreverent and refreshingly candid with attitudes, stars, fashion and sass. Great interviews. Published ten times a year.

Variety, 5700 Wilshire Blvd, Suite 120, Los Angeles, CA 90036. www.variety.com. The world's foremost entertainment industry newspaper (daily and weekly).

Useful Addresses
Directors Guild of America, 7920 Sunset Blvd, Los Angeles, CA 90046. Tel: (1 310) 289 2000. Fax: 289 2029. www.dga.org.
Independent Feature Project, 104 W 29th St, 12th Floor, New York, NY 10001. Tel: (1 212) 465 8200. Fax: 465 8525. ifpny@ifp.org. www.ifp.org.

International Documentary Association, 1201 W 5th St, Suite M320, Los Angeles, CA 90017-1461. Tel: (1 213) 534 3600. Fax: 534 3610. info@documentary.org. www.documentary.org.

Motion Picture Association of America, 15503 Ventura Blvd, Encino, CA 91436. Tel: (1 818) 995 6600. Fax: 382 1784. www.mpaa.org.

ShoWest, 770 Broadway, 5th Floor, New York, NY 10003-9595. Tel: (1 646) 654 7680. Fax: 654 7693. rsunshine@vnuexpo.com. www.showest.com.

URUGUAY
All Tel/Fax numbers begin (598 2)

Archive
Cinemateca Uruguaya, Lorenzo Carnelli 1311, 11200 Montevideo. Tel: 418 2460. Fax: 419 4572. cinemuy@chasque.net. www.cinemateca.org.uy.

Useful Addresses
Asociación de Críticos de Cine del Uruguay (ACCU), Canelones 1280, Montevideo. Tel: 622 0085. Fax: 908 3904. criticosuruguay@yahoo.com.
Asociación de Productores y Realizadores de Cine y Video del Uruguay (ASOPROD), Maldonado 1792, Montevideo. Tel: 418 7998. info@asoprod.org.uy. www.asoprod.org.uy.
Fondo Para el Fomento y Desarrollo de la Producción Audiovisual Nacional (FONA), Palacio Municipal, Piso 1º, Montevideo. Tel: 902 3775. fona@prensa.imm.gub.uy.

www.montevideo.gub.uy/cultura/c_fona. htm.
Instituto Nacional del Audiovisual (INA), Reconquista 535, 8º Piso, 11100 Montevideo. Tel/Fax: 915 7489/916 2632. ina@mec.gub.uy. www.mec.gub.uy/ina.

ZIMBABWE
All Tel/Fax numbers begin (263 4)

Archive
National Archives of Zimbabwe, Borrowdale Road, Gunhill, Private Bag 7729, Causeway, Harare. Tel: 792 741. archives@gta.gov.zw. www.gta.gov.zw.

Magazine
Africa Film & TV, 10 Jewry St, Winchester, Hants, SO23 8RZ, United Kingdom. Tel: (44 1962) 861 518. Fax: 863 516. www.africafilmtv.com. Contact: Russell Honeyman, Publishing Editor.

Useful Addresses
African Script Development Fund, 43 Selous Ave, Harare. Tel: 724 673. Fax: 733 404. asdf@mweb.co.zw. www.icon.co.zw/asdf.
Media for Development Trust (MFD), 19 Van Praagh Ave Milton Park PO Box 6755, Harare. Tel: 701 323/4. Fax: 729 066. mfd@mango.zw. www.mfd.co.zw. Contact: John Riber.
Zimbabwe Broadcasting Corporation. Broadcasting Center, Pockets Hill, PO Box HG444, Highlands, Harare. Tel: 498 630. Fax: 498 613. info@zbc.co.zw. www.zbc.co.zw.
Zimmedia, 26 Cork Rd, Harare. Tel: 708 426. Fax: 708 425. info@zimmedia.com. www.zimmedia.com.

Index to Advertisers